Early Education Curriculum

A Child's Connection to the World

FOURTH
EDITION

Join us on the web at

EarlyChildEd.delmar.com

Early Education Curriculum
A Child's Connection to the World

FOURTH EDITION

Hilda L. Jackman

THOMSON
DELMAR LEARNING

Australia Canada Mexico Singapore Spain United Kingdom United States

THOMSON
DELMAR LEARNING

Early Education Curriculum: A Child's Connection to the World, Fourth Edition
by Hilda L. Jackman

**Vice President,
Career Education SBU:**
Dawn Gerrain

Director of Learning Solutions:
John Fedor

Managing Editor:
Robert L. Serenka, Jr.

Acquisitions Editor:
Christopher Shortt

Associate Project Manager:
Anne Orgren

Editorial Assistant:
Alison Archambault

**Director of Content and Media
Production:**
Wendy A. Troeger

Production Manager:
Mark Bernard

Content Project Manager:
Angela Iula

Technology Project Manager:
Sandy Charette

Director of Marketing:
Wendy E. Mapstone

Senior Channel Manager:
Kristin McNary

Marketing Coordinator:
Scott A. Chrysler

Art Director:
Dave Arsenault

Interior Illustrations:
Laurent Linn

For permission to use material from this text or product, submit a request online at http://www.thomsonrights.com
Any additional questions about permissions can be submitted by email to thomsonrights@thomson.com

Library of Congress Cataloging-in-Publication Data

Jackman, Hilda L.
  Early education curriculum: a child's connection to the world/Hilda L. Jackman —4th ed.
    p. cm.
  Includes bibliographical references and index.
    ISBN-13: 978-1-4283-2246-2
    ISBN-10: 1-4283-2246-9
  1. Early childhood education–Curricula–United States. 2. Curriculum planning–United States. 3. Interdisciplinary approach in education–United States. 4. Early childhood education–Activity programs–United States. I. Title.

  LB1139.4.J33 2009
  372.19–dc22

2007043981

NOTICE TO THE READER

Publisher does not warrant or guarantee any of the products described herein or perform any independent analysis in connection with any of the product information contained herein. Publisher does not assume, and expressly disclaims, any obligation to obtain and include information other than that provided to it by the manufacturer.

The reader is expressly warned to consider and adopt all safety precautions that might be indicated by the activities herein and to avoid all potential hazards. By following the instructions contained herein, the reader willingly assumes all risks in connection with such instructions.

The Publisher makes no representation or warranties of any kind, including but not limited to, the warranties of fitness for particular purpose or merchantability, nor are any such representations implied with respect to the material set forth herein, and the publisher takes no responsibility with respect to such material. The Publisher shall not be liable for any special, consequential, or exemplary damages resulting, in whole or part, from the readers' use of, or reliance upon, this material.

The authors and Thomson Delmar Learning affirm that the Web site URLs referenced herein were accurate at the time of printing. However, due to the fluid nature of the Internet, we cannot guarantee their accuracy for the life of the edition.

This book is lovingly dedicated

to my granddaughters Cambria and Rachel

and to the men in my life:

my husband, Phil, my sons,

Stephen and Larry,

my brother, Rick. . .

and, as always, to my nephew Jared.

CONTENTS

PART ONE

CREATING THE ENVIRONMENT THAT SUPPORTS CURRICULUM AND CONNECTS CHILDREN

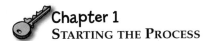

Chapter 1
STARTING THE PROCESS 2

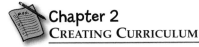

Chapter 2
CREATING CURRICULUM 36

PART TWO
DISCOVERING AND EXPANDING THE
EARLY EDUCATION CURRICULUM

PREFACE

Many times while writing this fourth edition of *Early Education Curriculum: A Child's Connection to the World*, I thought about why I wrote this book in the first place. In the beginning, I wrote the text I wished I had when I first began teaching early childhood courses on curriculum development. With each new edition the text continues to be an outgrowth of my forty-plus-year commitment to young children and the adults who guide them through their early childhood years. With this fourth edition, my focus remains the same: *the children* and the dedicated early childhood teachers who contribute daily to improve the lives of children everywhere.

Today the outside world of fast-paced living, work responsibilities, ever-changing technology, assessment requirements, violence, stress, and the how-to, what-for, and should-haves are constantly pushing against what teachers know and want to do for young children and their families. Therefore, we should listen to the children and concentrate our efforts on their development, needs, abilities, interests, and cultural diversity as we plan our early childhood curriculum.

In this fourth edition, interconnecting philosophies are still underscored. The first advocates that curriculum be *child centered and child initiated*, that it is sensitive to, and supportive of, the development of young children, individually and in a group, emphasizing acceptance of all children. This includes acceptance of diversity, individual differences, and special needs. The second focus is on the *curriculum* itself, which provides for all of a child's development by planning experiences that build upon what children already know and are able to do. The third philosophy to this text is to encourage children *to learn by doing*. This encourages experimentation, self-control, and the building of a positive self-image ("I can do it myself!"). The fourth recognizes the importance of *cultural context* in the development and learning of young children. Growing up as members of families and communities, children come to us with rich backgrounds of cultural experiences. Now, more than ever, the curriculum should promote opportunities to support a child's cultural and linguistic diversity. The fifth belief advocates developing a learning environment that invites *creativity*. This provides opportunities for unevaluated discovery and activity, while promoting acceptance and respect for one another's creations. This also helps one to develop an awareness that the process of creative thinking is complex. The sixth concept involves reciprocal *relationships between teachers and families*. Positive communication between home and school is crucial to providing a consistent and beneficial experience for young children. The seventh philosophy recommends that curriculum facilitate *physical activity and play* by integrating movement within activities throughout the day. Each of these philosophies allows children to make choices and is nourished by play. With less time and opportunity for children to play, it is critical for us to encourage and support play in all our early childhood programs.

All chapters of the text are separate and complete, while at the same time connecting to other chapters to form curriculum as a whole for children from infancy to age eight. This allows each instructor to use the chapters in any sequence. This approach is helpful in meeting the individual needs of the teacher, the student, and ultimately the children.

This book is designed for a beginning student as well as an experienced teacher looking for current early childhood philosophies, curriculum resources, fresh ideas, or insights. It can be used by those in two-year college or four-year university early education curriculum courses, graduate classes, mini/fast-track courses, and workshop/seminar courses for continuing education of teachers. It is also applicable for students working toward the Child Development Associate credential or any professional working with children and families.

HOW TO USE THIS BOOK

The text is divided into two parts. Part One, "Creating the Environment That Supports Curriculum and Connects Children," presents the elements of the foundation of early education curriculum. Chapter 1, "Starting the Process," presents early childhood historical information, learning, and developmental theories of early childhood education; strategies for organizing instruction, with emphasis on developmentally, individually, culturally, and creatively appropriate practices; the importance of play in the lives of children; the planning process; ways to include diverse ages, groupings, and individual differences; and communication with parents. Chapter 2, "Creating Curriculum," offers examples of curriculum models and programs; explains the process of curriculum development, including multicultural, anti-bias, and special needs considerations; presents developmentally appropriate early learning environments, indoor and outdoor; develops concepts and skills, themes, specific lesson and activity plans, guidance guidelines, and a plan of observation, assessment and evaluation based on different ages and individual differences. Both chapters begin with chapter Objectives and an Overview and end with an Afterview, Key Terms List, Exploration activities, References, and Additional Readings and Resources. These two chapters form the foundation for the remaining chapters.

Part Two, "Discovering and Expanding the Early Education Curriculum," explores each curriculum area in depth, taking into consideration the individual child, group of children, process of setting up appropriate environments, special subject content, and integration of all curricula. Each chapter presents developmentally appropriate activities for each age group and encourages self-esteem and creativity development.

The content chapters offer chapter Objectives, an Overview, guidance tips for teachers, multicultural/anti-bias activities, observation, assessment, and evaluation suggestions, technology information, activities to encourage family participation and support, an Afterview, Key Terms List, Exploration assignments, References, and Additional Readings and Resources to aid students in obtaining additional information on the chapter's topics.

The content chapters reflect the current emphasis on literacy, math, science, and social studies.

Chapter 3   Language and Literacy

Chapter 4   Literature

Chapter 5   Math

Chapter 6   Science

Chapter 7   Social Studies

Chapter 8   Art

Chapter 9   Sensory Centers

Chapter 10 Music and Movement

Chapter 11 Puppets

Chapter 12 Dramatic Play and Creative Dramatics

 Use the Inspiration® 8 Software on the front-of-the-book CD to create curriculum webs and other curriculum materials.

TEXTWIDE EMPHASIS

This book is designed to help students build knowledge with each chapter. Concepts are introduced in a specific chapter, then reviewed for elaboration and application throughout the text. Topics are approached developmentally and placed appropriately within the curriculum area where students can benefit from its content. Each topic becomes a part of the entire curriculum. New research, new or revised perspectives in the field, and new professional positions are all integrated into this fourth edition.

Some of these topics are:

- a young child's growth and development, including brain development
- expanded guidance techniques
- use of technology in early childhood
- observation, assessment, and evaluation
- importance of play
- health, safety, nutrition, and obesity prevention
- updated children's book lists
- transition activities
- open-ended explorations
- developmentally appropriate activities
- special needs adaptations and modification
- importance of family support and participation

NEW TO THIS EDITION

Updated national standards: National standards in literacy, mathematics, science, social studies, and music are included as they relate to specific standards. Essential recommendations and position papers of the National Association for the Education of Young Children (NAEYC) and Association of Childhood Education International (ACEI) are included as well.

Front-of-the-book CD: Newly created for the fourth edition, this CD offers numerous lesson and activity plans, checklists, observation/assessment forms, puppet patterns, room arrangement diagrams, curriculum webs, and more. Blank forms help students to successfully develop their own lesson and activity plans, while the inclusion of Inspiration® 8 software is an essential tool for curriculum web development.

Observation, Assessment, and Evaluation: Specific observation/assessment guidelines and tools are in this new edition. These highly effective assessment forms and suggestions will be used throughout the early childhood curriculum.

Full-color addition: Concepts surrounding the early childhood outdoor environment are enhanced with new color photos, text, and developmentally appropriate curriculum activities.

Technology: New information of developmentally appropriate ways to use different types of technology as part of the early childhood curriculum are included in this edition.

Anecdotes: Additional anecdotes from early childhood teachers, called "Why I Teach Young Children," are included throughout the text.

Historical Information: New to Chapter 1 is the historical highlights timeline of early childhood education and professional organizations.

Chapter Objectives: Each chapter begins with easy-to-understand objectives.

Key Terms and Glossary: Important terms have been updated and are listed in bold print within each chapter. They are in alphabetical order at the end of each chapter and again in the glossary at the back of the book.

Quotes: The words of early childhood professionals throughout the book are chosen carefully to extend each chapter's information base and present current theories and practices from many points of view.

Photos and Illustrations: Visual images offer another way of understanding the concepts presented in this book. New photographs and captions, depicting the ethnic diversity in classrooms today, have been added.

Guidance Guidelines: Renewed emphasis has been placed on guidance techniques, both verbal and nonverbal. There are helpful "Tips for Teachers" throughout the text and in the color insert.

Expanded Web Links: For each chapter, Web links are provided for additional reference, research, and information relative to the specific chapter content. Additional Web links are emphasized in Appendix C, "Resources for Teachers, with Internet Web Site Listings." These helpful Web sites have been selected for pertinent information for educators and students. Appendix D offers the home pages of professional organizations and associations.

The author and Thomson Delmar Learning affirm that the Web site URLs referenced herein were accurate at the time of printing. However, due to the fluid nature of the Internet, we cannot guarantee their accuracy for the life of the edition.

Updated Appendices: The appendices are designed to give teachers practical information that can be used across the curriculum. Appendix B, "My Community," is an integrated curriculum theme with activities. All appendices include updated and new resources.

More Features to Look For: Expanded information is provided on themes, projects, and webs plus additional discussion on bicultural, bilingual influences, and ways to help young children and their families. All of the features in this fourth edition are created to provide a resource of ideas, methods, suggested practices, and guidance goals that will give teachers and students guidelines to create and enrich their own curriculum.

ANCILLARIES

The following ancillary materials are available to accompany the fourth edition of *Early Education Curriculum: A Child's Connection to the World:*

 Front-of-the-book CD
This CD is new to this edition. It includes additional puppet patterns, extra room arrangement diagrams, newly created lesson and activity plans, checklists, blank forms of lesson and activity plans, observation/assessment forms, and curriculum webs especially created on Inspiration® 8 software for this CD. Also included on this CD is a 120-day trial version of Inspiration® 8 software, which can be used to build curriculum webs and more.

Instructor's Manual

The updated instructor's manual provides chapter summaries, chapter competencies, extensive topics for class discussions, additional student exploration activities, and activity sheets or checklists. It also includes guidelines for student observation of, and participation with, children.

e-Resource

The new e-Resource component is geared to provide instructors with all the tools they need on one convenient CD-ROM. Instructors will find that this resource provides them with a turnkey solution to help them by making available:

- An electronic version of the Instructor's Manual, including Microsoft Word versions of the Student Activity Plans that can be filled in electronically.
- A computerized test bank composed of hundreds of true/false, multiple choice, matching, and short answer questions. Instructors can use the computerized test bank software to create sample quizzes for students. Refer to the *CTB User's Guide* for more information on how to create and post quizzes to your school's Internet or Intranet.
- Power Point slides for each book chapter.
- A directory of Web links referenced throughout the text and ancillaries.

WebTutor™

The WebTutor™ to accompany the fourth edition of *Early Education Curriculum: A Child's Connection to the World* allows you to take learning beyond the classroom. This Online Courseware is designed to complement the text and benefits students in that it enables them to manage their time more effectively, prepare for exams, organize their notes, and more. Special features related to chapter content include:

- Chapter Learning Objectives
- Online Course Preparation
- Study Sheets
- Glossary
- Discussion Topics
- Frequently Asked Questions
- Online Class Notes
- Online Chapter Quizzes
- Web Links

Printing features allow students to print their own customized study guides.

A benefit for instructors as well as students, the WebTutor™ allows for online discussion with the instructor and other class members, real-time chat to enable virtual office hours and encourage collaborative learning environments, a calendar of syllabus information for easy reference, email connections to facilitate communication among classmates and between students and instructors, and customization tools that help educators tailor their course to fit their needs by adding or changing content.

WebTutor™ allows you to extend your reach beyond the classroom and is available on either the WebCT™ or Blackboard platform.

Online Companion™

The Online Companion to accompany the fourth edition of *Early Education Curriculum: A Child's Connection to the World*, is your link to early childhood education curriculum development on the Internet. Additional activities and explorations for each chapter will assist students in learning more about the content. Web links and review questions specifically related to chapter content are also included.

The Online Companion™ icon appears at the end of each chapter to prompt you to go on-line and take advantage of the many features provided. This offers exploration in early childhood education curriculum in a larger context.

You can find the Online Companion™ at www. earlychilded.delmar.com

Professional Enhancement Text

A new supplement to accompany this text is the *Curriculum in Early Education Professional Enhancement* handbook for students. This resource, which is part of Delmar Learning's Early Childhood Education Professional Enhancement series, focuses on key topics of interest for future early childhood directors, teachers, and caregivers. Becoming a teacher is a process of continuing to grow, learn, reflect, and discover through experience. The Professional Enhancement text helps tomorrow's teachers along their way. Students will keep this informational supplement and use it for years to come in their early childhood practices.

The *Curriculum in Early Education Professional Enhancement* text provides you with:

- developmental milestones by age and by skill, accompanied by developmental alerts
- suggested play materials for children
- basic program equipment and materials for an early childhood center
- observation and assessment methods
- suggestions for creating curriculum and lesson plans
- guidelines for developmentally appropriate practice
- additional professional development resources for teachers

ACKNOWLEDGMENTS

REVIEWER ACKNOWLEDGMENTS

The author and publisher would like to extend their gratitude to the following early childhood reviewers. Their knowledge of and dedication to the early childhood field has been a tremendous asset to this text.

Betsy-Tom Brown
Halifax Community College, NC

Beverlyn Cain
Elizabeth City State University, NC

Leann Curry, M.Ed.
Midwestern State University, TX

Susan Davies
Ivy Tech Community College, IN

Sylvia L. Dietrich, Ph.D.
Western Kentucky University, KY

Patricia Dilko, MPA
Canada College, CA

Mary Harder
Edison College, FL

Karen L. Hutchinson, EdD
University of Texas at San Antonio, TX

Anne C. Lindsay, Ph.D.
University of Arkansas at Little Rock, AR

Catherine Mogharreban
Southern Illinois University, IL

Barbara E. Schwartz, Ph.D.
New York University, NY

Kellie Jo Sullivan
Brazosport College, TX

Cindy Waters
Upper Iowa University, IA

Becky Wyatt
Murray State College, OK

ADDITIONAL ACKNOWLEDGMENTS

The author gratefully acknowledges the contributions of the many individuals who helped make this book possible. A very special THANK YOU goes to **Janet Galantay,** my friend and colleague, who has been there throughout all the editions of this text. As an outstanding early childhood professional and lab school director, her contribution to this edition has been invaluable. Other generous friends who have spent their professional lives pursuing all that is best for children and who are most willing to share their expertise are **Jo Eklof** and **Bea Wolf,** whose musical creativity and commitment to, and respect of, children and the world we live in are expressed in their songs and writings; **Carmen Osbahr ("Rosita")** and **Caroll Spinney ("Big Bird"** and **"Oscar the Grouch")** of *Sesame Street,* who contributed to Chapter 11; **Bonnie Rubinstein,** friend, talented early childhood professional and director of the Temple Shalom Preschool was always there for me when I asked, "Do you have a minute to talk?"; the early childhood teachers at Temple Shalom Preschool in Dallas, who welcomed me into their classrooms to observe and record the developmentally appropriate activities occurring daily with their delightful children and who shared their personal experiences for "Why I Teach Young Children." A big thank you to the teachers at the Collin College Child Development Lab School in Plano, who also contributed their personal experiences for "Why I Teach Young Children." Special recognition must go to my son, **Laurent Linn,** for his wondrous illustrations, which demonstrate his love and understanding of children and give depth and meaning to what I have tried to communicate in words.

My most special gratitude, love, and respect go to my husband, **Phil Jackman,** my "in-house editor" for his love, patience, encouragement, and participation in this project. As always, without him, this book would not have been possible.

To my son, **Stephen Linn,** who is always there with much-needed additional support and reassurance, a heartfelt "thank you."

With deep appreciation and many thanks to instructors, students, and colleagues who continue to use *Early Education Curriculum* in their classes.

And to **Anne Orgren** and the editorial and production staff at Delmar Learning, a huge THANK YOU for your assistance, encouragement, and guidance.

ABOUT THE AUTHOR

Hilda Jackman brings to her authorship a background rich in experience and achievement as it relates to the education of young children. Long before she became professor emerita with the Dallas County Community College District and Professor-Coordinator of the Brookhaven Child Development/Early Childhood program, she pioneered children's television programming in the Dallas–Fort Worth area as a writer, producer, and puppeteer. She went on to earn a master of science degree in Early Childhood Education at The University of North Texas and for many years was a teacher of young children (infants through kindergarten) and director of several Child Development programs. When Brookhaven College opened, Hilda was selected to establish the Child Development/Early Childhood Program and the Parent-Child Study Center. During her twenty years at Brookhaven, besides writing curriculum and teaching, she helped establish the first Certificate Program in Texas to train nannies, developed multicultural/anti-bias curriculum courses, and consulted with business and industry on child care. Since retiring from college teaching, Hilda continues to act as a mentor, presents workshops and staff development seminars, consults, and stays active in the National Association for the Education of Young Children (NAEYC), Texas Association for the Education of Young Children (TAEYC), and other professional organizations. She is also the author of *Sing Me a Story! Tell Me a Song! Creative Thematic Activities for Teachers of Young Children* (2005), also published by Thomson Delmar Learning.

Hilda is the mother of two adult sons. Most recently, she is the very proud grandmother of twin granddaughters, shown in the photo above.

This book is lovingly dedicated to **Cambria** and **Rachel** and to the men in my life: my husband, **Phil**, my sons, **Stephen** and **Larry,** my brother, **Rick**. . . . and, as always, to my nephew **Jared.**

TO THE STUDENT

Welcome to the world of early education. I am glad you are here. Our profession needs caring, committed individuals to encourage and support children through their early years.

Each of you has a different reason for wanting to be in an early childhood classroom. Some of you are just beginning. Others are experienced teachers. No matter what type of program or what age group you work with, it is important that you understand the development of young children, help them connect with the changing world of their families, and promote developmentally appropriate practices in early education environments and curriculum.

This text is designed to be a practical guide to help you develop a curriculum appropriate for young children. Based on the knowledge of current research, theory, and developmentally appropriate activities found in this text, you can develop your own curriculum.

 Use the Inspiration® 8 software included in the front-of-the-book CD to create curriculum webs. Write lesson and activity plans using the forms in the CD as well. I hope this new CD will help you develop appropriate curriculum for young children.

Your experiences with young children are most important to your academic and professional development. I encourage you to use this curriculum text to stimulate your own creativity and knowledge of children. Mix and match, add to, and redesign the ideas and activities presented. Take the time to enjoy the uniqueness of each individual child, as well as the group of children, as they explore and interact with the curriculum.

It is also important to remember that professional ethics and confidentiality are concerns that are inseparable from all observation, assessment, and participation activities. It is crucial that you deal with each child and/or adult without prejudice or partiality and refrain from imposing your own views or values upon children or adults.

I hope this text will prove helpful to you as you strive to make a difference in the lives of young children and their families. We are all in this profession together, and, like the children, we too are growing and developing.

—HILDA L. JACKMAN

PART ONE

Creating the Environment that Supports Curriculum and Connects Children

I stand outside the classroom, teacher,
At the doorstep to the world.
I want to see it all,
To hear and feel and taste it all.
I stand here, teacher,
With eager eyes and heart and mind.
Will you open the door?

— Janet Galantay
(Reprinted with permission)

CHAPTER 1

STARTING THE PROCESS

OBJECTIVES

AFTER STUDYING THIS CHAPTER, YOU SHOULD BE ABLE TO:

- Discuss why historical information is important to early childhood education.

- Define and outline the theories of Erik Erikson, Jean Piaget, Lev Vygotsky, and Howard Gardner.

- Identify developmentally appropriate practice, including child development and learning, individual strengths, interests, and needs.

- State why the recent exploration of brain function holds essential information for early childhood educators, parents, and young children.

- Recognize the importance of racial and cultural identity in the development of young children.

- Discuss the importance of play in the lives of young children and describe the developmental stages of play.

- Explain the process of planning and implementing a developmentally appropriate environment for young children, including communicating with parents.

OVERVIEW

Please think of the children <u>first</u>. If you ever have anything to do with their entertainment, their food, their toys, their custody, their day or night care, their health care, their education—listen to the children, learn about them, learn from them. <u>Think of the children first.</u>

These words of Fred Rogers (2003) are meaningful to us as students and teachers. Children must be at the center of all we do. As adults who genuinely care about them, we should honor the uniqueness of each child and the child's family. Give them teachers with commitment, training, experience, and knowledge about child development and how children learn. "Children come into the world eager to learn. . . . There can be no question that the environment in which a child grows up has a powerful impact on how the child develops and what the child learns" (Bowman, Donovan, & Burns, 2000).

As you read this chapter, its focus on making the environment and the curriculum child-centered will be apparent. This chapter extends this philosophy by studying historical aspects of early education, learning and developmental theories, developmentally appropriate practices (DAP), social and cultural contexts, creative appropriateness, importance of play for young children, curriculum planning, early childhood schedules and routines, and communicating with parents. Also included are ideas to enhance instruction and activities that respect a child's culture, language, and learning style. Additionally, in-depth attention should be paid to language development, cognition, physical development, and social and emotional competence.

EARLY CHILDHOOD EDUCATION

The field of early care and education has changed profoundly in the last decade. In some ways many longtime early childhood educators find it nearly unrecognizable. Standards and guidelines abound. Increasing numbers of early childhood programs are required to address state early learning standards (or guidelines) that will soon include three-year-olds and next, perhaps, even infants and toddlers. (Freeman & Feeney, 2006)

With this in mind it's important to look back at our profession to see how changes produced new ways to help children and families. Historical information gives us an opportunity to see how past generations viewed children and their acquisition of knowledge, based on religious, ethnic, political, and economic pressures of the times. Almy (cited in Greenberg, 2000) believes that "it's most important not to leave behind everything we already know about children as we go on learning new things. . . . New knowledge should build on prior knowledge, not erase and replace it."

Exploring the storied history and philosophy of early childhood education presents us with significant individuals and far-reaching developments that have impacted and influenced our thinking. "Knowing that early childhood philosophy has deep roots can be an inspiration and helps teachers develop professional expression" (Gordon & Browne, 2008). Figure 1–1 is a timeline of historical highlights of early childhood education.

The professional organizations mentioned in the timeline are all striving to improve the field of early childhood education. Their efforts emphasize the importance of **advocacy,** an attitude that encourages professionals, parents, and other caring adults to work together on behalf of young children.

advocacy
An attitude that encourages professionals, parents, and other caring adults to work together on behalf of young children.

1900s	In the early 1900s Patty Smith Hill created a curriculum that provided the foundation for kindergartens in the United States. She also founded the laboratory school at Columbia University Teachers College, which became the model for training early childhood educators, and began organizing a professional organization of early childhood educators (Isbell & Raines, 2007).
1910s	The development of the nursery school was conceived by two sisters, Margaret and Rachel McMillan, who first introduced their philosophy to America in 1910 and watched as their "nurture schools" grew. During the 1930s and 1940s nursery schools continued to spread throughout the United States reflecting the principles of a child-centered approach (Gordon & Browne, 2007; Spodek & Saracho, 1994).
1920s	During the 1920s more than one-half the households in the United States had at least one other adult living there besides the two parents, such as an aunt, uncle, or grandparent. At the same time, nursery schools linked to child development and psychology were available, while day nurseries focused on meeting the needs of poor and immigrant families (NAEYC, 2001).
1930s	The Depression of the 1930s produced an economic and social crisis in the United States. Out of this came the Works Progress Administration (WPA) nurseries. These child care facilities were designed "to develop physical and mental well-being of preschool children in needy unemployed families or neglected or underprivileged homes. . . . Almost two thousand WPA nursery schools were in operation by 1935" (NAEYC, 2001).
1940s	In response to World War II in the 1940s, the Lanham Act was passed by Congress to allow public funds to be used for child care. Nursery schools and day care centers were opened as millions of women went to work for the war effort. All families, regardless of income level, were eligible. Between 1943 and 1945, Kaiser Shipyards used Lanham Act funds to open child care centers for its employees. These became the largest centers in the country and functioned twenty-four hours a day all year long, offering quality care and comprehensive services to families. Once the war ended, however, the workers left and the centers closed (Gordon & Browne, 2004; NAEYC, 2001; Spodek & Saracho, 1994).
1960s	The rest of the twentieth century represents an active time in the formation of early childhood education (Essa, 2007). In the early 1960s the High/Scope Perry Preschool Project began. This program was originally designed to serve at-risk children from impoverished neighborhoods. It has developed into a landmark long-term study of the effects of high quality early care and education on low-income three- and four-year olds (Wiekart & Schweinhart, 2007). (More information on this can be found in Chapter 2 of this text.)
1964	NANE, the National Committee on Nursery Schools (established in 1929), became the National Association for the Education of Young Children (NAEYC). In 2007, NAEYC membership has grown to over 100,000 and counting.
1965	As part of the Economic Opportunity Act's "War on Poverty," project Head Start was funded to counteract the effects of poverty among children. (More information on this can be found in Chapter 2 of this text.)

(continues)

FIGURE 1–1
Timeline of Historical Highlights.

1970	The National Black Child Development Institute (NBCDI) in Washington, D.C., was created. This nonprofit organization has continued to provide and support programs, workshops, and resources for African-American children, their parents, and communities (NBCDI, 2002).
1971	The Child Development Associate (CDA) was created as part of the U.S. Department of Health, Education, and Welfare. In 1985 NAEYC became the administrator of the CDA Credential. Then, in 1989, the Council for Professional Recognition, as a separate organization, assumed the responsibility for the CDA Credential (NAEYC, 2001).
1973	The Children's Defense Fund in Washington, D.C., was founded by Marian Wright Edelman. Currently, their website gives early childhood professionals, advocates, families, and every member of our society essential information that can make a difference in children's lives (Children's Defense Fund, 2007).
1975	The Education for All Handicapped Children Act was passed by Congress. In 1997, this Act was reauthorized and strengthened to include early childhood services. It is now known as the Individuals with Disabilities Education Act (IDEA). (More information on this act can be found in Chapter 2 of this text.)
1982	The National Association for Family Day Care was established. As the profession of family child care changed, so did the focus of this organization. In 1994, it became the National Association of Family Child Care (NAFCC), with the goal of providing assistance for developing leadership, professionalism, and quality for family child care providers. NAFCC has published Quality Standards for NAFCC Accreditation. (NAFCC, 2007).
1984	NAEYC publishes a report entitled "Developmentally Appropriate Practices" which outlines what is meant by "quality" work with young children, infancy through age eight (Gordon & Browne, 2007).
1992	The Association of Childhood Education International (ACEI) celebrated its centennial, having begun as the International Kindergarten Union in 1892 in Saratoga Springs, N.Y. ACEI is now the oldest professional association of its type in the United States with members in over 40 countries(ACEI, 2007).
2000s	In the last part of the 20th century Reggio Emilia, an educational approach established in Italy in 1946, has influenced early childhood thinking around the world (Essa, 2007; Gordon & Browne, 2007). More information about this curriculum model can be found in Chapter 2 of this text.
2001	The No Child Left Behind Act of 2001, signed into law on January 8, 2002, has placed far more emphasis than ever before on program accountability and assessment. At the core of the NCLB Act are a number or measures designed to drive broad gains in student achievement and to hold states and schools more accountable for student progress in grades 3-8 (Essa, 2007; U.S. Department of Education, 2001).

FIGURE 1–1
Timeline of Historical Highlights.

Advocacy takes place at many different levels—from families who approach their child's teacher or program director to ask for an arts program, to teachers who approach the school board to request additional funding for books to help their students meet rigorous academic standards, to groups of business leaders who form coalitions with early childhood caregivers, to professional associations who create opportunities to educate policymakers about a particular problem that young children face. At all levels of advocacy, caring adults take a stand on behalf of children. (Robinson & Stark, 2002)

It is also essential for teachers to use every resource available to them, such as having membership in local, state, and national professional organizations. Attending meetings, workshops, and conferences offers opportunities for networking with other teachers. Reading professional journals keeps one up-to-date with current information as well. (See Appendix C for a comprehensive listing of professional organizations and their Web sites.)

Learning and Developmental Theories of Early Childhood Education

developmental theories
Principles that examine children's growth, behavior, and process of learning.

theory
A systematic statement of principles and beliefs that are created to explain a group of facts that have been repeatedly tested or widely accepted.

As we continue to consider the influences that have contributed to the field of early childhood education, it is beneficial to review the **developmental theories** that examine children's growth, behavior, and process of learning. A **theory** refers to a systematic statement of principles and beliefs created to explain a phenomenon or group of facts that have been repeatedly tested or are widely accepted. "The foundation for all curricula is developmental theory or beliefs about how children develop and learn. These beliefs guide our view of teaching and supporting children as learners" (Catron & Allen, 2003).

The following are a few of the most influential theories and the individuals who developed them.

PSYCHOSOCIAL THEORY. *Erik Erikson* (1902–1994), over five decades, made significant contributions to psychoanalysis, personality theory, education practice, and social anthropology.

Erikson recognized growth and development to be continuous throughout an individual's life. His eight **psychosocial** stages describe the interaction between an individual's social-emotional condition and the interpersonal environment. His stages of development help us understand the importance of allowing children to play out their feelings in an environment of acceptance. The first four stages are relevant to early childhood educators.

Erik Erikson

psychosocial
Erikson's eight stages that describe the interaction between an individual's social-emotional condition and the interpersonal environment.

1. *Basic Trust vs. Mistrust* (birth to 1 year). This developmental stage is important to an infant's learning that people can be depended upon and that the child can depend upon himself. Love and acceptance are important for the child to learn that the world is a safe place in which to live. This foundation of trust will be developed if the infant's needs are met. This is observable when the infant babbles, coos, laughs, crawls, pulls up, and is comfortable with the environment.
2. *Autonomy vs. Shame and Doubt* (second year). This stage helps a child develop a basic sense of self-control and independence. The child is growing rapidly. It is significant during this stage that the toddler has opportunities to do things for himself. This is observable when a toddler feeds and dresses himself, and generally has an "I can do it myself" attitude that is accepted and reinforced by the adults in his life. Putting on and taking off "dress-up" clothes also demonstrates this.
3. *Initiative vs. Guilt* (3 to 5 years). During this stage of life, children are becoming interested in exploring and are ready to learn. Children need to express their natural curiosity and creativity through opportunities in the environment. This stage of development is observable by watching how children demonstrate body control and motor skills while riding a tricycle and running. Initiative is reinforced when

children are given freedom to engage in fantasy and other dramatic play activities. Social roles in dramatic play continue to show children identifying with adult roles. They enjoy making adult situations conform to their notion of the ways things are. Roles can be reversed and new roles can be tried out.

4. *Industry vs. Inferiority* (6 to 11 years). At this stage of life, the child is ready for challenges of new and exciting ideas. The child needs opportunities for accomplishment in physical, intellectual, and social development. This is observable by watching older children during creative dramatics activities. They improvise their own dialogue, play the scenes, and evaluate the results. This is informal and demonstrates individual and group imagination, problem solving, critical thinking, and cooperation with others.

The last four of Erikson's psychosocial stages follow the individual from the teenage years through the rest of the life span.

5. *Identity vs. Role Diffusion* (12 to 18 years).
6. *Intimacy vs. Isolation* (young adulthood).
7. *Generative vs. Stagnation* (adult middle years).
8. *Ego Integrity vs. Despair* (older years). (Erikson, 1963)

> *Erik Erikson's work and wisdom have profoundly shaped the field of child development. What comes through most strongly in Erikson's work is his empathy and respect for children— and for their parents and the societies in which they live. . . . Erikson's work has more than withstood the test of time; it continues to inform and inspire the fields of child development, life-span studies, anthropology, history, sociology, and others. (Stott, 1994)*

COGNITIVE DEVELOPMENT THEORY. Cognitive development is described as the intellectual acquisition of information, facts, or data and includes reasoning, understanding, problem solving, and language acquisition. Much of what is known about cognitive development has come from the work of *Jean Piaget* (1896–1980). He introduced the study of children's thinking and was the first to describe how each child creates his own mental image of the world, based on his encounters with the environment. "Piaget suggested that a child's system of thought develops through a series of stages common to all children of all cultures" (Spodek & Saracho, 1994).

A careful consideration of Piaget's concepts, along with close observation of children, helps teachers provide appropriate environments and experiences. Piaget believed that **learning,** or change in behavior, occurs as children construct knowledge through active *exploration* and *discovery* in their physical and social environments. He also asserted that learning happens through the dual process of assimilation and accommodation. **Assimilation** is a process that occurs when a child handles, sees, or otherwise experiences something. (See Figure 1–2.) He adds this information to existing schemata. A **schema** (plural, *schemata*) is an integrated way of thinking or mental images. "We constantly create, refine, change, modify, organize, and reorganize our schemata" (Essa, 2007). **Accommodation** occurs when a schema is modified as a result of experience. (See Figure 1–3.) **Equilibrium** happens when there is a balance between assimilation and accommodation. According to Piaget, this continues until new information causes the process to begin again (Piaget, 1926).

Cognitive development is divided into four stages by Piaget:

1. *Sensorimotor stage* (birth to about 2 years). During this time children grow from helpless newborns to children who are able to walk and talk. Infants begin learning through the use of their sensory system and reflexes. Gradually these reflex behaviors are changed and new behaviors develop. Babies enjoy repeating behaviors. Often something unexpected happens during repetitions and a new behavior is discovered. They then try to repeat the new behavior. Throughout the sensorimotor

---

cognitive development

The mental process that focuses on how children's intelligence, thinking abilities, and language acquisition emerge through distinct ages; Piaget's study of children's thinking, involving creating their own mental image of the world, based on encounters with the environment.

learning

Change in behavior or cognition that occurs as children construct knowledge through active exploration and discovery in their physical and social environments.

assimilation

Piaget's process of cognitive development, which occurs when a child handles, sees, or otherwise experiences something.

Jean Piaget

schema

An integrated way of thinking or of forming mental images.

accommodation

Piaget's theory of modification of existing cognitive information. Cognitive schemes are changed to accommodate new experiences or information.

equilibrium

A balance of one's cognitive schemes and information gathered from the environment; assimilation and accommodation.

FIGURE 1–2
Example of Piaget's concept of assimilation.

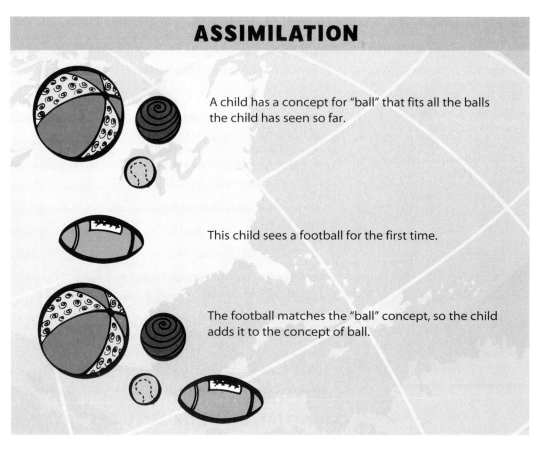

ASSIMILATION

A child has a concept for "ball" that fits all the balls the child has seen so far.

This child sees a football for the first time.

The football matches the "ball" concept, so the child adds it to the concept of ball.

FIGURE 1–3
Example of Piaget's concept of accommodation.

ACCOMODATION

A child has a concept for "dog" that includes all animals with four legs.

This child sees a cat for the first time and calls it a "dog." When the child realizes the cat does not fit "dog," he may create a new category for "cat."

As the child matures, the process of accommodation will enable him to create a super-concept, or a broader category, which would include both the cat and the dog–such as "animal."

object permanence

A mature state of perceptual development. According to Piaget's theory, a baby thinks that objects, including people, cease to exist the moment he stops seeing them. An older child starts to search for the missing object or person.

egocentric

Individuals that think about the world only in relation to themselves.

symbolic thinking

Symbols or mental representations are formed, allowing children to solve problems by thinking before acting.

stage, infants are developing the concept of **object permanence.** According to Piaget's theory, a baby thinks that objects, including people, cease to exist the moment he stops seeing them. For example, if an object that has left returns, the infant considers it a new, though identical, object.

2. *Preoperational stage* (about 2 to 7 years). Piaget believed that children's thinking during this stage is **egocentric,** that is, they think about the world only in relation to themselves. Along with this, the preoperational period is characterized by **symbolic thinking.** Symbols or mental representations are formed, allowing children to solve problems by thinking before acting. They begin to enjoy pretend play. As thinking emerges as verbal expression, language acquisition proceeds rapidly. Intellectual and language development blend together. The more a child uses all his senses and broadens his experiences, the more he has to think and talk about.

3. *Concrete Operations stage* (about 7 to 12 years). During this stage children are developing concepts of number, relationships, and processes, as well as thinking problems through mentally. Logical thought requires actual physical objects or events. Piaget explains,

Manipulation of materials is crucial. In order to think, children in the concrete stage need to have objects in front of them that are easy to handle, or else be able to visualize objects that have been handled and that are easily imagined without any real effort.

Teachers should select materials that make the child become conscious of a problem and look for the solution himself. And, if he generalizes too broadly, then provide additional materials where counter-examples will guide him to see where he must refine his solution. It's the materials he should learn from. (Piaget, 1961)

4. *Formal Operations stage* (12 years through adulthood). The individual reasons logically and moves from concrete manipulations to abstract thinking. The ability to hypothesize and think about what might be rather than what is usually occurs during this stage.

Each of these stages involves a period of formation and a period of attainment. Each builds on the development of the preceding stage. Teachers and parents should provide appropriate environments and ask appropriate questions, moving from simple to complex and from concrete to abstract.

For exploration of other Piagetian concepts, see the section on play in this chapter and Chapter 5, "Math."

SOCIOCULTURAL THEORY. Over the past decade, the educational theories of Russian developmental psychologist *Lev Vygotsky* (1896–1934) have been translated and made available in the United States. Vygotsky asserted that a child's learning development is affected by his culture, including the culture of family environment. He focused on the whole child and incorporated ideas of culture and values into child development, particularly the development of language and self-identity. "Because Vygotsky regarded language as a critical bridge between the sociocultural world and individual mental functioning, he viewed the acquisition of language as the most significant milestone in children's cognitive development" (Berk & Winsler, 1995). It is from language that the child constructs reality.

Much of what a child learns comes from the culture around him. In addition, interactions with teachers, parents, and more experienced peers contribute significantly to a child's intellectual development. Vygotsky believed that a difference exists between what a child can do on his own and what he can do with help. Vygotsky called this difference the **zone of proximal development.** In other words, the "zone" is the range of potential each child has for learning, with that learning being shaped by the social environment in which it takes place. This potential ability is greater than the actual ability of the individual when the learning is facilitated by someone with greater expertise (Wertsch, 1991).

Lev Vygotsky

zone of proximal development

The range of potential each child has for learning, with that learning being shaped by the social environment in which it takes place.

According to Vygotsky (1978), "[C]hildren first develop lower mental functions such as simple perceptions, associative learning, and involuntary attention. Through social interactions with more knowledgeable others, such as more advanced peers and adults, children eventually develop higher mental functions such as language, logic, problem-solving skills, moral reasoning, and memory schemas."

For teachers of young children, the zone of proximal development may be used to provide a theoretical base from which to understand cooperative learning. In the culture of the classroom, this can translate into small-group instruction in which students work together to solve problems. This approach encourages children to *construct* their own knowledge while engaging in activities that build and rebuild, or construct, ideas based on previous experiences. In addition, the role of the teacher "includes both designing an educative environment and collaborating with children by scaffolding their efforts to master new skills. From this perspective, Vygotsky-based teaching is *activity centered,* since it emphasizes creating opportunities for children to engage in culturally meaningful opportunities with the guidance of teachers and peers" (Berk & Winsler, 1995). This kind of teaching emphasizes **scaffolding,** which occurs as the teacher (adult) continually adjusts the level of help offered in response to the child's level of performance. Scaffolding can help instill the skills necessary for independent problem solving in the future.

For exploration of another major Vygotskian concept, see the section on play in this chapter.

MULTIPLE INTELLIGENCES THEORY. *Howard Gardner (1943–   ),* a psychologist and professor at Harvard Graduate School of Education, is also a researcher who has studied the mind and brain with particular reference to learning and education. He has challenged the view that something called "intelligence" can be objectively measured and reduced to a single number or "IQ" score. In fact, Gardner's definition of intelligence is multifaceted. His ongoing research, Project Zero, at Harvard suggests that an individual is not born with all of the intelligence he will ever have. Rather, intelligence can be learned and improved upon throughout a lifetime.

Gardner identifies his cross-cultural exploration of the ways individuals are intelligent as **multiple intelligences.** His philosophy also proposes that one form of intelligence is not better than another; all are equally valuable and viable. Gardner's theory also suggests that "each child not only learns quite differently, but possesses varying amounts of strengths in the eight identified intelligences" (Miller, 2002).

The following explanations of Gardner's Multiple Intelligences are adapted from Gardner (1983, 1993), Hine (1996), Nicholson-Nelson (1998), and Wilkins (1996).

1. *Verbal-Linguistic Intelligence:* From the babbling of infancy to the toddler's simple sentences, the ability to use language and words continues to grow throughout early childhood. Whether written or spoken, it develops with sensitivity to the order and rhythm of words. The learning environment should include a language- and print-rich classroom with opportunities for reading, writing, speaking, and creative writing. Children who are accomplished in verbal-linguistic abilities enjoy reading, writing, telling stories, playing word games, and communicating effectively.

2. *Logical-Mathematical Intelligence:* Starting with babies inspecting their world to the recognition of similar characteristics of objects by toddlers, the ability to categorize and to use numbers, patterns, sequencing, and cause and effect to solve problems continues to develop and grow throughout early childhood. The learning environment should offer opportunities to relate math and science to real life situations while providing activities that make math and problem solving fun, relevant, and challenging. Children who are adept in logical-mathematical abilities learn through asking questions in a logical manner, making connections between pieces of information, exploring, and developing strong problem-solving and reasoning skills.

scaffolding
The adjustable support the teacher offers in response to the child's level of performance.

Howard Gardner

multiple intelligences
Gardner's theory, which proposes that one form of intelligence is not better than another; all eight are equally valuable and viable.

Creating visual images with shape, color, and form opens up new understanding for young children.

3. *Musical-Rhythmic Intelligence:* Starting with the prenatal awareness of noises and rhythms and, later, imitations of sounds and pitches, a child soon develops the ability to produce and recognize simple and then complex songs and to perceive pitch, tone, and rhythmic pattern. He becomes immersed in the music and sounds of the world. The learning environment should provide opportunities for singing, listening, movement activities, sound awareness, and musical instrument appreciation and practice, while emphasizing cultural awareness through music. Children who are strong in musical-rhythmic abilities think in rhythms and melodies; enjoy listening to music, singing, dancing, humming, and playing musical instruments; and exhibit a sensitivity to environmental sounds.

4. *Visual-Spatial Intelligence:* From the infant's ability to discriminate among the faces around him to the toddler's first steps, the facility to perceive the visual world with a great deal of understanding continues throughout early childhood. Creating visual images with shape, color, and form opens up new understanding. The learning environment should be a graphic-rich classroom that encourages opportunities for visual processing as well as thinking and planning in three dimensions. Children who are highly capable in visual-spatial abilities think in images and pictures; like to draw, design, and create things; and often see things from different points of view.

5. *Bodily-Kinesthetic Intelligence:* From an infant's looking for and grasping different objects to the strength and coordination of an older child, the ability to use the body for self-expression develops through information gained from muscles, sensations, reflexes, coordination, and movement. The learning environment should reflect opportunities for physical challenges throughout the day, not just outdoors but indoors as well. The classroom should facilitate tactile experiences and the use of manipulatives in math, science, and language arts. Children who are resourceful in bodily-kinesthetic abilities learn through moving, doing, and touching. They enjoy physical activities, such as those involving hand-eye coordination and hands-on experiments.

6. *Interpersonal Intelligence:* From an infant's bonding with his parents to the meaningful relationships with others outside the family, the ability to understand other people and their actions, moods, and feelings develops as young children deal with person-to-person relationships and communication. The learning environment should provide opportunities for children to relate to others by cooperatively

participating, sharing, negotiating, and communicating in groups or with individuals. Children who show interpersonal abilities learn through listening, cooperating in shared projects, demonstrating leadership skills, seeing things from other perspectives, and organizing and negotiating group activities.

7. *Intrapersonal Intelligence:* Starting with a baby's realization that he is a separate person from his mother, his ability to understand himself grows throughout early childhood and at the same time helps him to identify his feelings, moods, strengths, and weaknesses. The learning environment provides plenty of space and time for self-reflection and working alone in a safe environment that encourages appropriate risk taking. Children who are accomplished in intrapersonal abilities learn through understanding their role in relationship to others, have a strong sense of self, and enjoy setting goals, planning, and working on self-paced projects, all of which involve having choices.

8. *Naturalist Intelligence:* A child's interest in seeing, smelling, and touching a flower, reacting to the sound of a bird, or playing with the family pet demonstrates his ability to recognize important distinctions in the natural world. The learning environment should offer opportunities for exploring outdoors and bringing the outdoors inside by providing field trips, books, visuals, objects, and materials relating to the natural world. Children who show naturalist abilities learn through observing nature, being sensitive to all features of the natural world, and enjoying books, visuals, and objects related to the world around them.

The Multiple Intelligences theory is a useful model for developing a systematic approach to nurturing and teaching children and honoring their individual needs and strengths within a classroom setting. As teachers of young children "we should help students to understand the world around them—the physical world, the biological world, the social world, the world of personal experiences" (Gardner, 2001).

The concept of multiple intelligences does not require discarding previous ideas. Teachers can supplement current appropriate activities with new ideas that will reach even more of their students. In fact, Gardner contends that teachers need to guide students into using their combination of intelligences to help them learn whatever they want to learn, as well as what teachers and society believe they have to learn.

The multiple intelligences approach provides a framework for us to identify how children learn to build on their strongest assets, to help them become more intelligent by exposing them to a variety of ways of learning, to better individualize for their interests and needs, and to use teaching strategies that make learning more appropriate, successful, and enjoyable for all children. Examples of using Gardner's Multiple Intelligences theory in the classroom can be found in the curriculum content chapters of this book. For further application of this and other theories, see the curriculum models and programs in Chapter 2.

early childhood education

The curriculum, programs, and settings that serve young children, from birth through the eighth year of life.

developmentally appropriate practice

The curriculum planning philosophy expressed by NAEYC that recognizes that each child learns and develops differently in physical, intellectual, cultural, emotional, and social growth.

DEVELOPMENTALLY APPROPRIATE PRACTICE

 Early childhood education refers to the programs and settings that serve young children from birth through the eighth year of life (Bredekamp & Copple, 1997). Children receiving early education may attend drop-in, half-day, full-day, before- and after-school programs, kindergarten, and primary classrooms that are publicly or privately funded in family child care homes, churches, child care centers, schools, and other community settings.

During these important years of birth to age eight, a child's physical, intellectual, emotional, and social growth should be supported within the home, child care facility, school, and community. Each child learns and develops differently. The philosophy of **developmentally appropriate practice** promotes this thinking and is identified by the National Association for the Education of Young Children (NAEYC) as

In a developmentally appropriate environment, teachers develop relationships with children that are consistent and supportive.

Children's eagerness to learn about the world and their place in it should be nurtured by a supportive environment and teachers who understand their development.

development
Systematic and adaptive changes in the body and mind.

the outcome of a process of teacher decision making that draws on at least three critical, interrelated bodies of knowledge: (1) what teachers know about how children develop and learn; (2) what teachers know about the individual children in their groups; and (3) knowledge of the social and cultural context in which those children live and learn. (Bredekamp & Copple, 1997)

Developmentally appropriate early education recognizes the social nature of learning, and it values cultural and linguistic diversity. Also included is the understanding that children need an environment that allows them to interact at their own level of development with a minimum amount of adult direction. A strong emphasis is placed on children learning to think critically, work together cooperatively, and solve problems. Because developmentally appropriate classrooms are not only age/stage appropriate but also individually appropriate, they will not all look alike. In order to enhance the quality of educational experiences for young children, developmentally appropriate practice is a framework for continuing to meet the diverse needs of all the children in our care. Kostelnik, Soderman, and Whirien (1999) explain, "The essence of developmental appropriateness is not simply what we do, but how we think—how we think about children and programs; what we value children doing and learning; how we define effectiveness and success." Throughout this book, developmentally appropriate practice will be discussed in relation to chapter content.

Child Development and Learning

 First, let us focus on what is developmentally occurring with young children, the variations in their development, and their developmental process for learning. **Development,** in relationship to early childhood education, can be defined as systematic and adaptive changes in the body and mind based on sequence and patterns of growth and maturity (Charlesworth, 2004; Watson, Watson, & Wilson, 2003). "Developmental trends occur in a similar fashion for all children. This does not, however, imply uniformity. On the contrary, individual differences due to genetic and experiential variations and differing cultural and social contexts have strong influences on development" (Bowman, Donovan, & Burns, 2000).

Infants are actively involved with their world.

As we think about development and learning, it's important to remember that the areas of physical, intellectual, emotional, and social growth may overlap, even as age-groups may.

Some children will exhibit certain characteristics and behaviors at earlier ages than their peers; others will take longer to acquire a given set of skills and concepts. . . . It is through close observation and interaction with the individual children in their classroom that skilled teachers assess where children are and so know how to best guide them (Copple & Bredekamp, 2006).

INFANTS. The early months of infancy are crucial in creating a foundation for all areas of development. Infants are actively involved with their world. They explore with all their senses (seeing, hearing, tasting, smelling, and feeling) and are acutely aware of their environment. "Their sense of belonging and ability to understand their world grow when there is continuity between the home and child care setting" (Bredekamp & Copple, 1997). Infants and the significant adults in their lives establish very special relationships that involve getting to know each other and adjusting to each other. What adults do can modify how infants behave (Watson, Watson, & Wilson, 2003).

Infants learn about their surroundings by physically moving around, through sensory exploration, and by social interaction. Gallagher (2005) continues this thought, "A typically developing child needs frequent opportunities for movement and interactions with people and objects. Fixed pieces of equipment such as playpens, high chairs, and bouncy seats provide little opportunities for varied and active experiences." As they are learning, the sight of the adult who feeds, holds, and comforts the infant is reinforced when that adult shows pleasure in caring for the infant. Emotional attachment develops as the child learns to expect that special person to make him feel good. The infant then seeks more contact with that adult. Even after crawling and walking have begun, the child frequently asks to be held. Honig (2002) explains further, "Research and clinical findings over the past decades confirm the connection to later emotional well-being of a secure attachment between each baby or young child and a warm, stable adult."

A happy moment between baby and caregiver — just look at those faces!

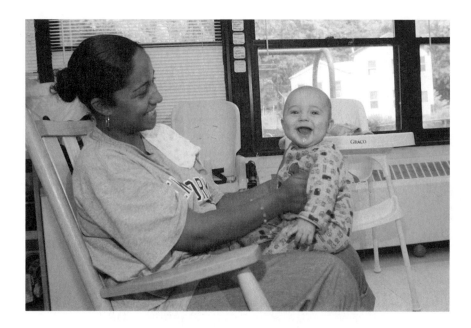

As teachers of the youngest children, we have a significant responsibility to the infants in our care. Decades of research by neuroscientists and others have found what we in early childhood education have been saying for years, namely, that a child's foundation for behavior and learning for the rest of his life is laid in the early years. The better the child's early nurturing, the better are his prospects for future development (Gabbard & Rodrigues, 2002).

Although it has been known for many years that most of a child's brain *cells* are formed in the prenatal stage, the brain is not completely developed at birth. Research indicates that important *neural (nerve) connections,* transferring information from one part of the body to another, occur and strengthen after birth. Further, by age three the child's brain is 90 percent adult size, and his experiences and nurturing—or the lack thereof—have shaped the basis for how he will function emotionally, intellectually, and socially for the rest of his life (Perry, 2002a; Zero to Three, 2002). Research continues to refine scientists' insight into brain development, such as "understanding of developmental periods of dramatic brain growth, information about regions of brain growth, and details on brain functions. We know that the brain has growth spurts during certain times of development, such as early childhood and adolescence" (Schore, cited in Gallaghter, 2005).

An important aspect of a young child's continued mental development is **self-regulation,** his growing natural ability to exercise control over physical and emotional needs in the face of changing circumstances. Shankoff & Phillips (cited in Gillespie & Seibel, 2006) believe that "the growth of self-regulation is a cornerstone of early childhood development and is visible in all areas of behavior." For example, by using consistent routines with infants, you are helping young children learn to self-regulate within the structure of a nurturing environment.

All of this, along with new and continuing exploration of brain function, from birth through the first 10 years of life, helps us understand more about the relationship between *nature* and *nurture.* "How humans develop and learn depends critically and continually on the interplay between nature (an individual's genetic endowment) and nurture (the nutrition, surroundings, care, stimulation, and teaching that are provided or withheld). Both are crucial" (Shore, 1997).

TODDLERS. Children in their second year of life grow and learn rapidly. "The toddler is a dynamo full of unlimited energy, enthusiasm, and curiosity. . . . The toddler begins this period with the limited abilities of an infant and ends with the relatively sophisticated skills of a young child" (Allen & Marotz, 2003). This is a time for development in mobility, autonomy, and **self-help skills,** the child learning what can be done for himself by his own effort or ability, such as washing and drying hands, and feeding or dressing himself. "Perhaps one of the best ways to nurture good feelings about self is to encourage toddlers' already strong interest in doing things for themselves" (Gestwicki, 2007). They try many tasks that are often too difficult for them. At this time, the safety of the environment is critical. As a teacher, you should expect this newfound independence and allow for trial and error. Children love to repeat and use these new skills over and over again (Essa, 2007).

As these active children become more independent, "their speech is limited, but their understanding of communication is beyond their speech. . . . Toddlers learn a great deal through imitation and especially from observing demonstrations accompanied by a verbal explanation" (Charlesworth, 2008). Chapter 3 emphasizes language and literacy development.

Appropriate teaching techniques require the building of trust between the children and the teacher, and between the children and their environment. This can develop only if there are safe, consistent, and child-centered surroundings that encourage success for both children and teacher. Further information on developmentally appropriate learning environments is continued in Chapter 2.

self-regulation

A child's natural ability to exercise control over physical and emotional behavior in the face of changing circumstances.

self-help skills

In early childhood, a child's ability to care of oneself, such as dressing, feeding, and toileting.

This is a time for rapid development as a toddler learns self-help skills.

Young children are full of enthusiasm and high energy.

THREE-, FOUR-, AND FIVE-YEAR-OLDS. Three-year-olds have a distinct period of development with added skills and challenges. They are anxious to try new things but get frustrated when they cannot do what they set out to do. With an enlarged vocabulary, they engage in more extensive conversations; and although they can play along with other children, they often find it difficult to cooperate in a game. The three-year-old enjoys fantasy and imaginative play, although the difference between fantasy and reality is not always clear.

Generally, the child's interest has become more sustained, but repetition is still important. He begins to enjoy looking at picture and story books, and has a better understanding of verbal cues. There is a continued need for exploration and experimentation. Teachers of three-year-olds need to respect their growing skills and competencies without forgetting just how recently they were acquired.

Four-year-olds are full of enthusiasm and high energy. The ability to do more things without help, along with increased large and small muscle control, allows the children to develop a greater self-confidence. Children of this age enjoy learning to do new things and like to have an adult's attention. At the same time, because they are so eager to learn and learn so fast, they can use a higher level of language (more and bigger words) than they really understand.

The four-year-old has broader and more diverse interests. He begins to understand his environment and benefits from field trips. His interest in others prompts him to ask searching questions about people and their relationships with others. He is interested in the letter carrier, the firefighter, the police officer, and everyone around him who performs various services.

The child is conscious of make-believe and begins to "be" other people or animals. He gradually builds a background for imaginative play. Essa (2007) explains, "Peers are becoming important. Play is a social activity more often than not, although fours enjoy solitary activities at times as well." As a teacher, when you interact with these active children, you will be bombarded with questions. Sometimes they will insist on trying to do things that are too difficult for them. Help them find many things that they *can do*. Observe the children and set up the environment to match their skills. More information on play is provided later in this chapter.

Five-year-olds are becoming more social; they have best friends and also enjoy playing with small groups of children. Their use of language, especially vocabulary, continues to grow along with the understanding that words can have several meanings. Experimentation with language is evident at this age.

Fives are more self-controlled, but family and teacher have the most influence on how they behave. They take responsibility very seriously and can accept suggestions and initiate action. With the increase of large and small muscle abilities, five-year-olds can run, jump, catch, throw, and use scissors, crayons, and markers easily.

Exploration of the environment is important to these children. They are learning about the world and their place in it. They act on their own and construct their own meaning. Each of their actions and interpretations is unique to them. They are developing an understanding of rules, limits, and cause and effect. The teacher's role is to allow all this to happen, while at the same time creating the appropriate environment, encouraging curiosity, and learning along with the children. With the current emphasis on expecting the five-year-old to enter kindergarten "ready to learn to read by the end of the year," kindergarten must not be turned into first grade. Instead, it "has to be a place for *every* child to grow and learn, in every dimension of development" (Graue, cited in Gullo, 2006).

SIX-, SEVEN-, AND EIGHT-YEAR-OLDS. The body growth of six-to-eight-year-olds is slower but steadier, and physical strength and ability are important to them. Their motor coordination begins to improve and playing games that require eye-hand coordination, such as baseball, becomes easier at this age. These children are able to think and learn in more complicated ways, both logically and systematically. They are developing the ability to concentrate their attention for longer periods of time.

Primary-age children have achieved many of the cognitive skills needed to enjoy playing board games with other children.

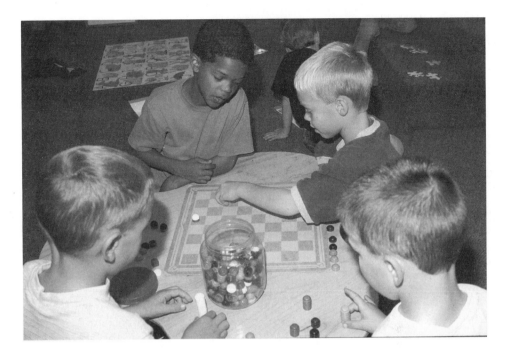

The language and communication development in these primary-grade children is dramatic. They move from oral self-expression to written self-expression. "During these years, children's receptive vocabulary increases not just by listening but by reading, and their expressive vocabulary expands from spoken to written communication" (Bredekamp & Copple, 1997). They are becoming more independent and have strong feelings about what they eat, wear, and do. The six-to-eights are extremely curious about their world, and they actively look for new things to do, see, and explore. They are making new friends, and these peers play a significant role in their lives as they take into consideration the viewpoints and needs of others.

Seefeldt and Barbour (1998) tell us, "They're developing the ability to see things from another perspective and are able to be more emphatic. At the same time, they're very sensitive and their feelings get hurt easily." As these primary-age children try out their new independence, they need teachers' and parents' guidance, affection, encouragement, and protection as much as, if not more than, ever.

Along with the home, church, and community, primary-grade schools and school-age care programs are among the key settings in which children's character is shaped. Therefore, the primary-grade years are an important time not only to support children's intellectual development but also to help them develop the ability to work collaboratively with peers; express tolerance, empathy, and caring for other people; function responsibly; and gain positive dispositions toward learning, such as curiosity, initiative, persistence, risk taking, and self-regulation. (Bredekamp and Copple, 1997)

Note: The additional references, readings, and resources listed at the end of this chapter offer additional in-depth information on the developmental process.

Individual Strengths, Interests, and Needs

Now let us examine individual appropriateness, which involves adapting an early childhood environment to meet a child's cultural and linguistic needs, as well as his individual strengths and interests. This includes providing each child with the time, opportunities, and resources to achieve individual goals of early education.

The teacher should support a positive sense of self-identity in each child. It is important for a teacher to provide many opportunities for teacher-child interaction. However, individual appropriateness should not result in the lowering of expectations.

It is important to include opportunities for interacting with the child's family as well. Communication between home and school offers consistent and beneficial experiences for young children and their families.
Gestwicki (2007) says it clearly:

> *Developmentally appropriate practice does not approach children as if they were equal members of an age grouping, but as unique individuals. . . . This knowledge [of specific uniqueness] primarily comes through relating and interacting with children and also their parents, who are important resources of knowledge about their children. Developmentally appropriate practice is based on parents' active involvement both as resources of knowledge and as decision makers about what is developmentally appropriate for their children.*

Including parents in the program will encourage their support and provide you more insight into their child. Communication with family members is discussed throughout this book. Suggestions on how teachers can work in partnership with families and communities are discussed later in this chapter.

By observing young children, gathering data about who they are, and developing awareness of their strengths, interests, and needs, you are starting to build a child-centered curriculum. You will discover that children benefit from being treated as individuals while being part of a class community. For curriculum and environments to be developmentally appropriate, they must be individually appropriate. Observation, assessment, and evaluation of curriculum and environments will be studied in the ensuing chapters of this book.

Social and Cultural Contexts

 Early childhood educators recognize the importance of cultural context in the development and learning of young children. Growing up as members of a family and community, children learn the rules of their culture—explicitly through direct teaching and implicitly through the behavior of those around them (Bredekamp & Copple, 1997). "Rules of development are the same for all children, but social contexts shape children's development into different configurations" (Bowman, 1994). To affirm these differences and similarities, an early education environment should encourage the exploration of gender, racial, and cultural identity, developmental abilities, and disabilities. To eliminate **bias**—any attitude, belief, or feeling that results in unfair treatment of an individual—and to create an **anti-bias** atmosphere, you need to actively challenge prejudice and stereotyping. **Prejudice** is an attitude, opinion, or idea that is preconceived or decided, usually unfavorably. **Stereotype** is an oversimplified generalization about a particular group, race, or sex, often with negative implications (Derman-Sparks & A.B.C. Task Force, 1989).

Children with learning, behavioral, or physical disabilities should be included in early childhood classrooms for at least a part of the day. "Just as knowledge of individual variation must be used in making decisions about typically developing children, so too must knowledge of typical child development be used in providing services for children with disabilities or developmental delays" (Bredekamp & Copple, 1997). (Multicultural/anti-bias and special needs considerations are discussed more fully in Chapter 2.)

Individual appropriateness requires the teacher/adult to try to put herself in the place of the child in the classroom. It means asking questions, such as:

⊕ What would make the environment comfortable for infants, toddlers, preschoolers, early school-age children, or children with ability differences?

---

bias

Any attitude, belief, or feeling that results in unfair treatment of an individual or group of individuals.

anti-bias

An attitude that actively challenges prejudice, stereotyping, and unfair treatment of an individual or group of individuals.

prejudice

An attitude, opinion, or idea that is preconceived or decided, usually unfavorably.

stereotype

An oversimplified generalization about a particular group, race, or sex, often with negative implications.

🌐 What kind of adult support would be appropriate?

🌐 What is planned to encourage parent participation?

🌐 What is being done to develop a child's sense of trust, sense of self, and feeling of control over the environment?

🌐 What should be happening to encourage positive self-concept development?

🌐 What would I see if I were at the child's level?

🌐 What kind of activities, supplies, and materials should be available?

🌐 What is occurring to support a child's need for privacy or "alone time"?

In answering these questions, take into account what is known about how young children develop and learn, and match that to the content and strategies they encounter in early education programs. Being reflective and carefully listening to what children have to say is also important. As we continue through this book, the activities discussed in all curriculum areas will be developmentally appropriate with an emphasis on meeting the needs of *all* children.

A child *needs* to be appreciated by the teacher and other significant adults. He needs to experience an environment that reflects back to the child an awareness of and appreciation for his individual and cultural differences. The results of these positive influences will stay with the child for a lifetime.

Creative Appropriateness

 Creativity is the process of doing, of bringing something new and imaginative into being. "Creativity is a combination of motivation, openness/flexibility, curiosity and autonomy as well as divergent thinking" (Mitchell, 2006).

Many times we hear people say that adults have to be retaught to be imaginative. Some ask why creativity dims with age. Others believe that the years between two and six are the crucial ones in which creativity develops and, if not cultivated then, is very hard to rekindle later in life. By encouraging their creativity when they are children, we can help them become adults who can solve problems creatively. "In reality everyone is creative in one way or another. No one is uncreative" (Mayesky, 2006).

Isbell and Raines (2007) believe:

> In a rapidly changing world, we must develop programs for young children that include the competencies they will need now and in the future. . . . The creative arts provide an avenue for learning and experiencing that is uniquely different. Their inclusion, during the early years of children's lives, establishes a rich foundation that adapts to change, provides joy, and inspires involvement.

For those of us in early education, Gordon and Browne (2008) extend the point of view even further. "The roots of creativity reach into infancy, for it is every individual's unique and creative process to explore and understand the world, searching to answer larger questions 'Who am I? What and where am I?, and Where am I going?'"

We should offer encouragement by providing opportunities for creativity to be expressed and by showing that we genuinely respect its expression. Children need to be in an inspiring environment, one that they help create and interact with. It is important that as teachers we understand the intrinsic quality of creativity. It can be destroyed by a teacher who does not appreciate the creative act or the child who expresses the act.

Mayesky (2006) helps us understand that "Teachers who allow children to go at their own pace and be self-directed in a relaxed atmosphere are fostering creative development. . . . The learning environment must also welcome exploration by elimination of conditions providing stress, and too strict time limits."

creativity

The process of doing, of bringing something new and imaginative into being.

In this text the importance of the *process* is often expressed. As it relates to creativity, the process is crucial. In fact, *the process is more important than the product.* With this in mind, the teacher's role is to:

🌐 Develop an awareness that the process of creative thinking is complex.

🌐 Celebrate and value each child's creativity.

🌐 Understand that there is no right or wrong way of doing things, only possibilities.

🌐 Understand that a child's personal creativity is doing something new, something he has never done before.

🌐 Recognize that all children are creative to some degree, and some children are more creative than others.

🌐 Recognize that some children are more creative in one area than another.

🌐 Provide extended, unhurried time for children to explore and create (creativity does not follow the clock).

🌐 Recognize that creativity may reflect an ability to think divergently or seek multiple solutions rather than a single solution to problems.

🌐 Arrange an appropriate classroom space for children to leave unfinished work to continue the next day.

🌐 Encourage children to engage in creative processing as they manipulate and play with objects, while remembering it may not result in a finished product.

🌐 Introduce children to new materials and techniques.

🌐 Supply extensive, imaginative, wonderful collections of resource materials that might be bought, found, or recycled.

🌐 Help parents to appreciate their child's creative abilities, with or without a finished product.

🌐 Offer encouragement for, and acceptance of, a certain amount of messiness, noise, and freedom.

🌐 Continue to experiment and test alternatives to determine what is best for your children and your classroom situation.

🌐 Understand that creative expression should flow through the entire curriculum.

(Adapted from Edwards & Springate, 1995; Isbell & Raines, 2007; Mayesky, 2006; and Schirrmacher, 2006.)

IMPORTANCE OF PLAY

play
A behavior that is self-motivated, freely chosen, process-oriented, and enjoyable.

DAP   Play is at the core of developmentally appropriate practice. **Play**—a behavior that is self-motivated, freely chosen, process oriented, and enjoyable—is a natural activity for children. It allows them the opportunity to create, invent, discover, and learn about their world. It provides children joy and understanding of themselves and others.

Free, spontaneous, and self-initiated play was once the norm for young children. This is no longer the case. . . . Both parents and early childhood educators, who once encouraged young children to choose their own activities, are being pressured to replace them with adult directed games, sports, and academic instruction. . . . When children have the opportunity to engage in true play, they are learning to consider options and make choices. (Elkind, 2002)

Children coming to early childhood programs and schools today typically have very little time or opportunity to engage in informal play. Jambor in 2000 stated that "This situation is the result of concerns of neighborhood violence, changing family structures, elimination of recess due to academic pressures, increased vehicle traffic, squeezed residential play space, unsafe and unchallenging playgrounds, and an increase in

In exuberant outdoor play there's a lot of learning going on!

sedentary lifestyle brought on by TV, videos, and, most recently, computers." Now we can add video games, iPods, cell phones, and other new devices to the mix.

With less time and opportunity for children to play, it is crucial for those of us in early childhood education to keep focused on what we can do to encourage and support play in our daily programs. As with all aspects of early childhood growth and development, young children go through a series of stages in the development of play. Each new experience offers opportunities for play exploration. Some types of play are characteristic of children at identifiable stages, but children can use many of these stages in varying degrees of sophistication as they get older.

Developmental Stages of Play

Children's observable behaviors that reflect social development and participation in play were first identified by Mildred Parten in 1932. She provided this landmark study that is still considered valid today (Essa, 2007; Gestwicki, 2007; Sluss, 2005). These stages of social play are described as follows.

Unoccupied behavior usually occurs during infancy and early toddlerhood. A child occupies himself by watching anything of momentary interest. Sometimes the child may not appear to be playing at all.

Onlooker play is sometimes observed in young toddlers or in children introduced to new situations. This play focuses on the activity rather than the environment. Onlookers place themselves within speaking distance of the activity. Although passive, they are very alert to the action around them.

Solitary play surfaces first for a toddler. The child actually engages in play activity alone at home but is within "earshot" of mother or another adult. In an early education setting, the child plays independently without regard to what other children are doing.

Parallel play can be observed in the older toddler and young three-year-old. A child this age is playing for the sake of playing. This child is within "earshot" and sight of another child and can be playing with the same toy but in a different way. Parallel play is the early stage of peer interaction, but the focus is on the object rather than another child.

Associative play finds the three- and four-year-old playing with other children in a group, but he drops in and out of play with minimal organization of activity. Two or three children use the same equipment and participate in the same activity, but each in his own way.

Cooperative play is organized for some purpose by the four-year-old and older child. This type of play requires group membership and reflects a child's growing capacity to accept and respond to ideas and actions not originally his own. Group play (social play) is the basis for ongoing relationships with people and requires sharing of things and ideas, organizing games and activities, and making friends. Another aspect of cooperative play is the emphasis on peers and moving away from the importance of adults in the life of a child. The six- to eight-year-old extends cooperative and symbolic play to include detailed planning and rule making. Leadership roles begin to emerge as play becomes serious.

According to Maxim (1997),

The patterns of play enjoyed in infancy develop into new patterns as children grow older and participate in play experiences. But the earlier patterns do not disappear as new behaviors emerge, and the new patterns are not just enhancements of the earlier ones. They bring maturity to children's play as new experiences are encountered.

THEORISTS AND PLAY. Erik Erikson (1963) emphasized the importance of play in helping children to develop cooperative relationships and gain mutual trust. He believed that children develop their "self-esteem and sense of empowerment by allowing them mastery of objects" (Tsao, 2002). Hughes (1999) explains further that Erikson thought "play can also have an ego-building function since it brings about the development of physical and social skills that enhance a child's self-esteem."

practice play or sensorimotor play

The stage in cognitive development during which the young child learns through repetitive sensory and motor play activities.

symbolic play

A type of play that allows the child to transfer objects into symbols (things that represent something else) and images into people, places, and events within his experiences. Symbolic play occurs during Piaget's preoperational stage (two to seven years). Superhero fantasy play is considered a type of symbolic play for a young child.

dramatic play

A type of creative, spontaneous play in which children use their imaginations to create and dramatize pretend characters, actions, or events.

According to the theory of Jean Piaget (1961), play provides opportunities for many types of learning in young children, with emphasis on developing representational language and thought. Piaget calls play during the first two years of life **practice play or sensorimotor play,** the stage in cognitive development during which the young child learns through repetitive sensory and motor play activities. (Smilansky, 1968, also calls this type of play *functional.*) In the beginning of Piaget's preoperational stage around the ages of two to four or five, **symbolic play** or **dramatic play** become observable in a young child by the way he spontaneously uses objects, images, and language. The use of the environment represents what is important to the child at that moment. This type of imaginative play allows the child to imitate realities of people, places, and events within his experiences, such as pretending to sleep while patting the baby doll to sleep, drinking "coffee" from an empty cup, and talking to imaginary friends. These imaginary friends allow children to work through anxieties in times of stress or change. In addition, symbolic play and language give children an outlet to practice new physical and mental activities for dealing with the world, such as practicing acceptable behaviors that they see around them so that they can act appropriately in different situations (Krissansen, 2002; Tsao, 2002). Superhero fantasy play is considered a type of symbolic play for a child. (Chapter 12 discusses dramatic play and creative dramatics for young children in greater depth.)

Piaget's third stage of play, ages five to eleven, is identified as games with rules. The roles of the children are clearly defined, the rules of the game are clear-cut, and behavior imitates reality (Sluss, 2005). With increased maturity, children arrive at a complete understanding of rules both in behavior and thought.

Lev Vygotsky's theory (1978) states that social experiences shape children's way of thinking and that social play offers children a way to interpret the world by focusing on rules that underlie all play activities and social interactions. "Even the simplest imaginative situations created by very young children always proceed in accord with social rules, although these rules are not laid down in advance" (Berk & Winsler, 1995). Vygotsky further states that supportive guidance from adults can "create a scaffold for children's learning, essential for moving children to higher levels of cognitive development" (Isbell & Raines, 2007). Play provides children with important insights into themselves and the communities in which they live.

TIPS FOR TEACHERS

Teachers have a responsibility to help children develop in their use of play. "Research on the brain demonstrates that play is a scaffold for development, a vehicle for increasing neural structures, and a means by which all children practice skills they will need later in life" (Isenberg & Quisenberry, 2002). We also should convey to parents the importance of play in the lives of young children. Play can be a valuable means of gauging a child's developmental progress. This information, in turn, can be communicated to parents. Other teacher responsibilities are to:

🌐 Create a positive and safe place for play.

🌐 Respect and encourage individual differences in play abilities.

🌐 Have patience with children and give them time to learn new play skills.

🌐 Introduce activities and materials appropriate for each child's age and stage of development.

🌐 Take a sincere interest in learning discoveries.

🌐 Provide a play environment that reflects attitudes and values of the surrounding culture.

🌐 Offer appropriate props from a child's culture that will help him make connections as he plays.

Introduce activities and materials appropriate for each child's age and stage of development.

WHY PLAY IS IMPORTANT

Play	inspires	Imagination
Imagination	inspires	Creativity
Creativity	inspires	Exploration
Exploration	inspires	Discovery
Discovery	inspires	Solving Problems
Solving Problems	inspires	New Skills
New Skills	inspires	Self-confidence
Self-confidence	inspires	Sense of Security
Sense of Security	inspires	More Play

🌐 Make available culturally diverse materials for all the children to enjoy and learn from as they play.

🌐 Encourage cooperation.

🌐 Allow children time without scheduled or *externally focused* activity. This offers an opportunity for children to be *internally focused* so that imagination and creativity can take over.

🌐 Take time to listen to children as they play and to observe how each child plays, what he plays with, who he plays with, and what the child *can* do.

The Association for Childhood Education International's (ACEI) position paper, "Play: Essential for All Children," sounds "A Call to Action" (2002). (See Figure 1–4.)

Childhood play has a key role in the development of self and identity. Understanding this, you can help the children in your care develop to their fullest potential. As you continue through the chapters of this text, you will find specific examples of how curriculum planning and implementation influence and strengthen childhood play.

Elkind (cited in Koralek, 2004) explains further:

As teachers of young children, we need to resist the pressures to transform play into work—into academic instruction. We encourage true play by making certain that we offer materials that leave room for the imagination—blocks, paints, paper to be cut and pasted—and that children have sufficient time to innovate with these materials. When we read to young children, we can ask them to make up their own stories or to give a different ending to the story they are hearing…. Most of all we need to adopt a playful attitude that will encourage our children to do the same.

goals

The general overall aims or overview of an early childhood program.

objectives

The specific purposes or teaching techniques that interpret the goals of planning, schedules, and routines. These objectives are designed to meet the physical, intellectual, social, emotional, and creative development of young children.

PROCESS OF PLANNING

Planning and scheduling are important in early education classrooms, including those with infants and toddlers. Detailed information about this process will follow in Chapter 2, but it is important to explore several guidelines at this point.

As teachers of young children, consider the following:

🌐 Long-range planning includes setting up goals and objectives. **Goals** help describe the general overall aims of the program. **Objectives** are more specific and relate to curriculum planning, schedules, and routines. Seefeldt and Barbour (1998) suggest, "The goals you select will be based on the nature of the children you teach, the values and goals of the community in which the children live, and your own values."

FIGURE 1–4
Reprinted with permission of J.P. Isenberg, N. Quisenberry, and the Association for Child-hood Education International. Copyright © 2002, Fall, by the Association.

A CALL TO ACTION

ACEI believes that all educators, parents, and policymakers must take the lead in articulating the need for play experiences in children's lives, including the curriculum. To assume strong advocacy roles, it is imperative that all educators, parents, and policymakers who work with or for children from infancy through adolescence fully understand play and its diverse forms. Equally important is the ability to use that knowledge to achieve what is best for children in all settings. This paper has argued strongly for legitimizing play as an appropriate activity in schools and other educational settings. Therefore, educators, families, and policymakers can and should:

Optimize brain functions by providing rich experiences that include a variety of learning materials, feedback, appropriate levels of challenge, and enough time to process information

Rethink and transform the nature of relationships and communication between adults and children

Make play a fundamental part of every school curriculum

Recognize, respect, and accept play in all its variations as worthwhile and valuable

Balance work and play to ensure that children reap the benefits of intrinsic motivation and experience sheer joy in their endeavors

Balance encouragement and opportunity to fulfill children's natural tendency and need to play; children will find the means to play if the environment affords an opportunity to do so

Create a climate of acceptance by respecting children's play choices, recognizing the cultural context in which play occurs, and providing many play options.

🌐 Goals and objectives should involve developmentally, individually, culturally, and creatively appropriate practices. They should consider the physical, intellectual, social, and emotional development of the children you are teaching.

🌐 The center or school in which you teach can offer a long-range plan that will help you see where you and the children fit into the total program.

Schedules and Routines

The schedule and routine components of planning can help create a framework of security for young children. "Children who are provided with a predictable schedule and secure environment are more likely to feel confident about exploring their world. . . . Through these explorations, children strengthen their connections to the people and environment around them" (Klein, 2002). The format becomes familiar to them, and they welcome the periods of self-selected activities, group time, outdoor play, resting, eating, and toileting. The establishment of trust that grows between teacher and parent is based on consistent daily contact and the well-being of the children.

schedule
The basic daily timeline of an early childhood program.

routines
The events that fit into the daily time frame of an early childhood program.

All early childhood programs include basic timelines, curricula, and activities that form the framework of the daily **schedule.** The events that fit into this time frame are the **routines.** The secret of classroom management is getting the children used to routines.

🌐 *Arrival* provides interaction time for the teacher, parent, and child. It also offers a smooth transition from home. This early morning ritual reinforces the trust, friendship, and consistency necessary to young children and their families.

The development of toileting skills and handwashing occurs as the young child matures.

🌐 *Departure* at the end of the day should also offer a relaxed transition for the child and family.

This is another time for sharing positive feedback with the parents and provides a consistent routine for the child.

🌐 *Mealtimes and snacks* are some of the nicest moments of the day when teachers and children sit down and eat together. "Snacks and meals are pleasant when they are orderly enough to focus on eating and casual enough to be a social experience" (Feeney, Christensen, & Moravcik, 2001). Self-help skills are developed as well when children pour their own juice and milk and help themselves family-style during meals. If children bring food from home, teachers need to give the parents culturally sensitive and nutritionally sound guidance concerning what food is appropriate for the children to bring.

🌐 *Diapering and toileting* are routines that are ongoing throughout the day as needed. The development of toileting skills and handwashing occurs as the young child matures. Adult handwashing and disinfecting diapering surfaces to prevent disease are other important daily routines.

🌐 *Rest or naptime* runs smoothly if teachers make the environment restful, soothing, and stress free. Consistency in how this routine is handled each day provides security to the children. The use of soft music, dim lights, and personal books or blankets encourages children to rest or sleep on their mats or cots. Older children need a short rest-time too. Sitting quietly with a book offers a quiet period during the day.

🌐 *Transitions,* such as cleanup, prepare the environment for the next activity. These times are part of your lesson plan and should be based on the developmental needs of the children. (A complete discussion of transition activities is included in Chapter 2.)

🌐 *Activity time* offers children a large block of time for them to self-select from a variety of activities. "A wide variety of well-planned activities should reinforce the objectives and theme of the curriculum. Each day's activities should also provide multiple opportunities for development of fine and gross motor, cognitive, creative, social, and language skills" (Essa, 2007). In addition, appropriate times for solitary moments, small and large group activities, indoor and outdoor play, along with a balance of active and quiet activities, should be provided.

🌐 *Outdoor activities* offer children many opportunities for growth and learning. To be developmentally appropriate, outdoor play requires the same planning, observation, and evaluation as indoor activities (Brewer, 2001). Large blocks of outdoor time should be scheduled and planned daily.

Figures 1–5, 1–6, and 1–7 are examples of infant, toddler, and three-to five-year-old schedules and routines appropriate for early education programs. Figure 1–8 illustrates how routines can be teachable moments in an environment for young children.

COMMUNICATION WITH PARENTS

It is the teacher's responsibility to keep the lines of communication open to families. It is the family's responsibility to be involved with their child's teacher and child care center or school. The following guidelines for developmentally appropriate practice, which offer suggestions on how teachers can work in partnership with families and communities, are adapted from Bredekamp and Copple (1997), and Gestwicki (2007).

1. Success in the education of young children must be built on a foundation of teamwork involving both teachers and families. It is not the teacher telling the parent what needs to be accomplished. It is both teachers and parents cooperatively

FIGURE 1–5
Example of a daily flexible schedule and routines for a group of infants.

INFANTS

(3–18 months)
Very Flexible Schedule and Routines

7:00	Morning arrival
	Greet parents and infants
	Put away bottles, food, and diaper supplies
	Spend individual time holding and talking to each child
8:00–9:00	Snack
	Younger infants: Individual cereal, fruit, formula, or juice. Younger infants have individual schedules that include feeding, diapering, and sleeping
	Older infants: Snack, cleanup, diapering, and looking at books
9:00–11:00	*Younger infants*: Individual play on floor, movement exercise, outdoor play, or take a walk in stroller
	Individual formula, juice, or water
	Talk to each child throughout the day
	Child sleeps when tired
	Older infants: Individual or group play, visit toddler playground, walk around center, or play in indoor playroom, read books, dramatic play, manipulatives, art, music and movement, and finger plays
11:00	*Older infants:* Lunch with formula, milk, juice, or water
	Talk to each child
11:30–12:30	Cleanup and prepare for naps: Lights dimmed, soft music, quiet play
12:30–2:00	Naptime
	Talk to and play quietly with infants who are awake
2:00–3:30	Quiet play with books and toys, individual exercises with each child
	Younger infants: Individual formula, juice, or water; soft snacks
	Older infants: snack
3:30–4:30	Individual play, group activities, outdoor play, walks
4:30–5:30	Prepare for going home read books, play on floor, and so on
	Talk to each parent

Diaper changes: As needed after snacks, after lunch, before and after naps, before departure, and changing of soiled diapers anytime during the day.

Note: All times are suggested ones. Times are sensitive to the needs of the children.

FIGURE 1–6
Example of a daily flexible schedule and routines for a group of toddlers.

TODDLERS

(18 months to 3 years)
Flexible Schedule and Routines

7:00	Morning arrival Greet children and parents, free play (children choose activities)
8:00–8:50	Center activities (art, manipulatives, blocks, dramatic play), spend individual time with each child or small group activity
8:50–9:00	Cleanup with song or poem or special individual time
9:00–9:30	Bathroom time (wash hands, change diapers, toileting, etc.), talk to each child Snack and time for washing hands and face
9:30–10:30	Outdoor play
10:30–10:40	Bathroom time (wash hands, change diapers, toileting), talk to each child
10:40–11:15	Center activities Guided exploration Large group activity of a story, finger plays, language activities, or music
11:10–11:30	Bathroom time, wash hands for lunch and change diapers if needed
11:30–Noon	Lunch
Noon–12:30	Bathroom time, brush teeth, and change diapers if needed
12:30–2:30	Quiet time with books and music while children finish in bathroom and get on their cots for naptime or rest
2:30–3:00	Wake-up time (put away cots and blankets , toileting, diaper change, washing, put on shoes), free play
3:00–3:15	Snack and clean up
3:15–3:30	Group time with story, song, flannelboard, or other language activity
3:30–4:30	Outdoor play, individual time with each child
4:30–4:45	Bathroom time
4:45–6:00	Quiet activities (books, puzzles, music), individual time with each child, playing games, singing, talking; prepare to go home

Note: This daily schedule is flexible, depending on the needs of the children and the weather.

Times are suggested ones and are compatible with the needs of the children

FIGURE 1–7
Example of a daily flexible schedule and routines for a group of three-, four-, and five-year-old children.

PRESCHOOLERS AND KINDERGARTNERS

Daily Schedule and Routines for Full Day Class
(three-, four-, and five-year-olds)

7:00–8:30	Arrival and free play, individual time with teacher and each child.
8:30–9:00	All centers are open for activity time
	Small groups rotating inside and outside play or continuation of centers
	Toileting and washing hands for snacks
	Snack and clean up
	Group time
	Centers and individual time with teacher to talk about what they did and what they want to do
10:15–10:30	Clean up to go outside
10:30–11:30	Indoor or outside play, walks, or small groups
11:30–11:45	Toileting, washing hands
	Any of the following activities: share time on cots with books, pictures (two children to a cot), quiet conversation or relaxing on cots, listening to music, finger plays, songs, stories, or sitting on carpet squares and reading books
11:45–12:15	Lunch
12:15–12:30	Finish lunch, toileting, washing hands, brushing teeth, getting settled on cots with music or story the teacher will read
12:30–12:45	Quiet time transition, resting, and quiet music
12:45–2:30	Naptime or rest, with provisions made for children who wake early or cannot sleep
2:30–3:00	Wake-up time, fold and put away cots and blankets, put on shoes, toileting, get ready for snack
	Snack and clean up
	Centers or individual time with teacher
	Cleanup and transition activity
4:00–4:30	Small groups or large group time
4:30–5:15	Indoor or outside play or small groups
5:15–6:00	Any of the following activities: quiet activities, table games, stories, songs, music
	Get ready to go home

Note: This schedule is flexible and subject to change. The needs of children and the weather will affect changes.

FIGURE 1–8
Every routine can be used as an opportunity for learning. (Source: Gordon & Browne, 2004)

ROUTINES: LEARNING OPPORTUNITIES

- Eating Teaches Health:
  Introduction to new and different foods, good nutritional habits
- Eating Teaches Social Skills:
  How to manage oneself in a group eating situation, focusing on eating and conversing, acceptable mealtime behavior and manners
- Eating Teaches Fine-Motor Skills:
  Pouring, handling spoons, forks, serving self, drinking, eating without spilling
- Eating Teaches Independence Skills:
  Finding and setting one's place, serving self, making choices, cleaning up at snack and lunch times
- Eating Teaches Individual Differences:
  Likes and dislikes, choices of food, pace of eating
- Resting and Sleeping Teach Health:
  Personal care skills; relaxation habits; internal balance and change of pace: alternating activity to allow body to rest
- Dressing Teaches Independence Skills:
  Self-awareness: size of clothes, comparisons between clothes for girls and boys, younger and older, larger and smaller children, and children in and out of diapers or training pants
  Self-esteem: caring for one's own body; choosing one's own clothes
- Dressing Teaches Fine-Motor Skills:
  How to manage snaps, buttons, zippers; handling all garments; maneuvering in and out of a snowsuit or jacket; matching hands and feet with mittens and boots or shoes
- Toileting Teaches Emotional Skills:
  Self-awareness: body functions, learning the names and physical sensations that go with body functions
  Self-identity: comparisons between girls and boys (sit versus stand)
  Self-esteem: caring for one's own body without guilt, fear, shame
  Human sexuality: in a natural setting, promotes healthy attitudes toward the body and its functions, and that adults can be accepting, open, and reassuring about the body and its care

sharing knowledge and beliefs about educating children and developing common goals. "Partnerships enrich both teachers' and families' relationships with children and bring together their mutual expertise for the benefit of the child" (Keyser, 2006).

2. Families are the primary educators of their own children. It is imperative that teachers respect that crucial role by maintaining open communication with parents, learning from them, and involving them in the education process.

3. There is a learning process that teachers and parents always face in the educational experience. The teacher is learning from the children and their families about the children's world apart from the early childhood setting, while family members are developing knowledge about the principles and techniques of early childhood education. Both are necessary and important. With increased communication, mutual respect emerges.

Encourage parents to share with you what they know about their children and what is important to them as parents.

4. Assessing the child's needs and progress must take into account the child's culture and environment. A teacher's failure to do so is likely to create a breakdown in the educational process.

5. The early childhood teacher is in a unique position to be an advocate by recognizing the special circumstances of a child and his family and to help link up with whatever community resources are available and appropriate for helping them.

Positive communication between home and school is crucial to providing a consistent and beneficial experience for young children. "Just as the teacher deals with each child as a unique individual by employing a variety of teaching guidance methods, so must a flexible approach be maintained in communicating with families to meet their individual requirements" (Essa, 2007).

Prior and Gerard (2007) continue with this thought, "Family involvement has been shown to lead to an increase in children's positive attitudes about school, improved attendance, and better homework habits. Children tend to see a connection between their homes and school when their parents are involved." In the busy and complex lives of parents and teachers alike, this connection between home and school is more important today than ever before.

Teachers and other staff members in early childhood settings should be responsive to cultural and language differences of the children and their families. Affirming and supporting diversity includes being perceptive about differences in caregiving, feeding, and other practices (Wortham, 2006).

Here are some additional suggestions for active communication with parents.

🌐 Provide an infant daily report (Figure 1–9).

🌐 Provide a toddler daily or weekly report (Figure 1–10).

🌐 Create bulletin boards with information regarding health and safety issues, family meetings, guest speakers, community resources and referrals, and tips for parents.

🌐 Provide parent letters discussing the goals, objectives, theme, and classroom activities. Offer suggestions for activities parents can do with children at home to extend or emphasize classroom experience.

FIGURE 1–9
Example of an infant
daily report.

INFANT DAILY REPORT

(Morning input from parents to teachers.)

My Name: _____ Date: _____

When I last ate: _____ Food:_____ Formula/Milk: _____

Time I woke up today: _____ Time I went to bed last night: _____ Hours slept: _____

Last diaper change: _____ Medication: Yes_____ No _____ (must sign in)

How I feel today: (circle one)   Great! OK Fussy Not well Feverish

Upset tummy Teething Diaper Rash

Today, my teachers should know: _____

(Teachers, input to parents at end of infant's day)

Feedings:	Naps:		Changes:
(Time & Description/Amount)	(Time Slept)	(Time)	(My Diaper D W BM)
_____	_____	_____	_____
_____	_____	_____	_____
_____	_____	_____	_____
_____	_____	_____	_____
_____	_____	_____	_____

My day at school:

Supply needs: (circle one) Clothes   Diapers   Formula   Food   Wipes   Other:
COMMENTS:

FIGURE 1–10
Example of a toddler
daily report.

TODDLER DAILY REPORT

Child's Name: _____ Date: _____ Teacher:_____

    Morning input from parents to teachers:

(*Note:* Weekly menu is posted on parent bulletin board.)

MORNING SNACK:	Child Ate:	well ( )	fair ( )
LUNCH:	Child Ate:	well ( )	fair ( )
AFTERNOON SNACK:	Child Ate:	well ( )	fair ( )

NAP:_____

DIAPER CHANGES: TOILET USE:

ACTIVITIES:

ITEMS NEEDED FROM HOME:

COMMENTS:

- ✪ Encourage parents to share with you what they know about their children and what is important to them as parents.
- ✪ Encourage families to visit the classroom. They should be as welcome as their child.
- ✪ Conduct parent-teacher conferences that focus on the accomplishments and needs of the individual child and that ensure privacy and confidentiality for the family.
- ✪ Provide multilingual written communications as needed.
- ✪ Provide opportunities for parents to volunteer.

✳ AFTERVIEW

Many influences, such as historical aspects of early childhood education, developmental theories, insightful educators, developmentally appropriate practices, and ongoing research have impacted and continue to impact our understanding of what is appropriate for the young children in our care. From them we learn that an early childhood program should be based on fulfilling the developmental needs of all children. It should be planned to meet each child's physical, intellectual, social, and emotional growth. Understanding the interrelationships among development, learning, and experiences is essential to providing the highest quality care and education for young children.

The program should be founded on the assumption that growth is a sequential process, that children pass through stages of development, and that children learn and grow through their play and by actively participating in the learning experiences offered. It should adapt to the developmental, individual, and cultural differences of the children.

As teachers, we need to offer age, individually, and creatively appropriate experiences and activities for each child. We should assist each child in growing to his fullest potential by recognizing each stage of development; by providing an environment that encourages the success of each child; by respecting the culture, language, and special needs of each child; and by welcoming family participation in the program.

As we plan for children and their families, we are saying: Welcome! This environment is safe and appropriate. We care, we will listen, we will share, and we will nurture you and recognize your uniqueness.

✳ KEY TERMS

accommodation	egocentric	scaffolding
advocacy	equilibrium	schedule
anti-bias	goals	schema
assimilation	learning	self-help skills
associative play	multiple intelligences	self-regulation
bias	object permanence	solitary play
cognitive development	objectives	stereotype
cooperative play	onlooker play	symbolic play
creativity	parallel play	symbolic thinking
development	play	theory
developmental theories	practice play or senso-	unoccupied behavior
developmentally appro-	rimotor play	zone of proximal
priate practice	prejudice	development
dramatic play	psychosocial	
early childhood education	routines	

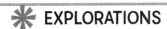 EXPLORATIONS

1. The number of early childhood programs has increased in response to the growing need for out-of-home care and education during the early years. Identify and discuss the indicators of the current need for child care and education, including changing lifestyles and family patterns. How is your local community responding to these needs of young children and their families? Give specific examples.

2. Think about your experiences with a teacher or teachers during your early years in school. Give an example in which the teacher encouraged your creativity. What about the teachers you had in junior high school? High school? How do you feel about your creativity now? What are some of the things you do to express your creativity? What will you do or what are you doing as a teacher to set up a creatively appropriate environment for young children?

3. It is common to hear a comment about a young child such as, "Oh, he's just playing." The implication is that what he's doing is not very important. From what you have learned about the developmental stages of play and from Parten's, Erikson's and Piaget's theories about the function of play for children, what is incorrect about this type of comment? Why do you think people tend to undervalue play?

4. Select a group of toddlers or kindergarten children. Observe them at play in their classroom and in their outdoor environment. Using the information on *play* in this chapter, describe what activities the children were involved in and what developmental stages of play you observed. How did the teacher plan for the children's play activities? Was it child-directed or teacher-directed play? Would you change anything if you were the teacher? Explain.

5. Visit an early childhood program. Select a classroom and look at its daily schedule and the routines within the schedule. Obtain a copy, if possible. Are the schedule and routines developmentally appropriate? Do they consider the needs of all the children? Explain your answers. Did the teacher follow the posted schedule and routines? What was changed and why? Would you change anything? Why or why not?

✳ REFERENCES

Allen, K. E., & Marotz, L. R. (2003). *Developmental profiles: Pre-birth through twelve* (4th ed.). Clifton Park, NY: Thomson Delmar Learning.

Association of Childhood Education International (ACEI). (2002). On-line at: *http://www.udel.edu/bateman/acei*

Berk, L. E., & Winsler, A. (1995). *Scaffolding children's learning: Vygotsky and early childhood education. Washington*, DC: NAEYC.

Bowman, B. (1994). The challenge of diversity. *Phi Delta Kappan, 76*(3), 218–225.

Bowman, B., Donovan, M. S., & Burns, M. S. (Eds.). (2000). *Eager to learn: Educating our preschoolers*. Washington, DC: National Academy Press.

Bredekamp, S., & Copple, C. (Eds.). (1997). *Developmentally appropriate practice in early childhood programs* (Rev. ed.). Washington, DC: NAEYC.

Brewer, J. (2001). *Introduction to early childhood education* (4th ed.). Boston: Allyn & Bacon.

Catron, C., & Allen, J. (2003). *Early childhood curriculum* (3rd ed.). Upper Saddle River, NJ: Merrill Prentice Hall.

Charlesworth, R. (2008). *Understanding child development* (7th ed.). Clifton Park, NY: Thomson Delmar Learning.

Children's Defense Fund. (2007). On-line at: *http://www.childrens defence.org*

Copple, C., & Bredekamp, S. (2006). *Basics of developmentally appropriate practices*. Washington, DC: NAEYC.

Derman-Sparks, L., & A.B.C. Task Force. (1989). *Anti-bias curriculum: Tools for empowering young children*. Washington, DC: NAEYC.

Edwards, C. P., & Springate, K. W. (1995, Fall). The lion comes out of the stone: Helping young children achieve their creative potential. *Dimensions of Early Childhood, 23*(4), 24–29.

Elkind, D. (2002, November–December). The connection between play and character. *Child Care Information Exchange, 148*, 41–42.

Erikson, E. (1963). *Childhood and society* (2nd ed.). New York: Norton.

Essa, E. L. (2007). *Introduction to early childhood education* (4th ed.). Clifton Park, NY: Thomson Delmar Learning.

Feeney, S., Christensen, D., & Moravcik, E. (2001). *Who am I in the lives of children?* (6th ed.). Upper Saddle River, NJ: Merrill.

Freeman, N. K., & Feeney, S. (2006, September). The New Face of Early Care and Education. *Young Children, 61*(5), 10–16.

Fromberg, D. P. (1998). Play issues in early childhood education. In C. Seefeldt (Ed.), *The early childhood curriculum: A review of current research* (2nd ed.). Upper Saddle River, NJ: Merrill.

Gabbard, C., & Rodrigues, L. (2002, May/June). Optimizing early brain and motor development through movement. *Early Childhood News, 14*(3), 32–38.

Gallagher, K. C. (2005, July). Brain research and early childhood development: A primer for developmentally appropriate practice. *Young Children, 60*(4), 12–20.

Gardner, H. (1983). *Frames of mind: The theory of multiple intelligences*. New York: Basic Books.

Gardner, H. (1993). *Multiple intelligences: The theory in practice*. New York: Basic Books.

Gardner, H. (2001). *An education for the future*. On-line at: *http://www.pz.harvard.edu/WhatsNew/Amsterdam.htm*

Gestwicki, C. (2007). *Developmentally appropriate practice: Curriculum and development in early education* (3rd ed.). Clifton Park, NY: Thomson Delmar Learning.

Gillespie, L. G., & Seibel, N. L. (2006, July). Self-regulation, a cornerstone of early childhood development. *Young Children, 61*(4), 34–39.

Gordon, A. M., & Browne, K. W. (2007). *Beginning Essentials in Early Childhood Education*. Clifton Park, NY: Thomson Delmar Learning.

Gordon, A. M., & Browne, K. W. (2008). *Beginnings and beyond* (7th ed.). Clifton Park, NY: Thomson Delmar Learning.

Greenberg, P. (2000, January). What wisdom should we take with us as we enter the new century?—An interview with Millie Almy. *Young Children, 55*(1), 6–10.

Gullo, D. F. (Ed.). (2006). *K today: Teaching and learning in the kindergarten year.* Washington, DC: NAEYC.

Hine, C. (1996, November–December). Developing multiple intelligences in young children. *Early Childhood News, 8*(6), 23–29.

Honig, A. S. (2002*). Secure relationships, Nurturing infant/toddler attachment in early care settings.* Washington, DC: NAEYC.

Hughes, F. P. (1999). *Children, play and development* (3rd ed.). Boston: Allyn & Bacon.

Isbell, R. T., & Raines, S. (2007). *Creativity and the arts with young children* (2nd ed.). Clifton Park, NY: Thomson Delmar Learning.

Isenberg, J. P., & Quisenberry, N. (2002). *Play: Essential for all children. A position paper.* Olney, MD: Association for Childhood Education International.

Jambor, T. (2000, Fall). Informal, real-life play: Building children's brain connections. *Dimensions of Early Childhood, 28*(4), 3–8.

Keyser, J. (2006). *From parents to partners.* St. Paul, MN: Redleaf Press & Washington, DC: NAEYC.

Klein, A. S. (2002, Spring). Infant & toddler care that recognized their competence. *Dimensions of Early Childhood, 30*(2), 11–17.

Koralek, D. (Ed.). (2004). *Spotlight on young children and play.* Washington, DC: NAEYC.

Kostelnik, M., Soderman, A., & Whirin, A. P. (1999). *Developmentally appropriate programs in early childhood education* (2nd ed.). Upper Saddle River, NJ: Merrill.

Krissansen, D. (2002, November–December). Getting along with imaginary friends. *Child Care Information Exchange, 148,* 51–53.

Maxim, G. W. (1997). *The very young* (5th ed.). Upper Saddle River, NJ: Merrill.

Mayesky, M. (2006). *Creative activities for young children* (8th ed.). Clifton Park, NY: Thomson Delmar Learning.

Miller, S. (2002, August–September). Supporting how children learn best: Using learning styles and multiple intelligences in your classrooms. *Early Childhood News, 14*(4), 48–52.

Mitchell, A. (2006, November). From our president. *Young Children, 61*(6), 6.

National Association for the Education of Young Children (NAEYC). (2001). *NAEYC at 75, 1926–2001.* Washington, DC: Author.

National Association for the Education of Young Children (NAEYC). (2002, January). Our promise for children. *Young Children, 57*(1), 56.

National Association of Family Child Care (NAFCC). (2002). On-line at: *http://www.nafcc.org*

National Black Child Development Institute (NBCDI). (2002). On-line at: *http://www.nbcdi.org*

Nicholson-Nelson, K. (1998). *Developing students' multiple intelligences.* New York: Scholastic Professional Books.

Perry, B. D. (2002a). *Biological relativity: Time and the developing child.* On-line at:*http://www.teacher.scholastic.com/professional/bruceperry/biological_relativity.htm*

Piaget, J. (1926). *The language and thought of the child.* New York: Harcourt Brace.

Piaget, J. (1961). *Play, dreams and imagination in childhood.* New York: Norton.

Prior, J., & Gerard, M. R. (2007). *Family involvement in early childhood education.* Clifton Park, NY: Thomson Delmar Learning.

Robinson, A., & Stark, D. R. (2002). *Advocates in action.* Washington, DC: NAEYC.

Rogers, F. (2003). *The world according to Mister Rogers: Important things to remember.* New York: Hyperion.

Rushton, S. P. (2001, September). Applying brain research to create developmentally appropriate learning environments. *Young Children, 56*(5), 76–82.

Schirrmacher, R. (2006). *Art and creative development for young children* (5th ed.). Clifton Park, NY: Thomson Delmar Learning.

Seefeldt, C., & Barbour, N. (1998). *Early childhood education* (4th ed.). Upper Saddle River, NJ: Merrill Prentice Hall.

Shore, R. (1997). *Rethinking the brain: New insights into early development.* New York: Families and Work Institute.

Sluss, D. J. (2005). *Supporting play: Birth through age eight.* Clifton Park, NY: Thomson Delmar Learning.

Smilansky, S. (1968). *The effects of sociodramatic play on disadvantaged children.* New York: John Wiley & Sons.

Spodek, B., & Saracho, O. N. (1994). *Right from the start: Teaching children ages three to eight.* Boston, MA: Allyn & Bacon.

Stott, F. (1994, September). In memoriam: Erik H. Erikson. *Young Children, 49*(6), 43.

Tsao, L. L. (2002, Summer). How much do we know about the importance of play in child development? *Childhood Education, 78*(4), 230–233.

Vygotsky, L. S. (1978). *Mind in society.* Cambridge, MA: Harvard University Press.

United States Department of Education. *No Child Left Behind Act of 2001.* On-line at: *http://www.highscope.org*

Watson, L., Watson, M., & Wilson, L. C. (2003). *Infants and toddlers* (5th ed.). Clifton Park, NY: Thomson Delmar Learning.

Weikart, D. P., & Schweinhart, L. J. (2007). *Perry Preschool project.* On-line at: *http://www.highscope.org*

Wertsch, J. V. (1991). *Voices of the mind.* Cambridge, MA: Harvard University Press.

Wilkins, D. (1996). *Multiple intelligences activities.* Huntington, CA: Teacher Created Materials, Inc.

Wortham, S. C. (2006). *Early childhood curriculum* (4th ed.). Upper Saddle River, NJ: Merrill Prentice Hall.

Zero to Three (2002*). Prenatal development.* On-line at: *http://www.zerotothree.org/brainwonders/care_prenatal.html*

✳ ADDITIONAL READINGS AND RESOURCES

Bodrova, E., Leong, D. J., & Henninger, M. (2000, Fall). Imaginative child-directed play: Leading the way in development and learning. *Dimensions in Early Childhood, 28*(4), 25–30.

Carlisle, A. (2001, November). Using the multiple intelligences theory to assess early childhood curricula. *Young Children, 56*(6), 77–83.

Christian, L. G. (2006, January). Understanding Families. *Young Children, 61*(1), 12–20.

Clements, R. (2000, Fall). Playworkers: Creating opportunities for children's play. *Dimensions of Early Childhood, 28*(4), 9–13.

Cooper, J. L., & Dever, M. T. (2001, May). Sociodramatic play as a vehicle for curriculum integration in first grade. *Young Children, 56*(3), 58–59.

Copple, C. (Ed.) (2003). *A world of difference.* Washington, DC: NAEYC.

Dombro, A. L., & Lerner, C. (2006, January). Sharing the care of infants and toddlers. *Young Children, 61*(1), 29–33.

Edwards, C. P., & Raikes, H. (2002, July). Extending the dance: Relationship-based approaches to infant/toddler care and education. *Young Children, 57*(4), 10–17.

Fromberg, D. P. (2002). *Play and meaning in early childhood education.* Boston: Allyn & Bacon.

Fromberg, D. P. (2006). Kindergarten education and early childhood teacher education in the United States: Status at the start of the 21st century. *Journal of Early Childhood Teacher Education, 27*(1), 65–85.

Gable, S. (2002, July). *Teacher-child relationships throughout the day.* Young Children, 57(4), 42–46.

Gestwicki, C. (2007). *Home, school and community relations* (6th ed.). Clifton Park, NY: Thomson Delmar Learning.

Grave, E. (2001, May). What's going on in the children's garden? Kindergarten today. *Young Children, 56*(3), 67–73.

Gronlund, G. (2006). *Make early learning standards come alive.* St. Paul, MN: Redleaf Press & Washington, DC: NAEYC.

Haugen, K. (2002, November–December). Time, trust, and tools: Opening doors to imagination for all children. *Child Care Information Exchange, 148,* 36–40.

NAEYC. (2005). *NAEYC early childhood program standards and accreditation criteria: The mark of quality in early childhood education.* Washington, DC: Author.

NAEYC. (2005, March). Why we care about the K in K–12. *Young Children, 60*(2), 54–56.

Peterson, K. (2002, January–February). Creating home-school partnerships. *Early Childhood News, 14*(4), 38–45.

Roskos, K. A., & Christie, J. F. (2002, March). "Knowing in the doing": Observing literacy learning in play. *Young Children, 57*(2), 46–54.

United States Department of Education. (2004). *No Child Left Behind: A toolkit for teachers.* (Rev. ed.). Jessup, MD: Education Publications Center. On-line at: *http://www.ed.gov/teachers/nclbguide/toolkittoc.html*

Van Hoorn, J., Nourot, P. M., Scales, B., & Alward, K. R. (2003). *Play at the center of curriculum.* Upper Saddle River, NJ: Prentice Hall.

For additional information on early education curriculum, visit our Web site at http://www.earlychilded.delmar.com

CHAPTER 2

CREATING CURRICULUM

OBJECTIVES

AFTER STUDYING THIS CHAPTER, YOU SHOULD BE ABLE TO:

- Define curriculum and discuss the process of curriculum development.

- Identify and describe early childhood curriculum models and theories.

- Develop awareness of, and sensitivity to, cultural diversity and provide a multicultural/anti-bias and inclusive educational environment in which all children can succeed.

- Understand how to guide children from inappropriate behavior to appropriate behavior through the use of developmentally appropriate guidance techniques.

- Observe, plan, and evaluate developmentally appropriate early childhood learning environments, indoors and outdoors, including equipment, materials, and supplies selection.

- Evaluate and integrate developmentally appropriate technology into an early childhood learning environment.

- Identify the importance of using themes, units, projects, and webs in curriculum development and specify curriculum areas appropriate for early education programs.

- Select and describe ways to use observation, assessment, and evaluation as part of the curriculum development process.

OVERVIEW

As we progress through this chapter, focusing on how to create a curriculum appropriate for young children, we once again emphasize the interconnecting philosophies of this text:

1. *Curriculum* is *child-centered* or *child-initiated* while being sensitive to, and supportive of, the development, age, and experiences of young children, individually and in a classroom community.
2. *Curriculum* provides for all of a *child's development* by planning experiences that build upon what children already know and are able to do.
3. *Curriculum* encourages children to *learn by doing* through experimentation, exploration, and discovery while building self-control and a positive self-image.
4. *Curriculum* includes appropriate supports and services for children with *special needs* in an inclusive environment.
5. *Curriculum* promotes opportunities to support each child's *diverse cultural and linguistic heritage.*
6. *Curriculum* invites *creativity* by providing opportunities for unevaluated discovery and activity while promoting tolerance and respect for each other's creation.
7. *Curriculum* facilitates *physical activity and play* by integrating movement within activities throughout the day.
8. *Curriculum* involves reciprocal *relationships between teachers and families.* Positive communication between home and school is crucial to providing a consistent and beneficial experience for young children.

This chapter illustrates how we develop an early education curriculum and all it encompasses, including classroom management techniques, appropriate practices for inclusion, arrangement of indoor and outdoor space, and selection of equipment and materials. The plan of observation, assessment, and evaluation discussed at the end of this chapter will help determine if developmentally appropriate curriculum goals and content have been achieved.

The National Association for the Education of Young Children (NAEYC) and the National Association of Early Childhood Specialists in State Departments of Education (NAECS/SDE) define curriculum as "an organized framework that delineates the content children are to learn, the processes through which children achieve the identified curricular goals, what teachers do to help children achieve these goals, and the context in which teaching and learning occur" (Bredekamp & Rosegrant, 1992). Additionally, for infants and toddlers, "every experience, and every minute in the day are a part of the infant and toddler curriculum. Diapering, feeding, washing, and comforting are elements of the curriculum, as are singing, playing, watching, and moving" (Watson, Watson, & Wilson, 2003).

Curriculum is a multilevel process that encompasses what happens in an early education classroom each day, reflecting the philosophy, goals, and objectives of the early childhood program. In an early education program, the **philosophy** expresses the basic principles, attitudes, and beliefs of the center or school. **Goals**—broad, general overviews of what children are expected to gain from the program—and **objectives**—specific teaching techniques or interpretations of the goals and meaningful descriptions of what is expected to be learned—are designed to meet the physical, intellectual, cultural, social, emotional, and creative development of each child.

We learn in so many different ways—all of them valid—too few of them acknowledged. Children make meaning about the world through song, music, movement, the arts, play, story, poetry, nature. How and what do they learn through constant drilling, worrisome test preparation, isolated skills disconnected from meaningful concepts and materials? (Chenfeld, 2001)

---

curriculum

A multileveled process that encompasses what happens in an early education classroom each day, reflecting the philosophy, goals, and objectives of the early childhood program.

philosophy

In an early childhood program, expresses the basic principles, attitudes, and beliefs of the center, school, or individual teacher.

goals

The general overall aims or overview of an early childhood program.

objectives

The specific purposes or teaching techniques that interpret the goals of planning, schedules, and routines, as well as meaningful descriptions of what is expected to be learned. These objectives are designed to meet the physical, intellectual, social, emotional, and creative development of young children.

As we continue focusing on the process of curriculum development, let us remember that whatever we do, say, plan, or assess must concentrate on developing a child's positive self-esteem. Valuing each child's cultural background, experiences, interests, and abilities is critical. The "I can do it!" feelings of competence strongly influence learning ability. This is true for all children, from the youngest infant to the preschooler or the eight-year-old. Figure 2–1 is a statement of commitment to all children.

PROCESS OF CURRICULUM DEVELOPMENT

 The *process* of curriculum development is *ongoing*. It is both planned and impromptu, written or unwritten. "Creating a good curriculum for young children is not simply a matter of practicing curriculum planning. It is a matter of understanding the process: how children interact with people and materials to learn" (Gordon & Browne, 2004). The selection of themes, projects, integrated curriculum areas, equipment, and materials is based on sound *child development* theories reinforcing the child's current stage of development and challenging her to move toward the next stage. As you begin this process of curriculum development, the first step is to set goals for learning based on the philosophy of the center/school and on the knowledge of the individual children in your classroom. Throughout this chapter and all the other chapters, we will be discussing the ongoing process of curriculum development culminating in the selection of topics and activities, writing of objectives, and planning for observation, assessment, and evaluation.

The use of the terms *inclusive* curriculum, *integrated* curriculum, and *emergent* curriculum in early childhood education explain further what is appropriate in developing curriculum for young children. **Inclusive curriculum** underscores the importance of individual differences and cultural diversity among young children, allowing for children to learn at their own pace and style. **Integrated curriculum** encourages young children to transfer knowledge and skills from one subject to another while using all aspects of their development. Gestwicki (2007) explains that "integrated curriculum helps children build meaningful connections when presented with new information, allows children to use knowledge and skills from one area to explore other subject areas, and allows teachers to negotiate the tricky balance

---

inclusive curriculum
Underscores the importance of individual differences and cultural diversity among young children.

integrated curriculum
Encourages young children to transfer knowledge and skills from one subject to another while using all aspects of their development.

FIGURE 2–1
Adapted from the "Statement of Commitment," *Code of Ethical Conduct and Statement of Commitment* (NAEYC, 1998). Reprinted with permission from the National Association for the Education of Young Children.

OUR PROMISE FOR CHILDREN

For the children and for our nation, I affirm my personal commitment to all young children and their families.

I promise to model behaviors that solve problems without resorting to aggression or violence and to teach tolerance and respect for differences.

I will serve as an advocate for children, families, and the early childhood profession.

I promise to maintain the highest standards of professional practice and ethical conduct.

I will be open to new ideas and value the suggestions of others while I continue to learn, grow, and contribute as an early childhood professional.

I know that my work makes a difference. I vow to help make the future bright, safe, and productive for all children.

emergent curriculum

A curriculum that emerges out of the interests and experiences of the children.

between standards and developmentally appropriate practice." **Emergent curriculum** emerges out of the interests and experiences of the children. This curriculum "is always open to new possibilities that were not thought of during the initial planning process" (Jones & Reynolds, 1992). It is also suggested that "teachers should allow plenty of time for conversation and should use the children's own reactions, comments, and questions as the basis for what they do next" (Lewin-Benham, 2006).

Examples of Curriculum Models and Programs

A curriculum model is a structure or organizational framework that is used to make decisions about everything from policies and priorities to teaching methods and assessment procedures. (Crosser, 2005).

As a teacher of young children, you will find many early childhood curriculum models and theories available today. It is important to identify curriculum approaches and resources that are based on the developmental and cultural needs and interests of the children in your classroom. Curriculum models are helpful to point out guidelines for planning and organizing experiences. However, keep in mind that no single model addresses all the developmental and cultural priorities, such as anti-bias, inclusion, emergent curriculum, and the project approach. The following overview of curriculum model examples were chosen because they continue to be identified by the early childhood profession, have been implemented in multiple locations, and "are accompanied by an extensive literature describing their educational objectives, content and structure, and assessment procedures" (Goffin, 2001). As teachers, we should continue to investigate other models and programs as well, looking for additional insights into early education curriculum.

MONTESSORI (1870–1952). These programs are based on Dr. Maria Montessori's original ideas, materials, and methods, which were designed to meet the needs of impoverished children in Italy. The Montessori method is the second curriculum model created expressly for early education (Goffin, 2001). (The first model was created by Friedrich Froebel in Germany, who began the kindergarten, or "garden for children," in the mid-1800s). In the United States today there exist a wide variation and interpretation of the Montessori principles. According to Dr. Montessori's philosophy, children learn best in a child-sized environment that is stimulating and inviting for their *absorbent minds,* one that offers beauty and order. Placed in that environment, the child may choose her own work—activities that have meaning and purpose for her. For example, to teach her students how to write, Montessori cut up large sandpaper letters and had the children trace them with their fingers, and later with pencil or chalk. Soon, the four-year-olds were able to write letters and then words, by themselves. The Montessori classroom was one of the first to emphasize a warm and comfortable environment based on independent learning. "Many of [Montessori's] once radical ideas—including the notions that children learn through hands-on activity, that the preschool years are a time of critical brain development, and that parents should be partners in their children's education—are now accepted wisdom" (Schute, 2002).

Children learn best in a child-sized environment that is stimulating and inviting.

After the child is introduced to the Montessori materials by a guide (teacher), she is free to use them whenever she likes, for as long as she wishes, undisturbed by others. The materials are *self-correcting.* If the child makes a mistake, she can see it for herself, without the need for an adult to point out her errors. Montessori materials are also *didactic,* designed to teach a specific lesson; focused on *daily living practical tasks* to promote self-help and environmental care skills; *sensorial,* planned to encourage children to learn through using their senses; and *conceptual,* or involving academic materials designed to develop the foundations of reading, writing, and math. Some examples of Montessori-type materials found in many early childhood classrooms today are:

puzzles—self-correcting

nesting or stacking cups, rings, or blocks—self-correcting

rough and smooth boards and fabrics—didactic and sensorial

containers and tops—self-correcting and practical life task

setting a table—practical life task

washing dishes—practical life task

sound or scent bottles—sensorial

sandpaper letters and numbers—sensorial and conceptual

measuring materials—conceptual

HEAD START. For 40 years Head Start has successfully served more than 22 million of America's poorest children (Children's Defense Fund, 2005). These programs are the largest publicly funded educational programs for infants and toddlers (Early Head Start) and preschool children. They include health and medical screening and treatment, required parent participation and involvement, and comprehensive services to families. "Today there are Head Start programs in every state and territory, in rural and urban sectors, on American Indian reservations, and in migrant areas" (Essa, 2007). From its inception in 1965, Head Start has sought to provide classroom-based and, most recently, home-based comprehensive developmental services for children from low-income families. Head Start's experience has shown that the needs of children vary from community to community and that to serve these needs most effectively, programs should be individualized, thus meeting the need of the community served and its ethnic and cultural characteristics (Head Start, 2003).

Developing a curriculum that continuously meets the needs of children is an important task for any Head Start program. The Head Start program performance standards define curriculum as a written plan that includes:

🌐 goals for children's development and learning

🌐 experiences through which they will achieve the goals

🌐 roles for staff and parents to help children achieve these goals

🌐 materials needed to support the implementation of a curriculum (U.S. Department of Health and Human Services, 2005).

Head Start programs have a low child-staff ratio, with 10 percent of the enrollment in each state available for children with special needs. Head Start provides staff at all levels and in all program areas with training and opportunities, such as the Child Development Associate (CDA) credential and related subjects at colleges and universities.

An essential part of every Head Start program is the involvement of parents in parent education, program planning, and operating activities. Head Start also addresses families' unmet needs (housing, job training, health care, emotional support, and family counseling) that may stand in the way of a child's full and healthy development.

Many different programs have been developed and evaluated as part of Head Start, and much research in early childhood education has been undertaken in Head Start programs. Thus, Head Start has been beneficial not only to the millions of children who have attended programs but also to the profession of early childhood education. (Brewer, 2001)

The original vision of Head Start has been improved and expanded for the new century as a model that challenges the effects of poverty and promotes physically and mentally healthy families. In 1994, Early Head Start was created to promote healthy prenatal outcomes, enhance the development of infants and toddlers, and encourage healthy family functioning while responding to the unique strengths and needs of each individual child and family. Early Head Start fulfilled a growing need that developed during this same period. Research on brain development revealed how crucial the first years of a child's life are to healthy development, the lack of infant and toddler care was desperately affecting most communities, and welfare reform was creating new child care needs. As Early Head Start continues to serve diverse families across the United States, with both center-based and home-based support, it is strengthening developmentally appropriate and culturally sensitive services for infants and toddlers (Essa, 2007).

The U.S. Congress continues to address the ongoing needs and funding requirements of Head Start. As advocates for young children and their families, we should continuously stay abreast of new developments.

BANK STREET. Founded in 1916 by Lucy Sprague Mitchell, this program continues to be an important model of early childhood education in the United States. Mitchell looked at education in a different way by developing a new type of educational experience for all children. Her essential component to reforming schools was shifting the focus to *child-centered learning.* Emphasis was on individual children and how they learn. "These ideas have carried Bank Street through growth and change over nearly ninety years of influencing the lives of children and the educational system" (Stavisky, 2002). Bank Street's *developmental interaction* method is dedicated to fostering all aspects of a child's development, the whole child, not simply to promoting specific learning. It also emphasizes the interaction between the child and the environment, as well as the interaction between the cognitive and affective areas of the child's development, thus underscoring that thinking and emotion are not separate but truly interactive. Children are creators of meaning. They work to understand the world they inhabit. The creation of meaning is the central task of childhood; if it is fostered by the adults who care for them, children will become learners for life (Bank Street School for Children, 2002).

At Bank Street School for Children, teachers arrange the classroom environment into distinct learning centers such as math, science, art, dramatic play, and music.

A developmentally appropriate environment encourages young children to develop self-help skills.

These centers, along with a variety of materials and experiences, relate to the ages and interests of the children in the group to encourage integrating the curriculum, making choices, taking risks, and accepting help. Teachers and children alike learn from and teach one another by building on shared experiences to develop meaningful relationships. This sharing extends to the families and communities.

> *The Bank Street approach is considered synonymous with open education, a term encompassing programs that operate on the premise that children, provided a well-conceived environment, are capable of selecting and learning from appropriate activities. The program does not aim to teach children a lot of new concepts, but rather to help them understand what they already know in more depth. (Essa, 2007)*

HIGH/SCOPE. Under the leadership of David Weikert, this educational approach began over 30 years ago as an intervention program for low-income, at-risk children. The High/Scope Perry Preschool Study is a landmark long-term study of the effects of high-quality early care and education on low-income three- and four-year-olds that followed the children to 40-year-old adults (High/Scope, 2005). Today the High/Scope program serves a full range of children—infant, toddler, preschool, elementary, and early adolescent—adapting to the special needs and conditions of their group, their setting, and their community. The High/Scope program has been successfully implemented in both urban and rural settings in the United States and around the world.

Active learning, High/Scope's central belief for all age levels emphasizes that children learn best through active experiences with people, materials, events, and ideas. Influenced by Jean Piaget's and Lev Vygotsky's theories of cognition and social interaction, this cognitively oriented model assists children in constructing their own knowledge from meaningful experiences. Materials are organized in each activity area so that children can get them out easily and put them away independently. In this kind of environment, children naturally engage in *key experiences*—activities that foster developmentally important skills and abilities (Hohmann, Banet, & Weikert, 1995).

A pioneer in conducting research and developing programs for young children, High/Scope implemented its first home visiting program for parents of infants over 40 years ago. It continues to focus on the development and needs of infants, toddlers, and families, while creating infant and toddler key experiences for teachers of this young age group (High/Scope Educational Research Foundation, 2005).

Teachers in a High/Scope program give children a sense of control over the events of the day by planning a consistent routine that allows children to anticipate what happens next. Central to this curriculum is the daily *plan-do-review* sequence in which the children, with the help of teachers, make a plan, carry it out, and then recall and reflect on the results of their chosen activities. Plan-do-review was developed to help *play* become more meaningful. Planning allows children to consider the what, where, when, how, and why of what they will be doing for the next time period. Doing means action, such as working with materials, interacting with other children, choosing, creating, and sharing, thus stimulating the children's thinking abilities through the application of skills to problem-solving tasks. Reviewing involves putting what one has done into words or pictures and sharing the representation with other children, teachers, or parents. Daily schedules provide for both large and small group interaction, a time for outside play, and time for the plan-do-review sequence of student-selected activities (Hohmann, Banet, & Weikert, 1995).

In addition to *plan-do-review,* the High/Scope approach emphasizes *key experiences* in which the children have plenty of time for active exploration in the classroom and the High/Scope *Child Observation Record* compiled from the daily recorded observations of the teacher. All of these are unique components of the High/Scope framework.

REGGIO EMILIA. Reggio Emilia, a small city in industrial northern Italy, established what is now called "the Reggio Emilia approach" shortly after World War II, when working parents helped to build new schools for their young children (New, 2000). Founded by Loris Malaguzzi, the early childhood schools of Reggio Emilia, Italy, have captured the attention of educators from all over the world. Inspired by John Dewey's progressive education movement, Lev Vygotsky's belief in the connection between culture and development, and Jean Piaget's theory of cognitive development, Malaguzzi developed his theory and philosophy of early childhood education from direct practice in schools for infants, toddlers, and preschoolers.

The teachers in Reggio Emilia are partners and collaborators in learning with the children and parents. The teachers become skilled observers of children in order to plan in *response to the children.* Each group of children is assigned co-teachers. There is no lead teacher or director of the school. A *pedigogista,* a person trained in early childhood education, meets with the teachers weekly. Every school has an *atelierista,* who is trained in the visual arts, working closely with teachers and children. *The hundred languages of children* is the term teachers use in referring to the process of children depicting their understanding through one of many symbolic languages, including drawing, sculpture, dramatic play, and writing. Teachers and children work together to solve any problems that arise. Children stay with the same teacher and group of children for three years (Albrecht, 1996; Gandini, 1993; New, 2000).

In 1987, The National Association for the Education of Young Children (NAEYC) introduced the first presentation on Reggio Emilia at the annual conference. Since then, inspired by the exhibition "The Hundred Languages of Children" and supported by delegations of educators who have seen the city and its early childhood classrooms firsthand, American interest in Reggio Emilia has grown at a remarkable pace (New, 2000). The Reggio Emilia approach is currently being adapted in early childhood classrooms throughout the United States, including many Head Start programs. Also, there is now a Reggio Emilia "track" of seminars at each NAEYC annual conference, as well as a network of educators, parents, and advocates who have formed the North American Reggio Emilia Alliance (NAREA).

Klein (2007b) recommends that in order to see whether a school is a good adaptation of the Reggio Approach, look for the following indicators:

1. Teachers reflect on their teaching practices.
2. Children are celebrated and seen as competent and capable.
3. Teachers realize it's an ongoing quest to capture what children are actually doing.
4. The use of documentation is evident, and it truly illustrates the children's explorations (e.g., capturing the process children go through to come up with ideas and examining children's thoughts).
5. The teachers seek to learn, not copy, Reggio educators and adapt their knowledge in the school.
6. Relationships are important, such as teachers with families, children with teachers, and teachers with teachers.

Bredekamp (1993) concludes that "The approach of Reggio Emilia educators is both old and new. Fundamentally the principles of Reggio Emilia schools are congruent with the principles of developmentally appropriate practice as described by NAEYC, presumably because both sets of principles share some of the same philosophical origins." See Figure 2–2 for concepts of the Reggio Emilia approach. Throughout this book you will find suggestions for incorporating Reggio Emilia principles into the curriculum.

FIGURE 2–2
Concepts of the Reggio Emilia Approach. (Source: Fraser & Gestwicki, 2002, p. 11)

GUIDING PRINCIPLES OF THE REGGIO EMILIA APPROACH

The following are some of the concepts of the Reggio Emilia Approach:
- the image of the child—the cornerstone of Reggio Emilia experiences conceptualizes an image of the child as competent, strong, inventive, and full of ideas with rights instead of needs
- environment as a third teacher—preparing an environment that acts as a third teacher carefully designed to facilitate the social constructions of understanding, and to document the life within the space
- relationships—seeing the importance of relationships physically in the way objects are displayed in the classroom; socially and emotionally in the interactions of the people in the environment; and intellectually in the approach to learning that is always seen in context and depends on co-construction of knowledge
- collaboration—working together at every level through collaboration among teachers, children and teachers, children and children, children and parents, and the larger community
- documentation—providing a verbal and visual trace of the children's experiences and work, and opportunities to revisit, reflect, and interpret
- progettazione—this difficult to translate Italian word means making flexible plans for the further investigation of ideas, and devising the means for carrying them out in collaboration with the children, parents, and, at times, the larger community
- provocation—listening closely to the children and devising a means for provoking further thought and action
- one hundred languages of children—encouraging children to make symbolic representations of their ideas and providing them with many different kinds of media for representing those ideas
- transparency—creating transparency through the light that infuses every space and in the mirrors, light tables, and glass jars that catch and reflect the light around the classroom; and metaphorically in the openness to ideas and theories from other parts of the world, and in the availability of information for parents and visitors

MULTICULTURAL/ANTI-BIAS CONSIDERATIONS

🌐 Twenty-eight percent of Head Start children speak a home language other than English.

🌐 By the year 2010, more than 30 percent of all school-age children will come from U.S. homes in which the primary language is not English.

🌐 By 2050, Hispanic and African American children under age five will outnumber non-Hispanic whites in the United States. (NAEYC, 2007).

You are, and will continue to be, an important person in the lives of these children. Your ability to understand and address their individual needs will help determine whether they have the knowledge and skills to succeed in school (Colbert, 2007). Each time you set up an appropriate, warm, supportive environment for young children, much of what you do is very familiar to you. At the same time, if you are exploring new ways to encompass each child's uniqueness, you may find many things that are unfamiliar to you. Exploring gender, culture, race/ethnicity, and different-abledness offers opportunities to develop new insights about yourself and the children in your care. You may feel comfortable and uncomfortable at the same time. It is important to understand that exploring and implementing a multicultural/anti-bias curriculum becomes a continuous journey of growth and change. As a teacher of young children, you should take, as one of the first steps in your exploration of multicultural education, the task of *discovering your own cultural uniqueness.* By reflecting on the culture and race/ethnicity of your family, you learn about yourself and about the culture of others as well.

Exploring your feelings about individuals who differ from you culturally, racially, or with special needs or disabilities is another step in the anti-bias curriculum development process. Discovering and coming to terms with your own feelings and attitudes will help you when these children join your group. Thus, **anti-bias** is an attitude that actively challenges prejudice, stereotyping, and unfair treatment of an individual or group of individuals. The inclusion of all children, whether they are differently abled or not, is a supporting principle of the anti-bias rationale. Ask yourself the following questions and then evaluate yourself by asking: Which of these issues have surfaced? What have I already accomplished? On what areas do I need to work?

anti-bias
An attitude that actively challenges prejudice, stereotyping, and unfair treatment of an individual or group of individuals.

- What differences among people or children make me feel uncomfortable?
- Do I have strong reactions to children from certain economic backgrounds, cultures, or races?
- How do I feel when children do not conform to my expectations about appropriate or acceptable behavior?
- Do I generally tend to prefer children of one sex?
- How do I react to families who have lifestyles that are very different from my own, and do these reactions influence my relationships or feelings about their children?
- When have I experienced or witnessed bias in my life, and how did I respond?
- How did I become aware of the various aspects of my identity and culture?

The *Anti-Bias Curriculum,* developed by Derman-Sparks and the A.B.C. Task Force (1989), is a comprehensive curriculum that offers helpful guidelines, activities, and materials that create an early education environment rich in possibilities for valuing differences and similarities. "Through anti-bias curriculum, teachers enable every child to achieve the ultimate goal of early childhood education: the development of each child to her or his fullest potential."

Cech (1991) explains, "At the center of each program is the child, and at the center of each child is culture." We must be sensitive to and respectful of the cultural background of each family member. The home and the center or school should develop a partnership to enable children to make an easy transition from known to unknown. We must support and retain the language and culture of the family as we add the language and culture of the early education program to each child's experiences.

Many children today are bicultural and bilingual. "The number of multiracial babies born since the 1970s has increased more than 260% compared to a 15% increase of single-race babies. . . . More than one million first generation biracial babies were born since 1989" (Wardle, 2001). West (2001) explains further, "Third culture children whose lives span two cultures, so-called for the third culture created within them, may hold two citizenships or hold citizenship in only one country but be born of parents representing two different races or ethnic groups." Increasing diversity means that as teachers and caregivers we must become more observant of individual children.

At the center of each program is the child, and at the center of each child is culture.

As teachers we must also be aware that some cultures emphasize a child's relationship to her group with group problem solving, rather than independence, individualism, and competition. In addition, some cultures value learning by active participation, while others encourage learning by observing and listening. "A simple but sometimes problematic cultural difference involves personal space. In cultures where people are often in crowded groups, children may sit and stand very close, touch a lot, and bump up against each other. This behavior may feel aggressive to children who aren't used to so much closeness and may require some guidance from the teacher. . . . It takes real sensitivity on the part of teachers and providers to decide how to handle behavior that is acceptable to one child within his family but considered aggressive by other children or by a teacher" (Gonzalez-Mena & Shareef, 2005). Therefore, we must give young children time to develop independence and accept responsibility within their own cultural framework. As teachers we should recognize our own defensiveness, continue to work on understanding, appreciating, and respecting differences, and developing patience with ourselves and the children. "The diversity of life is astounding, and the world is more complex than ever before. Our children will experience more new ideas, people, and change than any other generation in history" (Perry, 2002).

Culture Is Learned

No one is born acculturated. You must learn the beliefs of your culture. Anthropologists and educators consider culture to be something that is learned and transmitted from generation to generation. Another dimension is the concept that culture is something that members of a group share in common. You are born to a group with rules. However, groups borrow and share with other groups. As a result, culture is ever-changing rather than static and fixed.

York (2003) believes, "Multicultural education is more than teaching information directly. It means providing a classroom that includes materials depicting people from many different places doing many different things. . . . It is also encouraging children to act, think, and talk like members of their own culture. It's helping children like themselves just the way they are." Cech (1991) explains further, "The choices the child makes form the language of that culture. . . . This cultural language may begin as early as conception, long before the child can say the word 'culture.'" In infant-toddler programs how you feed, diaper, hold, talk to, and interact with each child is relevant to anti-bias curriculum. Teachers and parents should be in agreement with how these basic needs are met (Gonzalez-Mena, 2001).

Each child brings her culture into the group. Some may be from a culture different from the teacher's or that of the dominant classroom culture. Perhaps one of the children is accustomed to eating with chopsticks at home. Offering chopsticks, as well as forks and spoons, for use during lunch or snack shows that you are sensitive to the child's culture. Because the child will also be interacting with your culture, she may sometimes eat with a fork and spoon. At the same time, other children may try eating with chopsticks. This is the beginning of multicultural education in its most basic form.

Culture, then, is the sum total of a child's or family's ways of living: their values or beliefs, language, patterns of thinking, appearance, and behavior. It includes the set of rules that govern a family's behavior and are passed or learned from one generation to the next. As we learn about other than our own, we should be careful not to assume that just because children or families are from a specific ethnic or racial group that they necessarily share a common cultural experience. Recognize differences *within cultures* and *within families* (Marshall, 2001).

A multicultural/anti-bias curriculum is one that actively challenges prejudice and stereotyping and represents an opportunity for the development of mutual respect,

culture

The sum total of a child's or family's ways of living: their values or beliefs, language, patterns of thinking, appearance, and behavior. These are passed or learned from one generation to the next.

Each child and each teacher adds their culture and their uniqueness to the group.

mutual sharing, and mutual understanding. It is crucial to establish an early education environment that enables children to make connections to their reality as well as the larger world, to develop positive self-esteem, and to receive approval, recognition, and success.

The curriculum is also based upon how we set up our environments to include culture. Levy (2007) explains:

🌐 Explicit communication involves the activities and themes you plan for the children, the artifacts you provide from other cultures/countries, the books you make available, the toys and games you choose, and how you actively present information to the children.

🌐 Implicit communication includes the background items that don't necessarily define your program but which are important parts of daily activities and the learning environment. The background music you choose, the name of your classroom, how you define groups of children, the way you interact with the children, what information you value, how you resolve conflict, and how you arrange the room are all examples of implicit communication.

Expanding learning experiences to include others helps young children develop values, respect, and a cultural sense of belonging. Suggestions for integrating multicultural/anti-bias content and materials into specific curriculum areas can be found in Chapters 3 through 12.

> *An anti-bias classroom can flourish regardless of the educational setting. The process, however, takes time and can only be implemented within the developmental capacities of children. For this reason, the anti-bias approach is best begun in infancy. . . . [This] approach is not an add-on; it is a way of learning that permeates every element of the curriculum, i.e., interactions and modeling, family involvement, community relationship, staffing, routines, and the physical environment. (Hall, 1999)*

As you continue to study curriculum development in this book, you will understand how the anti-bias approach can flow through every element of the early childhood curriculum. (See Figure 2–3 for guidelines for a multicultural anti-bias environment.)

FIGURE 2–3
Guidelines for a multi-cultural anti-bias environment.

GUIDELINES FOR A MULTICULTURAL ANTI-BIAS ENVIRONMENT

The following guidelines can help you provide a developmentally appropriate, multicultural/anti-bias environment for young children.

- Be sensitive to, and respectful of, each child's cultural learning style without stereotyping. Include content about ethnic groups in all areas of the curriculum.
- Use differences in language and culture as a foundation for learning. Identify staff members or other adults from the community to serve as role models to help develop language learning and cultural activities.
- Communicate with parents to clarify home and school values about socialization and children's cultural and racial identities.
- Involve parents in the planning and implementation of activities.
- Model acceptance and appreciation of all cultures.
- Adapt curriculum materials to make them more relevant to all your children, and offer accurate information about different cultural groups in contemporary society.
- Ensure that the environment contains abundant images that reflect diverse abilities and current racial, ethnic, gender, and economic diversity.
- Make the necessary instructional and environmental adaptations (when possible) to meet the needs of children with special needs.
- Discuss cultural, racial, physical, and language differences *and* similarities honestly with children. Children are aware of differences in color, language, gender, and physical ability at a very young age.
- Provide opportunities for children to reinforce and validate their own racial and ethnic identities. Help children develop pride in their language, and their skin, hair, and eye color. Place value on the uniqueness of each individual.
- Help children find alternative ways or words to deal with racism and racial stereotypes.
- Focus curriculum material about cultures on similarities *and* differences, such as eating, clothing, shelters, celebrations, and music. Global awareness of similarities and differences builds understanding and respect.
- Provide opportunities to ask children questions about the activities/materials to assess their knowledge and help them to construct new knowledge. Allow time for children to practice changing perspectives.

(Adapted from Essa, 2007; Derman-Sparks & A.B.C. Task Force, 1989; Feng, 1994; Gonzalez-Mena, 2001; Marshall, 2001; Spodek & Saracho, 1994; York, 2003).

Special Needs Considerations

SN Recommended practices for serving young children with special needs and their families have changed dramatically in recent years and are continuing to evolve (Davis, Kilgo, & Gamel-McCormick, 1998). Children with learning, behavioral, or physical disabilities are now included in early childhood classrooms. **Inclusion** efforts reflect the blending of practices from early childhood education and early childhood special education. Miller (1996) explains, "Inclusion means that children with special needs are totally integrated into the activity of the classroom. . . . Effective inclusion is characterized by its virtual invisibility. Children with disabilities are not clustered into groups of persons with similar disabilities . . . children in an inclusive classroom are children with and without disabilities." Allen and Schwartz (2005) clarify further, "Inclusion is not about a place, or an instructional strategy or a curriculum; inclusion is about belonging, being valued, and having choices. Inclusion is

inclusion

Reflective of the blending of practices from early childhood education and early childhood special education.

Wide pathways help all children move comfortably, including those in wheelchairs.

about accepting and valuing human diversity and providing the necessary support so that all children and their families can participate successfully in the program of their choice."

According to Public Law 94–142, 1975 (amended to PL 99–457, 1986, and further amended in PL 102–119, 1991, and reauthorized in 1997 to PL–105–17), children with disabilities should be placed in the *least restrictive environment.* This means an environment that is as close as possible to the environment designed for nondisabled children, while remaining appropriate for their special needs (Spodek & Saracho, 1994). The environmental arrangement requires a teacher to prepare and organize materials and activities in learning centers and make appropriate adaptations for young children with disabilities (Davis, Kilgo, & Gamel-McCormick, 1998).

In agreement with the Individuals with Disabilities Education Act (IDEA) public laws, a written individualized family services plan (IFSP) that identifies the needs and goals of young children and their families must be developed for children ages birth to three in an early childhood setting. Klein, Cook, Richardson-Gibbs (2001) and Gargiulo and Kilgo (2000) identify several key activities that are expected to occur in the IFSP process. These include the following:

- In accordance with each individual state's criteria, *eligibility* must be determined for each child. This involves sharing, gathering, and exchanging information between families and staff.

- To assist families in making choices, *assessment* of the family's resources, priorities, and concerns, as well as the child's strengths, is made. A statement of the infant's or toddler's present levels of physical, cognitive, communication, social or emotional, and adaptive development should also be included.

- At a meeting, conducted in the native language of the family, *development* of the initial IFSP document is accomplished. At this point, a service coordinator is designated.

- To *implement* and *monitor* the IFSP document, the service coordinator is responsible for coordinating, facilitating, and monitoring the timely delivery of early intervention services with a review of the IFSP every six months and a full evaluation annually.

- Identify the steps to *support* the *transition* of the toddler with a disability to services provided under Part B (preschool).

An individualized education plan (IEP) is the legal document that must be written for a child with special needs over the age of three and his family, specifying learning objectives that are part of regular classroom activities and routines (Spafford, Itzo Pesce, & Grosser, 1998). "Current federal guidelines require children who will receive any special education services to be seen for a diagnostic study by members of a multidisciplinary team before services can begin" (Klein, Cook, & Richardson-Gibbs, 2001). How much help is provided by professionals in special education or related services depends on the needs of the children and on state and local resources (McCormick & Feeney, 1995). These specialists, together with the family and the early childhood teacher, function as a team.

Klein, Cook, & Richardson-Gibbs (2001) and Gargiulo & Kilgo (2000) expand on what the written IEP must include:

- A statement of the child's present levels of educational performance
- A statement of annual goals and related short-term behavioral objectives
- A statement of the specific special education and related services to be provided to the child
- The extent to which the child will be able to participate in regular education programs

Link the needs of each child with developmentally appropriate instructional practices.

🌐 The supporting services needed within the regular program

🌐 The projected dates and duration of services

🌐 The objective criteria and evaluation procedures, as well as how progress toward annual goals will be measured and a statement of how student's parents (guardians) will be regularly informed of such progress

Edmiaston, Dolezal, Doolittle, Erikson, & Merritt (2000) explain some of what an appropriate IEP framework *should include,* but usually does not:

🌐 Provide a potential framework for identifying goals for all children in early childhood classrooms.

🌐 Identify the goals and objectives that are necessary for young children with disabilities to function successfully in early childhood classrooms in which developmentally appropriate practice guides children's learning.

🌐 Focus on the whole child as an individual.

🌐 Link individual evaluations of children with developmentally appropriate instructional practices.

🌐 Revise IEP goals and objectives as necessary throughout the year to best fit the needs of the child.

It is crucial to be aware of the special needs that families of children with disabilities have and determine how the early childhood program can help meet these needs. As a teacher, you need to be sensitive to the various reactions that parents may experience, such as grief, guilt, anger, and even disregard of their child's special need. It is important to acknowledge and accept their reactions by listening, providing practical advice, and offering information on community resources that can be of help (Essa, 2007). Services to families must be individualized with regard for their cultures, strengths, values, skills, expectations, and needs. You should help them believe that they can cope with challenges and be successful in gaining the necessary resources and services (Wolery & Wilburs, 1994). See the Inclusion Adaptations Checklist, Figure 2–4, for further clarification.

INCLUSIVE ENVIRONMENT. Establishing an inclusive environment in an early childhood program should reflect and be sensitive to the diversity of all the children

Child's Name: _____   Date: _____

INCLUSION ADAPTATIONS CHECKLIST
CHECK ADAPTATIONS ANTICIPATED FOR THIS CHILD

PERSONNEL
_____ No extra support necessary
_____ Part-time extra support (specific parts of day)
_____ Full-time extra support (1:1 aide)

PHYSICAL ASSISTANCE
_____ No physical help necessary
_____ Physical help as needed
_____ Partial physical help
_____ Full physical help

CURRICULUM
_____ Adapt for lower cognitive level
_____ Adapt for vision impairments
_____ Adapt for hearing impairments
_____ Adapt for physical handicaps

PACING AND AMOUNT OF TIME PER ACTIVITIES
_____ Same pace and time as all other children
_____ Less time than other children (e.g., less attention)
_____ More time than other children (e.g., goes slower)
_____ Slower pacing necessary for understanding (e.g., more wait time for comprehension and/or action)

HIERARCHY OF PROMPTS
_____ Full physical help to complete activities
_____ Partial physical help to complete activities
_____ Direct verbal reminders to complete activities (e.g., "Sit down")
_____ Indirect verbal reminders to complete activities (e.g., "What do you need to do?")
_____ Gestures to complete activities (e.g., pointing)

ENVIRONMENT
_____ Seating adaptations (e.g., chairs too high, child does better sitting next to specific peers, etc.)
_____ Reduce/minimize distractions or stimulation
_____ Define limits (e.g., physical and/or behavioral)

BEHAVIOR
_____ Define limits (e.g., physical and/or behavior)
_____ Use positive reinforcement
_____ Determine behavior plans through use of ABC (antecedent, behavior, consequences)

FIGURE 2–4
Inclusions Adaptations Checklist. (Source: Klein, Cook, & Richardson-Gibbs, 2001, p. 110)

and their families. Each child, whether one with special needs or not, should be viewed as an individual with unique characteristics, strengths, and needs.

> *Children with special needs are often able to use most of the curriculum materials typically found in early childhood classrooms. They too need their life mirrored in the school setting with dolls, books, and play accessories that signify acceptance and belonging. (Gordon & Browne, 2007).*

Note: See the Checklist for Room Arrangement, Figure 2–11, and the front-of-the-book CD to help you, as a teacher, determine what you have done and what you need to do to create a developmentally appropriate early childhood environment, one that includes multicultural/anti-bias and special needs considerations. Adaptations and modifications of the classroom environment and curriculum will be discussed in each of the ensuing chapters of this book, Chapters 3–12.

Managing the Environment with Appropriate Guidance Techniques

Management in early education, including infant and toddler programs, is a direct result of understanding child development, establishing a philosophy, determining goals and objectives, and applying appropriate guidance techniques. This includes the personal philosophy of the teacher and the overall philosophy of the early education program. Inclusion of both indoor and outdoor environments is involved. The **environment** represents all the conditions and surroundings affecting the children and adults in an early childhood setting. "The environment is the stage on which children play out the themes of childhood: their interests, triumphs, problems, and concerns" (Gordon & Browne, 2008).

environment

In an early childhood setting, the conditions and surroundings affecting children and adults.

The arrangement of indoor and outdoor space requires *planning* for each individual child and group of children, *understanding prior experiences and development* of the children, and supporting the formation of trust, independence and creativity in the children. If the children feel they belong and their needs are being met, appropriate behavior usually follows.

Set clear, consistent, and fair limits for classroom and playground behavior, guide younger children toward appropriate ways to relate to others and to function in a group environment, and help older children set their own limits. Setting limits means security for young children. It is appropriate to remind children of the rules and listen when they express their feelings and frustrations. The National Association for the Education of Young Children, in the brochure *Helping Children Learn Self-Control* (2000), suggests, "The rules should be kept simple, few in number, clear, truly necessary, and reasonable for the age of the child." Whenever possible, explain the reason for the rule. For example, "The water stays in the water table so the floor will not be wet. Someone could fall on the wet floor." Remember, too, that as a teacher, you should model good behavior. You must follow the rules you expect the children to follow.

Many times children experience intense and dramatic emotions. A part of early education management is to help children deal effectively with the outward expression of their feelings. Help the individual child identify what she is feeling, place a limit on her behavior, and give the child an appropriate outlet for that feeling. For example, "I know you are angry with Jared, but I cannot let you hit him. You may hit the play dough instead." "Use your words to tell Shirley how you feel."

Try to explain children's behavior to each other. "I think Larry wants to play with you." "I think Stephen needs to play by himself for a while." Also, try to use suggestion or redirection rather than the word *don't*. It is helpful to say "Sand stays in the sandbox!" rather than "Don't throw the sand!" Tell children what you expect them to do in a positive manner. (See Figure 2–5.)

FIGURE 2–5
Appropriate verbal
guidance can help
young children develop
self-confidence and re-
spect for others.

APPROPRIATE VERBAL GUIDANCE WITH YOUNG CHILDREN

Practice saying "DO," not "DON'T." Focus on the positive. Use clear, short, meaningful phrases that encourage and offer positive suggestions to the child.

SAY THIS:	INSTEAD OF SAYING:
"Thank you for sitting down when you slide."	"Don't stand up when you slide."
"Please keep the puzzle on the table."	"Don't dump the puzzle pieces on the floor."
"Please turn the book pages carefully."	"Don't tear the book!"
"Thank you for talking in a quiet voice."	"Don't shout!"
"Please wipe your brush on the side of the paint cup."	"Don't drip paint on the floor."
"It's time to go inside. I have something to show you."	"Shall we go inside?"
"You need to turn off the faucet after you wash your hands."	"Don't waste the water."
"Please give me the ball to hold while you're climbing."	"Don't climb with that ball."

Handle spills and mishaps as a natural part of a child's day. By saying "Juanita, please get some paper towels to clean up the milk" and "I'll help you clean that up," you preserve a child's self-concept while allowing her responsibility for herself. See Figure 2–6 for suggestions on how to develop responsibility and independence.

The following guidance techniques are additional suggestions to think about as we deal with challenging behaviors of children in our classrooms:

🌐 Remember to address the behavior, not the child, when a behavior occurs that is not appropriate. Our goal should be to help guide the child from inappropriate behavior to appropriate behavior. Redirection, getting them interested in something else, is a nonthreatening way to achieve this.

🌐 "Teachers, parents, and child care providers quite often are trapped by the idea that if something does not work the first time, then it will never work. Children eventually change a behavior when they finally comprehend and remember that the action will quickly and consistently be stopped or redirected" (Miller, 2007). As teachers, we should remind ourselves that in order for children to behave appropriately, there must be *consistency* in both our expectations and our applications of rules.

🌐 "In learning new skills and concepts of any kind, children make mistakes. Under the right circumstances, errors in the cognitive domain are accepted as part of the learning experience. Correction when given, is responsible to the child's development and experience" (Gartrell, 2007).

🌐 Ask yourself: Is this behavior a signal of the onset of a new developmental stage? Some difficulties occur in infancy, toddlerhood, and early childhood at such times. Give a child choices, use humor, and be firm but supportive (Reinsberg, 1999).

🌐 Vance and Weaver (2002) have developed a problem-solving guidance approach that has worked for them in their early childhood classrooms for many years. They suggest *class meetings*.

Such meetings are not something you try once a week for a few weeks and then decide whether they are working. We recommend that teachers use this approach regularly for at least three months. . . . During class meeting a child, who needs help resolving a conflict, presents her view of the problem. The other children involved in the incident give their perspectives. With guidance from the teacher and suggestions from the rest of the class, the children involved work out a solution they can all accept. From their experiences in class meetings, children learn that honesty is valued, feelings are respected, and classmates care about each other.

This type of problem solving can encourage preschoolers and primary-age children to internalize this technique. Then, hopefully, when incidents occur, the children can solve their problems without a teacher's assistance.

⊕ Remember to communicate with parents. Teacher-family interaction creates a consistent and beneficial experience for young children. Our cultural values profoundly influence our perceptions about what guidance practices are most appropriate for children. Parents oftentimes assume that other parents naturally share the same underlying beliefs about how children should be disciplined (Miller, 2007). It is important that you, as the teacher, clarify what appropriate behavior is expected of the children in your care. If a child's behavior creates problems, open discussions between home and school are important.

FIGURE 2–6
Suggested guidance guidelines for young children.

GUIDANCE GUIDELINES FOR DEVELOPING RESPONSIBILITY AND INDEPENDENCE

- Arrange the environment to allow children access to age-appropriate toys, materials, supplies, learning centers, the restroom, etc.
- Expect children to do things for themselves, while understanding what their capabilities are. Do not expect more of them than they can give. Be patient and give the children time.
- Encourage self-help skills such as self-feeding and toileting, while planning opportunities for learning new skills, especially first attempts by children to do things for themselves. Keep in mind cultural values of independence versus interdependence.
- Give positive reinforcement for children's independent behaviors. It is the effort that counts, not the outcome.
- Offer simple yet consistent guidelines for the group and the individual child. Be sure your expectations are in line with the children's abilities and cultural expectations.
- Offer choices and then respect the child's preference and wishes. Suggest an easier or better way to do something when necessary, but leave the final decision up to the child.
- Allow and encourage children to participate in planning. Sometimes a child will come up with a better idea than the adult does.
- Allow children the privilege of learning through their mistakes without feeling guilty for having made a mistake. Be sensitive enough to know when not to help.
- Show each child that you trust and have confidence in her.
- Help each child change inappropriate behavior to appropriate behavior by using consistent, positive guidance techniques.
- Model appropriate behaviors for children so that they can be guided to attain the same behaviors.
- Avoid using words that would shame the children or cause them to doubt their competence.
- Support children when they feel frustrated and need security as they strive for independence.

Teacher-family interaction creates a consistent and beneficial experience for young children.

🌐 *Model* expected behavior and demonstrate *self-control*. Name feelings. Teach acceptable ways to express feelings. All of these actions can further show children how to be kind to and considerate of others.

🌐 As a teacher, you need to develop a support system for yourself. Create a teaching team that can help each other when children have crises or long-term needs.

Look for additional guidance suggestions throughout this book.

Setting limits, anticipating, and preparing for behavior difficulties are only part of a teacher's responsibility. Ensuring safety and preventing accidents in the environment for young children must also be considered at all times and in everything we do with and for young children. "Health and safety are not external patches or optional aspects of programs. Regardless of the limits imposed by funding, staffing, physical or curricular constraints, the health component should be an integrated part of the daily program activity" (Aronson, 2002). Indoor and outdoor safety is essential for all children. Preparation and prevention are critical to child safety. Catron and Allen (2003) remind us, "Only when safety is ensured, needs are met, and problems are prevented or diminished can the staff turn their full attention to implementing the program goals and objectives for enhancing children's growth and development." In Figure 2–7, Marotz, Cross, and Rush (2005) suggest a safety checklist for indoor and outdoor environments.

Arrangement of the Early Childhood Learning Environment

The indoor environment should invite you to "come on in." If you do not feel a positive welcoming, it is a signal that something probably needs changing. "It is important to remember, however, not to change everything at once. When making changes, think about what will appeal to you and the children and see where it takes you. Also think about the various areas and materials in the classroom and the type of behaviors and activities you wish to foster. If something is not functional or attractive, be brave enough to let it go" (Klein, 2007a).

INDOOR AREAS SAFETY CHECKLIST

1. A minimum of 35 square feet of usable space is available per child
2. Room temperature is between 68°–85° F (20°–29.4° C)
3. Rooms have good ventilation
   a. windows and doors have screens
   b. mechanical ventilation systems in working order
4. There are two exits in all rooms occupied by children
5. Carpets and draperies are fire-retardant
6. Rooms are well lighted
7. Glass doors and low windows are constructed of safety glass
8. Walls and floors of classrooms, bathrooms, and kitchen appear clean; floors are swept daily, bathroom fixtures are scrubbed at least every other day
9. Tables and chairs are child sized
10. Electrical outlets are covered with safety caps
11. Smoke detectors are located in appropriate places and in working order
12. Furniture, activities and equipment are set up so that doorways and pathways are kept clear
13. Play equipment and materials are stored in designated areas; they are inspected frequently and are safe for children's use
14. Large pieces of equipment, e.g., lockers, piano, bookshelves, are firmly anchored to the floor or wall
15. Cleaners, chemicals and other poisonous substances are locked up
16. If stairways are used
    a. a handrail is placed at children's height
    b. stairs are free of toys and clutter
    c. stairs are well lighted
    d. stairs are covered with a nonslip surface
17. Bathroom areas
    a. toilets and washbasins are in working order
    b. one toilet and washbasin available for every 10–12 children; potty chairs provided for children in toilet training
    c. water temperature is no higher than 120° F (48.8° C)
    d. powdered or liquid soap is used for handwashing
    e. individual or paper towels are used for each child
    f. diapering tables or mats are cleaned after each use
18. At least one fire extinguisher is available and located in a convenient place; extinguisher is checked annually by fire-testing specialists
19. Premises are free from rodents and/or undesirable insects
20. Food preparation areas are maintained according to strict sanitary standards
21. At least one individual on the premises is trained in emergency first aid and CPR; first aid supplies are readily available
22. All medications are stored in a locked cabinet or box
23. Fire and storm/disaster drills are conducted on a monthly basis
24. Security measures (plans, vigilant staff, key pads, locked doors, video cameras) are in place to protect children from unauthorized visitors.

OUTDOOR AREAS SAFETY CHECKLIST

1. Play areas are located away from heavy traffic, loud noises and sources of chemical contamination
2. Play areas are located adjacent to premises or within safe walking distance
3. Play areas are well drained
4. Bathroom facilities and drinking fountain easily accessible
5. A variety of play surfaces, e.g., grass, concrete, sand are available; there is a balance of sunny areas and shady areas
6. Play equipment is in good condition, e.g., no broken or rusty parts, missing pieces, splinters, sharp edges, frayed rope
7. Selection of play equipment is appropriate for children's ages
8. Soft ground covers present in sufficient amounts under large, climbing equipment; area is free of sharp debris
9. Large pieces of equipment are stable and anchored in the ground
10. Equipment is placed sufficiently far apart to allow a smooth flow of traffic and adequate supervision
11. Play areas are enclosed by a fence at least four feet high, with a gate and a workable lock for children's security and safety
12. There are no poisonous plants, shrubs, or trees in the area
13. Chemicals, insecticides, paints and gasoline products are stored in a locked cabinet
14. Grounds are maintained on a regular basis and are free of debris; grass is mowed; broken equipment is removed
15. Wading or swimming pools are always supervised; water is drained when not in use

FIGURE 2–7

A safety checklist for early childhood indoor and outdoor environments. (Source: Marotz, Cross & Rush, 2005, 6th ed., pp. 199–200.)

Arranging appropriate indoor and outdoor areas in an early education program is significant to curriculum development. This is an extension of classroom management and part of a teacher's strategy to accomplish the learning goals and objectives. Organization of the outdoor environment, like the indoor classroom, should set limits with reasonable, appropriate rules that are consistently reinforced to promote appropriate behavior. Teachers and children spend many hours in the classroom and on the playground. The extra time you spend to organize, plan for the needs of the children, and plan effective and efficient use of space will aid you in creating a developmentally appropriate learning environment.

INDOOR LEARNING ENVIRONMENT.

> *Although we talk about the environment in terms of the materials, equipment, and enhancements that create it, what we are trying to create is less tangible than the pieces we use to create it. It is the way a room feels in its entirety, the way it looks but also the way it smells and sounds, the way the air moves through it, whether it is warm or cold, whether it invites us to linger or encourages us to pass quickly through. . . . The environment sets the stage for children's living at school, as the primary aesthetic experience. (Wurm, 2005).*

Children need to feel that they belong. The environment should tell the children "we care about you." For example, have a personal space or "cubbie" for each child with her name or photo. In a shared space, each child needs to know there is one place that belongs to her. Display children's art, special projects, pictures, and bulletin boards at their eye level. These wall areas should be a visual extension of what is happening in the classroom. Ideas suggested by the children and their involvement in the final product should be part of the creative process of assembling the bulletin board. Reflect the interests of the children in all that you do.

Think about how you use color in the classroom. Try to express an anti-bias atmosphere. Primary colors and colors of the rainbow are used most often, but you should be sure to include brown and black as well. Many times we send a message that these colors are not aesthetically equal to other colors (Thomson, 1993).

The characteristics of a responsive, organized classroom offer a variety of well-defined **learning centers**, sometimes called interest centers, zones, clusters, or activity centers, where materials and supplies are combined around special groupings and common activities. These centers support children's learning and enable them to explore, experiment, and interact with the environment at their own rate of development.

Arranging and organizing the space for preschool, kindergarten, and primary classes becomes more specific and complex. The following learning centers are suggested for early education classrooms and outdoor areas (many of these can be combined or expanded):

learning centers
Well-defined curriculum areas (sometimes called interest centers, zones, clusters, or activity centers) where materials and supplies are combined around special groupings and common activities.

- Books, language, literacy, listening, and writing center
- Dramatic play, home living area, or puppet center
- Art center
- Sensory activities with manipulatives; woodworking; cooking; water, sand, and mud play
- Blocks
- Music and movement
- Science, discovery, and nature
- Math and manipulatives
- Social studies/multicultural
- Computers/technology center

The learning centers involve hands-on experiences with a variety of materials. These materials and supplies have a direct correlation to a particular objective, theme, lesson plan, or concept being introduced. Well-planned, continuous introduction and rotation of new materials stimulate interest. The learning centers make possible individual and small group instruction while providing an opportunity for the children to make choices in many different areas. The placement of the centers is important for balancing the number of noisy and quiet activities. How many of the areas are used at the same time depends on what is happening in relationship to the schedule, routines, and lesson plans. Sometimes specific learning centers may be closed to allow for expansion of other centers, for reasons relating to guidance and discipline, or because the size of the room necessitates rotation of activities. Also, the ages of the children and regulatory requirements will affect the numbers and types of learning centers available in an early education setting. Chapters 3 through 12 offer specific curriculum activities and a rationale for each learning center.

The clearly arranged spaces and classroom design assist children in setting their own pace and making choices that will help them to be more self-directed, which in turn will improve their self-control. (See Figures 2–8, 2–9, 2–10, and 2–11 for suggested room arrangements for infants, toddlers, and preschoolers. Additional room arrangement diagrams and a room arrangement checklist are in the front-of-the-book CD.)

The environment tells children how to act and respond. Children are more likely to follow classroom rules when the environment reinforces these: For instance, if it is important for reasons of safety that children not run inside, classroom furnishings should be arranged in a way that makes walking, rather than running, natural (Essa, 2007 and Isbell, 2007).

For children with special needs, additional environmental conditions should be considered. Allen and Schwartz (2005) explain that "effective early education is based on the principle that children are children, regardless of their abilities. All children have the same needs, though the needs may be more pronounced in some. For example:

FIGURE 2–8
A suggested room arrangement diagram for infants.

SAMPLE INFANT ROOM ARRANGEMENT

FIGURE 2–9
A suggested room arrangement diagram for toddlers.

SAMPLE TODDLER ROOM ARRANGEMENT

FIGURE 2–10
A suggested room arrangement diagram for preschoolers.

SAMPLE PRESCHOOL ROOM ARRANGEMENT

A CHECKLIST FOR ROOM ARRANGEMENT

_____ Does your arrangement support the goals and objectives you have set up for your indoor environment and outdoor area?

_____ Are the learning centers well defined? Can they be restructured for special needs?

_____ Is there enough space for the activity to take place, but not too much open space to encourage running?

_____ Is each center located in the best possible place in the room? Are windows used for appropriate centers?

_____ Are water play and art centers located near water sources? Do you have hooks near your art table for children to hang up paint smocks?

_____ Are noisy and quiet centers separated?

_____ Is protection from "traffic" given to centers that need it so that traffic flow does not interrupt children's play?

_____ Can both children and teacher move about freely?

_____ Are there wide pathways available for children with wheelchairs?

_____ Is the room uncluttered but still warm and inviting?

_____ Is there clear visibility so you can see all the children?

_____ Are equipment and furniture movable and is the arrangement flexible according to changing needs? When you convert your room for lunch or nap, do you do it the same way every day to encourage your children to feel comfortable and secure?

_____ Is the furniture appropriate for the physical size of the children? To promote independence are hooks, wash basins, toilets, and drinking facilities easily reached by the children? Can they all be child-operared?

_____ Is the environment flexible to accommodate children with special needs?

_____ Are bathroom facilities convenient?

_____ Are electrical outlets available in the right place? Are they covered when not in use?

_____ Is lighting adequate? Is the temperature of the classroom comfortable for the children?

_____ Are the materials and supplies for each center visible to and available for use by the children? Are directions clear and age appropriate? Do the materials stimulate a child's natural curiosity?

_____ Is the number of children per center controlled? Does the arrangement or a visual clue suggest the desired number of children?

_____ Are materials limited in each center to offer choices that are not overwhelming but still offer enough materials for all?

_____ Does each center offer visual clues for placement of materials and equipment while encouraging cleanup? Are storage containers labeled with objects, pictures, photographs, or outlines of the contents? Are labels written in languages other than English?

_____ Are the learning centers organized and attractive and appropriate for young children? Do they reflect cultural diversity free of stereotyping? Do the cultures represented visually reflect the multicultural reality of the world rather than your classroom reality?

_____ Does the arrangement within the learning center promote social skills while encouraging cooperative group learning or individual learning?

_____ Is there a space for a child to have some alone time?

_____ Are pictures and bulletin boards placed at the eye level of children? Do they display the children's projects appropriately and attractively?

_____ Does each child have individual space for storage (cubbie)?

_____ Is the environment welcoming to parents as they enter the classroom?

FIGURE 2–11

A checklist for room arrangement in an early childhood environment that includes developmentally appropriate and special needs considerations.

🌐 Moving about safely—in an environment free from clutter, slippery floors, or rumpled rugs—contributes to the safety and security of every child. For children with limited vision or physical problems, an environment free of obstacles protects against serious injury.

🌐 Minimizing clutter and confusion enhances the ability of all young children to concentrate on the tasks at hand. For children with attention or learning disorders, reducing distractions may be the best way to promote learning."

Exploring their physical environment comprises a great deal of the curriculum for mobile infants and toddlers. For them, a safe and healthy environment offers major activity areas designed for eating, sleeping, diapering, and playing. Caring for and playing with a few infants or toddlers at a time are the focus of these areas. Rocking chairs or gliders are a must. Babies enjoy rocking while being fed or comforted. If possible, sleeping should be in a separate room or quiet place away from active areas. These young children explore and interact with their environment through their senses; therefore, opportunities for open-ended exploration, visible and accessible materials, and safe possibilities for grasping, reaching, pushing, and pulling should be available. Mirrors add enjoyment for children during diapering and washing time.

Developmentally appropriate toddler programs are not a scaled down version of appropriate preschool programs. For toddlers, the addition of a toileting area is necessary. Their play areas can be more specific, such as ones with blocks, books, and large and small muscle activities. They also need space where they can play alone or be onlookers as others play.

OUTDOOR LEARNING ENVIRONMENT. The outdoor environment should invite you to "come on out." "The running, jumping, skipping, shrieking, and laughing of children at play is almost contagious in its expression of well-being" (Garvey, 1990).

Planning a balanced and varied outdoor environment, according to Catron and Allen (2003), "involves understanding children's perceptual motor development, incorporating outdoor activities into lesson plans, and regularly altering the outdoor environment to enhance opportunities for skill development." For example, taking inside activities outside opens the door for many creative learning activities. These activities can also encourage independence and socialization. Planning also includes a process for developing curriculum for the outdoors in a way that parallels what teachers do indoors.

> Simple experiences with nature can be very powerful opportunities for teaching and learning with very young children. Observing and talking about the many sensory aspects of nature—the sounds and smells of wind and rain, changing colors of the seasons, the tastes of fruits, vegetables, and herbs—inspire interest and appreciation of the beauty of nature. (Torquati & Barber, 2005).

An outdoor space for infants can be as simple as placing a blanket or mat in an unused section of a larger playground, or it can be an area with appropriate infant-sized equipment. The importance is that infants have access to the outdoors where they can experience the change in temperature, color, smell, sounds, and textures (Reynolds, 2002).

As a part of learning, children explore and test the environments, and so the playground, like the indoor classroom, must have limits. Fences, mandated by licensing requirements, set the parameters, and the teacher sets reasonable and appropriate rules that are consistently enforced. For example, "We sit on the slides and come down feet first."

Safety is the first priority. At least two adults should be supervising the playground at all times. McCracken (2000) advises, "Outdoor time requires adults who are playful, have sharp senses and quick reactions, and who will closely observe children. Save reading, resting, parent conferences, team meetings, and even casual conversations with other adults for more appropriate occasions. Your attentive eyes can prevent an injury."

Outdoor play is an essential part of the overall primary grade curriculum. Play reflects and enhances all areas of children's development, yet today outdoor recess is in jeopardy in many schools. Recess is increasingly viewed as the most useless of activities. Nonetheless, the available research suggests that recess can play an essential role in the learning, social development, and health of elementary school children. Recess may be the only opportunity for some children to engage in social interactions with other children. It is most important for educators and parents to become effective advocates for recess time (Jarrett, 2002; Tyler, 2000; Wellhousen, 2002).

Sutterby and Frost (2002) also emphasize that "opportunities for outdoor play aren't what they used to be, and children are suffering as a result. . . . Lack of exercise and poor eating habits are leading to declining levels of fitness among children and increased levels of childhood obesity. . . . The reduction in recess and physical education at schools is linked to increases in sedentary activity at home." As teachers of young children, we should enthusiastically encourage and participate in outdoor activities that motivate young children to become more active. (See Figure 2–12.)

As you continue to plan outdoor spaces for play and learning, think back to when you were a child. What were your favorite outdoor play settings? They probably included dirt, water, flowers, trees, places to be alone, places to climb, places to hide, places to build, and plenty of unstructured playing time with your friends. As teachers, we have the opportunity to give the children in our care these same activities in safe, creative, stimulating, and developmentally appropriate play environments.

(See the eight-page color insert for more information and photos of developmentally appropriate outdoor play. Chapter 10 also suggests other activities for outdoors.)

Criteria for Equipment, Materials, and Supplies Selection

The selection of indoor equipment (furniture and other large and expensive equipment), materials (smaller items such as puzzles, books, toys), and supplies (consumables such

Outdoor play is an essential part of the overall early childhood curriculum.

FIGURE 2–12
Call to Action: Preventing a continued increase in childhood obesity.

CALL TO ACTION
CHILDHOOD OBESITY

- *Estimates show that 15 percent of all children in the United States are overweight.* (National Institute of Environmental Health Sciences, 2007).
- *"It is probably not a coincidence that childhood obesity is on the rise at a time when some elementary schools are reducing or eliminating recess and critics are calling for preschools to spend time focusing on academics and drills"* (Ginsberg, 2006).
- *On average, children spend 5.5 hours a day watching TV, using the Internet, and playing video games. Children that watch more than 5 hours of television per day are 4.6 times more likely to be overweight.* (The Kaiser Family Foundation, 2004).
- *"The rising number of children identified as overweight or obese is deemed a critical concern as overweight and obese children are at risk for serious medical ailments . . . . social-emotional development can also be impaired"* (Greaser & Whyte, 2004 in Simpson & Gaus, 2006).

With these thoughts in mind, it is important for teachers to find out more about childhood obesity. This is our Call to Action. Visit the following Web sites to become more familiar with the facts and to find out what you can do to be proactive in addressing the needs of children and preventing a further increase in childhood obesity.

Action for Healthy Kids: http://www.actionforhealthykids.org
American Dietetic Association: http://www.eatright.org
American Obesity Association: http://www.obesity.org
The Center for Health and Care in Schools: http://www.healthinschools.org
Food and Nutrition Information Center: http://www.fnic.nal.usda.gov
Kids Health: http://www.KidsHealth.org
American Alliance for Health, Physical Education, Recreation and Dance:
    http://www.aahperd.org
The National Institutes of Health Obesity Research: http://obesityresearch.nih.gov
National PTA: http://www.pta.org
The Center for Health and Care in Schools: http://www.healthinschools.org
USDA Food Pyramid: http://www.mypyramid.org
U.S. Department of Health & Human Services: http://www.surgeongeneral.gov
Click on "Reports and Publications," then find the section "Calls to Action on Public Health Issues," and then click on "The Surgeon General's Call To Action To Prevent and Decrease Overweight and Obesity (2001)."

as paint, paper, glue) should be developmentally appropriate for the children in each classroom. Items must be child-size, nontoxic, aesthetically appealing, sturdy with rounded corners and edges, easy to maintain, and not easily broken. Many activities can be done on the floor, so the floor covering must be "child-proof " and made of linoleum, tile, or carpeting that can take spills and hard wear. Tables can serve as art, manipulative, and eating places. Boys and girls need experiences with the same kinds and variety of learning materials. Soft toys, big and comfy pillows, and furnishings that fit the children's size, abilities, and interests should also be included.

Arrange the environment to allow children access to materials, supplies, and learning centers. Labels, signs, and other kinds of print around the room offer visual guidance for children.

The Bank Street College of Education (1992) emphasizes the importance of including sensory materials in the selection for young children, especially toddlers. The use of

Store labeled materials in places that will make it easy for the children to use them and replace them.

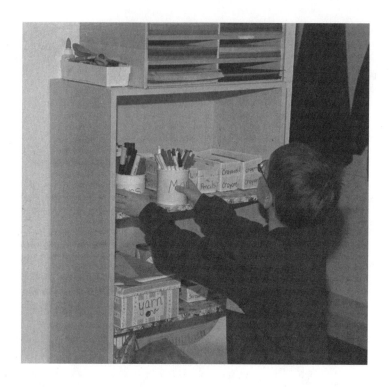

"tactile materials (things you can feel) is a full-body experience for toddlers—they will be up to their armpits in shaving cream or finger paint and will often want to paint with their hands instead of brushes."

In the outdoor area, play structures are lower and wider for those young children who need time to climb up or down. The design, according to Frost (1992), "should 1) allow a wide range of movement; 2) stimulate the senses; 3) offer novelty, variety, and challenge; and 4) be safe and comfortable."

The selection of outdoor equipment and materials emphasizes safety, durability, and age appropriateness for all children. The outdoor space should contribute to physical, intellectual, creative, emotional, and social development and offer a variety of stimulation for play and exploration. The design should also offer ramps and tracks that accommodate wheelchairs and adapted vehicles, giving proper attention to slope, width, types of surface, and direct and safe accessibility to play and structures (Frost, 1992). The surfaces should offer textures and colors, such as a hard-surfaced area for games and wheeled toys, a large soft grassy area with trees, a garden area, organic loose material such as play bark/wood chips and pine bark mulch, inorganic loose material such as sand and pea gravel, and rubber or foam mats.

The following are suggestions for equipment selection:

- permanent climbers
- take-apart climbers for older children to rearrange
- sturdy wooden crates and barrels
- railroad ties surrounding sand box
- tire swings with holes punched in several places for drainage (steelbelted tires are not appropriate)
- slides
- inner tubes
- balance beam
- tricycles, wagons, other wheeled toys

Selection of outdoor equipment should always emphasize safety, durability, and age appropriateness for all children.

 plastic hoops

 rubber balls of various sizes

 mounted steering wheel

 sturdy cardboard boxes

 equipment and materials that eliminate head entrapment points

You should think creatively of new ways to bring the indoor activities outside, and the outdoor activities inside, while at the same time keeping in mind the skills to be developed: body awareness, coordination, balance, large and small muscle development, encouragement of spontaneous and creative play, awareness of nature and the environment, and development of positive self-esteem and autonomy (Johnson, Christie, & Yawkey, 1987).

Technology and Young Children

TECH *Computers, as we have seen, have found their place into the preschool setting, taking their place beside the finger paints, play dough, books, and other media found within the early learning environment. (Mayesky, 2006).*

Computers, along with developmentally appropriate software, inexpensive cameras, digital cameras, videos, age-appropriate video games, interactive CDs, digital videodiscs (DVDs), and cassette tape recorders can make a unique contribution to the education of young children. As with any learning resource available, *how* technology is used is more important than *if* technology is used at all. Integrating computers and other technology into an early childhood classroom can enrich a cooperative, project-based, hands-on curriculum (Anderson, 2000).

Connecting with families through technology can also be successful. Ray and Shelton (2004) tell us, "At the beginning of the year, a first grade teacher requested e-mail addresses of family, friends, and school alumni who would like to be a part of an e-pal project. Those who responded received regular newsletters via e-mail, including photographs of the children engaged in activities, information about what the children learned and samples of children's work." The project produced increased involvement with families and the children's appreciation for family and cultural diversity also improved. Although technology should never replace direct contact with families it can offer an alternative way to communicate.

The following technology "Tips for Teachers" can get you thinking about using these resources in your classroom:

- Good teaching practices must always be the guiding goal when selecting and using new technologies.
- Select technology that reflects and reinforces all educational goals.
- Planning is important. Use technology only after adequate professional development on the appropriate use of computer hardware and software.
- Choose software carefully. Pick high-quality research-based computer applications that make unique contributions to children's learning. Choosing appropriate software is similar to choosing appropriate books for the classrooms—teachers constantly make judgments about what is age-appropriate, individually appropriate, and culturally appropriate.
- Use software that provides open-ended activities and problem-solving experiences.
- Link technology activities with hands-on classroom materials.
- Use appropriate technology that can improve children's thinking ability and help them develop good relationships with peers.
- Computers help primary-age children cooperatively plan, revise, and discuss, as well as focusing on spelling, punctuation, spacing, text meaning, and style.
- Work together with parents to promote appropriate use of technology at home.
- Use suitable technology tools that encourage learning activities that are self-paced and driven by the child's own interests and abilities.
- Make sure children with special needs are accepted and supported at the computer.

(Adapted from Clements & Sarama, 2003; Southern Early Childhood Association (SECA), 2000b; and NAEYC, 1996).

Further discussion of developmentally appropriate technology is included in each of the remaining chapters of this book. Considerations for selection of appropriate software for young children can be found in Chapter 9, "Sensory Centers."

For our primary-age children, Charlesworth (2008) says:

Hopefully, learning to focus on a task, make independent decisions, and maintain curiosity and creativity will enable today's young children to deal with our increasingly complex technological environment in the future.

THEMES, UNITS, PROJECTS, AND WEBS

You will find that the core of curriculum development is your capability, as a teacher of young children, to integrate the children's needs, interests, and abilities with your conceptual plan for implementing goals and objectives. As discussed earlier in this chapter, emergent curriculum themes actually *emerge* from the interests of the children and adults in the program with no specific time frame for the learning to unfold (Essa, 2007; Jones & Nimmo, 1994). Themes, units, projects, and curriculum webs will aid you in developing a child-centered, emergent curriculum approach.

Themes and Units

Thematic curriculum is curriculum that focuses on one topic or theme at a time. This is a process for managing curriculum while achieving developmental appropriateness. Integrated curriculum is intertwined with the thematic approach and enables the teacher to tie in the observations, interests, and abilities of the children to major content areas of language and literacy, dramatic play, art, sensory centers, music and movement, math, science, and social studies with curriculum direction and expansion initiated by the children.

Many educators use the terms *theme* and *unit* interchangeably. This book presents a **theme** as a broad concept or topic, such as "Magnificent Me," "Seasons," "My Community," "Friendship," and "The Environment." This approach can be used to introduce children to activities that require active exploration, problem solving, and acquisition of a specific concept or skill. A **unit** is a section of the curriculum that you determine to be important for the children to know more about and is based on the unifying theme around which activities are planned. This is often offered as an activity planned for a particular learning center.

Developing a list of themes is usually the first phase. This is useful as you move toward developing a lesson plan and the activities that fit within this plan. Remember to remain flexible and responsive to the children, including being adaptable to the varying developmental stages and experiences within the group. Your theme planning should merge play with child-directed and teacher-initiated experiences.

Here are some examples of themes that have proven to be favorites. These can be modified to fit any age group:

- Magnificent Me
- My Family and Me
- My Community
- Families
- Friendship
- Caring and Sharing
- The Seasons
- Weather
- My Five Senses
- Colors and Shapes in Our World
- Textures
- Things That Grow
- The Environment
- Plants and Gardening
- Animals
- Pets
- Cars, Trucks, and Buses
- Airplanes, Trains, and Tracks

theme

A broad concept or topic that enables the development of a lesson plan and the activities that fit within this curriculum plan.

unit

A section of the curriculum based on the unifying theme around which activities are planned.

Basic Concepts for Developing Thematic Curriculum

1. Themes and activities should reflect the philosophy suggested by the National Association for the Education of Young Children (NAEYC) for Developmentally Appropriate Practice (DAP) in Early Childhood Programs, such as: the critical role

of teachers in understanding and supporting children's development and learning; the concept of classrooms or groups of children as communities of learners; the importance of each child in the group; and the significant role of families in early childhood education.

2. Themes and activities should take into consideration the age, stage of development, and experiences of young children.

3. Themes and activities should emphasize and integrate different aspects of development and learning.

4. Themes and activities should be developmentally appropriate and underscore the importance of individual differences and cultural diversity among young children. This allows children to learn at their own pace and style.

5. Themes and activities should encourage the development of positive self-esteem and a sense of "I can do it" in young children.

6. Activities should be easily adaptable to large group, small group, or individual instruction.

    See Appendix B for an example of an integrated curriculum theme with activities: *My Community*.

Projects

A **project** is an in-depth investigation of a topic worth learning more about. This is usually undertaken by a small group of children within a class, sometimes by an entire class, or individually by an older child. This approach involves children applying skills, asking questions, making decisions and choices, and assuming responsibility. Projects may last for a few days or for extended periods of time. Some examples of project work include

> *drawing, writing, reading, recording observations, and interviewing experts. The information gathered is summarized and represented in the form of graphs, charts, diagrams, paintings and drawings, murals, models and other constructions, and reports to peers and parents. In the early years, an important component of a project is dramatic play, in which new understanding is expressed and new vocabulary is used. (Katz, 1994)*

The first phase in beginning the project process is to choose a topic, such as pets, cars, flowers, or the grocery store. Sometimes children have ideas for a topic, and sometimes a teacher chooses a theme based on the children's experiences (Gandini, 1993). Develop a topic web as a visual approach to the project. This web can also provide assistance for documenting the progress of the project (see Figure 2–13). The topic should allow the integration of a range of subject areas, including social studies, science, and language arts, as well as literacy and math skills (Katz, 1994).

Chard (2001) suggests the following criteria be used "to discriminate among different possible topics of study that depend on how children learn best, the basic social values we expect children to live by, and what we understand the role of the school to be in educating children." These criteria can be expressed in the form of questions about the value of studying any given topic. For example, how can study of this topic

- build on what children already know?
- help children to make better sense of the world they live in?
- help children to understand one another better?
- enable children to understand the value of literacy and numeracy in real life contexts?

🌐 encourage children to seek sources of information outside school?

🌐 facilitate communication with parents?

(Chard, 2001)

Progressing to the second phase involves investigating and developing the topic based on children's questions and directions. This continues with exploring sites, objects, or events of the project while collecting data, making observations, making models, and using Internet resources.

In the third phase, as interest reaches its maximum point, end the project by reviewing what you and the children have learned and participate in a culminating group activity. Throughout the project process, families act as partners in the children's learning. With you as their guide, everyone takes an exciting exploration together.

Helm and Katz's (2001) use of the project approach explores how early childhood professionals can apply project work to meet the challenges they encounter in their classrooms. They offer these comments:

🌐 Projects provide contexts in which children's curiosity can be expressed purposefully, and that enable them to experience the joy of self-motivated learning.

🌐 Teachers and children embark on these learning adventures together.

🌐 Parents also become involved and interested in the children's projects.

🌐 The use of technology by teachers and children during the project is beneficial.

🌐 Projects are helpful to children who are learning English and native-English-speaking children who are learning second languages. Children get meaning from hands-on experiences, demonstrations, and role-playing as well as from language.

🌐 Projects can be done in classrooms where children have special needs, both in self-contained classrooms and others with full inclusion. Teachers determine interests through observation, encourage verbalization from children who are not verbal, and support children by offering a multitude of ways to investigate.

FIGURE 2–13
An example of a thematic web.

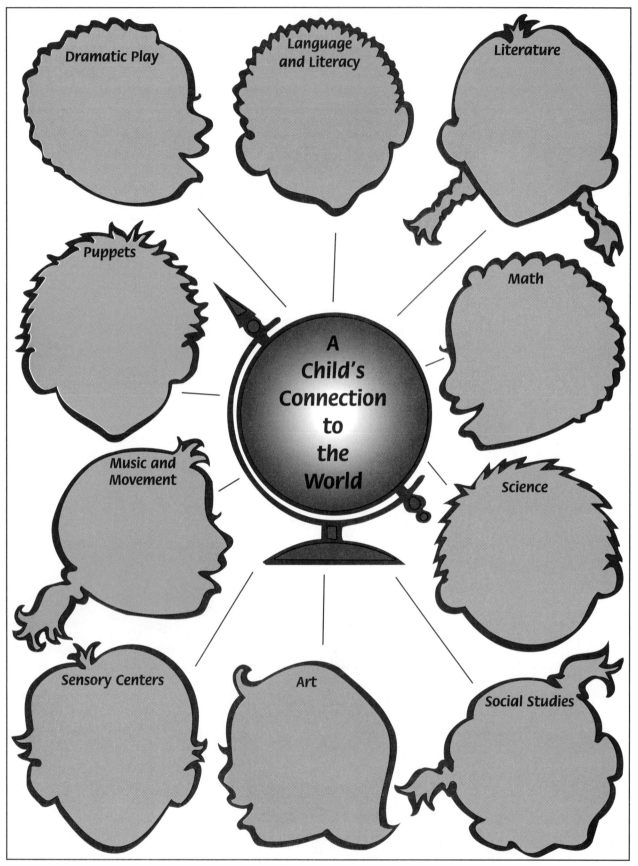

FIGURE 2–14
A curriculum planning web worksheet.

Webs

A **curriculum web** integrates various learning activities. This visual process offers flexibility for you and the children. You can move in different directions, design learning activities that integrate various curriculum areas in special ways, and extend the thematic planning and/or project chosen. "Webbing" helps develop the scope and content of the theme.

To produce a thematic web, you have the choice of brainstorming a single idea or topic by yourself, with a colleague, or with the children. Then record the ideas in an expanding web. This becomes a visual illustration of what could be included in a theme or unit or project approach to the curriculum, You can then put the elements of the web into planned daily activities, with the children actively investigating, initiating, questioning, and creating. For an infant, toddler, or child with special needs, have the individual child be the center of the theme (web) in order to plan activities for that child.

Figures 2–13 and 2–14 are examples of a curriculum planning web. The worksheet in Figure 2–14 is used throughout the text to demonstrate the application of learning center activities. Other examples of a thematic web can be found in Chapter 9 and Appendix B.

In the front-of-the-book CD, additional curriculum webs are created using the software *Inspiration®* 8. See the student CD for a trial version of *Inspiration®* 8 software. You can create your own curriculum webs and more.

LESSON PLANS

The **lesson plan** is an outgrowth of theme selection, brainstorming/webbing, and selection of projects and activities. This involves making a series of choices based on the developmental stages, learning styles, and interests of the children; the goals and objectives of the program; and the availability of materials, supplies, and resources.

As you plan for the weekly, biweekly, or monthly period, think about the following:

🌐 A classroom that is well planned, attractive, and organized provides an environment that facilitates learning and becomes a part of the learning program itself.

The lesson plan offers opportunities for small group activity times.

It is helpful to schedule a specific teacher planning time during each week. This allows you time to reflect on your observations of the children, what is working, what needs to be changed, and what additional materials and supplies are needed.

It is helpful to develop a planning form, such as a written lesson plan worksheet. This will clarify your thinking and aid you in articulating your rationale for what you plan to do. It can also be posted for parents, teacher-assistants, and substitute teachers to see and refer to. (See Figures 2–15, 2–16, and 2–17 for lesson plans of infants, toddlers, and preschool children. The activities included in these plans are in Chapters 3–12.) Blank lesson plan worksheets can be found in Appendix A and in the front-of-the-book CD for this book along with additional lesson plans, as well as examples of lesson plans for individual children.

The lesson plan allows for planning the emergent curriculum theme or unit, concepts to be explored, skills to be developed, individual activities and large or small group activity times to be created, integration of the learning centers and curriculum areas, and preparation for special activities or field trips.

It is helpful for you to develop a "things to remember" form for writing down items or materials to prepare or gather before the children arrive. It also allows you to write down ideas that come to mind to be used at another time. You will find that many new or remembered ideas come to mind during this special planning time.

Remember to plan for "a rainy day." Unexpected events, such as bad weather, can require you to have on hand materials and supplies for new activities to be implemented at a moment's notice. A new puppet, book, game, flannelboard story, song, or art activity are examples of activities you can put in a special box to use for such an occasion.

As you plan, develop a checklist for yourself that includes the following questions:

What do the children already know? How can I build on that? What have they thought of ?

Is the theme or activity appropriate for the age and stage of development of the children?

Are the selections too general or too broad?

Are there too many or too few activities?

Are multicultural and anti-bias activities included?

Is the lesson plan flexible enough to allow for unexpected events or spontaneous moments?

Is there a wide selection of books, songs, finger plays, and so on?

Are the units of instruction open-ended, allowing for exploration and learning opportunities to occur?

As the children learn at their own pace about the world around them, they are organizing, manipulating, experimenting, communicating, and trying out different roles. To help children initiate their activities, trust the value of play experiences and spontaneous moments. If all of this is happening in your early childhood environment, then independent thinking and creative responding will happen.

Sample INFANT LESSON PLAN (12-18 Months)

TEACHER(S):   DATES: THEME: Magnificent Me!

CENTERS & ACTIVITIES	MONDAY	TUESDAY	WEDNESDAY	THURSDAY	FRIDAY
SENSORY: ART, MUSIC, TACTILE ACTIVITIES	Scribble with multicultural crayons. Make banana/raisin snack.	Sing "Name Song". Use large soft blocks.	Sing "If You're Happy and You Know it" with jingle bells.	Watch or chase bubbles floating to music. Play with play dough.	Cover table with white sheet & use non-toxic markers.
COGNITIVE & LANGUAGE ACTIVITIES	Sing "I Have Two Ears" and read Yellow Ball.	Show and talk about family pictures. Read My Family	Play "Pat-a-Cake" with jingle bells. Read the book Pat-a-Cake	Play "Peek-A-Boo" and read the book Peek-A-Boo.	Play "Where's _____? There s/he is!"
SMALL MUSCLE & LARGE MUSCLE ACTIVITIES	Push & pull toys	Roll ball back & forth, crawl on soft rug	Drop (wooden) clothespins into a container one at a time	Crawl up soft foam incline	Stack bean bags
SELF-AWARENESS, SELF-HELP ACTIVITIES	Make faces into a mirror	Play Peek-A-Boo in mirror	"Jack Frost", fingerplay naming parts of body	Sing "Rock-a-Bye Baby" with soft babydolls.	"This is the Way We Wash Our Hands"
SPECIAL ACTIVITIES	Take stroller walk	Play on a quilt outdoors	Hang wind chimes near window or vent and listen to them.	Sing or chant "Roll the ball to _____. Roll it back to me.	Visit from grandparents (if possible)
BOOKS OF THE WEEK	Peek-a-Boo (Ahlberg), Pat-a-Cake (Kemp), Yellow Ball (Bang), I Hear (Isadora), I See (Isadora), I Touch (Oxenbury), My Family (Ostarch), Baby Says (Steptoe)				
SPECIAL NOTES	Dramatic play with soft multicultural baby dolls and blankets. Multicultural music and song tapes.				

FIGURE 2–15
An infant lesson plan worksheet.

Sample TODDLER LESSON PLAN

TEACHER(S): ___ DATES: ___ THEME: Magnificent Me!

CONCEPTS: I am special & wonderful! I'm learning to do many things. SKILLS: Self-Help, Language, Social

DAY	LARGE GROUP ACTIVITIES	SMALL GROUP ACTIVITIES
MONDAY	Sing "I'm a Special Person and So Are You"	Practice dressing with dress-up clothes
TUESDAY	Read A Baby Just Like Me while sitting on a cozy quilt	Bathe baby dolls in warm soapy water (use no-tear baby shampoo), pat dry
WEDNESDAY	Read My Feet Wiggle toes together	Take off and sort shoes, then put your own back on
THURSDAY	Read Caps For Sale while wearing caps from dramatic play	Add caps to the pile of shoes, sort, put on, then look in the mirror
FRIDAY	Read together "Una Casita Roja (The Little Red House)"	Use small, unbreakable hand mirror "___, ___, who do you see?"

SENSORY ACTIVITIES
Sand box toys
Colored water in water table
Play dough in various skin colors

MUSIC ACTIVITIES
Sing "Rock-a-Bye Baby" to dolls
Sing "If You're Happy & You Know It..."
Listen to multicultural music & dance.

ART ACTIVITIES
Scribble on sheet-covered table
Put torn paper on sticky-backed paper
Foot & hand prints with paint

DRAMATIC PLAY / HOME LIVING & PUPPETS
Play kitchen with dishes, aprons, dress-up clothes include hats, full-length mirror, family puppets

SELF-AWARENESS, SELF-ESTEEM, SELF-HELP ACTIVITIES
Dress self, put on shoes and caps
Serve and pour at meals

LANGUAGE ACTIVITIES
"Humpty Dumpty" finger play
Discuss torn paper: color, feel, sizes
Flannel board "Una Casita Roja"

MOVEMENT / OUTDOOR ACTIVITIES
Chase bubbles
Push and pull toys, trikes
Climbing structure

SMALL MUSCLE / MANIPULATIVE ACTIVITIES
Cut & tear paper in tactile table
Puzzles of babies & families
Small figures & doll house

TRANSITIONS
"If your name is ___, then go to ___, (the door, etc.)"
"Name Song"

BOOKS OF THE WEEK:
Here Are My Hands, To Baby With Love, Making Friends, Where's the Baby?, On Mother's Lap, The Napping House

ACTIVITIES / NOTES:
Take a walk in the neighborhood
Visit from grandparents (if possible)
Cut up apples and eat.

FIGURE 2–16
A toddler lesson plan worksheet.

Sample PRESCHOOL-KINDERGARTEN LESSON PLAN

TEACHER(S):

DATES:

THEME: Magnificent Me!

CONCEPTS: I am unique, special, and part of a family

SKILLS: Prewriting, writing, measuring, graphing, problem-solving, and-awareness of similarities/differences

CENTERS & ACTIVITIES	MONDAY	TUESDAY	WEDNESDAY	THURSDAY	FRIDAY
MORNING GROUP ACTIVITY	Sing "Good Morning." Introduce "My Body."	Take individual instant photos. Introduce "My ends."	Read On the Day You Were Born. Introduce "My Family."	Make breadsticks formed in initials. Introduce "My Home."	Healthy snack chart: finish & discuss.
AFTERNOON GROUP ACTIVITY	Identify body parts and what they do.	Animal friends: share stuffed animals and/or pets.	Chart birthdays of the children and family members.	Read How My Parents Learned to Eat.	Bring and share something about yourself.
LANGUAGE & LITERACY	Begin "All About Me" books.	Write about photo and put into "Me" book with photo.	Add family photo to book. Write or draw about photo.	Write class story about field trip experience.	Finish "All About Me" books and share. Finish class story.
ART	Make life-sized self-portraits.	Make thumbprint and footprint pictures.	Make puppet papercup family pop-ups.	Make kitchen gadget puppets.	Mix playdough to match skin color.
MUSIC & MOVEMENT	"Name Song" Body parts move to music.	Sing "I'm A Special Person and So Are You" and "Friends Go Marching."	Beanbag toss and Kitchen marching band.	Sing "So Many Ways to Say Good Morning" and dance.	Dance in hats with streamers to music.
DRAMATIC PLAY HOME LIVING	Home living center with a full mirror and baby pictures of children.	Add phones, paper, and pencils for message-taking.	Bathe baby dolls in warm sudsy water. Add stuffed animals to area.	Add a Wok and other cookware to center.	Add hats to dress-up clothes.
MATH MANIPULATIVE	Measure and record height of each child.	Graph the children's heights.	Use puzzles of family celebrations.	Gather items from home and play "What's missing?"	Estimate number of pennies in a jar, then count them.
SCIENCE & DISCOVERY	Listen to heart with stethoscope. Examine picture or model of skeleton.	Magnifying glasses to see thumbprints. Exploring shadows.	Food colors, eye droppers, and ice trays.	Weigh on scales for "Me" book. "What's That Sound?"	Magnets and what sinks, what floats?

BLOCKS
Add: people figures, animal figures, boxes, houses, cars

OUTDOOR/LARGE MUSCLE
Nature walk: obstacle course on playground Hop, run, skip, jump

TRANSITIONS
Puppet helper of the day Variations on "Name Song"

SENSORY CENTERS
Water table with warm, soapy water Multicultural skin colored playdough. Healthy snacks "Tasting Tray"

SOCIAL STUDIES
Invite family members to visit. Field Trip to grocery store. We are all alike. We are all different.

BOOKS OF THE WEEK
My Five Senses, Big Friend, Little Friend, Mommy's Office, William's Doll

SPECIAL ACTIVITIES & NOTES

Field trip to grocery store. Children decide which healthy snacks to buy. Explain decisions.

Week-long project: Make chart or diagram re: food groups. Prepare and eat snacks. Write class story.

FIGURE 2–17
A preschool-kindergarten lesson plan worksheet.

Activity Plans

Using an activity plan format as you set up learning centers will help you focus on clearly describing the activity, objectives, concepts, skills, space and materials needed, step-by-step procedure, guidance and limits for expected behavior, and the evaluation and follow-up.

The presentation of an activity works on many levels. Fortson and Reiff (1995), in their discussion of continuous goals for teaching and learning, help us understand that "The way we present materials, lead activities, and guide discussions makes an enormous difference in whether children use independent thinking and exercise powers of thought, feeling, and expression." Hopefully each activity will encourage children to solve problems, complete a project, and develop an eagerness to learn more.

When writing measurable objectives for an activity, describe "the precise quality of change in knowledge, behavior, attitude, or value that can be expected from the learner upon completion of the learning experiences" (Redican, Olsen, & Baffi, 1993 and in Marotz, Cross, & Rush, 2005). For example, the child will be able to demonstrate math concepts such as one-to-one-correspondence, counting, and measuring. The key word in this objective is *demonstrate.*

Other examples of measurable terms are:

- compare
- demonstrate
- describe
- explain
- identify
- list
- match
- recognize
- write

The activity plan worksheet (Figure 2–18) is a suggested format that can be used to help you plan activities. Multiple activity plan examples are included in Chapters 3 through 12 and in the front-of-the-book CD of this book.

TRANSITIONS

Transitions are activities/learning experiences that move children from one activity to another. They are also teaching and guidance techniques. A sensitive teacher determines in advance the transition times in the daily program so that the children avoid lining up or waiting their turn, and the change of pace will not be jarring or interruptive to them.

Children need time to adjust to change; therefore, as a teacher you should use a transition activity to direct children from

- a self-initiated to a teacher-directed activity.
- an active to a quiet activity or from quiet to active play.
- cleanup and toileting to snack time.
- lunch to naptime.
- outside to inside or inside to outside play.

In addition, for the younger child, transitions can be used to help them adjust to arriving and then separating from mommy or daddy, learning to listen, sitting down, and joining in a small group activity for a brief time. For older children, transition activities can be used for getting attention, giving directions, gathering the group, and helping them understand the sequence of events or when events change without warning.

transitions

Activities or learning experiences that move children from one activity to another.

ACTIVITY PLAN WORKSHEET

Date of activity:_____

Children's age group:_____

Number of children in this group (large group, small group, or individual activity):_____

Learning center to be used:_____

Name of Activity and Brief Description

Purpose/Objectives of Activity

(Concepts, skills, awareness, or attitudes you have designed the activity to teach or develop. Describe in measurable objectives.)

Space and Materials Needed

Procedure

(Step-by-step description of the activity. Tips for getting started: describe what you will say or do to get the children interested in the activity, and let them know what they will be doing. Describe the activity in the sequential order you will use with the children. Where will this activity take place? Plan for ending the activity. How will you help the children make a smooth transition to the next activity?)

Guidance

Establish necessary limits for behavior and boundaries of activity. Anticipate problems that may develop during this activity and consider ways to handle them.

Evaluation and Follow-Up

What was the children's response? What worked well? What didn't work? How could this activity be changed to make it effective or more appropriate? List possible activities that would extend or give practice to the objectives of this activity.

FIGURE 2–18
An activity plan worksheet.

When the children get used to the schedule and routines of the day, the number of transitions used can be reduced. Children who are free to choose their play and activities will develop their own natural transitions as their interests and curiosity direct.

Examples of Transition Activities

🌐 Use a record or tape, or sing a song such as "The Hokey Pokey," where children can join the group as they finish with cleanup.

🌐 After group time, ask all children who are wearing red to stand up. Continue calling various colors until all the children are standing. Then give directions to the next activity.

🌐 Prepare a set of flannelboard circles with each child's name on one. Place name side down on flannelboard, and take off one at a time while saying the child's name. When the child's name is called she chooses a song, finger play, or activity for the group to do.

🌐 Use rhythm instruments to accompany a song you are singing. Let the children take turns using these instruments. As each child finishes her turn, she chooses a learning center to go to.

🌐 Children gather quickly when you play the autoharp, guitar, or other instrument. Let a few children strum the instrument while you are waiting for others to gather.

🌐 Pretend that one child is the engine on a train. As that child "chugs" around the room, other children join the train by putting their hands on the shoulders of the child ahead.

When all children are part of the train, then "chug" along outdoors.

⊕ Play "Simon Says." On the last direction, Simon says, "Sit down." You are now ready for a story or other quiet activity.

⊕ Play directional games such as "Touch your nose, turn around, sit down." Start with simple directions and get more complicated as the children are able to follow through on two and three directions.

⊕ Gently remind children when it is time to begin to complete their activities. A simple blinking of the overhead lights will let them know it is time to clean up.

⊕ Help children move toward closure of the daily activities. Put things away and gradually close down the centers. Then read or tell a story until all the children have been picked up.

PLAN OF OBSERVATION, ASSESSMENT, AND EVALUATION

The process of curriculum development is one of continuous planning, implementing, observing, assessing, and evaluating. A curriculum is planned to meet the needs of the individual children in the group by defining philosophy, goals, and measurable, meaningful objectives.

Observation is taking in information and objectively interpreting it for meaning. Ahola & Kovacik (2007) explain that ". . . watching children is not the same as observing them, and that only by observing the developing child can we truly understand him. . . . Why observe? The answer to this is very basic. We observe a child in order to understand the true nature of the child."

The following methods for observing and recording are often used in the assessment and evaluation process:

Anecdotal record: A brief, informal narrative account describing an incident of a child's behavior that is important to the observer. It may apply to a specific child or to a group of children. Anecdotes describe the beginning and ending times of the observation, an objective, and a factual account of what occurred (telling how it happened, when and where it happened, and what was said and done). Anecdotal records come only from direct observation, and are written down promptly and accurately (Essa, 2007). "The anecdotal record allows us to view the child's behavior within the contexts in which it is happening" (Ahola & Kovacik, 2007).

Checklist: A record of direct observation that involves selecting from a previously prepared list the statement that best describes the behavior observed, the conditions present, growth and development, or the equipment, supplies, and materials available. "They are intended to reflect common activities and expectations in classrooms that are structured around developmentally appropriate activities and are based on national, state, and local standards" Meisels, (2000). Checklists are easy to use and helpful in planning for individual or group needs.

Reflective Log or Diary: A teacher's or administrator's record of the most significant happenings, usually made at the end of the day or during an uninterrupted block of time. This includes what stood out as important facts to remember for the day, written in as much detail as possible.

Case study: A way of collecting and organizing all of the information gathered from various sources, including observations of and interviews with the child, to provide insights into the behavior of the individual child studied. Interpretations and recommendations are included. The main purposes for this detailed observational record are to discover causes and effects of behavior, child development research, and to plan for the individual child.

Portfolio assessment: This method is based on a systematic collection of information about a child's ongoing development and the child's work gathered by both the child and teacher over time from all available sources. A portfolio is a collection

---

observation

The process of observing various aspects of an early childhood program by taking in information and interpreting it for meaning.

anecdotal record

A brief, informal narrative account describing an incident of a child's behavior that is important to the observer.

checklist

A record of direct observation that involves selecting from a previously prepared list the statement that best describes the behavior observed, the conditions present, or the equipment, supplies, and materials available.

reflective log or diary

A teacher or administrator's record of the most significant happenings, usually made at the end of the day or during an uninterrupted block of time.

case study

A way of collecting and organizing all of the information gathered from various sources to provide insights into the behavior of the child studied.

portfolio assessment

An evaluation method based on a systematic collection of information about a child and the child's work, gathered by both the child and teacher over time from all available sources.

of child-produced material, such as "works-in-progress," creative drawings, paintings, and dictated stories; lists of books and stories read; product samples showing a child's strengths and skills; samples of a child's self-initiated "work"; audio and video tapes; teacher objectives for the child, observations and anecdotal records, developmental checklists, and parent interviews; and parents' comments. Teacher comments on each portfolio sample can help document what the child knows, can do, and how she does it. Portfolios can be a file folder or an accordion-type folder for each child (Batzle, 1992; Hendrick; 2003). Portfolio information helps the teacher "construct a well-rounded and authentic picture of each child so you are better able to plan your program, to build on individualized strengths, and to support each child's growth. . . . Because you want portfolios to be integrated into your daily program, they need to be within children's easy reach. Children enjoy looking back through their work, and browsing and reflection are important parts of this process" (Cohen, 1999).

 Note: A sample portfolio assessment checklist and multiple observation forms are in the front-of-the-book CD accompanying this book (see Figure 2–19).

OBSERVING YOUNG CHILDREN GUIDELINES

Reasons for observing children:
- To gain knowledge of age-appropriate behaviors
- To gain knowledge of individual differences
- To become aware of the total environment and influences on children
- To identify specific strengths and difficult areas for individual children
- To gather data to plan for individual children
- To gain understanding of children—the stages of physical, intellectual, emotional, social, and language development
- To gain an appreciation of young children—their abilities, interests, perceptions, and personalities
- To gain knowledge of how children learn
- To identify how individual children react/relate to a group situation
- To become aware of positive (pro-social) and negative (anti-social) behaviors of young children

Guidelines for recording the behavior of young children:
- Remember that all information is confidential
- Observe quietly with little or no interaction with the child (children) being observed
- Record objective observations in a clear, precise, and useful manner
- Think of the child and respect her as she is, not as you think she should be
- Be familiar as possible with the age group before beginning to observe
- Use the speaker's exact words when recording conversation

Guidelines for interpreting the behavior of a young child:
- To identify consistent patterns of behavior for a particular child over a specific period of time
- To document patterns of behavior with specific examples of such behavior
- To identify areas of difficulty and developmental delays as well as age-appropriate and accelerated development
- To remember not to make assumptions about the child's family life as the cause of her behavior at school/center
- To remember not to make assumptions about the child's behavior away from the school/center

FIGURE 2–19
Observing young children guidelines.

assessment

The collection of information or data on young children through observation and record keeping of what they do and how they do it as a basis for making educational decisions.

Assessment refers to the collection of information or data collecting. "Assessment is the process of observing, recording, and otherwise documenting the work children do and how they do it, as a basis for a variety of educational decisions that affect the child. Assessment is integral to curriculum and instruction" (NAEYC & NAECS/SDE, 1991). Assessment must also serve in ways that enhance opportunities for optimal growth, development, and learning (SECA, 2000a). In many states early childhood educators are finding that state standards are guiding assessment.

The National Association for the Education of Young Children (NAEYC) and National Association of Early Childhood Specialists in State Departments of Education (NAECS/SDE) in 2003 updated their joint position statement on Curriculum, Assessment, and Program Evaluation. Concerning assessment they stated:

Make ethical, appropriate, valid and reliable assessment a central part of all early childhood programs. To assess young children's strengths, progress, and needs, use assessment methods that are developmentally appropriate, culturally and linguistically responsive, tied to children's daily activities, supported by professional development, inclusive of families, and connected to specific, beneficial purposes: (1) making sound decisions about teaching and learning, (2) identifying significant concerns that may require focused intervention for individual children, and (3) helping programs improve their educational and developmental interventions.

In general, assessment of any kind should relate "to the goals and objectives of the program, and the results of the assessment should guide planning and teaching" (Crosser, 2005). Standardized testing has prompted early childhood educators to find better ways to access children, particularly those with special needs. One way that has been shown to be very valuable is called *play-based* assessment (Ahola & Kovacik, 2007). Zero to Three (2005) defines play-based assessment as:

A form of developmental assessment that involves observation of how a child plays alone with peers, or with parents or other familiar caregivers, in free play or in special games. This type of assessment can be helpful because play is a natural way for children to show what they can do, how they feel, how they learn new things, and how they behave with familiar people.

An effective assessment should collect information necessary to make important decisions about a child's developmental and educational needs. Curriculum and assessment together can provide instruction and activities that support the development of appropriate skills for each individual child in your classroom.

evaluation

The process of determining whether the philosophy, goals, and objectives of the early childhood program have been met.

Evaluation is the process of determining whether the philosophy, goals, and objectives of the program have been met. Interpretations and decisions are made based on the collected information. Assessment and evaluation are closely related and can happen simultaneously. Gordon and Browne (2008) explain further, "Evaluation is a continuous process. It is at once a definition, an assessment, and a plan. . . . In its simplest form, evaluation is a process of appraisal." Informal and formal evaluation of a program should include the indoor and outdoor environments, schedule, routines, the curriculum as a whole, themes, lesson plans, activities, performances of the children, and the teacher's role. Ongoing evaluation is part of the curriculum process. Evaluation provides feedback concerning the effectiveness of the program, the goals and objectives, the teaching approach, the observation cycle, and once again the evaluation process.

You will find suggestions for observation, assessment, and evaluation in each of the following chapters of this book. Hopefully, this will help you link observation, assessment, and evaluation with planning and curriculum.

✳ AFTERVIEW

A child-centered early education environment focuses on children playing and learning. As we know, young children develop and learn in a variety of ways. As teachers we have the responsibility to understand the cultural influences and developmental characteristics of young children, to extend and support children's ideas and interests, and to provide appropriate learning activities and guidance techniques to meet their needs. The children acquire the skills, concepts, and knowledge of the curriculum through rich and varied interaction with peers, teachers, and materials. As a teacher, you prepare and organize a developmentally, individually, and culturally appropriate classroom to provide children with a range of high-quality learning experiences. This is based on curricular goals and objectives, age-appropriate practices, children's interests, and instructional needs.

Young children entering our programs are naturally curious about their environment and are eager to explore and learn about their world. Classroom arrangements and materials directly affect children's learning and self-esteem. A developmentally appropriate classroom should give children the opportunity to select activities from a variety of centers that are interesting and meaningful. The learning centers allow the children to create situations using both the real world and their fantasy world to solve problems and express creative ideas. The selection of open-ended materials for these centers encourage children to freely explore, experiment, and create.

Effective early education classrooms involve children in multisensory and multicultural experiences in a variety of settings, including independent activities, small group activities, and large group projects. Children are encouraged to talk about and share their experiences with their peers and adults. An early education environment is truly an active one when children are engaged in learning and play.

✳ KEY TERMS

anecdotal record	environment	observation
anti-bias	evaluation	philosophy
assessment	goals	portfolio assessment
case study	inclusion	project
checklist	inclusive curriculum	reflective log or diary
culture	integrated curriculum	theme
curriculum	learning centers	transitions
curriculum web	lesson plan	unit
emergent curriculum	objectives	

✳ EXPLORATIONS

1. If an appropriate curriculum is *child centered* or *child initiated*, doesn't this conflict with the idea that a teacher plans experiences and guides the child's learning? Explain your answer.

2. Interview a teacher from one of the model programs discussed in this chapter, such as Montessori or Head Start. Ask the teacher to describe the philosophy of the school; how she develops curriculum to meet the abilities, interests, and needs of the children in her class; and how she assesses or evaluates the development of the children and the program itself.

3. Keep a journal or notebook for one week on multicultural/anti-bias and inclusion activities you observed or culturally related activities that you personally experienced. List the date, event, and what you learned or experienced for each entry. Your listings can report your observations in an early education classroom; present a synopsis of articles you read in newspapers, magazines, or journals; or describe ethnic events you attended, new ethnic foods you ate, or a multicultural resource center or museum you visited in your community. Turn in your journal or notebook to your instructor, and discuss your findings with your classmates or colleagues.

4. You are the director of a small child care center and a benefactor wants to donate a substantial sum of money earmarked strictly for computers, peripheral equipment, and software. However, you are

aware that your playground equipment is minimal and in bad repair, plus your indoor facilities need improvements. The benefactor is insistent that the technology equipment must be purchased. What is your response? Why?

5. Based on the information from this chapter and from observing an early education classroom, create a diagram of a room arrangement for a classroom of three-, four-, and five-year-olds. Include doors, windows, furniture, sources of electricity, water, and so on. Label each learning center. Use "A Checklist for Room Arrangement" (Figure 2–11) to test the validity of your diagram. Explain how your room arrangement will impact the behavior of the children in this room.

✳ REFERENCES

Ahola, D., & Kovacik, A. (2007). *Observing and understanding child development: A child study manual.* Clifton Park, NY: Thomson Delmar Learning.

Albrecht, K. (1996, Fall). Reggio Emilia: Four key ideas. *Texas Child Care, 20*(2), 2–8.

Allen, K. E., & Schwartz, I. S. (2005). *The exceptional child: Inclusion in early childhood education* (4th ed.). Clifton Park, NY: Thomson Delmar Learning.

Anderson, G. T. (2000, March). Computers in a developmentally appropriate curriculum. *Young Children, 55*(2), 90–93.

Aronson, S. S. (Ed.). (2002). *Healthy young children* (4th ed.). Washington, DC: NAEYC.

Bank Street College of Education (1992). *Exploration with young children.* Mt. Rainier, MD: Gryphon House.

Bank Street School for Children. (2002). *Bank Street School for Children's Parent Handbook.* New York: Author.

Batzle, J. (1992). *Portfolio assessment and evaluation.* Cypress, CA: Creative Teaching Press.

Bredekamp, S. (1993, November). Reflections on Reggio Emilia. *Young Children, 49*(1), 13–17.

Bredekamp, S., & Rosegrant, T. (Eds). (1992). *Reaching potentials: Appropriate curriculum and assessment for young children* (Vol. 1). Washington, DC: NAEYC.

Brewer, J. (2001). *Introduction to early childhood education* (4th ed.). Boston: Allyn & Bacon.

Catron, C. E., & Allen, J. (2003). *Early childhood curriculum* (3rd ed.). Upper Saddle River, NJ: Merrill.

Cech, M. (1991). *Globalchild: Multicultural resources for young children.* Menlo Park, CA: Addison-Wesley.

Chard, S. (2001). *Project approach.* On-line at: http://www.projectapproach.com

Charlesworth, R. (2008). *Understanding child development* (7th ed.). Clifton Park, NY: Thomson Delmar Learning.

Chenfeld, M. B. (2001). *Oy! Education.* On-line at: http://www.pdkintl.org

Children's Defense Fund. (2005). On-line at: http://www.childrensdefense.org

Clements, D. H., & Sarama, J. (2003, November). Young children and technology: What does the research say? *Young Children, 58*(6), 34–40.

Cohen, L. (1999, February). The power of portfolios. *Early Childhood Today, 13*(5), 31–33.

Colbert, J. (2007). *Bridging differences with understanding: Helping immigrant children be more ready to learn.* On-line at: http://www.earlychildhoodnews.com

Crosser, S. (2005). *What do we know about early childhood education? Research based practice.* Clifton Park, NY: Thomson Delmar Learning.

Davis, M., Kilgo, J., & Gamel-McCormick, M. (1998). *Young children with special needs: A developmentally appropriate approach.* Boston: Allyn & Bacon.

Derman-Sparks, L., & A.B.C. Task Force (1989). *Anti-bias curriculum: Tools for empowering young children.* Washington, DC: NAEYC.

Edmiaston, R., Dolezal, V., Doolittle, C., Erikson, C., & Merritt, S. (2000, July). Developing individualized education programs for children in inclusive settings: A developmental appropriate framework. *Young Children, 55*(4), 36–41.

Essa, E. L. (2007). *Introduction to early childhood education* (5th ed.). Clifton Park, NY: Thomson Delmar Learning.

Essa, E. (1999). *A practical guide to solving preschool behavior problems.* (4th ed.). Clifton Park, NY: Thomson Delmar Learning.

Feng, J. (1994). Asian-American children: What teachers should know. (Report No. EDO-PS-94-4). *ERIC Digest.* Urbana, IL: ERIC Clearinghouse on Elementary and Early Childhood Education.

Fortson, L. R., & Reiff, J. C. (1995). *Early childhood curriculum.* Boston: Allyn & Bacon.

Frost, J. L. (1992). *Play and playscapes.* Clifton Park, NY: Thomson Delmar Learning.

Gandini, L. (1993, November). Fundamentals of the Reggio Emilia approach to early childhood education. *Young Children, 49*(1), 4–8.

Gargiulo, R., & Kilgo, J. L. (2000). *Young children with special needs: An introduction to early childhood special education.* Clifton Park, NY: Thomson Delmar Learning.

Gartrell, D. J. (2003). *A guidance approach for the encouraging classroom* (3rd ed.). Clifton Park, NY: Thomson Delmar Learning.

Garvey, C. (1990). *Play.* Cambridge, MA: Harvard University Press.

Gestwicki, C. (2007). *Developmentally appropriate practice: Curriculum and development in early education* (3rd ed.). Clifton Park, NY: Thomson Delmar Learning.

Ginsberg, M. R. (2006, May). Observations and reflections. *Young Children, 61*(3), 64.

Goffin, S. G. (2001). *Curriculum models and early childhood education* (2nd ed.). Upper Saddle River, NJ: Merrill.

Gonzalez-Mena, J., & Shareef, I. (2005, November). Discussing diverse perspectives on guidance. *Young Children, 60*(6), 34–38.

Gonzalez-Mena, J. (2001). *Multicultural issues in child care* (3rd ed.). New York: McGraw-Hill.

Gordon, A.M., & Browne, K. W. (2007). *Beginning essentials in early childhood education.* Clifton Park, NY: Thomson Delmar Learning.

Gordon, A. M., & Browne, K. W. (2008). *Beginnings and beyond* (7th ed.). Clifton Park, NY: Thomson Delmar Learning.

Hall, N. S. (1999). *Creative resources for the anti-bias classroom.* Clifton Park, NY: Thomson Delmar Learning.

Head Start (2003). *Head Start: A child development program* [Brochure]. Washington, DC: U.S. Department of Health and Human Services.

Helm, J. H., & Katz, L. (2001). *Young investigators: The project approach in the early years.* New York: Teachers College Press, Washington, DC: NAEYC.

Hendrick, J. (2003). Total learning (6th ed.). Upper Saddle River, NJ: Merrill Prentice Hall.

High/Scope Educational Research Foundation. (2003). *Professional development programs.* Ypsilanti, MI: Author.

Hohmann, M., Banet, B., & Weikert, D. P. (1995). *Young children in action: A manual for preschool educators* (2nd ed.). Ypsilanti, MI: The High/Scope Press.

Isbell, R. (2007). *An environment that positively impacts young children.* On-line at: http://www.earlychildhoodnews.com

Jarrett, O. S. (2002, July). Research in elementary school: What does research say? (Report No. EDO-PS-02-5). *ERIC Digest.* Urbana, IL: ERIC Clearinghouse on Elementary and Early Childhood Education.

Johnson, J. E., Christie, J. F., & Yawkey, T. D. (1987). *Play and early childhood development.* Glenville, IL: Scott, Foresman and Company.

Jones, E., & Reynolds, G. (1992). *The play's the thing: Teachers' roles in children's play.* New York: Teachers' College Press.

Jones, E., & Nimmo, J. (1994). *Emergent curriculum.* Washington, DC: NAEYC.

The Kaiser Family Foundation. (2004, February). *Role of media in childhood.* On-line at: http://www.kff.org

Katz, L. G. (1994). The project approach (Report No. EDO-PS94-6). *ERIC Digest.* Urbana, IL: ERIC Clearinghouse on Elementary and Early Childhood Education.

Klein, A. S. (2007a). *Creating peaceful environmental designs for the classroom.* On-line at: http://www.earlychildhoodnews.com

Klein, A. S. (2007b). *Different approaches to teaching: Comparing three preschool programs.* On-line at: http://www.earlychildhoodnews.com

Klein, M. D., Cook, R. E., & Richardson-Gibbs, A. M. (2001). *Strategies for including children with special needs in early childcare settings.* Clifton Park, NY: Thomson Delmar Learning.

Levy, A. (2007). *Culture in the classroom.* On-line at: http://www.earlychildhoodnews.com

Lewin-Benham, A. (2006, March). One teacher, 20 preschoolers, and a goldfish. *Young Children, 61*(2), 28–34.

Lowman, L. H., & Ruhman, L. H. (1998, May). Simply sensational spaces. *Young Children, 53*(3), 11–17.

Marotz, L. R., Cross, M. Z., & Rush, J. M.. (2005). *Health, safety, and nutrition for the young child* (6th ed.). Clifton Park, NY: Thomson Delmar Learning.

Marshall, H. H. (2001, November). Cultural influences on the development of self-concept. *Young Children, 56*(6), 19–25.

Mayesky, M. (2006). *Creative activities for young children* (8th ed.). Clifton Park, NY: Thomson Delmar Learning.

McCracken, J. B. (2000). *Playgrounds safe and sound* [Brochure]. Washington, DC: NAEYC.

Meisels, S. J. (2000). *Performance assessment in early childhood education.* Urbana, Il: ERIC.

Miller, D. F. (2007). *Positive child guidance* (5th ed.). Clifton Park, NY: Thomson Delmar Learning.

Miller, R. (1996). *The developmentally appropriate inclusive classroom in early education.* Clifton Park, NY: Thomson Delmar Learning.

National Association for the Education of Young Children. (NAEYC). (2007). *Where we stand. Many languages, many cultures. Respecting and responding to diversity.* On-line at: http://www.naeyc.org

National Association for the Education of Young Children. (NAEYC). (2000). *Helping children learn self-control.* [Brochure]. Washington, DC: Author.

National Association for the Education of Young Children. (NAEYC). (1998). Our promise for children: Statement of commitment. *Young Children, 57*(1), 56.

National Association for the Education of Young Children. (NAEYC). (1996). *Technology in early childhood programs.* On-line at: http://www.naeyc.org/resources/eyly/1996/09a.htm

National Association for the Education of Young Children (NAEYC) & National Association of Early Childhood Specialists in State Departments of Education (NAECS/SDE). (2003). Joint Position Statement. Early childhood curriculum, assessment, and program evaluation: Building an effective, accountable system in programs for children birth through age 8. On-line at: http://www.naeyc.org

National Association for the Education of Young Children (NAEYC) & National Association of Early Childhood Specialists in State Departments of Education (NAECS/SDE). (1991, March). Joint Position Statement. Guidelines for appropriate curriculum content and assessment in programs serving children ages 3 through 8. *Young Children, 46*(3), 21–38.

National Institute of Environmental Health (2007). *Obesity and the environment.* On-line at: http://obesityresearch.nih.gov

New, R. S. (2000). Reggio Emilia: Catalyst for change and conversation (Report No. EDO-PS-00-15). *ERIC Digest.* Urbana, IL: ERIC Clearinghouse on Elementary and Early Childhood Education.

Perry, B. D. (2002, November–December). A different world. *Parent and Child, 10*(3), 47–49.

Ratcliff, N. (2001, September). Use the environment to prevent discipline problems and support learning. *Young Children, 56*(5), 84–88.

Ray, J.A., & Shelton, D. (2004, May). E-pals: Connecting with families through technology. *Young children 59*(3), 30–32.

Redican, K., Olsen, L., & Baffi, C. (1993). Organization of school health problems. Dubuque, IA: Brown & Benchmark.

Reinsberg, J. (1999). *Understanding behavior: A key to discipline.* On-line at: http://www.naeyc.org/ece/1999/ll.asp

Reynolds, E. (2002). *Infant environments.* On-line at: http://www.earlychildhood.com

Schute, N. (2002, September). Madam Montessori. *Smithsonian, 33*(6), 70–74.

Simpson, C. G., & Gaus, M. D. (2006, Fall). Childhood obesity: A teacher's approach to battling a growing epidemic. *TAEYC Early Years, 28*(2), 2–9.

Southern Early Childhood Association (SECA). (2000a). *Assessing development and learning in young children.* On-line at: http://www.southernearlychildhood.org/position_assessment.html

Southern Early Childhood Association (SECA). (2000b). *Supporting learning with technology in the early childhood classroom.* On-line at: http://www.southernearlychildhood.org/position_technology.html

Spafford, C. S., Itzo Pesce, A. J. I., & Grosser, G. S. (1998). *The cyclopedic education dictionary.* Clifton Park, NY: Thomson Delmar Learning.

Spodek, B., & Saracho, O. N. (1994). *Right from the start: Teaching ages three to eight.* Boston: Allyn & Bacon.

Stavisky, K. (2002, Fall). A richness of purpose in teacher education: A Bank Street tradition. *Street Scenes, Bank Street College of Education, 10*(1), 1.

Sutterby, J. A., & Frost, J. L. (2002, May). Making playgrounds fit for children and children fit on playgrounds. *Young Children, 57*(3), 36–41.

Thomson, B. J. (1993). *Words can hurt you: The beginning of anti-bias education.* Menlo Park, CA: Addison Wesley.

Torquati, J., & Barber. J. (2005, May). Dancing with trees: Infants and toddlers in the garden. *Young Children, 60*(3), 40–46.

Tyler, V. (2000, Fall). Why recess? *Dimensions of Early Childhood, 28*(4), 21–24.

U. S. Department of Health and Human Services. (2005). On-line at: http://eclkc.ohs.acf.hhs.gov

Vance, E., & Weaver, P. J. (2002). *Class meetings: Young children solving problems together.* Washington, DC: NAEYC.

Wardle, F. (2001, November). Supporting multiracial and multiethnic children and their families. *Young Children, 56*(6), 38–39.

Watson, L. D., Watson, M. A., & Wilson, L. C. (2003). *Infants and toddlers: Curriculum and teaching* (5th ed.). Clifton Park, NY: Thomson Delmar Learning.

Wellhousen, K. (2002). *Outdoor play every day.* Clifton Park, NY: Thomson Delmar Learning.

West, M. M. (2001, November). Teaching the third culture child. *Young Children, 56*(6), 27–32.

Wolery, M., & Wilbers, J. (1994). (Eds.). *Including children with special needs in early childhood programs.* Washington, DC: NAEYC.

Wurm, J. P. *Working in the reggio way.* (2005). St. Paul, MN: Redleaf Press & Washington, DC: NAEYC.

York, S. (2003). *Roots and wings.* (Rev. ed.). St. Paul, MN: Redleaf Press.

Zero to Three. National Center for Infants, Toddlers and Families. (2005). On-line at: http://www.zerotothree.com

✳ ADDITIONAL READINGS AND RESOURCES

Balaban, N. (2006, November). Easing the separation process for infants, toddlers, and families. *Young Children, 61*(6), 14–18.

Bewick, C. J., & Kostelnik, M. (2004, May). Educating early childhood teachers about computers. *Young Children, 59*(3), 26–29.

Bolenbaugh, S. (2000, July). Activity-based developmental learning in a collaborative first-grade classroom. *Young Children, 55*(4), 30–32.

Bowe, F. G. (2004). *Birth to eight: Early childhood special education* (3rd ed.). Clifton Park, NY: Thomson Delmar Learning.

Collins, E. N., & McGaha, C. G. (2002, Summer). Create rewarding circle time by working with toddlers, not against them. *Childhood Education, 78*(4), 194–199.

Copple, C. (Ed). (2003). *A world of difference.* Washington, DC: NAEYC.

Cowles, M. (2006, Fall). Creating emotionally safe and supportive environments for children. *Dimensions of Early Childhood, 34*(3), 36–38.

Curtis, D., & Carter, M. (2003). *Designs for living and learning.* St. Paul, MN: Redleaf Press.

Debord, L. L., Heseness, R. C., Moore, N., Cosco, N., & McGinnis, J. R. (2002, May). Paying attention to the outdoor environment is as important as preparing the indoor environment, *Young Children, 57*(3), 32–35.

Edwards, C. P., Gandini, L., & Forman, G. E. (Eds.). (1998). *The hundred languages of children: The Reggio Emilia approach—Advanced reflections.* (2nd ed.). Greenwich, CT: Ablex Publishing.

Fenton, A. (2005, March). Collaborative steps: Paving the way to kindergarten for young children with disabilities. *Young Children, 60*(2), 32–37.

Flicker, E. S., & Hoffman, J. A. (2002, September). Developmental discipline in the early childhood classroom. *Young Children, 57*(5), 82–89.

Flynn, L. L., & Kieff, J. (2002, May). Including everyone in outdoor play. *Young Children, 57*(3), 20–26.

French, K., & Cain, H. M. (2006, May). Including a young child with spina bifida. *Young Children, 61*(3), 78–84.

Friedman, S., & Soltero, M. F. (2006, July). Following a child's lead. Emergent curriculum for infants and toddlers. *Beyond the Journal.* On-line at: http://www.naeyc.org

Gartrell, D. (2002, March). Replacing time out: Part Two—Using guidance to maintain an encouraging classroom. *Young Children, 57*(2), 36–43.

Hannon, J. H. (2000, November). Children are more than test results: Learning to like Matthew. *Young Children, 55*(6), 24–28.

Hatch, J. A. (2005). *Teaching in the new kindergarten.* Clifton Park, NY: Thomson Delmar Learning.

Helm, J. (2006). Projects that power young minds: Why child-initiated projects should be central in the early grades. *Educational Leadership, 62*(1), 59–62.

Helm, J. H., & Beneke, S. (Eds.). (2003). *The power of projects.* New York: Teachers College Press, Washington, DC: NAEYC.

Kohn, A. (2001, September). Five reasons to stop saying "Good job"! *Young Children, 56*(5), 24–28.

Koralek, D. (Ed.). (2007). *Spotlight on young children and families.* Washington, DC: NAEYC.

Koralek, D. (2002, May). Outdoor settings for play and learning. *Young Children, 57*(3), 8–9.

Matthews, H., & Ewen, D. (2006). *Reaching all children: Understanding early care and education participation among immigrant families.* Washington, DC: Center for Law and Social Policy.

McGinnis, J. R. (2002, May). Enriching the outdoor environment. *Young Children, 57*(3), 28–30.

McLean, D. (2002, Winter). Helping Aaron navigate: Including children with physical disabilities. *Dimensions of Early Childhood, 30*(1), 9–15.

Moore, M. R. (2002, Fall). An American's journey to kindergarten's birthplace. *Childhood Education, 79*(1), 15–20.

Mulligan, S. A. (2003, November). Assistive technology: Supporting the participation of children with disabilities. *Young Children, 58*(6), 50–53.

Murphy, K. L., De Pasquale, R., & McNamara, E. (2003, November). Meaningful connections: Using technology in primary classrooms. *Young Children, 58*(6), 12–18.

Okagaki, L., & Diamond, K. E. (2000, May). Research in review: Responding to cultural and linguistic differences in the beliefs and practices of families with young children. *Young Children, 55*(3), 74–79.

Prevesse, K. (2002, March–April). Guidance and discipline strategies for young children: Time-out is out. *Early Childhood News, 14*(2), 12–16.

Richey, D. D., & Wheeler, J. (2000). *Inclusive early childhood education.* Clifton Park, NY: Thomson Delmar Learning.

Sorrels, B., Norris, D., & Sheeran, L. (2005, Spring/Summer). Curriculum is a verb, not a noun. *Dimensions of Early Childhood, 33*(2), 3–10.

Wein, C. A., Stacey, S., Keating, B. H., Rowlings, J., & Cameron, H. (2002, January). The doll project: Handmade dolls as a framework for emergent curriculum. *Young Children, 57*(1), 33–38.

For additional information on early education curriculum, visit our Web site at http://www.earlychilded.delmar.com

PART TWO

DISCOVERING AND EXPANDING THE EARLY EDUCATION CURRICULUM

A child is sunshine,
Sparkling in every step she takes.
A child is laughter,
Filling the air with sounds he makes.
A child sees beauty,
Wonder, and excitement everywhere
And freely offers
A vision of joy, to treasure, to share.

— HILDA JACKMAN
(REPRINTED WITH PERMISSION)

CHAPTER 3

LANGUAGE AND LITERACY

OBJECTIVES

AFTER STUDYING THIS CHAPTER, YOU SHOULD BE ABLE TO:

- 🌐 Discuss language development in young children and relate stages of child development to literacy development.

- 🌐 Define and give examples of developmentally appropriate ways to support emergent literacy at home and in an early education program.

- 🌐 State why it is extremely important to respect and meet the needs of bilingual and bicultural young children.

- 🌐 Describe reading and writing development as well as organizing and planning for integrated language and literacy experiences.

- 🌐 Understand how to use assessment to support literacy learning in an early childhood classroom.

- 🌐 Design a developmentally appropriate language arts center, including selection of materials, supplies, and technology.

- 🌐 Create and present flannelboard and other literacy activities appropriate for young children.

OVERVIEW

As human beings, we have the desire to communicate with others. We do this in many ways. A smile communicates a friendly feeling; a clenched fist transmits anger; tears show happiness or sorrow. From the first days of life, a baby expresses pain or hunger by cries or actions. Gradually, the infant adds expressions of pleasure and smiles when a familiar person comes near. Then, the little one begins to reach out to be picked up.

A baby eventually learns the words of his parents. If the parents speak English, the baby will learn to speak English. If the baby spends a lot of time around significant adults who speak Spanish, Japanese, Hebrew, or any other language, the infant will learn the language of the people around him.

The process of learning a language is important. It is one of the most important skills a child develops. The development of oral language is a natural accomplishment. Usually, a child learns the rules of language at an early age without formal instruction. A child learns language by listening and speaking. He learns language by using it. Learning to talk, like learning to walk, requires time for development and practice in everyday situations. During the first few years of life, listening and speaking constitute a large part of a child's experience with language.

According to recent brain research, we now understand that there are "windows of opportunity" or critical periods in a young child's life when he can "easily acquire a new language because the brain cells that process language are in the process of being wired, and are therefore especially responsive to experience. . . . How a brain develops hinges on a complex interplay between the genes you're born with and the experiences you have. . . . By the time children reach age three, their brains are twice as active as those of adults" (Shore, 1997).

Fleming (2002) explains, "Each child has more than 50,000 nerve pathways that can carry sounds of the human voice from the ears to the brain. The brain encodes the words and actually rearranges its brain cells into connections or networks to produce language." Therefore, infants and toddlers need experiences with caring adults "who offer many one-on-one, face to face interactions with them to support their oral language development and lay the foundation for later literacy learning" (Neuman, Copple, & Bredekamp, 2000).

Emergent literacy in young children is a process of developing awareness about reading and writing before they can actually read or write. Their emergent literacy skills are the building blocks for later reading, writing, and communicating.

Helping you, the teacher, promote appropriate language and literacy environments is the intent of this chapter. Understanding language and literacy development in young children, encouraging family support, and setting up a developmentally appropriate environment to strengthen and extend this development will also be examined. (Chapter 4, "Literature," is a continuation of the language arts program introduced in this chapter.)

EARLY LANGUAGE AND LITERACY DEVELOPMENT

Language can be defined as human speech, the written symbols for speech, or any means of communicating. **Language development** follows a predictable sequence. It is related, but not tied to, chronological age. This developmental process includes both sending and receiving information. *It is important to remember that language is learned through use.*

Literacy, the ability to read and write, gives one the command of a native language for the purpose of communicating. This involves skills in listening, speaking, reading, and writing. The excitement of learning to read and write, hopefully, will be as rewarding as a child's first words and first steps.

---

emergent literacy

A process of developing awareness about reading and writing before young children can read or write.

language

Human speech, the written symbols for speech, or any means of communicating.

language development

Developmental process of a predictable sequence that includes both sending and receiving information. It is related, but not tied, to chronological age.

literacy

The ability to read and write, which gives one the command of a native language for the purpose of communicating.

Long before babies can speak, they listen to sounds and words. They hear differences in voices and sounds. Infants will turn their heads in the direction of a particular sound. Friendly verbal interaction with and encouragement from nurturing adults help a baby form his first words out of randomly babbled sounds. An infant learns quickly that communicating is worthwhile because it results in action on the part of others.

Gestwicki (2007) develops this idea further when she states: "In reality it is through the same social relationships that introduce infants to the emotions of love and trust, and to the behavior of people in their environment, that babies learn language as part of the complex system of communication they will use throughout their lives."

Language Development of Young Children

Children learn language through predictable stages of development. As with many other aspects of child development, individual differences are apparent in the development and use of language.

Baby's cry: This form of communication varies in pitch and intensity and relates to stimuli such as hunger, discomfort, or fear. Just as adults respond differently to a baby's cry (some touch, some talk), the baby's response varies as well. An infant can stop crying, then smile, or laugh in reaction to an adult's facial expression, to words spoken, or to being held.

Cooing: These are the sounds made when an infant's basic needs are met and he is relaxed, content, or stimulated by what is seen or heard. A baby derives a great deal of pleasure from practicing and listening to his own gurgling and cooing.

Smiling and laughing: Babies seem to be smiling when they are only a few days old. Some smile in their sleep, possibly through inner motivations. Adult facial, auditory, or motor stimuli can also be a source of smiles. "An infant's early laughter is usually full of squeals, howls, hoots, giggles, and grins" (Machado, 2007).

Babbling: These early random sounds made by an infant are a repetition of sequences of clear, alternating consonant and vowel sounds. This vocalization will eventually be combined into words, such as *baba* for bottle and *wawa* for water.

Association: A baby begins to get some idea of the meaning of a few words at about six to nine months. An association between the sounds an infant makes and the meanings of these sounds starts to become clear. When an adult begins to recognize and interpret these sounds, another level of communication has been reached. Playing "peek-a-boo" and "pat-a-cake" are fun to do and help the child develop an association between sounds and meanings.

Fields and Spangler (2000) explain further:

Before the first year is over, babies have narrowed their utterances from all the possible sounds to those significant in their environment. Babies in Mexico will trill the r sound, while babies in Germany will practice guttural sounds they hear, and English speaking babies will learn neither. Before long, they all begin to make the sounds of their language in combinations that mean something specific. As soon as they acquire this ability to communicate with words, they begin to string them together for even greater results.

One-word usage: Many first words are completely original, private words of the child. They may be sequences of sounds or intonations used on a consistent basis. "The physical organs need to function in a delicate unison, and the child must reach a certain level of mental maturity. At around the age of 12 months, the speech centers of the brain are poised to produce what is perhaps the most magical moment of childhood: the first word which marks the flowering of language" (Machado, 2007). In the early stages of language development, a word, such as *hot* or *no*, often stands for a whole object or an experience. The one-word stage also uses a word to get something or some action from others, such as *go, down,* or *mine.* Getting the appropriate response, approval, and smiles from adults encourages the child to make the sounds again and again. Language is a two-way process. Reaction is an important feedback to action. Although a child can speak only in "one-word sentences," he can understand more complex sentences and can react to what others are saying. From this point on, the child has progressed from receptive language, that is, listening and understanding, to the period of expressive language, that is, speaking.

Recall: A child's ability to remember an object named even when the object is not visible is helped by the touching, grasping, and tasting of the object. Responding to his name, identifying family members, and watching, pointing to, and naming an object usually occur toward the end of the first year. Recall is sometimes called "sign-language" communication, such as when a child holds up her arms to be picked up.

Telegraphic speech: The two-word sentence is the next step in the development of language of the young child. This speech helps a child express wishes and feelings, and ask questions. "Many words are omitted because of the child's limited ability to express and remember large segments of information" (Machado, 2007). The child repeats words over and over, such as *all gone, drink milk,* or *throw ball.* It is important to talk and listen to a toddler. This is a critical language-growth period, because the young child is processing, testing, and remembering language. See Figure 3–1 for toddler language characteristics.

Multiword speech: When a young child reaches the stage of adult-like speech with longer sentences and almost all of the words present, he asks questions and understands the answers. The child can express feelings and tell others what he wants. At the same time, the child can understand the words of other people and absorb new knowledge. The child's vocabulary increases; and the repetition of songs, stories, and poems comes more easily. Words become important tools of learning, and they help a young child grow socially. Children talk together, and friendships grow. Thus, it becomes obvious that oral language is the foundation of early literacy.

Allen and Schwartz (2005) remind us that our knowledge of the language acquisition and development of young children will help us understand that speech and language irregularities come and go and appear to be self-correcting unless the child is pressured. We also need to be aware of early warning signs that a child could be having some difficulty.

A child is developing an awareness of reading and writing before he can actually read or write.

FIGURE 3–1
Toddler language
characteristics. (Source:
Machado, 2007, p. 61)

TODDLER LANGUAGE CHARACTERISTICS

- Uses two- to five-word sentences.
  "Baby down."
  "Baby boom boom."
  "No like."
  "No like kitty."
  "Me dink all gone."
  "See me dink all gone."
- Uses verbs.
  "Dolly cry."
  "Me going."
  "Wanna cookie."
- Uses prepositions.
  "In car."
  "Up me go."
- Adds plurals.
  "Birdies sing."
  "Gotta big doggies."
  "Bears in dat."
- Uses pronouns.
  "Me big boy."
  "He bad."

- Uses articles.
  "The ball gone."
  "Gimme a candy."
- Uses conjunctions.
  "Me and gamma."
- Uses negatives.
  "Don't wanna."
  "He no go."
- Runs words together.
  "Allgone," "gotta," "gimme," "lookee."
- Asks questions.
  "Wa dat?"
  "Why she sleep?"
- Does not use letter sounds or mispronounces spoken words.
  "Iceam," "choo" (for shoe), "member" (for remember), "canny" (for candy).
- Sings songs.
- Tells simple stories.
- Repeats words and phrases.
- Enjoys word and movement activities.

A number of young children have problems speaking or learning the language; some children have trouble with both. Problems may range from developmentally normal delays and dysfluencies to serious problems requiring the services of a speech and language specialist. An undiagnosed hearing loss is always a possibility and needs to be ruled out first in diagnosing a language delay or impairment in a young child. (Allen & Schwartz, 2005)

Literacy Development of Young Children

literacy development
A lifelong process that begins at birth and includes listening, speaking, reading, and writing.

As previously indicated, **literacy development,** a lifelong process that begins at birth, includes listening, speaking, reading, and writing. Listening is a prerequisite to speaking. Learning to speak is an important step toward learning to read.

Bank Street College (2002) helps us understand even more about literacy development.

Literacy learning is circular; learners may move forward in some areas and seem to step back as they consolidate understanding in others. Thus, reading and writing may not develop evenly. A child may be fluent in one area and emergent in another. Ultimately, however, whatever the timetable or path, the goals are the same for all:

🌐 *To become fluent and efficient readers and writers who can make sense of and convey meaning in written language;*

🌐 *To become thinkers and communicators who are actively reviewing and analyzing information;*

🌐 *To enjoy reading and writing; and*

🌐 *To feel successful as users of literacy for a variety of purposes.*

Researchers also believe children learn about reading and writing through *play*. As a teacher of young children, you see this happening every day. You have observed children learning to talk, read, or write when they are playing "peek-a-boo," engaging in nonsense speech play, listening to and singing familiar jingles and rhymes, scribbling, pretending, and using objects as symbols. Because literacy is a continuous process, children are working on all aspects of oral and written language at the same time.

Understanding what is developmentally appropriate for young children can help you recognize what is important in the development of oral and written language. Here are a few suggestions for guiding children into letter recognition (Hill-Clarke & Cooley, 2002; National Institute for Literacy, 2002; Wasik, 2001):

- Begin with a child's name. Learning to recognize and produce his name is an appropriate activity for learning the alphabet.
- As a child continues to recognize his name, he begins to see the similarity between letters in his name and letters in words in the environment.
- Introducing alphabet books and reading storybooks can also create additional awareness of letters.
- The alphabet can easily become part of any thematic activity.
- The letter-of-the-week can also extend the connection of the alphabet if it is done appropriately and as part of the curriculum.

Researchers and educators are also deliberating the phonics versus whole language approaches to literacy. **Phonics** is the relationship between the letters of written language and the sounds of spoken language. Phonics emphasizes the sound-symbol relationship or "sounding out" unfamiliar syllables and words. In addition, Neuman and colleagues (2000) inform us that

> *phonological awareness refers to the whole spectrum from primitive awareness of speech sounds and rhythms to rhyme awareness and sound similarities, and at the highest level, awareness of syllables and phonemes. Phonemes are the smallest units in speech, for instance, the /b/, /a/, and /t/ sounds that make up the word bat. Becoming attentive to the sound structure of language—becoming phonologically or phonemically aware—is an "ear" skill, unlike phonics, which is the relation between letters and sounds in written words.*

As teachers you can emphasize the sounds of language by providing opportunities for children to practice with the **phonemes,** the smallest unit of speech, as well as helping them write the letter-sound relationships they know by using them in words, sentences, messages, and their own stories. **Whole language** introduces literacy by building on what children already know about oral language, reading, and writing while highlighting experiences and meaningful language rather than isolated skill development. National Association for the Education of Young Children (NAEYC) suggests a balanced view that involves teaching phonics not separately but in context, so that children make connections between letters and sounds that are meaningful to them (Bredekamp & Copple, 1997). When children sing nursery rhymes, jingles, and songs, they are playing with and exploring the sounds of language. **Rhyming** is the ability to hear two words that end the same way, a beginning concept of **phonological awareness,** the awareness and the ability to hear and identify these individual sounds and spoken word, and development of listening skills. See Figure 3–2 for a suggested list of books that emphasize rhyming.

In 1997, in response to a congressional directive, a National Reading Panel (NRP) was convened by the National Institute of Child Health and Human Development (NICH). The NICH's report, in part, was based on the 1998 study of the research on learning to read by Snow and her colleagues. The research concluded that children need a balanced reading program that provides for both skills in understanding letter/sound relationships and experiences with literature and language. The NICH recommendations were incorporated in the federal 2001 No Child Left Behind Act. (Charlesworth, 2008; Epstein, 2007). See Figure 3–3.

phonics

The relationship between the letters of written language and the sounds of spoken language.

phonemes

The smallest units of speech.

whole language

A view of literacy and learning that builds on what children already know about oral language, reading, and writing while emphasizing meaningful language rather than isolated skill development.

rhyming

The ability to auditorily distinguish two words that end the same way.

phonological awareness

The ability to hear and identify individual sounds and spoken words.

Wasik, 2006, helps us understand another important aspect of language development, *vocabulary.* "Learning new words allows children to accurately label objects and people, learn new concepts, and communicate with others. In addition, vocabulary development is closely linked to children's progress in school and, in particular, their success in learning to read." Teachers can display the words children learn by developing *word walls.* See Chapter 4 for ideas on how to set up a word wall in a classroom for young children.

Each child who comes to you has already been busy, actively creating his own definition of what it means to interact in a literate society (Canizares, 2002). Through shared reading experiences, writing their names, and playing games related to their letter discoveries, they are developing literacy skills at their own pace. You are building on what children already know and can do, while creating a developmentally appropriate language and literacy environment when you:

🌐 Talk to children, even while diapering or feeding them.

🌐 Talk to children in standard spoken language, not baby talk. Speak clearly and give simple explanations.

🌐 Reinforce a child's native language. Understand that every child's language or dialect is worthy of respect as a valid system for communication.

FIGURE 3–2
Suggested list of books that emphasize rhyming.

BOOKS THAT EMPHASIZE RHYMING

Brown, M. W. (1994). *Four fur feet.* New York: Hyperion.

Ghigna, C. (1995). *Riddle rhymes.* New York: Hyperion.

Graham, J. B. (1999). *"Flicker Flash."* Illus. by N. Davis. New York: Houghton Mifflin.

Hopkins, L. B. (2001). *Marvelous math: A book of poems.* Illus. by K. Barbour. New York: Aladdin.

Lewison, W. (1992). *"Buzz" said the bee.* New York: Scholastic.

Martin, B., & Archambault, J. (1989). *Chicka Chicka ABC.* Illus. by L. Ehlert. New York: Simon & Schuster.

Prelutsky, J. (2002). *The frog wore red suspenders.* Illus. by P. Mathers. New York: Greenwillow.

Sierra, J. (2000). *"There's a zoo in Room 22."* Illus. by B. Saltzberg. New York: Harcourt.

Trapani, I. (1997). *I'm a little teapot.* Watertown, MA: Charlesbridge Publishing.

Shared reading experiences give young children opportunities to develop literacy skills.

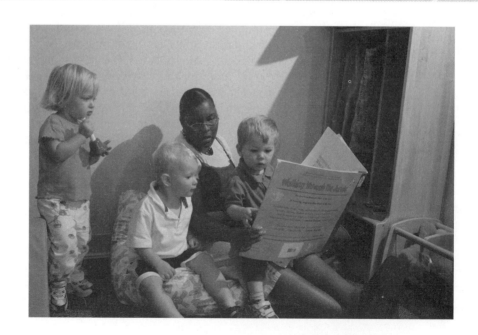

FIGURE 3–3
The components of reading instruction. (Source: Charlesworth, 2008, p. 409)

THE FACTS ABOUT READING ACCORDING TO THE NATIONAL READING PANEL

According to the study done by the National Reading Panel (No Child Left Behind, 2002), five key components of reading instruction have been scientifically proven to work:

1. **Phonemic awareness:** the ability to hear and identify individual sounds and spoken words
2. **Phonics:** the relationship between the letters of written language and the sounds of spoken language
3. **Fluency:** the capacity to read text accurately and quickly
4. **Vocabulary:** the words students must know to communicate effectively
5. **Comprehension:** the ability to understand and gain meaning from what has been read

Books in sign language, Braille, and a variety of languages can be explored with yong children.
Source: Sign Language poster, Copyright School Speciality Publishing, used with permission. (Photograph Copyright Thomson Delmar Learning.)

- Speak in a voice that helps children listen—not too fast or too soft.
- Encourage children to talk to you.
- Enable children to use language to communicate their thoughts about ideas and problems that are real and important to them.
- Listen when children talk to you. Give children your full attention when they speak. Be on their level and make eye contact. Use nonverbal communication, such as eye-to-eye contact, smiling, and holding a child's finger or hand to reinforce that you are listening. Be patient.
- Use children's names frequently.
- Allow time and opportunity for children to listen and talk freely without interruption.
- Play music for children to listen to. Provide different types of music in the environment, such as tapes or CDs of lullabies, songs from many cultures, and classical music.
- Sing songs. Make up songs with the children.
- Play finger plays, which offer a combination of stories, poems, directions, songs, and hand movements. Finger plays also offer a transition into a story or activity.
- Read or tell stories to children. Make a wide selection of books available to children. Be sure there are books in a variety of languages, including Braille and sign language. (Chapter 4, "Literature," offers detailed information.)
- Offer shared book experiences with repeated readings of the same story, so the children themselves are encouraged to read and reread. Also, children enjoy the repetition of familiar phrases and rhythms.
- Enhance children's concept of and exposure to print. "Some teachers use Big Books to help children distinguish many print features, including the fact that print (rather than pictures) carries the meaning of the story, that the strings of letters between spaces are words and in print correspond to the oral version, and that reading progresses from left to right and top to bottom" (IRA & NAEYC, 1999).
- Take walks and listen to the sounds of the environment. Talk about what you see and hear. Write down what the children say and then put their words in a classroom book or on a large sheet of paper posted on an easel or a wall.

🌐 Play listening games to develop sound awareness, such as clapping hands in a fast or slow tempo; then have children repeat the clapping as they heard it. Audio tape the games, and then play them back to the children to see if they can associate the taped claps with the ones they did.

🌐 Encourage children to use and expand language and literacy in all learning centers.

"Literacy experiences should be prevalent in every primary classroom, incorporated into every area of the curriculum. Learning to read and write must be viewed as a developmental process, not a set of skills to be mastered" (Miels, 2001). Additional and specific examples of language and literary developmental activities are presented at the end of this chapter. As stated earlier, in a developmentally appropriate setting, speaking, listening, reading, and writing are integrated into or combined with other curriculum areas. You will find examples of this throughout the chapters of this book.

SHARING LITERACY: ENCOURAGING FAMILY SUPPORT

As previously stated, family members are a child's primary teachers of language. They are the first people a child hears speak, the first adults spoken to, and the most important people a child will communicate with throughout his life. Awareness of the importance of parents and other significant family members to a child's language and literacy development is one of the first steps in working with parents. It is also helpful to let family members know how valued their efforts are. Express to them how much you appreciate their interactions with you. Let them know what you are doing in the early childhood program. Point out ways they can contribute to or extend language and literacy development at home with their child.

Some teachers find it helpful to send notes home periodically. This chapter includes a sample letter that can be sent home, once a week, as a special "language link" from you to the parents, which might include the following suggestions:

Read to your child. Read books, stories, magazines, comic strips, and poems. Have children's books around the house for your children. Some can be purchased and some can be checked out from the library. Read them often, and add to them regularly. These are the books we are reading in class this week. (You could list several books with the author's and illustrator's names, such as *Family Pictures, Cuadros de Familia,* by Carmen Lomas Garza; *I Love My Family,* by Wade Hudson; *On Mother's Lap,* by Ann Herbert Scott, illustrated by Glo Coalson; *Friday Night Is Papa Night,* by Ruth A. Sonneborn, illustrated by Emily A. McCully; and *The Day of Ahmed's Secret,* by Florence P. Heide and Judith H. Gilliland, illustrated by Ted Lewin.)

Talk about the illustrator or photographer. Look at the pictures in the book you are sharing with your child. Can "Larry" think or guess what the story will be about? If it is a picture book, let your child tell you about the pictures or photographs. You will help him use pictures or other clues for reading comprehension. (You might then tell the parent something such as: "We are looking at Tana Hoban this week. Her wonderful photographs are in these books: *Shapes, Shapes, Shapes; I Read Signs; Of Colors and Things;* and *26 Letters and 99 Cents.*")

More suggestions follow:

🌐 Have a regular story time before or after meals or at bedtime. It will help both you and your child relax and share some private time together.

🌐 Look at the book cover together. Use the words *front cover, back cover, title, author, illustrator, top, bottom, left, right.* This exposes your child to reading vocabulary.

🌐 Read all kinds of signs, labels, restaurant menus, and calendars to your child. Point out print on home equipment and products, and items of print used in your daily life. Point out signs when you are out riding together.

Reading a book with daddy is a favorite language activity for a young child.

🌐 Let your child see you reading newspapers, magazines, books, and letters. Reading together and sharing stories is a family affair. Enjoy it and do it often!

🌐 Talk to your child. Listen to what your child has to say. Provide uninterrupted time for communicating.

🌐 Do activities together, then talk about it. This includes routine shopping, worship services, the zoo, museums, movies, television viewing, and sports activities.

🌐 Sing to, and with, your child. Music is a wonderful way to make family activities even better.

🌐 Surround your child with opportunities to play with words. Provide a variety of things to write with: chalk, crayons, pencils, markers, and all kinds of paper.

🌐 Encourage your child to draw. Besides clarifying thoughts and ideas, drawing tells stories and expresses feelings. It also reinforces the motor skills your child needs for writing.

🌐 Tell family stories. Encourage your child to ask questions. Let him tell a family story of his own.

🌐 How's the "art gallery" coming along? Post your child's scribbles and drawings on the refrigerator or the wall in his room. This gives all the family members a chance to look at his efforts. It is fun to add your own drawings.

🌐 Write to your child. Put notes in lunchboxes, in book bags, under pillows, in pockets, on the refrigerator. Your child will look forward to "being surprised."

🌐 Let your child see you write. When you write a letter, let him write a letter, too. When you send a birthday card, let him add some scribbles.

(Adapted from Machado, 2007; U.S. Department of Education, 2002; and personal experiences and conversations with early education teachers.)

Figure 3–4 is a suggestion for a letter to be sent home with the children in your program. The younger children can add illustrations. The older children can write their own letter to explain about stories read at the center or school. It is important for the child to have "ownership" of the letter. However, some teachers prefer to send letters home that are informational and written from the teacher to the parent. Select the technique you prefer, as long as the parents receive something in writing. This, along with verbal communication, connects the parent to the teacher and the school.

If the parents speak a language other than English, get someone to help you translate your letter into the native language. Send both copies home with the child.

Teachers must always keep in mind . . . that the writing they see in the classroom tells only part of the story of a child's capabilities. The drawing and writing that children do at home can add rich information to the overall picture of children's literacy development. . . . Enlisting parents and other primary caregivers as partners in assessing and supporting preschoolers'

FIGURE 3–4
An example of a letter to send home with the children. Younger children can add drawings to the letter. Older children can write their own letters.

Dear Family
(or whatever the child calls his parents using the language spoken at home),

We have been reading stories. We enjoy acting out the stories we read. One of our favorites is The Very Hungry Caterpillar by Eric Carle. We like to tell the story over and over in our own words. We move around as we tell the story. We can be whatever we want to be: the caterpillar, the apple, the pear, the ice cream cone, the leaf, or the butterfly. Sometimes we don't use any words. This is called pantomime. It's fun.

Can we act out some of the stories we read at home? You can choose what part you want to be.

Child's name

writing development helps everyone involved develop a better understanding of how a child understands the functions, forms, and meanings of written language. (Schickedanz & Casbergue, 2004).

RESPECTING A CHILD'S BILINGUAL, BICULTURAL WORLD

M/A-B You may now have or eventually will have young children in your classroom who speak languages other than English and whose country of origin is not the United States.

Changing demographics of young children in the United States: more children and families who speak languages other than English and more children representing many diverse cultures in our classrooms. . . . We must learn how language develops, know about the many cultures of children and families in our programs and adapt our practices to best serve children. (Mitchell, 2006).

According to Helm and Beneke (2003), "In classrooms all across the United States there are second-language learners. These children may be in regular classrooms, transitional bilingual programs, or pull-out English as a second-language (ESL) programs for children acquiring English."

The following stages are adapted from Hernandez (1995); Ramsey (1987); Hickman-Davis (2002); and Espiritu, Meier, Villazana-Price, & Wong (2002):

🌐 *The Preproduction or Silent Stage:* A child's initial response to a new language is to listen to or "take in" the language rather than to speak it. The length of this particular stage will vary from child to child. During this period, music, movement, dramatic play, and art activities are appropriate. Reading books aloud to the child can offer a one-on-one experience with a teacher as well. Do not rush children through this nonverbal period.

🌐 *Early Production Stage:* At this stage, children have limited verbalization and growing comprehension. Occasionally asking questions that require a "yes" or "no" answer from the child will give a teacher an informal assessment of what the child is understanding. Speech can also be encouraged by asking questions that ask for the labeling of familiar objects ("What is this?") or finishing a statement ("We are eating . . ." "The color of this crayon is . . ."). This can be accomplished easily in informal conversations with the child. Group time, classroom games, outdoor play, and one-on-one activities will provide ample opportunities in which you can guide children through this stage. At the beginning, English language learners will have to mentally translate the question into their native language, formulate a response, then mentally translate the response back into English. This takes time.

🌐 *Expansion of Production Stage:* This is the speech emergence and expansion stage. With this comes increased comprehension and the ability to speak in simple sentences. Encourage the child to talk about his family and friends. Motivate him to describe, using his words, what he is experiencing with his five senses. Finger plays, songs, and rhymes are useful in stimulating the child toward using his new language.

Throughout the process of a child's language acquisition, your role will be to understand the whole child. Give "opportunities to exhibit skills and not assume that because the child doesn't speak the new language that he or she doesn't have the ability to function" (Hernandez, 1995). You should appreciate the countless ways in which children learn and do not rely on a set curriculum for teaching oral language or literacy. Instead, "learn from the children and adopt their curricula to allow for group preferences and individual variations" (Genishi, 2002).

Be sensitive and encourage the child to communicate in his own way during social interaction with other children. "Independent play and outdoor play offer excellent opportunities for children to interact with each other in the comfortable language. A caregiver [teacher] must give verbal as well as nonverbal support to Limited English Proficient children in both languages" (Schiller & Bermudez, 1988). Emphasize the child's strengths, and help to build his positive self-concept. Provide consistent and continual modeling of English and whenever possible allow the child to speak his primary language as well as English.

It is important to understand that accepting a child's language is part of accepting a child. The children in the classroom will model your behavior. Children can be very accepting and caring of each other. They communicate by gestures or by taking a child's hand and leading him to an activity, many times without your guidance.

Children will feel more successful if you involve their parents in activities and understand the different learning styles each child may have. The celebration of many cultural holidays at the school that include the family members of *all* the children in your class offers positive reinforcement. Invite them to visit the classroom and share their language with the children. Maintain personal contact with the child's family throughout the year. "Instead of the teacher being viewed as the sole expert, there is a reciprocal exchange where parents are valued as resources" (Ramsey, 1987).

Parents can help you identify some basic words used in the child's language, especially those that are important to the child. *Be sure to use the child's correct name and not an "Americanized" one. Use the name often and pronounce it correctly.* (Listen carefully to the parent's pronunciation and imitate it.)

At first and if possible, have a family member or someone who speaks the child's native language available to help the child learn the routines and expectations, as well as the new language. If another child in the class speaks the language, interaction between the two should be encouraged (Essa, 2007).

In a developmentally appropriate language and literacy environment, writing is an important part of a child's literacy development.

ORGANIZING AND PLANNING FOR INTEGRATED LANGUAGE AND LITERACY EXPERIENCES

To focus on reading alone disregards the importance of children's experiences with writing. Reading and writing skills develop simultaneously and are interconnected. Progress in one fuels development of the other (Mayer, 2007).

As previously discussed, throughout a child's life listening, speaking, reading, and writing are a prominent part of a child's world. As the significant adults in a child's life, we should ensure that the environment surrounding each child be the very best it can be—developmentally, individually, and creatively. When this occurs, children use and expand their language in almost every activity and curriculum area in which they participate.

As you plan the physical space for the language and literacy activities, you should keep in mind that how you design this area will affect the choices children make in their selection of activities. This part of the environment, sometimes called the language arts center, should be arranged so children can use this area independently or in small groups.

We should remember too, that the physical classroom space should allow children to move from center to center, from large group to small group and from small group to individual choice activities as well (Bobys, 2000). All of this is carefully orchestrated by the teacher, with selection of language and literacy activities by the children as the ultimate goal.

As with everything in an early childhood environment, the organization and focus is on creating a child-centered space. For infants and toddlers, the surroundings should be sensory-rich—bright colors everywhere, the air full of soft music, words

When you plan the physical space for language and literacy activities, how you design this area will affect the choices children make in their selection of activities.

from around the world being spoken, songs being sung, books being read, drawings being scribbled, and textures within reach.

You will find the language arts center is most effective when it

- is set in a part of the room that is quiet with little traffic, but is accessible from any other center.
- invites the children to use every inch of table, floor, and wall space.
- displays things at the children's eye level.
- attracts them to listen, look, think, write, draw, and read.
- includes materials, supplies, and equipment that offer explorative and developmentally appropriate hands-on experiences for young children.

The language arts center should be an environment that is soft. This can be accomplished by having a carpet, rug, or carpet squares on the floor; by adding large pillows and beanbag chairs; and by adding some "creative spaces," such as enormous stuffed animals with large laps for children to sit on or an old-fashioned bathtub filled with pillows of all sizes and colors for an individual child to spend some alone time reading a book or listening to a tape.

The center also should have good lighting and easy access to child-size tables, chairs, and bookcases that are arranged for group or individual use. Include both "stand-up" (chalkboard, easels, murals, window, clipboards) and "sit-down" (tables, lap desks, floor) writing places.

SETTING UP A LANGUAGE AND LITERACY ENVIRONMENT

Policy makers now regard preschool as foundational in helping children become successful readers and writers. State and national standards for early education, being implemented across the country, emphasizes early experiences with print as important for children's later literacy development (Mayer, 2007).

Children should have access to listening, reading, and writing materials in every learning center. Many of the items usually placed in the language arts center can be duplicated in other centers. When children want to write, copy, or draw, the "tools" should be available. Offer pressure-free experimentation with writing, and encourage children to write often. Remember that children's first writing attempts appear as scribbling. Help them when you feel they need it. For example, "This is how I write your name. How do you write your name?"

Emergent writing means that children begin to understand that writing is a form of communication, and their marks on paper convey a message (Mayer, 2007). "Writing is an important part of a child's literacy development. Pretend writing should be as meaningful to young children as pretend reading, so that there will be no fear of writing later on. Writing should be a natural, enjoyable, successful part of play" (Levine in Love, Burns, & Buell, 2007).

Offer pressure-free experimentation with writing and encourage children to write often.

Encourage children to learn written language in the same energetic and interactive ways they learn oral language. Invite children to experiment with language in any way they choose, and accept whatever the child "writes," such as lists, creative calendars, children's dictation, posters, signs, labels, songs, and "creative" spelling. Materials should be available at all times for children to use for writing. They should be separated into appropriate, brightly colored containers to make it easy for children to choose what they need. The use and care of the materials should be discussed each time something new is added to the learning center. The classroom should also be print-rich. Identification of words in the environment appears to be one of the first steps in learning to read. Signs, logos, and labels can be used as valuable literacy learning tools. Include environmental print in children's home language as well as English. Young children are aware of logos/trademarks of their favorite fast food restaurants, the products they eat or use, and the signs around their neighborhoods. "It is suggested that environmental print can be used as the springboard for learning other factors inherent in being able to read such as phonics and phonemic awareness" (Charlesworth, 2008).

In addition, Prior and Gerard (2004) explain further, "Adult instruction is the key element to effectively using environmental print to teach beginning reading skills. When an adult draws attention to the letters and sounds in environmental print words, children are more likely to transfer this knowledge to decontextualized print or text without graphics."

A print-rich literacy environment includes the following:

- examples of signs, labels, and logos from product packaging (e.g., cereal boxes, toothpaste boxes, fast food containers, store bags, magazines, or newspapers)
- photographic images taken around the school's neighborhood, such as street signs
- all types of books that are displayed attractively and within easy access of the children, including big books placed on story easels or on laundry drying racks
- books and journals made and written by individual children
- class collaborative projects that offer language-experience stories
- magazines and newspapers appropriate for young children
- recorded stories
- message boards
- calendars
- rebus and symbol charts and graphs
- story props for retelling stories
- alphabet charts and vocabulary posters
- a wide variety of pictures depicting life around the world

- labels on materials, on supplies, on equipment, and in learning centers throughout the room and outdoors
- lists of all kinds
- children's names displayed
- child dictation or writing and drawings displayed

It is important to remember that the *process* should be the emphasis of the children's activities; however, this process produces many outcomes and you will need to do something appropriate with "all that writing." Here are a few suggestions: Have the children take home the items they select; take the items the children select and place them around the room; place some of the writings in a child's folder or portfolio; or mail others to family members and friends.

Observation and Assessment

"Implement curriculum that is thoughtfully planned, challenging, engaging, developmentally appropriate, culturally and linguistically responsive, comprehensive and likely to promote positive outcomes for all young children" (NAEYC & NAECS/SDF, 2003). Then, from the curriculum goals and objectives, teachers now have a context for observation. Observations are the foundations for assessment.

Use assessment to support learning in the early childhood classroom. Select useful information about children's knowledge, skills, and progress by observing, documenting, and reviewing children's language and literacy work over time. "The most powerful outcome of ongoing assessment is the positive relationship teachers can build with each child. Every child is different, but the one thing every child needs is to feel accepted and appreciated. . . . A system of ongoing assessment also helps the teachers build a relationship with each child's family" (Dodge, Heroman, Charles, & Maiorca, 2004).

Neuman and colleagues (2000) emphasize that

> *assessment should support children's development and literacy learning. Good assessment helps to identify children's strengths, needs, and progress toward specific learning goals. . . . Good assessment uses a variety of tools, including collection of children's work (drawings, paintings, writings), and records of conversation and interviews with children. . . . The core of assessment is daily observation. Watching children's ongoing life in the classroom enables teachers to capture children's performance in real activities rather than those contrived to isolate specific skills.*

Here are some suggestions for assessment collection of children's language and literacy activities and projects:

- written language as collected in captions on drawings, labels, or child-made books
- items that indicate a child's learning style and interests
- spoken language as collected in anecdotal notes or on audio and videotapes
- musical expressions such as made-up songs and dances
- webs, lists of words, or other records of vocabulary
- multiple examples of how a child expresses ideas
- multiple examples of a child's self-portrait, even if it shows scribbling
- multiple examples of anecdotal records of language and literacy skill development
- culture and language included as part of the assessment process (source for materials that can be individualized to one's needs: CLAS, the Early Childhood Research Institute on Culturally and Linguistically Appropriate Services; on-line at: *http://clas.uiuc.edu*)

(Adapted from Helm, Beneke, & Steinheimer, 1998; Gober, 2002; Santos, 2004; and conversations with early education teachers.)

See Figure 3–5 as an example of an appropriate assessment checklist.

Refer to Chapter 2 for an explanation of other appropriate assessment tools in early childhood education, as well as the CD that accompanies this book.

Literacy and Learning with Technology

TECH   The use of technology in an early childhood setting requires that each of us as early childhood educators should learn as much as we can about technology issues and trends. "This knowledge can help us make informed decisions about technology use and support our efforts to prepare today's young children for their future" (Blagojevic, 2003).

Technology can bring different learning opportunities to the language/literacy curriculum. With the computer, changing the font size or color, manipulating touch screens or switches, or using simple or multi-task software helps children access the curriculum and contribute their ideas. For example:

> The children work together to create their own book—"Our Favorite Things." Children have a variety of ways they can represent their thoughts in different learning areas, including finger painting and use of the computer center. A software program is open and allows children to choose items from a picture library or to create a composition representing their favorite things. . . . They may decide to use the drawing component of the program to create an original drawing. (Blagojevic, 2003)

This activity or project can continue by adding digital photographs that the children take themselves or with the help of their family members. For younger children, write or type their dictated comments about the photographs to put in their books of "Our Favorite Things." These photos and comments can be included in the children's portfolios as evidence in language growth and connections between speaking, listening, and writing (DeMarie & Ethridge, 2006). Another extension could be for the children to take photographs and to interview the staff of the center/school for another book to share with parents and children in other classes.

Think about using technology often. Technology in early childhood can enrich and expand the literacy and language experiences of young children and their families.

TIPS AND ACTIVITIES

Figure 3–6 is a suggested list of what to place in the language arts center, including things to write with, to write on, and to write in.

There are many techniques you can use to place items promoting language and literacy around the room. Some we have already discussed in this chapter. The following suggested activities are additional ones that teachers of young children have found to be developmentally and multiculturally appropriate, as well as lots of fun to do.

Flannelboard Activities

Often teachers hear a child say: "Tell it again." One of the ways to tell or extend a story effectively is with the use of a **flannelboard**.

> As children use flannelboard activities to retell a new or familiar story they represent oral and written language in picture form, thereby gaining structures for later abstract thinking. Young children's symbolic play signals the development of representational thought (Piaget) and has been recognized as critical in the development of abstract thought (Vygotsky). . . . Using flannelboards with primary grade children provides a natural connection to process writing. Students enjoy writing and rehearsing their own scripts. (Short, Harris, & Fairchild, 2001)

Flannelboard

Used as a prop to tell or extend a story effectively.

As children of all ages listen to the storyteller, their visual attention is focused on the characters and movement taking place on the flannelboard.

Child _____ Age _____ Grade _____

School _____ Teacher _____

What Children Can Do	Assessment Dates	Comments
Goals for Preschool: Awareness and Exploration ● Enjoys listening to and discussing storybooks ● Understands that print carries a message ● Engages in reading and writing attempts ● Identifies labels and signs in the environment ● Participates in rhyming games ● Identifies some letters and makes some letter-sound connections ● Uses known letters or approximations of letters to represents written language **Goals for Kindergarten: Experimental Reading and Writing** ● Enjoys being read to and retells simple narrative stories or informational texts ● Uses descriptive language to explain and explore ● Recognizes letters and most letter-sound connections ● Show familiarity with rhyming and with beginning sounds ● Understands basic concepts of print, such as left-to-right orientation and starting at the top of the page ● Understands that spoken words can match written words ● Begins to write letters of the alphabet and some high frequency words, such as their names, family names, or words such as cat, dog, and so on. **Goals for First Grade: Early Reading and Writing** ● Reads and retells familiar stories ● When comprehension breaks down, uses a variety of strategies, such as rereading, predicting, questioning, and contextualizing ● Initiates using writing and reading for his or her own purposes ● Can read orally with reasonable fluency		*(continues)*

FIGURE 3–5

This list is not exhaustive and any individual child may be at different levels of development in different areas. (Source: Charlesworth, 2008, pp. 426–427)

What Children Can Do	Assessment Dates	Comments
● Identifies new words through letter-sound associations, word parts, and context		
● Identifies an increasing number of words by sight		
● Can sound out and represent all the major sounds in a spelling word		
● Writes about personally meaningful topics		
● Attempts to use some punctuation and capitalization		
Goals for Second Grade: Transitional Reading and Writing		
● Reads with greater fluency		
● When comprehension breaks down, uses strategies more efficiently		
● Uses strategies more efficiently to decode new words		
● Sight vocabulary increases		
● Writes about an increasing range of topics to fit different audiences		
● Uses common letter patterns and critical features to spell words		
● Punctuates simple sentences correctly and proofreads own work		
● Spends time each day reading		
● Uses reading to research topics		
Goals for Third Grade: Independent and Productive Reading and Writing		
● Reads fluently and enjoys reading		
● Uses a range of strategies when drawing meaning from the text		
● When encounters unknown words, uses word identification strategies appropriately and automatically		
● Recognizes and discusses elements of different text structures		
● Makes critical connections between texts		
● Writes expressively in different forms, such as stories, poems, and reports		
● Uses a rich variety of vocabulary that is appropriate to different text forms		
● Can revise and edit own writing during and after composing		
● Spells word correctly in final written drafts		

FIGURE 3–5

This list is not exhaustive and any individual child may be at different levels of development in different areas. (Source: Charlesworth, 2008, pp. 426–427)

FIGURE 3–6
A list of language arts center materials and supplies.

- Pencils, pens, and chalk of various sizes and colors
- Crayons of various sizes, colors, and thicknesses
- Markers of various colors, fine tipped, thick tipped, washable, permanent, and scented
- Magnetic letters and numbers
- Typewriter
- Computer
- Toy or nonworking telephone
- Toy microphone
- Paper of various sizes, colors, and textures; lined and unlined paper; drawing paper; construction paper; and scraps
- Cardboard and posterboard
- Stationery
- Journals
- Note pads
- Index cards
- Envelopes
- Graph paper
- Post-its
- Order forms
- Business forms
- Large and individual chalkboards, dry erase boards, and magic slates
- Carbon paper
- Finger paints
- Pencil sharpener
- Rulers
- Tape
- Glue
- Scissors
- Stapler
- Stickers
- Date stamp and pad
- Other donated office stamps and pads
- Paper clips
- Hole punch
- Brads
- Maps and globes
- Pictionaries and dictionaries
- Message board
- Folders and notebooks
- Old newspapers and magazines

A good flannelboard activity

- attracts attention.
- stimulates interest.
- is flexible in use.
- frees a teacher's hands.
- adds texture to the activity.
- is a visual prop for a story, song, or poem that does not have illustrations.
- improves communication.
- dramatizes concepts.
- is easily made and easily stored.

Other important aspects of this type of activity are as follows:

- The children can help the teacher tell the story by placing the pieces on the board at the appropriate time in the story.
- After the teacher tells the story, the flannelboard and character pieces can be placed in any activity center or curriculum area.
- The children or individual child can then tell the story to each other or make up another story to relate to the flannelboard pieces.
- Flannelboard figures can be touched, held, and moved, forming a bridge between the real and the abstract.

FRONT   BACK

CARDBOARD or PLYWOOD

FLANNEL COVERING

FLANNEL STAPLED TO-BACK

FOLD-OUT SUPPORTS

HINGES

YARN or TWINE

You can purchase a commercial flannelboard or you can make your own. Select plywood, masonite, or any wood-based board for durability. Styrofoam board, heavy cardboard, display board, and prestretched artist's canvas are more lightweight and easier to carry but not as durable. The board may be freestanding or placed on an easel, on a chalkboard tray, or on a chair. Smaller, individual boards can be placed in the language arts center for children to use by themselves or with a friend.

Flannel cloth is usually the best material to use for covering the base. It has excellent adhering qualities and is lightweight and colorful. Felt cloth also can be used with good results, as can most fuzzy textured material. Velour (material used for making house robes and blankets) stretches slightly to cover the board, maintains its texture, and is available in an assortment of colors.

An almost unlimited variety of materials for use with flannelboard activities can be obtained easily and inexpensively. The most commonly used items are nonwoven interfacing material from the fabric store, felt, and heavy flannel. When selecting materials to be used for flannelboards, it is important to be sure the adhesive quality of the material is great enough to support its own weight or the weight of the item to which it will be attached.

Some of the resources for finding flannelboard poems, stories, and figures are: teachers of young children, commercial activity sets, and shapes and figures traced from books, magazines, photographs, illustrations, pictures, and drawings. (See Appendix A for puppet and flannelboard characters introduced in this text and Appendix C for a listing of teacher resources.) Be creative and draw some yourself.

Color can be added to the flannelboard set pieces with permanent felt markers, crayons, and paints. It is fun to accent the figures with wiggly eyes and imitation fur fabric. You will find it helpful to trace with tissue paper. For easy storage, use a folder with pockets, a large mailing envelope, a manila folder with the story stapled inside (make a pocket of tag board or construction paper to hold the pieces), or large plastic household bags. (See illustration.)

WHY I TEACH YOUNG CHILDREN

As an early childhood educator of many years, certain memories never leave. The memories help me remember how literal children are. This also helps me remember how to speak to children so that they understand what I am saying. For example, I was introducing a three-year-old class to community helpers. One of the activities relating to mail carriers was to learn our home address. Each child made a crayon picture on manila paper that we folded in thirds. I sat with each child individually to write out his or her *address*. We mailed the letters and I said that in a few days they would receive it as a present since their address was on the drawing.

After a few days had passed, one of the parents came to tell me that I had made her daughter very angry. She said that when the mail came, her daughter had ripped open the paper and then in an angry voice said, "Where is my red dress? Mrs. Rubinstein told me she was sending me a *red dress*."

—Bonnie Rubinstein

The following are suggested books that are appropriate for early childhood flannelboard stories:

Aliki. (1989). *My five senses.* New York: HarperCollins.

Carle, E. (1981). *The very hungry caterpillar.* New York: Philomel.

Ehlert, L. (1997). *Color farm.* (Board Book). New York: HarperCollins.

Martin, B., Jr. (1967). *Brown bear, brown bear, what do you see?* Illustrated by E. Carle. New York: Henry Holt.

Martin, B., Jr., & Archambault, J. (1988). *Listen to the rain.* Illustrated by J. Endicott. New York: Henry Holt.

McQueen, L. (1995). *The little red hen/La gallinita roja.* New York: Scholastic.

Shaw, C. G. (1947). *It looked like spilt milk.* New York: HarperTrophy.

Group Time Activities

Group time presents an opportunity for listening, speaking, vocabulary development, and cognitive and social activities. Here are a few helpful hints for successful group time activities:

- Organize activities ahead of time, plan carefully, and think about what is going to happen before, during, and after.
- Have realistic expectations of the children and be flexible.
- Select a time and place where a few children can be involved or where others can join in when they finish cleaning up. Be able to accommodate the entire group.
- Select developmentally and culturally appropriate activities that relate to the children's experiences.
- Guide children in and out of group time with appropriate transitions.
- Change the pace often and include a variety of activities.

Group time offers an opportunity for quality interaction time among children and adults.

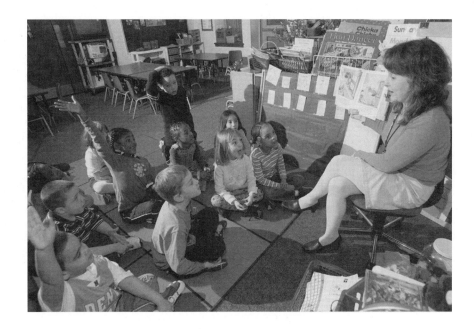

🌐 Encourage listening and discussing skills. Respond to a child's meaning even if his words are not correct words. Model the appropriate words when you clarify what he has said.

🌐 Anticipate problems and take steps to avoid them by explaining expected behaviors to the children.

🌐 Acknowledge and reinforce *appropriate* behavior.

🌐 Give clear, simple directions.

🌐 Respond to each individual child as well as to the group.

🌐 Maintain physical and emotional closeness.

🌐 Anticipate a "good" stopping point, or stop before the children lose interest.

🌐 Be prepared with an extra activity in case what you have planned does not work or the activity time needs to be extended.

🌐 Evaluate and make needed changes for next time.

🌐 Enjoy the children.

Appropriate group time activities are finger plays, poetry, songs, stories, flannel-board activities, and sensory activities. These should be developmentally appropriate and reflect multicultural/anti-bias content.

The following activity, "HOP-HOP!" illustrates a musical finger play activity that toddlers and preschoolers enjoy doing.

The story of *A Little Red House (Una Casita Roja)* is an example of another appropriate group activity. It can be told in group time, then repeated by using flannelboard pieces (Appendix A). Follow-up activities can be: Put the flannelboard pieces and the written story in the language arts center, have a special cooking center set up so children can find their own "little red house," and then make applesauce.

Putting the applesauce recipe on a **rebus chart** (Figure 3–7) is another way to integrate literacy into the curriculum. The rebus chart offers visual picture signs and directions to help children make sense of any activity, that is, read left to right, top to bottom, and recognize letters and symbols. This helps put children in charge of their own learning. For older children, placing the rebus chart in a learning center helps them work independently without teacher direction. This chart is friendly and helpful to children whose native language is not English (Jurek & MacDonald, 1994).

rebus chart
Visual pictures, such as signs, illustrations, and directions, to help children make sense of any activity.

HOP-HOP!
(FINGER PLAY ACTIVITY WITH SONG)
(Suitable for Ages Toddler—Three)

Teacher: Let's tell a story together. Our hands can help.
First, make a fist, like this:

(Teacher makes a fist and continues to model for the children all the actions that follow.)

Now, hold up two fingers *(index and middle fingers)*.
See, we have a bunny! These are his ears. *(Wiggle fingers.)*
Wiggle, wiggle, wiggle, it's Robby Rabbit! Can he hop? *(Make hopping motions.)*
Up and down, up and down—good!
Now, make another bunny with your other hand.
This is Reba Rabbit. Wiggle her ears—wiggle, wiggle, wiggle.
Now we have two bunnies. Can they both hop? Good!
Let them hop behind your back and hide.
Now we can begin our story.
Everyone sings softly: "Ta-dah!"

Children: Ta-dah!

Teacher: *(Bringing one hand forward with hopping motion)*
Here comes Robby Rabbit—wiggle, wiggle, wiggle!
And here comes Reba Rabbit! (Other hand) Wiggle, wiggle, wiggle!
(Bunnies face one another. When they speak, their ears wiggle. Reba's voice should be pitched higher than Robby's.)

Teacher: Robby Rabbit says, "Hello!"

Reba: Hello Robby! How are you?

Reba: I'm fine.

(Both bunnies gasp and begin to tremble.)

Teacher: Now they're both so scared that they hop behind you and hide.
Do you want to see them again? Sing, "Ta-dah!"

(Repeat the whole procedure through Reba's line, "I'm fine!" This time, only Reba begins to tremble.)

Teacher: Reba is so scared, she hops behind you to hide again. But
Robby Rabbit is not scared. He sings this song:

(Robby hops and sings:)

Reproduced by permission of B. Wolf

Language Activity

The following is a language activity for toddlers that encourages self-esteem and language development while developing awareness and appreciation of differences:

At group time, after reading Bill Martin and Eric Carle's Brown Bear, Brown Bear, What Do You See? *(1967, New York: Henry Holt), sit on the floor with the children seated in a circle with you. Pull a small (unbreakable) hand mirror from your pocket. Pass the mirror from child to child.*

SONG TO ACCOMPANY HIP-HOP!*

Hop, hop, hop! Here comes Rob- by Rab- bit! Hop, hop, hop!

Mov- in' right a- long. Hop, hop, hop! Hap- py lit- tle bun- ny!

Hop, hop, hop! Sing- in' a hap- py song!

TEACHER: Like this -- bring out Reba Rabbit --- hop, hop, hop!

Now we have two bunnies again. Let them hop and sing together:

Spring's a love- ly time of year, full of joy, full of cheer!

Spring- time flow- ers all are here, and so are al- ler- gies!

Reproduced by permission of B. Wolf
Copyright B. Wolf - 1993

A LITTLE RED HOUSE
(Una Casita Roja)

Once upon a time, there was a little girl named Maria. Maria had her favorite toys, and she had a big back yard with a garden where she liked to play. One day, she was tired of doing the things she usually did, and she wanted to do something different.

So, Maria went to her mother and asked, "Mamá, what can I do?"

Maria's mother thought for a minute, and then she said, "I know what you can do. You can try to find a little red house, *una casita roja,* with no windows and no doors, but with a star, *una estrella,* inside."

"Mamá, is there really such a thing as a little red house, *una casita roja,* with no windows and no doors, but with a star, *una estrella,* inside? How can I find something like that?" asked Maria.

Yes, *sí*, Maria, there is," answered her mother,"and I know that you can find it, if you look."

Maria thought and thought about what her mother had said, but she didn't know where to find a house like that. So, she went to her big brother, Paco, and asked him,"Paco, do you know where I can find a little red house, *una casita roja*, with no windows and no doors, but with a star, *una estrella*, inside?"

"Maria," Paco said,"I have never heard of a little red house, *una casita roja*, with no windows and no doors, but with a star, *una estrella*, inside. I cannot help you. Why don't you go and ask Papá?"

So, she went to the back yard, where her father was working in the garden, and asked him, "Papá, do you know where I can find a little red house, *una casita roja*, with no windows and no doors, but with a star, *una estrella*, inside?"

Papá looked at Maria, and smiled, and said,"Our house is red, *roja*, but it has doors and windows, and I don't think there is a star, *una estrella*, inside. I'm afraid I can't help you, Maria."

Maria was getting a little tired of looking by now, so she sat down in her favorite back yard spot, under the apple tree, to rest and to think. Her cat, Chica, came and sat in her lap. Maria stroked Chica's soft fur and asked,"Chica, do you know where I can find a little red house, *una casita roja*, with no windows and no doors, but with a star, *una estrella*, inside?" Chica didn't answer. She just went on purring her soft purr.

Maria thought to herself,"I'm not having much luck. I might as well ask the wind." So she did."Señor Wind, can you help me? I am looking for a little red house, *una casita roja*, with no windows and no doors, but with a star, *una estrella*, inside." Just then, the wind began to blow gently, and down from the tree fell a bright, shiny red apple. Maria picked up the apple, and went to find her mother to tell her that she just could not find the little red house, *una casita roja*.

When Maria's mother saw her walking in the door with the apple, she said,"Maria, I see you found the little red house, *una casita roja*, with no windows and no doors, but with a star, *una estrella*, inside." Maria was puzzled, but followed her mother into the kitchen, where she took out a knife, and cut the apple in half, and …

THERE WAS THE STAR! (*UNA ESTRELLA!*) ★

(Cut the apple through the center perpendicular to the core.)

una—oo′ na	*casita*—cas ee′ ta	*roja*—ro′ ha
estrella—ess tray′ ya	*señor*—seen yore′	*sí*—see

By Janet Galantay
Reprinted with permission

Here is the recipe for applesauce:

Applesauce
6 apples
$1/2$ cup water
1 teaspoon lemon juice
sugar, to taste
$1/8$ teaspoon cinnamon
Peel apples. Remove core. Cut up apples. Add water, lemon juice, and sugar. Cook until tender. Add cinnamon. Press through a colander. Then eat!

APPLE SAUCE

Peel six apples .

Remove cores and cut them up.

Add ½ cup water,

Sugar to taste and

One teaspoon lemon juice.

Cook until tender.

Add   ⅛ teaspoon cinnamon.

Press through a colander. THEN EAT!

FIGURE 3–7
Rebus chart of applesauce recipe.

Teacher: *"Janet, Janet" what do you see?* (Child looks into mirror.)
Child: I see "Janet" looking at me.

> Continue to pass the mirror around the circle until all the children have had a turn.

> Another time you can have the children look into the mirror and say "I see a boy *with* brown hair *looking at me.*"—"I see a girl *with* brown eyes *looking at me.*"—or—"I see a boy *with* brown skin *looking at me.*"

Additional Activities

Following are additional activities that may be used to promote language and literacy development.

- *Writing with Water:* Take a bucket of water and several large and small paintbrushes outside. The children can "write" on or "paint" the sidewalk, the building walls, the tricycles, the wagons, and the fence. This activity helps develop large muscle control, and at the same time provides the beginnings of literacy development. It is easy and fun, too.

- *Labeling:* Encourage the children to label things in the classroom as well as outdoors. Start the labeling yourself and let the children help. Listen to the children and let them label what they think needs labeling. This will help them "read the room." (The children love to use Post-its to label things and they can change them whenever *they* want to.) It is also fun to make floor signs, such as traffic signs that say "enter," "exit," "stop," and "go."

- *Writing to Others:* Have the children write thank-you letters or notes to community members who visit the class and to those visited during field trips.

- *Story Starters:* Have the children tell you a story about when they were babies, or what happens when the wind blows, or what sounds they hear and sights they see. Use a tape or video recorder to capture their storytelling. Older children can write and illustrate their own big book based on the story.

- *Birthday Celebration:* Create a birthday celebration center once a month that lasts a week. Stock it with paper to make birthday cards; markers, and crayons; old birthday card fronts; and scraps of lace, yarn, fabric, stickers, and birthday words. Use *happy birthday* from other languages, such as, *joyeux anniversaire* (French) and *feliz cumpleaños* (Spanish). Children can make cards for family members and classmates. This is a wonderful way to promote thoughtfulness, socialization, language, writing, reading, and creativity. Extend this activity by making a "Birthday Book" of the class. (If a child's family does not celebrate birthdays, the child does not have to visit this particular learning center.)

- *Journal Writing:* Motivate the children to write or copy the words to songs, finger plays, and recipes in their journals.

- *Dictionaries:* Promote opportunities for the children to go for "word walks" around the classroom and copy words from labels, books, and so on. They learn name recognition by writing their classmates' names in their dictionary. This helps the children to become more aware of print and identifies early alphabetizing or sequencing. Also have actual dictionaries around (Bobys, 2000).

Figure 3–8 is the curriculum planning web worksheet, with language and literacy activities added. This worksheet, with appropriate additions, is included in the ensuing chapters to illustrate how you could complete the lesson plan.

Refer to the front-of-the-book CD for additional suggestions for activity plan worksheets, curriculum web examples, and interactive curriculum webs. *Inspiration®* *8* is the software used for creating the webs. See the student CD for a trial version of *Inspiration® 8* software. You can create your own curriculum webs.

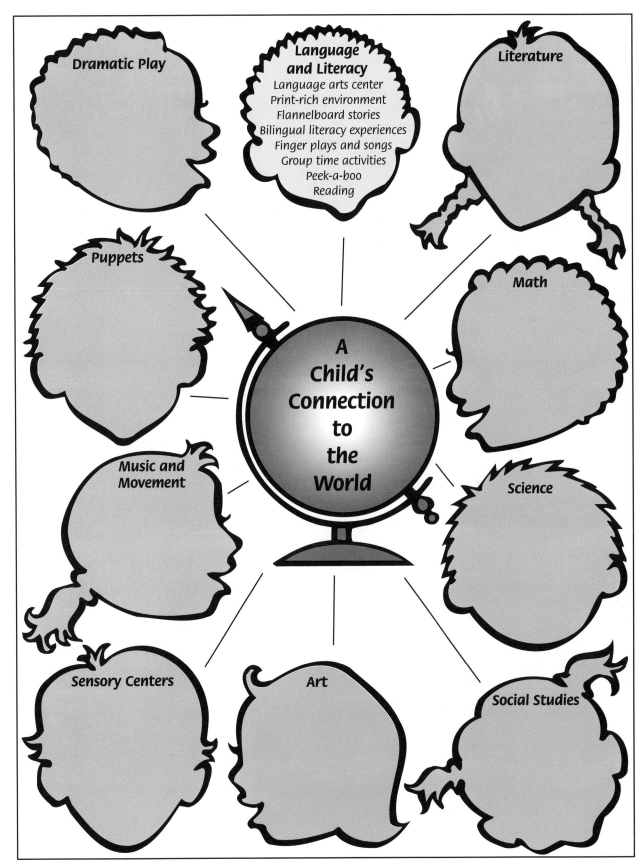

FIGURE 3–8
A curriculum planning web worksheet with language and literacy activities added.

✳ AFTERVIEW

Through language and literacy, a child

- 🌐 develops listening skills.
- 🌐 develops the concept of print.
- 🌐 recognizes that print is talk on paper.
- 🌐 acquires verbal comprehension and association skills.
- 🌐 develops letter recognition skills.
- 🌐 practices scribbling; drawing; and making letters, numbers, and words.
- 🌐 recognizes and differentiates between shapes, sizes, signs, and sounds.
- 🌐 experiments with word formation.
- 🌐 learns left-to-right progression.
- 🌐 uses new vocabulary in everyday communication.
- 🌐 strengthens visual memory.

- 🌐 interprets pictures.
- 🌐 recognizes sequencing of pictures and illustrations.
- 🌐 practices storytelling and dictation of stories, while imagining events and situations.
- 🌐 develops the ability to recall stories and experiences.
- 🌐 practices writing and illustrating an original story or book.
- 🌐 learns about other cultures and broadens concepts and experiences about life.
- 🌐 acquires the ability to use technology with language and written activities.

✳ KEY TERMS

emergent literacy	literacy	phonological awareness
flannelboard	literacy development	rebus chart
language	phonemes	rhyming
language development	phonics	whole language

✳ EXPLORATIONS

1. Select an early education classroom and observe for at least one hour. Describe, in writing, six language and literacy activities the children were involved in at the time of your observation. What did you learn from this observation?

2. Select and plan a language activity for young children. Specify which age group this activity is planned for: infants, toddlers, preschoolers, or primary-age children. In writing, list objectives, materials needed, step-by-step procedures for presenting this activity, follow-up activities, and evaluation guidelines. (Use the activity plan worksheet in Chapter 2.) Prepare this activity and demonstrate it during class or with a group of children.

3. Visit an early childhood classroom where there are children who speak more than one language. Describe, in writing, the following:

   - 🌐 How did the teacher interact with the children?
   - 🌐 Which stage or stages of language acquisition did you observe?

   - 🌐 What social interaction between the children did you observe?
   - 🌐 What activities of the children did you observe?
   - 🌐 What languages were evident in written materials in the classroom?
   - 🌐 What languages were spoken by the adults in the classroom?
   - 🌐 What was done in the classroom to support the language and literacy development of a multilingual group of children? Explain.
   - 🌐 What did you learn from this observation?

4. Select a classmate or colleague as a partner. Share ideas on games and activities to extend a child's vocabulary. Discuss ways to use or adapt these games to extend the vocabulary of children who speak other languages or dialects. Then, develop one activity that helps a child learn new words and appropriate language usage. If possible, share your activity with a group of young children. Evaluate its appropriateness

and effectiveness. Did it accomplish your objectives? Explain.

5. Based on the information in this chapter and on your observations of early education environments, design a language and literacy learning center. Sketch a floor plan showing where materials, supplies, and equipment are placed.

✳ REFERENCES

Allen, K. E., & Schwartz, I. S. (2005). *The exceptional child: Inclusion in early childhood education* (4th ed.). Clifton Park, NY: Thomson Delmar Learning.

Bank Street College. (2002). *Early literacy development.* On-line at: http://www.bankstreet.edu/literacyguide

Blagojevic, B. (2003, November). Funding technology does it make cents? *Young Children, 58*(6), 28–33.

Bobys, A. R. (2000, July). What does emerging literacy look like? *Young Children, 55*(4), 20–22.

Bredekamp, S., & Copple, C. (Eds.). (1997). *Developmentally appropriate practice in early childhood programs.* (Rev. ed.). Washington, DC: NAEYC.

Canizares, S. (2002, December). Why reading together is essential. *Scholastic Parent and Child, 10*(3), 32.

Charlesworth, R. (2008). *Understanding Child Development* (7th ed.) Clifton Park, NY: Thomson Delmar Learning.

DeMarie, D., & Ethridge, E. A. (2006, January). Children's images of preschool: The power of photography. *Young Children, 61*(1), 101–104.

Dodge, D. T., Heroman, C., Charles, J., & Maiorca, J. (2004, January). Beyond outcomes: How ongoing assessment supports children's learning, and leads to meaningful curriculum. *Young Children, 59*(1), 21–28.

Epstein, A. S. (2007). *The intentional teacher: Choosing the best strategies for young children's learning.* Washington, DC: NAEYC.

Espiritu, E., Meier, D., Villazana-Price, N., & Wong, M. K. (2002, September). A collaborative project on language and literacy learning. *Young Children, 57*(5), 71–78.

Essa, E. L. (2007). *Introduction to early childhood education* (4th ed.). Clifton Park, NY: Thomson Delmar Learning.

Fields, M. V., & Spangler, K. L. (2000). *Let's begin reading right: Developmentally appropriate literacy* (4th ed.). Upper Saddle River, NJ: Merrill.

Fleming, B. (2002). *Brain keys language development.* On-line at: http://www.nncc.org/release/brain.language.html

Genishi, C. (2002, July). Young English language learners—Resourceful in the classroom. *Young Children, 57*(4), 66–72.

Gestwicki, C. (2007). *Developmentally appropriate practice: Curriculum and development in early education* (2nd ed.). Clifton Park, NY: Thomson Delmar Learning.

Gober, S. Y. (2002). *Six simple ways to assess young children.* Clifton Park, NY: Thomson Delmar Learning.

Helm, J., & Beneke, S. (Eds.). (2003). *The power of projects: Meeting contemporary challenges in early childhood classrooms.* New York: Teachers College Press; Washington, DC: NAEYC.

Helm, J., Beneke, S., & Steinheimer, K. (1998). *Windows on learning: Documenting young children's work.* New York: Teachers College Press.

Hernandez, A. (1995, July–August). Language acquisition: What to expect. *Instructor, 105*(1), 56–57.

Hickman-Davis, P. (2002, Spring). "Cuando no hablan Ingles": Helping young children learn English as a second language. *Dimensions of Early Childhood, 30*(2), 3–10.

Hill-Clarke, K., & Cooley, S. M. (2002, Fall). Promoting early literacy in the natural environment. *Dimensions of Early Childhood, 30*(4), 10–16.

International Reading Association (IRA) & National Association for the Education of Young Children (NAEYC). (1999). *A joint position paper: Learning to read and write, developmentally appropriate practice for young children.* [Booklet].Washington, DC: NAEYC.

Jurek, D., & MacDonald, S. (1994, Spring). Using rebuses with young children. *Dimensions of Early Childhood, 22*(3), 17–20.

Love, A., Burns, M. S., & Buell, M. J. (2007, January). Writing empowering literacy. *Young Children, 62*(1), 12–19.

Machado, J. M. (2007). *Early childhood experiences in language arts* (8th ed.). Clifton Park, NY: Thomson Delmar Learning.

Mayer, K. (2007, January). Emerging knowledge about emergent writing. *Young Children, 62*(1), 34–40.

Miels, J. C. (2001, March). Abby Bear deserves to be heard: Setting early writers free. *Young Children, 56*(2), 36–41.

Mitchell, A. (2006, September). From Our President. *Young Children, 61*(5), p. 4.

National Association for the Education of Young Children (NAEYC) & National Association of Early Childhood Specialists/State Departments of Education (NAECS/SDE). (2003). Joint Position Statement: Early childhood curriculum, assessment, and program evaluation. On-line at: http://www.naeyc.org

National Institute for Literacy. (2002). *Partnership for reading.* On-line at: http://www.nifl.gov/partnershipforreading

Neuman, S. B., Copple, C., & Bredekamp, S. (2000). *Learning to read and write.* Washington, DC: NAEYC.

Oken-Wright, P. (1998, March). Transition to writing: Drawing as a scaffold for emergent writers. *Young Children, 53*(2), 76–81.

Prior. J., & Gerad, M. R. (2004). *Environmental print in the classroom: Meaningful connections for learning to read.* Newark, DE: International Reading Association.

Ramsey, P. G. (1987). *Teaching and learning in a diverse world: Multicultural education for young children.* New York: Teachers College Press.

Santos, R. M. (2004, January). Ensuring culturally and linguistically appropriate assessment of young children. *Young Children, 59*(1), 48–50.

Schickendanz, J. A., & Casbergue, R. M. (2004). *Writing in preschool.* Newark, DE: International Reading Association.

Schiller, P., & Bermudez, A. B. (1988, Winter). Working with non-English speaking children. *Texas Child Care, 12*(3), 3–8.

Shore, R. (1997). *Rethinking the brain.* New York: Families & Work Institute.

Short, R. A., Harris, T. T., & Fairchild, S. H. (2001, Spring). "Once upon a time": Telling stories with flannelboards. *Dimensions of Early Childhood, 29*(2), 3–9.

Snow, C. E., Burns, M. S., & Griffin, P., (Eds.). (1998). *Preventing reading difficulties in Young children.* A Report of the Committee on the Prevention of Reading Difficulties in Young Children, National Research Council. Washington, DC: National Academy of Sciences.

United States Department of Education. (2002). *Helping your child become a reader: No child left behind.* Washington, DC: Author.

United States Department of Education. (2002). On-line at: http://www.nochildleftbehind.gov

Wasik, B. A. (2006, November). Building vocabulary one word at a time. *Young Children, 61*(6), 70–77.

Wasik, B. A. (2001, January). Teaching the alphabet to young children. *Young Children, 56*(1), 34–40.

✳ ADDITIONAL READINGS AND RESOURCES

Ada, A. F. (2003). *A magical encounter: Latino children's literature in the classroom.* Boston, MA: Allyn & Bacon.

Armington, D. (1997). *The living classroom: Writing, reading, and beyond.* Washington, DC: NAEYC.

Brock, C. (2001). Serving English language learners: Placing learners learning on center stage. *Language Arts, 78*(5), 467–475.

Bucar, D. (2002, January). Teaching reading in first grade. *Young Children, 57*(1), 72–79.

Dickinson, D. K., & Tabors, P. O. (2002, March). Fostering language and literacy in classrooms and homes. *Young Children, 57*(2), 10–18.

Guang-Lea, L. (2002, Spring). Three strategies to promote young children's literacy development. *Young Children, 30*(2), 27–31.

Houle, A., & Krogness, A. (2001, September). The wonders of word walls. *Young Children, 56*(5), 56–57.

Koralek, D. (2002, March). The power of conversations: Supporting children's language learning. *Young Children, 57*(2), 8–9.

Lamme, L. L. (2002, Fall). Reading good books: Priming the pump for literacy development. *Dimensions of Early Childhood, 30*(4), 17–21.

McGee, L. M. (2002, Fall). Preschool literacy programs. *Dimensions in Early Childhood, 30*(4), 22–26.

Meier, D. R. (2000). *Scribble scrabble: Learning to read and write with diverse teachers, children, and families.* New York: Teachers College Press.

Morrow, L. M. (2002). *Organization and management of the language arts block.* New York: Guilford Press.

Novick, R. (2002, May). Learning to read the heart: Nurturing emotional literacy. *Young Children 57*(3), 84–89.

Okagaki, L., & Diamond, K. (2000, May). Responding to cultural and linguistic differences in the beliefs and practices of families with young children. *Young Children, 55*(3), 74–80.

Ordonez-Jasis, R., & Ortiz, R. W. (2007). Reading their worlds: Working with diverse families to enhance children's early literacy development. In D. Koralek (Ed.), *Spotlight on young children and their families,* 44–49. Washington, DC: NAEYC.

Owocki, G., & Goodman, Y. (2002). *Kidwatching: Documenting children's literacy development.* Portsmouth, NH: Heinemann.

Pattnaik, J. (2003, Fall). Multicultural literacy starts at home. *Childhood Education, 80*(1), 18–24.

Petersen, D. (2000, July). Using transitions to promote literacy in preschool and primary classrooms. *Young Children, 55*(4), 16–22.

Reisner, T. (2001, March). Learning to teach reading in a developmentally appropriate kindergarten. *Young Children, 56*(2), 44–48.

Reynolds, M. R., & Milner, S. (1998, Winter). Preschoolers on camera: Using videos to explore emergent literacy. *Dimensions of Early Childhood, 26*(1), 23–24.

Riojas-Cortez, M. (2001, Winter). It's all about talking: Oral languages development in a bilingual classroom. *Dimensions of Early Childhood, 29*(1), 11–15.

Roller, C. M. (Ed.). (2002). *Comprehensive reading instruction across the grade levels: A collection of papers from the Reading Research 2001 Conference.* Newark, DE: International Reading Association.

Ross-Degnan, L. (2002, November–December). J is for Jamal: The teacher's role in supporting young children's writing. *Early Childhood News, 14*(6), 32–34.

Schickedanz, J. A. (1999). *Much more than the ABC's: The early stages of reading and writing.* Washington, DC: NAEYC.

Selman, R. (2001, May). Talktime: Programming communicative interaction into the toddler day. *Young Children, 56*(3), 15–18.

Thornburg, K. (2001, September). What does it look like and what does it take? Supporting early literacy. White House summit on early childhood cognitive development. *Young Children, 56*(5), 56–57.

White, M. (2002, May). A lesson in listening. *Young Children, 57*(3), 43.

For additional information on early education curriculum, visit our Web site at http://www.earlychilded.delmar.com

CHAPTER 4

LITERATURE

OBJECTIVES

AFTER STUDYING THIS CHAPTER, YOU SHOULD BE ABLE TO:

- Discuss children's literature in relationship to literacy development.
- Explore the purposes and values of children's books.
- Identify types and genres of books for children and discuss children's book awards.
- Develop criteria for selecting appropriate books for infants, toddlers, preschoolers, and primary-grade children.
- Select and share appropriate literature with young children and their families.
- Describe the process of integrating literature into other curriculum areas.
- Discuss activities that encourage children to be authors and illustrators.
- Expand skills as a storyteller and observe, plan, present, and evaluate developmentally appropriate children's literature activities.

OVERVIEW

Children's literature is a wondrous and exciting part of early education curriculum. Most of us can still recall favorite childhood stories that were read or told to us by a loving adult. Books have a way of connecting us to others. They put us in a different time and place and capture our imaginations and our hearts. That is the thrust of this chapter: connecting children to literature by developing ideas and ways of making literature an integral and stimulating part of the early education curriculum.

Where you place the book center, whether it is for two children or a special, private place for one child, indicates how much importance you place on a child's interacting with books and stories. When and how often you read a book to the group or an individual child points this out as well. Is it always at the same time each day or in the same location? Are you spontaneous? Sometimes do you just *feel* like telling a story, reading a book, or developing an activity? Being flexible and creating on-the-spot activities with children's suggestions are just as important and worthwhile as having planned activities.

These interactions with children through books help us enfold literature into language and literacy development. The language of literature provides the child with vivid, imaginative, well-ordered words—words to think about, to listen to, and to try out and make her own. Oral language relates to reading and writing. It is a part of the development of both. The child who hears stories all through childhood learns language and structure and develops attitudes and concepts about the printed word (Morrow, 1989).

Early education emphasizes reading and writing opportunities *across the curriculum.* Sawyer (2004) explains further, "Integrating each of the content areas with literature brings a cohesiveness to the program and the classroom. It also lends stability, an important component of early childhood education. Yet, integration of content areas still allows wonderful things to happen in the classroom." (See Chapter 3, "Language and Literacy," for additional information.)

In support of children, the International Reading Association (IRA) and the National Council of Teachers of English (NCTE) have developed and updated their 12 Standards for the English Language Arts (2007):

> *The vision guiding these standards is that all students must have the opportunities and resources to develop the language skills they need to pursue life's goals and to participate fully as informed, productive members of society. These standards assume that literacy growth begins before children enter school as they experience and experiment with literacy activities—reading and writing, and associating spoken words with their graphic representations. Recognizing this fact, these standards encourage the development of curriculum and instruction that make productive use of the emerging literacy abilities that children bring to school.*

To view the complete standards, visit http://www.readwritethink.org and click on the "Standards" button. The IRA and NCTE Web sites (linked to the Standards page at http://www.readwritethink.org) also contain more information, including the complete standards.

Literature can reflect the joy, pleasure, sadness, and expectations that are experienced in a child's life. "Each story changes with the voice that tells it, each picture with the eyes that see it" (Thomas, 1998). Throughout a child's discovery of literature in all its forms, there should be encouragement by the significant adults the child encounters. A lifelong love of literature will be the result.

literature

All the writings (prose and verse) of a people, country, or period, including those written especially for children.

CHILDREN'S LITERATURE AND LITERACY DEVELOPMENT

Our cultural history is tied to literature. (Arnoff, 2003).

Literature, in its simplest sense, is all the writings (prose and verse) of a people, country, or period, including those written especially for children.

Children's literature can be defined in many ways. By looking at purposes, values, types, and genres of books for early education, we can define what literature is for young children. The material comes from many sources in both language and illustrated materials.

Using literature to foster the development of understanding requires that we focus our use of books on more than just teaching children to read. We must also use books as tools for helping children learn about the world. Through books, children can explore science, social studies and math concepts, develop multicultural understandings, learn how to do and make things, and learn more about topics of personal interest. (Owocki, 2001).

Young children develop visual literacy skills even before they can read. As teachers we can encourage this by helping them to use illustrations to decode meaning from the text and to challenge them to describe, compare, and value both visual and written communication. Furthermore, by starting with the literal and concrete, children begin to think about what they see in an illustration and, in turn, describe what they think will happen next in the book they are reading. Aesthetics can be emphasized to young children when teachers focus on line, color, and shape, as well as evaluate the illustrations for strength, mood, and feeling.

According to Strickland (2002), today's informed early childhood educator should understand and be able to build upon the following principles in order to support young children's literacy development:

🌐 Children's language and culture have a direct influence on their learning.

🌐 Learning to read and write is a complex process.

🌐 Language and literacy development are interdependent and interactive. What children know about communication through talk is used to build understandings about reading and writing.

🌐 Children learn best when teachers understand and address the variability among them.

🌐 Children learn best when teachers understand the developmental continuum of reading and writing, are skilled in a variety of strategies to help children achieve, and know how to monitor children's learning in terms of challenging but achievable goals.

Literacy development also can be encouraged by using Vygotsky's (1986) theory of *scaffolding*. This occurs as the teacher (adult) continually adjusts the level of help offered in response to the child's level of performance. For example:

Shared work—the teacher, in a leadership role, selects and shares a book with the children.

Guided work—the teacher guides and encourages the students on an as-needed basis as they explore children's literature, such as helping them to draw illustrations of stories read to them.

Independent work—by this time children are embarking on their own responses to literature that interests them, the teacher being only minimally supportive, such as five-year-olds doing a puppet version of a favorite story. (Adapted from Bickler, 1999, in Jalongo, 2004).

PURPOSES AND VALUES OF CHILDREN'S BOOKS

As we explore the many purposes of including children's books in early childhood classrooms and homes, it is crucial to understand their fundamental role in the learning experience. Because learning is basically the process of associating that which is new with that which is already known, stories can be a powerful tool to accomplish it. A book introduces a child to something new, which can give her greater understanding of the world and create an excitement to know more.

In addition, Sawyer (2004); Huck, Hepler, & Hickman (1993); and Owocki (2001) have suggested the following purposes and values of children's books:

- provide sheer enjoyment for a child
- help develop a child's imagination
- help a child find meaning in life
- offer a child time to reflect on experiences that relate to real life
- help a child reinforce discoveries about the world
- give a child opportunities to reread parts enjoyed or not understood
- introduce a child to many kinds of learning through the enjoyment of books
- help a child develop processes and skills
- help a child focus on predicting outcomes, drawing conclusions, and solving problems
- encourage a child to develop a curiosity about learning and life
- help a child build a foundation for learning to read
- give a child exciting experiences with books and with language
- provide a means for a child to listen to others
- give a child an awareness of and sensitivity to others
- help a child appreciate the writing and illustrations in books
- enable a child to build a foundation for the use and care of books

It is important for teachers and parents of young children to share with each other what they think the purposes are of creating an environment filled with books as part of a child's life. Open communication can offer a partnership to enrich relationships for everyone.

TYPES AND GENRES OF BOOKS FOR CHILDREN

genre
Category used to classify literary works, usually by form, technique, or content.

Before a teacher, parent, or other significant adult selects books for children, understanding about the many *types* and *genres* of books available is essential. **Genre** is a category used to classify literary works, usually by form, technique, or content.

format

The overall arrangement of the way a book is put together, such as size, shape, paper quality, colors, and content of each page.

A book's **format** is the overall arrangement, or the way the book is put together, involving factors such as size, shape, paper quality, colors, and content of each page. Isbell and Raines (2003), Machado (2007), and many other children's literature experts believe that teachers and parents should select books from a wide variety of genres and types. This is fairly easy when you are working with adult literature, which falls into familiar categories, such as fiction, nonfiction, poetry, and prose. But with children's literature in all of its many varieties, the labeling is much more difficult.

Although several systems are used to group children's books, educators do not always agree on how a given book might be labeled or placed. Many books do not neatly fit any category or may fit more than one. Nevertheless, most books relating to children's literature fall into the categories that follow. (See Figure 4–1 for children's literature information on the Internet.) The types of literature are listed with specific characteristics that identify each kind of book. For clarity and organization, the types or categories of children's books are arranged in alphabetical order.

Alphabet Books

alphabet books

Simple stories based on the alphabet that present letter identification and one-object picture association.

Alphabet books are books based on the alphabet that

- offer simple stories.
- present letter identification and one-object picture association.
- offer paired words and objects with matching illustrations.
- have a consistent theme.
- present opportunities to discover names and association of alphabet letters that are easily identified.
- provide emergent readers with opportunities for oral and written language development.

FIGURE 4–1
Suggested children's literature Internet Web sites.

CHILDREN'S LITERATURE WEB SITES

- Alma Flor Ada Web site – http://almaflorada.com
- American Library Association – http://www.ala.org
- Carol Hurst's Children's Literature – http://www.carolhurst.com
- Center for the Study of Books in Spanish for Children and Adolescents – http://www.csusm.edu/csb
- Children's Book Council – http://www.cbcbooks.org
- Denise Fleming Web site – http://www.denisefleming.com
- Education World – http://www.education-world.com
- Eric Carle Web site – http://www.eric-carle.com
- Gail Gibbons Web site – http://www.gailgibbons.com
- Jan Brett Web site – http://www.janbrett.com
- Laura Numeroff Web site – http://www.lauranumeroff.com
- The Literacy Center – http://www.literacycenter.net

Internet Resources for the Children to Explore:
- The Children's Digital Library – pages full of stories and activities, including a Spanish version – http://www.storyplace.org
- KIDS – illustrate a story, poetry in pictures, meet the illustrators – http://www.rif.org
- Poetry – poetry playground – http://www.poetry4kids.com
- Scholastic Web site for children – http://www.scholastic.com

Beginning-to-Read Books

beginning-to-read books
Predictable books that are easy to read and present words that are simple and repetitive.

Beginning-to-read books may also be referred to as easy-to-read books. These books

- present words that are simple and repetitive.
- have short sentences.
- are usually predictable.
- are designed to be read by the emergent reader.

Big Books

big books
Oversized books that present extra-large text and illustrations.

Big books may also be called oversized, giant, or jumbo books. Big books

- present extra-large text and illustrations.
- allow teachers to share books with a group of children easily.
- are mass published, so many popular titles are available in this format.

Board Books

board books
First books for infants and toddlers made of laminated heavy cardboard.

Board books are usually the first books for infants and toddlers because they are made of heavy cardboard and are laminated. Board books

- offer ease of page turning for children learning to handle books.
- are sometimes referred to as minibooks because they are small and can easily be picked up by a young child.
- have simple illustrations.

Concept Books

concept books
Books that present themes, ideas, or concepts with specific examples. They also identify and clarify abstractions, such as color or shape, and help with vocabulary development.

Concept books have been identified as a young child's first informational book. These books

- present themes, ideas, or concepts with specific examples.
- identify and clarify abstractions, such as color or shape.
- help with vocabulary development.
- include alphabet and counting books as favorite types of concept books.

Counting Books

counting books
Books that describe simple numeral and picture associations, and often tell a story. They show representations of numbers in more than one format and vary from simple to complex.

Counting books are books based on counting and numeral recognition. These books

- describe simple numeral and picture association.
- often tell a story.
- offer one-to-one correspondence illustrations.
- show representations of numbers in more than one format.
- vary from simple to complex.
- present illustrations that are consistent in adding to understanding for young children.

Folk Literature

folk literature
Tales that come from the oral tradition of storytelling that appeal to the child's sense of fantasy.

Folk literature may also be called folk tales, fairy tales, fables, tall tales, myths, and legends. These tales

- come from the oral tradition of storytelling.

- appeal to the child's sense of fantasy.
- teach value systems.
- offer language that is appealing to children and create strong visual images.
- are available in picture book format.
- connect with other cultures and countries because they retell traditional stories that are shared from generation to generation. (Some specific examples include: Hans Christian Andersen's original and adapted stories, which are modern fairy tales; fables, which present explicit morals with animals speaking as humans; myths, which describe the creation of the world and nature; and legends, which are based on the actions of a single hero. Story collectors, such as the Grimm brothers, wrote down stories from the oral tradition.)

Informational Books

informational books
Books that offer nonfiction for emergent readers by providing accurate facts about people and subject matter.

Informational books offer nonfiction for emergent readers. They also

- explore new ideas.
- answer "why" and "how."
- stimulate and expand individual or group interest.
- give accurate facts about people (biographies) and subject matter.

Interaction Books

interaction books
Books used to stimulate imagination by using some device for involving young readers, such as pop-ups, fold-outs, scratch and sniff, pasting, puzzle pictures, humor, and riddles.

Interaction books are sometimes called novelty, toy, or participation books. These books

- use some device for involving young readers, such as pop-ups, foldouts, scratch and sniff, pasting, puzzle pictures, humor, and riddles.
- provide audiocassettes or CDs.
- stimulate imagination.
- can be designed in different sizes and shapes for exploring and touching.

Mother Goose and Nursery Rhymes

Mother Goose and nursery rhyme books
Books passed from generation to generation and known by children all over the world. These are often a child's first introduction to literature.

Mother Goose and nursery rhyme books are often a child's first introduction to literature. These books

- are known by children all over the world.
- are passed from generation to generation.
- offer varied illustrations of the rhymes.
- appeal to infants and toddlers.

Multicultural Books

multicultural books
Books that develop awareness of and sensitivity to other cultures. They also help to increase positive attitudes toward similarities and differences in people.

Multicultural books are also referred to as cross-cultural or culturally diverse books. These books

- develop awareness of and sensitivity to other cultures.
- increase positive attitudes toward similarities and differences in people.
- offer accurate portrayals and rich details of individual and group heritage.
- can extend to seasonal and holiday books (a separate listing of *anti-bias literature* that promotes gender equity and the importance of the inclusion of children with special needs may include multicultural books as well).

Picture Books or Picture Story Books

Picture books are often referred to as the most popular type of children's literature. These books

picture books
Books written in a direct style that tell a simple story with illustrations complementing the text.

- are written in a direct style that tells a simple story.
- offer varied illustrations that complement and associate closely with the text.
- are written especially for adults to share with children.
- are uniquely appropriate for the young child.

Poetry

Poetry is overlooked many times as part of children's literature. Poetry

poetry
A form of literature that contributes imaginative rhyme, rhythm, and sound.

- can be one book, one poem, or a collection of poems.
- contributes imaginative rhyme, rhythm, and sound.
- is another way to present culture, country, and language.
- stimulates imagery and feelings.
- is pleasing and can relate to life in terms that children can understand.

Predictable Books

Predictable books contain familiar and repetitive sequences. These books

predictable books
Books that contain familiar and repetitive sequences.

- describe events that are repeated or added to as the story continues.
- permit successful guessing of what happens next.
- supply opportunities for children to read along.
- build self-confidence.
- encourage children to read naturally.

Realistic Literature

Sometimes called bibliotherapy or therapeutic literature, **realistic literature** deals with real-life issues. These books

realistic literature
A form of literature that helps children cope with common, actual experiences by offering positive solutions and insights.

- help children cope with common, actual experiences.
- offer positive solutions and insights.
- encourage talking about a child's feelings.
- are often tied in with anti-bias literature that relates to children with special needs.

Reference Books

Reference books emphasize individualized learning through special topic books, picture dictionaries, and encyclopedias. They also encourage older children to find a resource that answers questions.

reference books
Books that emphasize individualized learning through special topic books, picture dictionaries, and encyclopedias.

Series Books

Series books are often written for primary-grade children. These books

series books
Books written for primary-grade children and built around a single character or group of characters.

- are built around a single character or group of characters.
- can introduce the concept of books written in chapter form.
- can be related to television characters that are familiar to children.

Teacher- and Child-Made Books

teacher- and child-made books
Books made by the teacher or child that encourage self-esteem, creativity, and the sharing of ideas. They also encourage children to articulate experiences.

Teacher- and child-made books are a part of developmentally appropriate early education classrooms. These books

- 🌐 encourage self-esteem, creativity, and sharing ideas with others.
- 🌐 reinforce group learning.
- 🌐 develop a child's understanding of authorship by seeing her name in print.
- 🌐 encourage children to articulate experiences.
- 🌐 invite children to use their imagination.

Wordless Picture Books

wordless picture books
Books that tell a story with visually appealing illustrations. These books promote creativity by encouraging a child to talk about experiences and use his or her imagination.

A young child develops language, reading skills, and meaning through the illustrations with **wordless picture books,** sometimes called stories without words. These books

- 🌐 help develop building blocks of language.
- 🌐 offer visually appealing illustrations.
- 🌐 aid in developing eye coordination.
- 🌐 present sequential action from page to page.
- 🌐 promote creativity by encouraging a child to talk about experiences.
- 🌐 use imagination.
- 🌐 invite older children to write a story about what is seen, with character descriptions and dialogue.

WHY I TEACH YOUNG CHILDREN

I teach to see the faces of the children who are so engrossed in an activity that one can physically see how much learning is taking place. This happens when the children can relate to the topic either through their own experiences or the experiences of their friends and/or teacher.

As an example, our pre-k class has been very involved learning about ocean life. I had just returned from a trip to the east coast of Florida where I saw a manatee slowly meandering through the water, very close to shore. It was eating seaweed as it swam along and almost seemed to turn its head to smile at the many observers on the beach. I took a digital photo of the manatee and, as librarian, was most eager to share my picture and experience with the children.

I showed the picture while telling my story but did not name the animal. No child could identify the picture, so I told them, and then read a book about manatees. The children did not make a sound. Their eyes were wide, their jaws were dropped, and there was no movement as I read. Afterwards, I asked them what they learned about manatees and wrote down what they said. They shared so much information which I am sure they will remember.

This was an example of how children learn through many types of experiences. They related to my story and it made the manatee seem real to them. It made me also realize that we are not just teachers while in our classrooms. We are teachers wherever life takes us and we can never pass up the opportunity to capture the moment.

—Bonnie Rubinstein

CHILDREN'S BOOK AWARDS

An understanding of who gives awards for outstanding children's literature and the nature of each award provides a guide to choosing books.

In 1938, Frederick G. Melcher, editor of *Publisher's Weekly*, established the Caldecott Award. This medal is awarded annually to the artist of "the most distinguished picture book for children" printed in the United States and published during the preceding year. It is named in honor of the English illustrator Randolph Caldecott (1846–1886), a nineteenth-century pioneer in the field of children's books. The selection is made by a committee, the members of which are either elected or appointed from the ranks of children's and school librarians who are members of the Association for Library Services to Children, a part of the American Library Association.

The Caldecott Award is presented at the same time as the Newbery Award. Named for John Newbery (1713–1767), the first English publisher of children's books, and established in 1922, the Newbery Award is for "the most distinguished contribution to American literature for children" published the preceding year. It honors the quality of the author's writing and is usually a book appropriate for older children who are more mature readers. Both the Caldecott and Newbery Awards are presented at the annual conference of the American Library Association.

The Hans Christian Andersen Medal, established in 1956, is given by the International Board on Books for Young People. This award is presented every two years to a living author and an illustrator in recognition of their entire body of work.

The International Reading Association Children's Book Award is given to new authors.

The Coretta Scott King Awards are presented to an African-American author and illustrator for "outstanding inspirational and educational contributions to literature for children." In addition, the National Jewish Book Awards and the Catholic Book Awards add to the list of over 100 awards made annually to recognize authors and illustrators of literature for children (Isbell & Raines, 2003; Huck, Hepler, & Hickman., 1993).

Use award books as a starting point for selecting literature. Personal evaluation and knowledge of individual children, their interests, and their needs should also be criteria for selection.

> *We can, through employment of picture books, bring a second and third teacher into the classroom. Authors and illustrators have done half our planning for us—and high-quality*

Select books that appeal to children and relate to their experiences.

planning it is too—and we can piggyback on their talent and industry and use their books to jumpstart our own imaginations. (J. Graham, 2000).

SELECTION OF BOOKS FOR YOUNG CHILDREN

Many developmentally appropriate books are available for use in early education. The following criteria should be considered when making selections for young children:

🌐 Select books for enjoyment.

🌐 Select books that encourage a child's capacity for laughter.

🌐 Choose durable books. Books are to be handled and used by children.

🌐 Select books with different styles of illustrations.

🌐 Consider the length of the story. Books should be age and developmentally appropriate.

🌐 Pick books that appeal to children and relate to their experiences.

🌐 Choose books that have an appealing story and style. Children like sound, rhythm, and repetition in their stories.

🌐 Avoid overly frightening, confusing stories.

🌐 Offer children a variety of writing styles and languages.

🌐 Choose books that appeal to a young child's senses. Enjoyment is found in books with descriptive words that make children taste, smell, and feel, as well as see and hear.

🌐 Use literature as a stimulus for activities that require children to use their senses in discovery or exploration.

🌐 Pick books that help children develop positive self-esteem by emphasizing the capabilities children have.

🌐 Share books that promote feelings of security.

🌐 Choose books that show characters seeing themselves positively.

🌐 Select books in which characters show emotions common to young children.

🌐 Read several books on the same topic to provide more than one perspective.

🌐 Introduce books that will expand vocabulary.

🌐 Present books that reinforce concepts already being acquired.

🌐 Select books that may help clarify misconceptions.

🌐 Select stories that have a plot in which there is action; for example, stories that tell what people did and what they said.

🌐 Enrich a child's experiences with literature by providing poetry selections and books of poems.

M/A-B Multicultural books for children should introduce a variety of family compositions, including single parents, grandparents who play key roles in nurturing children, and extended families who share a home and each other's lives (Reading Is Fundamental, 2007).

🌐 Include a wide variety of multicultural books. There are many that present the uniqueness of a present-day culture as seen through the eyes of a child.

🌐 Select books that do not stereotype people according to gender, ethnic background, culture, age, or types of work.

🌐 Minority characters should be shown as independent thinkers who can face challenges and solve problems. Select books with well-developed characters.

⊕ Illustrations should not use stereotypical caricatures of a group's physical features.

⊕ Look for accuracy in stories.

⊕ Share literature from other countries to expand children's global awareness.

 The Reading Is Fundamental (RIF) organization (2007) suggests the following guidelines in the selection of books that include children with special needs:

⊕ Choose books that show differently—abled people in active and interactive roles. Be sure that some books have a person with special needs as the main character.

⊕ Read those books that regard children with disabilities as children first. Pick those that approach special needs children as being more like other children than different.

⊕ Make positive reading experiences a priority for children with disabilities. Read books to children that have characters with disabilities similar to theirs.

⊕ Make use of technology by individualizing instruction for each student and match programming to student learning styles.

⊕ Partner with families on reading strategies.

RECOMMENDED BOOKS

The examples of representative books have been divided into two lists: one suggests books for age and developmental appropriateness, and the other is a thematic list of children's books. Some duplications will be found in the two listings. These are books that were suggested over and over again by teachers of young children, are used as examples of quality literature by educators in the field, or have been selected as personal favorites and current discoveries. (You can add favorites of your own to these. Ask colleagues, librarians, and parents to suggest additional titles and authors.)

It is important for infants to interact with books.

Age and Developmentally Appropriate Children's Books

INFANTS. When you hold an infant in your lap and share a special story or book, you are making a difference in that child's life. When you set up the special places in the infant room for reading or telling a story or for singing a nursery rhyme, include pillows, stuffed animals, quilts, and mats. Sawyer (2004) points out that "babies sit on laps, crawl about, and listen in various positions and in various places." It is important for infants to interact with the books. For them, that means chewing on the pages, touching and looking at them in unique ways, and making them a part of their "personal turf." Schickendanz (1999) tells us,

Choose durable books. Books are to be handled and used by children.

> Older babies will enjoy a special book nook. Crawlers and walkers can get to an area where attractively arranged books are easy to reach. . . . A book nook for babies can be made by standing some books up on the [carpeted] floor and laying others flat nearby. Because the opened and standing books can be seen from a distance, they will catch the children's attention.

See Figure 4–2 for suggested books for infants.

TODDLERS. The special place for story time in the toddler room should be surrounded with colorful pillows, carpet squares, and other comfortable spots available for these young children to listen to, participate with, and enjoy books. Small groupings offer the children a chance to turn the page, point to, and identify things, while sharing their choice of books with the teacher and each other. For those toddlers who enjoy one-on-one time with a teacher and a favorite book, sitting in a rocking chair fulfills this need in a special way.

Story time outdoors on a big quilt, under a tree, and surrounded by grass can be exciting and appropriate for toddlers, too. Bredekamp and Copple (1997) explain, "Two-year-olds are learning to produce language rapidly. They need simple books, pictures, puzzles, music, and time and space for active play such as jumping, running, and

Ahlberg, A., & Ahlberg, J. (1981). *Peek-a-boo.* New York: Viking.

Brown, M. W. (1991, First Board Book Edition). *Goodnight moon.* Illustrated by Clement Hurd. New York: HarperCollins.

Cowell, C. (2003). *What shall we do with the boo-hoo baby?* New York: Scholastic.

de Paola, T. (1985). *Tomie de Paola's Mother Goose.* New York: Putnam.

Greenfield, E. (1991). *Daddy and I.* Illustrated by Jan Spivey Gilchrist. New York: Black Butterfly Children's Books and Readers Publishing Inc.

Hale, S. (1990). *Mary had a little lamb.* Illustrated by Tomie de Paola. New York: Scholastic.

Hathon, E. (1993). *Soft as a kitten.* New York: Grossett & Dunlap, Inc.

Hoban, T. (1993). *Black on white.* New York: Greenwillow.

Hoban, T. (1993). *White on black.* New York: Greenwillow.

Kubler, A. (2000, Board Book Edition). *My new baby.* New York: Child's Play International.

Krauss, R. (1993, First Board Book Edition). *The carrot seed.* Illustrated by Crockett Johnson. New York: HarperCollins.

Kunhardt, D. (1962). *Pat the bunny.* Racine, WI: Western.

Lavis, S. (2001). *Cock-a-doodle-doo! A farm yard counting book.* (Board Book). New York: Ragged Bears Books.

Marzollo, J. (2002). *Baby's alphabet.* Photographs by N. Sheehan. Brookfield, CT: Roaring Brook Press.

Rescek, S. (2006, Padded Board Book). *Twinkle, Twinkle Little Star and other favorite nursery rhymes.* New York: Tiger Tales.

Shaw, C. G. (1993, First Board Book Edition). *It looked like spilt milk.* New York: HarperCollins.

Steptoe, J. (1988). *Baby says.* New York: Lothrop, Lee & Shepard.

Watson, C. (1983). *Catch me and kiss me and say it again.* New York: Philomel.

FIGURE 4–2
Suggested books for infants.

dancing." Physically enjoying the story is important for these children. See Figure 4–3 for suggested books for toddlers.

THREE-, FOUR-, AND FIVE-YEAR-OLDS.
The story center, library, or book center should be one of the most inviting and exciting learning centers or curriculum areas in a classroom for preschoolers. Huck, Hepler, & Hickman (1993) found in their research that many times the library corners are the least frequently chosen area and that "To fully take advantage of young children's active natures, we must reexamine the size, arrangement, and contents of the library area."

For this age child, many comfortable reading spaces should be provided, such as a soft rug; a big, empty "refrigerator-size" box with pillows to sit on and "windows" cut in the box to look out; and child-size tables and chairs set up with a variety of books, magazines, catalogs, newspapers, and books with audiotapes, blank paper, and writing instruments.

As teachers, you should read aloud to your three-, four-, and five-year-olds every day. Plan activities that integrate listening, speaking, reading, and writing. It is also important for you to continue to read to individual children if they ask you to, because preschool children still need this special time with a significant adult.

> *The magic of book reading is amplified when children are on a lap. . . . Children become active participants when they point to specific things in pictures, turn the pages, ask questions, and make comments. The lap reading experience is vital for children to acquire "book language," "story sense," and a host of other early reading knowledge. . . . Although instruction is helpful, what children most need in order to learn how to ride horseback, is to get up in the saddle and ride. To learn how to skate, they must lace up their skates and give skating a try. To learn to read, children need exposure to a lot of good books and a mentor who can read with them and coach them along the way. (Lamme, 2002)*

Young children enjoy alone time with a book of their choice.

(Review Chapter 3 for suggestions of physical space arrangement and activity plans for setting up the library, literature, or literacy center.) See Figure 4–4 for suggested books for three-, four-, and five-year-olds.

Asch, F. (1998). *Barnyard lullaby*. New York: Simon & Schuster.

Boynton, S. (2004, Lap-size Board Book). *The going to bed book*. New York: Little Simon.

Carle, E. (1996). *Have you seen my cat?* New York: Little Simon.

Dyer, J. (1998). *Animal crackers: Bedtime*. (Board Book). Boston: Little, Brown & Company.

Emberly, R. (2002). *My clothes/Mi ropa*. Boston: Little, Brown & Company.

Emberly, R. (2000). *My colors/Mis colores*. Boston: Little, Brown & Company.

Fleming, D. (1998). *Mama cat has three kittens*. New York: Henry Holt.

Fox, M. (1993). *Time for bed*. Illustrated by J. Dyer. San Diego, CA: Gulliver Books.

Gentieu, P. (2000). *Grow! Babies!* New York: Crown.

Martin, B., Jr. (1983). *Brown bear, brown bear, what do you see?* Illustrated by E. Carle. New York: Henry Holt.

Martin, B., Jr. (2004, Big Book). *Panda Bear, Panda Bear, What do you see?* Illustrated by E. Carle. New York: Henry Holt.

Marzollo, J. (2000). *Papa papa*. (Board Book). Illustrated by L. Regan. New York: HarperCollins.

Omerod, J. (1994). *To baby with love*. New York: Lothrop, Lee & Shepard Books.

Oxenbury, H. (1992). *Mother's helper*. New York: Dial.

Raposo, J. (2001). *Imagination song*. Illustrated by L. Linn. New York: Random House.

Winter, S. (1994). *A baby just like me*. New York: Dorling Kindersley.

Wood, A. (2000, Board Book Edition). *The napping house*. Illustrated by D. Wood. New York: Red Wagon Books.

FIGURE 4–3
Suggested books for toddlers.

Aliki. (2000). *All by myself.* New York: HarperCollins.

Brown, M. W. (2002). *Buenas noches, Luna/Good night moon.* Illustrated by C. Hurd. Translated by T. Mlawer. New York: Harper Festival.

Curtis, J. L. (1998). *Today I feel silly: And other moods that make my day.* Illustrated by L. Cornell. New York: HarperCollins.

dePaola, T. (1983). *The legend of the bluebonnet.* New York: Putnam.

Dr. Seuss. (1992). *Huevos verdas con jamon/Green eggs and ham.* Translated by A. Marcuse. New York: Lectorum.

Ehlert, L. (2002). *In my world.* New York: Harcourt.

Ehlert, L. (2000). *Market day: A story told with folk art.* New York: Harcourt.

Fleming, D. (2007, Big Book Edition). *In the small, small pond.* New York: Henry Holt.

Hoban, T. (1999). *Construction zone.* New York: Greenwillow.

Katz, K. (2004, Big Book Edition). *The color of us.* New York: Henry Holt.

Louie, T. O. (2002). *Raymond's perfect present.* Illustrated by S. Wang. New York: Lee & Low.

Martin, B., Jr. (1993). *Polar bear, polar bear, what do you hear?* Illustrated by E. Carle. New York: Henry Holt.

Martin, B., Jr., & Archambault, J. (1988). *Listen to the rain.* Illustrated by J. Endicott. New York: Henry Holt.

Miller, M. (1994). *My five senses.* New York: Simon & Schuster.

Numeroff, L. (2002). *If you take a mouse to school.* Illustrated by F. Bond. New York: HarperCollins.

Reitano, J. (1998). *What if zebras lost their stripes?* New York: Scholastic.

Rohmann, E. (2003). *My friend rabbit.* New York: Roaring Brook Press.

Wilson-Max, K. (1997). *Big red fire truck.* (Liftflap edition). New York: Cartwheel Books.

Yee, W. H. (2007). *Who likes rain?* New York: Henry Holt.

FIGURE 4–4
Suggested books for three-, four-, and five-year-olds.

SIX-, SEVEN-, AND EIGHT-YEAR-OLDS. Computers, movies, television shows, video games, and music videos pose a challenge to teachers, librarians, and parents trying to capture the reading attention of six-, seven-, and eight-year-olds. As a result, literature for this age reflects the addition of topics grounded in real-life issues. Illustrations are more complex and artistic, and a greater diversity is available.

As a teacher, you should provide many opportunities for reading and writing in the primary classroom. Bredekamp and Copple (1997) point out several ways to make the environment developmentally appropriate. Set up a "tempting library area for browsing through books, reading silently, or sharing a book with a friend; a listening station; and places to practice writing stories and to play math and language games."

The more emphasis you place on the importance of books in the lives of six-, seven-, and eight-year-olds, the more important literature will be to the children. As with all ages, *read aloud* to them as often as you can. Let them tell you and others about what they have read, and encourage open-ended questioning by everyone. Encourage parents to continue reading aloud to their children, too.

When visitors come to your classroom, have them tell a story or read to the children. Inviting parents, grandparents, community volunteers, other teachers, or staff to read provides another dimension. See Figure 4–5 for suggested books for six-, seven-, and eight-year-olds.

Thematic Selection of Children's Books

Many teachers find that using a thematic approach to literature selection gives them more individuality in curriculum development. The thematic strategy leads children to activities that suggest active exploration, problem solving, and

There should be plenty of time to share a book with a friend.

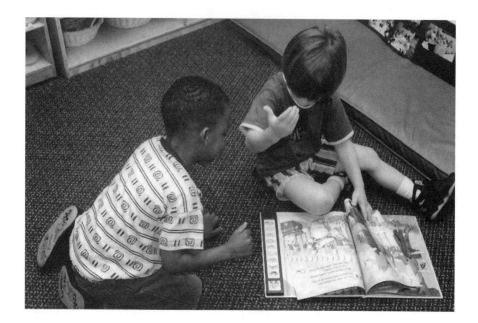

Andrews-Goebel, N. (2002). *The pot that Juan built.* Illustrated by D. Diaz. New York: Lee & Low.

Angelou, M. (1994). *My painted house, my friendly chicken, and me.* Photographs by M. Courtney-Clarke. New York: Clarkson Potter.

Banks, B. (2001). *A gift from the sea.* Illustrated by G. Hallensleben. New York: Frances Foster Books.

Dillion, L., & Dillion, D. (2003). *Rap a tap tap*: Here's Bojangles, think of that. New York: Bluesky Press.

Dorros, A. (1991). *Tonight is carnival.* Illustrated with arpilleras sewn by the Club de Madres Virgen del Carmen of Lima, Peru. New York: Dutton.

Giles, A. (2001). *Giraffes can't dance.* Illustrated by G. Parker. New York: Orchard Books.

Goodall, J. (2001). *The chimpanzees that I love: Saving their world and ours.* New York: Scholastic.

George, L. B. (1995). *In the woods: Who's been here?* New York: Greenwillow.

Kerley, B. (2002). *A cool drink of water.* Washington, DC: National Geographic.

Kroll, V. (1993). *A carp for Kimiko.* Illustrated by Katherine Roundtree. Watertown, MA: Charlesbridge.

Neuschwander, C. (2007). *Patterns in Peru: An Adventure in patterning.* Illustrated by B. Lango. New York: Henry Holt.

Taback, S. (2002). *This is the house that Jack built.* New York: Putnam.

FIGURE 4–5
Suggested books for six-, seven-, and eight-year-olds.

the acquisition of specific concepts or skills. Themes can be weekly, biweekly, or monthly. Select the theme that relates to the children in your class according to their experiences and their age and stage of development. (Review Chapter 2 for specific explanations of themes, units, projects, and webs.) Then, select the literature that will emphasize, explain, and extend the theme. See Figure 4–6 for books about friendship.

Glazer (2000) suggests that:

> *Books with characteristics in common can be grouped together into units that focus on a single item, describe similar content or represent literature of a particular genre or by a particular author or illustrator. . . . [C]onsider a variety of titles, but narrow the selection to those books which best fit your purposes, and include only those which you actually plan to use.*

Aliki. (1995). *Best friends together again*. New York: Greenwillow.

Bunnett, R. (1992). *Friends in the park*. Photographs by Carl Sahloff. New York: Checkerboard Press.

Cain, J. (2001). *The way I feel*. New York: Scholastic.

Hague, M. (2007). *Animal Friends: A collection of poems for children*. New York: Henry Holt.

Holt, K.W. (2007). *Skinny brown dog*. Illustrated by D. Saaf. New York: Henry Holt.

Kellogg, S. (1990). *Best Friends*. New York: Dial.

Kroll, V. (2000). *New friends, stuck-like-glue friends*. Grand Rapids, MI: Eerdman's.

Marxhausen, J. (1990). *Some of my best friends are trees*. St. Louis, MO: Concordia.

McCarty, P. (2007). *Hondo & Fabian*. New York: Henry Holt.

Morris, A. (1990). *Loving*. Photographs by Ken Heyman. New York: Lothrop, Lee, & Shepard,

Palacco, P. (1992). *Mrs. Katz and Tush*. New York: Bantam Books.

Rogers, F. (1987). *Making friends*. New York: Putnam

Russo, M. (1992). *Alex is my friend*. New York: Greenwillow.

Sunico, R. C. (1991). *Two friends, one world*. New York: Cacho Publishing House, Inc.

Tafuri, N. (2000). *Will you be my friend?* New York: Scholastic.

Ziefert, H. (2001). *39 uses for a friend*. New York: Penguin Putnam.

FIGURE 4–6
Suggested books for the theme "Friendship."

INTEGRATING LITERATURE INTO OTHER CURRICULUM AREAS

Currently, in classrooms throughout the country, literature-based instruction is "what's happening." The connection between literature and the other curriculum areas, as Machado (2007) explains, "includes reading aloud to children, making use of informational books, and encouraging children's response to books using drama, art, and child-dictated writing."

Sawyer (2004) explains literature-integrated units as being "taught around a general theme or a key idea. . . . One may wish to develop a theme around a single book. . . . The focus may also be in a content area such as science, social studies, basic concepts, or holidays."

Nelsen and Nelsen-Parish (2002) suggest other ways of connecting books to areas of the curriculum.

Reproductions and retellings are children's responses to literature through art, music, and drama, using their own language. In a reproduction, children make language come to life as they interact with the original text. A retelling is a summary of a story in the children's words. It is an effective tool for teaching children to recognize and organize story elements.

Glazer (2000) presents another way of looking at integrating curriculum:

Children should be guided to perceive literature as a body of work rather than as separate and unrelated stories and poems. If you group books for presentation, you set the stage for children to see the relationships among books, to notice the recurring structural patterns of literature.

"Putting literature around the room" can be done realistically by creatively decorating containers for books with bright contact paper, wallpaper, or children's drawings and by placing baskets of books in every learning activity center. For example, books relating to houses and buildings can be put in the block center; those dealing with shapes and colors can be put in the art center; and books concerning gardening, fish, and turtles can be near the sand and water table. See Figure 4–7 for suggested books about the natural environment.

WHY I TEACH YOUNG CHILDREN

It is the little things that make teaching so wonderful. The smiles when a child feels successful. The hugs they give that tell you they feel safe. The words they repeat while working or playing that show you they remember what you said. The sheer enjoyment on their faces when you read a book to them or they "read" to you. You know they feel loved, not when you help them, but when they reach their hands out to you when they think you need a helping hand.

—Stephanie Shiller

Appelt, K. (2005). *Miss Ladybird's wildflowers: How a First Lady changed America.* Illustrated by J. F. Hein. New York: HarperCollins.

Bang, M. (1997). *Common Ground: Water, earth, and air.* New York: Scholastic.

Buchanan, K. (1991). *This house is made of mud.* Illustrated by L. Tracey. New York: Northland Publishing.

Carle, E. (1990). *The very quiet cricket.* New York: Philomel.

Cassedy, S. & Kunihiro, S. (1992). *Red dragonfly on my shoulder.* New York: Harper/Collins.

Donald, R. L. (2002). *Air Pollution.* (True Books). New York: Children's Press.

Donald, R. L. (2002). *Water Pollution.* (True Books). New York: Children's Press.

Dorros. A. (1997), *A tree is growing.* Illustrated by S. D. Schindler. New York: Scholastic.

Earth Works Group. (1990). *50 simple things kids can do to save the earth.* New York: Andrews & McMell.

Harlow, R. (2002). *Garbage and recycling.* New York: Kingfisher.

Leavell, C. & Cravotta, N. (2005). *The tree farmer.* New York: VSP Books.

Martin, B., Jr., & Sampson, M. R. (2006). *I love our earth.* Watertown. MA: Charlesbridge Publishers.

Rockwell, A. (2000). *Our earth.* New York: Voyager Books.

FIGURE 4–7
Suggested books for the theme "Natural Environment."

Encourage children to write and illustrate their own books.

Activities That Encourage Children to Become Authors and Illustrators

One of the most stimulating child-centered activities a teacher can use is having the children write original books or one-page stories. "In a collaborative classroom project, each child contributes a unique individual piece to the collaborative process—especially the collaborative bookmaking process—in your classroom" (Spann, 1997). You can help the youngest children put their artwork together in the form of a book, using string or rings to do so; for older children, pair them as "book buddies" or "book partners" to write and illustrate their own books. Some teacher preparation or assistance may be needed or requested. Machado (2007) presents the values of books authored by children or their teachers:

- They promote interest in the classroom book collection.
- They help children see connections between spoken and written words.
- The material is based on the interests of both the children and the teacher.
- They personalize book reading.
- They prompt self-expression.
- They stimulate creativity.
- They build feelings of competence and self-worth.

Children (and teachers) as authors and illustrators can be emphasized in many ways. Having children make book covers for their books can affirm the importance of all books. In the writing or art center, provide paper, wallpaper, or contact paper that will cover a child's favorite book. The child can decorate the cover and write the title, author, and illustrator as well.

How about a "Let's Pretend Book"? In the dramatic play area have a camera (digital, video, or disposable type) ready for children to take pictures of what is going on in the grocery store, pet shop, post office, or whatever the area represents for that week. These are then placed on sheets of paper to be made into a book by the children and the teacher. The children can tell or dictate the story of who they were pretending to be. Visually and concretely, this helps children understand that their words and actions make stories and books.

Reading Is Fundamental (RIF) (2007) suggests that looking at and understanding both words and pictures demands a higher cognitive level than merely seeing that words and pictures are there. Teachers should develop many opportunities for children to become illustrators, such as:

- Have children author a book without illustrations and then author the same story, including illustrations.
- Have children develop a traditional storybook in which the text and illustrations are mutually supportive.
- Encourage children to try their hand at authoring and illustrating a wordless picture book.
- Help children see the relationship between a book's meaning and its art.

As with any child-directed activity, the teacher prepares materials and space in advance and is available to offer assistance. Suggestions for putting the book together can come from the teacher as well, with the children putting the book together with yarn, staples, masking tape, metal rings, or brads. The size and shape of the cover and pages of the book can be another creative element, such as books shaped to match the current curriculum theme or children's interests. Also, books can be in the shape of a bird, butterfly, car, bus, animal, fish, vegetable, and so on.

Keep in mind that however and whenever you mix and match literature with other curriculum areas, all activities should benefit the children developmentally, individually, and creatively. (There are specific examples at the end of this chapter. See Developmentally Appropriate Activities for Young Children.) See Figure 4–8 for suggested authors, illustrators, and photographers of children's books to share with the children. See Figure 4–9 for information about the Eric Carle Museum of Picture Book Art.

Teachers as Storytellers

"Throughout the world, in every culture, people have told stories," says Jimmy Neil Smith, executive director of the National Association for the Preservation and Perpetuation of Storytelling. The oral tradition was once the primary method for passing history and culture from one generation to the next. Eventually it became unpopular. "This may have been due," he continues, "to books and print media, radio, television and computerization. They fill us with images that were once the province of the oral tradition," concludes Mr. Smith (quoted in Schnedler, 1994). Sawyer (2004) agrees. "At one time, storytelling was the dominant method for sharing a culture's heritage with the next generation."

FIGURE 4–8
Suggested list of authors, illustrators, and photographers of books for young children.

Aliki	Lois Ehlert	Jerry Pinkney
Byron Barton	Denise Fleming	Patricia Polacco
Jan Brett	Gail Gibbons	Anne F. Rockwell
Eric Carle	Ken Heyman	Allan Say
Donald Crews	Ron Hirschi	Vera Williams
Tomie dePaola	Tana Hoban	Ken Wilson-Max
Arthur Dorros	Ann Morris	

FIGURE 4–9
The Eric Carle Museum of Picture Book Art.

THE ERIC CARLE MUSEUM OF PICTURE BOOK ART

By sharing a book, an adult shows a child, "I have time for you, I care for you—therefore I read to you. By reading together, we also give children an early taste of beauty. We clothe children, we feed children—and we read to children. It's part of growing up. It's culture, the human spirit" (Carle quoted in Brozowsky, 2002).

- The Eric Carle Museum of Picture Book Art, which celebrates the art of the picture book, opened to the public November 22, 2002, in Amherst, Massachusetts.
- Conceived by Carle, the museum is 44,000 square feet, situated in a 7.5 acre apple orchard next to Hampshire College campus.
- The museum collection includes picture book art from around the world and has at its core the work of Eric Carle.
- It is designed to do what picture books always have done: create intimate moments between adults and children as they talk with each other about what they see and feel. Museum Director Nick Clark (quoted in Brozowsky, 2002) explains: "With the great books, there is a pace and a magic. But it's not just the book. You remember that you were snuggling with somebody."
- You can visit the museum on-line at: http://www.picturebookart.org

A story is one of the means by which children make sense of their world and organize events, experiences, and facts. A teacher *telling* a story without a book and using changes in pitch, tone, and dramatic flair; using puppets, props, toys, songs, flannelboard pictures, and finger plays; or drawing a story while it is being told can captivate and entertain a small or large group of children. This unique way of presenting children's literature encourages children to tell their own stories or retell the stories back to the teachers.

"Storytelling is perhaps the most powerful way that human beings organize experience"(Engel, 1996/1997). Im, Parlakian, and Osborn (2007) tell us, "Adults can tell stories through language, but infants and toddlers tell their stories with a flick of their eyes, the point of a finger, or a coo. . . . Remember that much of infant and toddler communication is nonverbal. Very young children need patient and willing listeners who can accurately read their cues . . . and respond appropriately."

It is helpful for the teacher to select stories with simple plots and small numbers of characters for the younger children. Older children like the challenge of remembering a complex plot with multiple characters.

Poetry

Teachers should read poetry to children often. Kindergarten and primary children can memorize a few poems of their choosing. Not only is this an enjoyable activity, it is also a valuable way to develop phonemic awareness and cognitive skills. Appreciation for poetry develops slowly, but the time and place for poetry is any time, any place. See Figure 4–10 for suggested poetry books for young children.

Have snack time become a "poetry break time." Start by reading a poem to the children during their snack. Then, on following days, let the children read or tell a poem to each other and the teacher after snack time. Adding a musical background, recorded or live, offers a different dimension to poetry reading.

Other activities can be to act out a poem, draw an illustration for a poem, include poetry at group time, pick a theme and make an illustrated booklet or exhibit of poems that relate to the theme, and create a "Poetry Line" (clothesline or thick yarn) stretched across the back of the room with poems attached.

The following examples of poems should be shared with young children. (You will find flannelboard characters for "Spring Showers" in Appendix A.) Figure 4–11, "Tongue Twisters for Young Children," is a different kind of poem. Children learn about language with this fun activity.

Agee, J. (1993). *Flapstick: Ten ridiculous rhymes with flaps.* New York: Dutton/Penguin.

Booth, D. (1990). *Voices on the wind: Poems for all seasons.* New York: Morrow Junior Books.

de Paola, T. (2004, Board Book). *Tomie's little book of poems.* New York: Putnam.

Ghigna, C. (1995). *Riddle rhymes.* New York: Hyperion.

Hoberman, M. A. (1993). *Fathers, mothers, sisters, brothers: A collection of family poems.* New York: Puffin Books.

Hopkins, L. B. (2001). *Marvelous math: A book of poems.* Illustrated by K. Barbour. New York: Aladdin.

Hudson, W. (1993). *Pass it on: African American poetry for children.* Illustrated by Floyd Cooper. New York: Scholastic.

Johnston, T. (1996). *Once in the country: Poems of a farm.* Illustrated by Thomas B. Allen. New York: Putnam.

Prelutsky, J. (2002). *The frog wore red suspenders: Rhymes.* Illustrated by Petra Mathers. New York: Greenwillow.

Wells, R. (2003, Board Book). *Read to your bunny.* New York: Cartwheel.

FIGURE 4–10
Suggested list of poetry books for young children.

ELEPHANT

The elephant is big.
The elephant is strong.
The elephant has a trunk which is very, very

L
O
N
G!!!!

Reproduced by permission of B. Wolf—1995
Copyright B. Wolf—1993

JACK FROST

Jack Frost nips at your nose,
tingles your fingers,
tickles your toes!
Jack Frost soon will be here—
riding the breeze—
painting the trees—
That's how we know that Winter is near!

Reproduced by permission of B. Wolf—1995
Copyright B. Wolf—1993

RAINDROPS

Listen, do you hear the rain
falling on my windowpane?

Raindrops
    dropping—
        falling—
           plopping—
raindrops
    splashing—
        thumping—
           dashing—
      down upon my window-
      pane!

Reproduced by permission of B. Wolf—1995
Copyright B. Wolf—1993

SPRING SHOWERS

The sunlight is shining down through the trees.
The flowers stir and sway in the breeze.
Then here come the clouds—crowds of clouds—
hurrying, scurrying, covering the sun.
The lightning flashes!
The thunder crashes!!
The flowers are happy, for now the rain has begun.
Listen!

Raindrops falling, Raindrops falling,

Rain falls with a lovely sound.
Rain is very fine, I think!
Rain falls on the thirsty ground, giving all the plants a drink.

Raindrops falling, Raindrops falling, down

And now the clouds all blow away—
leaving a bright, sunshiny day.
And all the flower faces glow;
and all the plants begin to grow,
s-t-r-e-t-c-h-i-n-g . . . r-e-a-c-h-i-n-g . . .

up . . . so . . . high . . .

t-r-y-i-n-g, . . . t-r-y-i-n-g . . .

to . . . touch . . . the . . . sky!

Now rainbows are sparkling over the trees.
The flowers stir and sway in the breeze.

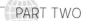

"WHAT A SPLASH!"

If all the lakes were one lake,
What a great lake that would be!
And if all the oceans were one ocean,
What a great sea that would be!
And if all the people were one person,
What a great person that would be!
And if the great person took a great jump
And jumped as high as could be,
And jumped into the great ocean
What a great splash that would be!

Philip Jackman

LOOKING AT THE WORLD

When I wake up
What do I do?
I open my eyes
Just like you.
    When I get up
    What do I see?
    I see my bedroom.
    It's all around me.
I go to the window
And look outside.
I see the world
So big and wide.
    It's filled with wonderful
    Things to see.
    Like the sun and flowers,
    Like grass and trees.
Like cars on the street,
Like clouds in the sky.
I love to watch
The world with my eyes.

Philip Jackman

FIGURE 4–11
Tongue twisters for
young children.

TONGUE TWISTERS FOR YOUNG CHILDREN

Busy buzzing bumble bees.
Papa, papa picked a pot of peas.

A flea and a fly flew up in a flue.
Said the flea, "Let us fly!"
Said the fly, "Let us flee!"
So they flew through a flaw in the flue.

Author Unknown

She sells sea shells by the seashore.
He sells shells at the sea shell store.

Which wristwatch is a Swiss wristwatch?

Mama, mama mashes marshmallows.
Mama, mama mashes marshmallows.
Mama, mama mashes marshmallows.
MMMMM!

Sharing Literature: Family-School Connection

Make reading to your child a part of every day. You can help parents understand that when reading books is a regular part of family life, they send their children a message that books are important, enjoyable, and full of new things to learn.

Part of a teacher's responsibility in early education is to effectively inform parents of this basic fact and to answer questions about ways for parents and their children to become involved with books. The following suggestions have been successful for some teachers of young children:

🌐 Find opportunities to suggest titles and authors of books for the child and the parents.

🌐 Give parents addresses of local libraries and list the story times.

MOUSE

I am a *little* mouse,
a teeny, tiny mouse.
I live in someone's house in a *tiny* hole in the wall.
That's where I find it best to build my cozy nest, so the
people in the house won't know I'm there at all.
I eat my *tiny, little* breakfast, and then a snack I munch;
and then, before I know it, I'm sitting down to lunch,
after which I take a *little* nap, before I have my tea.
And just when tea is over, it's dinner time, you see.
What a treat for me!
Oh, what fun it is to be a *teeny, tiny mouse—*
the smallest little mouse,
and live in someone's house in a *tiny* hole in the wall.
That's where I find it best to build my cozy nest
so the people in the house won't know I'm there at all.
in *my tiny hole in the wall.*

Reproduced by permission of B. Wolf—1995
Copyright B. Wolf—1993

🌐 Suggest local bookstores that specialize in or offer a large selection of children's literature.

🌐 Send home a list of the books that are going to be or have been read to the children. Personalize the information with a special note about a book their child especially enjoyed.

🌐 Set up a parent-lending library at your school. Supply a bright-colored folder or large envelope in which the borrowed book can be returned.

🌐 Encourage parents to read a story to their child at the end of the day before going home from the child care setting. This helps both parent and child make a relaxed transition.

🌐 For older children, ask parents to allow a block of time in the evening to have a child read to the parent and encourage parents to read aloud to the child as well.

🌐 Ask parents to be role models by letting their children see that they read books. Talk about what they read and what the children read.

🌐 Suggest that a special place for the children's books be provided at home.

🌐 Have parents provide children's reading material in the families' home language and encourage adults to read to their children in that language.

🌐 Encourage parents to give books as gifts to let their child know that the parents think books are important and special.

🌐 Read more than books. Use grocery shopping to encourage reading. Read whatever is close at hand, anything and everything: magazines, cards, newspapers, milk cartons, cereal boxes, street signs, and signs in stores.

🌐 Encourage parents to limit television time, watch less television on school nights, read about things they see together that interest the child, and view children's books on video.

🌐 Promote cooking with their children, reading recipes, and making a family cookbook of favorite recipes.

The more a teacher includes the child's parents or caregivers in the literature experience, the more a child can see how books are related to everyday life. Children enjoy the connection of parent and teacher. See Figure 4–12 for suggested books to nurture inclusion.

TIPS FOR TEACHERS

A common teacher misconception is that sharing picture books is a separate activity to be reserved for a storytime of a few minutes a day. Actually, teachers who are successful in promoting literacy infuse picture books into their entire program by making their classrooms and centers places where books are shared, recommended, connected with all curricular areas, and supportive of the goals of diversity. (Jalongo, 2004).

When reading aloud to a group of children:

🌐 Start the process by selecting an appropriate piece of literature for your age group.

🌐 Read through the story several times before reading aloud to the children. Practice your presentation.

🌐 Plan the appropriate time, place, and purpose for the story time. Alternate small group and large group activities.

🌐 Make sure everyone is comfortable.

Brown, T. (1995, Reprint Edition). *Someone special, just like you.* Photographs by F. Oritz. New York: Henry Holt.

Bunnett, R. (2006, Reprint Edition). *Friends at school.* Photographs by M. Brown. New York: Star Bright.

Cowen-Fletcher, J. (1996). *Mama zooms.* New York: Scholastic.

Dwight, L. (1998). *We can do it!* New York: Star Bright.

Ely, L. (2004). *Looking after Louis.* Illustrated by P. Dunbar. Chicago, IL: Albert Whitman & Company.

Girnis, M. (2000). *A B C for you and me.* Photographs by S.L. Green. Chicago, IL: Albert Whitman & Company.

Girnis, M. (2001). *123 for you and me.* Photographs by S.L. Green, Chicago, IL: Albert Whitman & Company.

Heelan, J. R. (2000). *The story of Taylor and his wheelchair.* Illustrated by N. Simmonds. New York: Peachtree Publishers & The Rehabilitation Institute of Chicago.

Lears. L. & Ritz, K. (1998). *Ian's walk: A story about autism.* Chicago, IL: Albert Whitman Company.

McMahon, P. (1995). *Listen for the bus: David's story.* New York: Boyds Mill Press.

Millman, I. (1996). *Moses goes to a concert.* New York: Farrar, Straus & Giroux.

Pitzer, M. W. (2004, Board Book). *I can, can you?* New York: Woodbine.

Powers, M. E. (1992). *Our teacher's in a wheelchair.* Chicago, IL: Albert Whitman & Company.

Rankin, L. (1998). *The handmade counting book.* New York: Dutton.

Thomas, P. (2005). *Don't call me special: A first look at disability.* Illustrated by L. Harker. New York: Barron's Educational.

Willis, J. & Ross, T. (2000). *Susan laughs.* New York: Henry Holt.

Woloson, E. (2003). *My friend, Isabelle.* Illustrated by B. Gough. New York: Woodbine.

FIGURE 4–12
Suggested books to nurture inclusion. Share these books with both children and parents.

🌐 Show the cover and read the title, author, and illustrator of the book.

🌐 Suggest things the children can look for or listen for during the story.

🌐 Try to maintain as much eye contact with the children as possible while you share the story.

🌐 Sit on the floor with the children or on a low chair.

Select age-appropriate stories and read to the children whenever they show an interest.

- Hold the book so that everyone in the group will be able to see the page. The use of big books can be effective.
- Use different voices for different characters. The children will enjoy your involvement with the story, and these "voices" help children to distinguish between characters.
- Ask children to make predictions about the plot, the characters, and the setting.
- Allow children to ask questions or make comments during the story.
- Ask questions about the story after you read it. Give all the children time to answer your questions and then to ask some of their own.

WORD WALLS

word wall

An alphabetically arranged display or chart of words that children have experienced throughout the school year.

In early childhood classrooms, a **word wall** is a tool children can use to discover new words while practicing and expanding their language skills. "It is an interactive ongoing display of words and/or parts of words used to teach spelling, reading and writing strategies, letter-sound correspondence, and more" (Wagstaff, 2005). The word wall is an alphabetically arranged display or chart of words that children have experienced. These words should be reviewed daily to help the children internalize them. As teachers we should collaboratively build word walls with the children. They choose words from meaningful contexts such as shared reading materials and oral language experiences, thereby reinforcing their growing vocabulary and special interests they have explored in each previous unit of study (Houle & Krogness, 2001).

Neuman, Copple, and Bredekamp (2000) emphasize: "To read, children must be able to distinguish the letters of the alphabet and to connect letters and letter clusters with sounds. To become proficient readers they need to be able to recognize many familiar words at a glance as well as decode words they don't know by sight."

The following are a few tips for teachers from Houle and Krogness (2001):

- Create the wall at the children's eye level in an accessible and highly visible area.
- Keep the wall simple and uncluttered for easy reference.
- Make sure there is ample room to add new words.
- Encourage children to help build the wall with words they wish to spell and/or words they know and want to add.
- Make your word walls interactive by attaching key words with Velcro strips, sticky tack, or pockets. This allows the children to go to the wall, remove a word, use it, and return it.
- For younger children, add pictures describing each word.

GUIDANCE GUIDELINES

G The following guidance techniques can be helpful to use during story time:

- When a child wants to leave the group during story time, gently encourage the child to stay, but do not insist. Sometimes a reassuring arm around the child will help.
- Young children are easily distracted. Listening as part of a group is a skill that must be learned. Begin with books that have only a few pages.
- Asking a child a question about what might happen next will help direct her attention back to the story.

🌐 While telling the story, whatever has to be said or done to handle a problem should be brief an interruption of the story as possible. (Sometimes interruptions can be an important part of the literature experience, if they offer focused discussion of the story or book.)

🌐 Be sure that the children have elbow and knee room. Be sure that everyone can see. For the habitual nudger or distractor, catching her attention might be achieved by inserting her name as part of the story.

🌐 It is helpful to include the children in the process by having them retell the story using their own words, joining in to repeat lines, or letting them add the flannelboard pieces as you tell the story. Using a puppet is effective in guiding the children through the story.

Figure 4–13 is the curriculum planning web worksheet with *literature* activities added. This worksheet with appropriate additions is included in each chapter.

ACTIVITY PLAN WORKSHEET

Developmentally Appropriate Activities for Young Children

Children's age group: Infants (3 to 18 months)

Name of Activity and Brief Description

Sharing nursery rhyme books with individual children
These are the books we will share:

Hoberman, M. A. (2003, Sing Along Stories). *Mary had a little lamb*. Illustrated by N. B. Westcott. New York: Little Brown Young Readers.

Lincoln, Ltd., Frances. (1991). *Polly put the kettle on*. Photographs by Anthea Sieveking. Hauppauge, NY: Barron's Educational Series Inc.

Wells, R. (2001, Board Book). *Twinkle, twinkle little star*. New York: Scholastic.

Purpose/Objectives of Activity

- to listen to a short story for the development of listening skills
- to look at books and rhymes
- to recognize and point out objects and familiar animals
- to turn pages
- to say words and sing rhymes

Space and Materials Needed

Rocking chair, floor, pillows, and books

Procedure

The following activities are mainly inside ones, carried on next to the bookshelf while the child sits on the adult's lap, on the floor, or in a rocking chair. These activities can also be taken outside and done while you are sitting on a blanket.

1. Let the child choose a book from the low shelf.
2. Read the book to the child. Point to what is going on in the pictures. See if the child will try to say a word or part of a word with you.
3. Do the finger plays for the rhymes, such as "Twinkle, Twinkle Little Star."
4. Repeat these finger plays or songs often during transition times.

Guidance

Usually this is a one-on-one activity, but other children in the group are welcomed to look at the pictures and encouraged to do the finger plays, too. If other children want a book read to them at the same time, have enough books on the shelf or nearby so they can look at them. Keep the stories short.

Evaluation and Follow-Up

These nursery rhyme books are popular with the infants, and so are the follow-up activities. Sing the nursery songs and do the rhymes often to encourage language and motor development. Play dough makes a great "Pat-a-Cake." Have a tea party for "Polly Put the Kettle On." Use cotton balls to make "Mary Had a Little Lamb." Eat muffins to relate to "Muffin Man," and do exercises (sit, stand up, and fall down) with "Humpty Dumpty." To achieve effectiveness in this activity, keep the stories short and do not mind when a child turns the page before you finish the rhyme. However, be sure there are plenty of books available, because a child this age does not share easily.

ACTIVITY PLAN WORKSHEET

Developmentally Appropriate Activities for Young Children

Children's age group: Toddlers (18 months to 3 years)

Name of Activity and Brief Description

Group time story and art activity
     This is the book we will share:

Ziefert, H., & Baruffi, A. (1992). *Where is Mommy's truck?* New York: HarperCollins.

     Reading this book offers children opportunities to lift the flaps and see exactly where mommy's truck is hiding. Teacher and children can spend a few minutes together talking about the people that drive trucks, big and small. Sometimes mommy and daddy drive a truck to work. Mommies and daddies go to many different kinds of jobs. By asking open-ended, short questions, toddlers can spend time one-on-one with the teacher and the book. After reading the book, the teacher will explain the art activity: car and truck painting. This activity will be available for any child to do with minimal assistance from the teacher, if needed. The children should direct the process.

Purpose/Objectives of Activity

- to practice small muscle skills
- to practice hand-eye coordination
- to demonstrate cause and effect
- to practice color recognition
- to demonstrate gender equity and recognition appropriate for toddlers

Space and Materials Needed

Indoor (or outdoor) table with or without chairs, individual sheets of paper, washable paint on a tray, and small cars and trucks

Procedure

1. Place cars and trucks on a tray with paint.
2. One child at a time (wearing a painting smock) rolls the cars and trucks through the paint

and then "car paints" on his sheet of paper. (If possible, have several places set up for this activity.)

3. The teacher talks to the child and asks questions throughout this activity, such as: "Can you drive the car and make some tracks?" "Show me how you can drive on the paper." "Does your car make some sounds?" "What color is your car or truck or the road you're making?"
4. At the end of the activity for each child, the teacher can say: "Your paper is full of roads and tracks." "Show me how you can wash your hands and hang your smock up." "What a great job!"

     Some children will participate in this activity in their own way. That is all right. It is the process that is important, not the product.

Guidance

Anticipating what a toddler might do, the teacher can easily use her words to guide the child. This encourages the child to "use her words." Examples: "Your car drives on the tray or on the paper." "Show me how you can sit on your bottom on the chair." "Your paper is so full of roads, now it is another friend's turn." "Would you like another piece of paper?"

     It is helpful to have another teacher or teacher assistant guiding the other children into activity centers while the teacher at the art table works one-on-one with a child.

Evaluation and Follow-Up

Were all the objectives met? When an older toddler is participating in the art activity, the teacher can suggest placement of the car on the tray or paper, such as back-and-forth or up-and-down. And at this point, other paint colors on additional trays can be added. This helps a child see how one road can cross another. To further extend the activity, add puzzles of cars and trucks to the manipulative center. Sing songs such as "Little Red Wagon" or "The Wheels on the Bus."

ACTIVITY PLAN WORKSHEET

Developmentally Appropriate Activities for Young Children

Children's age group: three-, four-, and five-year-olds

Name of Activity and Brief Description

Group time story and cooking activity

These are the books we will share:

Dooley, N. (1995). *Everybody bakes bread*. Illustrated by P. J. Thornton. New York: Carolrhoda.

Gershator, D. (1998). *Bread is for eating*. New York: Henry Holt.

Morris, A. (1989). *Bread, bread, bread*. Photographs by Ken Heyman. New York: Lothrop, Lee & Shepard.

Paulsen, G. (1998, Reprint Edition). *The tortilla factory*. New York: Voyager.

After reading the books, invite the children to go to the snack table. The teacher has provided a "tasting party" of different types of bread. Blunt table knives for spreading butter or margarine and jam or jelly are available for the children.

The teacher (with her teacher assistant) explains how she plans to let any child who wants to help with the cooking activity.

Purpose/Objectives of Activity

- to introduce the concepts that people all over the world eat bread and that bread comes in many different shapes, sizes, and colors
- to recognize that some families serve bread for various festivities and ceremonies
- to ask open-ended questions about the type of bread each child eats at home, such as: "Which is your favorite type of bread?" "Have you ever eaten corn bread?"
- to introduce children to different ingredients
- to provide opportunities for measuring, pouring, sifting, stirring, and baking
- to practice a cooking activity and to involve children in the process of doing, thinking, talking, and asking

Space and Materials Needed

Large low table, small chairs, mixing bowls, ingredients, measuring cup, measuring spoons, large spoon for stirring, muffin pan, paper muffin cup liners, oven tray, blunt plastic knives, butter or margarine, jam or jelly, variety of breads to taste, recipe, and book to introduce activity

Procedure

1. At group time, read the book *Bread, Bread, Bread* or *Bread is for Eating*.
2. Ask open-ended questions about the families shown in the photographs in the book, the children's families, what kind of bread they eat at home, and which is their favorite.
3. Children go to the large table for snack time. They taste all kinds of bread, margarine, and jam.
4. The teacher explains the activity choices for the day. Making corn bread muffins is one of the activities. Three children and the teacher will make the first batch. Later the teacher will make some more corn bread with another three children. The corn bread muffins will be the afternoon snack.
5. The children and the teacher wash their hands and the table, put on smocks, put out the cooking utensils and ingredients, and read the recipe together. (The teacher has printed the recipe on a large poster with both illustrations and words.)

CORN BREAD

(1) 1 cup flour	(5) 1/2 teaspoon salt
(2) 1 cup cornmeal	(6) 1 egg
(3) 1/4 cup sugar	(7) 1 cup milk
(4) 4 teaspoons baking powder	(8) 1/4 cup cooking oil

Sift together #1, 2, 3, 4, and 5. Add #6, 7, and 8. Beat until smooth. Pour into a greased pan and bake for 20 minutes at 425 degrees.

Guidance

Anticipating what could occur, the teachers prepare to help children understand why they cannot taste the ingredients that are measured to go into the corn bread. There will be time when the muffins are cooking for them to taste the ingredients. (Put some ingredients aside for small tastes. Exclude the raw egg. Then, talk about pre- and post-baking.) Remind the children of safety factors when using utensils. Supervise closely. Provide sponges and soap and water for cleanup and child-size brooms for sweeping.

(continues)

ACTIVITY PLAN WORKSHEET (CONTINUED)

Evaluation and Follow-Up

After this specific activity, the children participated with open-ended questions. One child talked about Yom Kippur and that her family is Jewish. That evening they would have a "feast" and eat *challah* bread, which was also one of the breads included in the tasting activity.

Extended activities might include:
- Read other books about bread.
- Take a field trip to a bakery or bagel shop.
- Relate bread to nutrition and the food groups.
- Bake other breads, such as *tortillas*.

CORN   BREAD

Sift together:

One cup flour, one cup cornmeal,

¼ cup sugar, 4 teaspoons baking powder,

and ½ teaspoon salt.

Add one egg, one cup milk and

¼ cup cooking oil. Beat until smooth.

Pour into a greased pan and bake
for 20 minutes at 425 degrees.

(continues)

ACTIVITY PLAN WORKSHEET (CONTINUED)

TORTILLAS
2 cups masa
1 cup water
Mix together. Roll into 1-inch balls. Press very flat, using waxed paper to keep from sticking. Cook in a greased electric skillet at 350 degrees. Turn when you can "slip" a spatula under, and cook on the other side until done.

Tortillas
Mix these ingredients in a bowl:

Two cups masa and one cup water

Roll into 1 inch balls.

Press flat using waxed paper to keep from sticking.

Fry in a greased electric skillet at 350 degrees.

Turn when you can "slip" a spatula under and cook on the other side until done.

ACTIVITY PLAN WORKSHEET

Developmentally Appropriate Activities for Young Children

Children's age group: Kindergarten

Name of Activity and Brief Description

Group time story, writing invitations, and making no-bake cookies

This is the book we will share:

de Regniers, B. S. (1999). *May I bring a friend?* Illustrated by Beni Montresor. New York: Atheneum.

This is an introduction for the theme "Friends and Families." After reading the book, continue discussing friends, the ones in the book as well as the friends in the class.

The teacher explains how during the week each child can write an invitation to her friend in the classroom to come to the party on Friday during afternoon snack time. Another activity will be to make cookies to share with their friends at the party.

Purpose/Objectives of Activity

- to introduce concepts that friends can be people or animals, and that friends are kind to each other
- to recognize that everyone can *be* a friend and *have* a friend at the same time
- to provide opportunities for cooperation, sharing, and kindness
- to practice math skill development: counting, measuring, number value, and quantity

Space and Materials Needed

Book to introduce the activity; various colored and textured papers; markers and crayons; pencils; scissors; paste; tape; rulers; large, low table; small chairs; mixing bowls; small plastic bags; rolling pins; cookie ingredients; recipe

Procedure

1. At group time, read the book *May I Bring a Friend?*
2. Ask open-ended questions about the animals in the book. Do the children have any pets at home? What kind of animals do they like? What animals have they seen at the zoo?
3. Explain the activity choices for the day. Making invitations for the "friend party" on Friday is one of the activities, and this center will be open for two children at a time until Thursday afternoon.
4. On Friday morning, the children give the invitations to their friends. (The teacher has asked each child to make just one invitation without a name on it.) The teacher then puts all of the invitations in a sack, and the children close their eyes and reach in to select one. Part of the fun is to see if the children get their own invitation or one that someone else made.
5. The no-bake cookies will be an activity choice for Friday morning. Two children at a time will make no-bake cookies until everyone has made some. (The teacher has printed the recipe on a large poster with both illustrations and words.)
6. The children and the teacher wash their hands and the table, put on smocks, put out the cooking utensils and ingredients, and read the recipe together.

GRAHAM CRACKER NO-BAKE COOKIES

1/2 cup raisins
1/2 cup chopped dates
2 tablespoons honey
graham crackers

Let the children pour raisins, dates, and honey into a mixing bowl. Place several graham crackers in a plastic bag. Children can crush these with a rolling pin. Add to honey-fruit mixture until dry enough to roll into balls. Eat at snack time!

Guidance

By limiting the number of children at the writing table and having fewer at a time participating in the cookie making, the teacher has anticipated many of the problems that could occur. This is a time when the teacher can talk about sharing and taking turns with friends.

As with all cooking activities, provide sponges, soap, and water for cleanup. It is helpful to have the teacher assistant moving around the room to supervise the other learning activities. This will give the teacher an opportunity to have some special one-on-one time with the other children.

(continues)

ACTIVITY PLAN WORKSHEET (CONTINUED)

Evaluation and Follow-Up

Were all the objectives met? Extended activities might include:

- Place the recipe poster in the writing center. This gives the children an opportunity to write out the recipe to take home.

- Make fingerprint paintings. Children can look at their own and those of their friends. Use the magnifying glass to look at the fingerprints. Are they alike? Are they different? How?

GRAHAM CRACKER NO-BAKE COOKIES

Pour ½ cup raisins, ½ cup chopped dates and two tablespoons honey in a mixing bowl. Place several graham crackers in a plastic bag. Crush crackers with a rolling pin. Add to honey—fruit mixture until dry enough to roll into balls. EAT AT SNACK TIME!

Additional Activity Plans are in the front-of-the-book CD.

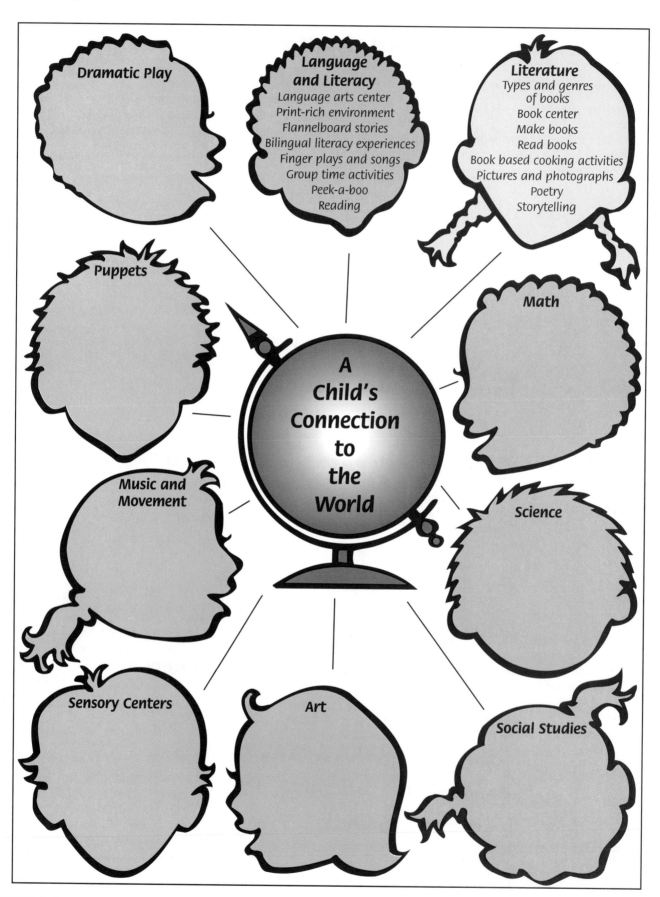

Dramatic Play

Language and Literacy
Language arts center
Print-rich environment
Flannelboard stories
Bilingual literacy experiences
Finger plays and songs
Group time activities
Peek-a-boo
Reading

Literature
Types and genres
of books
Book center
Make books
Read books
Book based cooking activities
Pictures and photographs
Poetry
Storytelling

Puppets

Math

A Child's Connection to the World

Music and Movement

Science

Sensory Centers

Art

Social Studies

FIGURE 4–13
A curriculum web worksheet with literature activities added.

✳ AFTERVIEW

Through books, a child

- 🌐 learns to listen to stories.
- 🌐 develops imagination and creativity.
- 🌐 gets new ideas and develops interests in many things.
- 🌐 adds to previous experiences.
- 🌐 learns more about the world and the people in it.
- 🌐 increases attention span.
- 🌐 attempts to read and write independently.
- 🌐 increases vocabulary and language skills.
- 🌐 develops the concept of print and the written word.
- 🌐 begins to take responsibility for the care of books.
- 🌐 enjoys quiet moments alone with her thoughts.
- 🌐 develops a lifelong interest in literature and reading.

✳ KEY TERMS

alphabet books
beginning-to-read books
big books
board books
concept books
counting books
folk literature
format

genre
informational books
interaction books
literature
Mother Goose and nursery
    rhyme books
multicultural books
picture books

poetry
predictable books
realistic literature
reference books
series books
teacher- and child-made books
word wall
wordless picture books

✳ EXPLORATIONS

1. Bring to class a selection of children's books that represent the types and genres of books described in this chapter. Discuss with other students which books are appropriate for infants, toddlers, preschoolers, and primary-grade children and why they are suitable. Read one book aloud and describe ways of extending this book for a class of young children.

2. Select one of the books listed in this chapter and make a flannelboard story out of it. Share it with a child or a group of young children. What worked well? What would you change? Was it easier or more difficult than you expected?

3. Create a book for young children. Complete an Activity Plan Worksheet, such as the one in this chapter, then read the book to a small group of young children. Observe their responses. What age group did you select? Was your book developmentally appropriate for that age group? Explain your answers and your evaluation.

4. Visit a library, an ethnic bookstore, or an early childhood classroom and observe during the time books or stories are being read or told to a group of children. Do the children focus visually on the storyteller? What questions do the children ask? Do they seem to understand the story? How can you tell? Does the story seem appropriate in content and vocabulary for young children? What kinds of things distract the children? What guidance techniques does the storyteller use in relating to inappropriate behavior?

5. How would you answer a parent who asked, "Of what possible value could a book be to an infant? She can't read or even understand what the pictures are about. Shouldn't you wait to expose her to books when she is older?" How would you go about explaining to the parent why infants should be exposed or introduced to books? How would you get the parent to do the same?

✳ REFERENCES

Arnoff, I. (2003). Reflection on children's literature. Working paper, New York University. In M. R. Jalongo, *Young Children and Picture Books*. Washington, DC: NAEYC.

Bredekamp, S., & Copple, C. (Eds.). (1997). *Developmentally appropriate practice in early childhood programs* (Rev. ed.). Washington, DC: National Association for the Education of Young Children.

Brozowsky, S. (2002, September 22). Why we love picture books. *Parade Magazine*, 12–13.

Engel, S. (1996/1997). The guy who went up the steep nicken: The emergence of storytelling during the first three years. *Zero to Three, 17*(3), 1,3–9. On-line at: http://www.zerotothree.org

Finazzo, D. A. (1997). *All for the children: Multicultural essentials of literature*. Clifton Park, NY: Thomson Delmar Learning.

Glazer, J. I. (2000). *Literature for young children* (4th ed.). Upper Saddle River, NJ: Merrill.

Graham, J. (2000, July). Creativity and picture books. *Reading, 34,* 61–69.

Houle, A., & Krogness, A. (2001, September). The wonder of word walls. *Young Children, 56*(5), 92–93.

Huck, C. S., Hepler, S., & Hickman, J. (1993). *Children's literature in the elementary school* (5th ed.). New York: Harcourt.

Im, J., Parlakian, R., & Osborn, C. A. (2007, January). Stories: Their powerful role in early language and literacy. *Young Children, 61*(1), 52–53.

Isbell, R. T., & Raines, S. C. (2003). *Creativity and the arts with young children*. Clifton Park, NY: Thomson Delmar Learning.

International Reading Association. (2007). On-line at: http://www.ira.org

Jalongo, M. R. (2004). *Young children and picture books* (2nd ed.). Washington, DC: NAEYC.

Lamme, L. L. (2002, Fall). Reading good books: Priming the pump for literacy development. *Dimensions of Early Childhood, 30*(4), 17–21.

Machado, J. M. (2007). *Early childhood language arts* (7th ed.). Clifton Park, NY: Thomson Delmar Learning.

Morrow, L. M. (1989). *Literacy development in the early years*. Upper Saddle River, NJ: Prentice Hall.

National Council of Teachers of English. (2007). On-line at: http://www.ncte.org

Nelsen, M., & Nelsen-Parish, J. (2002). *Peak with books: An early childhood resource for balanced literacy* (3rd ed.). Clifton Park, NY: Thomson Delmar Learning.

Neuman, S. B., Copple, C., & Bredekamp, S. (2000). *Learning to read and write: Developmentally appropriate practices for young children*. Washington, DC: NAEYC.

Owocki, G. (2001). *Make way for literacy! Teaching the way young children learn*. Portsmouth, NH: Heineman; Washington, DC: NAEYC.

Reading Is Fundamental (RIF). (2007). On-line at: http://www.rif.org

Sawyer, W. E. (2004). *Growing up with literature* (4th ed.). Clifton Park, NY: Thomson Delmar Learning.

Schickendanz, J. A. (1999). *Much more than ABC's: The early stages of reading and writing*. Washington, DC: NAEYC.

Schnedler, M. (1994, August 14). Finding new ways to spin old yarns. *Dallas Morning News*.

Spann, M. B. (1997). *30 Collaborative books for your class to make and share*. New York: Scholastic.

Strickland, D. S. (2002). Bridging the gap for African American children. In B. Bowman (Ed.), *Love to read: Essays in developing and enhancing early literacy skills of African American children*. Washington, DC: National Black Child Development Institute, Inc.

Thomas, M. (1998). *Free to be you and me*. New York: McGraw Hill.

Vygotsky, L. S. (1986). *Thought and language*. Cambridge, MA: MIT Press.

Wagstaff, J. (2005, March). Word walls that work. *Instructor*. On-line at: http://content.scholastic.com/browse/article.jsp? id=4380

✳ ADDITIONAL READINGS AND RESOURCES

Ada, A. F. (2003). *A magical encounter: Latino children's literature in the classroom*. Boston, MA: Allyn & Bacon.

Collins, E. N., & McGaha, C. G. (2002, Summer). Creating rewarding circle times by working with toddlers, not against them. *Childhood Education, 78*(4), 194–199.

Courtney, A. M., & Montano, M. (2006, March). Teaching comprehension from the start: One first grade classroom. *Young Children, 61*(2), 68–74.

Creech, N., & Bhavnagri, N. (2002, Summer). Teaching elements of story through drama to 1st graders: Child development frameworks. *Childhood Education, 78*(4), 219–223.

Derman-Sparks, L., & A.B.C. Task Force (1989). *Anti-bias curriculum: Tools for empowering young children*. Washington, DC: NAEYC.

Isbell, R. T. (2002, March). Telling and retelling stories: Learning language and literacy. *Young Children, 57*(2), 26–30.

Isbell, R. T., & Raines, S. (2007). *Creativity and the arts with young children* (2nd ed.). Clifton Park, NY: Thomson Delmar Learning.

Jones, C. G. (2003, Winter). Choosing good books for toddlers. *Dimensions of Early Childhood, 3*(1), 29–36.

Mazzeo, D. A., & M. R. Jones. (2002, Summer). Children's literature that encourages the identity development of interracial children. *Dimensions of Early Childhood, 30*(3), 13–20.

McCarthey, S. J. (2000). Home-school connections: A review of the literature. *Journal of Educational Research, 93*(3), 145–153.

Ortiz, R.W., & Ordonez-Jasis, R. (2005). Leyendo Juntos—Reading together: New directions for Latino parent early literacy involvement. *Reading Teacher, 59*(2), 110–121.

Prudhoe, C. M. (2003, Fall). Picture books and the art of collage. *Childhood Education. 80*(1), 6–11.

Swope, S. (2005). *I am a pencil: A teacher, his kids, and their world of stories*. New York: Henry Holt.

For additional information on early education curriculum, visit our Web site at http://www.earlychilded.delmar.com

CHAPTER 5

MATH

OVERVIEW

Mathematics is everywhere! We are involved with math concepts from infancy onward. Much of what we do as part of our everyday lives relates to mathematics: telling time with clocks and watches, cooking and eating, getting dressed, watching a basketball game, and planning our lives by the calendar (electronic or otherwise). Daily activities involve problem solving, one-to-one correspondence, classifying, measuring, and sequencing. This is true for children, too.

As you progress through this chapter, the approach to setting up the developmentally appropriate math center will parallel the approach to, and interconnect with, all the content areas in this book. The math-rich environment is built on basic math concepts, the children's developmental level (individually and collectively), and their interests.

"In today's high-tech, increasingly connected world, it is important that young children build confidence in their ability to do mathematics" (Furner & Berman, 2003). Providing hands-on, developmentally appropriate math experiences in a safe and trustworthy environment gives children opportunities to develop math awareness and understanding. "The best way to teach children is in a purposeful manner—in a context that has a purpose to the child" (Baroody, 2000). This is very different from the rote learning, rigid rules, workbooks, and flash cards many of us grew up with. The goal for children today is to focus on conceptual math, not pencil-and-paper figuring.

The new view of math is relaxed and comfortable for the teacher and the children.

Children need to acquire basic skills and concepts *first* to live in our world, which is exploding with information and continuously changing.

Young children continually construct mathematical ideas based on their experiences with their environment, their interactions with adults and other children, and their daily observations. These constructed ideas are unique to each child and vary greatly among children the same age. (Copley, 2000)

It is also important to understand that the *acquisition of math skills and concepts occurs in stages over time*, as with all growth and development in young children. "Researchers are in the beginning stages of learning how infants and toddlers build the skills they will one day use for mathematics. We know that infants and toddlers begin to notice relationships as they start to classify, seriate (put objects in order based on number and size), compare and order objects" (Geist, 2003). Repetition is meaningful during this process. Children need to rethink and practice what they know as they continue to add new skills and concepts. Making the environment, both indoors and outdoors, available for young children to experience the world and their place in it will encourage them to understand that mathematics is everywhere!

CONCEPT DEVELOPMENT IN YOUNG CHILDREN

Early childhood is a period when children actively engage in acquiring fundamental concepts and learning fundamental skills. Concepts are the building blocks of knowledge; they allow people to organize and categorize information. . . . Concepts can be applied to the solution of new problems that are met in everyday experience. (Charlesworth & Lind, 2007).

When child development and mathematics are mentioned together, Jean Piaget and Lev Vygotsky come to mind.

Jean Piaget pioneered the study of children's thinking (cognitive growth and development) and described how each child creates his own mental image or knowledge of the world, based on his encounters with the environment. Piaget called this

A young child needs to rethink and practice what she knows as she continues to add new skills and concepts.

physical knowledge

Learning about objects in the environment and their characteristics, such as color, weight, and size.

Logico-Mathematical knowledge

Includes relationships constructed in order to make sense out of the world and to organize information, such as counting and classification.

physical knowledge or learning about objects in the environment and their characteristics, such as color, weight, and size. Piaget's **Logico-Mathematical knowledge** is the type that includes relationships each individual constructs in order to make sense out of the world and to organize information, such as classification, counting, and comparing (Charlesworth & Lind, 2007).

Like Piaget, Lev Vygotsky also studied children's thinking. He contributed significant insight into the way we learn from those around us, especially those who have more skill. He believed that we develop ways of cooperating and communicating, as well as exhibiting new capacities to plan and to think ahead (Charlesworth & Lind, 2007). "Vygotsky was intrigued not only by the skills and understanding that children possess, but also by the skills and understanding they're on the verge of possessing, also known as the zone of proximal development" (Bank Street, 2002). Refer to Chapter 1 for additional information.

Howard Gardner includes logical/mathematical thinking in his research relating to multiple intelligences, sometimes referred to as "different ways of knowing." Children strong in this form of intelligence think conceptually in logical and numerical patterns, making connections between pieces of information. Young children who excel in Logical-Mathematical intelligence have strong problem-solving and reasoning skills and ask questions in a logical manner. They thrive in logical and consistent sequencing of daily schedules and routines (Gardner, 1993; Nicholson-Nelson, 1998). Review Chapter 1 for information on all of Gardner's multiple intelligences.

When you observe children, you become aware of how they think (problem solve) and talk (communicate) about what they are discovering. **Concept development** is fostered by *solving problems* or figuring things out. Constructing knowledge by making mistakes is part of this process as well.

A curriculum that accommodates a variety of developmental levels as well as individual differences in young children sets the stage for problem-solving opportunities

concept development

The construction of knowledge through solving problems and experiencing the results, while being actively involved with the environment.

Tell me mathematics, and I will forget;

Show me mathematics and I may remember;

Involve me . . . and I will understand mathematics.

(Williams quoted in Furner & Berman, 2003)

(Bredekamp & Copple, 1997). This, too, is a process. Beginning with the needs and interests of the children; the development of themes, lesson plans, and webs; and providing time, space, and materials, encourages problem solving.

MATH LANGUAGE OF EARLY CHILDHOOD

Young children understand math in relationship to how it affects them. The infant discovers the shape of the object by putting it in his mouth and holding on to it. The toddler can let you know he is two years old by trying to show you two fingers. The three-year-old likes to sing a number song, while the four-year-old counts "one twothreefourfivesix." The five-year-old shows you how tall his block building is, and the school-age child wants to win at the board game he is playing. All these children are using *math language*. See Figure 5–1 for examples of math language used by the National Council of Teachers of Mathematics.

In the beginning, children can say the names of numbers in order. They remember the *words*, but they do not understand the *meaning* of what they are saying. This number sense evolves during the first eight years of a child's life. How you set up the early education environment will determine how often the child has opportunities to develop number sense and logical ways of thinking about time, space, and other mathematical ideas.

For young children, infants and toddlers especially, the schedules and routines of the day become a consistent sequence of events. This regular predictable pattern helps put order to things, which is part of the process of math learning. When you frequently sing number songs and finger plays, read number books, share number flannelboard stories, and repeat numerals, you are placing math in the environment and making it part of the day's routine.

"All decisions regarding mathematics curriculum and teaching practices should be grounded in knowledge of children's development and learning across all interrelated areas—cognitive, linguistic, physical, and social-emotional" (National Association for the Education of Young Children [NAEYC] and National Council of Teachers of Mathematics [NCTM], 2002). With this in mind, as teachers you should plan environments that build on children's curiosity and enthusiasm and encourage them to discover math concepts in the process of play.

Richardson (2000) explains, "Mathematics can provide children with ways to understand and appreciate the world around them and enrich rather than narrow children's experiences." The following discussions of math concepts, processes, and skills are based on recommendations from NCTM's *Principles and Standards for School Mathematics* (2000).

FIGURE 5–1

Examples of math language used by the National Council of Teachers of Mathematics (NCTM) Curriculum Standards Goals, 2000.

EXAMPLES OF MATH LANGUAGE

1. *Numbers and Operations* includes counting, one-to-one correspondence, classifying and sorting, part-whole relationships, comparison, recognizing and writing numerals, and place value.
2. *Patterns, Functions, and Algebra* includes use of symbols and order.
3. *Geometry and Spatial Sense* includes analyzing, exploring, and investigating shapes and structures.
4. *Measurement* includes recognizing and comparing attributes of length, volume, weight, and time.
5. *Data Analysis and Probability* includes collecting and organizing data about individuals and the environment.
6. *Problem Solving* includes reasoning, communication, connections, and representation.

Numbers and Operations

Number sense is a concept and *counting* is a skill that children use often in their everyday activities. "Number sense develops over time as children engage in activities that encourage them to think about, explore, and discuss mathematical ideas. Teachers and the classroom environments they create are fundamental in developing children's number sense" (White, 2002).

Because the development of number concepts does not occur in one lesson, theme, or even one year, we should understand that it is a continuous process that provides the foundation for much more of what is taught in mathematics for young children (Copley, 2000; Texas Education Agency, 1998). The most effective and developmentally appropriate way to work toward number sense and all the NCTM Standards is to *begin wherever the child is.* "Any other strategy simply wastes the child's time and prevents the development of the essential foundational understandings and skills needed for future success" (Richardson, 2000).

COUNTING. Count anything and everything! Count real things to help children use their own experience with objects to better understand numbers. Throughout the day sing number songs, repeat finger-plays and rhymes, share number flannelboard stories, and read books that include counting. Counting with young children starts with **rote counting,** the ability to recite names of numerals in order. **Rational counting** requires children to match each numeral name, in order, to an object in a group. "To count objects accurately the child must know the numeral names in the correct order and be able to coordinate eyes, hands, speech, and memory" (Charlesworth & Lind, 2007).

> *Researchers have determined that finger counting plays an important role in the development of mathematical understanding of young children. Using fingers to count, compare, and perform simple operations can provide children with a basis for understanding numbers up to 10. (Copley, 2000)*

One-to-One Correspondence

One-to-one correspondence is based on the premise that each object has the value of one. One-to-one correspondence is established when one object is paired with one other object or a group of objects is paired with another group of equal number. The assigning of a number name (one, two, three, etc.) to each object helps children place the objects in a one-to-one correspondence. Children show an awareness of this relationship daily.

The following are examples of this awareness:

- Language is important to toddlers, so a teacher touching and counting aloud (one child, one book, one block, one doll) is expressing one-to-one correspondence. A child is learning self-help skills and one-to-one correspondence when he puts one arm into a coat sleeve.
- For preschoolers and older children, activities such as putting one peg in one hole, setting the table with one napkin for each child, or putting one sock on one foot is one-to-one correspondence. Giving a child four pennies and asking him to put one penny in each of four cups also demonstrates one-to-one correspondence.

Classifying and Sorting

Children grouping objects by a common *attribute* or characteristic, such as size, shape, or color, are **classifying and sorting**. These children are interacting with the environment, using visual discrimination, and manipulating real objects.

---

number sense
A concept that develops over time as children think about, explore, and discuss mathematical ideas.

rote counting
The ability to recite names of numerals in order.

rational counting
Requires matching each numeral name, in order, to an object in a group.

one-to-one correspondence
The pairing of one object to another object or one group of objects to another group of equal number.

classifying and sorting
Grouping objects by a common characteristic, such as size, shape, or color.

Sorting activities allow teachers to naturally introduce the language of mathematics with words such as more, few, many, most, least, and none to describe children's collections. Once children complete a sorting activity, they are often interested in how groups relate to each other. Children may be overheard saying, "This group has more" or "This group is bigger." (White, 2002)

As a teacher, your role is to extend the children's concepts about the material's attributes.

The following are some examples:

🌐 Infants learn about shapes through using their hands, mouth, and eyes. They are discovering that some toys are easier to hold, while others roll better.

🌐 During late infancy, babies grasp an important developmental concept—object permanence. "This realization is key for learning and is especially important for developing thinking and number skills. Once toddlers grasp object constancy, sorting by size and color is within reach" (Poole, 1998).

🌐 Toddlers begin noticing alike and different when they sort colored blocks into blues and reds or big and little ones. It is important to remember to keep concepts simple and consistent for toddlers. For example, have all the blue and red blocks they are sorting be the same size and shape so the children are dealing only with the concept of color. Simple puzzles also help toddlers begin to develop classification skills.

🌐 Preschool children begin by sorting objects with one characteristic or quality. They enjoy sorting buttons, plastic animals, wooden beads, and shells. Provide a muffin tin (see Figure 5–2), plastic cups, or an empty, clean egg carton for the sorted objects. For older preschoolers, classifying becomes more involved by isolating a set from a collection, such as counting children and sorting them into boys and girls, and then observing which children are wearing stripes and which are not.

🌐 Primary-grade children use more complex concepts by sorting sets into subsets and looking at what materials objects are made of (wood, plastic, metal) or what function they have (forks, knives, spoons). Older children can explain to you their rule for making the sorting decision.

FIGURE 5–2
Classifying and sorting objects by a common characteristic.

---

pattern

A sequence of colors, objects, sounds, stories, or movements that repeats in the same order over and over again.

Patterns, Functions, and Algebra

Patterning is another way for children to see order in their world. A **pattern** is a sequence of numbers, colors, objects, sounds, shapes, or movements that repeat, in the same order or arrangement, over and over again. "Patterns serve as the cornerstone of algebraic thinking. . . . Recognizing, describing, extending, and translating patterns encourage children to think in terms of algebraic problem solving (Taylor-Cox, 2003).

Copley (2000) explains, "Mathematics is the science and language of patterns. Thinking about patterns helps children make sense of mathematics." Some examples follow:

🌐 For infants, patterning is recognizing the human face with eyes, nose, and mouth in a specific place. For older infants, looking in a mirror helps them place their face in the same pattern.

🌐 Toddlers asking for the same book to be read again and again soon begin to "read" the story along with the teacher. They are placing the events of the story in a sequencing pattern.

🌐 For preschoolers and older children, stringing beads or putting pegs in a pegboard in a specific pattern, such as blue, red, green, and yellow, is visual patterning. The younger children can duplicate the pattern and the older children can duplicate and extend it.

Patterning is another way for children to see order in their world.

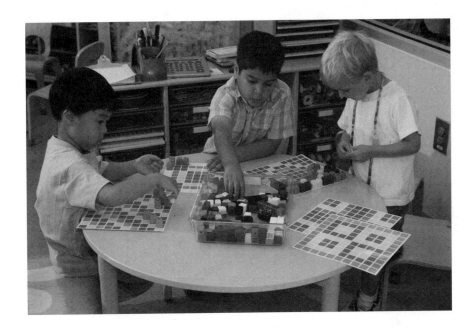

Auditory patterning is repeating or singing sounds (such as soft, loud, soft, loud, soft) over and over again and then having the children repeat the sequence. You can do this with tactile patterning by creating a texture board with articles that are smooth, rough, smooth, rough, smooth.

🌐 Instead of talking about a pattern, the teacher "reads" the pattern using simple vocabulary: *circle, square, circle, square, circle, square* or *a, b, a, b, a, b.* Create a pattern physically: *jump, jump, clap, clap, jump, jump, clap, clap* (Copley, 2000).

🌐 See Figure 5–3 for a shape pattern flannelboard activity.

🌐 With linking cubes the plus-one pattern can be visually shared with children.

Not only do young children need many experiences with repeating patterns, they also can work with growing patterns that increase (or decrease) by a constant amount. The simplest of all growing patterns increases by one and begins with a small number. For example, 1, 2, 3, 4, 5, 6 . . . is a growing pattern based on a constant change of plus one. This is best understood by young children through concrete representation. (Taylor-Cox, 2003)

Seriation

According to the National Council of Teachers of Mathematics (NCTM), "Standard 13 provides that students recognize, extend, and create a wide variety of patterns." Underlying the concept of patterning are the concepts of comparing, ordering, and seriation (Charlesworth and Lind, 2007).

Seriation or ordering of objects is based on the ability to place them in logical sequence, such as smallest to largest. "Simple seriation involves concrete objects; for instance, arranging objects from longest to shortest or widest to narrowest. Sensory seriation can include ordering sounds from loudest to softest, tastes from sweetest to sourest, or colors from darkest to lightest. Seriation can also relate to time sequences; for example, what happened first, second, third, and so forth" (Essa, 2007).

Geometry and Spatial Sense

Geometry is the area of mathematics that involves shape, size, space, position, direction, and movement, and describes and classifies the physical world we live in (Fromboluti & Rinck, 1999).

seriation

Seriation or ordering of objects is based on the ability to place them in logical sequence, such as smallest to largest or shortest to tallest.

geometry

The area of mathematics that involves shape, size, space, position, direction, and movement.

Geometry offers students an aspect of mathematical thinking that is different from, but connected to the world of numbers. As students become familiar with shape, structure, location, and transformations and as they develop spatial reasoning, they lay the foundations for understanding not only their spatial world but also mathematics in art, science and social studies. (NCTM, 2000)

spatial sense

Comparisons that help children develop an awareness of themselves in relation to people and objects in space, such as exploration using blocks and boxes.

See Figure 5–3.

Spatial sense is a child's awareness of himself in relation to the people and objects around him. Games and movement activities can be the keys to spatial relationship awareness, such as location/position (on/off, over/under), direction/movement (up/down, forward/ backward, in/out, in front of/in back of, around/through), and distance (near/far, close/far from). See Figure 5–4.

Manipulating shapes in space introduces children to vocabulary words. In addition, "distinguishing between letters of the alphabet involves attention to shape and position. In art, spatial relationships and geometric forms are critical elements in both two-dimensional and three-dimensional creations" (Copley, 2000). Other examples are filling and emptying, such as playing in the sandbox; fitting things together and taking

FIGURE 5–3

Real objects and abstract shapes have one-, two-, or three-dimensional features that can be examined and compared.

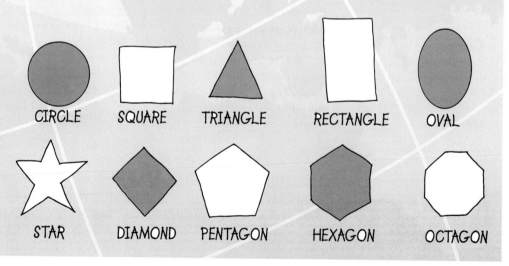

SHAPE PATTERNS

This is a small group activity.

● Put a large flannelboard and shapes of many sizes and colors in the math center. You can also have small individual flannelboards, chalkboards, and chalk there as well.

● Ask the children to choose partners. The pairs of children will take turns with other pairs at the large flannelboard.

● On a large card set up a simple pattern. Ask the children to arrange the same pattern on the flannelboard. For example, place a circle, square, another circle, and a triangle.

● Continue holding up patterns for the children to duplicate. Increase the difficulty of each pattern. (A square, two circles, a star, two triangles, a rectangle, an oval, and two more rectangles.)

● For older children, add colors and sizes to the shape patterns. Add new shapes, such as the pentagon, hexagon, and octagon.

● Leave the flannelboard(s) and shapes in the math center for the children to create patterns by themselves.

CIRCLE SQUARE TRIANGLE RECTANGLE OVAL

STAR DIAMOND PENTAGON HEXAGON OCTAGON

FIGURE 5–4
Helping children
understand spatial
relationships.

them apart, such as Legos and boxes with lids; and setting things in motion, such as things that roll and spin (High/Scope, 2003).

"Imagine, for example, the wealth of concepts relating to *space, position, time, sound, rhythm, body parts, and body control* a child might grasp through a group activity involving music and rhythmic movement" (Fortson & Reiff, 1995). Toddlers and young preschoolers enjoy moving streamers in time with the music. You can help increase spatial awareness by saying, "move your streamer over your head or in front of you." You are encouraging them to change the arrangement of space they are in.

Play the "hide an object" game with preschoolers. For example, hide a block or a beanbag somewhere in the room. Let the children guess if you have hidden it over, under, on top of, and so on. The child who guesses where the object is hidden becomes "it" and hides the object for the other children to guess where it is. The children are thinking in images and pictures. They are finding the object that has been placed in space and out of sight. Older children extend spatial relationships to board games where they count squares and move forward or backward on the game board. They are exploring a new spatial layout and varying the arrangement of the game pieces in space.

Appropriate software is available for children to learn more about spatial relationships using the computer, but first, it is critical that they understand the basic math concepts used in the relationships. Math language of early childhood overlaps, interconnects, and involves all the senses. No matter what terminology is used, children are counting, classifying, thinking, reasoning, comparing, measuring, problem solving, and learning about math naturally as they play.

Measurement

According to NCTM's Standards (2000), "Measurement is one of the most widely used applications of mathematics. It bridges two main areas of school mathematics—geometry and number." **Measurement** is finding the length, height, and weight of an object using units like inches, feet, and pounds. Offer children activities to identify and compare attributes of length (longer, shorter), capacity (holds more, holds less), weight (heavier, lighter), and temperature (colder, warmer). Time is measured using hours, minutes, and seconds by reading time on both digital and analog clocks.

Measurement is an important way for young children to look for relationships in the real world. Through playing, imitating, and learning to use standard units of measurements, young children explore and discover measurement. By practicing measurement, they will learn how big or little things are and how to figure that out.

Many daily activities involve measurement. Here are a few examples: cooking, matching objects, comparing sizes of containers at the sand and water table, measuring the number of steps it takes to get somewhere, comparing and ordering

measurement
Finding the length, height, and weight of an object using units like inches, feet, and pounds.

objects according to their length using terms such as longer and shorter, estimating and measuring length to the nearest inch and foot, and linking cubes to find objects that are shorter or longer than ten linking cubes.

Data Analysis and Probability

Questions that cannot be answered by direct observation can often be assessed by gathering data. Data can be organized, represented, and summarized in a variety of ways. Using graphs and charts, children can discover how to organize and interpret information and see relationships. Graphing and charting offer children a way to show and see information and can make it easier to make predictions about related events. Ask the children questions that require collection and organization of data, and then display relevant data to answer the questions (NCTM, 2000). Examples of this are: (1) children asking questions about their environment and then gathering data about themselves and their surroundings, and (2) sorting and classifying objects according to their attributes and organizing data about the objects (Charlesworth & Lind, 2007).

Figure 5–5 offers a variety of suggestions for getting children to think and talk about math.

FIGURE 5–5
Math questions teachers should ask.

MATH QUESTIONS TEACHERS SHOULD ASK

After asking questions, listen to the child's answers. This will give you insight into what each child knows and does not know. The following questions help young children to visualize math as well as thinking and talking about math.

How can we make 7 feet? How can we make 5 elbows? How can we make 12 fingers?

How many Xs go in the empty square?

How can we make this shape pattern longer? Shorter?

Problem Solving

Problem solving is critical to being able to do all other aspects of mathematics. Children learn that there are many different ways to solve a problem and that more than one answer is possible.

"Problem solving is natural to young children because the world is new to them, and they can exhibit curiosity, intelligence, and flexibility as they face new situations" (NCTM, 2000).

Many early childhood educators and researchers emphasize the importance of problem solving in helping children clarify and strengthen their math understandings. As Charlesworth and Lind (2007) point out:

> The development of problem-solving skills is a long-term activity; it is not learned in one lesson. It must be focused on the process of problem-solving, not just the answer. Therefore, you must provide children with problem-solving situations and observe how they meet them. . . . Behavior noted can be recorded with anecdotal records or checklist.
>
> Problem solving and reasoning are the heart of mathematics. . . . While content represents the what of early childhood mathematics education, the processes—problem solving, reasoning, communication, connections, and representation—make it possible for children to acquire content knowledge. . . . Children's development and use of these processes are among the most long-lasting and important achievements of mathematics education. (NAEYC and NCTM, 2002).

In 2006, The National Council of Teachers of Mathematics introduced *Curriculum Focal Points*, an extension of their *Principles and Standards Goals (2000)*. "*Focal Points* present a way to bring focus to the teaching, learning, and assessing of mathematics. They provide a framework for designing and organizing curricular expectations and assessments. Collectively they describe an approach that can be used in developing a mathematics curriculum for prekindergarten through grade 8" (NCTM, 2006).

In addition, the focal points are intended as a first step toward a national discussion on how to bring consistency and coherence to the mathematics curricula used in the United States (NCTM Press Release, September, 2006).

Math awareness continues outside. It is fun to experience the math concept of a circle when you can crawl through it.

MATH EXPERIENCES IN AN EARLY CHILDHOOD ENVIRONMENT

Math awareness continues outdoors, too.

- Toddlers enjoy play structures that are lower and wider and allow them opportunities to climb up and down. The wheels on the tricycles are round and the sandpile is a square.

- Preschool children can look for rough and smooth objects to compare and count. They like to weave crepe paper or ribbon through a chain link fence to create a pattern and count how many times they toss a beanbag back and forth to each other.

- Older children can take chalk and make a giant hopscotch area with numerals from 0 to 20 as well as measure and record rainfall using a clear container with 1/4-in., 1/2-in., and 1-in. markings.

- You can help the children collect boxes, small to large, and set up an outdoor obstacle course for them to crawl through, around, over, and under. This will also help the children order their movements to reach a particular goal.

⊕Line up two rows of smooth stones with each row having six stones. Space the stones farther apart in one row. Ask the children if one row has more or less than the other. Most preschoolers will answer that the longer row has more rocks than the other. When children reach the developmental stage of knowing that both rows have the same amount of stones, no matter how they are spaced, they are also practicing the concept of conservation or "the ability to retain the original picture in the mind when material has been changed in its arrangement in space" (Charlesworth & Lind, 2007).

Ask open-ended questions to learn more about children's thinking, such as, "Which of the cups do you think will hold the most sand?"; "How many circles can you find in our room?"; "How many steps do you think it will take to go from the tricycle to the sandbox?"; or "What can we use to measure the length of the art table?" You will get a lot of wonderful answers. Expect and accept whatever the children say. This will guide you as you evaluate where you and the children go next.

Folder and Lotto Games

Folder games and lotto games are additional ways of including math in the classroom. Older children can match numerals, identify sets, and recognize objects that are alike and different.

The following folder game can be available when children celebrate their birthdays. This will give them something concrete to help identify how old they are. You can also weigh and measure the children on their birthdays.

Take an ordinary folder, open it, and place 10 figures of birthday cakes in two rows of four and one row of two. The cakes are all alike, except for the number of candles and large dots on each cake. On separate square pieces of construction paper or tagboard, make individual cakes with the same number of candles that correspond to those in the folder. You may want to add the written numeral to match the number of candles and dots. This will give the children an opportunity to match "how many candles each cake has" with several visual clues. Laminate or cover all the items of the folder game with clear contact paper. To keep materials organized, make a pocket on the back of the folder to hold the pieces of the game. This can be a plastic bag or a paper pocket that is glued or taped onto the folder. To extend this activity, make flannelboard characters that represent the birthday cakes and candles. The children can place the correct number of candles to match the number of dots on each cake. See Figure 5–6. (The flannelboard characters are included in Appendix A.)

To make a lotto game (bingo or matching), take two identical pieces of cardboard or tagboard and line both pieces in the same way to make as many squares as you want. Leave one piece of cardboard whole. (This is the game board.) Cut the other piece up into equal squares (the game pieces). Draw or paste pairs of identical pictures or stickers, one to each cut-up square and one to each square of the large card. Laminate or cover all the lotto game pieces with clear contact paper. Make a pocket on the back of the whole lotto card, as you did with the folder game. This will help to keep all the game pieces organized and together. See Figure 5–7.

Other general math activities can include talking to the children about their addresses and phone numbers; asking children to bring you supplies, such as five sheets of red construction paper, three paintbrushes, and two small bottles of glue; and letting the children count the number of children present in the classroom, figuring out how many are missing, then naming those who are absent.

FIGURE 5–6
Example of a folder
game.

FIGURE 5–7
Example of a lotto game.

INTEGRATING MATH WITH OTHER CURRICULUM AREAS

Math concepts are better understood when they are a part of the daily activities. Other curriculum areas can include math easily and successfully. In addition, according to NAEYC and NCTM (2002):

> Young children do not perceive their world as if it were divided into separate cubbyholes such as "mathematics" or "literacy." Likewise, effective practice does not limit mathematics to one specified period or time of day. Rather, early childhood teachers help children develop

mathematical knowledge throughout the day and across the curriculum. The classroom environment is organized so that children can investigate mathematics through many types of hands-on experiences (Wortham, 2007).

Math and Science

Math and science are like a two-piece puzzle. They fit together to make a whole, but each piece is important by itself. That is why these two curriculum areas are separate chapters in this book. Chapter 6, the next chapter, covers the science curriculum in early childhood. Here are several suggestions on how to use math concepts and relate them to the science center and theme.

- Sort collections of shells, magnets, leaves, seeds, and rocks. Classify them according to size.

- Use a thermometer and ask open-ended questions, such as, "What happens when you put the thermometer into hot water?" or "What happens when you put it in cold water?"

- Older children can graph the daily temperature. This can extend the daily calendar activity of marking the day of the week and month of the year.

- Have children count the number of legs on insects. Use both pictures and real insects, if possible.

- Plants offer opportunities for children to keep a chart or graph of the days or times plants should be watered and how much they have grown.

- Children's literature can create strategies to integrate math and science concepts in the curriculum. "Nearly any topic of interest can be developed using books, real-life artifacts, and related hands-on learning experiences" (Benson & Downing, 1999).

- *Planting a Rainbow* (1988) and *Growing Vegetable Soup* (1987), both by Lois Ehlert, are two books that integrate math and science in an exciting way. "Gardens in all their colors, shapes, and sizes offer linkages with many books that support a wide variety of activities, and of course more thinking, problem solving, and questioning" (Hinnant, 1999).

Cooking

One of the most delightful ways to invite children into the world of math is through cooking. Ask a young child playing in the dramatic play area to explain the ingredients

---

WHY I TEACH YOUNG CHILDREN

I will always remember a little girl I observed several years ago. She was learning about subtraction in her second grade class. The teacher, knowing that we all learn better with concrete examples, brought in donuts. The children had set up a "donut bakery" in the classroom. The girl was "buying" the donuts and was supposed to figure out how much change she should get from her $1.00 bill. Instead, she told the "baker" to *"keep the change."* She took her donuts and left. (The teacher also learned a lesson that day.)

The above observation came to my mind yesterday, when four-year old Dylan was telling me all about his mommy and daddy's anniversary. I asked him how long his mom and dad had been married. His answer was, *"Forever."* Young children do tell us exactly where they are, mathematically.

—Bonnie Rubinstein

Invite children into the world of math through cooking.

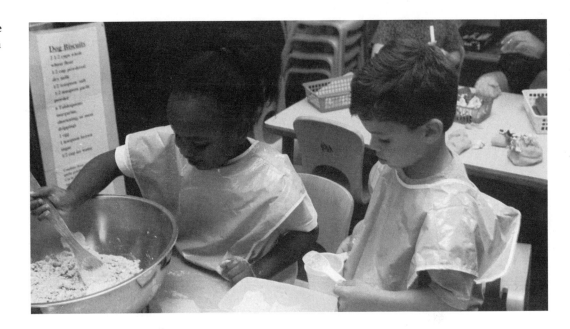

of the imaginary cake he is baking, and the answer will probably be something like this: "I put in 20 cups of sugar, a bunch of flour, two eggs (one for each hand), and mix 'em all up and put it in the stove for ten minutes." Even though their numbers may be inaccurate, it shows that they are aware of quantities in recipes.

Extend both the dramatic play and math. Let the children bake an actual cake. Just think about the ways you can help children clarify math concepts through experiences with cooking. You are involving children with counting, one-to-one correspondence, fractions, time, temperature, weight, shapes, sizes, amounts, measurements, reading a recipe, and following a sequence.

Here's an easy cake recipe, and all you do is "dump" everything together: Put 1 can of fruit, including juice, into a buttered cake pan. Dump 1 box of cake mix over the fruit. Chop up 1 stick of butter or margarine. Dump these pieces on the top of the cake mix. Bake at 350 degrees for 30 to 40 minutes. Then divide into servings, one for each child, and eat!

You can also make *pretzels* and *cheese* shapes. Children really enjoy making these. You will need:

14-ounce block of cheddar cheese
package of stick pretzels

1. Wash hands.
2. Cut cheese into various shapes.
3. Put ends of pretzels into the cheese shapes.
4. Eat and talk about the shapes the children are eating.

Incorporating math concepts into snacktime is another way to make math more meaningful. Developmentally appropriate math lessons occur every day in my prekindergarten classroom since I converted our former teacher-directed group snacktime to a self-serve center open through the middle of the morning. Enthusiastic children eagerly count and measure their own portions and construct useful early math concepts with immediate personal relevance. (Meriwether, 1997)

Art

Children need to relate math to themselves, and adding art projects to the math activities will help them do this. For example, make an "All About Me" book, poster, or chart. Include the child's weight, height, and shoe size or foot outline at the beginning of the year, during the year, and at the end of the year. This offers a child a concrete way to compare his stages of growth. This is also another way to do assessment.

Another art and math activity is to draw an outline around a child's body on a large piece of white butcher paper or brown wrapping paper. The younger child will need you to do it, but the older child can select a partner to do it. Each child can then weigh himself on a scale in the classroom, measure different parts of her body, and record the results on the drawing. Next, the child can add finishing art to the drawing by adding facial features, hair, clothing, and shoes.

Language, Literacy, and Literature

> *Teachers and parents have begun to realize that mathematics truly is everywhere. As, more and more, we consciously include critical thinking, problem solving, and communication as important goals within the mathematics curriculum, so we have become aware that children's literature holds countless creative opportunities for working towards these goals. (Wright, 2002)*

For language, literacy, and literature development, select math books of all types and genres to read to the children, or have the children read and discuss during group time. Here are a few to get you started:

Accorsi, W. (1999). *10 button book.* New York: Workman Publishing.

Anno, M. (1999). *Anno's mysterious multiplying jar.* New York: Putnam.

Beinstein, P. (2002). *Count with Dora.* New York: Simon Spotlight.

Cline-Ransome, L. (2002). *Quilt counting.* Illustrated by J. E. Ransome. New York: SeaStar Books.

Dorros, A. (2000). *Ten go tango.* Illustrated by E. A. McCully. New York: HarperCollins.

Ehlert, L. (1990). *Fish eyes: A book you can count on.* New York: Scholastic.

Falconer, I. (2002). *Olivia counts.* New York: Atheneum.

Harris, T. (2000). *100 days of School.* Illustrated by B. G. Johnson. New York: Millbrook.

Hoban, T. (2000). *Cubes, cones, cylinders, and spheres.* New York: Greenwillow.

Pallotta, J. (2002). *Apple fractions.* Illustrated by R. Bolster. New York: Cartwheel Books.

Tang, G. (2002). *Math for all seasons.* Illustrated by H. Briggs. New York: Scholastic.

Turner, P. (1999). *Among the odds and evens: A tale of adventure.* Illustrated by W. Turner. New York: Farrar, Straus & Giroux.

Wells, R. (2000). *Emily's first 100 days of school.* Winnipeg, Manitoba, Canada: Hyperion Press.

Williams, R. L. (2001). *The coin counting book.* Watertown, MA: Charlesbridge Publishing.

MANIPULATIVES

manipulatives
Toys and materials that enable young children to gain the fine motor control they need to accomplish tasks important to their growth and development.

> *Math manipulatives are meaningful to children and the reasons that children engage in these activities are specific and real. . . .They need to touch things and move them, as they relate a sense of number to the objects. (Diffily, Donaldson, & Sassman, 2001).*

Copley (2000) agrees,"[R]esearch strongly supports the use of a wide variety of manipulatives to help children understand geometric shapes and develop spatial sense." Using **manipulatives** (toys and materials) also enables young children to gain

An early childhood manipulative area should offer a quiet place for an individual child to practice using his small muscles with materials especially designed for him.

the fine motor control they need to accomplish tasks important to their growth and development. Essa (2007) explains, "Manipulatives are sensory materials, involving visual and tactile discrimination; they require skill in coordinating the eyes with what the hands can do." Seo (2003) comments, "The ways children use objects are often very different from those that we intend or define. Math manipulatives are just objects until children use them to think about mathematical ideas."

The manipulative center should be a quiet place for an individual child or several children at a time to practice using their small muscles with materials especially designed for them, such as puzzles, pegboards with pegs, and board games. Within this area, children experience the freedom to explore materials, become problem solvers, and develop their own thoughts.

Purposes and Objectives

When you plan opportunities to develop small muscle skills, you will encourage children to:

🌐 make choices.

🌐 develop self-discipline and self-esteem by working independently and successfully completing a task.

🌐 participate cooperatively with others in completing a task.

🌐 use open-ended materials that develop creativity.

🌐 develop skills in patterning, sequencing, matching, pairing, comparing, classifying, and differentiating by color, size, and shape.

🌐 strengthen small muscle control, hand-hand coordination, and hand-eye coordination.

🌐 develop readiness skills and explore basic concepts in a variety of curriculum areas.

🌐 develop concentration skills.

The Teacher's Role

Careful selection of materials and planning to meet the developmental needs of the children are the most important responsibilities for you as a teacher. A variety of materials that give the children choices should be considered for the manipulative center.

In setting up the center, choose child-size tables and chairs, accessible shelves, and enough room for the children to play with the manipulatives on the floor, if they choose. It is also important to teach children how the manipulatives should be used, shared, and put away. Make sure the puzzles have all the pieces, the games are complete, and the table blocks are kept in clearly labeled containers. There should be enough toys and materials available for the number of children who choose to be in the manipulative center. As you have done before, give visual cues with pictures and numbers that let the children know how many can be in the center at one time.

Ask yourself these questions when you select manipulatives for young children:

🌐 Are they safe?

🌐 Are the ones with small parts used by older children only?

🌐 Are they durable and long-lasting? Manipulatives are meant to be handled.

🌐 Are these toys, games, and materials adaptable to many uses, or are they limited to one?

🌐 Are they culturally diverse and nonsexist?

Long periods of time for play and enriched environments and materials (including manipulatives, such as blocks and Legos) that invite mathematical thinking are critical for developing children's mathematics ideas and skills. By closely observing children's play, teachers can meaningfully intervene as needed to further children's learning. (Sarama & Clements, 2006).

Manipulative Toys, Games, and Materials

Self-correcting, structured toys include the following:

- counters—Unifix cubes®, base-10 blocks, plastic animal shapes, Popsicle sticks, straws, and beads in various colors and sizes
- puzzles—wooden, wooden pieces with handles, rubber inset, and sturdy cardboard; puzzles with larger and fewer pieces are for younger children
- stacking, nesting, and sorting boxes/blocks
- self-help skill forms (buttoning, zipping, and tying)

Open-ended or construction toys have no right or wrong way to put them together or play with them. They include:

- sewing cards with yarn
- snap blocks
- magnetic blocks, numbers, and letters
- small, wooden table blocks
- parquetry blocks
- pattern blocks
- Legos®
- pegs and pegboards—for younger children, use those that have large holes and pegs; for older children, use those that have smaller holes and pegs
- wooden beads—larger ones for younger children; yarn or sturdy string for stringing (older children often string the beads in intricate patterns)

Table games and materials are used for classifying, sorting, and matching. They include:

- board games
- lotto
- bingo
- dominos with pictures for young children
- checkers
- Chinese checkers with marbles for older children
- coins from many countries
- ethnic fabric squares
- buttons
- shells
- Styrofoam pieces
- texture board with matching pieces
- plastic containers and jars with lids
- flannelboard with flannelboard pieces
- multicultural puppets and small dolls to dress

Rhythm and Rhyme

Young children enjoy number rhythm and rhymes. The following are two traditional ones that are still popular.

ONE POTATO

One potato	Four potato	Six potato	Eight potato
Two potato	Five potato	Seven potato	Nine potato
Three potato	Six potato	Eight potato	Ten potato
FOUR	MORE	SHOUT	OUT

ONE, TWO, BUCKLE MY SHOE

1, 2,
Buckle my shoe;
  3, 4,
  Shut the door;
    5, 6,
    Pick up sticks;
      7, 8,
      Lay them straight;
        9, 10,
        Let's say it again.

—Author unknown

MATERIALS FOR DEVELOPING MATH CONCEPTS

As we know, young children are interested in math. Their natural curiosity is evident in their everyday play and work. The role of teachers and parents is to provide children with the appropriate words, materials, and resources to explore their interests and scaffold new levels of understanding (Epstein, 2003).

The following materials offer children many ways to develop their understanding of math concepts:

- balances, weights, scales
- bingo cards
- calendar
- calculators
- cans or egg cartons, with numbers on them to put a matching number of objects into
- children's socks, shoes, mittens, and gloves, to match in pairs
- clocks with numbers (*not* digital)
- computer programs that allow children to recognize and create series and patterns
- geometric boards (geoboards): to manipulate rubber bands or elastic loopers to form shapes or designs
- magnetic board with plastic numerals
- measuring cups, spoons, and pitchers
- milk cartons to demonstrate liquid measures and relationships between half-pints, pints, quarts, and gallons
- number strips and counting boards
- objects to count, sort, and classify, such as buttons, paper clips, pennies, colored cubes, bottle caps, aluminum washers, colored plastic clothespins, empty spools, shells, Popsicle or craft sticks, keys, bread tags, and nuts and bolts
- rulers, yardsticks, and measuring tapes

WHY I TEACH YOUNG CHILDREN

I had been talking about shapes with the children in my preschool class. We had explored and counted squares, circles, triangles, and even some three-dimensional shapes, such as cones, cubes, and spheres. The children had really enjoyed pointing out the different shapes throughout the day, and even commented on the shapes of the foods they had for lunch. During nap time, I sat in the quiet classroom and reflected on the events of the day. I got out a pad of paper and a pen and began walking quietly around the room, making a list of the areas that I felt needed to be changed the next day. One little girl, Avery, was not yet asleep, quietly watched me from her cot. When I got to her side of the room, she looked up at me and quietly asked, "Ms. Janet, what are you doing?" I whispered back to her, "Well, Avery, we are having a work day tomorrow, and I just wanted to see what shape this room was in." She looked at me with an expression on her face that told me she thought I'd said something completely ridiculous and said, "Can't you see it's a square!" I struggled to keep a straight face when I told her she was right and didn't she feel good about knowing her shapes so well. Those are the moments that make teaching young children special.

—Janet Galantay

- sandpaper numerals
- shape puzzles and flannelboard characters, such as circle, square, rectangle, triangle, cone, sphere, cube, cylinder, oval, diamond, star, and heart
- storage containers in graduated sizes
- table games, such as parquetry blocks, pattern blocks, card games, and dominos
- telephones
- thermometers (outside)
- timer
- unit, hollow, shape, and table blocks, which offer opportunities to learn about balance, measurement and estimation, width, height, length and dimensionality, size relationships, and how shapes fit into space
- wooden pegboard and pegs

TIPS FOR TEACHERS

As you plan, facilitate, observe, and evaluate the math activities in your early education classroom, think about the following:

- Let the children know it is acceptable not to have an immediate answer to the math activity on which they are working. Let them know that there may be more than one way to solve a problem or complete a task.
- Let the children make mistakes and correct them themselves.
- Hand pieces of a manipulative toy one by one to a child who is easily distracted when playing or completing a task. For example, start with objects to count or a puzzle.
- Break down a cooking project into its parts when a child is overwhelmed. Describe the steps in clear terms, first we do this, then we do that. Use rebus charts to help with the explanation.

🌐 Encourage collective or cooperative problem solving, which builds positive self-esteem.

🌐 Allow time for trying out new ideas and taking risks.

🌐 Guide the children to develop math skills needed for the new changing information age of sophisticated machines, technology, computers, and calculators.

🌐 Allow math materials to be moved to other curriculum centers. Spontaneity and creativity are exciting and important!

TECHNOLOGY IN THE MATHEMATICS PROGRAM

TECH Calculators and computers are part of a young child's world. They are now a given resource in learning mathematics (Wortham, 2007). Kostelnik, Soderman, and Whiren (2007) suggest, "Although young children need to learn to estimate and calculate problems mentally (mental math), they must eventually learn to do paper-and-pencil math and to use a calculator. Each of them should have access to a calculator, and the calculators they are given should have easy-to-read numbers found directly on the keys, and easy-to-depress keys." Teachers must also learn to use the calculator appropriately with children.

Computers provide games and simulation that aid problem-solving and skill building for young children when they practice with developmentally appropriate software. Software for teaching math is being developed at a rapid rate. Educators should review and evaluate software carefully before using it with young children. NCTM (2000) proposed, "Technology is essential in teaching and learning mathematics; it influences the mathematics that is taught and enhances students' learning."

Technology use that is connected to what children already know and can build upon leads to greater motivation and self-direction. Loss of creativity can be a problem if children use drill-and-practice software. Open-ended software—software that provides opportunities to discover, make choices, and find out the impact of decisions—encourages exploration, imagination, and problem solving (Northwest Regional Educational Laboratory, 2001).

Computers provide games and simulation that can aid problem solving and skill building.

Children working at the computer solve problems together, talk about what they are doing, help and teach friends, and create rules for cooperation. In fact, they prefer working on the computer with a friend to doing it alone. (Epstein, 2007).

OBSERVATION, ASSESSMENT, AND EVALUATION

A Support children's learning by thoughtfully and continually assessing all children's mathematical knowledge, skills, and strategies. Assessment is an ongoing process to determine a child's strengths and needs. Support teacher planning by using the information and insights you gain to evaluate your teaching techniques and curriculum.

Assessment is crucial to effective teaching. . . . Child observation, documentation of children's talk, interviews, collections of children's work over time, the use of open-ended questions, and appropriate performance assessments to illuminate children's thinking are positive approaches to assessing mathematical strength and needs. Careful assessment is especially important when planning for ethnically, culturally, and linguistically diverse young children and for children with special needs or disabilities. (NAEYC & NCTM, 2002)

One form of assessment that can be used often and successfully is the *anecdotal record*. This will provide a helpful description of what a child does during an observational period. It is an attempt to record a specific episode that is of particular interest or concern. Gober (2002) comments, "Anecdotal records (notes) work well alone or with other assessment methods such as documentation for checklists and parent interviews. . . . Children of all ages should be observed for anecdotal records. Be sure to keep anecdotal records on *all* children. . . . When you keep these notes over an entire year, they provide an objective picture of how that child has grown or changed." Charlesworth and Lind (2007) explain further, "Recording observations can become a habit and provides an additional tool in assessing children's learning and your teaching strategies. Anecdotes are also invaluable resources for parent conferences."

Using Figure 5–8, the "Anecdotal Record Worksheet," offers one way to take notes on what you observe. This should be done first without including your opinions.

FIGURE 5–8
This anecdotal record worksheet will help with observations that are part of the assessment process.

ANECDOTAL RECORD WORKSHEET

Date of observation
Beginning time:

Observation (factual/objective)
(Suggestions of what to include: Date of observation. Description of the situation or activity. What is happening? Description of what the child is doing. Location of the child? Who else is near the child? Description of the child's body movements. What is the child, children, or adult saying? What changes occur between the beginning and the end of the observation?)

Comments (opinion/subjective)
(Suggestions of what to include: your interpretations, opinions, and conclusions of what you observe. How interested is the child in what he is doing? Is the child really being included in what is happening? What do you think the child is feeling? Was any guidance, positive or negative, offered? Describe.)

Ending time of
observation:

You can separate your subjective thoughts and include them in a separate column. The more you observe, the better an observer you will become. Information gained from this observation should be used to support the development of the child. Also, think about how to use your observations to effect changes in the classroom and the curriculum. (The front-of-the-book CD offers additional anecdotal record/observation forms.)

SHARING MATH: ENCOURAGING FAMILY SUPPORT

"As teachers, we must communicate to parents how much they have already participated in their children's mathematical knowledge merely by living life with them and serving as examples. Research, of course, also supports parent interests and involvement in children's acquisition of math concepts" (Prior & Gerard, 2007).

Young children enjoy assisting Mom or Dad in the kitchen or helping to sort the laundry. You can help the parents understand that these experiences offer their children math activities.

Following are a few ways to explain this to the family members. Hopefully, this will get parents started in asking you questions about what else they can do at home. They may even start observing the schedule, routines, and activities that are occurring daily in their child's classroom.

Number Songs

The following songs offer additional appropriate activities for you to do with the children. Both of these offer opportunities to add puppets, flannelboard characters, finger plays, or whatever else the children suggest. "Birds on the Rooftop" can also be used as a transitional song—have the children "fly" from one activity to another.

Figure 5–9 is the curriculum planning web worksheet with math activities added. This worksheet, with appropriate additions, is included in each chapter.

MATH AT HOME

Your child will learn to sort and classify objects by helping you with the clean laundry. He could start with sorting clothes by color. He could help put all the white clothes in one pile and the dark clothes in another pile. He can learn to sort and classify items by types, putting the shirts in one pile, the sheets in another pile, and the towels in another pile. Start simply and then go to the complex sorting. For example, sorting socks gives practice in pairing by color, size, and design. Putting rough jeans in one pile and soft bedclothes in another pile offers sorting and classifying of items by texture.

Your child can learn math concepts in the kitchen, too. He can learn number concepts when helping you to set the table. How many people will be at breakfast or dinner? How many knives will you need? How many forks? How many spoons?

Your child also learns spatial concepts by setting the table. The fork goes next to the plate on the left. The knife goes next to the plate on the right. He learns about the sequence of your meal time. First, you set the table. Next, you eat your dinner. Last, you wash the dishes. Keep the steps to three at first, and gradually add more steps. This sequencing helps your child recognize the pattern or sequence of events in the world around him.

Children learning these basic concepts in early childhood will be able to understand and adjust to the growing technology that is and will be a part of their lives. They will likely be the ones who will one day help explain to us how to successfully use the latest technology.

ACTIVITY PLAN WORKSHEET

Developmentally Appropriate and Multicultural/Anti-Bias Activities

Children's age group: appropriate for two- and three-year-olds

Name of Activity and Brief Description

The flannelboard shape game is designed to help young children become aware of shapes, begin to identify them by name, and look for shapes in their environment.

Purpose/Objectives of Activity

- develop shape awareness and recognition
- identify shapes
- enhance matching ability
- recognize equal amounts
- sort and classify objects by shape and sizes
- develop fine motor skills
- offer tactile learning experience

Space and Materials Needed

This activity can be done on the floor during circle time or at a table during small group time with a flannelboard and felt pieces cut into shapes (circles, squares, triangles, and rectangles) of various colors and sizes. These shape pieces should be sizes that two- and three-year-olds can manipulate. Also, cut a large version of each shape from cardboard, construction paper, or felt.

Procedure

1. Introduce the activity by placing one shape at a time on the flannelboard. Ask the children if they can name the shape. Discuss the properties of each shape with the children; for example, the triangle has three sides and three corners. Say, "count with me." as you point to each side.
2. Continue placing shapes on the flannelboard and repeating the above procedure until all the small shapes are displayed.
3. Below the flannelboard, place the large shapes that you cut out.
4. Ask the children to match the shape by taking a small shape from the flannelboard and placing it on the larger piece that it matches. Help the younger children take just one shape at a time from the flannelboard and guide them to place it on the proper large shape.
5. Encourage them to continue matching shapes until *they* decide the activity is over, usually by wandering off to another center.

Guidance

Anticipating the sometimes short attention span of the children in the group, the teacher should be fully prepared before beginning the activity. If the majority of the children are not interested in the activity, give them a choice of going to another center while you interact with the children who are interested. If one child takes two or three shapes at a time, give the other children two shapes as well. Then guide the children to take turns with their two shapes and make this a positive, not confrontational, time.

Evaluation and Follow-Up

Were all the objectives met? Did the activity hold the children's attention? Were they able to do the activity? What will you change if you do it again?

Extend the activity by leaving the flannelboard and shapes out for the children to use throughout the day. Also, take a shape walk around the room and around the center/school. Point out the shapes they see every day. See how many shapes the children recognize.

Make shape cookies with the children using shape cookie cutters. Later the children can use the cookie cutters to make shapes with play-dough. Read children's books relating to math, such as *Shapes, shapes, shapes* by Tana Hoban (1986). New York: Greenwillow.

ACTIVITY PLAN WORKSHEET

Developmentally Appropriate and Multicultural/Anti-Bias Activities

Children's age group: appropriate for older preschool, kindergarten, and school-age children

Name of Activity and Brief Description

The Name Game is designed for the children to find opportunities to measure, count, and have fun with their names.

Purpose/Objectives of Activity

- build math connections
- develop an awareness that math is everywhere
- develop math concepts, such as one-to-one correspondence, counting, and measuring
- encourage cooperative problem solving
- become aware of similarities and differences in names
- recognize the importance of names and learn names from other cultures
- increase listening skills and encourage language development

Space and Materials Needed

This activity can be done in the math center, the art center, on the floor, or anywhere that the children can use rulers, measuring tape, pencils, crayons, markers, and paper.

Procedure

1. At group time introduce the activity. Briefly talk about names. Ask the children if they have ever thought about the number of letters in their names. Have they ever counted the letters? Have they ever measured their names?
2. Using your name as an example, you can demonstrate what you want them to do. Show your name printed on a piece of paper. Have the children count the number of letters in your name. Then place a ruler along the bottom of your name and measure how many inches long your name is.
3. Explain that this is what you would like for them to do with their names. They can do it now, or they can do it another time. They get to choose. Count how many want to do it now and how many want to do it later. Add the two numbers together to figure out how many children are in class today.
4. Use a transitional activity, such as: the child whose first name begins with A goes to a center of his choice or begins the name activity. Continue through the alphabet until all the children have selected what they want to do.
5. You can then observe who needs assistance in getting started and who does not need any help.

Guidance

In anticipating what the children might do, remember to guide them through this activity. Let them work together to problem solve. The children will probably discover for themselves that some names are shorter than others and compare the shortest name with the longest one. You may need to facilitate, especially with the younger children.

Some children may not want to participate in this activity. That is acceptable. Guide them into another activity center.

Evaluation and Follow-Up

Were all the objectives met? Did the younger children participate for a short or long period of time? How much did the children discover? Did they share and problem solve together? What would you leave the same and what would you change the next time you did this activity with the children?

Extend this activity by having children assign a color to each letter. When they use crayons and markers to "decorate" their names, they are adding another dimension to the activity. The next day at group time have the children rhyme their name with another word. Then go around the circle and have the children try to say all the rhymes together.

COUNTING IS FUN

Words and Music by Jo Eklof

BIRDS ON THE ROOFTOP*

Words and Music by Jo Eklof

(Adding) One lit-tle bird on the roof-top, chirp-ing, chirp-ing, flut-ter-ing its wings!
Two lit-tle birds   their
(Sub-   Ten
tracting) Nine

Soon it was joined by an-oth-er, and there were two lit-tle birds on the roof-top!
Soon they were   three (etc.)
One flew a-way to the for-est,   nine
One flew a-way to the corn-field,   eight (etc.)

(Repeat as necessary to match
number of birds desired.)

Reproduced by B. Wolf—1995
Copyright © B. Wolf—1993

✳ AFTERVIEW

Through math activities, a child

🌐 relates life experiences to math.

🌐 develops number concepts through concrete experiences.

🌐 develops number sense.

🌐 learns one-to-one correspondence.

🌐 sorts and classifies objects by size, shape, color, and texture.

🌐 identifies shapes and numerals.

🌐 explores spatial relationships and develops math language.

🌐 experiments with concepts of volume, weight, and measurement.

🌐 recognizes patterns, a skill that develops into algebraic problem solving.

🌐 learns how to interpret the calendar and the clock.

🌐 has opportunities to make comparisons and to see relationships of concrete objects.

🌐 develops problem-solving skills through experimentation.

🌐 learns to cooperate with others.

🌐 continues with language development by incorporating math vocabulary, such as less than, greater than, and equal.

✳ KEY TERMS

classifying and sorting
concept development
geometry
Logico-Mathematical knowledge
manipulatives

measurement
number sense
one-to-one correspondence
pattern
physical knowledge

rational counting
rote counting
seriation
spatial sense

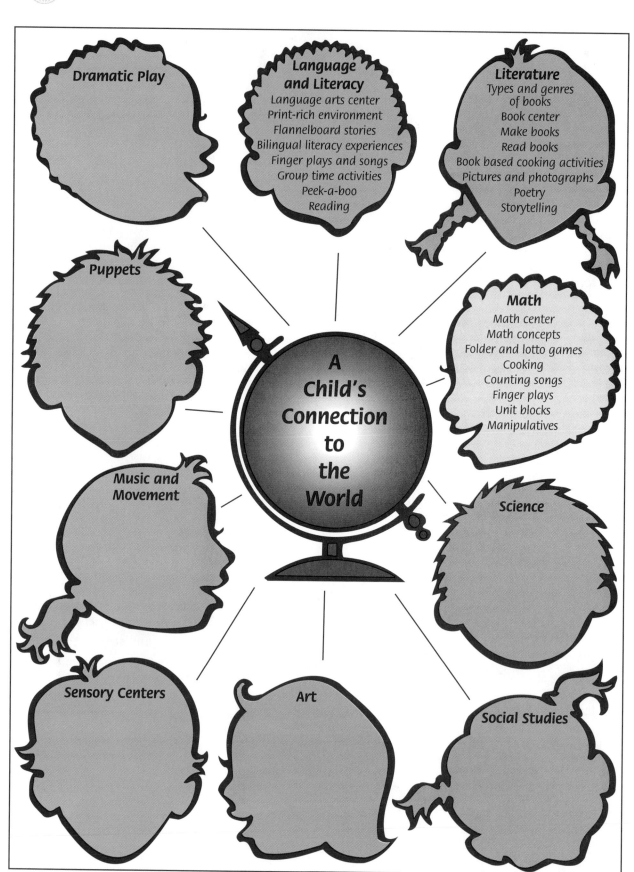

FIGURE 5–9
A curriculum planning web worksheet with math activities added.

✳ EXPLORATIONS

1. What is meant by the statement *"number sense* is a concept, and *counting* is a skill"? Which of these terms is more fundamental? Does that mean that the other is unimportant?

2. Interview two teachers who teach kindergarten or primary-grade children. Have them explain what math skills and concepts are important for the age children they teach. Have them describe their math program. If possible, observe the children in the classroom doing some of the math activities. How will you use the information gained from these interviews and observations?

3. After visiting a library and/or a bookstore, select five children's books that relate to math concepts for young children. Discuss your selections and explain how you would use each book with the children.

4. Select and plan a math activity for young children. Specify which age group this activity is planned for: infants, toddlers, preschoolers, or primary-age children. Write a list of objectives, materials needed, step-by-step procedures for presenting this activity, follow-up activities, and evaluation guidelines. (Use the activity plan worksheet in Chapter 2.)

5. Based on the information in this chapter and on your observations of early education environments, describe how you would introduce one-to-one correspondence, classifying and sorting, patterns, spatial relationships, and other math concepts to a group of preschoolers. Put these descriptions in writing and share them with a classmate or colleague.

✳ REFERENCES

Bank Street. (2002). *Mathematics*. On-line at: http://www.bankstreetcorner.com/develop_practices.shtml

Baroody, A. J. (2000, July). Does mathematics instruction for three- to five-year olds really make sense?—Research in review. *Young Children, 55*(4), 61–67.

Benson, T. R., & Downing, J. E. (1999, Spring). Rejuvenate math and science—Revisit children's literature. *Dimensions of Early Childhood, 27*(2), 9–15.

Bredekamp, S., & Copple, C. (Eds.). (1997). *Developmentally appropriate practice in early childhood programs* (Rev. ed.). Washington, DC: NAEYC.

Charlesworth, R., & Lind, K. K. (2007). *Math and science for young children* (5th ed.). Clifton Park, NY: Thomson Delmar Learning.

Copley, J. V. (2000). *The young child and mathematics*. Washington, DC: NAEYC; Reston, VA: National Council of Teachers of Mathematics.

Diffily, D., Donaldson, E., & Sassman, C. (2001). *Early Childhood Learning Centers*. New York: Scholastic.

Epstein, A. S. (2007). *The intentional teacher: Choosing the best strategies for young children's learning*. Washington, DC: NAEYC.

Epstein, A. S. (2003, Summer). Early math: The next big thing. *High/Scope Resource, A Magazine for Educators*, pp. 5–10.

Essa, E. L. (2007). *Introduction to early childhood education*. (5th ed.). Clifton Park, NY: Thomson Delmar Learning.

Fortson, L. R., & Reiff, J. C. (1995). *Early childhood curriculum*. Boston: Allyn & Bacon.

Fromboluti, C. S., & Rinck, N. (1999). *Early childhood: Where learning begins, mathematics*. Washington, DC: U.S. Department of Education. On-line at: http://www.ed.gov/pubs/EarlyMath/whatis.html

Furner, J. M., & Berman, B. T. (2003, Spring). Math anxiety: Overcoming a major obstacle to the improvement of student math performance. *Childhood Education, 79*(3), 170–174.

Gardner, H. (1993). *Multiple intelligences: The theory in practice*. New York: Basic Books.

Geist, E. (2003, January). Infants and toddlers exploring mathematics. *Young Children, 58*(1), 10–12.

Gober, S. (2002). *Six simple ways to assess young children*. Clifton Park, NY: Thomson Delmar Learning.

Hinnant, H. A. (1999, March). Growing gardens and mathematicians: More books and math for young children. *Young Children, 54*(2), 23–26.

Kostelnik, M. J., Soderman, A. K., & Whiren, A. P. (2007). *Developmentally Appropriate Curriculum*. (4th ed.). Upper Saddle, NJ: Prentice Hall.

Meriwether, L. (1997, July). Math at the snack table. *Young Children, 52*(5), 69–73.

National Association for the Education of Young Children (NAEYC), & National Council of Teachers of Mathematics (NCTM). (2002). *Joint position paper—Early childhood mathematics: Promoting good beginnings*. Washington, DC: NAEYC; Reston, VA: NCTM.

National Council of Teachers of Mathematics. (2000). *Principles and standards for school mathematics*. Reston, VA: Author. On-line at: http://www.nctm.org

Nicholson-Nelson, K. (1998). *Developing students' multiple intelligences*. New York: Scholastic.

Northwest Regional Educational Laboratory. (2001, June). *Technology in Early Childhood Education*. On-line at: http://www.nwrel.org

Poole, C. (1998, January). The path to math. *Early Childhood Today, 12*(4), 13–14.

Prior, J., & Gerard, M. R. (2007). *Family involvement in early childhood education*. Clifton Park, NY: Thomson Delmar Learning.

Richardson, K. (2000). Mathematics standards for pre-kindergarten through grade 2. (Report EDO-PS-00-11) *Eric Digest*. Urbana, IL: ERIC Clearinghouse on Elementary and Early Childhood Education.

Sarama, J., & Clements, D. H. (2006, September). Mathematics in kindergarten. *Young Children, 61*(5), 38–41.

Seo, K. H. (2003, January). What children's play tells us about teaching mathematics. *Young Children, 58*(1), 10–12.

Taylor-Cox, J. (2003, January). Algebra in the early years? Yes! *Young Children, 58*(1), 14–21.

Texas Education Agency. (1998). *Essential knowledge and skills*. On-line at: http://www.tea.state.tx.us/curriculum/early/prekguide.html

White, D. Y. (2002, Summer). Developing number sense in prekindergarten and kindergarten children. *ACEI Focus on PreK and K Newsletter, 14*(4), 1–5.

Wortham, S. C. (2007). *Early childhood curriculum: Developmental bases for learning and teaching*. (4th ed.). Upper Saddle, NJ: Prentice Hall.

Wright, C. (2002). *Integrating mathematics and literature*. On-line at: http://www.bankstreetcorner.com/mathematics_literature.shtml

✳ ADDITIONAL READINGS AND RESOURCES

Carlisle, A. (2001, November). Using the multiple intelligences theory to assess early childhood curricula. *Young Children, 56*(6), 77–83.

Clements, D. H. (2001). Mathematics in the preschool. *Teaching Children Mathematics, 7,* 270–275.

Cozza, B., & Fiascki, C. (2002, Winter). "What is that noise?" Integrating purposeful talk and reflective thinking in math. *Dimensions of Early Childhood, 30*(1), 23–29.

Cutler, K. M., Gilkerson, D., Parrott, S., & Bowne, M. T. (2003, January). Developing math games based on children's literature. *Young Children, 58*(1), 22–27.

Denton, K., & West, J. (2002). *Children's reading and mathematics achievement in kindergarten and first grade.* Washington, DC: National Center for Educational Statistics.

Diezmann, C., & Yelland, N. J. (2000). Developing mathematical literacy in the early childhood years. In N. J. Yelland (Ed.), *Promoting meaningful leaning.* Washington, DC: NAEYC.

Fagan, J. & Palm, G. (2004). *Fathers and early childhood programs.* Clifton Park, NY: Thomson Delmar Learning.

Guha, S. (2002, May). Integrating mathematics for young children through play. *Young Children, 57*(3), 90–92.

Kamii, C. (2003, September). Modifying a board game to foster kindergartners' Logico-Mathematical thinking. *Young Children, 58*(5), 20–26.

Kato, Y., Honda, M., & Kamii, C. (2006, July). Kindergartners play lining up the 5s: A card game to encourage logico-mathematical thinking. *Young Children, 61*(4), 82–88.

Kilpatrick, J., Swafford, J., & Findell, B. (2001). *Adding it up: Helping children learn mathematics.* Washington, DC: National Academy Press.

National Association for the Education of Young Children (NAEYC) and National Council of the Teachers of Mathematics (NCTM). (2002, July). Math experiences that count. *Young Children, 57*(4), 60–62.

Schoenfeld, A. H. (2002). Making mathematics work for all children: Issues of standards, testing, and equity. *Educational Researcher, 31,* 13–25.

Tomlin, C. (2006, January and February). 10 Easy and fun ways to promote math skills. *Early Childhood News,* p. 10.

Trafton, P. R., & Andrews, A. (2002). *Little kids—Powerful problem solvers: Math stories from a kindergarten classroom.* Portsmouth, NH: Heinemann.

Worsley, M., Beneke, S., & Helm, J. H. (2003, January). The pizza project: Planning and integrating math standards in project work. *Young Children, 58*(1), 44–50.

For additional information on early education curriculum, visit our Web site at http://www.earlychilded.delmar.com

CHAPTER 6

SCIENCE

OBJECTIVES

AFTER STUDYING THIS CHAPTER, YOU SHOULD BE ABLE TO:

- 🌐 Identify and discuss scientific process skills and concepts for young children based on the National Science Education Standards.

- 🌐 Describe ways to create a scientific environment for young children.

- 🌐 List appropriate science materials and equipment to include in an early childhood classroom.

- 🌐 Discuss the concepts included in nutrition education for young children and plan developmentally appropriate nutrition activities.

- 🌐 Identify and give examples of ecology in the early education environment.

- 🌐 Explain why the study of animals is part of science education for young children.

- 🌐 Identify appropriate multicultural/anti-bias activities and other developmentally appropriate science activities.

- 🌐 Explore anecdotal record observations to aid in assessing children's science learning.

OVERVIEW

The science curriculum in an early childhood environment should shout "Please touch! Please explore!" We must nourish young children's excitement about learning and encourage them to ask, "What would happen if . . . ?," then give them the materials to find out the answers. These active encounters help children define basic concepts and stimulate natural curiosity, exploration, and discovery.

As we discuss throughout this text, all children learn about the world around them through their senses. Infants and toddlers, as well as preschoolers and primary children, base their scientific knowledge on what they see, hear, taste, smell, and touch. A developmentally appropriate science curriculum expands on this basic fact of child growth and development by stimulating observation, inquiry, interest, and verbalization.

As a teacher, you will also observe, question, predict, experiment, and verify many scientific occurrences along with the children. That is what science in early childhood is all about: setting the environmental stage for finding out about the world. Encourage young children to want to know, "What's in *my* environment? What effect do *I* have? What changes can *I* make?" Attitudes are formed early. We should nurture young children's natural curiosity and their need to know *why,* which will, in turn, encourage future scientific exploration and enthusiasm.

As you brainstorm ways to make exploration and discovery take place, you will come to realize that "we should view science as an ongoing part of the total curriculum, woven into daily activities and routines" (Colker, 2002). Part of this encouragement can be to spontaneously and creatively change the physical environment (indoor room arrangement) when the children initiate and motivate the changes, and to take advantage of what is happening in the outdoor environment. Materials that can be manipulated and reconstructed should be included. Plenty of time should be allowed so that questions can be asked, assumptions can be explored, and ideas can be expanded. This can provide the spark for a lifelong love of science.

Continue to display your own enthusiasm for science and discovery in our world. Ziemer (1987) offers us a stimulating way to do this:

> When you look up to the highest branches of an oak tree on an early summer morning, you may not be thinking of scientific principles operating to get nutrients from the soil, up the trunk, and out to every newly forming leaf and embryo acorn. But you have an awareness

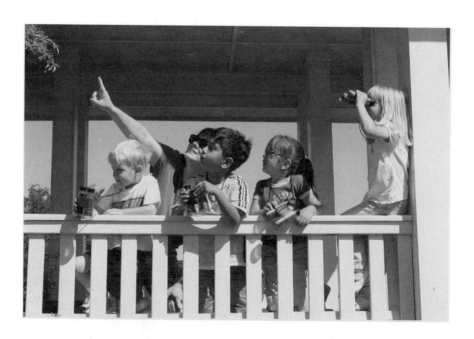

of it, and guiding your small students to be aware also is part of teaching science. Ask wondering questions: "I wonder what makes the leaves so green." "I wonder how long it took this tree to grow so tall." . . . We may not be teaching facts, but we are teaching curiosity.

BASIC SCIENTIFIC PROCESS SKILLS AND CONCEPTS FOR YOUNG CHILDREN

Science is a combination of both *process skills* (*how* children learn) and *content* (*what* children learn) (Dodge, Colker, & Heroman, 2000). **Process skills** allow children to process new information through concrete experiences. These build on and overlap each other (Charlesworth & Lind, 2007). These process skills are also known as *inquiry* skills. An **inquiry** is a questioning process that can be developed in young children. The opposite of rote learning, it encourages their natural curiosity and exploration.

In 1996, the National Research Council published the *National Science Education Standards*, which were designed to support the development of a scientifically literate society. Martin (2001) explains, "The ability to understand science and technology in its day-to-day context is called scientific literacy, and the development of scientific literacy is the basic goal of all science education."

> *From the earliest grades, students should experience science in a form that engages them in the active construction of ideas and explanations that enhance their opportunities to develop abilities of doing science. Teaching science as inquiry provides teachers with the opportunity to develop student abilities and to enrich student understanding of science. Students should do science in ways that are within their developmental capabilities. . . . Full inquiry involves asking a simple question, completing an investigation, answering the question, and presenting the results to others. (National Research Council, 1996)*

The science curriculum content for young children responds to their need to learn about the world around them. As teachers, you know that children learn by doing. Therefore, the best way to learn science is to do science. "The science curriculum can be predominantly child centered and child initiated because knowledge is acquired best through firsthand investigation and experimentation" (Wortham, 2006).

The core of all science is observation. From the starting point of observing, children continue their investigation by comparing, classifying, measuring, communicating, inferring, and predicting. As a teacher, you should teach less and experience more by observing how eagerly the children use their senses to discover, to think about their experiences, and to talk about what they have seen and done. You will be learning right along with the children as you reinforce their curiosity and natural interests. Children learn science "within the context of both past experiences and present environment. . . . Teaching strategies involve a cooperative atmosphere where children and teachers are co-inquirers in the problem-solving process" (Desouza & Staley, 2002).

Essa (2007) believes, "Science concepts need to be concrete and observable. A concept that is abstract and not within the realm of children's experiences is not appropriate." Wortham (2007) suggests, "Children learn science concepts in a social milieu. While observing and working with other children in learning centers, cooperative groups, and paired activities, children exchange ideas, engage in science projects, and discuss their findings." Accordingly, based on the National Research Council standards, the fundamental science concepts and knowledge should be determined by what the children see and do each day and their developmental growth. The suggested categories are:

🌐 **Life science**—the study of living things, people, plants, and animals, including the functions and parts of living organisms (the children and their bodies, for example).

process skills
The abilities to process new information through concrete experiences.

inquiry
A questioning process that encourages curiosity and exploration. The opposite of rote learning.

life science
The study of living things, people, plants, and animals.

ecology
The study of living things in relation to their environment and to each other.

physical science
The sciences (physics, chemistry, geology, meteorology, and astronomy) that relate to nonliving materials.

chemistry
The science dealing with the composition and transformations of substances.

earth and space science
The study of earth materials, objects in the sky, and changes in the earth and sky.

geology
The study of the earth, such as rocks and shells.

meteorology
The science of weather and atmosphere.

astronomy
The study of the universe beyond the earth's atmosphere, such as sun, moon, planets, and stars.

🌐 **Ecology**—the relationship between living things and their environment and each other (caring for classroom plants and animals helps young children understand this concept).

🌐 **Physical science**—the study of nonliving materials. It includes the study of matter (solids, liquids, and gases) and energy (light, heat, sound, electricity, motion, and magnetism) and their laws, such as gravity (an infant dropping a spoon from a high chair), balance (a child building an unbalanced block tower that falls), and **chemistry**, the science dealing with the composition and transformations of substances (such as those that occur in cooking).

🌐 **Earth and space science**—the study of earth materials, objects in the sky, and changes in the earth and sky. It includes **geology**, the study of the earth, such as rocks and shells (for example, comparing a container of dirt from the playground with a container of dirt from a child's backyard); **meteorology**—the science of weather and atmosphere; and **astronomy**— the study of the universe beyond the earth's atmosphere, such as the sun, moon, planets, and stars.

Young children enjoy pushing on levers, making bulbs light, working with magnets, using a string-and-can telephone, and changing matter. This is the study of physical science— forces, motion, energy, and machines. . . . Keep in mind that children are growing up in a technological world. They interact daily with technology. It is likely that future lifestyles and job opportunities may depend on skills related to the realm of physical science. (Charlesworth & Lind, 2007)

Methods of Discovery

[T]he visions of both state and national standards serve to validate our belief that science is an ongoing process that requires children to be able to construct their own knowledge. . . . Learning is not a race for information; it is a walk of discovery. (Buchanan & Rios, 2004)

Give children many open-ended opportunities to investigate, self-discover, and problem solve. Use the "hands-on, minds-on" approach that Grieshaber and Diezmann (2000) suggest. Find out what children know at the beginning of any scientific investigation. Ask the children questions and listen carefully to their answers. Work with the children to identify particular areas in which they want to further their understanding about the topic. Then, in small groups, the children decide how the investigation will proceed. Continue by actually investigating, exploring, and discovering. Examples of observation and exploration activities follow.

🌐 Sensory exploration outdoors can include touching the bark of a tree or the grass, seeing the birds building nests or leaves blowing, hearing the sounds carried by the wind or the honking of a car horn nearby, smelling freshly cut grass or the fragrance of flowers, and tasting the vegetables grown in the school garden they helped to plant.

🌐 Investigating the properties of items can be done using a magnifying glass to examine shells, rocks, feathers, or objects discovered on a nature walk.

🌐 Children can problem solve while predicting or guessing which items will float or sink in a container filled with water.

🌐 Using their naturalist intelligence, children can discriminate among living things (plants and animals) as well as develop sensitivity to the features of the natural world (clouds, rock configurations). "Some people from an early age are extremely good at recognizing and classifying artifacts. For example, we all know kids who, at age 3 or 4, are better at recognizing dinosaurs than most adults" (Gardner, 1997).

WHY I TEACH YOUNG CHILDREN

One morning, Sammi came bounding across the classroom to me calling, "Come and look!" I followed her across the room, where she pointed to the window. She was bursting with excitement. Expecting to see no less than an elephant on the playground or a hot air balloon caught in the tree, I looked out, and saw nothing different. A quick glance at Sammi told me that it was still there, and I looked again. I saw nothing. She must have realized my inability to share her excitement, and lifted a tiny finger to the window, and said, "There." Then I saw *it*. On the outside of the windowpane was the tiniest spider I'd ever seen. Thank you, Sammi, for reminding me about the little things in life.

—Janet Galantay

Give children many open-ended opportunities to question, to compare similarities and differences, and to use trial-and-error to try out their theories. Experimentation, verification, and discovery activities follow.

- With a teacher's supervision, children can experiment with cooking and discover how certain foods change through the cooking process as well as what happens when foods are mixed together.

- Tasting different foods gives children a hands-on experience and at the same time enables them to discover the similarities and differences of ingredients such as flour, salt, and sugar.

- Classifying leaves by comparing their color, type, and vein structure offers another way to distinguish the similarities and differences of nature.

- Investigate a varied assortment of magnets with the children. Supply enough for each child to have one. What happens when the children select a magnet and attempt to pick up items from a tray filled with toothpicks, plastic straws, marbles, pencils, crayons, pieces of paper, cloth, shells, hairpins, small screws, keys, scissors, buttons, brads, paperclips, and pebbles? Which items did the magnet pick up? Which ones did it not pick up? Sort them into two piles. Why did it pick up some and not others? What conclusions can the children draw from this experiment? (Magnets attract objects made of metal.) Was the horseshoe magnet stronger or weaker than the magnetic wand or other magnets? Add new items and ask the children to predict if a magnet will pick them up. Keep this activity in the science center for the children to continue with their investigation. (Adapted from Allen, 2007).

- Give children many open-ended possibilities to concretely demonstrate their discoveries. Reproducing and reworking what they observe and remember helps the children and the teacher learn together. Recording and communicating activities follow.

- Children's drawings, paintings, charts, tape recordings, and/or discussions can record their scientific experiences.

- Children can mark off days on a calendar as they watch the silkworms go through their life cycles or predict how long it will take acorns that they planted to grow.

- The children can then reflect on what they might do next.

- Church (2006) clarifies why it is so important for children to experiment. "This is when children test out their predictions and try out their ideas. The key to this step is to provide plenty of different materials and TIME to explore. Provide materials for free exploration in your science area so children can visit and revisit them on their own—which is how children conduct their own version of an 'independent study.' For example, How can we test if light will shine through a leaf? How many different leaves can we test? What places can we put plants to see if they will grow?"

CREATING A SCIENTIFIC ENVIRONMENT

Fraser and Gestwicki (2002) remind us that we should prepare an environment that allows the child to be actively engaged in the process of learning. "Given this belief in the active exploration of young children, the space must encourage investigations and be open to change to respond to the demands of active learners."

> *Children notice everything in their world—icicles on the roof, the zigzag path of a ladybug, the dancing dust caught in the sunlight. As early childhood educators, we want to provide experiences that allow children to closely examine what interests them, although this often may mean rearranging instructional plans to take advantage of teachable moments. (Kupetz & Twiest, 2000)*

The following areas of inquiry should get you and the children started.

Investigate Water

🌐 Indoors or outdoors, place water in the water table or a large plastic tub. Let the children select which color they want the water to be. Add several drops of food coloring to the water. Also be sure to have plastic pouring and measuring containers along with funnels and spray bottles.

🌐 Later add boats, corks, sponges, rocks, pieces of wood, large marbles, keys, feathers, and pine cones. What sinks? What floats? Guide the children in making a chart of what items sink and what items float. Ask the children why they think some things stay above water and others settle to the bottom? For example, the air holes in a sponge make it float. When the children squeeze the sponge under the water they can see bubbles of air come out of the sponge.

Children learn by doing. Therefore, the best way to learn science is to do science.

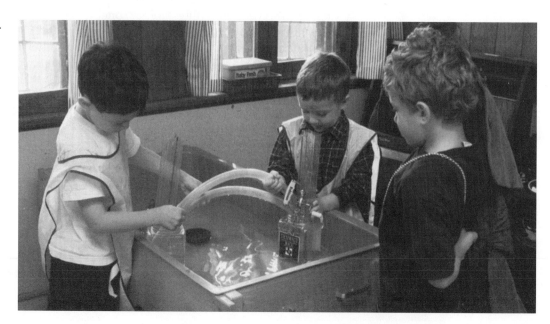

What happens when they let go of the squeezed sponge? What other items can the children add?

🌐 What happens to the items that sink or float in water when you add sugar, salt, oil, or sand to the water?

🌐 Place plain water and one or two eggbeaters in the water table or tub. What happens when the children "beat the water"? Have them add liquid dish detergent, and then beat the water. Now what happens? (The water can then be used to wash the doll dishes from the dramatic play area.)

🌐 Fill a sink full of water and notice how, when you pull the plug, the water always swirls down the drain in the same *clockwise spiral.* (This is because of the rotation of the earth. South of the equator, it goes in the opposite direction.) This can be fascinating to young children. Follow up this activity by looking at a globe and demonstrating how the world turns.

🌐 Introduce the children to absorption and evaporation by having them dampen cloth rags and paper towels with water, then hang them in the sun to dry. What happens to the water? Does the cloth or the paper dry faster? Why?

🌐 Making and blowing bubbles are delightful additions to water investigation. They float on air, glimmer with color, change shape, and pop! Why do bubbles pop? To make bubbles, mix one part liquid dish detergent to five parts water in a shallow tub or pan. Plastic circles on a handle or circles made with pipe cleaners work fine for making bubbles. Let the children experiment with blowing bubbles or moving the bubble ring in any manner they can think of to make bubbles.

🌐 See how water magnifies pebbles in a glass jar.

🌐 Taste water, then add salt or sugar or both. Discuss what this tastes like. What else will the children want to add?

🌐 Examine how water takes the shape of the container it is in.

🌐 Boil water in a pan on a hot plate (with close teacher supervision). Discuss the steam that forms.

🌐 Guide children on how to change a liquid into a solid, and then reverse the process. First place the water in a small, sealable plastic bag, and then freeze it. Next let them watch the ice melt. Encourage the children to predict how long they think it will take the water to freeze and then how long to melt. Actively discuss the changes in the water.

Chapter 9 offers additional activities.

An early childhood science environment is everywhere.

Discover Rainbows

🌐 Set the scene for activities relating to rainbows by introducing a prism (a triangular piece of glass that breaks up a ray of light into a colored spectrum). This can be purchased inexpensively. Glass beads can be used as well. (Parents may even have other glass costume jewelry that can be used.) Whatever you choose, tape this "rainbow-making" glass onto a window of the classroom that faces the outdoors to catch the sunlight. Let the children locate the rainbow by themselves. This rainbow will mean more to them if they make the discovery. How many colors do they see? Have they seen a rainbow before? When? Do they remember how many colors it had? Encourage the children to draw the rainbow. What colors do they choose?

🌐 Create other rainbows with the children by taking a shallow bowl of water out into some bright sunshine. Place a drop or two of oil on the surface of the water. How many colors do the children see? Are they the same colors as the prism rainbow? If you stir the water with a stick, do the colors change?

Look! Even snails have shadows.

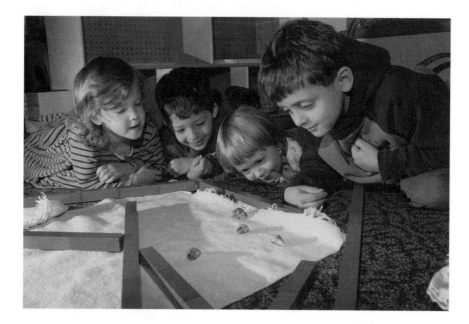

On a sunny day, you can help children find a rainbow by spraying water across the sun's rays with a garden hose or a spray bottle. The rays of the sun contain all the colors mixed together, but the water acts as a prism and separates the colors. Are they the same colors as the other rainbows the children discovered?

Explore Shadows

What is a shadow? It is fun to find out what the children will answer. Can they offer suggestions about how to produce a shadow? Try out their predictions. Are shadows created? If they have difficulty, you might guide them by suggesting that one child holds her hand in front of a bright light. (Shade is a dark place that light cannot reach. A shadow is the shape cast by whatever is in front of the light.) The shadow of an object gets bigger when you move the object closer to the light.

Let the children experiment with different objects in the room to find out which ones cast shadows and which ones do not. They can make a chart of the items.

Refer to Chapter 11 and have the children make shadow puppets and share them with each other.

Extend "shadow play" into dramatic play or music and movement activities.

The children can outline their shadows in chalk outside on the sidewalk. They can measure how long or how short their shadows are. Try this at different times during the day. Do the shadows change?

Take the children on a nature walk and look for shadows that the plants, trees, buildings, or cars make. They can come back and create shadow drawings or write a story of what they discovered during their explorations.

Here are some suggestions of books to read to the children and then place in the book center:

Dodd, A.W. (1994). *Footprints and shadows.* New York: Scott Foresman.

Gomi, T. (1981). *Shadows.* San Francisco: Heian International.

Hoban, T. (1990). *Shadows and reflections.* New York: Greenwillow.

Keats, E. J. (1964). *Whistle for Willie.* New York: Viking Press.

Robinson, L. (1998). *William and the magic ring: A shadowcasting bedtime story.* Boston, MA: Museum of Fine Arts.

Focus on Nature

For a teacher, it is exciting to share the natural world with young children. They are eager for active firsthand experiences.

> If teachers hope children will use their senses to explore the natural world, they need to encourage real contact with the world. From the feel of oozing mud or jagged tree bark to the smell of freshly cut hay or decaying leaves; from the visual experience of a hovering hummingbird to the repetitive sound of a calling cricket; from the taste of a crisp, sweet apple to the bitter bite of a sour grape—nothing offers the variety in sights, sounds, tastes, textures, and smells as well as nature. (Kupetz & Twiest, 2000)

AIR. Can the children taste or see air? Can they feel it? How? On the playground, guide the children to experience how the wind (moving air) can come from different directions. Children can experiment with wind streamers, windsocks, wind chimes, and bubbles. You might read the following book as an introduction or extension to other activities relating to air:

De Coteau Orie, Sandra. (1995). *Did you hear the wind sing your name?* Illustrated by Christopher Canyon. New York: Walker.

NATURE WALK. There are opportunities for many discoveries to take place during a walk around the children's natural environment. Before you go for a walk, encourage the children to make binoculars. Tape together two toilet paper rolls or a paper towel roll cut in two. Place holes in one end of the rolls and attach a piece of yarn or string to make a neck strap. Looking for bird nests and watching butterflies or birds fly are only samples of the many things the children can look at through their binoculars (Figure 6–1).

Each child can also make an individual nature walk "collection bag" (see Figure 6–2). Construct it with folded construction paper or tagboard and lace it with yarn that is left long enough to serve as a shoulder strap (Ziemer, 1987). Construct a classroom book with pages made out of sturdy cardboard and fastened together with rings. The children glue or tape items that they found on the nature walk onto the pages. Then place it in the book center for the children to enjoy.

Humphryes (2000) adds a special word for teachers. "Children have a tendency to want to take home everything they find. Explain to them that the balance of nature is very delicate and that everything in nature has a purpose (for example, a seed pod holds the seeds for next year's plants, a piece of bark may be home to many insects). Encourage their collections to something they have not collected before. . . . In general, *find, examine,* and *return.*" Fresh leaves can be pressed easily by placing them between sheets of newspaper, which are then sandwiched between two pieces of cardboard and secured tightly with rubber bands. After a week, the leaves can be removed and glued into a scrapbook (see Figure 6–2) or displayed in other ways in the classroom.

GROW GRASS. Go on a "science search" in which children look for different kinds of grass growing around their environment. In the classroom provide grass seeds for the children to plant. The quickest and easiest way to germinate the seeds is to place a damp sponge in a pie pan of water and sprinkle the seeds on the sponge. These seeds usually grow almost anywhere as long as they are watered regularly and have sunlight. (It is fun to cut the sponges into different shapes and watch the grass grow into a circle, triangle, or heart shape.) This is another way for children to observe nature firsthand. An alternative way to grow grass is to fill a plastic cup (which the children can decorate to look like a face) with dirt or potting soil. Sprinkle the grass seeds on the dirt, then water. The children really enjoy watching "the hair" grow.

FIGURE 6–1
This illustrates child-made binoculars.

COLLECTION BAG

NATURE BOOK

FIGURE 6–2
These are examples of a collection bag and nature book.

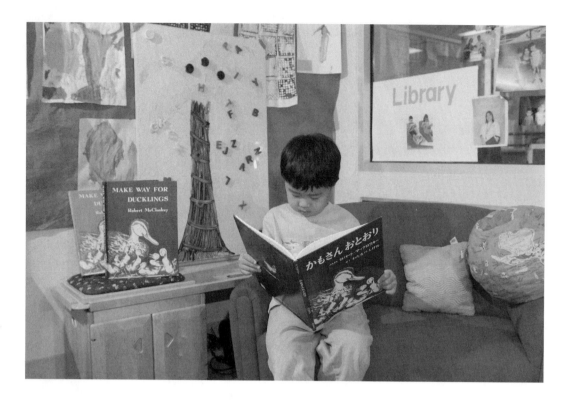

GARDENS. "Gardening is a wonderful activity for young children. As they plan, plant, and take care of plants, they learn valuable concepts and skills that will help them later in life. They learn science as they observe the life cycle of plants, math as they count and sort seeds, and language as they read seed packets and planting instructions. And there is a sense of pride that develops when children nurture a seed into a full grown plant" (Durkin & Perez, 1999). The children can plant an indoor garden (flowers and/or vegetables) in the sand and water table or in a window box. If there is a protected space outdoors, they can plant a garden there. This activity is another way to encourage children to take active responsibility for living things.

See Figure 6–3 for some suggestions of books on nature to read to the children and then place these in a basket in the science center as well as in the book center.

SUGGESTED SCIENCE MATERIALS AND EQUIPMENT

Many materials in a science center can be donated and many can be recycled. Some equipment can be purchased inexpensively. Figure 6–4 lists suggested materials and equipment that are appropriate for early education science investigations. (Only some of the items will be appropriate for infants and toddlers; you will need to be very cautious in what you select.)

NUTRITION IN EARLY EDUCATION

Why do you think nutrition education in an early childhood classroom is necessary or important? Essa (2007) comments, "Because food is a basic human need and so often provides great pleasure, nutrition education and cooking experiences should be an integral part of the curriculum. . . . You will need to tailor nutrition concepts to the ages and ability levels of the children, your own knowledge about

FIGURE 6–3
Books on outdoor experiences help keep children's curiosity alive while extending their investigation of nature.

NATURE BOOKS FOR YOUNG CHILDREN

Cheng, C., & Woolman, S. (2000). *One child*. New York: Crocodile Books.
Cole, H. (1998). *I took a walk*. New York: Greenwillow.
Dorros, A. (1997). *A tree is growing*. New York: Scholastic.
Ehlert, L. (1998). *Planting a rainbow*. New York: Harcourt.
Florian, D. (2001). *Lizards, frogs, and polliwogs*. New York: Harcourt.
Gibbons, G. (1991). *From seed to plant*. New York: Holiday House.
Goodall, J. (2001). *The chimpanzees that I love: Saving their world and ours*.
  New York: Scholastic.
Howard, E. (1993). *The big seed*. New York: Simon & Schuster.
National Wildlife Foundation. (1998). *Trees are terrific*. New York: McGraw-Hill.
Radley, G. (2001). *Vanishing from grasslands and deserts*. Illustrated by
  J. Sherlock. Minneapolis, MN: Carolrhoda Books.
Rockwell, A. (1999). *One bean*. Illustrated by M. Halsey. New York: Walker.

nutrition, and the depth which you plan to approach the subject." Introducing nutrition concepts at an early age can influence a lifetime of food choices and balances.

FIGURE 6–4
A list of science materials and equipment.

Aluminum foil pans	Pinecones
Aquarium with contents and supplies	Pipe cleaners
Ant farm	Plants
Binoculars	Plastic bottles, jars, and trays
Batteries, wires, bulbs	Prisms
Bird house and bird feeders	Pulleys and levers
Collection boxes and collecting net	Rain gauge
Color paddles	Rock and seashell collections
Compass	Rulers, tape measure, and
Corks, plugs, and stoppers	yard stick
Digital camera	Scales
Disposable cameras	Seeds and seed catalogs
Dried plants, such as flowers and grasses	Sieves, sifters, and funnels
Eggbeaters and wire whip	Shallow pans
Eye droppers	Smelling jars and sound jars
Feathers	Soil samples, such as clay, sand, and
Flashlights	loam
Food coloring	Stethoscope
Fossils	Sundial
Garden hose	Tape recorder and cassettes
Keys and locks	Telescope
Kitchen timer	Terrarium
Magnets, such as bar and horseshoe	Thermometers, both indoor and
types	outdoor type
Magnifying glasses and tripod	Tongs and tweezers
magnifier stand, microscope,	Watering cans
and slides measuring	Waxed paper and foil
materials	X-rays (Parents who are doctors or
Observation sheets and science	veterinarians often will give
journals	teachers old ones.)

nutrition

The study of food and how it is used in the body.

nutrients

The chemical substances with specific uses in the body.

Nutrition is the study of food and how it is used by the body. **Nutrients** are chemical substances with specific uses in the body (Marotz, Cross, & Rush, 2005). The body has three main uses for nutrients: as sources of energy, as materials for the growth and maintenance of body tissue, and to regulate body processes.

Marotz, Cross, and Rush (2005) present the following nutritional concepts relating to young children:

- Children must have food to grow and to have healthy bodies.
- Nutrients come from foods. It is these nutrients that allow children to grow and be healthy.
- A variety of foods need to be eaten each day. No one food gives all of the needed nutrients. Children should be exposed to and encouraged to accept a variety of foods from each of the food groups suggested by the Food Guide Pyramid.
- Foods must be carefully handled before they are eaten to ensure that they are healthful and safe.
- Snacks should contribute to the child's daily food needs and educational experiences.

The U. S. Department of Agriculture (USDA) offers a wealth of information designed to introduce children to foods and their impact on our bodies.

See Figures 6–5 and 6–6. For more information and activities for you and the children, visit the (USDA) Web site: http://www.mypyramid.gov.

Before you begin any of these activities:

- Review the food allergies of the children. Provide alternatives for those children who are allergic to certain foods or who are unable to participate in some of the activities.
- Be sensitive to the beliefs of the families in your program concerning foods. Some families may have restrictions on what foods they can or cannot eat.
- Take plenty of time to introduce foods to children.
- Plan how to introduce the activities and how to plan appropriate transitions out of each activity.
- Remember to have the children wash their hands before and after each activity.

Review Chapter 2 for information on preventing childhood obesity. This is our "Call to Action." We should help children and their families make better food choices.

FIGURE 6–5
United States Department of Agriculture (USDA) Food Pyramid.

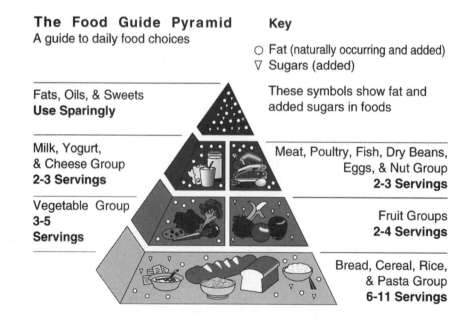

The Food Guide Pyramid
A guide to daily food choices

Key

○ Fat (naturally occurring and added)
▽ Sugars (added)

These symbols show fat and added sugars in foods

Fats, Oils, & Sweets
Use Sparingly

Milk, Yogurt, & Cheese Group
2-3 Servings

Meat, Poultry, Fish, Dry Beans, Eggs, & Nut Group
2-3 Servings

Vegetable Group
3-5 Servings

Fruit Groups
2-4 Servings

Bread, Cereal, Rice, & Pasta Group
6-11 Servings

FIGURE 6–6
My Pyramid – USDA's
new food guidance.

EXTENDED SCIENCE ACTIVITIES

The following activities extend over a period of time. This will demonstrate to the children that many scientific investigations take time to evolve and that some are unpredictable. These experiments can also offer a concrete way to introduce the children to edible plant parts.

- Roots—Carrots, potatoes, turnips, radishes, and beets are the roots of plants.
- Stems—Celery and asparagus are examples of the stems of plants that connect the roots with the leaves.
- Leaf—Lettuce, spinach, cabbage, and parsley are the leaves of the plants.
- Flower—Broccoli and cauliflower are examples of the flowers of plants.
- Vegetable/fruit—Tomatoes and squash are examples of the "fruit" of plants.

Try the following activities.

CARROT TOP GARDEN

CARROT TOP GARDEN. After cutting the tops off of three or four carrots, the children place them in a shallow pan or dish. The carrot tops should be sitting in 1/4 inch of water and watered daily, a task that could be performed by the "plant helper" of the day. (A child can use a ruler to determine exactly how much 1/4 inch is.)

The children can predict how many days it will take the carrot tops to sprout new green foliage. Guide them into making a chart or graph that shows them how correct their predictions were. If some of the tops do not sprout, ask the children *why* they think they did not.

This is a great opportunity to read Ruth Krauss's 1988 book, *The Carrot Seed* (illustrated by Crockett Johnson).

SWEET POTATO
"EXPERIMENT"

ROOTING A SWEET POTATO. This is another experiment children enjoy doing. Push toothpicks halfway into a sweet potato. Then place the potato in a glass or jar of water with the toothpicks resting on the top rim. Be sure the end of the potato is immersed in water. The plant helper can be responsible to see that the bottom of the potato is *always* immersed in water. Place the potato where it will receive enough light. (Put another sweet potato in a dark spot of the room so the children can see what happens to the potato's growth without adequate light.) See Figure 6–7 for illustrations of a carrot top garden and rooting a sweet potato.

FIGURE 6–7
This illustrates the rooting of a carrot garden and a sweet potato.

The children can create a group art activity by drawing the sweet potato and adding to it over the time it takes for roots to grow out of the sides and bottom of the potato and the leaves to grow out of the top. A "before and after" drawing is interesting, too.

THIRSTY CELERY. This science experience demonstrates how plants get their water. Fill two tall, clear plastic glasses with water. Let the children put a few drops of red food coloring in one glass and drops of blue food coloring in the other. Put a piece of celery into each of the glasses, being careful to make a fresh cut at the base of the celery stalks before you place them in the water. Ask the children to watch the celery and record what happens. They can do this with a drawing or verbally with a tape recorder. Over the next few days, the colored water should travel up the stalk and into the leaves. Ask the children what happened to the celery. Why do they think this happened?

MINI GREENHOUSE. This indoor gardening activity can expand children's under-standing of how things grow. The needed materials are: ½ egg carton per student, 6 cotton balls per student, and seeds—birdseed, radish seeds, or grass seeds. Guide the children into putting the cotton balls in the carton. Place 3 seeds on top of each cotton ball. Saturate the cotton with water and close the lid. Set in a warm spot. Check daily, use an eyedropper to keep cotton wet. When green leaves appear, open the lid of the egg carton. What has happened? What will happen next? What should be done to keep the plants alive? Provide blank books for children to use as observation logs and encourage them to record plant growth through drawing. They can use the classroom camera to take photos to show what is happening day by day or week by week.

SEEDS. Several weeks ahead of the time you plan to introduce this activity, gather all kinds of seeds. Encourage the children to place the seeds in a line from the smallest to the largest. Discuss the texture of the seeds. Ask them to guess what would grow from the seeds if they were planted? Make a rebus chart for planting seeds. (An example of a rebus chart is in Chapter 3.) Give each child a small planting pot and ask them to fill these with the potting soil you have provided, then water each one. Place a number on each pot. During the next few weeks, the children will take care of the plants, as well as measure the growth of each plant and make a graph showing the progress. During this time, you and the children can try to figure out what kind of plants you have planted. Look up the leaf structure on the computer or in gardening books. This activity can be the starting point for a project approach (an in-depth investigation) of seeds by several children or an individual child.

Here is another activity that can extend the focus on seeds. Set up a tray with different fruits and vegetables, such as apples, cucumbers, oranges, plums, and green peppers. Allow the students to manipulate the items on the tray. Cut open one fruit and one vegetable. Ask the children what is inside these that is the same? (Seeds) Cut open the rest of the fruits and vegetables. Place each fruit and each vegetable seed on a separate paper plate labeled with a picture of each. Give the children a small taste of each fruit and each vegetable. Have they tasted any of them before? In what ways are seeds of each different? Both you and the children will continue asking and answering questions. Days later, the children may think of something else they want to know. You are actually planting "seeds" of interest and inquiry with all of these explorations.

ORANGE JUICE. To reinforce the science of nutrition, have the children make their own orange juice. This helps the youngest ones connect the actual fruit with the juice. Many children think that orange juice always comes in a carton or bottle at the gro-cery store. Ask each child to place one-half of an orange in a zip-lock bag. Zip the seal closed. Have the children squeeze the orange. (You may have to help.) This will pro-duce juice. Then, they open the bag and take out the half, being careful not to spill the juice. Close the bag, leaving only enough of an opening for the child to insert a straw into the bag. Then, she can drink and enjoy! (Chapter 9, Sensory Centers, offers more activities that relate to nutrition and cooking.)

Children develop responsibility when they take care of their plants.

ECOLOGY IN THE EARLY EDUCATION ENVIRONMENT

Early involvement with the environment will help foster a sense of appreciation and caring in a generation of children who will then make a difference in how our future world is treated. "We should emphasize the environment and the role humans play in consuming or protecting the Earth's riches. Humans affect their environments, and vice versa. Each child's interactions with the world affect not only the child but the world" (Rivkin, 1992).

What are the environmental problems that confront us today? Some of these are air and water pollution, too much garbage, global warming, the depletion of the ozone layer, and the destruction of the forests. Our responsibility as teachers is to guide the children by demonstrating our concern about "sound environmental practices such as recycling, composting and, above all, thrift" (Petrash, 1992).

As defined earlier in this chapter, ecology is the study of living things in relation to their environment and to one another. The environment is everything that surrounds us. We human beings change the environment with our actions and reactions. In addition, everything in nature is constantly changing, and change in one area can cause changes in another.

There are several approaches you can take in your early childhood curriculum planning that will include the changing environment and what we can do to protect it. One suggestion is to select the theme "Things in Nature That Are Always Changing." Using this thematic method, you can introduce the children to changing seasons, specific weather changes, night changing into day, and the changes that take place with the individual child.

We will serve our children well when we turn their attention to the stones, the grasses and flowers, the trees and animals by finding meaningful and creative ways to allow nature to enter our classrooms and play areas, and by bringing our children out into nature as much as possible. A loving relationship with nature will not only promote health for our planet but health for our children as well. (Petrash, 1992)

Some activities that focus on ecology include:

PLANT AND GARDEN AT DIFFERENT TIMES OF THE YEAR. In some places it is warm all year round, and plants there grow well at any time. In places where the ground freezes in winter, you will have to wait for warmer weather to garden outdoors, but indoor planting can work well. You can start plants in a collection of cans, grow a tree in a tub, or plant seeds in cracks in the concrete.

MAKE A COMPOST PILE. The children can place leaves, plant cuttings, and food scraps in the compost bin or pile. Then they can use the compost when they plant a garden in the spring. This can be a cooperative experience with one or two other classes. Children enjoy participating with other children in the center or school.

CATCH RAIN WATER IN A CONTAINER AND RECYCLE IT TO WATER THE PLANTS. Filter the rain water through a fine sieve, such as a tea strainer. This will provide an opportunity for the children to see what pollutants rainwater collects, in addition to providing clean rain water to water the indoor plants and vegetables.

ADOPT-A-TREE OR PLANT-A-TREE. The children can select a tree on the playground or in a nearby park to "adopt" as their tree to take care of and to observe throughout the year. Sometimes children prefer to plant a tree of their own on the playground or in a tub. Whatever choice is made can lead to an environmental discussion when you ask the question, "What do you think the tree takes from the environment, and what does it give to the environment?"

Plants in an early childhood environment give each child an opportunity to learn something about the growth and needs of plants.

Look at what's going on! Exciting scientific problem-solving, creativity, cooperation and group discovery.

It is helpful to invite a parent who knows a lot about trees or a professional gardener to visit the class to answer their questions and advise the children in their selections. In addition, a field trip to a garden shop can motivate the children. Giving young children the responsibility to take care of the tree can be a significant factor in encouraging them to take care of the environment.

After they select the tree and identify what kind it is, they can make drawings of it, take photos of their tree in different seasons, and compare it to other trees. They will also find it interesting to examine the bark, leaves, and bugs on the tree with a magnifying glass and observe and identify which birds like their tree. Children enjoy hanging a bird house or a bird feeder in their tree and watching the activity it attracts.

RECYCLE AND CONSERVE MATERIALS AND NATURAL RESOURCES.
The children can recycle newspapers, other types of paper, aluminum, glass, some plastics, and clothing. Find out about the recycling projects in your community and get the children and their families involved.

Try fixing broken items in the classroom instead of buying new things or throwing old things away. Encourage the children to stop wasting water. Have them turn off the water while brushing their teeth or washing their hands, instead of letting it run.

GROCERY SACKS AND NEWSPAPERS CAN BE PLACED AT THE EASELS.
Provide one or both along with paints for the children to paint on. To make newspaper logs for the block center, take a section of newspaper and roll into a tight roll. Use tape to hold the "logs." These can then be used to build towers, fences, and so forth.

STRESS THE IMPORTANCE OF NOT LITTERING.
Trash should be placed in a trash container. Because littering can be dangerous and unhealthy, the children should be shown how to avoid littering and to participate in cleaning up instead.

EARTH DAY IS APRIL 22.
Make party hats out of newspaper and grocery bags. Bake an Earth Day cake decorated to look like the planet earth. Cut out eco-cookies in natural shapes, such as birds, leaves, and trees. Have the children go on a "pick up trash walk." Celebrate with an environmental musical band. Provide recycled materials for the children to make instruments, and have a parade!

ASK THE CHILDREN OPEN-ENDED QUESTIONS. THESE WILL HELP THEM THINK ABOUT WHY IT IS IMPORTANT TO TAKE CARE OF OUR ENVIRONMENT:

What would happen if everyone threw trash on the ground?

What do you think would happen if we poured polluted water into clean water?

Why do we recycle?

What would happen if we cut down trees instead of planting them?

Why do you think plants are important to us?

What are ways we can help the environment at home?

ANIMALS IN THE EARLY EDUCATION CLASSROOM

The world of animals inspires wonder and curiosity in young children. You can guide the children into drawing pictures of their experiences with animals, moths, butterflies, and ants. Extend this by making puppets of the animals they draw.

For language development, the children can bring in their favorite stuffed animals and talk about them during group time. Play music and have a parade of stuffed animals. Read books aloud and place in the book center books that relate to animals, moths, butterflies, and ants. For example:

Aliki. (1997). *My visit to the zoo.* New York: HarperCollins.

Carle, E. (1981). *The very hungry caterpillar.* New York: Philomel.

Cassle, B., & Pallotta, J. (1995). *The butterfly alphabet book.* Illustrated by M. Astrella. Watertown, MA: Charlesbridge.

Ehlert, L. (1997). *Color zoo.* New York: HarperCollins.

Flanagan, A. K. (1998). *Buying a pet from Ms. Chavez.* Chicago: Children's Press.

Fowler, A. (1998). *Inside an ant colony.* Chicago: Children's Press.

Hague, M. (2007). *Animal friends: A collection of poems for children.* New York: Henry Holt.

Horenstein, H. (1994). *My mom's a vet.* Cambridge, MA: Candlewick.

Keats, E. J. (2001, Reprint). *Pet show.* New York: Puffin.

Martin, B., Jr. (1997). *Polar bear, polar bear, what do you hear?* (Board Book). Illustrated by E. Carle. New York: Henry Holt.

Priddy, R. (2002). *My big animal book.* New York: Priddy Bicknell Books.

Ryder, J. (2007). *Toad by the road.* Illustrated by M. Kneen. New York: Henry Holt.

Sayre, A. P. (2007) *Hush,, little puppy.* Illustrated by S. Winter. New York: Henry Holt.

See "The Animals in Our World" on pages 202–203.

▬ THE ANIMALS IN OUR WORLD ▬

As an animal lover and a wildlife rehabilitator, I have come to the conclusion that there are two categories of animals—not good or bad, but rather, touchable and untouchable. Touchable are those we know and with whom we have a relationship. I have spent many wonderful hours with my very special domesticated animals. We have learned to love and trust each other. I have the responsibility to see that all their needs are met.

Untouchable animals are those we do not know, who will probably be frightened of us and will do whatever they need to do to protect themselves. These animals, which are not domesticated, are born to be free. It is not fair to put them in a cage. They deserve to live as nature intended them to live. Because they are not used to people, they will be frightened and potentially very dangerous. They can also have diseases that *you, the children, or your pets* can catch, such as distemper or rabies. Enjoy watching and listening to them, but LEAVE THEM ALONE!

Occasionally, one comes upon an animal that looks as though it needs help; either it is injured or in some way unable to care for itself. It is important to know when and when not to rescue it.

What Not To Do

- *Do not* "rescue" an animal that does not need help. Most "orphaned" animals are not orphaned at all. The parent is usually hiding nearby, afraid to attend to its offspring when people are present. If you can see a nest from which a baby has fallen, it is best to place the baby back in the nest. Despite myths to the contrary, the scent of human hands will not disturb the parents and they will usually care for their returned offspring.

- *Do not* be tempted to raise an orphaned animal yourself. Federal and state laws prohibit the possession of most nondomesticated animals—and with good reason. These creatures need special care, far different from domestic animals. Wildlife rehabilitators are trained to provide that care.

What To Do

- *Do rescue an animal if the parent is known to be dead and the baby is too young to survive on its own, or if the animal is injured or in obvious danger.*

- Emergency care can be given if you have determined that the animal really needs care. Put on a pair of gloves *before* you touch it. For your safety and the animal's well-being, handle it as little as possible. Place it in a covered box with air holes for ventilation. The box should be just a little larger than the animal. Put the box in a dark, quiet room away from the children (and pets), and free from drafts.

- Do *not* feed it or give it liquids. The wrong food or wrong feeding method can do more harm than good. These animals have special diets and, as babies, must be fed often. For example, some baby birds must be fed every 20 or 30 minutes during the day and some baby mammals must be fed during the night.

- *These* babies need to learn from their parents what kind of animal they are and how to take care of themselves (just like human babies). Contact a wildlife rehabilitator *immediately.* A rehabilitator can be found through your state Parks and Wildlife Department or other private organizations in your community. They have been trained to care for these orphans during the early stages of life and to reintroduce them to their natural environment.

MOVE IT OUTDOORS!

DEVELOPMENTALLY APPROPRIATE CURRICULUM FOR YOUNG CHILDREN

Open the door to outside play and learning. Planning includes a process for developing curriculum for the outdoors in a way that parallels what teachers do indoors. The playground should encourage active play and exploration, offer blocks of time for uninterrupted play, provide safe equipment to develop motor skills, and have appropriate adult supervision. Organization of the outdoor environment, like the indoor classroom, should set limits with reasonable, appropriate rules that are consistently reinforced to promote appropriate behavior.

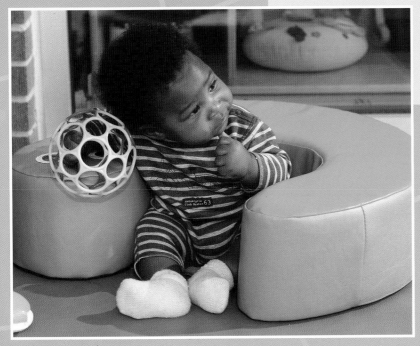

❮ Infants, like all young children, are curious about their outside world!

Children enjoy the space and freedom offered by outdoor activities. They can run, shout, stretch big muscles, and expand their imaginations.

Sand play offers children a unique sensory activity that lets them experience their world in a different way. Sand, water, or mud play can be an individual or small group activity. There is no right or wrong way to play with these multi-sensory materials.

How would you encourage this spontaneity?

How would you support children's exploration of and play?

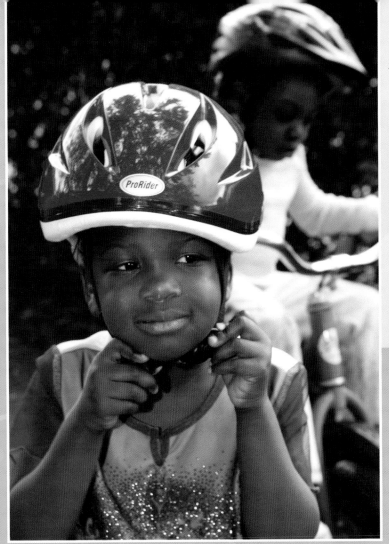

Young children playing outside can practice their newly discovered physical skills in a safe environment. They are exuberant riding tricycles, pushing along on scooters, tossing balls, climbing up and sliding down the slide, again and again.

Promote a bike/trike safety campaign.

Time spent outdoors contributes to a young child's fitness and appropriate weight. Overweight children have problems that go beyond physical appearances. The prevention of obesity is crucial to the health status of children. Children being active when they are young can influence them for a lifetime.

As a child, what were your favorite outdoor activities? Are they still your favorites?

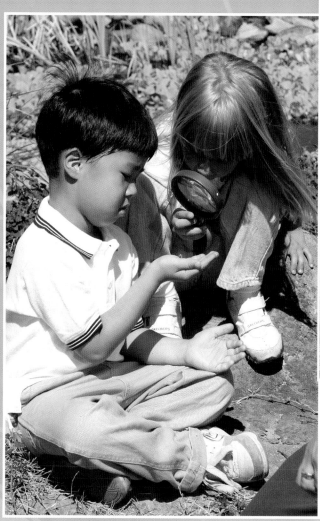

The outdoor learning environment should promote social interaction, cooperation, and inquiry. Give the children time, opportunities, and resources to develop independence and creative thinking.

Can you think of ways to encourage collaboration and cooperation within groups of young children engaged in outdoor play?

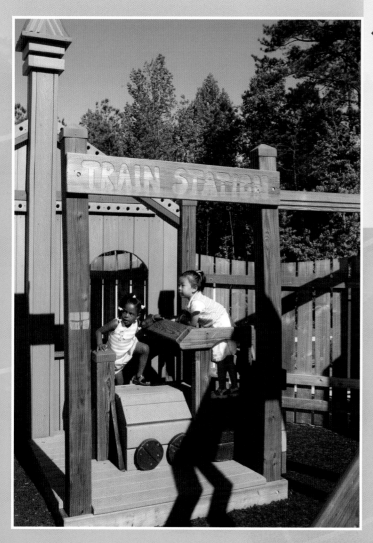

Provide chances on the playground for dramatic play that will give children the possibilities for practicing social skills. They can try on different roles and experiment with different themes.

Many other creative learning activities are appropriate to take outdoors. For example, spread a blanket on the grass and bring out a basket of books; set up parachute play; bring music outside; take blocks out in the open air; tape a long sheet of paper on the fence for mural painting; and remember to bring out easels, paints, crayons, and chalk.

◀ It is always fun to share snack time outdoors too.

What other meaningful, creative activities can you add to expand outdoor play?

A variety of play surfaces and a balance of sunny and shady areas help create safe outdoor surroundings for young children. In addition, these self-directed, open-ended activities help children feel positive about themselves. ▶

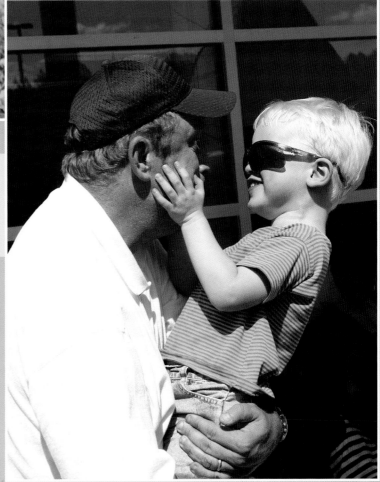

◀ Exchange positive information with families at arrival and departure. Invite them to join the children in their outdoor play.

What about conducting a parent-teacher conference while walking around the playground or sitting under a tree?

What would you do to establish a partnership with families?

CLASSROOM ANIMALS (CONTINUED)

We, as teachers of the future citizens of the world, have opportunities everyday to instill in our children a love and respect for themselves and for all the people, animals, and plants with whom we share our world.

There are many interesting learning exhibits you can have in your classroom. While visiting classrooms, I have seen some wonderful science centers with plants and animals, but have also, at times, been very saddened by sights of animals being poorly fed or improperly housed. Before you get any animal, be sure you understand and are prepared to meet its needs. Get answers to the following questions:

- What kind of enclosure should it have?
- What kind of food does it require?
- What temperature must it have?
- Is there any kind of special light it needs?
- Should it be kept with another animal?
- Is it safe for children to handle it?
- Does it need any special veterinarian care?
- Does it meet your state licensing requirements? (Some states require documentation that shows animals requiring vaccinations have been vaccinated according to state and local requirements. Some also require that parents must be advised when animals are present in the classroom or school.)

Along with animals that are commonly found in centers and can be displayed safely and effectively (small rodents, such as gerbils and hamsters, frogs, fish, birds, and turtles) you might try some of the following:

- *Earthworms*—You'll need a large plastic or glass jar, sand or loose moist soil, cloth cover, damp leaves or grass, and a dozen or so earthworms. (You can look for earthworms after a spring rain or buy them from a local bait shop.)

Place a layer of pebbles in the jar, then fill it with sand or loose moist soil. Put in some earthworms. Keep the soil moist but not wet. The children can feed the worms damp leaves and grass clippings. Be sure to cover the container with a dark cloth to shield the worms from light, because they are used to being in the dark ground.

The children can observe how the worms burrow tunnels in the soil. They can also carefully place a worm on a table to watch its movements (with teacher supervision). Note the difference between its back and underside. Using a magnifying glass, count the rings on its body. Notice the worm's reaction to various stimuli: light, sound, types of food, and soil.

After viewing the worms for awhile, the children can return them to their garden or playground. Earthworms are very important for healthy soil. They loosen it so that air and water can get to plant roots as well as fertilize the soil.

- *Silkworms*—You'll need a terrarium, mulberry leaves, and silkworm eggs or larvae. Many early childhood centers and schools store the eggs laid in one season in a small bottle in a refrigerator until the next season. When the mulberry leaves are on the trees, these eggs are placed in a terrarium with the leaves. (Network with other colleagues to get your supply of silkworm eggs.)

The silkworm (like all other moths and butterflies) undergoes a complete metamorphosis. *There are four stages of development: egg, larva, pupa, and adult moth.* One female silkworm moth can lay from 300 to 400 eggs. In about 10 days, cream to light green colored caterpillars hatch from the eggs and eat voraciously on mulberry leaves for about 30 days. Be sure you have access to mulberry leaves that have not been sprayed with insecticide. (Many parents can help supply the mulberry leaves.)

A cocoon will then be constructed from a single fiber of silk, which could be up to one quarter mile long! It takes about 3 days to complete the cocoon. Inside the cocoon, the silkworm metamorphoses into a cream-colored moth, which will not eat, rarely flies, and lives only a few days. One ounce of silkworm eggs produces 30,000 larvae, which can spin approximately 100 pounds of silk! (As you can see, you need only a few eggs to get started.) Introducing children to silkworms offers a very special way to help them understand what a life cycle is.

- *Butterflies*—The following company will ship butterflies directly to your center or school. Butterfly Garden is available from Insect Lore Products, P.O. Box 1535, Shafter, CA 93263, http://www.insectlore.com. Children can watch the metamorphosis of larva to chrysalides to butterflies, then have the fun of releasing the butterflies back into nature.
- *Ants*—Commercially sold ant farms are widely available in stores selling educational materials. It is fascinating to watch these little creatures dig tunnels, drag food, and interrelate with each other.

—By Jo Eklof

Jo is an educator, wildlife rehabilitator, songwriter, and performer. Many of her songs are shared with you throughout this book.

A frog inspires wonder and curiosity in young children.

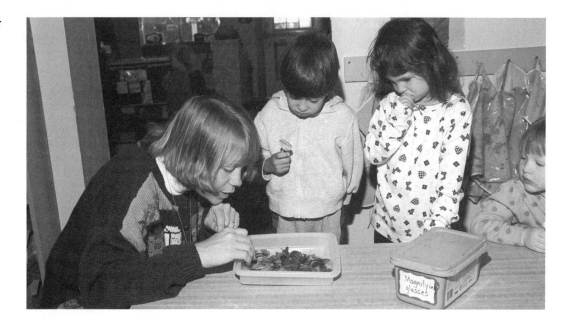

SHARING SCIENCE: ENCOURAGING FAMILY SUPPORT

Many of the activities in this chapter can be shared with parents so that science can become a family affair. Help them understand that children are *natural* scientists discovering their world. Send information and suggestions home. Begin with general ideas as to what parents can do with their children, and then show them specific activities that are ongoing in the classroom. For example, they also can grow a carrot-top garden or root a sweet potato at home with their child, as well as do the following.

- Look at science experiences all around you. Observe plants, insects, animals, rocks, and sunsets with your child.
- Go for a walk outside in the park or in the woods and talk about the natural things you and your child see.
- Feel a tree. Talk about the parts of the tree.
- Collect all kinds of things—from shells to sticks to rocks. Talk about where they came from.
- Help your child use her senses—sight, smell, touch, hearing, and taste—to explore the world around her. Look at leaves, smell them, and rub your fingers across their tops and undersides. Compare one kind of leaf with another, and look for changes over time.
- As your child begins to talk about plants in her environment, she can observe their growth by taking care of plants at school and at home. Together learn the names of plants, flowers, shrubs, fruits, vegetables, and trees.
- Explain what items you recycle. Share some of these with us at school: plastic containers, egg cartons, paper towel and bathroom tissue rolls, samples and end-cuts from wallpaper, fabric, floor tile, framing materials, and newspapers.

Family involvement in nutrition education is important so that children receive reinforced messages at home. According to Marotz, Cross, and Rush (2005) and Aronson (2002), here are some suggestions to involve families:

- Ask them to assist in planning menus.
- Place weekly menus on the parent board, as well as suggestions for foods that provide nutritional additions to each menu.

WHY I TEACH YOUNG CHILDREN

While teaching a unit about our bodies to a group of three-year-olds, I decided to show them a small doll house. We looked at all of the different rooms. I told them that our hearts had different rooms also called chambers. The next day, a mom came in and told me that her daughter had come home and told her, "I learned that I have a four bedroom heart!"

—Bonnie Rubinstein

🌐 Provide a report on the food experiences done in class and ask the families for feedback on their child's reaction to these experiences.

🌐 Invite families to attend a potluck (food sharing) dinner and bring special ethnic or traditional foods unique to their culture.

🌐 Help in developing guidelines for acceptable foods that families could bring to the center/school to celebrate a birthday or other holiday.

🌐 Help families understand how they can foster positive eating habits at home. Encourage good eating behaviors, such as always sitting down for snacks and meals.

🌐 Discuss ways to prevent obesity and why it is important to do so.

🌐 Remind families about ways to involve their child with food in the home, such as helping prepare food with age-appropriate safe kitchen tasks and sharing in cleanup activities.

TIPS FOR TEACHERS

Science is not just a body of knowledge. It is a way of thinking so teachers need not worry about feeling "prepared enough" to teach science. Teachers simply need to observe and explore along with the children. (Diffily, Donaldson, & Sassman, 2001)

🌐 Provide hands-on experiences that make science a part of every child's day.

🌐 Preserve and value a child's natural curiosity.

🌐 Avoid "telling" children about a scientific activity that they themselves cannot observe or experiment with. Relying on teacher information *only* is not useful or appropriate for children, as we have discussed throughout this chapter.

🌐 If you have difficulty with setting up a science environment, identify an individual interest or area of the real world you would like to know more about. Set up your early education classroom so that you can discover and learn things *along with the children.* Start with one of the science inquiries suggested in this chapter.

🌐 Allow the children to control the time spent on experimenting with appropriate materials. Children need time to try out ideas, to discover, to make mistakes and learn from them, and to learn from one another.

🌐 Some adaptations of materials may be necessary to help children with special needs, such as providing additional tactile cues for visually impaired children and helping those with hearing impairments experience sound by feeling the vibrations of tuning forks, guitar strings, or rubber bands stretched across a cigar box (Brewer, 2004).

Ask open-ended questions, and give children plenty of time to answer questions. This helps children to observe carefully and encourages them to put their ideas into words.
(What does a feather look like? How does the sky look when it is going to rain?)

 Allow for across-the-curriculum integration of activities.

DEVELOPMENTALLY APPROPRIATE AND MULTICULTURAL/ANTI-BIAS ACTIVITIES

DAP To introduce an awareness of the different environments in various parts of the world, read books to the children, display objects and artifacts from different cultures, and show photographs of faraway places like the rainforests in Central and South America, the deserts in the Middle East and Africa, and the rivers around the world. Keep a globe or a map of the world available for the children to find the areas discussed. Encourage them to draw or write about *their* world as *they* see it. Provide them with disposable cameras to take photographs that illustrate what they see. This activity can also stimulate further investigations of the children's homes, backyards, neighborhoods, and school environments. Photographs are useful devices for developing diversity recognition and science teaching and learning. Children begin to see patterns and make connections between their own personal explorations and discoveries and what is outside in the world at large. Photos can be instrumental in helping them do this (Hoisington, 2002).

Brewer (2004) offers us another reminder: "Teachers should make sure they know enough about the cultures of children in their classrooms that they do not engage the students in activities that will be offensive. For example, some cultures would be disturbed by studies of plants or animals that have symbolic meaning in their particular cultures. The key is to understand the various communities of the children well enough that you can avoid offending them."

Visit agencies and organizations in your community that offer resources and information relating to various cultures. As you gather materials and facts, ask the parents of children in your class for specific examples of what would be inappropriate to their culture. Continue to be aware of, and sensitive to, the many elements in each child's world.

Poetry, flannelboard stories, dramatic play, music, and movement offer additional opportunities for young children to become more aware of the world around them and their place in it. The poem and songs, on pages 207–209, are creative ways for the children to share their appreciation of the world and each other. (Flannelboard characters for the poem "Seeds" can be found in Appendix A.)

OBSERVATION, ASSESSMENT, AND EVALUATION

 Consistent with the goals for sciencing, evaluations of children's attitudes, skills, and knowledge should focus on the process, be based on multiple sources of information, and be ongoing. . . . To use this information, teachers should be relatively consistent in their conversations with the children and systematically record these observations of each child (Kilmer & Hofman, 1995).

As explained in Chapter 5, the anecdotal record process of assessment is one of the developmentally appropriate ways teachers can evaluate a child's learning. Review the process of keeping anecdotal records described in Chapter 5. Use the Anecdotal Record/Observation Form, Figure 6–8, to record your observation.

Chalufour & Worth (2004) offer the following key elements to assessment that are helpful to documenting children's inquiry skills and growing understanding of the science concepts.

FIGURE 6–8

Anecdotal Record/ Observation Form. (This form can be found on the CD that accompanies this text. Additional anecdotal record/observation forms are available on the front-of-the-book CD of this text.)

ANECDOTAL RECORD/OBSERVATION FORM

CHILD'S NAME	LOCATION
DATE	TEACHER
TIME AT START OF OBSERVATION	DEVELOPMENTAL DOMAIN (circle or underline all that apply)
TIME AT END OF OBSERVATION	Language Social/Emotional Small Motor Large Motor Cognitive
OBSERVATION	COMMENTS

🌐 Collecting data. Spend at least ten minutes three times a week collecting different kinds of data that capture children's level of engagement and their science understandings including written observations, photographs, videotapes, audiotapes, and samples of their other work.

🌐 Analyzing data regularly. Time spent reflecting on your collection of documents will help you understand the growing skills and understandings of each child in your class. The more kinds of documents you have, the fuller picture you will have of each individual.

🌐 Drawing conclusions and making decisions. Analysis of the documents you have collected will help you make the important connections between your teaching and the children's learning. Use your analysis of children's growth to consider what your next steps should be with individual children and the group.

Figure 6–9 is the curriculum planning web worksheet with science activities added. This worksheet, with appropriate additions, is included in each chapter.

SEEDS

The little seeds are sleeping under their blanket made of earth.
They dream until the rainclouds cover the sky;
then all the little seeds begin to sigh,
"We are thirsty! We're thirsty!
We need some rain to drink!"
And now there are raindrops falling, raindrops falling,

and all the little seeds are busy drinking up all the
raindrops falling, raindrops falling, and soon ———

the little seeds begin to grow ———
s l o w l y . . . s l o w l y -.-.-.
and some turn into flowers-.-.-.
and others turn into trees,
and many turn into good things to eat!
And all of them are beautiful;

they're very beautiful, reaching up so high

as they try to touch the sky!

*Reproduced by permission of B. Wolf—1995
Copyright B. Wolf—1993

LET'S HANDLE OUR WORLD WITH CARE

Words and Music by Jo Eklof

Let's han-dle our world with care. Our world is meant to
share. It's home to me. It's home to you. It's home to ev-'ry-
bo-dy, too. What do we need to do? Let's han-dle our world with care.

I'M SO GLAD THAT YOU LIVE IN THE WORLD WITH ME

Words and Music by Jo Eklof

WHAT A LUCKY DAY
Words and Music by Jo Eklof

Additional verses

What a lucky day it was for me. Do you know that? Today is the day that I got to see a cat.
It meow-meowed here and it meow-meowed there as I went on my way.
Oh boy, it was a very very very lucky day.

What a lucky day it was for me.   Please take my word. Today is the day that I got to see a bird.
It flapp-flapped here and it flap-flapped there as I went on my way.
Oh boy, it was a very very very lucky day.

What a lucky day it was for me. Make no mistake. Today is the day that I got to see a snake.
It wiggled here and it wiggled there as I went on my way.
Oh boy, it was a very very very lucky day.

Everyday is lucky. The world is a beautiful place. It's full of wonderful things that put smiles on my face.
I look and learn and listen and then go on my way.
Everyday is a very very very lucky day.

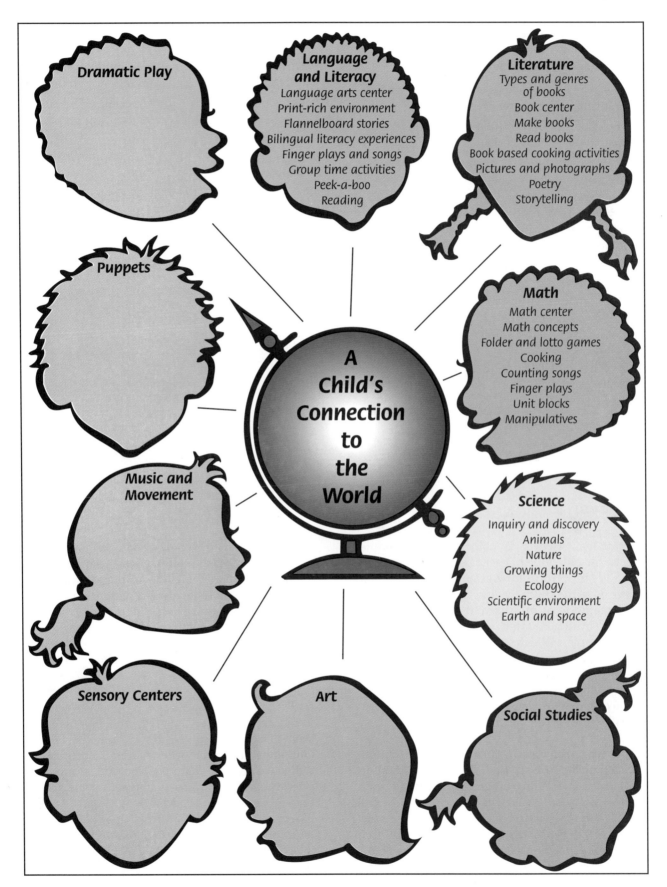

Dramatic Play

Language and Literacy
Language arts center
Print-rich environment
Flannelboard stories
Bilingual literacy experiences
Finger plays and songs
Group time activities
Peek-a-boo
Reading

Literature
Types and genres of books
Book center
Make books
Read books
Book based cooking activities
Pictures and photographs
Poetry
Storytelling

Puppets

Math
Math center
Math concepts
Folder and lotto games
Cooking
Counting songs
Finger plays
Unit blocks
Manipulatives

A Child's Connection to the World

Music and Movement

Science
Inquiry and discovery
Animals
Nature
Growing things
Ecology
Scientific environment
Earth and space

Sensory Centers

Art

Social Studies

FIGURE 6–9
A curriculum planning web worksheet with science activities added.

✳ AFTERVIEW

Through science activities, a child

- ❂ enjoys sensory experiences and uses the senses to gain information about the world.
- ❂ becomes more aware of life and physical sciences, and earth and space sciences.
- ❂ sharpens her curiosity, formulates and evaluates predictions, gathers simple data, and draws conclusions.
- ❂ investigates nutrition and discovers the nature of food, the origin of food, the physical properties of food, and how food changes from one state or form to another.
- ❂ observes nature and develops an appreciation of natural beauty.
- ❂ learns to care for plants.

- ❂ learns to care for animals and develops sympathy and tenderness through association with pets.
- ❂ learns that the earth is very special.
- ❂ realizes that the earth is our home and that we need to take care of it.
- ❂ understands that the earth belongs to all living creatures.
- ❂ learns that every living thing must have water to live.
- ❂ discovers how growing things enrich the environment.
- ❂ realizes that recycling is important to protecting our world.
- ❂ learns ways to help clean up litter.
- ❂ develops ways to preserve and conserve our natural resources.

✳ KEY TERMS

astronomy	geology	nutrients
chemistry	inquiry	nutrition
earth and space science	life science	physical science
ecology	meteorology	process skills

✳ EXPLORATIONS

1. Select at least two early childhood classrooms. Observe for one hour in each. Describe objectively (factually) in writing how science activities were introduced to the children.
   Which methods of inquiry and process skills (as described in this chapter) were used? Explain by giving examples. Which science activities happened indoors and which ones occurred outdoors? Was there a science learning center as part of the room arrangement? Explain. Describe at least four activities you observed. What are your subjective (opinion) thoughts about early education science activities once you have completed this assignment?

2. Find out what materials are collected in your community and how they are recycled. Then, using this information, plan a recycling program appropriate for a preschool classroom. What will you recycle? How will you collect the discarded materials? What are your objectives? What projects can you and the children do to reuse the materials instead of discarding them? Share your plan with another classmate or colleague.

3. With another classmate, conduct a science activity with a group of preschoolers. For example, compare how sand and water flow through sieves. This helps

children extend the concept of flow to dry as well as to wet. This also reinforces the scientific method of investigation. While one adult is involved with the children, the other should record what the children are doing and saying. Afterward, evaluate the activity. Were the children actively involved? What should stay the same? What should change? How would the activity change if planned for a group of toddlers?

4. Select two of the activities suggested in this chapter, such as the carrot-top garden, rooting a sweet potato, thirsty celery, or growing grass, and experiment with them at home. Then plan how you will arrange the environment, what transitions into the activities you will use, and what materials you will supply for the scientific investigations as you set up the activities for a group of young children.

5. Based on the information from this chapter, write a letter on science activities to give to the parents of the children in your class. Be creative. Explain what science projects you and the children are doing. Give suggestions for extended activities the parents can do with their children. Describe other ways to communicate with parents.

✳ REFERENCES

Allen, M. (2007). Look, think, discover: Adding the wonder of science to the early childhood classroom. On-line at: http://www.earlychildhoodnews.com

Aronson, S. S. (2002). (Ed.). *Healthy young children.* Washington DC: NAEYC.

Brewer, J. A. (2004). *Introduction to early childhood education* (4th ed.). Boston: Allyn & Bacon.

Buchanan, B. L., & Rios, J. M. (2004, May). Teaching science to kindergartners. *Young Children, 59*(3), 82–87.

Chalufour, I. & Worth, K. (2004). *Building structures with young children: The young scientist series.* St. Paul, MN: Redleaf Press & Washington, DC: NAEYC.

Charlesworth, R., & Lind, K. K. (2007). *Math and science for young children* (5th ed.). Clifton Park, NY: Thomson Delmar Learning.

Church, E. B. (2006). Scientific thinking: Step by step. On-line at: http://www.scholastic.com

Colker, L. J. (2002, September). Teaching and learning about science. *Young Children, 57*(5), 10–11.

Desouza, J. M., & Staley, L. M. (2002, Winter). The Reggio Emilia philosophy inspires scientific inquiry. *Dimensions of Early Childhood, 30*(1), 3–8.

Diffily, D., Donaldson, E., & Sassman, C. (2001). *Early childhood learning centers.* New York: Scholastic.

Dodge, D. T., Colker, L. J., & Heroman, C. (2000). *Creative curriculum for early childhood: Connecting content, teaching, and learning* (3rd ed.). Washington, DC: Teaching Strategies.

Durkin, L., & Perez, J. (1999, March). Gardening activities. *Early Childhood News, 11*(2), 58–59, 61.

Eklof, J. (2003). *Animals in the classroom.* Dallas, TX: Miss Jo Publications.

Essa, E. (2007). *Introduction to early childhood education* (5th ed.). Clifton Park, NY: Thomson Delmar Learning.

Fraser, S., & Gestwicki, C. (2002). *Authentic childhood: Exploring Reggio Emilia in the classroom.* Clifton Park, NY: Thomson Delmar Learning.

Gardner, H. (1997). Teaching for multiple intelligences. *Educational Leadership, 55*(1), 9–12.

Grieshaber, S., & Diezmann, C. (2000). The challenge of teaching and learning science with young children. In N. J. Yelland (Ed.), *Promoting meaningful learning.* Washington, DC: NAEYC.

Hoisington, C. (2002, September). Using photographs to support children's science inquiry. *Young Children, 57*(5), 26–32.

Humphryes, J. (2000, March). Exploring nature with children. *Young Children, 55*(2), 6–13.

Kilmer, S. J., & Hofman, H. (1995). Teaching early childhood curriculum and assessment. In S. Bredekamp & T. Rosegrant (Eds.), *Reaching potentials: Appropriate curriculum and assessment for young children.* Washington, DC: NAEYC.

Kupetz, B. N., & Twiest, M. M. (2000, January). Nature, literature, and young children: A natural combination. *Young Children, 55*(1), 59–63.

Marotz, L. R., Cross, M. Z., & Rush, J. M. (2005). *Health, safety, and nutrition.* (6th ed.). Clifton Park: NY: Thomson Delmar Learning.

Martin, D. J. (2001). *Constructing early childhood science.* Clifton Park, NY: Thomson Delmar Learning.

National Research Council. (1996). *National Science Education Standards (NSES).* Washington, DC: National Academy Press.

Petrash, C. (1992). *Earthways.* Mt. Rainier, MD: Gryphon House.

Rivkin, M. (Ed.). (1992, May). Science is a way of life. *Young Children, 47*(4), 4–8.

Wortham, S. C. (2006). *Early childhood curriculum: Development bases for learning and teaching.* (4th ed.). Upper Saddle River, NJ; Pearson Prentice Hall.

Ziemer, M. (1987, September). Science and the early childhood curriculum. *Young Children, 42*(6), 44–51.

✳ ADDITIONAL READINGS AND RESOURCES

Basile, C., & White, C. (2000, Summer). Environmental education: A walk in the park is just the beginning. *Dimensions of Early Childhood, 28*(3), 3–7.

Bellows, L., & Anderson, J. (2006, May). The food friends: Encouraging preschoolers to try new foods. *Young Children, 61*(3), 37–38.

Bernath, P., and Masi, W. (2006, May). Smart school snacks: A comprehensive preschool nutrition education program. *Young Children, 61*(3), 20–24.

Conezio, K., & French, L. (2002, September). Science in the preschool classroom: Capitalizing on children's fascination with the everyday world to foster language and literacy development. *Young Children, 57*(5), 12–18.

Danoff-Burg, J. A. (2002, September). Be a bee and other approaches to introducing young children to entomology. *Young Children, 57*(5), 42–46.

Egertson, H. A. (2006, November). In praise of butterflies: Linking self-esteem and learning. *Young Children, 61*(6), 58–60.

Jackman, H. L. (2001, January/February). Science experiences in early childhood. *Early Childhood News, 13*(1), 32–34.

Jones, J., & Courtney, R. (2002, September). Documenting early science learning. *Young Children, 57*(5), 34–40.

Kemple, K. M., & Johnson, C. A. (2002, Summer). From the inside out: Nurturing aesthetic response to nature in the primary grades. *Childhood Education, 78*(4), 210–218.

Moriarty, R. F. (2002, September). Helping teachers develop as facilitators of three- to five-year-olds' science inquiry. *Young Children, 57*(5), 20–24.

Redleaf, R., & Robertson, A. (1999). *Learn and play the recycle way.* St. Paul, MN: Redleaf Press.

Ross, M. E. (2000, March). Science their way. *Young Children, 55*(2), 6–13.

Worth, K., & Grollman, S. (2003). *Worms, shadows, and whirlpools: Science in the early childhood classroom.* Portsmouth, NH: Heinemann; Newton, MA: EDC; and Washington, DC: NAEYC.

For additional information on early education curriculum, visit our Web site at http://www.earlychilded.delmar.com

CHAPTER 7

SOCIAL STUDIES

OBJECTIVES

AFTER STUDYING THIS CHAPTER, YOU SHOULD BE ABLE TO:

- Identify the core of social studies—the social sciences.
- Recognize the National Council for the Social Studies (NCSS) Curriculum Standards and explain their importance in early education curriculum development.
- Outline the goals of early education social studies.
- Describe activities that support the goals.
- Discuss how to create partnerships with families and the community.
- Specify types of field trips and discuss how to plan for these.
- Identify developmentally appropriate and multicultural/anti-bias activities.

OVERVIEW

Social studies, like all the content chapters in this book, is a developmentally appropriate link in the early childhood curriculum chain. Social studies emphasizes ways to provide care and education for each child by focusing on the child, the child's family, the community, the nation, and the world. Young children are enthusiastic as they gain understanding of the many aspects of their cultural and environmental world.

Seefeldt (2001) emphasizes:

> *The field of social studies is uniquely suited to prepare children with the knowledge, skills, and attitudes they need to participate in, and contribute to, the small democracies of their homes, their preschool or primary groups, and their immediate neighborhoods today, as well as to become functioning citizens of society in general in the future.*

Social studies, like math and science, needs to be experienced firsthand by the children. To have this happen, children need to be taken out into the world of people as well as have the world brought to them in the classroom (Feeney, Christensen, & Moravcik, 2001). Through interactions with children's families and the community, you can assist children in learning about the core of social studies—the **social sciences.** Individually they are the following: **anthropology,** the study of the way people live, such as their beliefs and customs; **sociology,** the study of group living, cooperation, and responsibilities; **history,** the study of what has happened in the life of a country or people; **geography,** the study of the earth's surface, and resources, and the concepts of direction, location, and distance; **economics,** the study of the production, distribution, and consumption of goods and services; and **psychology,** the study of the mind, emotions, and behavioral processes; and other areas of study such as environmental science, art, and current events. (Specific activities relating to the social sciences will be discussed as we continue through this chapter.)

Children today are aware at a very young age about aspects of all the social sciences. They are experiencing moving to and living in different places or knowing family members and friends who have. Many travel on a regular basis and have access to the Internet, television, video games, movies, books, and magazines that introduce them to an ever-changing world.

With all of this in mind, your role as an early childhood teacher continues to be nurturing, valuing, and accepting of the children and families in your care, both individually and as a group. Supportive adults in a supportive environment allow children to release their feelings, ask questions and expect appropriate answers, solve problems, and resolve conflicts. As you continue through this chapter, you will understand how social studies follows the path through the preschool years of a child's own life, to those of his family, school, neighborhood, then branching off during the primary years to his state, nation, and then the larger world or global community.

---

social sciences

The core of social studies: anthropology, sociology, history, geography, economics, and psychology.

anthropology

The study of the way people live, such as their beliefs and customs.

sociology

The study of group living, cooperation, and responsibilities.

history

The study of what has happened in the life of a country or people.

geography

The study of the earth's surface, resources, and the concepts of direction, location, and distance.

economics

The study of the production, distribution, and consumption of goods and services.

psychology

The study of the mind, emotions, and behavioral processes.

DEVELOPMENTALLY APPROPRIATE PRACTICE AND THE NATIONAL COUNCIL FOR THE SOCIAL STUDIES CURRICULUM STANDARDS

 Using a developmentally appropriate practice model (Bredekamp & Copple, 1997), teachers can develop the natural social studies curriculum, as suggested by Mindes (2005):

- Build on what children already know.
- Develop concepts and processes of social studies rather than focusing on isolated facts.
- Provide hands-on activities.

🌐 Use relevant social studies throughout the year.

🌐 Capitalize on child interest.

Wortham (2006) continues the discussion, "Throughout the school year, students and teachers work together in setting learning goals and classroom rules and solving social problems that arise in the classroom. Choices are made about what and how they will learn, particularly when planning projects or thematic units."

The National Council for the Social Studies (NCSS) curriculum standards are organized into ten thematic strands based on the social sciences and designed to act as a framework for social studies curriculum while guiding the development of worthwhile learning experiences in early education. The ten themes are listed below with explanations adapted from Kostelnik, Soderman, and Whiren (2007), Mindes (2005), Wallace (2006), and Wortham (2006).

🌐 CULTURE—Through activities in the classroom, children develop knowledge of their own culture and the culture of others. A child's culture is a fundamental building block in the development of a child's identity. During the preschool years children explore the concepts of likenesses and differences to help them understand themselves and others.

🌐 TIME, CONTINUITY, AND CHANGE—Important to the lives of young children is their personal history and that of their family. The social studies curriculum should include experiences that provide for the study of ways human beings view themselves in and over time.

🌐 PEOPLE, PLACES, AND ENVIRONMENTS—Where things are in the children's near environment is important information for them to have as they move further from home. Younger children draw upon immediate personal experiences as a basis for exploring geographic concepts and skills. They are also concerned about the use and misuse of the environment.

🌐 INDIVIDUAL DEVELOPMENT AND IDENTITY—The self, the family, and the community are most important to young children. A sense of belonging, and the ability to take care of themselves and their own needs impact children in the early years. For the youngest citizens, infants and toddlers, content focuses on self-development in the social world. In the preschool and primary years, social studies offer a structure for broad theme-based content.

🌐 INDIVIDUALS, GROUPS, AND INSTITUTIONS—Children belong to many groups—family, class, after-school activity groups, congregations, and so forth. This NCSS standard is better suited to older children in their studies.

🌐 POWER, AUTHORITY, AND GOVERNANCE—This standard is also better suited for the older grades to investigate. The concepts are too abstract for young children.

🌐 PRODUCTION, DISTRIBUTION, AND CONSUMPTION—Children can be made aware of the diverse kinds of work adults engage in by talking to them and observing them at work. Prekindergarten and kindergarten children can develop an understanding of how goods and services are produced, distributed, and consumed through social studies projects.

🌐 SCIENCE, TECHNOLOGY, AND SOCIETY—Social studies for young children can introduce the concept that technology influences their lives and their families through household appliances, television, video and audio tapes, digital cameras, computers, automobiles, trucks, railroads, airplanes, and ships. Activities that encourage further study can be accomplished individually or with small or large groups.

🌐 GLOBAL CONNECTIONS—This NCSS curriculum standard is designed for older children to show the interconnectedness of the world. Global education is abstract, so it is less appropriate for young children.

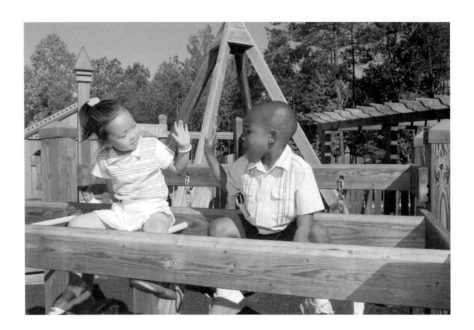

🌐 CIVIC IDEALS AND PRACTICES—Children have opportunities to practice aspects of democratic living when they learn to understand the rules that govern the classroom and when they become involved in making some of the rules themselves.

GOALS OF EARLY EDUCATION SOCIAL STUDIES

The goals for social studies focus on expanding children's horizons and teaching the elements of citizenship in a democratic society. The ultimate goal is to produce individuals who feel good about themselves and develop the necessary concepts and skills to make worthwhile contributions to society through thinking and decision making. (Kostelnik, Soderman, and Whiren, 2007).

According to the National Council for the Social Studies (1994), "today's social studies teaching requires a new vision. Because events happening in other parts of the world impact our lives every day, and because our increasing cultural diversity has transformed our social values and traditions, children need to develop an awareness and a sense of what exists beyond our national frontiers."

Robles de Melendez, Beck, and Fletcher (2000) state the aims of the social studies curriculum:

🌐 *Individual identity:* Pride in oneself, in one's abilities and innate potential, and in the cultural background to which one belongs.

🌐 *National identity:* Recognition of one's role in a democratic country, in this case, the United States of America.

🌐 *Global identity:* An awareness of being a part of the world.

"Community begins in the classroom. For most young children, being a 'classmate'—at day care, at a place of worship, or at school—constitutes their first active participation in an ongoing social structure outside the family. The vision of community that the classroom provides can color a child's ideas and expectations about equity, cooperation, and citizenship for a lifetime" (Teaching Tolerance Project, 1997)

The social studies curriculum emphasizes basic goals that encourage children to become self-reliant, contributing members of their society, namely, the family, the classroom, and the community. These goals encourage children to make choices, act independently, and develop a sense of responsibility and respect for themselves and others. In addition, Seefeldt (2001) believes that in "an early childhood program, children are not just preparing to become members of a democratic society but actually are citizens of a democracy. Within the democratic environment of an early childhood program, children practice principles of democracy."

The following goals help us focus on the core of the social studies curriculum. They are adapted from various sources (Day, 1994; Mayesky, 2006; Seefeldt, 2001; Taylor, 1999), and from conversations with early education teachers.

🌐 *To develop a child's positive self-concept:* A child's understanding and appreciation of himself must come first, before learning to appreciate and relate to others. From infancy on, a child is learning to adjust and accept himself in the family and the larger community. Curriculum activities to emphasize this goal should relate to a child's developing sense of autonomy and his place in the world.

🌐 *To further an understanding of a child's role in the family:* As the child learns about himself, he is also learning about his family. Knowing about the family history, where family members lived before, and the family's values, attitudes, customs, celebrations, and occupations all contributes to a child's sense of belonging. That, in turn, helps him to solidify a positive self-concept. Activities should offer opportunities for a child to talk about and identify things about himself and his family.

🌐 *To develop an awareness of a child's own cultural heritage as well as the traditions of others:* Continuing in the classroom what the child is experiencing in the home environment requires a teacher to communicate openly and often with the child's family. It also means that a teacher should start where the child is with his language, customs, traditions, and values and build on his growth toward self-understanding and acceptance.

🌐 *To provide an inclusive, multicultural classroom environment:* This should reflect the lives and interests of the children, families, and teacher who live in the immediate environment, as well as foster a respect for people everywhere. Social study activities should blend this diversity into the theme, lesson plans, and daily activities *throughout the year.* An appreciation of different ideas, physical appearances, ways and behaviors will result.

🌐 *To understand the need for rules and laws:* Starting with the rules of the family, the child begins to understand the limits placed on him within his environment at a very young age. Conflicts often occur as the child's sense of independence clashes with the rules of the home and classroom. To minimize these encounters, the child should participate in setting the rules.

Howard Gardner's theory of *multiple intelligences* (tools for learning, problem solving, self-definition, human interaction, and creativity), as well as Lev Vygotsky's *sociocultural theory* (influences and interactions from culture and social groups) and Jean Piaget's *cognitive development theory* (information and exploration gathered from the physical and social environment) can all be social studies factors in assisting teachers to guide young children into experiencing and building knowledge. (Review Chapter 1 for additional information on Piaget, Vygotsky, and Gardner.)

As teachers, we are daily role models for young children. By incorporating the goals for social studies into our activities, we can create a supportive environment for the children and their families. We can emphasize an anti-bias approach that influences children to respect and appreciate differences and similarities among people. See Figure 7–1. (All chapters of this book extend this philosophy. Review Chapter 2 for additional multicultural/anti-bias considerations.)

FIGURE 7–1
Social studies activities offer an understanding of people around the world.

WHY I TEACH YOUNG CHILDREN

I have been a teacher for more than twenty years. I have taught in three different countries and have worked with children of many nationalities. In all of the diversity I have seen and experienced among the children, one thing stays common: they can all be taught the love of learning. By reading to them, we give them the gift of love for reading and writing. By giving them opportunities to create, we help them become creative, and by modeling positive behaviors and interactions with others, we give them social tools to help them function in the world. With love and patience, we have the opportunity to enable the children we teach to have better lives as they grow into adults. What a pivotal role teachers play in touching the future of the world!

—Susy Mathews

ACTIVITIES THAT SUPPORT THE GOALS

As children interact with materials, ideas, peers, and adults, young children gain new and individualized insights about their realities. In the case of social studies, where children are in the process of developing knowledge about social phenomena, the optimal environment is a classroom that replicates society. In an active classroom environment, opportunities abound for children to look at reality through the classroom. (Robles de Melendez, Beck, and Fletcher, 2000)

The social studies curriculum is connected to all learning centers in an early education environment. Rather than create a separate center for social studies activities, the teacher needs to integrate these projects into all other learning centers. When

Social studies is connected to all learning centers in an early education environment.

using the project approach, children are building on what they know. At the same time, they are practicing cooperative learning; developing opportunities for observation, reading, writing, interviewing, and inquiry; and using multiple learning domains (Mindes, 2006). Many of the activities described in the other chapters can become part of the social studies curriculum. The following are some additional suggestions to get you started:

🌐 Appropriate *themes* to encourage the development of authentic self-esteem are "Magnificent Me" or "All About Me." Extensions of this can be "Me and My Family," "Me and My Friends," or "Me and My Community." (See Appendix B for a complete thematic, integrated curriculum for "My Community.")

🌐 After making life-size body outlines of themselves, the children can make individual *handprints* and *footprints* with tempera or fingerpaints. This body-awareness activity is time tested, according to Helen H. Johnson (1994):

> *What brilliant teacher first conceived the notion of young children painting their own life-size self-portraits? The activity never fails to capture and hold attention through all its stages: outlining oneself on butcher paper; painting in one's hair, features and clothing; cutting out the final two-dimensional Me.*

🌐 Children can dictate stories about themselves to the teacher or create an "I like" book from drawings and pictures they cut from magazines. These very meaningful activities can be introduced at group time and continued in the language and art centers.

🌐 Plan for the social studies curriculum to include topics that relate specifically to a child's family. For infants and toddlers, creating an atmosphere that makes them feel safe, secure, and special while they are away from home is most important. Activities for all children can include creating an individual or class scrapbook with photographs of family members and pets and magazine pictures depicting toys and home furnishings. Preschoolers can make craft stick puppets, coloring and designing one puppet for each family member. (Refer to Chapter 11.)

Social studies provides opportunities for children to learn about themselves and others.

As a teacher, you can help a child to identify his role in the family and understand how families change over time. Placement in the family may change due to adoption, birth, marriage, divorce, or the death of a family member. Figure 7–2 suggests some books dealing with these themes that you can share with the children.

It is important for children to feel good about themselves and their families. As you continue to prepare your classroom to reflect this attitude, consider the following: What members are in a child's family? How many family members (or others) live in a child's home? What ages are they? What are the roles of family members, both inside and outside the home? What do family members do together? What holidays or events do they celebrate? How are they celebrated? What is the family's history and ethnic background? What changes has the family experienced? Knowing this about each child's family will help you plan appropriate activities for the children in your class (Cunningham, 1994).

An exciting social studies theme can be "Homes." Stretch your and the children's interest and creativity by investigating information about all kinds of shelters for humans and animals. What types of habitats do the following live in: birds, rabbits, turtles, dogs, horses, and cows? Think of all the residences people live in, such as apartments, houses, duplexes, trailers, hotels, and tents. What are they made of, besides wood, brick, stone, and ice? Examine what climate and location have to do with determining how a house is built. Gather books, pictures, computers, and computer software to illustrate concretely what you are talking about. The children can even experiment with building models of some of these residences with blocks, pieces of fabric, scrap wood, boxes, and other materials.

FIGURE 7–2

Plan for the social studies curriculum to include books relating to a child's family.

BOOKS ABOUT FAMILIES

Cole, J. (1997). *I'm a big brother*. New York: Morrow.

Cole, J. (1997). *I'm a big sister*. New York: Morrow.

Feldman, E. B. (1996). *Birthdays! Celebrating life around the world*. Moraga, CA: Bridgewater.

Fletcher, R. (1990). *Relatively speaking: Poems about family*. New York: Orchard.

Garza, C. L. (1990). *Family pictures—Cuadros de familia*. San Francisco: Children's Book Press.

Greenfield, E. (1991). *Daddy and I*. Illustrated by J. A. Gilcrest. New York: Black Butterfly Board Books.

Hickcox, R. (1998). *Great grandmother's treasure*. New York: Dial.

Hudson, W. (1993). *I love my family*. New York: Scholastic.

Karkowsky, N. (1989). *Grandma's soup*. Illustrated by S. O. Haas. Rockville, MD: Kar-Ben Copies Inc.

Kroll, V. (1993). *A carp for Kimiko*. Illustrated by K. Roundtree. Watertown, MA: Charlesbridge Publishing.

Leunn, N. (1998). *A gift for Abuelita*. Flagstaff, AZ: Northland.

Low, A. (1999). *Mommy's briefcase*. New York: Scholastic.

Morris, A. (1990). *Loving*. Photographs by K. Heyman. New York: Lothrop, Lee & Shepard Books.

Newman, L. (2007). *Daddy's Song*. Illustrated by K. Ritz. New York: Henry Holt.

Ostarch, J., and Nex, A. (1993). *My family*. Los Angeles: Price Stern Sloan.

Scott, A. H. (1992). *On Mother's lap*. Illustrated by G. Coalson. New York: Clarion Books.

Williams, V. B. (1982). *A chair for my mother*. New York: Mulberry Books.

Yaccarino, D. (2007). *Every Friday*. New York: Henry Holt.

Cooperative caring for pets in the classroom teaches children social responsibility.

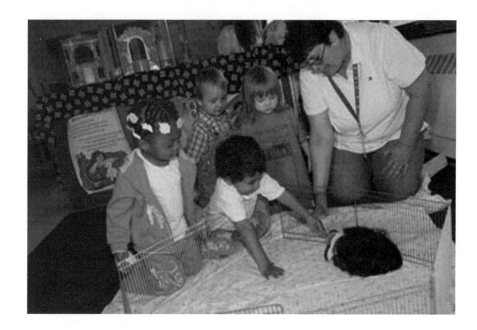

⊕ Taking a social studies viewpoint can become a process you can apply to most curriculum themes. Ramsey (1987) suggests a multicultural approach to learning about pets that could include the following activities and topics:

Caring for pets: social responsibility

Cooperative care of a classroom pet

Similarities among all pets

Diversity of pets

Learning about pets belonging to people in the classroom

Friendships, despite differences, between people and pets

Names of animals in other languages

Pets in other places

Communicating with pets

Animals communicating with each other

Protecting the rights of pets

Different ways that animals feed, clean, and care for their young

Working to change conditions that are harmful to animals

This social sciences/social studies approach can also be used with other topics, such as different ways of cooking and eating, types of clothing, kinds of occupations and work roles, weather conditions, and how people in the world are transported from one place to another.

⊕ Another social studies activity relates to maps or place awareness. The main objective is to introduce children to a map as a picture that shows places and things, where they are located, and how to get from one to another. Young children can usually understand this concept by working with puzzles or by drawing maps of their rooms at home, the classroom, or the playground. Map making is an abstract concept, so the activities should be fairly simple. Keep a globe and other types of maps available to provide visual answers to children's questions about places in the world. Children can use these also as props in their dramatic play activities.

FIGURE 7–3
Map making
opportunities for
children are an
important part of early
education social studies
activities.

It is important to
establish partnership
with parents.

FIGURE 7–4
Use these books to
offer an introduction
to the concept of story
mapping.

🌐 Create an opportunity for the children to make a three-dimensional map (model) of the classroom, their bedroom (see Figure 7–3), or the playground. Clear a large space of classroom floor where the children can construct their map. Place a large piece of cardboard, such as the side of a large box, on the floor. Gather materials, such as pipe cleaners, Styrofoam pieces, small counting cubes, crayons, markers, glue, and various types and colors of paper. The children will let you know what other materials they need during the creative process. They can work cooperatively in small groups to make their map. This activity may take several days or weeks to complete. Let the children make the decision as to when it is time to stop working on and playing with this activity.

🌐 Another type of mapping relates to children's literature. Wallace (2006) introduces the concept of *story mapping*. "The use of story maps is a great introduction to mapping skills with young children. As with most activities we do with young children, there are multiple purposes and outcomes of this activity. . . we are giving them strategies for increasing comprehension of a story, of understanding story elements. . . of using multiple modalities to learn and show what they have learned, and frequently to work cooperatively with other students."
Wallace suggests the following steps:

1. Begin with a book familiar to the children. Choose one you have read to them before.
2. Discuss and chart the different places the main character goes.
3. Have the children, either individually or in pairs or small groups, illustrate the locations.
4. Cut out and label each picture.
5. In sequential order of the locations, glue the illustrations on a large piece of paper. This becomes a very graphic way to introduce children to a map of the locations reached by the main character of the story.

Depending on the books you select, the children can become the main character of the book and make the map of where he traveled. Figure 7–4 is a selection of books, from the basic fairy tales to stories that travel the world.

🌐 "Timelines are used to represent data in chronological or sequential order. This technique offers visual aid for children by helping them begin to think in terms of sequence and chronology" (Wallace, 2006). Introduce primary-age children to personal time lines starting with the year they were born through the present. For each year the student will include at least one event that happened in the world or in his or her personal life (Seto, 1999). This can be an activity to be shared with families. The children can bring photographs from home relating to each year or ask their parents to write about what they remember from each year.

BOOKS FOR STORY MAPPING

Dooley, N. (1991). *Everybody cooks rice.* Illustrated by P. J. Thornton. Minneapolis, MN: Carolrhoda Books.
Galdone, P. (2001). *The gingerbread boy.* New York: Clarion.
Galdone, P. (2001). *Little red hen.* New York: Clarion.
Gilliland, J. H. (1990). *The day of Ahmed's secret.* Illustrated by T. Lewin. New York: Lothrop, Lee & Shepard.
Gresko, M. S. (2000). *A ticket to Israel.* Minneapolis, MN: Carolrhoda Books.
Johnson, C. (1955/1983). *Harold and the purple crayon.* New York: HarperTrophy.
Sis, P. (2000). *Madlenka.* New York: Groundwood Books. (Available in English and Spanish).

SHARING SOCIAL STUDIES: CREATING PARTNERSHIPS WITH FAMILIES AND THE COMMUNITY

As you establish partnerships with parents, it is important to continuously assess their needs and interests and use this knowledge to involve the parents as active partners in the lives of the children at the center or school. The families of today offer new challenges to early childhood educators. "Frequently, teachers find themselves in situations that were rare only a few years ago. Dealing with a variety of family structures, coping with increased occurrences of family violence, and witnessing strained parental relationships are difficult dimensions of this field" (Stamp & Groves, 1994).

Knowing this, we should relate to the families of our children with a commitment to accept their individual differences. We should acknowledge and respect children's home language and **culture** (National Association for the Education of Young Children [NAEYC] 1996). We should maintain positive interactions with them while communicating our goals of a child-centered, developmentally appropriate curriculum.

Get parental input as you plan activities and services. If the parents help to set the priorities and agenda, your planned activities will better meet their needs. The following are some examples of how to communicate with parents to maximize their involvement:

culture
The sum total of a child's or family's ways of living: their values or beliefs, language, patterns of thinking, appearance, and behavior. These are passed or learned from one generation to the next.

🌐 With parents of an infant or toddler, you will need to spend a lot of time making them feel comfortable in leaving their child with you. It is most important to build a sense of trust, and this takes time. Show them that you will communicate with them through daily notes and conversations. Let them know that there will be a period of adjustment for their child as well as for them. Explain that during this time, it might be helpful if their child brought a "security" toy or blanket. The parents can also call during the day to check on how their child is doing, if this will help them feel more at ease. All these suggestions can open lines of communication between you and the family members.

🌐 Place a parent bulletin board or information sheet on the door of your classroom. For family members who bring and pick up the child each day, this offers a consistent place to look for messages and items of interest. Change materials often.

🌐 Post weekly lesson plans on the classroom door to keep the parents up-to-date on the curriculum. This sends a signal that you want the parents to be fully aware of the daily activities of their children.

Invite parents to visit and to participate in classroom activities with their child.

■ WHY I TEACH YOUNG CHILDREN ■

Sherry and Tom (both one-year-olds) were playing side by side in the classroom, when suddenly Sherry pulled Tom's hair. I watched as Tom went to grab what I thought was going to be Sherry's hair, but was very much surprised to see him hug her instead.

He was crying and hugging her at the same time. This happened a couple of times over the next few days, and each time Sherry pulled Tom's hair, he would hug her. Soon, Sherry stopped pulling his hair. I couldn't have taught Sherry the lesson she learned any better than Tom did.

These children never cease to amaze me.

—Marilyn Parker

🌐 The weekly menu of lunch and snacks should also be posted for parents to see, as required by licensing regulations in most states.

🌐 A newsletter is another way to get parents involved. Some enjoy receiving it, whereas others are interested in taking the responsibility for writing it or collecting information to be in the newsletter. The teacher can contribute facts about what is happening in the classroom, suggestions for children's books and videos, parenting articles, and children's art.

🌐 Some teachers use audiocassettes instead of newsletters. "Children record current happenings on a cassette tape and several copies are circulated until all parents have heard them. This method allows busy parents to listen on the drive to work or school. Parents who cannot read also have access to classroom news" (Silliman & Royston, 1990). If there are non–English-speaking parents in your class, have a family or community member record or translate the information into their language.

🌐 Have a family breakfast, potluck supper, or picnic on the playground. Food always adds to the welcoming environment of family-school activities.

🌐 An open house or family meeting is a time for sharing with parents what their children are doing and what they are learning. This is an excellent opportunity to talk about the importance of play and other developmentally appropriate learning experiences. Be prepared to answer questions. Give family members an opportunity to take part in some of the activities the children have been doing. Set up materials and supplies in each learning center so that they can "learn by doing," the same as the children. Read a story to the parents or have them participate in a music and movement activity.

🌐 Once or twice a year, plan parent-teacher conferences to discuss their child's developmental progress. Plan both day and evening conferences to accommodate the parents' work schedules.

🌐 Invite family members to share their interests, talents, and occupations with the children in the class. This offers another way to make parent involvement special and unique.

Creating partnerships with community members and resources can be helpful. One of the most important groups of individuals to invite into your classroom consists of older members of the families of children in your class as well as other senior adults in the community. Intergenerational programs offer many ways to connect young children with the history and family customs of their own or other cultures.

There is much to be gained from contact with elders, yet some children either do not have grandparents and/or great-grandparents or don't see them often enough to understand

A walking trip around the early childhood area is short in duration and less tiring for the children.

the joy of listening to their stories. Interacting with older adults teaches children about the abundant wisdom, talent, and love elders possess. (Church, 1994)

After the visit or visits, it is important to keep in touch with the older adults. The children can establish a pen pal relationship, send frequent drawings, or dictate stories on audiocassettes to send to their new friends. Many times the children will receive replies that they can share with their classmates.

FIELD TRIPS AS CONCRETE EXPERIENCES IN EARLY EDUCATION

Another way of connecting the child to the community is through taking field trips with the children in your class. Such trips are an enriching part of early education curriculum that add a special dimension to classroom learning by providing firsthand experience that books, pictures, or discussions alone cannot provide. Young children need to see, hear, feel, taste, and touch their world to connect words and ideas to locations and people within their community.

Types of Field Trips

There are different types of field trips to consider. Leipzig (1993), Seefeldt (2001), and Redleaf (1983) suggest the following.

A WALKING TRIP AROUND A FAMILIAR ROOM. This trip offers infants and toddlers an opportunity to notice and learn the names of everything in the room. It can then be extended to another room until the children feel comfortable exploring and noticing things in the entire building or house.

A WALKING TRIP AROUND THE NEIGHBORHOOD. This is the natural extension of the room walk, and there are advantages to neighborhood field trips. They are free, and you do not have to arrange for cars or buses. They are short in duration and less tiring for the children. There is not a rush to meet schedules, so the children can make discoveries, their questions can be answered, and learning can occur. Repeated trips around the neighborhood offer chances to learn something new each time you visit the same places. (First take a walk without the children. Look at things from a child's point of view. Find connections that can be natural outgrowths of classroom activities.)

TAKING A SMALL GROUP OF CHILDREN AT ONE TIME ON A MINI-FIELD TRIP. Once the children become used to taking turns, go on a mini-trip. There are frequent opportunities to do so. There usually is no difficulty in planning trips for a specific purpose with a small group of children.

SPECIFIC-PURPOSE FIELD TRIPS. This type of field trip can be as simple as a neighborhood walk to go bird-watching or to record sounds around the neighborhood. It can be a short trip to the grocery store to get carrots and celery to go into the vegetable soup the children are making or down the block to see the new house being built.

MAJOR FIELD TRIPS. These are often taken by the entire class to a community location. This type requires additional adults and travel arrangements for cars, a van, or a bus. (This type of field trip is discussed in more detail as you read through the rest of this chapter.)

Planning for a Successful Field Trip

Many child care centers and schools are not taking as many field trips as they once did for reasons that include tightening of the budget and remaining concerns of the

September 11, 2001, tragedy. For those of you who are still planning field trips, careful planning is most important.

Making decisions about what an appropriate field trip should provide, selecting the site, visiting the location, planning for the trip, taking the trip, preparing follow-up activities, and evaluating the trip are all parts of the *process*. Think about the following guidelines as you plan field trips for young children.

Appropriate field trips provide:

- opportunities to clarify misconceptions young children have about places and people in the community.
- concrete experiences for the children.
- sensory activities outside the classroom.
- occasions to discover firsthand examples of "real life" work settings.
- contact with adult work models.
- opportunities to gather information and observe multiple environments.
- reinforcement and extension of concepts already learned, while developing new concepts.
- a common core of experiences for play and problem-solving activities.

An appropriate site should:

- be safe for young children to visit.
- be fairly close by so that the children have only a short car trip or bus ride.
- not be too fatiguing for the children.
- not be too crowded or noisy.
- offer the children sensory experiences.
- offer genuine learning experiences through participation.

Before you step out of the classroom door with the children, you should:

- visit the field trip site *yourself*.
- talk to the contact person who will be there on the day you and the children visit and call that individual for verification the day before the field trip.

🌐explain how many children and adults will be coming and the ages of the children; arrange for a time when the site is not too crowded.

🌐explain the children's need to be able to explore, see, and touch.

🌐find out the site's rules and regulations.

🌐find out where the bathrooms are located.

🌐find out accommodations for children with special needs, if applicable.

🌐determine arrangements for lunch or snack.

🌐walk around the location and look for dangerous places.

🌐set up the length of the visit, date, and time.

🌐get brochures, posters, and any other information to share with the children during pretrip discussions.

Prepare the children for the trip by:

🌐giving them an idea of what to expect.

🌐reading books; showing films, pictures, and posters; and talking about the planned trip.

🌐involving them in the planning of the trip.

🌐reminding them of the rules of expected behavior.

🌐reminding them that during the field trip they are not to talk to or go with anyone other than the people on the field trip.

🌐selecting a partner or buddy for each child and explaining how important it is to stay with their partner.

🌐telling them what to do if they get separated from the group.

Prepare the parents for the trip by:

🌐having the parent or guardian sign a walking field trip permission form at the beginning of the year, so that you can take the children on spontaneous walks around the neighborhood. (Figure 7–5 is an example of a walking trip permission form.)

🌐having the parent or guardian sign a field trip form for major types of field trips a week before the trip is to be taken (Figure 7–6 is an example of a field trip permission form).

🌐sending information home to parents explaining the field trip, its purpose, and other details.

🌐involving parent volunteers to accompany you and the children (one adult for every two or three children is advised. For older children, one adult for every

FIGURE 7–5

Walking trip permission form.

I give my permission for my child (child's name) to take part in any walking field trip around the neighborhood immediately surrounding the (center or school name). This permission is valid for the entire year (year date).

(signature of parent or guardian)

(date)

FIGURE 7–6
Field trip permission
form.

Dear Parent,

We will be going on a field trip to (name of site) on (day–date–time–return time). We will travel by (mode of transportation).

If you give permission for your child to go on this field trip, please sign this form in the space provided below.

(Child's name)

(Signature of parent or guardian)

(date)

Cost (if any) to be paid to the center (or school) by (date) in the amount of (amount).

five or six children seems to work well. You will need to decide what child/adult ratio is best for you and the children.)

🌐 explaining the emergency procedures and assuring them that all of the adults going on the trip understand the procedures.

🌐 explaining that arrangements have been made for any child who does not have permission to go on the trip to visit another class during the duration of the field trip.

Taking the Field Trip

Consider the following guidelines when you and the children take the field trip:

🌐 Take at least one fully charged cell phone with you.

🌐 Be sure that the drivers of cars, vans, or buses have a map with simple, precise directions on how to get to the field trip location.

🌐 Prepare a trip kit containing bottled water and paper cups, a basic first-aid kit, and several wet washcloths in individual, self-seal bags.

🌐 Keep the most apprehensive children close to you.

🌐 Take the time to see things along the way.

🌐 Listen to the children to find out what they do and do not know. Talk to them; ask open-ended questions and answer their questions.

🌐 Count "heads" often throughout the trip.

🌐 It is helpful if the children wear T-shirts or name tags with the center's or school's name on them. It is best not to put the child's name where it is visible, because a stranger calling the child's name may pull him away from the group.

🌐 Enjoy the field trip!

Follow-Up to and Assessment of the Field Trip

There should be many opportunities for follow-up activities. Here are a few suggestions:

🌐 Have the children write thank-you notes or draw pictures to send to the parent volunteers and the field site guides or managers who helped make the field trip successful.

A field trip is all about discovery!

◉ Encourage group discussions with the children on what they liked best or what they remember about the trip.

◉ Expand lesson plans to include follow-up activities.

◉ Deepen the children's understanding and recall through follow-up activities: dictate or write stories, draw pictures, create songs and poems, make puppet characters, and draw maps. Add related props and materials to the dramatic play, block, and other learning centers.

◉ Clarify and build upon what the children have seen, heard, experienced, and shared.

◉ Get written evaluations from all of the adults participating in the trip. Did the activity fulfill the trip's goals and objectives? How could the activity be changed to make it effective or more appropriate?

Suggested Field Trips

Children's museums provide a safe harbor in a scary, busy, and complicated world. They offer children the gift of playing freely in an inviting and complex environment and of playing with new things and people in time-tested ways. These positive play experiences are changing children's lives, not merely by what they learn during a museum visit, but by helping them believe in their own powers to learn, to succeed, to make their own choices, to get along with other people, to make their own discoveries, and to know that they are interesting people with good ideas. (Sinker & Russell, 1998)

David Elkind, a noted early childhood educator, observed in 2001 that "it is interesting that the number of children's museums has increased as the sociological, psychological and physical spaces for children have decreased." At the turn of the twentieth century (1899), the first museum for children opened in Brooklyn, New York. Now, in the twenty-first century, there are about 250 children's museums, with approximately 100 more in the planning stage. There are over 400 children's museums around the world.

The national goals of a children's museum work hand-in-hand with each local museum. A children's museum is a place dedicated to children, their families, and educators, where children learn to be proud of their own families and heritage and develop a better understanding of their classmates' and neighbors' cultures. It also serves as an extension of the classroom for educators and a place for parents to "get down on the floor" and play with their children while spending time together. (See Figure 7–7 for an example of an exhibit that invites young children to explore and learn.)

See Appendix C for a suggested list of children's museums, with their Web sites.

The following field trip sites are only suggestions. You know your community best and can make the most appropriate selection of places to visit with the children. If you choose not to take any trips outside the center or school, many individuals connected to the organizations or institutions mentioned will make presentations, bring exhibits or animals, and interact with the children.

Teachers will find that making a card file of possible field trip sites can be helpful. It is easy to add to or correct. Place the information on an index card, color coding each type of location. After you complete a visit to the site to see if it is appropriate for the children in your class, you can make notations on the card for easy reference. Figure 7–8 is a suggested index card form.

FIGURE 7–7
Dallas Children's Museum Exhibit: Paint Studio. Courtesy of Dallas Children's Museum.

SUGGESTIONS OF PLACES TO VISIT

Aquarium	Farmer's market	Puppet show
Arboretum	Fire department	Science museum
Art museum	Library	Sports field or arena
Bird-watching site	Museum of natural history	Wildlife sanctuary
Children's museum	Newspaper	Zoo
Children's theater	Pet shop	
City Hall	Planetarium	

FIGURE 7–8
Index card site form.

NAME OF POSSIBLE SITE/LOCATION

Address: _____

Phone: _____

Contact: _____

Days and hours open: _____

Length of tour or presentation: _____

What the tour or presentation consists of: _____

_____

Size of group permitted: _____

Ages of children: _____

Adult/child ratio required: _____

How early do reservations need to be made: _____

Special notes: _____

TIPS FOR TEACHERS

It is helpful to have a checklist to complete on the day of the field trip. This should be filled out completely by you. Not only will this give you an opportunity to double-check all of your preparations, but it is also written documentation that you are in compliance with state and/or school requirements for taking children away from the center or school. (See Figure 7–9.)

1. Notification of field trip was posted in a prominent place for the parents to see at least 48 hours before the planned trip. Name, address, and phone number of where we are going was clearly stated. Name of contact person was listed. Times of departure and return were clearly stated.

Yes _____ No _____

2. Field trip permission forms, specifically for this trip, have been signed by each child's parent or guardian. These permission forms are on file in the director's or administrator's office.

Yes _____ No _____

3. Only adults, 18 years of age or older, are counted as part of the child/adult ratio. Requirements have been met for the number of adults to accompany the children, including the teachers.

Yes _____ No _____

4. The medical emergency consent form signed by the parent or guardian for each child is being taken on the field trip, as well as the emergency phone numbers for each child's family and a written list of children in the group taking the field trip. This information should be put in the vehicle transporting the child.

Yes _____ No _____

5. An emergency first-aid kit is in each vehicle going on the trip.

Yes _____ No _____

6. There is an adult trained in first aid and another adult trained in CPR going on the field trip.

Yes _____ No _____

7. Arrangements for lunch or snack have been made. They are the following:

8. The driver(s) of the bus (van or cars) is/are:
   The driver's license number of each is:
   The license plate number of each vehicle is:

9. Names of adults going on trip:

10. Names of children going on trip:

11. Departure time: _____ Return time: _____

12. Additional information:

FIGURE 7–9
Teacher checklist for field trip.

DEVELOPMENTALLY APPROPRIATE AND MULTICULTURAL/ ANTI-BIAS ACTIVITIES

 Connect the social studies curriculum to the theme of "Self and Family" to assist children in learning the values, cultural traditions, and history of families.

Family Quilts

An effective way to accomplish this goal is to introduce children to quilts. Throughout the history of many countries, you will find quilting, an ancient craft. In American pioneer days, families and friends got together to make quilts for special occasions, such as weddings, births, and farewells to families moving West. This tradition continues today, and the act of quilting brings many adults together in friendship and sharing.

SUGGESTED BOOKS ARE

Bolton, J. (1994). *My grandmother's patchwork quilt. A book and pocketful of patchwork pieces.* New York: Doubleday Book for Young Readers.

Coerr, E. (1989). *The Josefina story quilt.* An I Can Read Book. Illustrated by B. Degen. New York: HarperTrophy.

Flournoy, V. (1985). *The patchwork quilt.* Illustrated by J. Pinkney. New York: Dial Books for Young Readers.

Franco, B. (1999). *Grandpa's quilt.* New York: Children's Press.

Hopkinson, D. (1993). *Sweet Clara and the freedom quilt.* Illustrated by J. Ransome. New York: Alfred A. Knopf.

Johnston, T., & de Paola, T. (1985). *The quilt story.* New York: Putnam.

Jonas, A. (1984). *The quilt.* New York: Greenwillow.

Polacco, P. (1988). *The keeping quilt.* New York: Simon and Schuster Books for Young Readers.

Waterstone, R. (1999). *The too much loved quilt.* Clarksville, TN: First Story.

The term *quilt* "refers to a fabric sandwich made of a top, bottom or backing, and a soft filler [batting] in between. The top consists of blocks arranged in a pattern. Each block may be a *patchwork,* that is—pieces of fabric cut in squares, rectangles, and other shapes and sewn together to form the block" (Parks, 1994).

Invite a quilter to visit your class. This individual can bring some handmade quilts and also show the children the three unfinished parts of a quilt—top, batting, and backing.

"The fascinating tradition of quilt-making can become an inclusive, engaging experience for children when the early childhood teacher considers a cross-curricular approach" (Helm, Huebner, & Long, 2000).

Your children may enjoy making a friendship quilt of single pieces of fabric or paper. To further illustrate this activity, there are several books that give information about family quilts. These selections offer opportunities for literature-based integrated curriculum. As you read one of the books during group time, pass a quilt around the circle of children. This is a tangible example of the abstract story you are reading. (Older children will be able to read the books by themselves or read them to younger children.)

These books, when shared with family members, stimulate the telling of family stories and, many times, the discovery of family quilts. The stories relate not only to families, but also to the multiple relationships within a family.

After you read the story, encourage the children to retell it by acting out the parts in small groups. You can extend the quilt to many learning centers. There are many projects that can promote the development of large and small muscle skills, as well as problem solving, socialization, cognitive development, language, and literacy abilities. The following are suggestions for these extended activities:

🌐 Develop a story or sequencing chart that diagrams the story line of the book. This can be a way of developing how the story can be reenacted.

🌐 Ask the children open-ended questions, such as "Do you have a quilt at your house?" "Would you like to make a paper quilt in the art center?" "Do you want to write your story about a quilt in the writing center?" "Would you help me collect fabric to make new squares for our class quilt?" "How do you think we can find the fabric?" "Who should we ask to help us?" "Would you like to make a quilt for the doll bed?"

🌐 Explore color in the science center. Children can mix colors, look through kaleidoscopes, or dye their own fabrics (Helm, Huebner, & Long, 2000).

🌐 Place a "quilt box" in the manipulative area containing an assortment of fabric squares (all the same size) with snaps or Velcro on each corner (top and bottom). A child can snap pieces together to make his own quilt, or several children can do this activity together. Some of the squares should have different patterns and shapes on the fabric.

🌐 Each child can design and paint a paper square for the classroom quilt. Patch the painted squares together with clear tape. Then place the completed quilt on the wall outside the classroom to share with the parents and other children.

🌐 Put washable paint of several skin-tone colors into individual shallow aluminum pans, and let each child make a single handprint on a piece of paper (white or yellow). Cut out each handprint and glue it onto a precut, individual square of construction paper. Let each child label his handprint with his name. Make holes in the corners of each square and use brightly colored yarn to lace the squares together. Hang this "quilt" in the classroom so that the children can daily enjoy seeing their art displayed.

🌐 "Our Family Quilt" in the form of a bulletin board can be made by mounting photographs of the children on squares of fabric. Add the children's dictated comments to the squares. A variation of this bulletin board can be to make a "Family Tree," with the photographs added as leaves of a tree.

🌐 During group time, discuss with the children activities that they enjoy doing with their families. They can draw pictures of what they like to do best.

Making the Class into a Neighborhood

Another, more complex social studies theme and series of activities is making the entire classroom into a neighborhood. This can be a creative follow-up to a walking trip around the neighborhood. It requires careful planning with the children to decide on how to do this, which will then indicate to the teacher what supplies, materials, and props will be needed for each area. Each learning activity center can be restructured into a part of the neighborhood, such as a home, construction site, fire station, grocery store, or other business establishment in the community. This all-encompassing plan benefits the physical, intellectual, social, emotional, and language development of all the children. The neighborhood concept connects children to their immediate world and brings about a feeling of community.

Figure 7–10 is the curriculum planning web worksheet with social studies activities added. This worksheet, with appropriate additions, is included in each chapter.

Children enjoy creating buildings designed like those in the neighborhood.

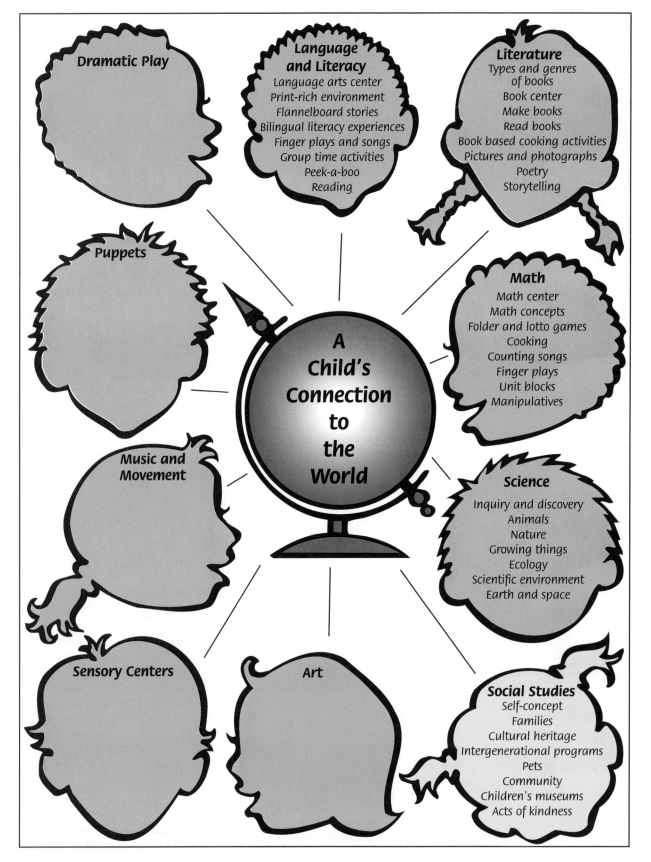

Dramatic Play

Language and Literacy
Language arts center
Print-rich environment
Flannelboard stories
Bilingual literacy experiences
Finger plays and songs
Group time activities
Peek-a-boo
Reading

Literature
Types and genres
of books
Book center
Make books
Read books
Book based cooking activities
Pictures and photographs
Poetry
Storytelling

Puppets

Math
Math center
Math concepts
Folder and lotto games
Cooking
Counting songs
Finger plays
Unit blocks
Manipulatives

A Child's Connection to the World

Music and Movement

Science
Inquiry and discovery
Animals
Nature
Growing things
Ecology
Scientific environment
Earth and space

Sensory Centers

Art

Social Studies
Self-concept
Families
Cultural heritage
Intergenerational programs
Pets
Community
Children's museums
Acts of kindness

FIGURE 7–10
A curriculum planning web worksheet with social studies activities added.

✳ AFTERVIEW

Through social studies activities, a child

🌐 learns about his world and his place in it.

🌐 identifies his family members and the multiple relationships within the family.

🌐 develops an awareness of his own cultural heritage as well as the traditions of others.

🌐 learns about other people who live in the world with him.

🌐 explores the geography, lifestyles, customs, and languages of other people.

🌐 explores his neighborhood and community and the resources within them.

🌐 participates in the democratic society of his classroom, school, and family.

🌐 has opportunities to learn firsthand about differences and similarities of classmates and other people in his world.

🌐 develops a positive self-concept and an acceptance of others.

🌐 participates in field trips within his neighborhood and wider community to learn about people, places, occupations, and resources.

✳ KEY TERMS

anthropology	geography	social sciences
culture	history	sociology
economics	psychology	

✳ EXPLORATIONS

1. Using the information in this chapter, survey the resources available in your community, and plan (on paper) an appropriate field trip for a group of preschoolers. Select a specific location, visit the site, and follow all the procedures of preparation as if you were actually going to take the children on the field trip. Share this information with your classmates or colleagues.

2. Invite a parent of a young child or other person from the community to share with your class his interests, occupations, talents, and other information about himself. If he is from another country, he can share his personal experiences, languages, and traditions. If the person is from a community organization, museum, or service agency that would be interesting to visit, find out what arrangements need to be made to take a group of children to visit that person where he works.

3. Observe an early education classroom that is participating in an intergenerational program. Describe what activities the older adult and the children were involved in. Interview the individual and get first-hand information about how the program works, what he thinks about participating in the program with young children, and what personal goals he is fulfilling. Share this information with the class or colleagues.

4. Select an early education classroom and observe for at least one hour. List at least ten items in the environment that relate to social studies activities, and describe one social studies activity in which the children were actively involved. How did the teacher introduce the activity, and what were his goals? If you are already teaching, evaluate your own classroom, list the items, and describe one social studies activity.

5. Visit a neighborhood with which you are not familiar. This can be residential or commercial or a combination of both. Write down everything you observe (objective). Write down everything you feel (subjective). Relate this to how a person coming to your community from another country or another state might feel when first visiting this neighborhood or coming to live here. Summarize your findings.

✳ REFERENCES

Bredekamp, S., & Copple, C. (Eds.). (1997). *Developmentally appropriate practice in early childhood programs.* (Rev. Ed.). Washington, DC: NAEYC.

Church, E. B. (1994, November–December). Learning from our elders. *Early Childhood Today, 9*(3), 40–41.

Cunningham, B. (1994, September). Portraying fathers and other men in the curriculum. *Young Children, 49*(6), 4–13.

Day, B. (1994). *Early childhood education* (4th ed.). Upper Saddle River, NJ: Merrill.

Elkind, D. (2001, Summer). A place for us: Children's museums in a child unfriendly world. *Hand to Hand: Newsletter of the Association of Children's Museums, 15*(2), 1–2, 6.

Feeney, S., Christensen, D., & Moravcik, E. (2001). *Who am I in the lives of children?* (6th ed.). Upper Saddle River, NJ: Merrill.

Helm, J., Huebner, A., & Long, B. (2000, May). Quiltmaking: A perfect project for preschool and primary. *Young Children, 55*(3), 44–49.

Johnson, H. H. (1994, September). The bodyworks: Inside me—Another approach to alike and different. *Young Children, 49*(6), 21–26.

Kostelnik, M. J., Soderman, A. K, & Whiren, A. P. (2007). *Developmentally appropriate curriculum: Best practices in early childhood education.* (4th ed.). Upper Saddle River, NJ: Prentice Hall.

Leipzig, J., (1993, May–June). Community field trips. *Pre-K Today, 78*(8), 44–51.

Mayesky, M. (2006). *Creative activities for young children* (8th ed.). Clifton Park, NY: Thomson Delmar Learning.

Mindes, G. (2006). Social studies in kindergarten. *K today: Teaching and learning in the kindergarten year.* Gullo, D. F. (Ed.). Washington, DC: NAEYC.

Mindes G. (2005, September). Social studies in today's early childhood curricula. *Young Children, 60*(5), 12–18.

National Association for the Education of Young Children (NAEYC). (1996, January). NAEYC position statement responding to linguistic and cultural diversity. *Young Children, 52*(2), 4–12.

National Council for the Social Studies. (1994). *Expectations for excellence: Social studies* (Bulletin 89). Washington, DC: Author. On-line at: http://www.socialstudies.org/standards

Parks, L. (Ed.). (1994, Spring). Make a friendship quilt. *Texas Child Care, 17*(4), 22–28.

Ramsey, P. G. (1987). *Teaching and learning in a diverse world.* New York: Teachers College Press.

Redleaf, R. (1983). *Open the door, let's explore: Neighborhood field trips for young children.* St. Paul, MN: Redleaf Press.

Robles de Melendez, W., Beck, V., & Fletcher, M. (2000). *Teaching social studies in early education.* Clifton Park, NY: Thomson Delmar Learning.

Seefeldt, C. (2001). *Social studies for the preschool–primary child* (6th ed.). Upper Saddle River, NJ: Merrill.

Seto, K. (1999). *Getting ready to teach second grade.* Torrance, CA: Frank Schaffer.

Silliman, B., & Royston, K. (1990, Fall). Working with parents. *Dimensions of Early Childhood, 19*(1), 15–18.

Sinker, M., & Russell, I. (1998, Summer). Describing for play. *Hand to Hand: Newsletter of the Association of Children's Museums, 12*(2), 3–4, 10.

Stamp, L. N., & Groves, M. M. (1994, Winter). Strengthening the ethic of care: Planning and supporting family involvement. *Dimensions of Early Childhood, 22*(2), 5–9.

Taylor, B. J. (1999). *A child goes forth* (9th ed.). Upper Saddle River, NJ: Merrill.

Teaching Tolerance Project. (1997). *Starting small.* Montgomery, AL: Southern Poverty Law Center.

Wallace, M. (2006). *Social studies: All day, everyday in the early childhood classroom.* Clifton Park, NY: Thomson Delmar Learning.

Wortham, S. C. (2006). *Early childhood curriculum: Developmental bases for learning and teaching.* (4th ed.). Upper Saddle River, NJ: Prentice Hall.

✳ ADDITIONAL READINGS AND RESOURCES

Briody, J., & McGarry, K. (2005, September). Using social studies to ease children's transitions. *Young Children, 60*(5), 38–42.

Cohen, L., & Blagojevic, B. (2002, September). Observing the whole child. *Early Childhood Today, 17*(1), 38–47.

D'Addesio, J., Grob, B., Furman, L., Hayes, K., & David, J. (2005, September). Learning about the world around us. *Young Children, 60*(5), 50–57.

Evitt, M. F. (2002, November–December). Raising a caring and compassionate child. *Parent and Child, 10*(3), 38–42.

Feeney, S., & Moravcik, E. (2005, September). Children's literature: A window to understanding self and others. *Young Children, 60*(5), 50–57.

Friedman, S. (2005, September). Social studies in action. *Young Children, 60*(5), 44–47.

Gestwicki, C. (2007). *Home, school, and community relations* (6th ed.). Clifton Park, NY: Thomson Delmar Learning.

Maxim, G. W. (2003, Fall). Let the fun begin! Dynamic social studies for the elementary school classroom. *Childhood Education, 80*(1), 2–5.

Root-Bernstein, M., & Root-Bernstein, R. (2001, Spring). Imagination and the museum. *Hand to Hand: Newsletter of the Association of Children's Museums, 16*(1), 2–4.

Washington, V. (2002, Summer). A vision shared. Hand to Hand: Newsletter of the Association of Children's Museums, 16(2), 7.

West, M. W. (2001, November). Teaching the third culture child. *Young Children, 56*(6), 27–32.

Whitin, P. (2001, September). Kindness in a jar. *Young Children, 56*(5), 18–22.

For additional information on early education curriculum, visit our Web site at http://www.earlychilded.delmar.com

CHAPTER 8

ART

OBJECTIVES

AFTER STUDYING THIS CHAPTER, YOU SHOULD BE ABLE TO:

- 🌐 Identify how art contributes to physical, cognitive, social, emotional, perceptual, and language development.

- 🌐 Discuss children's developmental stages in art.

- 🌐 Describe how a teacher establishes an environment for creative expression and experimentation.

- 🌐 Identify guidance guidelines for art in an early childhood classroom.

- 🌐 Explain why an aesthetic environment is important for young children and include tips for displaying their art.

- 🌐 Identify and give examples of the forms of art that are developmentally appropriate for early childhood children, including multicultural/anti-bias activities.

- 🌐 Explore adaptations for special needs and the use of technology in conjunction with art for young children.

- 🌐 Summarize how children's artistic growth can be assessed, with emphasis on portfolio authentic assessment.

OVERVIEW

As we begin this chapter, it is important to understand that a child's art—or artwork, as some educators call it—belongs to the child. Her awareness that she can produce something is critical to a child's development of a sense of self (Baghban, 2007). No adult interpretations or descriptions can, or should, describe what a child has created. This is part of the child's own process of communication and creativity.

Fortson and Reiff (1995) explain further:

> *When a young child brings to you, a teacher or parent, something made through desire, effort, and originality (a scribbled drawing, a bulky shape squeezed out of clay, or a splash of bold colors), this child is intuitively attempting to bring into being a type of relationship that lies at the very core of living. When bringing to you a "creation," however simple or strange, this child is unconsciously saying, "Here is a part of myself I am giving you."*

The first time a child makes a mark with a crayon, dips a brush into paint, or glues colored circles onto paper is the birth of a *creative process.* A child's blank sheet of paper soon becomes a creation that never existed before. This sensory event involving paints, crayons, and glue enables the child to freely experience the sheer pleasure of getting to know herself in a new way—through self-expression, "a way of communicating nonverbally with others" (Libby, 2000).

Art is *fundamental* to the growth of a child and an integration of many skills and basic experiences that begin at home and are continued and expanded in early childhood programs. **Art** is *visual* communication through the elements of color, line, shape, and texture instead of words. Smith, Fucigna, Kennedy, and Lord (1993) call it "graphic language." Art is *developmental,* and its contributions can be seen in physical, cognitive, social, and emotional development.

Physical development involves children using large muscles (gross motor development) in activities such as easel painting or clay pounding; manipulating small muscles (fine motor development) in actions such as fingerpainting or cutting; developing eye-hand coordination (using eyes and hands at the same time) through involvement with all types of materials; and acquiring self-help skills (gaining control over what the body can do) by freely manipulating materials to create expressions in art.

Cognitive development relates to children making art forms that represent and clarify how they see the world; finding new ways to problem solve with art materials and supplies; experimenting with cause and effect by asking, "What happens if?"; comparing sizes and shapes; and predicting outcomes through their involvement with art activities. All of these projects actively stimulate cognitive development for young children.

Social and emotional development in art consists of children developing positive images of themselves; expressing personality and individualism; representing imagination and fantasy; establishing enjoyable relationships with others; and expressing feelings by using as their "vocabulary" paints, paper, pencils, chalk, clay, fabrics, and other media while participating in developmentally appropriate art activities.

Language development is included in cognitive and social development as children clarify color, size, shape, texture, and patterns while talking about their art and the art of others. For example, when a toddler picks out a piece of velvet from the art materials box and asks you to "'sof ' it," in her stage of telegraphic speech she is saying to you, "Touch it and feel how soft it is!" Older children are introduced to new words when they pound the clay, make brush strokes, create a design, and make an arrangement of lines and patterns. Koster (2005) believes that "art is the first written language."

Perceptual development occurs when children use their senses to learn about the nature of objects, actions, and events. Koster (2005) explains,

---

art

Visual communication through the elements of color, line, shape, and texture instead of words.

physical development

Type of development involving children using large muscles, manipulating small muscles, developing eye-hand coordination, and acquiring self-help skills.

cognitive development

The mental process that focuses on how children's intelligence, thinking abilities, and language acquisition emerge through distinct ages; Piaget's study of children's thinking, involving creating their own mental image of the world, based on encounters with the environment.

social and emotional development

Type of development consisting of children developing positive images of themselves, expressing personality and individualism, representing imagination and fantasy, establishing enjoyable relationships with others, and expressing feelings.

language development

Developmental process of a predictable sequence that includes both sending and receiving information. It is related, but not tied, to chronological age.

perceptual development

Type of development in which children use their senses to learn about the nature of objects, action, and events.

Teachers need to provide experiences that are sensually rich and varied, and which require children to use their perceptual abilities in many different ways. Observational and visual perception skills are heightened as children use their senses to study the patterns, colors, textures, and shapes found in nature and in the artwork of others.

As we continue through this chapter, we will look at how the developmental stages relate to specific art activities for infants, toddlers, preschoolers, and primary school children. Creating an environment that values artistic expression and encourages children's creativity and experimentation is the focus of your role as teacher, facilitator, and observer. As one child suggested, "Let's do some arting today!"

CHILDREN'S DEVELOPMENTAL STAGES IN ART

"Stages in artistic development do not have discrete beginnings and endings in the developmental sequence, but rather children exhibit a tendency to move back and forth between stages as they learn and grow" (Taunton & Colbert, 2000). This includes not only the physical, cognitive, social, emotional, perceptual, and language development of each child; it also accounts for "social, cultural, religious, individual and environmental factors in tracing the development of child art" (Schirrmacher, 2006).

A teacher can recognize characteristics that are identifiable to help in understanding the needs and interests of the children in an early childhood program. Understanding what has come before helps in knowing what to look for as the child matures.

[Howard] Gardner's writings [1983] have stimulated new interest in the arts and their importance in the development of children. The theory of multiple intelligence recognizes that children may be talented in specific areas and learn in different ways. For some children, art may be the way they learn the best; for others, it may be a new way to experience the world. (Isbell & Raines, 2007)

Infants and Toddlers

Art is a sensory experience for infants and toddlers. The child uses her entire body when interacting with the art materials. The enjoyment for the child comes from this exploration.

Scribbling with crayons is more enjoyable with a friend.

Think about safety and appropriateness when selecting supplies and materials for this age. Younger children may be overwhelmed or overstimulated at first by too many choices, so start slowly and add items a few at a time. Crayons, fingerpaints, paints, paper, play dough, and water play should be available. The child needs opportunities to poke, pat, pound, shake, taste, smell, and scribble.

Transitions into and out of art activities are very important. The younger the child, the more verbal and visual clues are needed to help her move from one activity to another.

Flexibility, both inside and on the playground, is needed. This age child loves to water paint on the floor, table, brick wall, and sidewalk. Opportunities for experiencing color (add food coloring to the water or play dough), texture (art materials box or texture board), and temperature (warm water, cold play dough) can encourage a child to participate.

Scribbling begins around age two, but as with all developmental stages, it can begin earlier or later. The important thing is to supply the opportunity. "*Scribbles* are the building blocks of children's art. From the moment the child discovers what it looks like and feels like to put these lines down on paper, he has found something he will never lose, he has found art" (Kellogg & O'Dell, 1967).

Kohl (2003) observes,

Once or one is never enough for most toddlers. Repeat activities over and over and allow toddlers to make one or many art projects. The more they create the more they learn. If it won't work today, try it tomorrow. Being flexible, supportive and nurturing is the key to working with toddlers.

Expect an older infant and toddler to explore and manipulate art materials, but do not expect them to produce a finished art product (Bredekamp & Copple, 1997). See Figures 8–1, 8–2, 8–3, and 8–4 for infant and toddler drawings.

When using their fine motor skills to rub a crayon on paper or to make lines in sand or across a frosted window, toddlers learn that they can leave marks on these surfaces through their actions. Toddlers are pleased with their abilities and motivated to continue exploring scribbling. (Baghban, 2007)

FIGURE 8–1
Drawing made by a
14-month-old child.

FIGURE 8–2
Drawing made by an 18-month-old child.

FIGURE 8–3
Drawing made by a child 2 years,
6 months old.

FIGURE 8–4
Drawing made by a child 2 years,
6 months old.

Preschoolers and Kindergartners

From her research of two million pieces of children's art from 30 countries (Baghban, 2007), Rhoda Kellogg believed that these scribbles are meaningful to a child and should be valued by the adults in their environment (Kellogg, 1959). Kellogg's "20 Basic Scribbles" (vertical, horizontal, diagonal, circular, curving, waving, zigzag lines, and dots) continue to be discovered by preschoolers. Their art also shows them passing through the Placement Stage (definite patterns of scribbles placed in the left half, right half, center, or all over the page), into the Shape and Design Stages (combinations of scribbles forming definite shapes and designs), and then into the Pictorial Stage (structured designs that begin to look like something adults have seen before) around ages four and five (Kellogg & O'Dell, 1967).

The child enjoys exploration and manipulation of materials. Watch for a younger preschool child to paint her hands, for example. An older child still enjoys sensory experiences but will demonstrate this by experimenting with the materials in new and unusual ways. It is important for the child to develop control over the process. A child may even tear up her work during the process.

Art represents feelings and perceptions of a child's world. A child draws pictures and writes to organize ideas and construct meaning from her experiences (Baghban, 2007). The child creates what is important to her. A child uses colors that please her, and these colors may bear little relation to the actual colors of the objects created. An older preschooler creates forms and shapes, chooses materials carefully, and looks at the materials in new ways.

> A respect for the personal nature of the child's artwork means the teacher does not direct the process, but allows the child to proceed and experiment in the ways she deems appropriate. The child is able to create and combine materials in ways that the teacher may have never imagined. (Isbell & Raines, 2007)

See Figures 8–5 and 8–6 for children's drawings. See Figure 8–7 for Kellogg's 20 scribbles.

A child enjoys using her imagination. Copying a model changes the whole experience for her. A child who has used coloring books tends to lose the capacity to create naturally and individualistically. (This is discussed more fully later in this chapter.)

FIGURE 8–5
Drawing made by a child 4 years,
7 months old.

FIGURE 8–6
Drawing made by a child 4 years,
8 months old.

FIGURE 8–7
Representations of the
20 types of scribbles
identified by Rhoda
Kellogg. (Source: Isbell
and Raines, 2007, p.110)

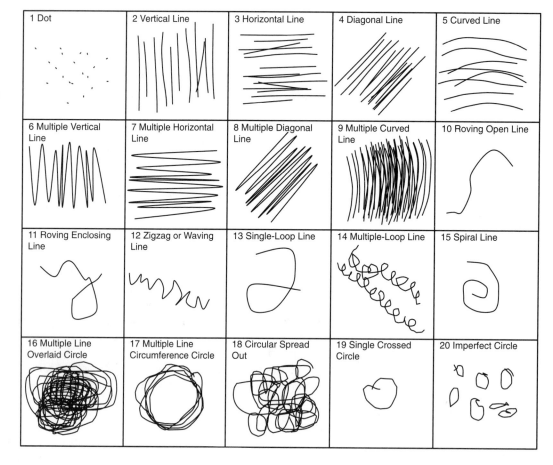

Five- to Eight-Year-Old Children

The child at this stage becomes more serious and focused in the art process. The child's early concrete experimenting and learning-by-doing art activities become a bridge to complex thinking. Realistic color and proportion are evident in the child's finished art. Careful planning is also becoming more apparent as part of the process. See Figures 8–8 and 8–9 for drawings.

FIGURE 8–8
Drawing made by a child
7 years, 5 months old.

FIGURE 8–9
Drawing made by a child 8 years,
10 months old.

The opinion of the adult observer becomes important. The child feels her art must be recognizable in both content and subject matter to the viewer. Often the child offers critical evaluation about her own work.

Schirrmacher (2006) explains further that primary children "want things to look right, to draw and paint things the way they appear in reality. They strive for photographic realism. . . . With increasing age, children become self-critical and succumb to peer pressure, internalizing hurtful comments which focus on their artistic shortcomings."

In a classroom situation, children will exhibit as many different levels of skill and creative ability as there are children in the room. If there is a child with a particular disability, he or she should be considered as just one more child in the room with a different skill level. (Libby, 2000)

TEACHER AS FACILITATOR AND OBSERVER

When you were young you probably had experiences, some of which were positive but some that were negative, concerning what teachers thought about *your* art. You should strive to be the kind of teacher the children in your care will remember as a positive and supportive influence in their lives.

In this chapter, as in all chapters of this book, you are asked to view what a child has created with different eyes than perhaps you have used before. Do not focus on the outcome or product: look at the process. Is the child participating, interacting, experimenting, exploring, and getting involved "up to the elbows"? This is what you should be observing as you plan, initiate, and evaluate the art center and art activities.

Your role as teacher is one of facilitator and observer. You set up the developmentally appropriate environment, furnish a variety of safe materials and supplies, provide opportunities for child-directed art experiences, and offer support and encouragement to the children as you observe their unique creations.

Approaching children's art from the perspective of facilitator can take any real or imagined pressures off of you *and* the children. For example, let the *children* decide whether to talk about their art or not talk about it. If they freely describe it and want you to write down a description, do so—otherwise *don't*.

Many times we try to get some response from the children and ask them to "Tell me about your picture" or "Tell me a story about what you're painting." This puts stress on the child to say what he or she thinks you want to hear. I overheard one child emphatically tell a teacher, "This is not a story! This is a picture to look at!" (That answer certainly made the teacher reflect on what she had asked the child.)

Make materials
available where
children can create
in an undisturbed
environment.

Some suggestions of what you could say should describe what you observe. Talk about the children's actions: "I see you used different colors in your picture." "You're feeling the fingerpaint, aren't you?" "You have a lot of dots on your paper today." "I see you covered the whole page." These statements and others like them do not ask for the child to "come up with an answer." This type of response from you offers affirmation and encouragement and avoids vague and extremely judgmental types of praise. "This is 'ART TALK' that infers 'show me' instead of 'tell me'" (Aulthouse, Johnson, & Mitchell, 2003).

Another part of your responsibility as a facilitator is to make materials available where children can create in an undisturbed environment. As you decide which activities and materials are appropriate, try them out yourself before you put them out for the children. This will enable you to introduce new supplies or materials comfortably and show the children how to use them appropriately. Once this is accomplished, step back and allow the children to investigate, explore, and try out the materials for themselves.

ESTABLISHING AN ENVIRONMENT FOR CREATIVE EXPRESSION AND EXPERIMENTATION

"An environment that nurtures artistic exploration is psychologically safe. It is a classroom where the teacher supports the children's creative efforts" (Isbell & Raines, 2007). "Creativity requires practice to flourish" (Schmirrmacher, 2006). *There is no right or wrong way to create!* We should value what the child is creating or attempting to create and provide many opportunities for her to do so. We should facilitate the development of creative thinkers and problem solvers. Setting up an appropriate art center is the first step in establishing this priority. "The simplest choices for teachers become major decisionmaking opportunities for children. What color paper to choose, what color crayons or paint, what shape and size of paper, which way to hold the paper are all options the child should have" (Szyba, 1999).

Young children learn by active involvement with people and by manipulating objects. It becomes clear that such activities as workbooks, worksheets, patterns, coloring books, stereotyped cutouts, and teacher-made models of art are not appropriate for young children (Bredekamp & Copple, 1997).

Lowenfeld (1972) explains further:

The art area should be
close to a sink for easy
cleanup.

In filling the outline drawings, children are regimented into the same type of activity, with no provision for their differences as individuals. . . . A child once conditioned to coloring books will have difficulties in enjoying the freedom of creating. The dependency which the coloring book creates is devastating.

For you as a teacher, you will find that making models and examples actually take more time and energy on your part than planning for developmentally appropriate art. The children will become more dependent on you to create patterns because they feel their creative expressions are not valued by you and therefore are unacceptable. Mayesky (2006) offers an additional thought:

If you do use an occasional model or example, it can function positively as a springboard to unlocking each child's own creative approach to a shared, common theme (or object). Many times, a brief look at one or two examples (which should not then be displayed for "copying" during the activity) can help motivate children to get started on making one of their own.

General Guidelines

As you plan or redesign your art center, provide *time, space,* and *materials* that allow children to work at their own pace without interference. The area should be large enough to accommodate the easels and art table. The art center should be a free-choice center, like the other centers in the classroom. The National Art Education Association (NAEA) states "We believe that children construct and reconstruct their own learning as they interact with their environment. This constructivist point of view places as much importance on *how* children think as on *what* children think" (quoted in Aulthouse, Johnson, & Mitchell, 2003).

- The art area should be close to a sink for easy cleanup. If this is not possible, place a bucket or plastic tub with warm soapy water nearby. Change the water often.
- Encourage the children to participate in all phases of an art activity, including preparation and cleanup. Have sponges and paper towels handy for the children to use. Protect the environment and the children so they do not have to be concerned about making a mess. Have smocks or aprons available for the children to wear during art activities.
- Continue to keep safety in mind as you select supplies and materials for the children to use in the art center. Select only nontoxic materials. Think carefully about using balloons in any project. They are fun but can be dangerous for young children, sometimes causing choking.
- It is important to think about using recycled materials, but a word of caution: *Do not reuse Styrofoam trays that have had meat or poultry on them.* Even after washing they may contain bacteria from the raw meat or poultry. Use clean, unused Styrofoam trays, which many grocery stores will give you at very little or no cost.
- Add several drops of liquid dishwashing soap to tempera paint. It washes out of clothes more easily and also prevents paint from chipping off the children's art when dry.
- A place for finished art should be provided. If they need to dry, plan ahead of time for a special drying place or hanging rack.
- Place the art center near a window, if possible, so the children can see outside while they are creating. Extend freedom of movement and free expression by allowing children to stand or sit at the art table as well as use the floor to spread out large sheets of paper for art activities.

- ⊙ Balance the activities: new with familiar, messy with clean, indoor with outdoor, large muscle and small muscle.
- ⊙ Children are fascinated by color, texture, shape, and design. You can attract the children to the art center by including activities that promote each of these. For example, invite the children to make a collage (pasting objects together onto a surface) of varying yellow colors found in magazines. This activity encourages preschoolers to cut, glue, look for, and discover that any color can have many shades.

Ⓖ Guidance Guidelines

"Good guidance begins with planning" (Hildebrand & Hearron, 1999). Clarify your goals and objectives for the art center and each art activity. Relate them to the theme and lesson plan when appropriate. (Review Chapter 2 for detailed information.)

Establish rules with the children concerning the care and use of art materials and limits within the art center. Guide them toward assuming responsibility for the use, care, and cleaning of materials and tools. Give visual and verbal clues as to the number of children allowed in the center at any given time. For example, put up a sign that shows three children with the numeral 3 written next to the figures of children (Figure 8–10).

Help children and their parents deal with being messy. Being messy is okay! Supply smocks or aprons on hooks near the art center. The children can be responsible for getting a smock, putting it on during an art activity, and putting it back when they have finished. Continue to repeat rules of the art center when necessary.

The type and number of materials supplied at one time should depend on the development and ages of the children involved in the activity as well as the number of children participating.

As you introduce each new activity or group of materials or supplies, explain the appropriate ways to use them. "[T]oo little structure can inhibit children's expression just as too-directed experience can. Children must clearly understand your expectations for the organized routines of working with art materials. Feeling *safe and stimulated* allows them to learn and grow" (Levinger & Mott, 1992).

For younger children, you will have to say, "Treat the paint (or the crayons, or the markers) gently," and probably repeat it many times. It is important to begin early to explain how art materials are to be used, and that they are not to be used to touch or hit others.

FIGURE 8–10
Visual clues help children understand rules and limits in the classroom.

Help all children learn to respect their own art and the art of others. Many times a cooperative art activity, such as painting a mural with each child having her own space on the paper, will demonstrate to a child how to focus on her own creation and not to interfere with others.

Give verbal or sound cues to let the children know when it will be time to clean up. Set a timer for five minutes and tell the children what you are doing. When it goes off, let them know it is time to clean up.

Use of Food in Art Projects

Using food in art activities with children is a continuing topic of discussion. Teachers and administrators are divided on this issue. I have found that not using food works better for the following reasons:

- It is difficult to justify using food when many parents are working long hours to put food on the table for their families. Food is expensive. Also, the casual use of food in art when many are homeless and hungry can be upsetting to some adults.

- The use of food in an art activity may offend some cultural groups who use that food item for religious or ethnic celebration (Schirrmacher, 2006).

- It is important *not* to use foods for art because toddlers are developing self-regulatory skills and must learn to distinguish between food and other objects that are not to be eaten (Bredekamp & Copple, 1997).

- Using cornstarch, flour, salt, and food coloring is acceptable because these are used in small amounts as additives to make play dough and other recipes for art.

- There are other alternatives for art projects. For example, instead of using macaroni, string together paper shapes with a hole punched in the middle or paper straws cut in various lengths. Sand or buttons can be glued instead of rice. Use cotton balls, Styrofoam, or toothpicks instead of beans for collages and textured art. It is fun to come up with other creative choices.

You will need to decide for yourself whether you want to use food in art projects or not. Consider your own values, economic factors, and the policies of your center or school.

Outdoor Environment

Take it all outdoors! Children enjoy the space and freedom offered by outdoor art activities. Take the easels, a table, long sheets of butcher paper, paints, and cleanup buckets outdoors. Let the children use chalk on the sidewalk; explore rocks, shells, flowers, trees, birds, and butterflies; go for walks and look for colors, textures, and shapes; and gather leaves for making rubbings or prints or for using as materials on paintings and collages.

> Nature excursions also can inspire creativity in artwork. Children can draw or paint pictures about their experiences. Collections of natural materials (berries for dyes; dried weed stalks for tracing or relief rubbings; acorns, seeds, sticks, and pebbles for collage) can be used to create artistic masterpieces. You may even find real clay to dig up and sculpt. (Humphryes, 2000)

If your playground has a chain link fence, it can be used as a drying area. Clothespins easily attach the paintings or murals to the fence. A safe drying area can also be arranged inside a large cardboard box. Plan for cleanup with buckets, hoses, and lots of paper towels. "Easy 'mess management' makes outdoor art inviting and enjoyable for everyone" (Jurek & MacDonald, 1990).

Chapter 9 offers additional ideas for outdoor activities with sand, water, and woodworking.

Aesthetic Environment

Jim Greenman (1987) captures the essence of environmental aesthetics in the following description:

> Imagine a room where there are bright splashes of color, often attached to moving bodies, and warm muted hues on carpet and walls. Sunshine catches the light of a prism in one corner, and there is a small patch of sunlight so bright you have to squint. There are soft indirect lights, shadows, and cool dark corners.
>
> There are hanging baskets of trailing green plants, flowers, pussy willows and cattails, angel hair and dried grasses. The beauty of life is captured by Monet and Wyeth and assorted four-year-olds.

aesthetic environment

An environment that cultivates an appreciation for beauty and a feeling of wonder and excitement of the world in which we live.

We can actively create such an **aesthetic environment** for children, one that cultivates an appreciation for beauty and a feeling of wonder and excitement of the world in which we live. We can do this by:

- designing indoor and outdoor environments to emphasize beauty, attention to detail, color, shape, textures, lines, and patterns in carefully thought-out space and arrangements.
- allowing time for looking at and talking about all kinds of art.
- providing beautiful books with all types of illustrations.
- introducing children to fine art by displaying prints of paintings and sculptures in the classroom (the water gardens of Monet, the mothers and children of Cassatt, the ballerinas of Degas, and the splashed action paintings of Pollock) and by visiting local galleries and museums.
- encouraging the aesthetic display of children's art in a classroom "museum," which offers an opportunity for the children to take turns being the **curator,** the person who decides what art to display and how to display it (Fox & Diffily, 2001).

curator

The person who decides what art to display and how to display it.

- hanging up objects that play with the light, including mobiles made of cellophane, papers, and children's art (Schirrmacher, 2006).
- including art, wall hangings, weavings, and tapestry from diverse cultures as part of the aesthetic room environment.
- exposing children to nature by allowing time to watch a spider spin a web or to look closely at a wildflower.

Young children enjoy the space and freedom offered by outdoor art activities.

🌐 supporting children's self-expression and creativity as they reflect the world around them.

🌐 involving and informing parents how art production and appreciation are integrated into curriculum areas and inviting them to participate in museum trips.

Additionally, Epstein (2001) emphasizes that:

> too often, early childhood practitioners limit art education to the making of art. But being artistic in the fullest sense also involves developing a sense of aesthetics. Enabling young children to appreciate art gives them another mode of learning through direct encounters with people (artists) and objects (the work they create).

INVOLVING CHILDREN IN ALL FORMS OF ART

Children involved with art develop sensory awareness, aesthetic appreciation, self-expression, and improve visual and motor coordination. The process of experimenting with and creating two- and three-dimensional projects from a variety of media connects children to another facet of their world.

Davidson (1996) tells us:

> When children are introduced to a new medium, they explore what can be done with it. The first time children use fingerpaints they will swish it, squish it, pile it in the middle, run it through their fingers, makes lines in it and experiment in other ways to see what they can do with this thick wet stuff. It is not until after this exploration that children will begin to use the materials imaginatively. . . . It is important to know what one can make a material do, to be in control of a material, before putting it to use as a tool to create something.

We see, time and again, a young preschooler put one color of paint on the easel paper and then place another color exactly on top of the first, and then continue this process until the result is a mass of "indescribable" color. The color is beautiful to the

WHY I TEACH YOUNG CHILDREN

It's natural instinct and craving for me to have young children in my life. Their laughter with each other keeps my days going and their curious natures keep me on my toes. Their expressions upon their new discoveries or a friend's hug, or solving the world's problems, like what color to make the play dough, remind me of the simple pleasures of life.

Their eyes let me see into their world. It's such a magical, exciting place to be. Teaching keeps what's important and real in my life.

— Bev Sandheinrich

child, and she has created it. This newfound ability to change color is important and exemplifies learning for the child. The older child paints masses of color next to each other and may surround the color with dots and shapes. Both exemplify the process of making art.

The emphasis throughout this chapter is on allowing appropriate time, space, and flexibility for creating; to give permission and responsibility to the children; and to nurture and value their creativity. This will provide children with many opportunities to move beyond investigation to using these materials in unique, imaginative, and individually creative ways.

Tearing, Cutting, and Gluing

Tearing, cutting, and gluing offer individual activities to young children and provide small muscle development and tactile experiences; offer opportunities for controlling scissors and direction of cutting for creative purposes; provide discovery of form, shapes, colors, sizes, and textures; develop eye-hand coordination; and encourage verbal communication and sharing.

Painting, in all its forms, provides opportunities for creative expression and developmental growth.

Let the children do the tearing, cutting, and gluing. Use white glue, school paste, flour and water paste, glue stick, masking tape, and clear tape. Pour white glue into small plastic squeeze bottles or pour small, individual amounts of glue into jar lids, small bowls, or other containers. Children can use cotton swabs or their fingers to manipulate and spread the glue. Supply a wet paper towel for each child to have at her place, or moisten a sponge that several children can share to wipe their fingers.

Children can tear and cut tissue paper, construction paper, fabric scraps, old greeting cards, wallpaper samples, newspapers, and catalogs. Glue these materials to construction paper, corrugated paper, all sizes of paper plates, index cards, box lids, brown wrapping paper, foil, or gift wrapping paper.

Painting

> *Painting, like talking and writing, is a way of expressing ideas and feelings. . . . Instead of words you use lines, colors, shapes, and arrangements. You can find these in every painting in the world. (New York Metropolitan Museum of Art, 1959)*

Painting, in all its forms, provides sensory experiences, allows for coordinated use of many body muscles, encourages language development, helps with the judgment of spatial relationships, provides an opportunity for manipulation and experimentation, develops form perception, is often a two-handed experience, and develops skill in handling a brush and other art materials and tools.

Painting develops skills that are used in reading and writing. The curves, patterns, and lines that children make are similar to letters and words. The awareness of spatial relationship and configurations on the page relates to reading skills. Distinguishing painted forms, lines, and patterns from the background requires the same discrimination as reading. When you read, you separate, or "pull out," letters from the background.

Organizing the art environment for painting will help make the activities successful for children. When fingerpainting, children can use the paint directly on the table top, on a table that is covered with butcher paper, or on individual pieces of paper. For younger children, place a spoonful or two of fingerpaint into plastic bags. Close the bags carefully and seal with tape to prevent leaks. Each process offers a different experience for children. They have direct sensory contact with the material. They create changeable patterns, designs, and shapes in a short amount of time while maintaining their interest for a long time. To preserve a table-top painting, blot the fingerpainting with a piece of butcher paper to get the reverse design that the child can keep.

Fingerpaints in many colors are commercially available. Selecting skin-tone colors offers young children another way to develop self-esteem. Other items to use as fingerpaints are toothpaste, cold cream, hand lotion, or wet sand.

Easel painting is popular with young children. Easels can be placed indoors or outdoors. If several are set up, place them close together. This encourages interaction and conversation between the painters. Easels should be the correct height for young children, washable, and sturdy, and should have a tray for holding containers of paint. You could also tape the easel paper to a wall indoors or a fence outdoors.

Furnish large sheets of easel paper or paper cut into different shapes, brushes (one for each color being used) in a wide variety of sizes, and a choice of colors. For younger children, it is helpful to start with one color at a time. Have them use the primary colors of red, blue, and yellow; the secondary colors of orange, purple, and green (the colors obtained by blending pairs of primary colors); and black, brown, and white. Mixing black or white with primary colors teaches pastel tints and grayed tones. Children quickly discover for themselves what happens when colors are mixed together.

To thicken paint, add liquid starch or cornstarch (children will need large brushes to paint with thick paint). A teaspoon of alcohol added to each pint of paint or a drop or two of oil of wintergreen will prevent the paint from souring.

Easel painting is popular with young children.

Young children enjoy spontaneous expression when painting on a mural or extra large piece of paper.

Before children start to paint, you may have to remind them to put on a smock or apron. After the children are through, let them wash the brushes with soap and water, shape them, and place them brush-end up in a container to dry. Additional things that can be used as brushes are paint rollers, pot scrubbers, sponges, feathers, toothbrushes, and fly swatters.

string painting

A type of painting that involves moving string dipped in paint around on paper to make a design.

String painting is another art activity that young children enjoy doing. If they want to move the string around the paper to make a design, you might first attach a button to one end of the string so that the children can hold the button to manipulate the string more easily.

They can also dip short lengths of string or yarn into bowls of paint mixed with a small amount of white glue (holding the string with a clothespin can help those children who do not want to get their fingers in the paint). They then lay the yarn or string onto a piece of construction paper to form a design. Children can vary the lengths of yarn, string, or twine to add texture to the painting. An extension of this activity for older children is to guide them into mixing four different shades of blue (or any other color) and then make a string painting with the various shades of color.

Children can fold a sheet of paper in half, then open it and place the paint-wet string on one side of the paper. Fold the other side of the paper over and hold it with one hand. Then gently pull the string through while holding the folded paper in place with the other hand. To complete this activity, younger children may need assistance from you or another child.

Children enjoy experimenting with object or gadget painting. Provide items such as kitchen utensils, forks, corks, sponges, pieces of wood, combs, and cookie cutters for dipping into paint or a paint pad (made by pouring thick tempera paint onto several layers of paper towels or a thin sponge). The children press the object down onto a piece of manila or colored construction paper. A unique print is the result.

Painting with feet offers another sensory experience for children. (This is an extension of hand painting.) Begin by covering the floor or outdoor sidewalk with newspaper, and then place long pieces of butcher paper or brown wrapping paper over the newspaper. Tape the corners so that the paper will stay in place. The children remove their shoes and socks and then stand at one end of the paper. Help them step into containers or tubs you have prepared with tempera paint. Paint is slippery, so you may need to assist some children as they walk on the paper. At the other end of the paper place a tub of warm, soapy water and some towels. After the children make their "feet design," they will end up by stepping into the tub of water (Figure 8–11). It makes a wonderful mural. This is a fun activity to do with parents as well. (I still remember the first time I did feet painting, when my oldest child was in preschool. It was a parent-child activity during an open house. I have used it many times since with children, parents, and teachers.)

Other types of painting for young children are fingerprint painting (walking fingers dipped in paint across paper), sand mixed with paint (gritty paint), salt and paint (sparkle paint), flour and paint (lumpy paint), ball or marble painting (dipped items rolled over paper placed in a box), painting on rocks, and painting with watercolors.

Crayons, Markers, and Chalk

Crayons and markers are familiar to most young children. They have used them at home and other places, such as at restaurants that welcome children to color on the paper table covering or on the children's menu. *Caution:* Young children should use only water-based markers, because permanent markers may contain toxic solvents. Chalk provides another type of drawing experience. All these materials are ready-to-use, easy to store, and require very little cleanup.

When using crayons, markers, and chalk, children utilize different types of muscular coordination than those they use to control a paintbrush or a finger. They also encourage exploration of what colors can do, provide an excellent prewriting experience, develop hand-eye coordination, and stimulate the imagination.

FIGURE 8–11
The feet-painting
process.

Scribbling, as discussed earlier in this chapter, is important to young children. Crayon scribbling is usually one of the first activities children enjoy doing over and over again. A sitting position makes it easier to control a crayon. Children often use pressure to make marks on the paper, so having large crayons available for younger children works well. Older children prefer the small crayons.

By starting with large sheets of paper, then moving on to all sizes, shapes, and textures of paper, you can extend the crayon scribbling and drawing activities. Using crayons on colored paper teaches children what happens when one color is applied to another.

Crayon rubbings can be introduced early in the year, then continued as the variety of objects to be rubbed changes throughout the year. To make a crayon rubbing of a texture, children place an object under newsprint or other type paper and rub with a crayon. (You might need to tape objects down on the table at first.) Rubbing the side of the crayon across the paper sometimes works best. Suggestions of objects to be rubbed: cardboard squares, circles, rectangles, triangles, and ovals; coins and leaves of various sizes and shapes; different textures of wallpaper; and bricks, tree barks, and sandpaper. (Let the children discover these and others.)

A favorite art activity of toddlers and preschoolers is to "draw a child." For the young ones, you can draw around each child lying on a large piece of paper. The older child chooses a partner, and they can draw around each other. Then each child colors herself. Face, hair, clothes, and shoes can be added with additional materials from the art materials scrap box (see Figure 8–12).

Crayon resist is an interesting art activity for older children. They can draw a picture on paper with light-colored crayons, then cover the picture with watercolors or thin tempera paint. The paint will cover all but the crayon markings. A variation of this project is for the children to place waxed paper over a sheet of white paper

crayon rubbings

Duplicating an object of texture by placing it under paper and rubbing over it with a crayon.

crayon resist

A type of art for older children that involves drawing a picture in light-colored crayons then covering the picture with watercolors or thin tempera paint. The paint will cover all but the crayon drawing.

FIGURE 8–12
An example of the "drawing a child" process.

and draw on it with a pencil, pressing wax lines and design into the bottom paper. They then remove the waxed paper and brush thin paint over the wax lines on the paper. A design of white lines will appear on the painted surface.

Younger children can develop their small muscle ability, which is necessary to hold and control a writing implement on their own, by using chalk. Offer them the opportunity to write with colored chalk on the sidewalk, on a large chalkboard placed inside or outside, or on small individual chalkboards.

For a wet chalk project (wet chalk provides an interesting texture different from dry chalk), have the children dip the chalk in a cup of water before writing on paper. Another way to do this is for the children to wet the paper, including paper plates, instead of the chalk. For big pictures and designs, sweep the sides of the chalk across the paper. The children can then mix the colors together by blending them with their fingers or with a tissue.

An additional way of using crayons, markers, and chalk is to attach these to an easel with yarn or string. The children can use these independently or can mix and match for self-discovery. Children can also copy printed words from books, rebus charts, and other printed material around the room. This will help with learning the left-to-right progression of letters in spelling and words for reading.

Three-Dimensional Materials

The sensory experience of handling and shaping a variety of materials encourages young children to experiment, explore, and discover original ways to create three-dimensional art. These activities can help children release emotional tensions and frustrations, work with their hands, develop small muscles, and provide opportunities to manipulate, construct, and learn about spatial relationships.

Three-dimensional art (having depth as well as height and width) is demonstrated through the use of play dough, clay, and "goop." These materials should be used on a surface that is easily cleaned and is large enough for children to have plenty of "elbow room." These materials should be soft enough for the children to manipulate easily, neither too wet nor too dry. Placing individual amounts of these materials on a tray, linoleum square, or manila folder for each child helps the children identify limits and gives them personal space. It is helpful to provide a bucket of water for the children to wash their hands when they are finished with the activity. This will keep the residue of the materials out of the sinks.

Play dough, clay, and goop are extremely valuable because the children are able to use the materials with their hands without having to learn how to manage a tool, such as a paintbrush. (Younger children do better with play dough because it is softer and easier to manipulate.) The children are concerned with managing the material and learning what they can do with it. You can add rolling pins, cookie cutters, or other

three-dimensional art
Any art form that has three sides. Play dough and clay are examples of three-dimensional materials.

accessories after the children have had a lot of time to handle and experience the feel of the clay or dough. Many classrooms have both commercial clay and play dough. In others, the teachers prefer to make these materials themselves. You might want to supply both to the children.

The following is the recipe for cooked play dough (do not eat). You can make this first and then give it to the younger children. You and the older children can make it together so they can see the process.

COOKED PLAY DOUGH

1 cup flour	1 tablespoon cooking oil
1/2 cup salt	2 teaspoons cream of tartar
1 cup water	

Mix the above ingredients. Heat and stir over low heat until the mixture forms a ball. Remove from heat and wrap in waxed paper to cool. Knead it well. Store in an airtight container. The dough will last much longer if kept in the refrigerator. Add food coloring, if desired. (Some teachers put the food coloring in before cooking; others add color after cooking so the children can see the change from white, to marbled, to the final color.) For more play dough, just double the recipe.

The following is the recipe for uncooked play dough (do not eat). For younger children, give it to them already made. Let the older children make it with your guidance.

UNCOOKED PLAY DOUGH

1 cup flour	food coloring (optional)
1/2 cup salt	1 tablespoon salad oil

Mix flour and salt. Add oil. Slowly add water until the mixture sticks together but does not feel sticky. Add more water if too stiff, add more flour if too sticky. Knead it well. Store in airtight container.

The recipe for goop follows.

GOOP

1/2 box to 1 box of cornstarch
water

Add water slowly to cornstarch until it is semifirm. Mix it with your hands (or let the children help you). You can feel and see the changes in the texture. Store covered in the refrigerator. As it becomes dry from storage and handling, simply add more water.

Other three-dimensional works of art can be made into the form of sculptures by adding the following materials: toothpicks, Styrofoam, boxes, pieces of wood, egg cartons, paper towels, and toilet paper rolls.

ART AS A STIMULUS FOR OTHER CURRICULUM AREAS

Try connecting art to everything you do. For example, children can listen to music and draw or paint in rhythm to the music. They can express in their creations how the music makes them feel. Verbal and nonverbal language is expressed through art. As pointed out earlier in this chapter, children learn to include an art vocabulary into their everyday conversations with other children and adults. They express and represent what they know through their art. The art activities discussed in this chapter also give children an understanding of themselves and others. Their study of artists and their visits to art galleries and museums help them relate to their community and to the world.

CHILDREN'S BOOKS FEATURING ART, ARTISTS, AND ILLUSTRATORS

These books for young children encourage them to create their own illustrations using a variety of techniques, as demonstrated by the artists and illustrators in the following examples:

Blake, Q. (2001). *Tell me a picture.* Brookfield, CT: Millbrook Press.

Carle, E. (2002). *The art of Eric Carle.* New York: Philomel

Carle, E. (1980). *The very hungry caterpillar.* New York: Collins World.

Ehlert, L. (1988). *Planting a Rainbow.* New York: Harcourt.

Ehlert, L. (1987). *Growing Vegetable Soup.* New York: Harcourt.

Muhlberger, R. (1993). *What makes a Degas a Degas?* New York: The Metropolitan Museum of Art and Viking.

Muhlberger, R. (1993). *What makes a Monet a Monet?* New York: The Metropolitan Museum of Art and Viking.

Muhlberger, R. (1993). *What makes Rembrandt a Rembrandt?* New York: The Metropolitan Museum of Art and Viking.

Muhlberger, R. (1993). *What makes a Van Gogh a Van Gogh?* New York: The Metropolitan Museum of Art and Viking.

Scieszka, J., & Smith, L. (2005). *Seen Art?* New York: Viking.

Venezia, M. (1990). Getting to know the world's greatest artists: Mary Cassatt. Chicago, IL: Children's Press.

Weitzman, J. P., & Glasser, R. P. (2002). *You can't take a balloon into the Museum of Fine Arts.* New York: Dial Books.

Williams, K. L. (1998). *Painted dreams.* New York: Lothrop, Lee & Shepard Books.

Wood, A. (2000). *The Napping House.* (Board Book). Illustrator: Don Wood. New York: Harcourt.

Williams (1995) suggests that math and art content can be combined on a regular basis. For example: the math concepts of problem solving, inventing patterns, measurement, sorting, and classifying relate to the art concepts of awareness of line and shape, decoration of line and pattern, and awareness of texture and changing shape.

Schirrmacher (2006) points out that children quantify art materials, equipment, and supplies by counting the number of brushes and jars of paint that are in use and by deciding which brushes have longer handles, which crayons are fatter, and which geometric shapes are being used in their art creations.

Many scientific principles have already been discussed in this chapter, including:

- discovering what a specific material can do and what the child can do to control it
- observing what happens when colors are mixed together
- noticing what happens when flour and water are combined
- experimenting with thick paint and thin paint
- discovering what happens when you press down hard or lightly with a brush or crayon on paper

🌐 observing what happens when paint is brushed over a crayon picture

🌐 determining what occurs when different ingredients are mixed together

🌐 setting up a "discovery table" with art materials such as paper of different shapes and colors, clay, and other art media that can be integrated into any subject that is being discussed in the classroom

Art activities are one of the best ways to promote literacy and brain development in early childhood. Early childhood is an especially important time for hands-on, self-directed learning. Art engages children's senses in open-ended play; develops cognitive, social-emotional, and multisensory skills; and provides children with authentic self-expression. (Reyner, 2002)

SHARING A CHILD'S ART: ENCOURAGING FAMILY SUPPORT

Another part of the teacher's role is to help parents understand that the many pages or examples of art the children bring home are the results of creative and imaginative processes—all of them from the children. If the family understands *why* art is valued in the early childhood setting, they can more easily offer support to their child at home.

You can also guide the parents into setting up a special place at home for their child to continue experimenting and creating with art. Send home suggestions and lists of what materials and supplies are appropriate as well as explanations of what she has been doing in the classroom. *Interpret the child's developmental progress to the parents, not what the child's art is or is not.*

As you share the children's art and activities with the families, ask each family to share with you. Invite them to bring in any of the art their children create at home. Some may want to take photographs at home showing the child and family member involved with the activity. Start a "Family Art" section on your parent bulletin board.

 ### Special Needs

It is important to explain to the families of a child with special needs how their child participates in art activities.

Because of the open-ended nature of well-designed art activities, children with special needs can participate fully in most art programs, often without many modifications. If necessary, changes can be made in the tools and environment to allow active participation. The other children also need to be encouraged to accept and support those with special needs. (Koster, 2005)

For example, Koster (2005), Schirrmacher (2006), and special needs educators suggest the following:

🌐 Put trays across wheelchairs.

🌐 Provide wheelchair-height tables.

🌐 Place a stool under the table so that a child sitting in a regular child-size chair who cannot reach the ground will be able to rest her feet on the stool and stabilize her body. This stability helps children more easily use their fine motor skills.

🌐 Wrap art tools such as crayons, markers, pencils, and brushes in foam hair curlers to improve grip.

🌐 Use scented crayons and markers.

🌐 Provide many tactile materials.

🌐 Tape papers to the table to keep them from wrinkling or moving when the children are using them.

🌐 Use contact paper or other sticky paper as the backing for collages. The child only has to put things on paper. This eliminates the difficulty of gluing and pasting for some children.

🌐 Lower the easel and give a child a chair if she has difficulty standing at an art easel.

🌐 Ensure access to appropriate technology for children with special needs, whom assistive technologies may be essential for successful inclusion.

🌐 Use computer voice-text software that allows children to both receive and produce written communication, either with words or symbols.

🌐 Use adaptive peripherals, usually special switches or hardware that plug into the computer. This can provide alternatives for children unable to use a mouse or keyboard.

TIPS FOR DISPLAYING CHILDREN'S ART

As you send the children's art home, remember to save some of the creations to place around the classroom, with the child's permission, of course. The early education environment should reflect the children, and a wonderful way to do this is to display their art. (This also actively creates an aesthetic environment, as previously discussed in this chapter.)

Your goal is not to display children's "best" work, but to represent all the styles and levels created in your room, from scribble shapes to detailed portraits. When you do this, you send a clear message that you truly respect children's individual artistic expressions. (Feinburg, 1993)

Children's display of prints.

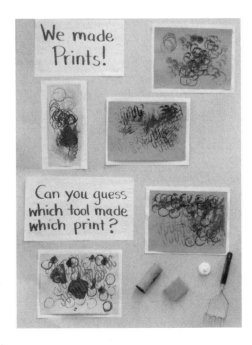

Displays show the parents what is happening in their child's classroom. Provide a place with wall and table displays outside the classroom in a hall or lobby for parents' enjoyment.

Art should be displayed at the child's eye level. Frame children's art attractively in a variety of ways using colored paper, wallpaper, or gift wrap as a background; rick-rack, fabric, or yarn to outline pictures; and a large group fingerpainting to serve as a mounting for individual art. Taking the time and effort to mat and frame the children's art is another way to show that you value what they have done.

Display all kinds of children's creations (clay models, Styrofoam structures, mobiles, wood sculpture, and collages). These kinds of art can be displayed on tables or shelves and arranged attractively on brightly colored paper. With permission, place the child's name in the upper left-hand corner to encourage left to right eye movement and to encourage the children to sign their art work. Change the art displays frequently. Let the children help decide when to change the selections and what to put up next. Arrange art in different kinds of groupings, such as several art items belonging to an individual child, several pictures that share the same colors, pictures with the same theme created from different media, and art connected to the theme or lesson plan of the week (see Figure 8–13).

FIGURE 8–13
A kiosk is a self-standing display with three or more sides.

An art kiosk is a workable solution to limited wall space. A kiosk is a self-standing display with three or more sides. It can be constructed of panels of sturdy cardboard, wood, or stacked cartons. It is space-efficient in that many pictures can be simultaneously displayed on a number of sides in a few feet of floor space. (Schirrmacher, 2006)

Feinburg (1993) sums it all up for us. "Just as photographs of children tell us much about what children look like on the outside, their art work tells us—boldly!—what they look like on the inside."

TECHNOLOGY

TECH   The use of technology in conjunction with art expands the classroom environment and creates new expressions for children's art. Aulthouse and colleagues (2003) suggest the following:

🌐 *Overhead projector:* Children can place color paddles, colored tissue paper, or cellophane on the overhead projector to find out what happens to light and color.

🌐 *Cameras:* Digital or inexpensive one time-use cameras can immediately document children's art activities. Taking photographs is yet another way for children to explore their world. Computers, printers, and scanners streamline this process and allow for flexibility with image size.

🌐 *Photocopier:* Children and teachers can also enlarge photographs on a color copier to display the pictures taken of their art.

🌐 *Videotapes:* These tapes of children's activities can show not only how children are engaged in art, but also how art can be integrated into all learning centers.

🌐 *Computer technology:* Children can use computers for word processing as they write and illustrate books. When selecting computer tools to use with art, it is important to use software that allows a child to design the art and control the creation of the pictures or illustrations. There are paint programs available for young children. Schirrmacher (2006) suggests, "Try viewing computer art as one component of your art program rather than as a replacement of all hands-on art experiences in your classroom."

Isbell and Raines (2007) help us understand how to choose appropriate software for art, especially with many different computer programs available for children.

1. The child is able to determine what will be drawn.
2. Options are available for creating lines, forms, colors, and making changes.
3. Different drawing tools can be used to change the texture, size, and proportion of the drawing.
4. The child's name and title/description can be added.

Different types of software have different effects. Open-ended programs foster cooperation and collaboration which, in turn, encourage children to be active participants. The pace should be set by the child and not the software program (Mayesky, 2006). (See Chapter 9, Sensory Centers, for more information relating to computers.)

DEVELOPMENTALLY APPROPRIATE AND MULTICULTURAL/ ANTI-BIAS ACTIVITIES

We could learn a lot from crayons…some are sharp, some are pretty, and some are dull. Some have weird names, and all are different colors, but they ALL have to live in the same box. (Anonymous)

A book, first introduced in 1955, that is one of the most popular ones for both children and teachers is Crockett Johnson's *Harold and the Purple Crayon.* You can use this imaginative story as a springboard for many art activities in an early childhood program. For example:

🌐 Read the book to the children at group time. Ask the children to think of other things Harold can do with his purple crayon. At the next group time introduce a flannelboard story that has Harold as the main character doing some of the things the children suggested.

🌐 In the art center place only purple items, such as crayons, markers, and construction paper. This is a creative way to introduce children to all the different shades of purple. Let the children experiment with paints and problem solve which ones to mix together to make purple. Also have purple play dough available for creative play.

🌐 For their snack you can serve purple grapes, or introduce the children to eggplant or other purple foods.

🌐 The children will also suggest other purple things to do.

For older children, you can use a self-awareness and self-expression activity called "The Me Bag" and suggested by Aronson (1995). Give the children a plain brown paper grocery bag to decorate any way they choose. They then are to take the bag home and fill it with things that are important to them, things they value and are proudest of. The next day they bring the bag back and talk about what is in it.

Aronson (1995) explains further:

> *Although each bag looks different, they all contain precious items. Children learn that the things that make them unique are as valuable as the things they have in common. They learn to appreciate differences rather than fear them. And they learn to see themselves as others might see them: as individuals with their own enthusiasms and cultural traditions, neither better nor worse than others.*

The following activities offer opportunities for sharing other cultures with the children in an early education program:

🌐 Each March 3, Japanese girls celebrate *Hina Matsuri* (HEE-nah maht-SOO-ree), or the Doll Festival. On this day the family's collection of ceremonial dolls, many of which are handed down from generation to generation, are placed on display. The girls themselves are also honored on this day (Milord, 1992).

🌐 Each May in Japan, the skies are filled with flying fish, carp-shaped windsocks hung high from bamboo poles in honor of young boys. This special occasion is called *Tango no sekku* (tahn-goh noh SEH-koo). It is celebrated on the fifth day of the fifth month (Milord, 1992).

Both of these special celebration days suggest exciting art projects in an early education classroom. The younger children can bring in their dolls or stuffed animals to share. Simple commercial kites or windsocks can be hung around the room to brighten the environment. Japanese music can be played in the background.

🌐 For preschoolers you can read the book *A Carp for Kimiko* (1993), by Virginia Kroll. Older children can read the book by themselves. This is a delightful story that deals with sharing and gender identity as well as traditional Japanese celebrations. This book discusses Children's Day, which is celebrated in May.

You can follow up with a cooperative group art activity of making kites. This incorporates problem solving, experimentation, creativity, planning, and sharing of responsibilities. You can start the process by asking the children to think about what makes a kite fly. What kind of a kite do they want to make? What materials will they need? Have a selection of books on kites and some suggestions for designs as well.

This activity can be the theme or lesson plan of the week. You will probably have to rearrange the room to accommodate the many aspects of the project going on at once. Figure 8–14 suggests a four-step process to make a paper cup windsock.

🌐 Other countries include dolls and kites in their cultures, for example, Russian *matrioshka* (mah-TROYSH-kah) nesting dolls. Koreans have many traditions involving kites. One is used in celebration of the new year. A bird-shaped kite is used to fly messages away. (Parents can be a great resource to help you learn about celebrations in their families.)

🌐 Remember to include skin-tone colors of crayons, markers, and construction paper; different colors of yarn to represent hair; and multicolors of play dough among the materials and supplies in the art center.

FIGURE 8–14
Making a paper cup windsock. The children will think of many different ways to make windsocks if you provide all kinds of materials for them.

STEP 1: Cut out the bottom of a paper cup (use the type that is not waxed on the outside).

STEP 2: Decorate with paint, markers, etc.

STEP 3: Glue long pieces of ribbon around bottom edge.

STEP 4: Hang with string and let it blow in the wind!

OBSERVATION, ASSESSMENT, AND EVALUATION

Art assessment can be described as authentic assessment because it visually documents a child's growth and development over time, using the child's art and explanations of her art in her own words. Each picture or piece of artwork shows where the child started at the beginning of the school year and where she is at the end of the year.

A **portfolio,** which is a collection of a child's work over time, is a record of the child's process of learning; how she thinks, questions, analyzes, synthesizes, and creates (Gober, 2002). Portfolios come in many shapes and sizes, such as expanding, accordion-type files, file folders, cardboard boxes, scrapbooks, three-ring binders, or unused pizza boxes.

Nilson (2001) in Koster (2005) clarifies how children's artistic growth can be assessed.

Portfolios, collections of the child's work and written observations are becoming an accepted form of documenting the child's progress. Written observations which are thorough, objective, regular, and done in the natural classroom environment are accurate measures of a child's progress.

You need to work out a routine with the children as to how the selection process of what goes in the portfolio will work. Some suggestions include: (a) You can take

portfolio
A collection of a child's work over time and a record of the child's process of learning.

one day per week, such as Friday, for the children to go through their weekly art and select one or two items they want to include. (b) You can also go through the art prior to or after the children have selected pieces to be included. (c) Art that is sent from home can be placed in each portfolio with date and explanation at any time. (d) It is important that children have an opportunity to choose and comment on each article of art, because it promotes self-evaluation and self-assessment. It is also good for the child's self-esteem for her to focus on all the things she can do and knows. (e) Keep in mind that each child's portfolio should be respected and confidential. (d) There is no right way to do portfolio saving. You have to try different ways and decide on which is right for you and the children in your class. (e) Write an end-of-the-year summary that you will keep and make a memory book of each child's artwork to send home.

 You will find a portfolio checklist, a portfolio sample form, and file folder labels for organizing an individual child's portfolio on the front-of-the-book CD included with this text.

Figure 8–15 is the curriculum planning web worksheet with art activities added. This worksheet with appropriate additions is included in each chapter.

✳ AFTERVIEW

Through art, a child

🌐 heightens an awareness of and appreciation for an aesthetic environment.

🌐 strengthens her self-expression, self-understanding, patience, and self-control.

🌐 acquires visual, spatial, and tactile awareness.

🌐 develops small and large muscles.

🌐 develops eye-hand coordination and hand-hand coordination.

🌐 experiments with color, line, form, shape, texture, size, balance, and configurations.

🌐 increases creative problem solving, decision making, and abstract thinking abilities.

🌐 experiments with different art media and recycled materials.

🌐 communicates ideas nonverbally.

🌐 releases emotional tensions and frustrations.

🌐 grows in social relationships.

🌐 increases vocabulary and language skills.

🌐 develops respect for artistic expressions of others.

✳ KEY TERMS

aesthetic environment
art
cognitive development
crayon resist
crayon rubbings

curator
language development
perceptual development
physical development
portfolio

social and emotional
   development
string painting
three-dimensional art

✳ EXPLORATIONS

1. Based on information in this chapter and your observations of early childhood environments, develop a list of appropriate materials and supplies to have available in the art center for young children. Are there materials that are new to you? Explain.

2. Collect at least ten examples of children's art (different ages, if possible). Determine what development stage each represents. What materials were used? Is it two- or three-dimensional art? Share these with others in your class. (Keep the children's names confidential.)

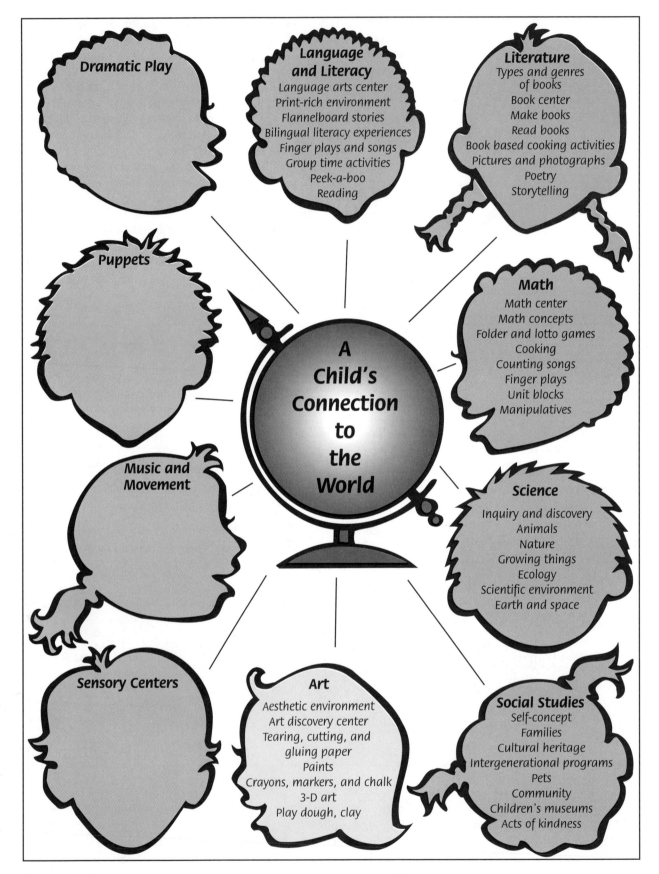

Dramatic Play

Language and Literacy
Language arts center
Print-rich environment
Flannelboard stories
Bilingual literacy experiences
Finger plays and songs
Group time activities
Peek-a-boo
Reading

Literature
Types and genres
of books
Book center
Make books
Read books
Book based cooking activities
Pictures and photographs
Poetry
Storytelling

Puppets

Math
Math center
Math concepts
Folder and lotto games
Cooking
Counting songs
Finger plays
Unit blocks
Manipulatives

Music and Movement

A Child's Connection to the World

Science
Inquiry and discovery
Animals
Nature
Growing things
Ecology
Scientific environment
Earth and space

Sensory Centers

Art
Aesthetic environment
Art discovery center
Tearing, cutting, and
gluing paper
Paints
Crayons, markers, and chalk
3-D art
Play dough, clay

Social Studies
Self-concept
Families
Cultural heritage
Intergenerational programs
Pets
Community
Children's museums
Acts of kindness

FIGURE 8–15

A curriculum planning web worksheet with art activities added.

3. Choose a partner or colleague and together complete the following "Art Brainstorming" activity:
   a. List five ways to use tempera paint.
   b. List five ways to use crayons.
   c. List five ways to use scissors.
   d. List five uses for glue.
   e. List five ways to make collages.
   f. List five uses for string.
   Discuss whether or not the activities are developmentally appropriate. If not, what could you do to make them appropriate? Review this chapter for assistance.

4. Select and plan an art activity for young children. Specify which age group this activity is planned for: infants, toddlers, preschoolers, or primary-age children. Write a list of objectives, materials needed, step-by-step procedures for presenting this activity, follow-up activities, and evaluation guidelines. (Use the activity plan worksheet in Chapter 2.) Prepare this activity and demonstrate it during class or with a group of children.

5. Select two early childhood classrooms and observe for at least one hour in each. Describe, in writing, six art activities you observed. Were these new to you? How did the teacher present the activities to the children? Which ones were child-directed? Were any of these teacher-directed? What transitions did the teacher use before and after the activities? What adaptations or modifications were made for special needs children? Will you use or have you used any of the six activities with children? Explain.

✳ REFERENCES

Aronson, D. (1995, Spring). The inside story. *Teaching Tolerance, 4*(1), 23–29.

Aulthouse, R., Johnson, M. H., & Mitchell, S. T. (2003). *The colors of learning: Integrating the visual arts into the early childhood curriculum.* New York: Teachers College Press; Washington, DC: NAEYC.

Baghban, M. (2007, January). Scribbles, labels, and stories: The role of drawing in the development of writing. *Young Children, 62*(1), 20–26.

Bredekamp, S., & Copple, C. (Eds.). (1997). *Developmentally appropriate practice in early childhood programs* (Rev. ed.). Washington, DC: NAEYC.

Davidson, J. I. (1996). *Emergent literacy and dramatic play in early education.* Clifton Park, NY: Thomson Delmar Learning.

Epstein, A. S. (2001, May). Thinking about art: Encouraging art appreciation in early childhood settings. *Young Children, 56*(3), 38–43.

Feinburg, S. G. (1993, October). Learning through art. *Early Childhood Today, 8*(2), 58–66, 72–73.

Fortson, L. R., & Reiff, J. C. (1995). *Early childhood curriculum.* Boston: Allyn & Bacon.

Fox, J. E., & Diffily, D. (2001, Winter). Integrating the visual arts—Building young children's knowledge skills and confidence. *Dimensions of Early Childhood, 29*(1), 3–10.

Gardner, H. (1983). *Frames of mind: The theory of multiple intelligences,* New York: Basic Books.

Gober, S. Y. (2002). *Six simple ways to assess young children.* Clifton Park, NY: Thomson Delmar Learning.

Greenman, J. (1987, November). Thinking about the aesthetics of children's environments. *Child Care Information Exchange, 58,* 9–12.

Hildebrand, V., & Hearron, P. F. (1999). *Guiding young children* (6th ed.). Upper Saddle River, NJ: Merrill.

Humphryes, J. (2000, March). Exploring nature with children. *Young Children, 55*(2), 16–20.

Isbell, R. T., & Raines, S. C. (2007). *Creativity and the arts with young children.* (2nd ed.). Clifton Park, NY: Thomson Delmar Learning.

Jurek, D., & MacDonald, S. (1990, May–June). Outdoor art: The sky's the limit. *Pre-K Today, 4*(8), 30–37.

Kellogg, R. (1959). *What children scribble and why.* Palo Alto, CA: National Press Books.

Kellogg, R., & O'Dell, S. (1967). *The psychology of children's art.* New York: Random House.

Kohl, M. A. (2003, Spring). Art with toddlers and twos? Face the fear! *Early Years, 25*(1), 2–3.

Koster, J. (2005). *Growing artists: Teaching art to young children* (3rd ed.). Clifton Park, NY: Thomson Delmar Learning.

Levinger, L., & Mott, A. M. (1992). Art in early childhood. In A. Mitchell & J. David (Eds.), *Explorations with young children: A curriculum guide from the Bank Street College of Education.* Mt. Rainier, MD: Gryphon House.

Libby, W. M. L. (2000). *Using art to make art: Creative activities using masterpieces.* Clifton Park, NY: Thomson Delmar Learning.

Lowenfeld, V. (1972). *Your child and his art: A guide for parents.* New York: Macmillan.

Mayesky, M. (2006). *Creative activities for young children* (8th ed.). Clifton Park, NY: Thomson Delmar Learning.

Milord, S. (1992). *Hands around the world.* Charlotte, VT: Williamson Publishing.

Nilson, B. (2004). Week by Week (3rd ed.). Clifton Park, NY: Thomson Delmar Learning.

Reyner, A. (2002, November–December). Creative connections. *Early Childhood News, 14*(6), 12.

Schirrmacher, R. (2006). *Art and creative development for young children* (5th ed.). Clifton Park, NY: Thomson Delmar Learning.

Smith, N. R., Fucigna, C., Kennedy, M., & Lord, L. (1993). *Experience and art* (2nd ed.). New York: Teachers College Press.

Szyba, C. M. (1999, January). Why do some teachers resist offering appropriate, open-ended art activities for young children? *Young Children, 54*(1), 16–20.

Taunton, M., & Colbert, C. (2000). Art in the early childhood classroom. In N. J. Yelland (Ed.), *Promoting meaningful learning.* Washington, DC: NAEYC.

The Metropolitan Museum of Art. (1959). *How to look at paintings: A guide for children.* New York: Author.

Williams, D. (1995). *Teaching mathematics through children's art.* Portsmouth, NH: Heinemann.

✳ ADDITIONAL READINGS AND RESOURCES

Damian, B. (2005, March). Rated 5 for five-year-olds. *Young Children, 60*(2), 50–53.

Fox, J. E. (2000, Fall). Constructive play in the art center. *Dimensions in Early Childhood, 28*(4), 15–20.

Gross, T., & Clemens, S. G. (2002, May). Painting a tragedy: Young children process the events of September 11. *Young Children, 57*(3), 44–51.

Jalongo, M. R. (2003, Summer). The child's right to creative thought. *Childhood Education, 79*(4), 218–228.

Mulcahey, C. (2002, January). Take-home art appreciation kits for kindergartners and their families. *Young Children, 57*(1), 80–88.

Oken-Wright, P. (1998, March). Transition to writing: Drawing as a scaffold for emergent writers. *Young Children, 53*(2), 76–81.

Riccio, L. L., Morton, K. C., & Colker, L. J. (2005, July). The SAIL effect: An arts-based charter school buoys children's learning. *Young Children, 60*(4), 42–49.

Sidelnick, M. A., & Snoboda, M. L. (2000). The bridge between drawing and writing: Hannah's story. *The Reading Teacher, 54*: 174–184.

Tarr, P. (2001, May). Aesthetic codes in early childhood classrooms: What art educators can learn from Reggio Emilia. *Art Education.* On-line at http://www.designshare.com/Research/Tarr/Aesthetic_Codes_3.htm

Warash, B. G., & Saab, J. F. (1999, Winter). Exploring the visual arts with young children. *Dimensions of Early Childhood, 27*(1), 11–15.

Zimmerman, E., & Zimmerman, L. (2000, November). Research in review—Art education and early childhood education: The young child as creator and meaning maker with a community context. *Young Children, 55*(6), 87–92.

For additional information on early education curriculum, visit our Web site at http://www.earlychilded.delmar.com

CHAPTER 9

SENSORY CENTERS

OBJECTIVES

AFTER STUDYING THIS CHAPTER, YOU SHOULD BE ABLE TO:

- Describe water, sand, and mud play activities and outline the purposes and objectives of these sensory activities.

- Identify the appropriate types of blocks for young children and discuss the developmental stages of block building.

- List the appropriate equipment and materials to have in the woodworking center and provide the purposes and objectives of this sensory area.

- Discuss acceptable cooking and creative food experiences in an early childhood classroom.

- Summarize why the use of technology by the children in early education programs is developmentally appropriate.

- Identify the teacher's role in each of the sensory curriculum areas.

- Discuss the importance of providing young children with opportunities to use and develop their five senses.

OVERVIEW

sensory experiences
Experiences that offer opportunities for free exploration in a variety of curriculum areas.

Young children learn through **sensory experiences** that offer them opportunities for free exploration in a variety of curriculum areas. Children learn best through repeated explorations, and the sensory area gives them multiple possibilities to do this. As you read this chapter, focus on how children see, hear, feel, touch, and taste the world around them. Observe carefully how the children in an early education setting make choices and react to the environment. Ask yourself if the classroom is "their room." Is it set up so that they can claim ownership? Is it giving them hands-on knowledge about their world?

Young children learn through their five senses. They have the ability to take in and make sense of information obtained from their senses. We have discussed this previously, and this chapter uses that information as a foundation on which to build additional developmentally appropriate experiences. The five *sensory centers* in the early childhood curriculum—water-sand-mud play, blocks, woodworking, cooking experiences, and computer-enhanced learning—can be indoors or outdoors, separate or a part of other learning centers. They can be changed easily as the children's developmental needs change, and they give children sensory involvement with their environment.

> *Children and adults inhabit different sensory worlds. Imagine a young infant's world of touch and taste—a world where you see and hear more than you look and listen—where you, in effect, think with your body and actions, and your whole body is your only means of reacting. (Gestwicki, 2007)*

The *quality* of the environment also contributes to the sensory development of children. Soft materials in the environment offer tactile sensory stimuli experiences. Softness creates the warmth and comfort young children need.

Miller (1996) extends our awareness by pointing out that

> *[s]ensory experiences are very accessible to all children. Very often children with special needs gravitate to sensory activities because of the ease with which they are able to be involved, because they might contain familiar elements and because they are able to exercise some control over the activity without becoming frustrated.*

These children are learning about their world through the senses of sight, smell, and touch.

Sand play is irresistible to young children.

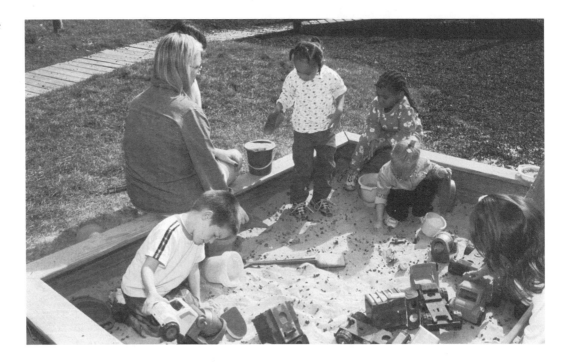

Isbell and Raines (2007) suggest that "providing interesting items to be enjoyed and examined help children become more focused on the beauty in the world around them. It helps children develop an awareness of the shades of color, texture, shapes, and design."

As you continue through this chapter, sharpen *your* sensory awareness and observe how the sensory centers interact and interconnect with the total curriculum.

WATER, SAND, AND MUD PLAY

Water, sand, and mud play can be an individual or a small group activity. Projects can be done indoors and outdoors. There is no right or wrong way to play with these multisensory materials. They are used in many different ways by the children using them. Even very young children enjoy splashing, pouring, squishing, and mixing. Water, sand, and mud can relate to any theme, lesson plan, or curriculum web.

Water play can be lively and at the same time relaxing. Young children enjoy running through a sprinkler, playing at the water table, bathing dolls in a plastic tub, filling and emptying water containers, and watering plants. It is fun, and children are naturally drawn to water play.

Stephenson (2001) clarifies the importance of outdoor water play for toddlers:

Looking through George's eyes revealed to me the wonder of this strange sloppy substance that uncontrollably slides through fingers and disappears irretrievably into sand. Babies spend many hours handling solid objects yet have relatively limited opportunities to experiment with liquids, so it is not surprising that water is such a deeply fascinating material.

Sand play is irresistible to young children. Starting with dry sand in the sandpile, sand tray, or sand table, children can spoon, pour, measure, dig, and shovel. They add props as they construct cities, farms, and airports, and they love to drive trucks through and over sandy roads.

Adding water to sand creates opportunities for additional sensory learning to take place. Combining props such as sunglasses, hats, towels, and an umbrella can turn the outdoor sand area into a beach. Have you tried adding live small crabs in a sand bucket to the "beach"? The children will be fascinated.

Give each child unstructured time to spend experimenting with sand.

Mud play is a sensory activity like no other. After a rain, the playground takes on an added dimension. It is special. "The water has transformed the everyday playground into a wonderland with endless possibilities. . . . Mix water and dirt and you get mud—ooey, gooey mud" (Betz, 1992). What you and the children do with the mud offers many possibilities. Try experimenting with a bucketful of mud. Make mud pies or "pizza," for example. Mix the mud to make paint. Brush the mud on different textures of paper. Dirt taken from different areas of the playground shows different pigmentations, which the children themselves will point out to you.

This child-centered activity of mud play offers children another way to experience their world. "When so much of our good earth is being covered with wall to wall concrete, it is imperative to save more than a spot of earth for growing children" (Hill, 1977).

Jensen and Bullard (2002) reminisce

about the pleasures of creating mud pies and mud sandwiches and holding tea parties with a variety of mud treats. We [remember] the deep sense of satisfaction in baking mud pies for the entire neighborhood. . . . Our children are affected by traffic, lack of space, and schedules that allow little time for outdoor play. . . . [As a result,] the idea of a dramatic play mud center outdoors [at a child care center or school] emerges from the interests of both children and adults.

Think about creating this activity area for your own child care center or school.

Purposes and Objectives

When you plan opportunities for children to develop and practice skills in the water, sand, and mud learning centers, you will encourage children to do the following:

PERFORM SIMPLE EXPERIMENTS. Predict whether objects will sink or float in plain water—try rocks, marbles, Styrofoam, ping-pong balls, coins, corks, and sponges. Add salt to the water to see whether the objects will sink or float. Explore various types of sand with magnets by running the magnet through the sand to see whether any grains stick to the magnet, or search for hidden metal objects buried in the sand. Discover how long it takes for water to evaporate outside on a hot or a cold day. Examine dirt using magnifying glasses and sifters.

MEASURE, COMPARE, AND PROBLEM SOLVE. Provide empty cardboard milk cartons, such as half-pint, pint, quart, and half-gallon containers, for children to pour from one carton to another to discover how much water each one holds. Measure equal amounts of wet and dry sand and put them on opposite sides of a balance scale to determine which is heavier. Use the mud puddle after a rain for the children to problem solve how to get the water out of the mud puddle.

PLAY CREATIVELY. Provide soapy water, sponges, and washable toys for the children to clean. Experiment with sand molds and determine whether dry sand or wet sand works best. Have boat races with children problem solving how to get their boats across the water-filled tub. (Hint: Children can either blow on the boats to make them move or pull them across with a string.) Make designs in the sand with sand combs made from pliable plastic containers such as clean bleach or detergent bottles. Put out buckets and sponges to scrub the playground equipment. Set up a "truck wash" for sand box construction toys.

DEVELOP NEW VOCABULARY. Introduce words such as pour, fill, flow, spray, squirt, splatter, empty, full, shallow, deep, measure, absorb, droplets, sift, sink, float, evaporate, melt, and dissolve.

DEMONSTRATE NEW CONCEPTS. Demonstrate how gravity causes water to flow downhill through tubes and funnels, how water takes the shape of its container, and how the liquid form of water can change into a solid by freezing in ice trays, paper cups, or milk cartons.

It is exciting when a child discovers how water takes the shape of its container.

The Teacher's Role

The following suggestions should be helpful to you in defining the teacher's role in water, sand, and mud play:

- Observe, ask open-ended questions, and make comments to show support and interest.
- Encourage children to talk about what they are doing and what is happening.
- Support children's exploration by providing space for messy activities and materials that can be fully explored without concern about waste (Feeney, Christensen, & Moravcik, 2001).
- Structure the centers so children have interesting and challenging materials to stimulate their water and sand play.
- Depending on the type and size of the area used for the water and sand activities, decide when and if you should limit the number of children playing at one time.
- Offer indoor and outdoor water play often. Limiting water play to one "water day" a week doesn't offer the children enough opportunities for exploration.
- Take your cues from the children on what to change and when to change it.
- Have smocks, aprons, and changes of clothes available for the children and the teacher too!
- Remember the safety and health rules of water, sand, and mud play: (1) Never leave children unattended around any type of water; (2) empty the water tub or table daily; (3) sanitize the water, wet sand toys, and tub each day with a fresh bleach solution of one tablespoon bleach to one quart of water in a spray bottle, then rinse with running water (Miller, 1994); and (4) check the sand and mud play areas each day for foreign objects, such as glass, that should be removed.
- Discuss with older children the importance of water and the shortages that will arise if we do not work to preserve this resource. Get the children's families involved, too.

Props and Materials

The following is a suggested list of props and materials to include in water, sand, and mud play. It is best to use dry, finely textured sand (available at toy stores and lumber or building supply stores). Use plastic props and containers, if possible, because metal will rust.

Suggested Props

Basters	Rotary eggbeaters
Eyedroppers	Spray bottles
Funnels	Cookie cutters
Measuring cups and spoons	Gelatin molds
Scoops	Salt shakers
Sieves	Scale
Colander	Sand timer
Straws	Sand combs
Slotted spoon	Spoons and shovels
Buckets, pails, and tubs	Bowls and pitchers
Magnifying glass	Paintbrushes
Plastic tubing	Sponges
Child-size brooms and dust pan	

Suggested Containers

Sand and water table	Outdoor sandpile
Wading pool	Wash tubs
Dishpan	Boxes
Bathtub	Infant tub

Suggested Substitutes for Sand

Seashells	Styrofoam pieces
Washed gravel	Birdseed
Cork pieces	

What fun! Toddlers and soap suds!

WHY I TEACH YOUNG CHILDREN

I can't imagine myself in any other profession. When you work with young children, you are reminded of their innocence and their unique outlook on life. You never know what you may say or do that will affect them for the rest of their lives. I never realized until Andrew, "the first-grader," stopped by for a visit. I had him in my class when he was three years old. I asked him if he remembered me. I really did not think he would because it had been over three years since I had seen him. He said he did remember me. He told me in such a sweet manner that I was still his favorite teacher ever! Andrew said I made him feel safe when his Mom was at work. He remembered that he could have his blanket anytime he needed it. At that moment, I was reminded how teachers leave lasting impressions no matter the age.

—Barbara Batista

BLOCKS

When you are setting up an early childhood environment, one of the first items you should purchase is blocks. Many teachers consider blocks to be the most used and the most useful materials in a program for young children. "They are the most versatile and open-ended of the nonconsumable materials in the early childhood setting, and well worth the investment of their price" (Petersen, 2003). Along with selecting blocks, you should plan carefully what type and quantity you choose, the way in which the blocks will be organized, and how you will arrange the physical environment to ensure developmentally appropriate activities with blocks.

Unit blocks are the most popular variety used in early education environments. Children continue to use them as they grow from infancy to primary-age. These sturdy hardwood blocks were designed by Carolyn Pratt in the early 1890s. The individual unit block is 13.8 inches by 2¾ inches by 5½ inches, and all other blocks are multiples or divisions of this basic size.

The cylinders and curved blocks are of similar width and thickness. Pratt's blocks were of

> smooth, natural-finish hardwood—free from details or color. In addition, she designed unpainted wooden people, 6 inches tall, in the form of family members and community workers, to be used with the unit blocks. She omitted painted details on any of her toys because she wanted children to apply their own imagination in their use of the materials. (Beaty, 1992)

Hollow blocks are also made of wood and are larger than unit blocks. "The basic square is 51.2 inches by 11 inches by 11 inches. There are five other pieces in a set: a half-square, a double square, two lengths of flat board, and a ramp. Hollow blocks are open on the sides so they can be carried more easily" (Dodge, Colker, & Heroman, 2002). Hollow blocks require additional space both indoors and outdoors for optimal use by the children (see Figure 9–2).

Other types of blocks appropriate for young children's play are: shoe-box size cardboard blocks, some of which are designed to look like bricks; small, wooden, colored ones that can be used as table blocks; log-type building blocks; interlocking blocks, such as Legos® or Bristle Blocks®; and foam blocks and large brightly colored lightweight blocks for infants' and toddlers' first experiences with block play.

unit blocks
Hardwood blocks used in early education environments, especially in block center play.

hollow blocks
Wooden blocks larger than unit blocks and open on the sides.

FIGURE 9–1
Unit blocks.

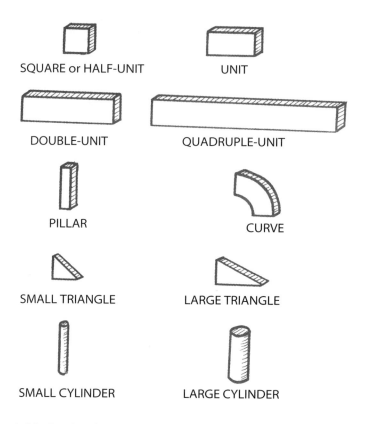

SQUARE or HALF-UNIT

UNIT

DOUBLE-UNIT

QUADRUPLE-UNIT

PILLAR

CURVE

SMALL TRIANGLE

LARGE TRIANGLE

SMALL CYLINDER

LARGE CYLINDER

The unit blocks should be placed on low shelves according to shape and size for organization and storage. Label the shelves with the outlines of the shapes and sizes of the different types of blocks. This assists children with cleanup and emphasizes classification. Place blocks other than the unit or hollow blocks in plastic containers or boxes clearly labeled for identification (see Figure 9–3).

Block play is noisy, so the center should be placed next to other active areas, such as dramatic play. The block area should be clearly defined on three sides. This offers protection and security for the children's activities. An area rug or carpeting should be on the floor to absorb some of the noise as well as to offer comfort to the children playing (Dodge, Colker, & Heroman, 2002).

> *If children are taught to build slightly away from the shelves, fighting and stress will be reduced as other youngsters also try to reach in for blocks. The construction area needs to be shielded from traffic to discourage children from delivering a kick at some treasured structure as they pass by. (Hendrick, 2003)*

FIGURE 9–2
Hollow blocks.

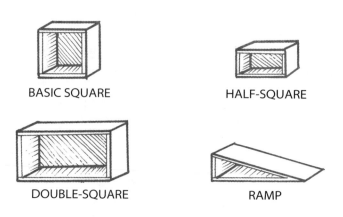

BASIC SQUARE

HALF-SQUARE

DOUBLE-SQUARE

RAMP

FIGURE 9–3
Visually label block
shelves to show the
children where and how
to replace the blocks.

Developmental Stages of Block Building

"Current interest in problem solving and brain research provides new support for integrating curriculum using blocks in both preschool and primary grades" (Starns, 2002). Harriet M. Johnson (1982) helps us understand that there are developmental stages in the way children use and play with blocks: First, children carry blocks from place to place. They are learning about how the blocks feel, how heavy they are, and how many they can carry at once (under two years of age).

Next, the children pile blocks one on top of another. In the beginning there is an irregular pattern to the stacking, then the blocks begin to form a tower, which often falls when additional blocks are added. Repetition of this activity will help children know how many blocks they can add before the tower will fall (toddlers).

At the same time children are making block towers, they are also trying to make block rows. They lay blocks close together, side by side or edge to edge (flat rows suggest roads, so adding small trucks and cars will be appropriate). The children may also space the blocks, alternating the sizes as they place them in rows (toddlers and three-year-olds).

Each of these steps in developmental block building includes repetition (see Figure 9–4). Practicing their accomplishments over and over is important to young children as they get more comfortable with using blocks. The next stage for children is bridging. This is observable by watching children set up two blocks, leaving space between them, and roofing that space with another block. Through repetition, the structures increase in elaboration and difficulty (three- and four-year-olds).

Enclosures made by children, sometimes simultaneously with bridging, put blocks together to enclose a space. Placing four blocks together so that a space is completely enclosed is not a simple task (two-, three-, and four-year-olds). Patterns and designs begin to appear when children feel comfortable enough with blocks to build balanced and decorative patterns (four-year-olds). Finally, representation occurs with the naming of block constructions and the combination of all elements of block building. Children (four-year-olds and older) demonstrate that they are aware of their world and their place in it with these structures (Hirsch, 1993).

The addition of miniature people representing various cultures, doll furniture, small animals, cars, trucks, boats, barges, canoes, sleds, airplanes, trains, and buses extends children's block play. For self-selection by the children, put each group of small items in clearly labeled (with pictures and words) plastic tubs or boxes near the unit blocks. This will also help with cleanup.

Books and pictures of different buildings from all around the world can stimulate children to build all kinds of structures. Older children create elaborate highways, bridges, and ramps. They add traffic signs, "Do Not Touch!" signs, and other kinds of labels.

FIGURE 9–4
Examples of the
developmental stages
of block building.

PILE   TOWER   ROWS

BRIDGING   ENCLOSURES

PATTERNS   REPRESENTATION

The teacher in this
classroom has provided
time, space, materials,
and freedom for
children to develop
creative experiences
with blocks.

Purposes and Objectives

When you provide time, space, materials, and freedom for children to gain sensory and creative experiences with blocks, you will encourage children to

- strengthen such perceptions of space as under, below, in front of, behind, above, inside, and outside.
- develop concepts of big/little, more than/less than, equal to, and taller/shorter.
- become aware of whole-part relationships.
- practice balancing, stabilizing, and matching skills.
- classify according to shapes, sizes, colors, textures, and types.
- develop symbolic representations as the blocks become whatever the children want them to be.
- create architectural forms by bridging and making tunnels, ramps, and grids.
- make use of imagery and recall by reproducing and recreating forms from past experiences.
- strengthen large and small muscle skills and eye-hand coordination.
- develop oral language skills.
- participate in cooperative block play with peers while combining ideas and solving problems.
- release emotions in an acceptable way.

The Teacher's Role

- Let the parents know what the children are accomplishing through their block play. Invite the parents to participate in the block center when they drop off or pick up their children. Provide opportunities for a family member who is in construction or architectural work to share his or her time and talent with the children.
- Observe developmental levels of the children. This knowledge will enable you to know when to introduce hollow blocks, other blocks, or accessories to the block center.
- Keep in mind the natural stages of block building as you support the children's efforts to gain confidence and to feel comfortable with blocks.
- Take photographs, often, of the block constructions. This offers an alternative to leaving the structures up for extra long periods of time if you do not have the space to do so. The children can have the photo to remember their special buildings. This will also help the children understand that you value their efforts. The photos can lead to children dictating stories about their creations. Perhaps they will recreate them in the art center as well.
- Set limits on the number of children in the block center at one time, and clearly label the rule (as discussed in Chapter 8). Define a few other basic rules, such as blocks are not for throwing or hitting. If the building project continues to grow, expand the space to another center so more children can be involved. This will eliminate some difficulties before they start. For example, put hard hats in the block center to indicate how many children can be in the block center at one time.
- Help children plan cooperatively and recognize the problems they have encountered and solved. This will contribute to positive self-esteem development.
- Remember blocks are for all ages. The primary-grade children will often surprise you with their exploration of structural engineering by testing the stability of their buildings. They use blocks to build simple machines, such as levers, pulleys, or rollers (Holliman, 1996).

During the years children are in the primary grades, their thinking abilities change considerably. . . . [D]evelopmental changes are reflected in primary age children's approach to constructive play and block-building activities. . . . Negotiation, problem-solving, and collaboration are characteristic of the social constructive play of primary-age children (Wellhausen & Kieff, 2001).

WOODWORKING

woodworking center
An activity center providing many different sensory and three-dimensional experiences.

The **woodworking center** in an early childhood environment is not new. It has been a part of a traditional early education classroom for a number of years. This activity center provides young children with many different sensory and three-dimensional experiences.

Unfortunately, in some settings the woodworking center is often nonexistent or underused. Think about how and when you can successfully incorporate carpentry into your curriculum. Boys and girls alike can develop physical, cognitive, social, and language skills through woodworking activities (see Figure 9–5).

Purposes and Objectives

When you include woodworking experiences in early education, you will encourage children to

FIGURE 9–5
The woodworking center provides sensory experiences for young children.

- develop and coordinate large and small muscles.
- improve eye-hand coordination.
- use wood as a medium of creative expression.
- communicate, plan, and work cooperatively with others.
- use woodworking as an emotional release and means of nonverbal expression.
- focus on the process while mastering the skills of sanding, gluing, hammering, nailing, sawing, and drilling to gain a sense of self-esteem.
- sharpen their senses through the smells, textures, and sounds of woodworking.
- learn to sustain interest and overcome frustration successfully.
- extend concepts of experimenting, creating, investigating, and problem solving into other areas of the curriculum.

Woodworking provides children with opportunities to become aware of textures and forms. Senses are sharpened as children explore the field of construction. Fingers explore many textures, ears pick out the sounds of different tools, noses test the different smells of various woods, and eyes see the many hues of wood. (Mayesky, 2006)

Figure 9–6 illustrates how woodworking equipment can be stored.

FIGURE 9–6
Children should properly replace woodworking tools after using them.

TOOL BOARD

The Teacher's Role

The following guidelines can assist you through planning, setting up, and evaluating a woodworking center for young children.

- Before beginning carpentry with real tools, plan for the children to have many spontaneous play experiences with bits of wood used as building blocks, match tools to shapes in puzzles, and in the math center pair up photos of tools, such as hammer and nails and screwdriver and screws.

- Be sure to allow plenty of time to explore.

- If you have not worked with tools or wood before, practice *before* you supervise the children. Ask a colleague or parent to share their knowledge with you and the children.

  Practice using all the tools yourself until you are comfortable with them. If you are a female teacher competently using tools, you become a role model, especially for girls.

- When starting, be sure you (or another teacher) are available the entire time to closely supervise the children. Limit the center to one child at a time. Add a second child later, when all children are comfortable with the tools.

- Place this center away from quiet centers. Many teachers like to take woodworking outdoors or into the hallway right outside the classroom door.

- Allow enough time for the children to explore the materials at their own pace.

- The woodworking center requires specific rules that are consistently reinforced:

  Goggles must be worn at all times.

  Tools must be kept at the workbench, and they are to be used for the purpose for which they are designed. (Help the children learn to use tools properly.) Return the tools to the tool kit or rack when finished.

  When two children are working at the workbench, let one stand on each side with plenty of space between them. Safety is always the first consideration when children are using tools. They must learn where to put their hands when hammering and sawing.

- Remember, it is the *process* that is important, not the result.

- To ensure success for children from the beginning, start with white glue and wood. Then gradually add hammers, roofing nails, soft wood, and a saw.

- If a child is using a hammer for the first time, you can pound several nails halfway into the wood to get him started. Roofing nails with large heads are the easiest for young children to use.

- Children may want to paint the projects they have made. Allow time for completion of this activity, too.

- Evaluate throughout each step of the process. Planning, initiating, and evaluating will help you and the children be successful in the woodworking center.

  Essa (2007) suggests additional guidelines:

  For very young children, wood can be replaced by thick styrofoam packing material, which is much softer and easier to saw. . . . Older preschoolers who have gained proficiency in using the tools and purposefully made objects in wood, will be interested in adding props. These should include round objects that suggest wheels, such as wooden spools, slices of large dowels, bottle caps, the metal ends from 6-ounce frozen juice containers, and a variety of other items.

A child should have plenty of time in the woodworking center to explore the materials at her own pace.

Equipment and Materials

Use *real* tools. They are much safer than toy ones. You may have to remind children to put on *safety goggles* before they start working with wood. A list of suggested equipment and materials follows:

Workbench—sturdy in construction, with vise or C-clamps attached, approximately 24 inches high or as high as the children's waists; a sturdy table can also be used.

Hammers—small claw hammers weighing 8 to 12 ounces.

Nails—roofing nails and assorted other sizes. The nails can be set out in small foil pie plates to keep the sizes from getting mixed up. The pie plates can be nailed to a long board to prevent spilling (Mayesky, 2006).

Soft wood—white pine, cedar, spruce, and redwood are light in weight and take nails easily. Lumber companies and construction sites are sources for soft wood scraps.

Glue.

Cross-cut saw—approximately 18 inches long.

Clamps.

Braces and bits.

Sandpaper or sanding sponges.

Ruler or square.

Pencils and paper.

Toolbox.

Pegboard tool rack or tool cabinet to store items.

Markers, crayons, and thinned tempera paint.

Screws and screwdrivers are difficult for young children to use. Perhaps you can add these to activities for older children along with wood files, planes, and levels.

COOKING AND CREATIVE FOOD EXPERIENCES

Cooking activities give children firsthand experiences that involve them in the process from planning to cleanup. A sense of accomplishment, the thrills of experimentation, and an awareness of taste, touch, and smell are all rewards of cooking experiences. Early positive encounters with food also help children gain the knowledge they will use to form lifelong eating habits. Cooking is fun! Just watch what infants and toddlers can do with a banana.

By including opportunities for children to cook, you offer additional times for them to practice math (comparing sizes, shapes, and measurements, one-to-one correspondence, fractions, and temperature), science (vegetables that are stems or roots, fruit that grows on trees, what happens to sugar on hot cereal), reading and writing (making lists and using recipes and rebus charts), social studies (learning more about their world and community resources), following directions, putting things in sequence, and learning to communicate and cooperate with each other.

You may find that some children will need to go through a similar "messing about" stage with any significantly new type of cooking material, just as they do when they first encounter a new art material. So be prepared to allow this exploratory period before you introduce any new type of cooking experience to young children (Colker, 2005).

Review the USDA *Food Guide Pyramid* that was introduced in Chapter 6. Place photos or posters of nutritious foods in the cooking activity area and where children eat meals and snacks. Include the colorful Food Guide Pyramid. "See if children can tell you when they are eating a food that is pictured on the posters. Talk about where the food fits into the food group sections of the Food Guide Pyramid" (Cryer, Harms, & Ray, 1996).

Cooking activities give children firsthand experiences that involve them in the entire process.

It is important that the cooking projects are appropriate for the children's age, interest, and understanding, and that these experiences value cultural diversity. Foods from other cultures offer opportunities for children to taste the different ingredients and flavors. This also helps to develop their understanding that many of the foods they eat are both different *and* similar to those eaten in other countries. On an even deeper level of understanding, children can relate to the fact that many of the foods eaten in the United States are greatly influenced by all the cultures represented in America today.

Principles of developmentally appropriate practice can link cooking-related activities at home to school activities. You could meet with parents to discuss relationships between family and classroom goals of working together. "Think of ways that children can become actively involved in planning dinner for the family. Children will benefit from learning to make choices and deciding which steps to take to complete the task" (Newman, 1995). Family members play a major role in teaching their children how to develop healthful eating habits that will last a lifetime.

Purposes and Objectives

When you include cooking activities in an early childhood environment, you will encourage children to

A child feels responsible, independent, and successful when involved in cooking activities.

🌐 feel responsible, independent, and successful.

🌐 learn about nutrition and the food groups.

🌐 work independently or cooperatively in small groups (the younger the children, the smaller the group should be).

🌐 complete tasks from preparation to cleanup.

🌐 learn about new foods and become aware of recipes from cultures other than their own.

🌐 learn about different careers that involve foods and cooking (farmers, truckers, grocers, bakers, and chefs, for example).

🌐 introduce new vocabulary and concepts, such as measure, melt, knead, shake, sift, spread, baste, peel, hull, grind, grate, chop, slice, and boil.

🌐 develop beginning reading skills with rebus charts and simple recipe cards.

🌐 learn math and science concepts.

- develop small and large muscle control and eye-hand coordination.
- extend cooking into dramatic play, puppetry, art, and other centers.

The Teacher's Role

- Plan cooking on days when you have another adult helping you, such as an assistant, a parent, or a volunteer. Supervision is critical to ensure safety for the children.
- Review the food allergies of the children. Provide alternative activities for those children who are allergic to certain foods.
- Be sensitive to the beliefs of the families in your program concerning foods. Some families may have restrictions on what foods they can or cannot eat.
- Integrate cooking opportunities into the theme and lesson plan. Cooking is a creative sensory activity and not necessarily a separate center. Plan appropriate transition activities into and out of each experience.
- Explain the limits and rules to the children, such as: their hands should be washed with soap and water before and after they prepare foods, smocks or aprons (not those used for art projects) should be worn while cooking, and fingers and utensils should be kept out of their mouths while they are cooking. Let the children help you establish other rules.
- At first, and with younger children, attempt food activities that require no cooking. The children can mix ingredients together and feel successful when they taste the snack.
- Washing fruits and vegetables before they cut and eat them provides additional opportunities for beginning cooks. Remember, all cooks need practice and support to succeed.
- When interacting with the children, use correct terms for foods, measurements, equipment, and processes. Repeating and explaining terms will help extend language skills.
- Take the time to discuss foods with the children. Allow them to smell the food and ingredients, taste small portions at various stages of preparation, and experience the feel of textures.
- Ample time should be available for children to complete the recipe, permitting them to learn from the process as well as the product.
- With older children, take time to explain the sequence of how things are grown, harvested, packaged, transported, placed in stores and markets, sold, transported to homes, cooked, and served. Allow time for you to answer the children's questions. Repeat this information in different ways, such as lotto games, matching games, reading books, making books, and field trips.

Equipment and Supplies

Use real kitchen utensils and equipment. A list of suggested supplies follows:

- Unbreakable nesting bowls for mixing
- Individual bowls for children
- Measuring cups and spoons
- Wooden stirring spoons
- Slotted spoons
- Unbreakable pitchers
- Rubber spatula
- Vegetable peelers

- Plastic grater
- Pastry brushes
- Wire whisks
- Funnel
- Tongs
- Rolling pins
- Hand eggbeater
- Potato masher
- Colander
- Sifter
- Hand squeezing orange juicer
- Plastic serrated knives (for younger children)
- Serrated steel knives and kitchen shears (for older children)
- Plastic cutting boards or trays
- Cookie cutters and cookie sheets
- Muffin tins
- Bread loaf pans and cake pans
- Airtight containers with lids
- Hot plate or electric skillet
- Toaster oven
- Electric wok
- Electric blender and/or mixer
- Can opener
- Timer
- Smocks or aprons (not the ones used in the art center)
- Hot pads and mitts or holders
- Sponges used just for cooking activities
- Paper towels and paper napkins
- Waxed paper, foil, plastic wrap, and plastic bags

Basic ingredients to keep on hand include:

Flour	Salt	Oil
Milk	Baking soda and powder	Vinegar
Sugar	Peanut butter	Bread
Cornstarch	Cornmeal	Honey

Sensory Snacks

- Dried fruits: apples, raisins, apricots, and pitted prunes. (Let the children spoon out the portions.)
- Bananas sliced in orange juice. (Let the children slice the bananas and drop them in their own bowls of orange juice.)
- Melon chunks. (Let the children feel, hold, and cut the fruit and then remove and plant the seeds.)
- Finger foods (that children can help prepare): cinnamon toast, cheese toast, popcorn, raw or cooked vegetables, hard cooked eggs (whole, half, quarters, slices), apple slices dipped in honey, tangerine wedges, pear sections, or plum pieces.

Snacks

Make the following recipes with the children.

BANANA SNACK

Bananas are a favorite food of infants. Older babies like to squeeze banana slices through their fingers and then taste them. For a change, let the children try to "cut" the banana into slices themselves by using craft sticks. Place a section of a banana in front of a child and demonstrate how this is done with each individual child. At first, hold the child's hand while placing the craft stick in it and gently "cutting down" on the banana. Remember to talk about what you are doing. This activity should be repeated several times while the child is gaining control over his muscles.

APPLESAUCE

6 apples   1 teaspoon lemon juice
1/2 cup water   1/8 teaspoon cinnamon
sugar to taste

Wash hands, then peel apples. Remove core from each apple. Cut up the apples and add water, sugar, and lemon juice. Put apple mixture in a pan, cover, and cook until tender on medium heat, approximately 15 to 20 minutes. Add cinnamon. Mash apples with a fork or potato masher, or press through a colander. Serve and eat!

SHAPE SANDWICHES

wheat or white sandwich bread
pimento cheese spread
small jar of pimentos
black olives

After washing hands, you and the children make sandwiches using the pimento cheese spread. With a star-shaped cookie cutter (or choose another shape), press out a sandwich. Decorate the individual shape sandwiches with pimento eyes and olive mouths. Enjoy!

FROSTED GRAHAM CRACKERS

1 cup powdered sugar   1 tablespoon milk
1/4 cup margarine   1 box graham crackers
food coloring   nuts or shredded coconut
1 teaspoon vanilla extract

Wash hands. Make this recipe several times with different small groups of children. Mix sugar, margarine, and two to three drops of food coloring. Mix vanilla and milk. Slowly add the vanilla-milk mixture, a drop or two at a time, to the sugar-margarine mixture until you have a spreading consistency. Spread over graham crackers. Decorate with chopped nuts or shredded coconut. Yum!

HAY STACKS SNACK

1 small package butterscotch chips
1 small package chocolate chips
1 6-ounce package of Chinese noodles

Wash hands. Melt the butterscotch and chocolate chips over low heat. Add the package of Chinese noodles. Place on waxed paper in large spoonfuls, and shape into balls. Let them set until cool. Eat and enjoy!

TECHNOLOGY IN EARLY CHILDHOOD PROGRAMS

TECH   As educators and parents think about the future,

they need to realize two things: technology is not going to go away and we are in the midst of a major sociocultural quantum shift. These technologies are revolutionizing the world our children will live in. So our task is to balance appropriate skill-development with technologies with the core principles and experiences necessary to raise healthy children. (Perry, 2002).

Throughout this book you will find suggestions for including technology in curriculum content. The National Association for the Education of Young Children's 1996 position statement on "Technology and Young Children, Ages 3 through 8" suggests some tips for professionals in evaluating computer programs:

1. Early childhood professionals must apply the principles of developmentally appropriate practice and appropriate curriculum and assessment when choosing technology for use in their classrooms or programs.
2. When used appropriately, technology can improve children's thinking ability and help them develop good relationships with peers.
3. Technology should be integrated into daily learning activities.
4. Teachers should work for equity in access to technology for all children and their families.
5. Technology has a powerful influence over children's learning: It must not teach them to stereotype or use violence to solve their problems.
6. Work together with parents to promote appropriate uses of technology. (NAEYC, 1996).

(NAEYC's position statement on "Technology and Young Children, Ages 3 through 8" is available on-line at: http://www.naeyc.org/resources/eyly/1996/09a.htm)

The role of computers in the early childhood curriculum should be that of uniquely adding to children's experiences (SECA, 1989). Buckleitner (1995) additionally cautions:

Computers are no substitute for running, jumping, playing with blocks, digging in the sand, and enjoying storybooks—all of which help foster intellectual development. However, if the right software is used the computer can be an excellent supplement to these traditional activities.

Young children interacting at computers engage at high levels of communication and cooperation.

If you offer the computer as another learning center for the children to choose, they will accomplish many of the same objectives that they do in other areas. The emphasis should be to encourage children to develop positive self-esteem while playing cooperatively with others. Placing two computers side by side can also accomplish this.

The children's response to computers will be within their developmental range. You should continue to offer children developmentally appropriate explorations of concepts through hands-on activities with concrete materials, then offer computer experiences that build on these explorations.

> *Computers empower young children. They enable them to become totally immersed in the joys of learning. The key is how computers are used. Selecting developmental software and websites is essential. . . . If computer experiences are not developmentally appropriate, children would be better served with no computer access. (Haugland, 2000).*

Purposes and Objectives

software
A set of instructions used to direct a computer to perform some activity.

The selection of **software** (a set of instructions used to direct a computer to perform some activity) will determine whether or not you are offering developmentally appropriate experiences to young children. Consider the following when you are making decisions:

- Select programs that present age-appropriate concepts, such as problem solving, making choices, predicting outcomes, creativity development, asking open-ended questions, and reading, writing, and language skill development.
- Give preference to the software that includes both printed instructions and graphic choices that make options clear to children. If you have a CD-ROM drive, the children can receive these instructions verbally. Touch pads and touch screens also offer opportunities to support the children.
- Make choices that allow one child to work independently or work as a partner with another child.
- The children should be able to use the software as a process. As we have stated previously, it is the process, not the product, that's important.
- Look closely at which programs offer opportunities for the children to develop patience while completing a software task and incorporate an exploratory mode—meaning that a child can *stop* any activity and move on to the next at any time, thereby setting his own pace.
- Look closely at software packages to be sure that you have the necessary equipment, computer memory, and materials to use the program.

Note: Select only those programs that you have screened, tested, and personally used prior to purchase. New ones are being produced every day.

The Teacher's Role

- Evaluate your own comfort level in the use of computers. Are you "computer literate"?
- Do you use and value what a computer can do? Do you take advantage of or seek out training opportunities? You should know about and use computers and the accompanying software before you set up a center for young children.
- Follow the same guidelines for setting up a computer center as you do in creating any developmentally appropriate learning center. "While a computer may attract much attention when it is first introduced, the novelty wears off and it becomes just another option" (Fischer & Gillespie, 2003).

Cameras—film, video, or digital—stimulate a young child's curiosity and encourage him to transfer his photographic images into the computer.

🌐 Place the center near another quiet one, such as the book center. Clearly define the center. Avoid lighting that will place a glare on the screen. Put the computer center against a wall with electric outlets so children will not trip over cables and cords.

🌐 Work with other teachers in finding local resources, both individuals and businesses, who can offer expertise and assistance to help you get started. Oftentimes parents will be able to give you guidance.

🌐 Make back-up copies of the program disks for the children to use, and keep the original software in a protected cabinet.

🌐 Considering the budget and appropriateness for the children, start with one computer for two children and then add others later.

🌐 Place the **hardware** (physical components of the computer system: monitor, keyboard, printer, disk drive, peripherals, electronic circuitry, mouse, etc.) on a child-size table. Have child-size chairs available so that two children at a time can share each computer. "Some teachers use an old piano bench, with shortened legs, instead of a single chair so that as many as three children can share the experience" (Buckleitner, 2002).

🌐 Guide children through the stages of becoming comfortable with a computer (clean hands and learning how to take care of the hardware and software). Limit the amount of time the children can spend at the computer center. You will be able to decide how much time is appropriate (15 to 30 minutes depending on the children's developmental level). Remember, a child's vision is still developing. Provide enough light in the area to reduce glare on the screen.

🌐 Talk to the children often so you will know what they are thinking. It is important to reflect on what they are doing and whether they feel successful or frustrated. Encourage vocabulary development by using correct terminology, such as monitor, disk, disk drive, mouse, keyboard, hardware, software, and cursor.

🌐 Provide extensions of classroom computer activities in other learning centers. Computer software should be interrelated in content to the theme, lesson plan, and other center activities.

🌐 Help parents understand that the computer is set up like all the curriculum centers in the classroom: The software programs are developmentally appropriate, the rules and limits are necessary, and the emphasis is on playing and learning both independently and cooperatively with others. Evaluate, evaluate, evaluate as you go along!

🌐 Read the current early education professional journals and magazines to see what is new in computers and software. Technology changes daily.

Bredekamp and Rosegrant (1994) give us their perspective on technology:

> *Technology—including video and audiotapes and, especially, computers—should not be abandoned because it has at times been misused or because mismatches have occurred in the past. The potentials of technology are far-reaching and ever-changing. The risk is for adults to become complacent, assuming that their current knowledge or experience is adequate. Technology is an area of the curriculum, as well as a tool for learning, in which teachers must demonstrate their own capacity for learning. If teachers themselves become models of exploration and inquiry, children are likely to follow.*

hardware

The physical components of the computer system, such as monitor, keyboard, mouse, and printer.

SHARING WITH FAMILIES: DEVELOPMENTALLY APPROPRIATE AND MULTICULTURAL/ANTI-BIAS ACTIVITIES

 By sharing experiences and activities with families, the teacher is encouraging them to know what is going on in their child's classroom. Increase this involvement by inviting parents and other family members to be resources for the children.

Differing types of activities for the sensory centers are suggested here. Figure 9–7 is a curriculum planning web using the children's book *My Five Senses* by Aliki as the theme. This web offers books, activities, and a special recipe.

Books Used in the Curriculum Web

Ahlberg, A., & Ahlberg, J. (1981). *Peek-a-boo.* New York: Viking.

Aliki. (1989). *My five senses.* New York: HarperTrophy.

Brown, M. (1947). *Stone soup.* New York: Aladdin Books.

Carle, E. (1990). *Pancakes! Pancakes!* New York: Scholastic.

de Paola, T. (1978). *Pancakes for breakfast.* New York: Harcourt Brace.

Dr. Seuss. (1960). *Green eggs and ham.* New York: Beginner Books.

Friedman, I. R. (1984). *How my parents learned to eat.* Illustrated by A. Say. Boston: Houghton Mifflin.

Haley, G. E. (1970). *A story, a story.* New York: Aladdin Books.

Hathon, E. (1993). *Soft as a kitten.* New York: Grossett & Dunlap.

Hoban, T. (1971). *Look again!* New York: Macmillan.

Hughes, S. (1985). *Noisy.* New York: Lothrop, Lee & Shepard Books.

Isadora, R. (1985). *I hear.* New York: Greenwillow.

Isadora, R. (1985). *I see.* New York: Greenwillow.

Kunhardt, D. (1962). *Pat the bunny.* Racine, WI: Western.

Martin, B. (1967). *Brown bear, brown bear, what do you see?* Illustrated by E. Carle. New York: Henry Holt.

Martin, B., & Archambault, J. (1988). *Listen to the rain.* Illustrated by J. Endicott. New York: Henry Holt.

Martin, B., & Archambault, J. (1987). *Knots on a counting rope.* Illustrated by T. Rand. New York: Henry Holt.

Morris, A. (1989). *Bread, bread, bread.* Photographs by K. Heyman. New York: Lothrop, Lee & Shepard Books.

Oxenbury, H. (1985). *I touch.* London: Walker Books.

Sendak, M. (1962). *Chicken soup with rice.* New York: Harper & Row.

Shaw, C. G. (1988). *It looked like spilt milk.* New York: Harper & Row.

Activities Suggested in the Five Senses Curriculum Web and Front-of-the-Book CD

The following activities involve all the senses. They are included in the curriculum web and are appropriate for young children to do. **(Note: Refer to the front-of-the-book CD for the additional curriculum webs of "the senses.")**

MAKING SANDPAPER. Provide cardstock, watery glue, paintbrushes, and containers of sand of various grades. Children first paint on one side of the cardstock with watery glue. Then they choose a grade of sand and sprinkle it on the card. Allow to dry overnight. When dry, the cards can be examined and touched by the children to compare how the different types of sand feel.

WHIP IT UP. Using a hand rotary eggbeater, dish pan, and liquid dishwashing detergent, children can turn the beaters and whip up bubbles in the individual dishpan or the sand and water table.

INDOOR RAINBOW. Fill a clear glass jar with water and set on a window sill in the bright sunlight. Place white paper on the floor to "capture the rainbow." The children can paint rainbows with watercolors.

MY FIVE SENSES
Sensory Texture Box
Nature walk—see, hear, smell,
and touch
Each child makes a "My Five
Senses" book
Puppet talks about the senses
Feel water, freeze it, then see and
feel it in a frozen-state
Build with blocks
Work puzzles
Eat finger foods
Woodworking center

I CAN TOUCH

Books:
Pat the Bunny
Soft as a Kitten
I Touch
Knots on a Counting Rope

Activities:
Make sandpaper
Find buried treasure in sand
"My favorite thing to touch"
Use a "feely box or bag"
Make mud pies

I CAN SEE

Books:
Peek-a-Boo
It Looked Like Spilt Milk
Look Again
A Story, A Story
I See
Brown Bear, Brown Bear, What Do
You See?

Activities:
"My favorite thing to see"
Whip it up
Indoor rainbow
Look at woodcuts
Use a magnifying glass
Make signs to label block buildings
Play "What's Missing?" or "Who's
Missing?" game

My Five Senses by Aliki

I CAN TASTE

Books:
Green Eggs and Ham
Pancakes! Pancakes!
Pancakes for Breakfast
Stone Soup
How My Parents Learned to Eat
Chicken Soup With Rice

Activities:
Why do we have a tongue?
"My favorite taste"
Make place mats
Have a tasting tray
If colors were foods, what would
they be?
Make "Stone Soup"

I CAN SMELL

Books:
Bread, Bread, Bread

Activities:
Bake bread; smell it
cooking
Why do we have a nose?
"My favorite smell"
Sniff "smell cards"
Smell fruits
Name different things that have
odors—try to describe
Take a "nose walk"

I CAN HEAR

Books:
I Hear
Listen to the Rain
Noisy

Activities:
"My Favorite Sound"
Use sound cans
Play and listen to musical
instruments
Listen to music
Listen to wind chimes
Listen to a tape of sounds and
guess the sound

FIGURE 9–7
A curriculum planning web using the children's book, *My Five Senses,* by Aliki.

LOOKING AT WOODCUTS. Woodcuts or woodblocks are among the oldest artistic media in both Western and Eastern cultures. Some of the earliest books for children were illustrated by black-and-white woodcuts.

To create a woodcut, an artist draws an image on a block of wood and cuts away the areas around the design. After rolling ink onto this raised surface, the artist presses the woodblock against paper, transferring the image from the block to the paper. (Norton, 1999)

Color prints require a different woodblock for each color in the picture. Gail Haley used woodcuts to illustrate her version of an African folktale, *A Story, A Story.*

Research local artists in your community to see if any of them have created woodcuts or woodblocks. Invite them to visit the class and demonstrate their art to the children. Perhaps the school-age children could make some of their own in the woodworking center.

SENSORY TEXTURE BOX. You can make this for the infants and toddlers *or* you and the older children can make one. Use an appliance box at least 3 feet square. Put several pounds of sand or gravel sacks in the bottom of the box to stabilize it. Close the box and tape down the flaps. Paint or decorate the box. Glue textured materials securely to the four sides of the box. Use sandpaper, cotton balls, egg cartons, kente cloth, silk flowers, foil, twigs, and other textured materials. This is a different kind of "texture board" for you and the children to enjoy in the classroom (adapted from Parks, 1994).

MAKE PLACE MATS. Make place mats for use at snack and meal time. Cut out colorful labels from food packaging, magazines, or construction paper. Glue these on a piece of paper and laminate. The children can share these, or each child can use the one he made.

LET'S USE ALL OUR SENSES. Set up a special "tasting tray" with foods that taste sweet, sour, salty, spicy, or bitter. Create "smell cards" using different spices and herbs secured to cards with white glue. (The glue does not have any odor.) Make "sound cans" by placing paper clips, beans, and so on, in empty plastic film containers. Make a "feely box or feely bag" filled with different items that emphasize shape and softness. Let the children feel an object and tell you what it feels like and what they think the items are without looking. Then they get to see if they guessed it or not.

Recipe Suggested in the Curriculum Web

See the rebus chart in Figure 9–8, the recipe and visual directions for Stone Soup. Source: Jackman, 2005, *Sing Me a Story! Tell Me a Song!* Back-of-the-book CD, Theme #13. (Review the rebus chart for applesauce in Chapter 3.)

STONE SOUP
(Read the story first. Have three clean rocks ready!)
    3 stalks of celery, chopped
    2 large carrots, chopped
    2 medium onions, chopped
    2 medium potatoes, chopped
    3 medium tomatoes, chopped
    1/2 teaspoon basil
    1/2 cup fresh parsley
    1 1/2 tablespoons salt
    1/2 teaspoon pepper

Everyone can chop or measure something. Put all the ingredients into a big pan on the stove. (An electric crock pot will work, too.) Add water to cover. Cook using low heat 2 to 3 hours. You can add rice (1 to 2 cups) to thicken.

STONE SOUP

Wash hands, Wash 3 clean rocks,

Chop and measure 3 stalks of celery, 2 large carrots,

2 medium onions, 2 medium potatoes, 3 medium tomatoes,

1/2 teaspoon basil, 1/2 cup fresh parsley,

1 1/2 tablespoon salt, and 1/2 teaspoon pepper.

Put all ingredients in a big pot and place on the stove.

Add water to cover the vegetables, Cook for 2 - 3 hours.

Add 1/2 cup rice to thicken the soup. ENJOY!

FIGURE 9–8
Rebus Chart, the recipe and visual directions for "Stone Soup." Source: Jackman, 2005, *Sing Me A Story! Tell Me A Song!*

The following songs can also be part of the sensory activities.

Figure 9–9 is the curriculum planning web worksheet with sensory activities added. This worksheet with appropriate additions is included in each chapter.

I HAVE TWO EARS

Words and Music by Jo Eklof

I have two ears to hear, hear, hear. I have a brain to think. I have two eyes to look, look, look. I have two lids to blink. I have a nose to sniff, sniff, sniff. I have some hands to touch. I have a mouth to give a smile and say, "I love you so much!

THERE'S A BRAND NEW HOLE IN MY MOUTH

Words and Music by Jo Eklof

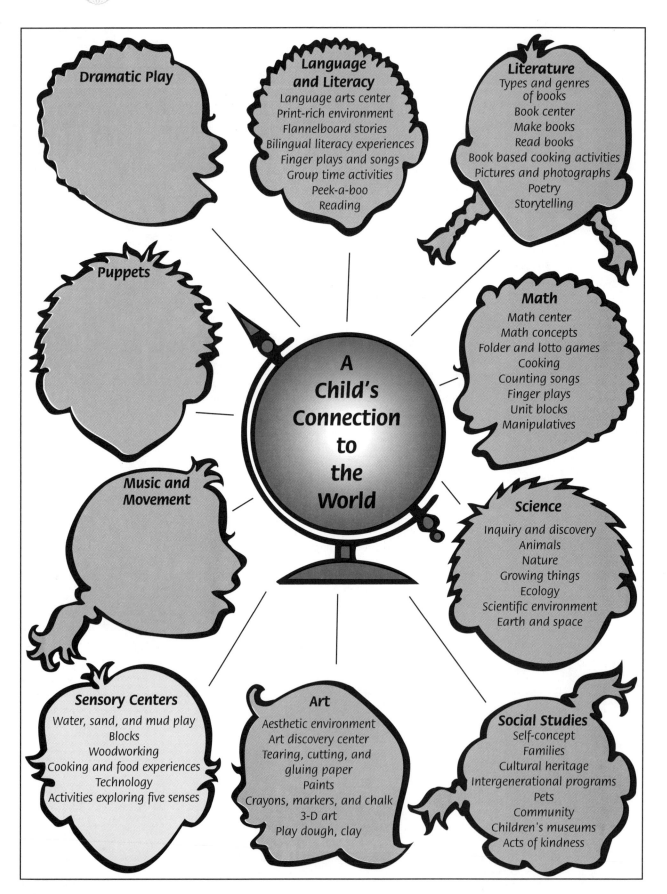

Dramatic Play

Language and Literacy
Language arts center
Print-rich environment
Flannelboard stories
Bilingual literacy experiences
Finger plays and songs
Group time activities
Peek-a-boo
Reading

Literature
Types and genres
of books
Book center
Make books
Read books
Book based cooking activities
Pictures and photographs
Poetry
Storytelling

Puppets

Math
Math center
Math concepts
Folder and lotto games
Cooking
Counting songs
Finger plays
Unit blocks
Manipulatives

Music and Movement

A Child's Connection to the World

Science
Inquiry and discovery
Animals
Nature
Growing things
Ecology
Scientific environment
Earth and space

Sensory Centers
Water, sand, and mud play
Blocks
Woodworking
Cooking and food experiences
Technology
Activities exploring five senses

Art
Aesthetic environment
Art discovery center
Tearing, cutting, and
gluing paper
Paints
Crayons, markers, and chalk
3-D art
Play dough, clay

Social Studies
Self-concept
Families
Cultural heritage
Intergenerational programs
Pets
Community
Children's museums
Acts of kindness

FIGURE 9–9
A curriculum planning web worksheet with sensory activities added.

✳ AFTERVIEW

Through sensory activities, a child

- 🌐 has opportunities to develop taste, olfactory, tactile, auditory, and visual skills.
- 🌐 develops perceptual discrimination by shape, size, color, detail, and design.
- 🌐 experiments with concepts of balance, leverage, volume, weights, and measurements.
- 🌐 learns that the parts make up the whole.
- 🌐 explores spatial relationships.
- 🌐 learns to solve problems.
- 🌐 practices reading and writing readiness activities.
- 🌐 develops strength and coordination of large and small muscles.

- 🌐 practices eye-hand and hand-hand coordination.
- 🌐 experiments with new materials and tools and learns to apply rules of safety.
- 🌐 enjoys a sense of achievement and self-control.
- 🌐 practices oral language by interaction with peers.
- 🌐 learns to work independently as well as cooperatively with others.
- 🌐 learns to complete a task and to be responsible for cleaning up after himself.
- 🌐 has opportunities to make choices.
- 🌐 expands his knowledge of the world.

✳ KEY TERMS

hardware
hollow blocks

sensory experiences
software

unit blocks
woodworking center

✳ EXPLORATIONS

1. What is meant by *sensory experiences* of young children? Why are these important in the growth and development of children? Explain.

2. Select an early education classroom and observe for at least one hour. Describe, in writing, six sensory activities the children were involved in at the time you were observing. What did you learn from this observation? Explain.

3. Select and plan a cooking or creative food experience for young children. Specify which age group this activity is planned for: infants, toddlers, preschoolers, or primary-age children. In writing, list objectives, materials needed, step-by-step procedures for presenting this activity, follow-up activities, and

evaluation guidelines. (A blank activity plan worksheet is available in the front-of-the-book CD.)

4. In developing cooking activities how might you use these activities to explore other cultures? Give six examples of cooking activities that would be useful for this purpose.

5. Select an early education classroom and observe for one hour. Describe, in writing, what happened in the block center during your observation. How many children were in the center at one time? Were these the same children for the entire hour you observed? How many boys? How many girls? What were they building? Describe the developmental stages you saw. What did you learn from this observation? Explain.

✳ REFERENCES

Beaty, J. J. (1992). *Preschool appropriate practices.* New York: Harcourt.

Betz, C. (1992, March). The happy medium. *Young Children, 47*(3), 34–35.

Bredekamp, S., & Rosegrant, T. (1994). Learning and teaching with technology. In J. L. Wright & D. Shade (Eds.). *Young children: Active learners in a technological age.* Washington, DC: NAEYC.

Buckleitner, W. (2002). *Sharing at the computer.* On-line at: *http://teacher.scholastic.com*

Buckleitner, W. (1995, Summer). Moving beyond the myths—Computers and children. *Scholastic Parent and Child,* 24–25.

Colker, L. J. (2005). *The cooking book: Fostering young children's learning and delight.* Washington, DC: NAEYC.

Cryer, D., Harms, T., & Ray, A. R. (1996). *Nutrition activities for preschoolers.* Menlo Park, CA: Addison-Wesley.

Dodge, D. T., Colker, L. J., & Heroman, C. (2002). *The creative curriculum for preschool* (4th ed.).Washington, DC: Teaching Strategies, Inc.

Essa, E. (2007). *Introduction to early childhood education* (5th ed.). Clifton Park, NY: Thomson Delmar Learning.

Feeney, S., Christensen, D., & Moravcik, E. (2001). *Who am I in the lives of children?* (6th ed.). Upper Saddle River, NJ: Merrill.

Fischer, M. A., & Gillespie, C. W. (2003, July). Computers and young children's development. *Young Children, 58*(4), 85–91.

Gestwicki, C. (2007). *Developmentally appropriate practice: Curriculum and development in early education* (3rd ed.). Clifton Park, NY: Thomson Delmar Learning.

Haugland, S. W. (2000, January). Early childhood classrooms in the 21st century: Using computers to maximize learning. *Young Children, 55*(1), 12–18.

Hendrick, J. (2003). *Total learning—Developmental curriculum for the young child* (6th ed.). Upper Saddle River, NJ: Merrill.

Hill, D. M. (1977). *Mud, sand, and water.* Washington, DC: NAEYC.

Hirsch, E. S. (Ed.). (1993). *The block book* (Rev. ed.). Washington, DC: NAEYC.

Holliday, L. (1996). *The complete guide to classroom centers.* Cypress, CA: Creative Teaching Press.

Isbell, R. T., & Raines, S. C. (2007). *Creativity and the arts with young children.* Clifton Park, NY: Thomson Delmar Learning.

Jackman, H. L. (2005). *Sing me a story! Tell me a song!* Clifton Park, NY: Thomson Delmar Learning.

Jensen, B. J., & Bullard, J. A. (2002, May). The mud center: Recapturing childhood. *Young Children, 57*(3), 16–19.

Johnson, H. M. (1982). *The act of block building.* New York: Bank Street.

Mayesky, M. (2006). *Creative activities for young children* (8th ed.). Clifton Park, NY: Thomson Delmar Learning.

Miller, R. (1996). *The developmentally appropriate inclusive classroom in early education.* Clifton Park, NY: Thomson Delmar Learning.

Miller, S. A. (1994, March). Sand and water around the room. *Early Childhood Today, 8*(6), 37–45.

National Association for the Education of Young Children. (1996). Technology and Young Children, Ages 3 through 8. (Position paper on technology and young children, on-line at: http://www.naeyc.org/resources/eyly/1996/09a.htm

Newman, R. (1995, Winter). Bringing the classroom into the kitchen: Lessons learned at home. *Childhood Education, 71*(2), 107–108.

Norton, D. E. (1999). *Through the eyes of a child—An introduction to children's literature* (5th ed.). Upper Saddle River, NJ: Merrill.

Parks, L. (1994, Fall). Make it with a box. *Texas Child Care, 18*(2), 22–28.

Perry, B. D. (2002). *Using technology in the early childhood classroom.* On-line at: http://teacher.scholastic.com/professional/bruceperry

Petersen, E. A. (2003). *Early childhood planning, methods, and materials* (2nd ed.). Boston: Allyn & Bacon.

Southern Early Childhood Association (SECA). (1989). *Appropriate uses of computers in the early childhood curriculum* [Brochure]. Little Rock, AR: Author.

Starns, L. (2002, Summer). Don't take the blocks away!—Block centers in preschool and primary classrooms. *The Early Years, 24*(2), 2–3.

Stephenson, A. (2001, May). What George taught me about toddlers and water. *Young Children, 57*(3), 10–14.

Wellhousen, K., & Kieff, J. (2001). *A constructivist approach to block play in early childhood.* Clifton Park, NY: Thomson Delmar Learning.

✳ ADDITIONAL READINGS AND RESOURCES

Alexander, N. P. (2000, Winter). Blocks and basics. *Dimensions of Early Childhood, 28*(1), 29–30.

Anderson, G. T. (2000, March). Computers in a developmentally appropriate curriculum. *Young Children, 55*(2), 90–93.

Bergen, D. (2002, Summer). Using technology in inclusive classrooms. *Childhood Education, 78*(4), 251–252.

Buckleitner, W. (2002, November–December). Teaching with technology. *Early Childhood Today, 17*(3), 12–13.

Buffington, J. (2002, May–June). Creative cooking. *Early Childhood News, 14*(3), 48–50.

Clements, D. H., & Sarama, J. (2003, November). Young children and technology: What does the research say? *Young Children, 58*(6), 34–40.

Cohen, L., & Blagojevic, B. (2002, September). Observing the whole child. *Early Childhood Today, 17*(1), 38–47.

Da Ros-Voseles, D., & Baldwin, V. (2002, Summer). In praise of sandboxes. *Dimensions of Early Childhood, 30*(3), 21–24.

Johnston, C. B. (1998, Spring). Four easels, five sand tables, and a billion blocks: Setting up an early childhood classroom. *Dimensions of Early Childhood, 26*(2), 24–27.

Johnston, L. L., Johnston, J. H., & Forde, J. (2001). *Use that computer! Teacher's guide for classroom success.* Nashville, TN: Incentive Publications.

Lasher, E., Abraham, C., & Joy, J. (2002, January–February). My five senses. *Early Childhood News, 14*(1), 28–31.

Levin, D. E. (1998). *Remote control childhood? Combating the hazards of media culture.* Washington, DC: NAEYC.

Marotz, L. R., Cross, M. Z., & Rush, J. M. (2005). *Health, safety, and nutrition* (6th ed.). Clifton Park, NY: Thomson Delmar Learning.

Murphy, K. L., DePasquale, R., & McNamara, E. (2003, November). Meaningful connections: Using technology in primary classrooms. *Young Children, 58*(6), 12–18.

Papert, S. (1999). *Mindstorms: Children, computers, and powerful ideas* (2nd ed.). New York: Basic Books.

Robertson, C. (2003). *Safety, nutrition, and health in early childhood education* (2nd ed.). Clifton Park, NY: Thomson Delmar Learning.

Simons, B. (2002, March). The sand tray. *Young Children, 57*(2), 8–9.

Stiles, G. (1999, March). Logging on! *Early Childhood Today, 13*(6), 8.

Young, D., & Behounek, L. M. (2006, March). Kindergartners use PowerPoint to lead their own parent-teacher conferences. *Young Children, 61*(2), 24–26.

For additional information on early education curriculum, visit our Web site at http://www.earlychilded.delmar.com

CHAPTER 10

MUSIC AND MOVEMENT

OBJECTIVES

AFTER STUDYING THIS CHAPTER, YOU SHOULD BE ABLE TO:

- Discuss why music and movement education is developmentally appropriate for young children.
- Define kinesthetics, locomotor, nonlocomotor, and manipulative movement skills.
- Describe musical experiences and activities that should be part of a music curriculum for young children.
- List the types of musical instruments that children can make from materials collected from home.
- Discuss how to set up an effective music center, including guidance techniques, that the children can enjoy throughout the day.
- Identify the types of music that children and teachers can enjoy together.
- List movement activities that teachers and children can enjoy together.

OVERVIEW

Hearing is the first sense to develop. Sometime between 20 and 30 weeks of gestation the human fetus can hear.

(Shore & Strasser, 2006)

tone
An individual musical sound.

rhythm
A sense of movement and patterns in music created by beats, the duration and volume of sounds, and the silences between sounds.

volume
The softness or loudness of sound.

tempo
A sense of slowness or rapidity in music.

"'Music' and 'the young child' are almost synonymous terms. They both invoke a sense of wonderment, enjoyment, laughter, movement, freedom, creativity, and expression" (Greenberg, 1979). A developmentally appropriate and creative classroom for young children has music and movement experiences woven into the daily curriculum. In fact, if you stop and listen to an active early childhood classroom, you will discover that it has a rhythmic pattern and beat all its own.

Unplanned, spontaneous moments occur daily in an early education environment. Young children hum, sing, clap hands, and move their bodies as they play and complete activities. Music, sound, and movement continuously contribute to the learning processes of young children. Human bodies function to rhythms (e.g., heartbeat, breathing), and children respond by moving. Music comes out of rhythm. "Music is one of our greatest inheritances as human beings. So global is the human experience of music that it has often been called the universal language of humankind" (Moomaw, 1984).

All humans come into the world with an innate capability for music. At a very early age, this capability is shaped by the music system of the culture in which a child is raised. That culture affects the construction of instruments, the way people sound when they sing, and even the way they hear sound. (Shelemay, 2001)

Music is a language, a means of communication. It is communicated through **tone, rhythm, volume,** range, **tempo,** and movement (Greenberg, 1979). Music can communicate feelings to children even when its cultural origin and language is foreign to them. Children are acquainted with music from birth. The tone of a mother's voice, the rhythm of a rocking chair, and the chanting of nonsense syllables are basic to a child's life. Before she knows words, an infant experiments with vocal sounds and understands tones and rhythms. "Early language learning is, in a sense, early music learning, since children learn both skills simultaneously" (Miche, 2002).

A child's involvement with music includes listening; creative activities related to singing, body movement, playing, and making instruments; and aesthetic examination.

Where does all this squirming energy come from? From the billions of active neurons hungry for stimulation and experience. I have come to appreciate the marvelous opportunities music and movement offer children for rich and varied learning experiences. (Palmer, 2001)

Music and movement are intertwined. They reinforce and strengthen each other. A child hears music, and she moves in response. A child's physical maturation process motivates her to move naturally in response to internal and external stimuli. Griss (1994) emphasizes that "children exposed to creative movement as a language for learning are becoming more aware of their own natural resources. They are expanding their concepts of creativity and of how they can use their own bodies."

In this chapter, we explore the ways music and movement can introduce concepts, foster growth in motor skills, reinforce and develop language skills, nourish positive self-esteem, encourage self-expression, and connect to other curriculum areas and chapters of this book.

MUSIC AND CREATIVE MOVEMENT EDUCATION FOR YOUNG CHILDREN

Music makes children want to clap hands, tap toes, beat drums, and dance. *Children learn best through acting upon what they experience.* Moving can be fun for its own sake and a way to enjoy music even more. Children express the music's aesthetic qualities through the movement of their bodies as they listen to, perform, and create music. "By using the body the child expresses what he *perceives* in the music, how he *feels* about the music, and what he *understands* in it" (Greenberg, 1979). Smith (2002) expands this thought even more.

> *Every child learns by moving, and every teacher can teach by moving with the children. In dance, children interpret ideas and feelings through the use of their bodies in an open-ended search for a unique movement vocabulary. Children are able to create their own dances just as they create their own stories.*

For young children in early education settings, including infants and toddlers, music and movement activities nurture the development of minds, bodies, emotions, and language. As you plan developmentally appropriate goals and objectives to encourage music and movement experiences, consider the following:

Include *physical development* activities that can help children gain increasing control over their large and small muscles, experiment with the movement of their bodies, and experience success in movement. Play, as discussed in Chapter 1 of this book, is the most developmentally appropriate activity in which young children engage. Researchers have validated this again and again. Still, today, recess and physical education are being cut from schools, not emphasized. Pica (2006) helps us understand even more how critical it is that young children have many opportunities during the day to PLAY. *Today the curriculum once considered appropriate for first and second grades is being taught to children in the kindergarten, and the kindergarten curriculum is foisted on children who are not yet five years old.*

Incorporate *intellectual growth* activities that can stimulate children to experiment with how sound is created through their voices or musical instruments, to recognize songs, and to explore melodies by varying tempo, rhythm, tone, and volume.

Include *listening* activities that make music a part of the daily environment by asking for a response, remembering a song or parts of a song, recognizing musical instruments, focusing on sound, and developing auditory discrimination. Every time a child engages in a music experience, she is listening.

Provide children with *socially and emotionally responsive* activities that energize, soothe, and enhance children's expression of feelings and sharpen their awareness of feelings for others. Music and movement experiences can also help children know and appreciate themselves and promote cultural identity and pride in themselves and others.

Give children opportunities to create new movements for action songs.

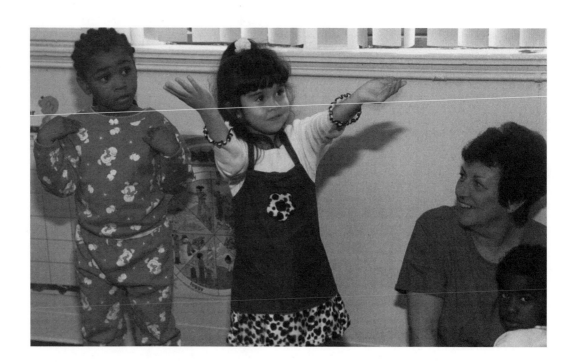

Include musical *language development* activities that encourage the acquisition and use of language to extend vocabulary, to learn word and sound patterns through singing and listening, and to describe musical happenings that can help children develop an appreciation for the music and language of diverse cultures. "The songs and music of childhood are a part of our cultural heritage. The folk songs and ballads that have survived to the present day and the regional tunes parents and teachers offer are part of each child's cultural literacy" (Machado, 2007).

Take advantage of music and movement opportunities that stimulate children's *creativity* and *uniqueness*. Give children musically creative group time by offering each child the opportunity to add to songs and finger plays and to create new movements for action songs. Each musical creation adds to the creativity of the whole group. Haines and Gerber (1996) suggest that children create to the sounds of their environment through active listening and through moving, singing, and playing percussion instruments. All these are integral to early childhood musical education.

LARGE AND SMALL MUSCLE DEVELOPMENT AND PHYSICAL FITNESS

Early education curriculum should include well-defined opportunities, both indoor and outdoor, for young children to develop motor skills. As discussed in previous chapters, setting up the environment and planning appropriate activities depends on the developmental skills, interests, and needs of the children.

Sanders (2002) has the following insight:

Young children learn through interaction with their environment. . . . [L]earning is moving. To learn how to climb, throw a ball, jump or do any other physical skill, children need a variety of practice opportunities over time and within many different contexts.

Large muscle (gross motor) development usually precedes small muscle (fine motor) development. For this chapter, we will focus on motor development that includes locomotor skills, large muscle activities, and physical fitness. Underlying all of this is the understanding that possibilities for exploration, creativity, and self-expression are included as part of the motor skill planning process.

Small muscle development is discussed in other chapters and includes such activities as turning pages of a book, finger plays, scribbling, drawing, writing, tearing, cutting, pouring, stringing beads, inserting pegs, pounding nails, and building with blocks. Involvement with music and movement projects can be very effective in furthering the development of small muscles.

Basic types of movement in young children, identified by Greenberg (1979) and expanded by Pica (2004), are locomotor, nonlocomotor, combination, and manipulative. All these actions need practice, encouragement, and an adult's understanding of individual growth patterns.

Locomotor movement (fundamental movement) is the ability to move the whole body from one place to another. This is demonstrated by crawling, creeping, walking, running, jumping, hopping, skipping, and climbing.

Nonlocomotor movement (axial or body movement) occurs when the feet remain stationary (as in standing, kneeling, sitting, or lying) while other parts of the body move. Examples are stretching, reaching, bending, twisting, bouncing, shaking, and clapping.

A combination of the previous two types of movement involves various motions that enhance coordination while giving children movement and rhythm combinations that occur simultaneously. This is demonstrated by walking and clapping at the same time or hopping and shaking (Greenberg, 1979).

Manipulative movement skills in the physical education field are described by Pica (2004) as "gross motor movements involving force imparted to or received from

locomotor movement
The ability to move the whole body from one place to another.

nonlocomotor movement
Occurs when the feet remain stationary (as in standing, kneeling, or sitting), while other parts of the body move.

manipulative movement
Large (gross) motor movements demonstrated by pulling, lifting, throwing, or kicking an object.

Plan and provide daily developmentally appropriate movement and exercise activities for the children.

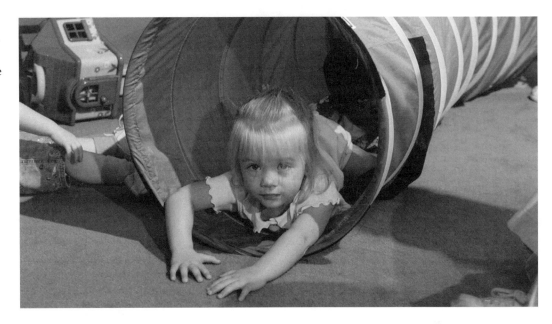

objects . . . [or] any gross motor skill in which an object is usually involved (manipulated)." This is demonstrated by pulling, pushing, lifting, striking, throwing, kicking, and ball catching.

Isbell and Raines (2007) add another important factor: **kinesthetics**—the use of the body to learn about physical capabilities, develop body awareness, and gain understanding of the world. Howard Gardner's (1983) theories of multiple intelligences describe bodily-kinesthetic intelligence as the ability to unite the body and mind in physical performance.

kinesthetics

The use of the body to learn about physical capabilities and to develop body awareness.

Opportunities for outdoor play aren't what they used to be, and children are suffering as a result. Health and education professionals are increasingly alarmed that lack of exercises and poor eating habits are leading declining levels of fitness among children and increased levels of childhood obesity. (Sutterby & Frost, 2002)

For you, as a teacher of young children, this means planning and providing daily developmentally appropriate movement and exercise activities for the children in your care. This specifies allowing time for movement exploration. Start with slow stretches to get their bodies "warmed up." For example, the children can touch their toes, then make circles with their arms, and finally stretch their arms way above their heads. You should demonstrate the importance of health and fitness by encouraging and participating with your actions as well as your words.

Locomotor, large muscle, and fitness activities can easily be combined with creative movement and music activities. There are no limits on how to accomplish this. You and the children together can discover wonderful things through movement and music!

TYPES OF MUSIC

A music curriculum for young children should include many opportunities to explore sound through singing, moving, listening, and playing instruments, as well as introductory experiences with verbalization and visualization of musical ideas. The music literature included in the curriculum should be of high quality and lasting value, including traditional children's songs, folk songs, classical music, and music from a variety of cultures, styles, and time periods (Music Educators National Conference [MENC], 1994).

The basic sources of music are the human voice, instruments, environmental sounds, and music from radio, television, videotapes, DVDs, audiocassettes, and CDs. As you use these sources to plan music experiences for young children, remember to connect them to their life experiences. See Figure 10–1 for basic terms.

Songs and Singing

Young children love to sing. Beginning in infancy and continuing on throughout their childhood, they are experimenting with their voices and the sounds that they can make. Billhartz (2007) helps us understand this even more:

> A young child will first attempt to sing by isolating parts of words or selected words from a larger song. If provided a rich array of singing experiences, children will begin with spoken and singsong inflection as toddlers, and then move to matching pitches and singing entire songs as older preschoolers. Although many children will not sing in a group setting or in front of another child or adult, they will sing during playtime. This is a perfectly developmental way for young children to respond. As children become more comfortable with their singing voices, they will begin to join in group singing activities.

Here are a few more musical items to think about:

🌐 Singing can be experienced alone or shared with others.

🌐 Songs encourage the children to make up new words and to move with the music. Neelly (2002) adds:

🌐 Singing with children throughout daily routines nurtures important learning connections.

🌐 Singing is a developmentally appropriate practice.

🌐 Enthusiastic teacher participation in singing encourages the development of children's innate musical ability.

> There is a whole generation that doesn't know nursery rhymes or traditional tunes. You and I have the responsibility and privilege of passing on our musical heritage and putting music back into children's lives. . . . Just open your mouth and SING! (Feldman, 2002)

There are many delightful and fun-filled songs to sing, such as the ones included in the developmentally appropriate activities at the end of this chapter and the following ones on page 305:

FIGURE 10–1
Basic musical terms.

---

melody
A sequence of tones of varying pitches organized in a rhythmically meaningful way.

pitch
The highness or lowness of a tone on a musical scale.

timbre
The unique tone quality of a voice or musical instrument.

Beat—An accent of sound or a continuing series of accents.

Melody—A sequence of tones of varying pitches organized in a rhythmically meaningful way.

Pitch—The highness or lowness of a tone on a musical scale.

Rhythm—A sense of movement and patterns in music created by beats, the duration and volume of sounds, and the silences between sounds.

Tempo—A sense of slowness or rapidity in music.

Timbre (TAM-bur)—The unique tone quality of a voice or musical instrument.

Tone—An individual musical sound.

Volume—The softness or loudness of sound.

- Songs that offer repetition and chorus, such as "Polly Put the Kettle On," "Mary Had a Little Lamb," and "Here We Go Round the Mulberry Bush."
- Songs with repeated words or phrases that can be treated like an echo, such as "Miss Mary Mack" and 'She'll Be Comin' 'round the Mountain."
- Songs that ask children to supply sound effects or animal noises, such as "If You're Happy and You Know It" and "Old MacDonald Had a Farm."
- Ballads or songs that tell a story, such as "Hush Little Baby," "Humpty Dumpty," and "Little Bo Peep."
- Question-and-answer songs or name games that help children make the transition from speaking to singing, such as "Do You Know the Muffin Man?"

Let us not forget how important a song can be to a young child—songs with words often give rise to spontaneous play as well as to wonderful moments of magic. When music is integral to a child's life, then it becomes central to a child's play. Play is a time when children are integrating new concepts and music may provide the anchor children need to remember and repeat what is being learned. (McGraw, 2002).

Using the Voice

When young children experiment with their voices and tongues, they can sound like musical instruments, animals, and the wind. Encourage the children to make some of these sounds:

whisper very quietly	cluck
talk very softly, then loudly	buzzz
whistle	growl
sneeze	bark
purr	snore
hum	cry

Choosing Classical Selections

Research tells us that classical music stimulates musical responses from young children.

Encourage children to use their voices to sound like musical instruments, animals, and the wind.

Whether they are "conducting," relaxing, listening, or moving creatively to these recorded musical works, children enjoy and can get caught up in them. "Because children's tastes are so variable, it is best if the teacher introduces a wide variety of orchestral and instrumental pieces and lets the children select those they particularly like" (Moomaw, 1984). Tapes and CDs are available in libraries or stores under many different labels and performing artists. Here are a few children's favorites:

🌐 Britten/*A Young Person's Guide to the Orchestra*

🌐 Copland/*Rodeo*

🌐 Dukas/*The Sorcerer's Apprentice*

🌐 Grofé/*Grand Canyon Suite*

🌐 Mozart/*Concerto for Flute, Harp, and Strings* (K. 299)

🌐 Prokofiev/*Peter and the Wolf*

🌐 Rimsky-Korsakov/*Flight of the Bumble Bee*

🌐 Rossini/*William Tell Overture*

🌐 Saint-Saëns/*Carnival of the Animals*

🌐 Strauss, R./*Till Eulenspiegel's Merry Pranks*

🌐 Stravinsky/*The Firebird*

🌐 Tchaikovsky/*The Nutcracker Suite*

🌐 Tchaikovsky/*The Sleeping Beauty*

Other Musical Experiences

As with language, children should not be deprived of the whole musical picture because they are too young to understand it. Children learn and understand a great deal more than they can speak about during their first years, but we would never think of not speaking to infants and toddlers just because they cannot speak. . . . Music deserves the same natural assimilation. (Andress & Walker, 1992)

When selecting songs, CDs, and tapes, include those you remember and enjoyed from your childhood. This will add a personal touch for you and the children. Also, select other music from chants, nursery tunes, American folk music, folk music from around the world, popular music, show tunes, country music, patriotic music, holiday and seasonal music, electronic experimental music, music for dancing and marching, rock music, and jazz.

For infants and toddlers, heavily orchestrated musical selections typically offer too much too soon. Gradually introduce this type of music into the environment. As you plan your music curriculum for all the developmental stages, remember that children are bombarded with sound (sound pollution) today. Background music in early childhood settings should be selective. Think about when and why you want to have music playing, and then choose it carefully.

MUSICAL INSTRUMENTS

Instruments of all kinds have value in the musical environment of young children. They should be encouraged to listen to the instrument, touch it, and experiment with making sounds and music on it. Have instruments of good quality that are well cared for, such as tambourines, wooden maracas, woodblocks, rhythm sticks, drums, finger cymbals, bells, triangles, and rain sticks. Teacher- and child-made instruments should always be included, as well as wind chimes, gongs, and music boxes.

"Invite a musician to play an instrument for the children, tell about it, and pass it around to be touched most respectfully. The children should have many listening experiences and exposures to many kinds of music and musical instruments" (Andress & Walker, 1992).

Types of Instruments

Usually the first instrument sounds a child hears and experiments with are those created in the home, such as banging on pots and pans (drums), jingling two spoons together (castanets), shaking a ring of metal measuring spoons (tambourine), banging two wooden spoons together (rhythm sticks), and crashing two lids or metal pie pans together (cymbals).

It is important for early education programs to encourage young children to continue this exploration of sounds and to broaden their understanding of musical instruments and the sounds they make. Percussion instruments are the ones most widely used in an early childhood setting. See Figure 10–2 for a list of musical instruments.

Dee Lillegard (1988), in *Percussion*, a volume in her Introduction to Musical Instruments series, tells us:

Percussion means hitting.

Bang on a can. Bang on a pan.

That's percussion.

Pound on a drum. Tap with your thumb.

That's percussion.

Musical instruments have many uses, actually. Everybody knows that music can be entertaining. But instruments can do more than please an audience. Around the world, they

FIGURE 10–2
List of musical instruments.

Percussion Instruments

Drums

Triangle

Cymbals

Tambourine

Xylophone

Chimes and bells

Castanets

Maracas

Claves

Glockenspiel

Piano

Wind Instruments

Flute

Piccolo

Oboe

Clarinet

Bassoon

Saxophones (soprano, tenor, and baritone)

String Instruments

(bowed)

Viola

Cello

Bass

Violin

(plucked)

Guitar

Mandolin

Ukulele

Harp

Banjo

Brass Instruments

Trumpet

Cornet

Bugle

Trombone

French horn

Tuba

play a big role in religion, celebration, communication, and even politics and war. In fact, you can travel anywhere on earth and you'll find musical instruments in almost every culture along the way. (Corbett, 1995)

Drums are used in the music and dances of many cultures, including African, Native American, Korean, and Thai (hand drums, tom-toms, and long ones carried on one shoulder with a strap). Maracas and claves sticks (short, polished hardwood sticks) are part of the Mexican and Caribbean musical heritage.

Other instruments also have been a part of ethnic music for centuries, such as the flute from Native American and African cultures and the bamboo flute from Chinese, Japanese, and Korean cultures. Stringed instruments, such as the Chinese *samisen*, the Japanese *koto* (a type of harp), and Thailand's *so sam sai*, add beautiful sounds to music selections (Allen, McNeill, & Schmidt, 1992).

Ask parents and community musicians to visit your class and share their music and musical instruments with the children. The combination of personal experiences and hands-on involvement with percussion, string, woodwind, and brass instruments will enrich the children *now*, during their formative years.

Introducing Musical Sounds and Instruments

We know that music is a spontaneous and joyous part of young children's lives. They hear it in the world around them and they respond by cooing, babbling, singing, dancing, and interpreting it in their individual ways from infancy onward. How we gather and keep the energy and interest of the children depends on how we include music in our daily curriculum.

Bea Wolf, composer and performer of children's music, suggests the following activities for sharing musical experiences with young children:

🌐 Introduce musical recordings that children can sway to. Have the children close their eyes and move their arms to the music. Ask them "What do you hear?" Listen to their response. Suggest that they sway their bodies with the music. A waltz tempo is easy to begin with, by swaying on the beat of 1 (1–2–3, 1–2–3, 1–2–3, etc.)

🌐 Select a favorite song and have the children clap to the rhythm of the music. They can clap their hands together, clap hands on knees, and clap hands on the floor. Often they will continue this activity on their own by humming, singing, and clapping to themselves throughout the day.

🌐 Wind chimes offer a delightful way to have the children focus on soft sounds. Group time can be a special time for children to listen closely as you share the sounds of several different kinds of wind chimes. Have each child listen closely to what these sound like. Then let them play the chimes gently by themselves.

🌐 Music boxes offer other unique sounds for children to listen to. Bring in several different sizes and types for the children to explore. Ask them to bring ones from home, too.

🌐 It is helpful to introduce musical instruments one at a time before combining all the instruments in conjunction with musical recordings. The *triangle* extends listening skills and shapes awareness. Shaking the *maracas* (use only one at first) invites children to shake their own rhythm, as does shaking the *jingle bells*, tap-tap-tapping and then rub-rub-rubbing with wooden sticks, shake-shake-shaking the tambourine, and beat-beat-beating the drums. Try having the children play the instruments to this beat: *sshhh-sshhh/ssh-ssh-ssh/sshhh-sshhh/ssh-ssh-ssh or 1–2/1–2–3/1–2/1–2–3.*

🌐 With preschoolers and older children it is fun to divide them into two groups facing each other with each child having an individual instrument. For example, one group has jingle bells, the other group has one maraca each. Play a recording of an instrumental musical selection. Explain to the children that you (or one of the children) will be the conductor and direct each group when to play individually or together. It is helpful to have the children sitting in groups at first. When the bells play, the maracas are placed gently on the floor; then when the maracas play, the bells are placed gently on the floor, so that the children can listen to their friends play. Then both groups can play together when the conductor directs them to do so.

🌐 Jingle bell instruments are fun to play along with the song "Jingle Bells," even in the month of June. Other songs are Stephen Foster's "Oh, Susanna" and lively folk songs such as "This Ole' Man" and "She'll Be Comin' 'round the Mountain."

🌐 Children five years and older enjoy discriminating between sounds and listening to the vibrations of various instruments. Introduce gongs and give the children time to experiment with them. Wooden sticks offer vibrations that sound differently. Place the serrated stick flat against the floor and rub it with the other stick. The floor becomes the amplifier. Different sounds are heard when sticks are placed on a carpeted floor and then on a noncarpeted floor.

Making Musical Instruments

Young children enjoy making their own musical instruments with materials collected from home, including:

🌐 rolls from bathroom tissue and paper towels

🌐 aluminum pie plates

🌐 paper plates

🌐 salt, cereal, and oatmeal boxes

🌐 large, round ice-cream cartons

🌐 bottle caps

🌐 spools

🌐 embroidery hoops

🌐 wooden blocks

The process of making musical instruments further extends the children's self-expression, their knowledge of how sounds can be made from their environment, and possibilities for hands-on experiences. This activity also combines language, art, science, math, social studies, and sensory learning opportunities (younger children will need guidance and supervision from the teacher). Some easy-to-make instruments include:

DRUMS. Children can make drums from salt or cereal boxes or from large ice-cream cartons. Glue the lid to the box or carton and decorate with markers and paint. Drums can be played by hitting or tapping with the fingers or with soft drum sticks made from pencils covered at one end with felt. See Figure 10–3.

TAMBOURINE. Take an aluminum pie plate or a heavy paper plate, punch several holes on the rim, and tie small bells or bottle caps with thin wire, string, or pipe cleaners to the plate in such a way that the bells hang freely. Then, shake to the musical **beat**. See Figure 10–4.

WOOD-BLOCK TAMBOURINE. The materials needed to make a wood-block tambourine are one block of wood (approximately ¾ inch by 1½ inches by 6 inches), six or more bottle caps, and nails with wide heads. Hammer a nail through the bottle caps partway into the wood block (Figure 10–5). Be sure the hole in the bottle cap is

FIGURE 10–3
Drum.

FIGURE 10–4
Tambourine.

FIGURE 10–5
Wood-block tambourine.

beat
An accent of sound or a continuing series of accents.

wide enough so the cap will slide freely along the nail. Any number of nails and bottle caps can be used.

SANDPAPER BLOCKS. Glue, staple, or thumbtack sandpaper to two wooden blocks (approximately 3 inches by 2 inches by 1 inch) on one 3-inch side of each block. On the opposite side, glue a spool or a small drawer handle. Try experimenting with sandpaper squares of different coarseness. Rub the sandpaper blocks together to make interesting sounds (when the squares wear out, replace them with fresh sandpaper). See Figure 10–6.

SHAKERS. Young children can make shakers from small boxes or clean plastic milk cartons of various sizes. (The handle is easy to hold onto.) Place clothespins, small pieces of wood, pebbles, dried beans, or birdseed in the container. Another type of shaker is made with paper plates. Take two paper plates and decorate them with crayons, markers, or paint. Place pebbles, dried beans, or birdseed between the two paper plates. Staple the plates together or sew them together with brightly colored yarn. Then, shake and shake to the rhythm of the music! See Figure 10–7.

WIND CHIMES. Wind chimes can be made from many different materials, such as various sizes of nails, scraps of metal, pieces of bamboo, or old silverware. Tie various lengths of string, evenly spaced, to a coat hanger or embroidery hoop. Tie nails to the strings, and adjust string lengths so that the nails strike each other when blown by the wind or gently swayed. For a variety of sounds, use pieces of several different sizes, and substitute silverware, pieces of bamboo, or scraps of metal for the nails. See Figure 10–8.

NAIL SCRAPER. Materials needed to make the nail scraper are a block of wood about 2 inches by 2 inches by 8 inches and nails of different sizes. Hammer a few nails of the same size into a block of wood so that they are all the same height. Leave a large space, then hammer some other size nails into the wood making these all the same height. Continue placing nails in the wood until there is no more room. To play this instrument, take a large nail and run it quickly along the row of nails. The different lengths of the nails will make different sounds. See Figure 10–9.

SHOE BOX GUITAR. This instrument is made by taking a shoe box and cutting a 2-inch oval hole on the top of the box. Stretch strong rubber bands lengthwise around the box. Place a pencil at one end of the top of the box under the rubber bands. Move the pencil to get different tones as the shoe box guitar is strummed or plucked with the fingers. See Figure 10–10 on page 311.

FLUTE. The children can make their flutes from bathroom tissue, paper towel, or wrapping paper cardboard tubes. Cut a circle of tissue paper or waxed paper and place over one end of the tube. Attach with a rubber band. Cut several small holes on the side of the tube. The children can hum into their flutes while they place their fingers on the holes to change the sound. See Figure 10–11 on page 311.

Storing and Caring for Instruments

All instruments, including those made by the children, should be treated with care. Guide the children into understanding that each instrument is to be cared for, handled carefully, and valued. *Musical instruments are not to be used as toys or weapons.*

Each type of instrument should be stored in a special storage place. According to Haines and Gerber (1996):

> *Instruments should never be dumped indiscriminately into a cardboard carton or piled in a basket or on a shelf. This is not good for the instrument or for the attitudes of children toward them. Attractive, accessible storage that the children can use independently should be provided. Damaged instruments should be discarded.*

FIGURE 10–6
Sandpaper blocks.

FIGURE 10–7
Examples of two types of musical shakers.

FIGURE 10–8
Wind chimes.

Figure 10–9
Nail scraper.

FIGURE 10–10
Shoebox guitar.

FIGURE 10–11
Flute.

FIGURE 10–12
Selected books about music and movement for children, teachers, and families.

SHARING WITH FAMILIES: MUSIC AND MOVEMENT ENVIRONMENTS AND ACTIVITIES

"Play is the primary vehicle for young children's growth, and developmentally appropriate early music experiences should occur in child-initiated, child-directed, teacher-supported play environments" (MENC, 1994). We should provide numerous music and movement activities that invite and encourage children to move around, especially because many children live in confined spaces. Integral to the success of these activities is well-planned space that is adaptable to a number of uses. Consider sound levels that will not interfere with the simultaneous activities of other groups or individuals. These spaces should not be confined to the outdoors or a large motor room. Classrooms should be arranged (or rearranged) to accommodate music and movement activities. See Figure 10–12 for music and movement books for children.

WHY I TEACH YOUNG CHILDREN

This is short, but it says it all.
I asked a 4-year-old to smile during dance class. She said, "When I dance, my body smiles!"

—Nancy Seale

Aliki. (2003). *Ah, music!* New York: HarperCollins.
Bassett, C. (2003). Walk like a bear, stand like a tree, run like the wind: Cool yoga, stretching and aerobic activities. New York: Nubod Concepts.
Carle, E. (1992). *Today is Monday.* New York: Scholastic.
Drew, H. (1993). *My first music book.* New York: Dorling-Kindersley.
Hayes, A. (1991). *Meet the orchestra.* Orlando, FL: Harcourt Brace.
Krull, K. (2003). *M is for music.* Illustrated by S. Innerst. New York: Harcourt.
Kuskin, K. (1982). *The philharmonic gets dressed.* New York: Harper & Row.
Lillegard, D. (1988). *Brass; percussion; strings; woodwinds.* An introduction to musical instruments (series). Chicago: Children's Press.
McMillan, B. (1987). *Step-by-step.* New York: Lothrop, Lee & Shepard Books.
Moss, L. (2003). *Music is.* Illustrated by P. Petit-Roulet. New York: Putnam.
Moss, L. (2001) *Our marching band.* Illustrated by B. Bluthenthal. New York: Putnam.
Rae, M. M. (1989). *The farmer in the dell.* New York: Scholastic.
Raffi. (1987). *Shake my sillies out.* New York: Crown.
Raschka, C. (1992). *Charlie Parker played be bop.* New York: Orchard Books.
Rounds, G. (1989). *Old MacDonald had a farm.* New York: Holiday House.
Rubin, M., & Daniel, A. (1992). *The orchestra.* Buffalo, NY: Firefly Books.
Sharma, E. (1993). *The voice, percussion, brass, woodwinds, strings* (Live music! series). Clifton Park, NY: Thomson Delmar Learning.
Wagrin, K. (2004). *M is for melody: A music alphabet.* New York: Sleeping Bear Press.
Wenig, M. (2003). *Yoga kids: Educating the whole child through yoga.* Photographs by S. Andrews. New York: Stewart, Tabori, & Chang.

Neelly (2001) quotes a music center sign in a prekindergarten classroom that invites the parents and other adults to join in:

There is a musician in every child. Here is a place where children explore, experiment, and extend their own knowledge about music and the qualities of sound. Children are encouraged to sing and dramatize songs, fingerplays, and rhymes either by themselves or with others.

"Simon Says Move Fingers, Hands, and Arms" Activity

Start this activity by explaining to the children that they will play a game by moving a part of their body without music, such as their fingers, hands, or arms. Later add music. This can be played as a "Simon Says" type of game. Introduce the movements first, a few at a time, suggesting only the movement exercises that are applicable to the age and stage of development of the children in your classroom. Remind the children to stay in their "own space." Let one of the children take your place, inserting the child's name to replace "Simon" or "Teacher Says." Accept whatever movement each individual child makes, unless it is inappropriate. The following are some examples:

- moving fingers and hands: bending, separating, stretching, curling, making fists
- moving arms: pushing, pulling, stretching, swinging
- moving feet and legs: stomping, kicking, crossing, and uncrossing
- moving elbows: touching, making circles
- moving head: bending, shaking, rolling, nodding
- moving eyes: opening; shutting; looking up, down, side to side, around
- nose: wiggling, breathing in and out
- mouth: opening wide, making shapes, shutting tight

Move the Body Activity

The following are exercises that require the children to move their whole bodies (with or without music or with a drum beat):

- Walk in the following ways: with arms swinging, without arms swinging, fast, slowly, with feet spread apart, heel to toe, on tip-toe, on heels, and with big steps.
- March in place with knees raised high.

Poem, Music, and Movement Activity

The following are several verses of a poem a kindergarten class of children helped me create. We tried to move like many animals and fly like a lot of birds before we decided on the ones included in the poem. The next day we tried to put the poem to music. Each child selected a part of the poem to sing and made up his or her own tune. This activity continued for several days as the children proceeded to think up new words and melodies. I recorded their wonderful songs and put the tape in the music center for them to listen to whenever they chose to do so. We also made a book of the poem, with the children drawing the illustrations. This went into the book center.

Here is the poem:

I can hop like a bunny.

I can spin like a top.

Hop, spin, Hop, hop, hop!

I can gallop like a horse.

I can jump like a clown.

Gallop, jump, Up and down!

Here is another verse the children created later:

I can bark like a dog. Arf ! Arf !

I can moo like a cow. Moo! Moo!

I can sound like a cat. Mee-ow!

I can hoot like an owl. Whoo! Whoo!

Obstacle Course Activity

Design an obstacle course for older children by setting up a path that leads around chairs and boxes, over piles of pillows, and through tunnels made of tables covered with blankets (or commercially made tunnels of varying lengths). For the younger children, set up an obstacle course with fewer parts.

Beanbag Activity

Use beanbags for many lively activities. They are easier for some children to catch than a ball. Ask the older children to experiment with how many different ways they can catch a beanbag, such as with one hand, two hands, their feet, or their head.

Set up several baskets into which children can practice throwing beanbags. Mark a tossing line on the floor with masking tape (or a wide chalk line, if the activity is played outdoors).

The children can take turns tossing beanbags into the basket. A variation of this game can be two teams tossing beanbags at the same time or moving the toss line up closer or farther back to make the activity easier or more difficult.

Make beanbags from colorful fabric or felt. The children can help you by deciding if they want them to be circles, squares, rectangles, triangles, or ovals. Fill the beanbags with bird seed, Styrofoam "peanuts," or dried beans.

Move with Scarves Activity

Moving with scarves (or any lightweight material) is another way for children to practice their creativity by moving and swaying to music. These scarves can encourage them to create stories through movement and act out stories using the scarves and other props.

CONNECTING MUSIC AND MOVEMENT WITH OTHER AREAS OF THE CURRICULUM

Many activities already mentioned in this chapter offer ways to connect music and movement experiences with other areas of the curriculum. It is important to think specifically about this when you select your theme and organize your lesson plan. Mayesky (2006) suggests,

> *When making lesson plans for the week, include music in at least two other curricular areas. For example, plan to play music during art activities, and note which selections you will use and on which day. Be sure to make a note to have the tape ready and the tape player set up for the days required. Then, plan to read a book at group time that relates to the new song(s) introduced that week.*

Indoors or outdoors, a parachute offers young children a unique experience in active body movement.

Music and movement are vital components of an early education environment. They contribute to language curriculum by introducing vocabulary, sound patterns, and literacy skills. Simple songs, such as question-and-answer songs or name games, can help children make the transition from speaking to singing. (Examples of this are included in the songs in this chapter; also see Figure 10–13.) They support social studies by bringing into the classroom music, musical instruments, and dances from around the world and creating a vibrant early childhood setting. Use the suggestions discussed in this chapter to stimulate your curriculum.

TIPS FOR TEACHERS

Music gets the whole child involved in the process of learning. Music activities prepare the brain for more difficult tasks needed later by preparing the brain to work from both hemispheres. (Harman, 2007).

"Of all the beautiful things in this world, there are few that surpass the images of music in childhood" (Campbell & Scott-Kassner, 1995). Use music as a transition from home to school and from school to home. Play recorded music of different types each day. Include this in your lesson plan and have information relating to the selection, artist performing the music, or instrument or orchestra featured. Share these musical moments with parents. The following are more suggestions:

🌐 Tape record the children singing their favorite songs or playing musical instruments. Share with their parents. You might also make copies of the tape for parents who want to learn the songs. (continued on next page.)

FIGURE 10–13
Selected musical audio tapes and CDs for children.

Children of the World. (1991). *Multicuitural rhythmic activities for preschool.* Long Branch, NJ: Kimbo.
Disney. (2005). *Here comes the ABCs.* New York: Disney Productions.
Eklof, J. (2000). *My favorite animal—Mi Animal Favorito; So many ways to say, "good morning"* (CD with picture song book). Dallas, TX: Miss Jo Publications.
Fiedler and the Boston Pops. (1986). *Favorites for children.* New York: RCA.
Grunsky, J. (1990). *Imaginary window.* Cypress, CA: Youngheart Music.
Henson, J. (1992). *A Sesame Street celebration.* New York: Sesame Workshop.
Ives, B. (1997). *Little White Duck and other favorites.* New York: Sony/Wonder.
Jenkins, E. (1997). *Multicultural children's songs; Counting games and rhythms for little ones; You'll sing a song and I'll sing a song.* Washington, DC: Smithsonian Folkway Records.
McGrath, B. (1998). *Sing along with Bob.* (Vols. 1 & 2). New York: Greengrass Enterprises.
Music for Little People/Various Artists. (1999). *A child's celebration of silliest songs.* New York: Music for Little People.
Palmer, H. (2000). *Early childhood classics—Old favorites with a new twist.* Freeport, NY: Educational Activities.
Raffi. (1998). *Rise and shine.* Willowdale, Canada: Troubadour Records Ltd.
Scelsa, G., & Millang, S. (1998). *Kids in motion.* Cypress, CA: Youngheart Music.
Seeger, P. (2000). *American folk, game, and activity songs.* New York: Folkway Records.
Sesame Workshop. (2003). *Songs from the Street: 35 years of music.* New York: Sony/Wonder.
Valeri, M. (1986). *Mi casa es su casa/My house is your house.* New York: Caedmon/Harper Audio.
Verve/Various Artists. (2004). *Jazz for kids.* New York: Verve Music Group.

🌐 Invite parents to participate in your music experiences. Ask them to think about songs that hold special cultural and family memories—songs they learned from their parents and grandparents when they were younger. Encourage them to bring musical instruments and music that are a part of their cultural heritage and share them with the children.

🌐 Use instruments as cues for transitions from one activity to another, such as cleanup time. Rotate which instruments you choose for this purpose for more variety.

🌐 Use a "singing hand puppet" as another transition activity. Sing songs the children are familiar with, ones that are included in the lesson plan.

🌐 Marching music is a wonderful way to move children from one activity to the next. Try it!

🌐 Observe and listen to the children. They will let you know what is working and what is not.

🌐 Ask children to provide sound effects for a story. The more music and rhythm is used and the more complex listening is experienced, the broader the foundation laid (Shore and Strasser 2006).

🌐 Use a variety of approaches in introducing songs. Use flannelboard characters, puppets, books, or simple props. Know the songs well yourself and sing them to the children several times while they listen. New songs should be sung to the children in their entirety, not phrase by phrase. Children pick up the tune and words naturally without having to be taught them. Incorporate simple actions into the songs. This offers visual clues to help children remember the words.

🌐 Rules (limits) should be developed and explained when you introduce musical instruments to the children. For example, "treat the instruments gently," "be careful not to touch anyone else with the instrument, stretch both arms out until you don't touch anyone else—this is your personal space," and "be careful not to hit instruments on the floor or anything else."

🌐 Enjoy singing songs, playing musical instruments, and movement activities. *Be involved! Be part of the activity!* The children pick up on your enthusiasm (or lack of it). Do not be concerned about your singing voice. Young children are not critical! They'll be so happy that you celebrate music with them.

Children need music every day and every year of their learning lives, and the more complex, the better! Continuing to listen to complex music throughout childhood and even adulthood is as important for brain development as learning to read letters and words. Music has much to offer our educational settings, even beyond simply touching our feelings. Music can touch our minds! (Shore & Strasser, 2006).

Each child picks up a teacher's enthusiasm when she joins in singing songs and playing musical instruments.

WHY I TEACH YOUNG CHILDREN

Having grown up in a family of teachers, this seemed to be my destiny. I love being around children and observing their natural curiosity and eagerness to know "why." After teaching for many years in different environments, these little people never cease to amaze me. I feel rewarded to provide them with learning experiences. Each day is special as they make me laugh and give me unconditional love in return.

—Julie Muchin

DEVELOPMENTALLY APPROPRIATE AND MULTICULTURAL/ ANTI-BIAS ACTIVITIES

Hildebrandt (1998) reminds us, "Just as children need to spend many hours listening to the language of their culture before they can talk, they need to listen to the music of their culture before they can sing and play. We need to continue to expose children to the music of their own culture as well as other cultures." Music is a universal language. "If as a caregiver you have a first language different from that of the infants and toddlers you care for, be sure to use the folk songs and lullaby songs of your people at naptimes" (Honig, 1995). Feel free to sing your songs to the children no matter what age you have in your class. They will be learning about you, and that is important.

Griss (1994) offers insight into the importance of dance as a multicultural activity for young children:

> *Dance provides a wonderful way to explore both the universality and particularity of human cultures. By learning ethnic dances and physically interpreting the poetry, literature, and folklores of diverse cultures, children develop deeper insights into the aesthetics and value systems of those cultures. Including multi-cultural dance in the curriculum also offers an excellent opportunity to invite professional artists to share their expertise with children.*

The following two groups of songs by Bea Wolf and Jo Eklof are some of the favorites requested by young children in early childhood settings. Once they and their teachers know these songs, they sing them often. These songs and stories offer a multitude of opportunities for stimulating creativity and enjoyment of music and movement activities. (Wolf and Eklof songs are included in many other chapters throughout this book. They are also listed in Appendix C, Teacher Resources.)

Figure 10–14 is the curriculum-planning web with music and movement activities added. This worksheet, with appropriate additions, is included in each chapter.

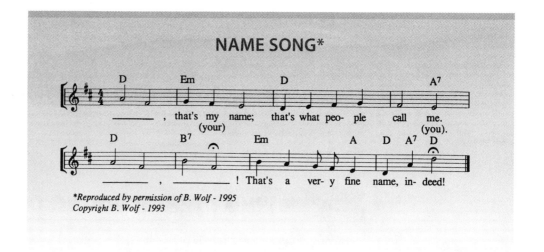

PUPPY DOG STORY

Once there was a puppy dog, as nice as he could be.
He thought he'd like a little playmate, just for company.
One day he saw a kitty who was playing in a tree.
He called to her, "Sweet kitty cat! Will you come play with me?"

And the puppy dog said, "Bow-wow!"
And the kitty cat said, "Meow!"
Then the puppy dog said, "Let's play!"
But the kitty cat said, "Go 'way!"

Then the puppy saw the kitty was afraid of him.
She thought that he would bite her,
so she climbed out on a limb!
But then the puppy told her he was gentle, good, and kind;
he'd be the nicest playmate anyone could ever find.
And the puppy dog said, "Bow-wow!"
And the kitty cat said, "Meow!"
Then the puppy dog said, "Let's play!"
And the kitty cat said, "Okay!"

The pup was very gentle, and the kitty wasn't rough,
and all the time they played
they never got into a huff!
Now the puppy and the kitty are the best of friends.
They play together every day,
and so our story ends,
with the puppy who says, "Bow-wow!",
and the kitty who says, "Meow!"
When the puppy dog says, "Let's play!",
then the kitty cat says, "Okay!"

SONG TO ACCOMPANY
PUPPY DOG STORY*

1.) Once there was a pup- py dog, as nice as he could
2.) Then the pup- py saw the kit- ty was a- fraid of
3.) pup was ver- y gen- tle, and the kit- ty was- n't

1.) be. He thought he'd like a lit- tle play- mate,
2.) him. She thought that he would bite her, so she
3.) rough, and all the time they played, they nev- er

1.) just for com- pan- y. One day he saw a
2.) climbed out on a limb. But then the pup- py
3.) got in- to a huff. Now the pup- py

1.) kit- ty who was play- ing in a tree; he
2.) told her he was gen- tle, good, and kind; he'd
3.) and the kit- ty are the best of friends. They

1.) called to her, "Sweet kit- ty cat, will you come play with
2.) be the ni- cest play- mate an- y- one could ev- er
3.) play to- geth- er ev'- ry day, and so our sto- ry

1.) me?" And the pup- py dog said, "Bow- wow!" And the
2.) find! And the pup- py dog said, "Bow- wow!" And the
3.) ends, with the pup- py who says, "Bow- wow!", and the

1.& 2.) kit- ty cat said, "me- ow!" Then the pup- py dog said, "Let's
3.) kit- ty who says, "Me- ow!" When the pup- py dog says, "Let's

1.
1.) play!" And the kit- ty cat said, "Go 'way!"
2.) play!" And the kit- ty cat said, "O- kay!" The

2.
3.) play!", then the kit- ty cat says, "O- kay!"

*Reproduced by permission of B. Wolf - 1995
Copyright B. Wolf - 1993

WINDSHIELD WIPERS

(activity song)

(Suitable for Two- to Five-Year-Olds—Entertainingly
Presents Concepts of Big/Little, Loud/Soft)

If children are old enough to understand, lead a short discussion about windshield wipers—when they are used and why. Then introduce the song and proceed to the following three activities:

Part 1: With children seated, explain that first we are going to be the windshield wipers on a very small car; therefore, we will use our small, soft voices to sing. As the song is sung, children use upraised index fingers and move hands in rhythm to simulate small windshield wipers.

Part 2: Explain that next we will be windshield wipers on a larger vehicle, such as a big car, or perhaps even a pickup truck. We will use medium voices for this, and we will make the windshield wipers by extending arms in front of us, bent at the elbows, with hands and fingers stretching up. Forearms, hands, and fingers then act as a unit to imitate wiper motions as song is sung. Children may perform this part of the activity either seated or standing.

Part 3: Now we are going to be windshield wipers on a *really* big vehicle, such as a bus. Children may wish to contribute their own examples of huge vehicles—fire trucks, eighteen wheelers, etc. We will become the largest windshield wipers we can be by standing, extending arms up as high as we can, and using our bodies from the waist up to simulate the wipers in motion. We will sing the song with our *very* loud voices!

SONG TO ACCOMPANY
WINDSHIELD WIPERS*

*Reproduced by permission of B. Wolf - 1995
Copyright B. Wolf - 1993

GOOD MORNING
Words and Music by Jo Eklof

Good morn - ing, good morn - ing, good morn - ing to you. To - day is full of won - der - ful things that we each get to do.

SO MANY WAYS TO SAY, "GOOD MORNING"
Words and Music by Jo Eklof

In Eng - lish we say, "Good morn - ing, good morn - ing, good morn - ing." In Eng - lish we say, "Good morn - ing, good morn - ing to you."

2. In Spanish we say, "Buenos Días." (buay-nos dé-as)
3. In Korean we say, "An nyung." (on yúng)
4. In French we say, "Bonjour." (bone-zhóor)
5. In Choctaw we say, "Holito." (hoe-lée-toe)
6. In Amharic we say, "Endmenaderachu." (end-men-a-dér-a-chew)
7. In Japanese we say, "Ohayo gozaimasu," (ohio-guy-zái-mus)
8. In Hindi we say, "Namasthe." (nah-móss-thay)
9. In German we say, "Guten morgen. (goo-ten mór-gen)
10. In Vietnamese we say, "Xin chao." (seen-chów)
11. However you say good morning, say it with a friendly smile.

SMILES AND HUGS AND I LOVE YOU'S
Words and Music by Jo Eklof

Smiles and hugs and I love you's, we need them eve - ry day. And the won-der-ful thing a - bout life is, we get back what we give a - way. Yes, we get back what we give a - way.

I'M A SPECIAL PERSON AND SO ARE YOU
Words and Music by Jo Eklof

Here's a lit - tle song that is fun to do, say, "I'm a spe - cial per - son and so are you." Say it with your (head) here's what you do, (nod), "I'm a spe - cial per - son and so are you."

Additional verses:

Eyes - blink..........
Tongue - click..........
Shoulders - hunch..........
Arms - flap..........
Hips - sway..........
Feet - jump..........
Now sit down - bump..........
Hands - clap..........
Now let's whisper - say (whisper)..........

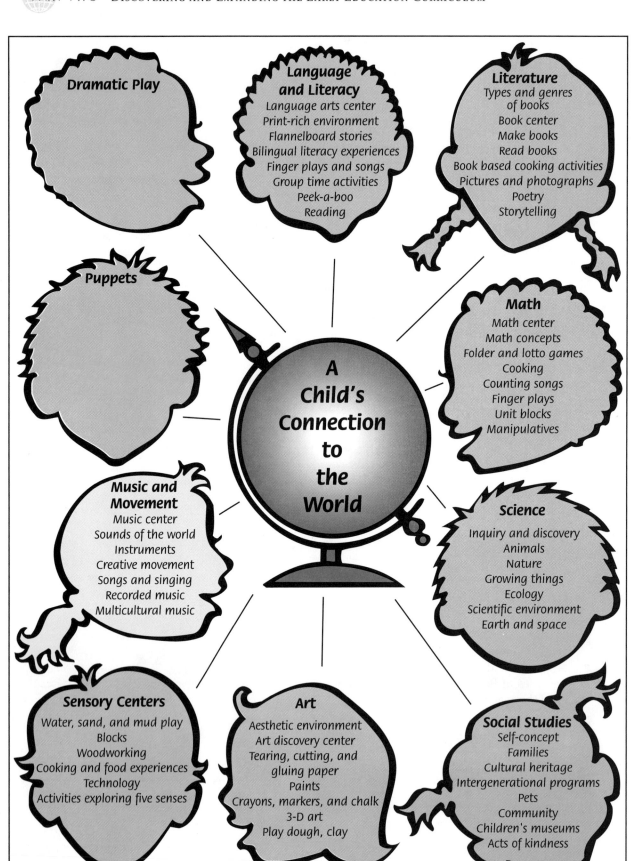

FIGURE 10–14

A curriculum planning web worksheet with music and movement activities added.

✳ AFTERVIEW

Through music and movement activities, a child

- 🌐 becomes sensitive to beauty and harmony.
- 🌐 validates creativity, individuality, and self-expression.
- 🌐 reinforces auditory, visual, and comprehension skills.
- 🌐 explores and differentiates sounds.
- 🌐 practices listening skills.
- 🌐 expands vocabulary and language development.
- 🌐 explores large and small muscle movement.
- 🌐 develops awareness of the body and how it works and moves.
- 🌐 has an opportunity to release energy and express emotions.
- 🌐 practices moving through space.
- 🌐 expresses herself freely through creative movement, playing musical instruments, and singing.
- 🌐 experiences a wide variety of music.
- 🌐 experiments with creating and performing music.
- 🌐 derives pleasure from musical experiences.
- 🌐 develops positive feelings about being part of a group and participates both as a leader and follower.
- 🌐 expresses pride in her ethnic heritage by using songs, dances, musical instruments, and recordings from her culture.

✳ KEY TERMS

beat	melody	tempo
kinesthetics	nonlocomotor movement	timbre
locomotor movement	pitch	tone
manipulative movement	rhythm	volume

✳ EXPLORATIONS

1. Select an early childhood classroom. Observe for at least one hour. In writing, describe any music and movement activities you observed. Did the children or the teacher initiate these activities? Describe some examples of how the children spontaneously approached these activities.

2. Describe a resource person and what that person might do on a visit to a classroom of young children that would enhance children's appreciation of movement and music. Indicate how you would prepare the children for the experience and what follow-up activities would you use.

3. In writing, discuss the ways musical instruments can be used in music activities with young children. Make one of the musical instruments suggested in this chapter. Introduce the use of the instrument to a group of children. Discuss why you chose this instrument. Did you achieve your objectives? What were the children's reactions? Were they stimulated to make this and other instruments? What would you do differently if you presented this activity again? Explain.

4. Select one of the songs in this chapter and create a flannelboard story to accompany this song. Present this song and story to a group of young children (toddlers or preschoolers). Evaluate the activity. What should be kept the same for the next time it is presented? What should be changed and why?

5. How useful are music and dance in developing multicultural awareness in young children? How could a teacher accomplish this? Give four examples of activities or experiences that would promote either or both.

※ REFERENCES

Allen, J., McNeill, E., & Schmidt, V. (1992). *Cultural awareness for children*. Menlo Park, CA: Addison-Wesley.

Andress, B. L., & Walker, L. M. (Eds.). (1992). *Readings in early childhood music education*. Reston, VA: Music Educators National Conference.

Billhartz, P. (2007). Let's make music. *Early Childhood News*. On-line at: http://www.earlychildhoodnews.com

Campbell, P. S., & Scott-Kassner, C. (1995). *Music in childhood*. New York: Schirmer Books.

Corbett, S. (1995). *A world of difference: Shake, rattle, and strum*. Chicago: Children's Press.

Feldman, J. (2002, Spring). Keep a song in your heart! *Early Years, 24*(1), 6–7.

Gardner, H. (1983). *Frames of mind: The theory of multiple intelligences*. New York: Basic Books.

Greenberg, M. (1979). *Your children need music*. Englewood Cliffs, NJ: Prentice Hall.

Griss, S. (1994, February). Creative movement: A language for learning. *Educational Leadership, 51*(5), 78–80.

Haines, B. J. E., & Gerber, L. L. (1996). *Leading young children to music* (5th ed.). Upper Saddle River, NJ: Merrill.

Harman, M. (2007). Music and movement: Instrumental in language development. *Early Childhood News*. On-line at: http://www.earlychildhoodnews.com

Hildebrandt, C. (1998, November). Creativity in music and early childhood. *Young Children, 53*(6), 68–74.

Honig, A. S. (1995, July). Singing with infants and toddlers. *Young Children, 50*(5), 72–78.

Isbell, R. T., & Raines, S. C. (2007). *Creativity and the arts with young children* (2nd ed.). Clifton Park, NY: Thomson Delmar Learning.

Lillegard, D. (1988). *Percussion*. (Introduction to Musical Instruments series). Chicago: Children's Press.

Machado, J. M. (2007). *Early childhood experiences in language arts* (8th ed.). Clifton Park, NY: Thomson Delmar Learning.

Mayesky, M. (2006). *Creative activities for young children* (8th ed.). Clifton Park, NY: Thomson Delmar Learning.

McGraw, G. (2002, Winter). Songs of childhood. *Early Childhood Connections*, Leadership Bulletin, Vol. 8, No.1. Greensboro, NC: Foundation for Music-Based Learning.

Miche, M. (2002). *Weaving music into young minds*. Clifton Park, NY: Thomson Delmar Learning.

Moomaw, S. (1984). *Discovering music in early childhood*. Boston: Allyn & Bacon.

Music Educators National Conference (MENC). (1994). *The school music program: A new vision* (Position Statement). Reston, VA: Author.

Neelly, L. P. (2002, July). Practical ways to improve singing in early childhood classrooms. *Young Children, 57*(4), 80–83.

Neelly, L. P. (2001, May). Developing appropriate music practice: Children learn what they live. *Young Children, 56*(3), 32–37.

Palmer, H. (2001, September). The music, movement, and learning connection. *Young Children, 56*(5), 13–17.

Pica, R. (2006). *A running start*. New York: Marlowe & Company.

Pica, R. (2004). *Experiences in movement: Birth to age 8* (3rd ed.). Clifton Park, NY: Thomson Delmar Learning.

Sanders, S. W. (2002). *Active for life: developmentally appropriate movement programs for young children*. Washington, DC: NAEYC.

Shelemay, K. (2001). *Music on the brain: Researchers explore the biology of music*. On-line at: http://www.news.harvard.edu/gazette/2001/03.22/04-music.html

Shore, R., & Strasser, J. (2006, March). Music for their minds. *Young Children, 61*(2), 62–67.

Smith, K. L. (2002, March). Dancing in the forest. *Young Children, 57*(2), 90–94.

Sutterby, J. A., & Frost, J. L. (2002, May). Making playgrounds fit for children and children fit on playgrounds. *Young Children, 57*(3), 36–41.

※ ADDITIONAL READINGS AND RESOURCES

Feierabend, J. M. (1995). *First steps in music for infants and toddlers*. Simsbury, CT: First Steps in Music, Inc.

Greenspan, S. I. (2002, November). Rhythm and timing: Important keys to learning. *Early Childhood Today, 17*(3), 34–35.

Humpal, M. E., & Wolf, J. (2003, March). Music in the inclusive environment. *Young Children, 58*(2), 103–107.

James, A. R. (2000, May). When I listen to the music. *Young Children, 55*(3), 36–37.

Marcon, R. A. (2003, January). The physical side of development. *Young Children, 58*(1), 80–87.

Moore, T. (2002, July). If you teach children, you can sing! *Young Children, 57*(4), 84–85.

Moravcik, E. (2000, July). Music all the livelong day. *Young Children, 55*(4), 27–29.

Pica, R. (2003, March–April). But we don't have room. *Early Childhood News, 15*(2), 24–26.

Ringgenberg, S. (2003, September). Music as a teaching tool: Creating story songs. *Young Children, 58*(5), 76–79.

Schilling, T., & McOmber, K. A. (2006, May). Tots in action on and beyond the playground. *Young Children, 61*(3), 34–36.

Staley, L., & Portman, P. A. (2000, January). Red Rover, Red Rover, it's time to move over! *Young Children, 55*(1), 67–72.

Steies, A. (2003, March–April). Childhood obesity: A new epidemic. *Early Childhood News, 15*(2), 15–23.

Wellhousen, K. (2002). Outdoor play every day: Innovative play concepts for early childhood. Clifton Park, NY: Thomson Delmar Learning.

For additional information on early education curriculum, visit our Web site at http://www.earlychilded.delmar.com

CHAPTER 11

PUPPETS

OBJECTIVES

AFTER STUDYING THIS CHAPTER, YOU SHOULD BE ABLE TO:

- 🌐 Plan for puppets in an early education classroom.
- 🌐 Describe and give examples of easy-to-make puppets that are appropriate for young children.
- 🌐 List the types of materials needed for children to make puppets.
- 🌐 Identify how to integrate puppets easily into an early childhood setting.
- 🌐 Connect puppets into curriculum areas both inside and outdoors.
- 🌐 Identify how puppets on television have influenced teachers and children.
- 🌐 Identify the teacher's role in puppet play.

OVERVIEW

Puppets can teach, entertain, and delight children and adults. Historically, puppetry has been described as a folk art, one produced by and for the people. Puppets have been around for thousands of years and are found virtually everywhere in the world, embedded in every continent and culture.

Raines and Isbell (1994) tell us:

> *Storytelling and puppetry are ancient forms of oral expression that developed historically in similar ways. The story told was passed from generation to generation and became a binding link for families and cultures. The puppeteer often augmented the storytelling by providing visualization and surprise elements to the story's presentation.*

"Puppets delight children and touch the hearts of adults. Increasingly, it is recognized that puppetry is a unique and innovative way to reach out to people of all ages. Puppets can entertain, inform, persuade and appeal. They are part of the world's ancient history, and at the same time, they are also part of the world's modern imagination" (UNICEF, 2007).

HISTORICAL VIEW OF PUPPETRY

puppetry
The art of making or operating puppets or producing puppet shows.

Indonesian Puppet.

No one knows exactly when the art of **puppetry** began. Were the first puppeteers primitive people casting shadows on darkened cave walls? Were the early priests and shamans who used puppets to celebrate important life cycle events some of the first puppeteers? Did the Egyptians invent the first puppet, as some historians have suggested? According to the Center for Puppetry Arts in Atlanta, Georgia, written documentation of puppetry's beginnings can be traced back to Asia, where it developed simultaneously in India and China in the ninth century B.C. In *Indonesia,* flat, leather *shadow puppets* and *three-dimensional rod puppets,* introduced centuries ago, are still used in performances today.

> *Vietnam is famous for its unique tradition of water puppetry which combines both rod and strings to manipulate the figures. The performance appears in a lake. The puppeteers are hidden in a structure resembling a Vietnamese communal house built in the middle of the lake. The puppets are attached to long bamboo rods and strings. When the audience views the show they see puppets acting on a watery stage with the puppeteer's house in the background. (Center for Puppetry Arts, 1994)*

Contreras, cited in Jalongo (2003), continues, "In the case of *Vietnam's water puppetry,* it is an expression of traditional values, a source of national pride, and for those outside the culture, a way of promoting intercultural understanding."

Puppetry also has roots in *Africa,* dating back to the fifth century B.C. *Puppet pageants* are still performed there for the entire community to celebrate important events, such as planting and harvest time.

In *Japan, Bunraku* originated in the sixteenth century. This is a highly refined form of rod puppetry, using three puppeteers to perform a single character. One controls the head and one arm; another, the second arm; and the third, the feet. The puppeteers usually dress in black, are visible behind each puppet, and possess great skill and coordination (Center for Puppetry Arts, 1994; Henson, 1994).

Hand puppets began appearing in *Europe* and *colonial America* in the mid-1700s. The *English Punch and Judy,* the most popular characters, were descendants of an *Italian puppet* named *Pulcinella.* Punch and Judy appeared in marketplaces, at community fairs, on the street, in town halls, at circuses, and in schools. Similar *puppets,* with different names, were also performing in *Germany, France, Russia, and Turkey.*

The *Mamulengo* tradition in puppetry can be found in *South America.* These puppeteers fuse the folk traditions of native populations and black culture, as well as draw

Japanese Bunraku
Puppet.

Punch and Judy
Puppets.

from colonial Hispanic and Portuguese influences when they present street puppet theater (Center for Puppetry Arts, 1994).

As you continue through this chapter, you will find ways for you and the children to create, enjoy, and develop skills by using this ancient form of folk art. You will find that the use of puppetry can enrich all the curriculum areas in your early education program. Most importantly, a child's positive self-esteem can be enhanced by using a puppet to mirror feelings, creativity, and learning processes. A child's connection to the world can be exciting when puppets are used.

PLANNING FOR PUPPETS IN EARLY EDUCATION

Children relate to puppets from their earliest years because they are used to making inanimate characters come to life. Children are puppeteers themselves from the first time they pick up a shoe, a squeezed-out half orange or a hairbrush and make it move and talk. Toys and dolls take an active role in children's play. They laugh and talk and argue. They put on personalities and take them off again. (UNICEF, 2007)

What exactly is a puppet? Cheryl Henson (1994), daughter of the late Jim Henson (the puppeteer who created the Muppets), explains, "A puppet is an object that appears to be alive when it's manipulated by a human hand. Some puppets look like dolls; others look like stuffed animals. Still others look like pieces of sculpture or even like piles of junk!"

For children in an early education program, a puppet is *whatever they say it is!* For young children, the discovery of themselves as puppeteers can be a wonderful discovery of themselves. Their excitement, enthusiasm, and imagination in creating and sharing puppets will become contagious to others, adults and children alike.

"Isenberg and Jalongo encourage the use of puppets as a nonthreatening device for improvisation and social collaboration or as a vehicle for building self-esteem and taking risks" (Esch & Long, 2002). Children can also explore the values of other cultures by recounting legends, folktales, or myths from around the world using puppets as storytellers.

For young children, the discovery of themselves as puppeteers can be wonderful.

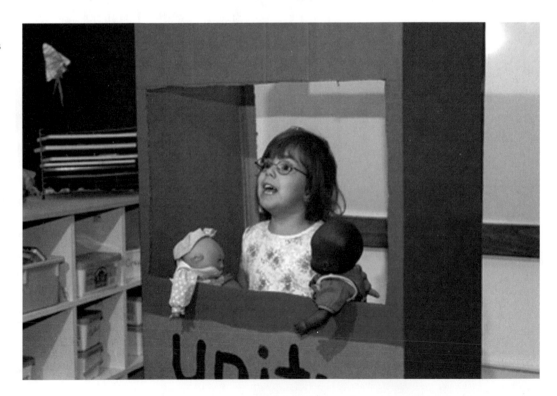

You and the children, together, should plan for and decide when and how to use puppets in your classroom. Here are some suggestions for getting started:

🌐 Begin by selecting a puppet for you, the teacher. Your first puppet, either one created by you or a ready-made commercial one, should become your special friend. Usually a hand puppet is the most comfortable; the more you use it, the more it fits like an old, favorite glove.

🌐 Identify why this particular puppet appeals to you. Does it remind you of a toy, doll, or puppet you had as a child? This discovery will help you decide on the puppet's name, personality, and voice. Remember, you do *not* have to be a ventriloquist.

🌐 Practice with your puppet. Watching yourself in the mirror might be useful in helping you decide how to use the puppet.

🌐 You do not need to use a stage or puppet theater. The personal interaction with a child or group of children is important.

🌐 Reinforce your own creativity and enjoyment of teaching. Let the puppet do for you what it does for a child: allow your imagination to flourish, your creative play to flow free, and your unique thoughts, feelings, and language to emerge.

🌐 Use puppets on a regular basis. As with any new or special materials you bring into the classroom or playground, demonstrate the appropriate use of the puppets.

🌐 Depending on the age of the children you teach, decide how often and how much you will use puppets. Usually, the younger the child, the more time you should take to make him feel comfortable with and trusting of the puppets. As with any toy or activity, use only safe materials.

🌐 For infants, having familiar stuffed toys and animals "talk to them" is a way of introducing puppets. Another way is to "walk" two of your fingers up a child's arm. Use a rhythmic, sing-song voice and say: "Here comes a little person walking up (child's name) arm. Now it's on your shoulder. Now it's on your neck. Tickle, tickle."

🌐 Take lots of time with toddlers. Start with finger plays and hand puppets. Leaving plenty of space between the puppet and the child usually helps this age child feel more comfortable.

🌐 Use puppets with your favorite finger plays, poems, songs, books, and flannel-board stories. Group time is a good opportunity to introduce puppets. When telling a familiar story, allow the children to hear the story several times. The retelling of the story allows you and the children to manipulate the puppets in a familiar setting. Children will eventually tell the story spontaneously and expand it in their own way *using puppets*.

Setting Up the Environment

By introducing children to different types of puppets, you can offer alternative learning experiences. These wonderful creations can tell a story, carry on a conversation, be a good listener, and entertain. While handling materials, manipulating, and organizing them, the *process*, as always, is the major focus.

> *When adults realize the most important aspect of creativity is the process, not the product, they will support the child's desire to experiment and create in individual ways. They will understand that the thing "made" is not nearly so important as what is happening in the process. (Fortson & Reiff, 1995)*

Young children can explore and stretch their abilities in all developmental areas through the process of creating and operating their puppets. They are:

🌐 experiencing the sheer joy of playing and fantasizing

🌐 developing positive self-images and independence

The introduction of the puppet activities can be done in three stages:

1. **Model the use of puppets during group time and in many curriculum areas.** By doing this, you, as the teacher, affirm the use of puppets. By demonstrating *nonviolent* behavior with puppets, you are showing the children how to enjoy them appropriately. Introduce them one at a time. As with any new activity, doing too much at one time can overstimulate the children.

2. **You and the children should create and use puppets together.** Allow children plenty of opportunities to practice with a variety of puppets before they begin to create their own. The guidance techniques you use will demonstrate additional and appropriate ways to enjoy puppets. Keep puppet construction, props, and stages very simple. Allow children to improvise, using their own creativity.

3. **Let individual children or a group of children make and interact with puppets through activities integrated into the lesson plan and the total curriculum.** The activities should be open-ended and allow children opportunities to extend the activities. Remember to make puppets accessible to children and give them time to explore with them. Provide the materials, but remember not to make a model for the children to copy. (The illustrations in this chapter and those in Appendix A are designed to give teachers *ideas* for making puppets, *not* to be used as models for the children to make.)

- using a safe and acceptable outlet for expressing themselves
- expanding vocabulary and communication skills
- improving social skills by sharing and cooperating and communicating ideas
- learning problem-solving skills and abstract thinking
- using fine motor skills
- practicing hand-eye coordination, hand-hand coordination, and muscle control

EASY-TO-MAKE PUPPETS

There are three basic categories of puppets: hand puppets, rod puppets, and marionettes.

Hand Puppets

hand puppets

Puppets that are put on the hand come in many types and varieties and are easy for young children to make and manipulate.

Hand puppets come in many types and varieties and are easy for young children to make and manipulate. Starting with finger puppets, the child gains ownership right away. It is fun to put two eyes, a nose, and a mouth on the child's thumb and fingers with a felt-tip pen. You will find some children do not want to wash their fingers after this activity. They like their puppets and want to keep them (see Figure 11–1).

Another kind of simple finger puppet can be made out of felt. Glue the two pieces together (as shown in the three-step illustration of Figure 11–2). Place eyes, a nose, and a mouth on the puppet. These can be easily manipulated by younger children and offer an unusual small muscle activity.

Other finger puppets can be made easily to illustrate shapes, numbers, nursery rhymes, or other concepts. You can first introduce them at group time, then put them in the manipulative center for the children to play with. By placing two fingers in one

Model the use of puppets during group time and in many curriculum areas.

FIGURE 11–1
Examples of finger puppets that are appropriate for young children.

FIGURE 11–2
Example of how to make finger puppets out of felt fabric.

of these, the child can add "legs" to make the puppet walk and dance. (See the three-step illustration in Figure 11–3.)

Basic hand, glove, and mitt puppets provide a close link between the puppet and the puppeteer. Toddlers, especially, enjoy this type of puppet. There are many commercially made examples, but the ones the teacher and children make are the most fun.

Figures 11–4 and 11–5 illustrate the easy-to-make basic design. The hand can be the whole body, with two fingers as the arms and one or two fingers operating the head. This hand puppet can be made easily from two pieces of felt or other fabric glued or sewn together and cut to fit a child's or an adult's hand. Eyes, nose, mouth, ears, hands, and hair can be attached with Velcro, glued, or sewn to the fabric. Felt squares of tan, beige, cream, brown, peach, and black can be used so a child can make a puppet that has his skin tone. (See Appendix A and front-of-the-book CD for basic patterns and new puppet patterns added.)

Rubber household gloves, which have a smooth surface, and garden gloves, which are available in many colors and designs, can be used to make another kind of hand puppet. This variety allows you to move all five fingers, independently as separate characters or together to make a creature, such as a "creepy crawler." Use double-stick tape on the rubber glove or sew small pieces of Velcro to the fingertips of the garden glove. Place the same kind of material on matching story pieces. This gives you and the children flexibility in creating hand puppets (see Figures 11–6 and 11–7).

STEP 1: Cut 2 finger puppet shapes out of felt (see Appendix A).

STEP 2: Glue the 2 shapes together along outside edges. Be sure to leave bottom open for finger.

STEP 3: Decorate with marker, glitter, cut shapes of felt, etc.

FIGURE 11–3
Example of how to make finger puppets out of cardboard.

STEP 1: Cut puppet figure out of cardboard or paper (see Appendix A).

STEP 2: Decorate with markers, paints, crayons, glitter, buttons, cut shapes of fabric, etc.

STEP 3: Play!

Ready-made mittens or household hot pad mitts can also be used to create another variety of hand puppets. Commercially crocheted puppets, usually representing animals, and sets of puppets are also available. Evaluate these carefully to be sure they are safe and appropriate for use with young children.

Think of all the finger plays, poems, songs, and stories you and the children can share with each other using sock puppets. These are probably the easiest puppets to make and use. Ask parents to donate unneeded children's socks in all sizes and colors. Once a child puts the sock on his hand, the puppet will "come to life." Add eyes made from buttons, commercial wiggly eyes, or anything you wish. Hair, made from yarn, string, steel wool, or cotton balls, and ears give extra personality to the character (see Figures 11–8 and 11–9).

Paper plate and paper bag puppets are some of the most fun to make and use. They are inexpensive, children can create more than one, and they are easily remade if they get torn. You and the children will design many kinds of paper puppets, but to get you started, a few examples follow.

FIGURE 11–4
Placement of the hand in a hand puppet.

FIGURE 11–5
Example of a completed hand puppet.

FIGURE 11–6
Example of a rubber glove puppet with finger characters.

FIGURE 11–7
Example of a "creepy crawler" puppet made from a glove.

Staple two paper plates together, leaving the bottom portion open for the puppeteer's hand. (You will find thin plates are easy for the children to handle.) Decorate this puppet, and it is ready to use!

A more complex type of puppet can be made by folding one paper plate in half and cutting another in half. Staple one of the cut halves to the back of the folded plate, leaving the bottom part open. Repeat this with the other half. The puppeteer's hand fits into the open part—fingers in the top, thumb in the bottom (Figure 11–10). This puppet can become any character. Add a construction paper body to give it a more complete look.

For a paper-bag, floppy-mouth puppet, use a small- or medium-size bag. Draw a puppet face on the bag or cut and glue one from a magazine. Use crayons, markers, paints, glue, yarn, cotton balls, or other material to finish the puppet. It is easy to work by placing your fingers inside the flap of the bag and moving them up and down.

Other paper puppets can be made from products such as paper cups or pudding, oatmeal, or small cereal boxes. Add these to the other creative materials in your puppet center for the children's exploration and experimentation.

FIGURE 11–8
The hand position for a sock puppet.

FIGURE 11–9
Example of a sock puppet.

FIGURE 11–10
Making of a paper plate puppet.

STEP 1: Staple two halves of a paper plate to a whole one.

STEP 2: Fold uncut plate in half and decorate face and mouth.

STEP 3: Add hair, ears, body, etc.

Stick or Rod Puppets

Stick or rod puppets are controlled by a single stick, such as a tongue depressor, dowel rod, paper towel roll, craft stick, or ice cream stick. An even smaller character might be placed on a paper straw. The figure itself can be cut from magazines, catalogs, and wrapping paper; traced from a pattern; or drawn by hand. Then it is glued to the stick or straw. Many card shops or toy stores have paper plates in the shape of animals. These make wonderful puppets when stapled to a dowel rod. These can be reinforced with tagboard and covered with contact paper or laminated.

A wooden spoon makes another delightful puppet. The bowl of the spoon makes a perfect head, and the handle becomes the body. Use felt-tip markers, crayons, or paint to make the face.

The "people puppet" (Figure 11–11) is made out of cardboard or tagboard and then attached to a stick or dowel rod. Encourage children to add eyes, a nose, a mouth, hair, clothes, and shoes. Multicultural or skin-toned paints, crayons, and construction paper should be available for the children to use. This promotes self-awareness and positive self-esteem. Another variation of the people puppet is one depicting a face (Figure 11–12). The children can cut out the eyes, then add a nose, a mouth, and hair. Attach a straw or craft stick to create a stick puppet or mask.

Make a paper plate and stick puppet combination. Staple or glue a paper plate—any size—onto a stick such as a tongue depressor, craft stick, or dowel rod. Put a happy, tearful, angry, or other emotional face on the puppet. You could make enough

FIGURE 11–11
Making a stick people puppet.

STEP 1: Cut out people puppet shape from cardboard (see Appendix A).

STEP 2: Decorate with paint, markers, crayons, cut shapes of paper, fabric, etc.

STEP 3: Glue stick to back of finished puppet.

FIGURE 11–12
Making a people mask puppet.

STEP 1: Cut face shapes from cardboard or paper (see Appendix A.)

STEP 2: Decorate with paint, markers, crayons, cut shapes of paper, fabric, etc.

STEP 3: Glue stick to back of decorated face shape.

STEP 4: Let it dry and then play!

of these to create a family of paper plate puppets, human or animal; the children will know what to do.

Marionettes

Marionettes, controlled by strings, offer an extra range of expression and full body movement. As teachers, we should appreciate the sophisticated skills needed to make and operate a marionette. In encouraging a school-ager who wants to make this type of puppet, the first question asked should be, "What do you want it to do?" It is important to think through and plan each step in the creation of a marionette. The "airplane control" is the simplest design to manipulate, usually with one string to the head and a string to each of the hands (Figure 11–13). Children need time to experiment and to experience the frustration of the puppet not working the first time it is tried. It is important to support them through the frustration. The failure and success of making and manipulating a marionette is part of their *process.* Maintenance and care of the marionette is also part of the experience. To avoid tangling the strings, it should be hung after it is used. Hanging marionettes make a distinctive classroom decoration.

Other Types of Puppets

Shadow puppets offer a visual dimension to puppetry that other types do not. Shown in a darkened room, they are held from below by rods against a translucent screen lit from behind. Puppeteers manipulate flat, cut-out silhouettes that the audience can see on the other side of the screen as moving figures. One of the simplest shadow animal puppets, a flying bird, is described by Cheryl Henson (1994):

All you need is a single light source—a standing lamp with the shade removed or a desk lamp tilted to the side. Interlock your thumbs and slowly flap your hands. When you pass them between the light source and a blank wall, the shadow they cast will look like a bird in flight.

Progression from this simple example to more complex shadow puppets will occur as older children discover creative ways to investigate and make these puppets (Figure 11–14).

Papier-mâché headed puppets are made with strips of newspaper soaked in a thick flour-and-water paste placed over a balloon, molded piece of clay, or foam ball. After drying, the "head" is cut in half to remove the clay or ball. Then the halves are glued back together. Paint facial features to create the puppet character. Make the neck long enough to hold fabric, which becomes the body of the puppet (Figure 11–15).

FIGURE 11–13
Example of a marionette.

marionettes
Puppets controlled by strings that offer an extra range of expression and full body movement.

shadow puppets
Puppets held from rods against a translucent screen lit from behind. These puppets offer a visual dimension that other types do not.

FIGURE 11–14
Example of a shadow hand puppet.

FIGURE 11–15
Making a papier mache puppet.

STEP 1: Cover ball in paper stripes soaked in flour paste.

STEP 2: When dry, cut in half to remove ball. Then glue halves together.

STEP 3: Cut a hole for finger, decorate, make a body and attach to head.

MATERIALS NEEDED

All of the various types of puppets can be made from a wide variety of materials. (Puppet patterns for teachers can be found in Appendix A and in the front-of-the-book CD with new puppet patterns added.) An easy way to collect these is to place a box in the classroom simply labeled, "Materials for Puppet Making." This keeps it visible for parents and children while reminding them that all kinds of things are needed. The following is a list of what needs to be gathered:

- 🌐 boxes—especially small cereal and salt boxes
- 🌐 buttons and wiggly eyes—especially the larger ones
- 🌐 clothespins
- 🌐 cloth scraps—felt, lace, cotton, towels, and washcloths in tan, beige, cream, brown, peach, and black
- 🌐 cotton balls, steel wool, sponges, pipe cleaners, corks, hair curlers
- 🌐 crayons, markers, pencils, pens, paints
- 🌐 egg cartons
- 🌐 feathers
- 🌐 gloves—cloth, garden-type, and rubber
- 🌐 leather scraps
- 🌐 magazines, catalogs, and newspapers

- office supplies—scissors, envelopes, paper clips, glue, brads, rubber bands, gummed labels and stickers, stapler and staples, and rulers
- paper products—cardboard; sandpaper; all sizes of paper bags, plates, and cups; towel and bathroom paper rolls; crepe paper; wrapping paper; tissue paper; wall paper; waxed paper; foil; straws; and construction paper in all colors representing skin tones, including tan, beige, cream, brown, black, and peach
- socks—especially those that will fit a child's hand and soccer socks for making adult-size puppets
- spools
- sticks—tongue depressors, ice cream sticks, craft sticks, yardsticks, toothpicks, and dowel rods
- Styrofoam balls and scraps
- tape—clear, masking, and double-stick types
- wooden spoons
- wood scraps—preferably already sanded smooth
- yarn, string, ribbons, and shoelaces

SUGGESTIONS FOR PLACEMENT AND STORAGE OF PUPPETS

Whether you offer a puppet center or puppets in every center, make it possible for the children to select and interact with any puppet they want to make or play with. The children should feel the freedom to move the puppets to another location to best meet their needs. Children are more likely to use puppets if the guidelines for use are clearly explained and if the puppets and puppet materials are organized and displayed attractively and accessibly.

At first, some children prefer just to examine the puppets and try them on to see how they feel. Others enjoy making puppets, and still others just like to play with ready-made puppets. Allow for individual and developmental preferences.

For the creative and spontaneous use of puppets, a stage is not necessary. As mentioned earlier, you, as a teacher, do not need to use a stage, and neither do the children. If you feel you need a creative boost, Hunt and Renfro (1982) suggest a story apron.

This is an ideal costume for you to wear as a puppeteller. It signals that Puppetime is about to begin, it provides a background for your story, poem, or song and it hides puppets and props

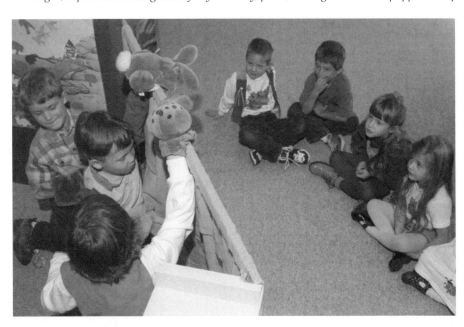

until you are ready to use them. . . . A general all-purpose story apron can be made by adding pockets to a store-bought apron or by creating your own custom-apron from selected fabric.

If the children insist on needing a stage for their puppets, here are some easy ways to provide one:

- Construct a puppet stage from a large packing carton. Cut the center out of the box to form a "stage opening."
- Drape a cloth over a piece of rope.
- Turn a small, sturdy table on its side so the children can "hide" behind it and show only the puppets, or use a table top draped in front with a sheet.
- Using a shower curtain rod, hang a piece of fabric low across an open doorway.
- Place two adult-size chairs back to back at a short distance. Drop a curtain or cloth over a yardstick placed between the chairs.
- Use a "gutted TV" (a television set from which the insides have been removed). This offers another dimension to a child's puppet play.

The following suggestions for the storage of puppets are used by many teachers and suggested by Hunt and Renfro (1982), Raines and Isbell (1994), and the author's personal preference:

- Hang a clothesline along a wall at child's eye and arm level, and use clothespins to clip the puppets to the line.
- Place the puppets on an accordion clothes rack.
- Clip the puppets to a multiple-skirt hanger.
- Store finger puppets and stick puppets in egg cartons or plastic bags.
- Store puppets in tiered hanging baskets.
- Use a shoe bag or shoe rack to organize puppets.
- Place shoe boxes or clear plastic boxes on low shelves.
- Store puppets in a toy box or chest.

A child might like to make a home for his very special puppet. Select a box into which the puppet will fit. Have the child decorate the box any way he chooses, including adding windows and a door. A scrap of soft material inside the box makes a bed for the puppet friend. The box can be placed in or near the child's cubbie.

CONNECTING PUPPETS TO CURRICULUM AREAS

It is helpful to brainstorm ideas with colleagues and classmates, but here are a few suggestions to stimulate your creativity:

- Puppets can speak in any language. This shows that all languages are valued. For example, Mister Number is a puppet that can count from one to twenty in many languages. Another puppet says only "yes and no" or "hello and goodbye," but does so in ten different languages. The puppet may speak only the language of the child talking or the child being spoken to. Multicultural puppets can also be used to introduce cultural celebrations.
- Expand the language arts center by adding puppets and props. A puppet with a microphone can encourage creative play. Puppets can even interview other puppets. Because the characters can be human, animal, or "Mr. and Ms. Anything," the questions asked can be about families, feelings, favorite foods, where you come from, or where you live. For older children, the questions can also concern current events, nutrition, math, science, or ecology.

🌐 Encourage storytelling with sock puppets representing "Billy Goats Gruff" by M. Brown, "The Little Red Hen" by P. Galdone, or characters from *Winnie the Pooh* by A. A. Milne and *The Velveteen Rabbit* by M. Williams. Use finger puppets or hand puppets to read the story books *Corduroy* by D. Freeman, *Leo the Late Bloomer* by R. Kraus, or *Horton Hatches the Egg* by Dr. Seuss (T. Geisel). Relating puppets to familiar stories can extend the retelling.

🌐 Add a puppet holding a toy telephone to the dramatic play center. This presents an additional dimension to telephone talk.

🌐 A puppet "helper of the day" can offer you a unique way to reinforce cooperation, cleanup rules, and problem solving. The puppet can ask the children questions, leading them to solve the existing problem instead of the teacher. This puppet character can help defuse many disputes and difficulties that occur in an early childhood setting.

🌐 Introducing a "listening puppet," one with big ears, can help you emphasize the importance of listening. One puppet might talk to or answer children only in song or verse. Perhaps another only dances. A very shy puppet who will not talk can learn to do so with help from the children.

🌐 Create some puppets for outdoor play. Have all types of clothing available for these puppet personalities. The children can select the appropriate clothes for the weather that day.

PUPPETS AND TELEVISION

Since the beginning of television, puppets have been a part of the daily viewing schedule. Local television stations usually began their day of live broadcasting with programs that featured puppets.

In the United States, eight great puppeteers introduced their creations to children who had never before seen puppets:

🌐 Edgar Bergen (1903–1978): a ventriloquist who entertained children and their parents with his wooden partners, Charlie McCarthy and Mortimer Snerd, on radio, stage, and television.

🌐 Bil Baird (1904–1987): puppeteered marionettes for over 60 years and created more than 3,000 puppets seen on stage, television, and film.

🌐 "Buffalo Bob" Smith (1917–1998): "Hey kids, what time is it?" "It's *Howdy Doody* time!" Hundreds of children, in the studio and at home, answered the question from 1947 to 1960 when "Buffalo Bob" and his marionette, Howdy Doody, a real-life but nontalking clown, Clarabell, and their friends entertained children during the early days of live television.

🌐 Burr Tilstrom (1917–1985): best known during the 1950s on television for his hand puppets Kukla and Ollie, along with Fran, a real human being who stood in front of the stage and interacted with the puppets.

🌐 Jim Henson (1937–1990): created the Muppets and to this day inspires children and families all over the world to laugh and learn together while enjoying *Sesame Street* and the Muppet movies and home videos.

🌐 Shari Lewis (1934–1998): innovative ventriloquist-puppeteer shared her endearing sock puppets Lamb Chop, Charlie Horse, and Hush Puppy with children and their parents for four decades in person and on television, the latest being *Lamb Chop's Play-Along* and *The Charlie Horse Music Pizza*.

🌐 Fred Rogers (1928–2003): Mister Rogers believed everyone is special, and his use of puppets in the Neighborhood of Make-Believe (King Friday and his friends) dealt with things that are important to young children. He was there through good times and bad times. He was there for teachers and parents as well. Mister

@ 2003 Seasame Workshop

For 38 years, and counting, Sesame Street has entertained and educated young children and their families. One of the most delightful and favorite puppet characters on television is Big Bird. Caroll Spinney is the talented and thoughtful puppeteer who, along with Jim Henson, gave birth to Big Bird and Oscar the Grouch. Spinney continues to give life to these two very special puppet individuals. The following is a conversation between the author (HJ), Caroll Spinney (CS), and Big Bird (BB).

HJ Why do you think puppets have become so successful for children's television?

CS There has been a change in the way puppets have been perceived. Jim Henson and his approach to puppets on television—this really isn't biased when I say it—was such a change. It just seems natural now. How else would you do it? Up to 1969 you couldn't sell puppets on television. It was cartoons and cartoons. TV saw puppets as "silly little things." Jim's approach was something that was more alive and more exciting. It succeeded in overwhelming cartooning. Cartoons are now enjoying the best age they've ever had. Every time you see puppets on TV now, they all look like something Jim made.

HJ Why do you think children respond so well to puppets, especially on TV? What is it about puppets that is better than cartoons?

CS My experience with "The Bird" is that he seems to live, talk, and include in his life those who

are watching. Cartoons are celluloid. They don't relate to you. They have their own life and you just observe.

The Muppets on *Sesame Street* "stroke the camera" all the time. The children all feel they're involved. It's something you can't do with cartoons, and if they do it, it's not spontaneous. We have the advantage with television and its immediacy. The puppets communicate more directly. Children identify with us. After 38 years, I still admire *Sesame Street*.

HJ Why do you think Oscar the Grouch has been so successful? Why do you think showing his kind of personality through a puppet instead of through a person makes it more appealing to you?

CS That's a good question, because I've always said I wouldn't walk across the street to talk to a "creep" like Oscar the Grouch. I'm amazed that I can play a character like that, because I'm appalled at things he says. I've even talked to the producers of *Sesame Street* and told them that he's rude. I asked, what is he teaching? I've decided he's not evil, he does have a heart. Oscar is really a grouch, but he's moral. We are trying to teach. I sometimes act like a censor or critic. I edit Oscar myself, it's instinctual. Perhaps it's a lot like teaching.

HJ   What makes Big Bird different? Why is he so loved and respected?

CS   He doesn't change. He's constant. It's his longevity. Big Bird is like a "teddy bear." He's a compassionate kid, as human as anyone on the show.

With *Sesame Street* there are elements of entertainment and teaching at the same time. We show the children that there's something worth looking at. We're not annoying. *Sesame Street* is a counterforce until the children are about seven years old. We're together until then.

HJ   Why do you think puppets are important in early childhood education? What can teachers do to introduce children to puppets?

CS   Introduce children to a good group of "live" puppeteers. Have them visit the classroom. It becomes more personal. Puppeteers of America [is] a good resource. [There are regional and community groups in most areas.]

Teachers should try puppets themselves. Give life to each puppet. There is a power of puppets to teach, to explore, and [to] learn. Have fun with puppets! Use puppets to get the children's attention. Have lots of puppets available. If I had been a teacher I would have had to use them all the time. Puppets give adults another way to relate to children. You can teach real humanity.

HJ   Now, I'd like for Big Bird to talk to the teachers. This is a question for you. You went to bird preschool, didn't you?

BB   Yes, I was with a bunch of sparrows.

HJ   What were some of your favorite things when you were in preschool?

BB   I built towers with blocks. Teacher had a big, yellow and white box full of wooden musical instruments like clackers and we asked the teacher when we could play with them. She always said "by-and-by," and we never did. I never did trust "by-and-by" as an answer anymore. The afternoon children she liked much better. They got to play with the instruments. It wasn't easy being only 3½ years old and 5 feet 11 inches. Now I'm 6 years old and 8 feet 2 inches tall.

HJ   If you could talk to the teachers, what would you tell them to teach the children?

BB   I remember asking Gordon, on *Sesame Street*, because he is very wise. He's a teacher. I asked him why did he do that. He said, "It's important to raise the children in the way they should go." Wouldn't it be smart to teach 'em about the good, nice stuff, not just about the bad stuff?

HJ   Why do you think it's important to go to school and meet friends?

BB   Because friends are important. They're the ones who make up the rest of the world besides me.

HJ   Anything else you'd like to say?

BB   Yes. When I grow up, I'm going to be a Professor-Bird.

HJ   Thank you both so much. I've enjoyed being on *Sesame Street* and visiting with you.

@ 2003 Seasame Workshop

Sesame Street has been broadcast in more than 140 countries around the world. Some countries air the original American show, whereas others create new versions in their own languages (Borgenicht, 1998). For example, in 1998 the Israeli/Palestinian co-production Rechov Sumsum/ Shara's Simsim began and China introduced Hu Hu Zhu. The children in Mexico enjoy Plaza Sesamo.

The charming Carmen Osbahr, who previously performed on Plaza Sesamo, is the puppeteer who gives voice and personality to Rosita on Sesame Street. Rosita, a delightful turquoise Muppet, speaks both English and Spanish, her native language. She's the first bilingual Muppet to ever appear on Sesame Street. The following is a conversation between the author (HJ), Carmen Osbahr (CO), and Rosita (R) when we met on Sesame Street.

HJ **Carmen, why do you think puppets are so successful for children's television?**

CO I grew up with puppets and television, *Sesame Street–Plaza Sesamo*. I think puppets have always been fun for children and grown-ups. With the introduction of puppets on television you are able to reach more people. Speaking as a puppeteer, you can be everything you want to be, go everywhere, and take the children watching along with you.

HJ **You mentioned that you were always interested in puppets. What were the puppets in Mexico?**

CO My parents used to take me to live shows. In kindergarten I remember my teachers, on Fridays at lunch, used to have these little theaters with

puppets and little sets to go with the stories they told. I remember *Capervsita Roja* (Little Red Riding Hood) and *La Bella Durmiente* (Sleeping Beauty). They were very simple, little "guignol" hand puppets. I think simple is best. I remember they changed the costumes with a little color and added different backgrounds. The teachers had fun too. I was just fascinated. Puppets were always around my life. I was 10 or 11 years old when *Plaza Sesamo* began. I was amazed.

HJ **Did you make puppets? When did you get started?**

CO I probably started in kindergarten. I remember doing the sock with the eyes glued on and making the puppet with the little ball head where we created our own little face. I'd go home and try to do more by myself.

HJ **Well, here's Rosita. Hi, Rosita.**

R HI! (Rosita uses a very big voice.)

HJ **Do you mind if I ask you some questions?**

R OKAY!

HJ **How old are you?**

R One, two, like this (holds up fingers). One, two, three, four, five, SIX! I just turned SIX! Uno, dos, tres, quatro, cinco, seis. I'm a six-year-old little monster. My whole name is Rosita, La Monstrua de las Cuevas—Rosita, the monster of the caves. See my wings? I can't fly, I don't know why I have them. I have my mommy, my daddy, my uncle Tito, my aunt Lola, and my cousin. I asked why do we all have wings and they don't know why because none of us can fly.

HJ **It's part of who you are.**

R YEAH! YEAH! (in a very big voice)

HJ **Do you go to school?**

R Yes, I do. I play. I have my friends. I run around, I sing a lot, and I learn my ABCs. I know how to count and I know all the colors, and I love my teacher, and that's it.

HJ **Do you help teach the other children about all those things in Spanish?**

R Yes, the ones that are curious, you know, but yeah, they like Mexican food, so I have to explain that that's an enchilada, and that's the mole, and of course to count in Spanish. Everybody knows how to count in Spanish.

HJ **Do you think you'll be a teacher when you grow up?**

R I never thought about it. Yeah, I will teach Spanish.

HJ **I think you'll be very good and you love to hug children . . .**

R Everybody, I love to hug everybody. I like to hug you.

HJ **Muchos gracias. How do you say my name Hilda in Spanish?**

R "Ilda" (whispering). In Spanish the H is silent. "Ilda." I want to sing to you. My song is Sing to the Sun.

Solecito que temprano,
Siempre me llenas de alegria y calor mi vida.
In English, I said:
The sun that comes out really early in the morning
Always brings me happiness and warms my life.
There's about 200 verses, but I only know one.
Well, I'm going to go play with my dolly, so I'll be around. 'Bye.

HJ **Good-bye, Rosita. I really enjoyed talking to you. Thank you again for the hug.**

R Mucho gracias. That means thank you!

HJ **Mucho gracias. Thank you.**

R No, thank you.

HJ **Let me know if you ever fly.**

R OKAY! I'll have my mommy send you an e-mail.

HJ **And mucho gracias to you too, Carmen.**

Rogers and his words will continue to inspire as we enjoy his videotaped television series and books. Visit the Family Communications Web site for information about the life and works of Fred Rogers, online at *http://www.fci.org*

🌐 Bob Keeshan (1927–2004): known to children and adults the world over as *Captain Kangaroo*. His children's network television program, with puppets Mr. Moose and Rabbit, ran from 1955–1984, plus an additional six years following on PBS. Why he chose the persona of the old captain, Keeshan explained: "I was impressed with the potential positive relationship between grandparents and grandchildren, so I chose an elderly character."

SHARING WITH FAMILIES: TAKING PUPPETS HOME

Getting parents involved with and enthusiastic about puppetry will take time and patience on your part. You might find the following suggestions helpful:

🌐 Send information home to parents about puppet presentations available in your community. It is important that children have opportunities to see live performances.

🌐 Figure 11–16 shows a letter to be sent home with the children in your program. The younger children can add illustrations to the letter. The older children can write their own letter to invite their families to a special evening at the center. If the parents speak a language other than English, ask someone to help you translate the letter into their native language. Send both copies home with the child.

🌐 Have an informal parents' meeting. After a light supper, including foods the children have made, the parents and children go to different learning centers in the room. This is a good time to introduce new or favorite activities. Set up the centers with materials and supplies for the families to make things together. One of the activities should be making puppets. Whatever the family group makes, they take home.

🌐 Offer a puppet lending library to the children and families. Display durable, commercially made puppets available for the families to sign out. Encourage parents to enjoy the puppets with their children. Supply a bright-colored sack or large envelope in which the borrowed puppet can be returned.

FIGURE 11–16
An example of a letter to send home with the children.

Dear Family

(or whatever the child calls his parent using the language spoken at home),

Please come visit my school on (date and time). We are cooking for you. We have planned some special things for you to do. One thing is to make puppets with me. We have been doing this and it's lots of fun. It will be lots of fun for you too. You can see my teacher and all my friends.

(Child's name)

TIPS FOR TEACHERS

The puppet can be whatever the puppeteer and the child make it. It can be the child's friend without demanding something in return. It can be a clown. It can be naughty and get into trouble without hurting anyone. It can say what the child thinks, feel what the child feels and share a child's sadness. It can show a child who knows poverty, hunger, war and loss that there can also be joy and love and a happy ending. A puppet can tell a child who rarely hears it that he is loved. A puppet can show a child that her father or mother can also be sad, and it can demonstrate the value of love, the futility of quarrel and the benefit of cooperation and support. (UNICEF, 2007)

Throughout this chapter, I have suggested guidance techniques and tips for introducing and using puppets. I have always used puppets in my teaching young children and adults, on television, and in the classroom. Puppet creations will become a valuable teaching tool for you. They can help you encourage appropriate behavior and speech. Once you feel comfortable in creating and using puppets yourself, you will discover that these wonderful characters can help you throughout the day. The more you use puppets, the more you will see for yourself how much children relate to and love puppets.

It is important for you to establish the following guidelines with the children in your classroom. These should affirm the children's creativity and promote puppetry. Explain that the children should

🌐 take all the time needed to make a puppet.

🌐 make the puppet their own way.

🌐 be creative and imaginative.

🌐 wait until *you* are ready.

🌐 please explore, experiment, and create.

Figure 11–17 is the curriculum planning web worksheet with puppet activities added. This worksheet with appropriate additions is included in each chapter.

WHY I TEACH YOUNG CHILDREN

"Mommy, mommy, come see. We have a surprise for you." My three-year-old son grabbed my hand and pulled me down the hall to his five-and-a-half-year-old brother's room. Both sons seated me in a chair facing them as they hid on one side of the bed. In a few seconds, up popped their hands, each holding a brightly colored rock. Then they proceeded to present a delightful "rock puppet show." Twenty-one years later my three-year-old son was making Muppets for Jim Henson.

—Hilda Jackman

ACTIVITY PLAN WORKSHEET

Developmentally Appropriate Activities

Children's age group: appropriate for toddlers if the activity is simplified; otherwise, the activity is appropriate for preschoolers and kindergarten children

Name of Activity and Brief Description

"Sound game with puppets and props"

Purpose/Objectives of Activity

● to listen to different sounds that promote auditory discrimination

(continues)

ACTIVITY PLAN WORKSHEET (CONTINUED)

- to recognize sounds in the environment
- to classify sounds
- to develop mental images of what is heard
- to recognize loud and soft sounds
- to recognize high and low sounds
- to listen to instructions

Space and Materials Needed

Depending on the number of children playing the game at one time, the area of floor space needed may be large or small. A puppet with attachable puppet ears is needed along with a cloth bag filled with objects having distinctive sounds, such as an eggbeater, a timer, a box of rice, some maracas, and a musical triangle.

Procedure

1. Have the children sit on the floor in a circle.
2. Attach large ears to "Ms. I Listen" puppet. (You can use the basic hand puppet suggested in Figure 11–4. The pattern can be found in Appendix A and in the front-of-the-book CD. Ears can be attached easily with Velcro.)
3. Use the puppet to introduce the activity by singing "Put Your Finger in the Air." End with "Put your finger on your ear and tell me what you hear."
4. Use the puppet to lead a discussion on why we have ears.
5. After discussion, use "Ms. I Listen" puppet to introduce the sound bag. Have her choose one child to be "it."
6. Give "it" the sound bag.
7. Have children stand, join hands, and circle clockwise, while the child who is "it" remains stationary outside the circle holding the sound bag.
8. The children continue circling until they hear "it" call "Stop!"
9. The child who is "it" chooses something from the sound bag and makes a sound with it. The child who has stopped directly in front of "it" must guess what is making the sound.
10. If he guesses correctly, he becomes "it" and changes places.
11. If the guess is incorrect, the teacher using the puppet guides the child into making the correct choice, and then he changes places with "it."
12. Continue until all items in the sound bag have been identified.
13. Use the puppet to direct children into the next activity.

Guidance

If possible, a small group of children should do this activity the first time it is presented. Once they know how the activity is played, they can then help the puppet, "Ms. I Listen," explain the game to the other children.

It is important to establish limits for behavior and boundaries of the activity.

It is helpful to anticipate problems that may develop during this activity and consider ways in which they may be handled. You know your group of children best. Therefore, use the guidance that will work best for your situation.

Evaluation and Follow-Up

Evaluate this activity to see whether the children were able to achieve the skills or understand the concepts presented. Consider how this activity could be changed to be more effective.

Follow-up activities could include attaching a large nose to the same puppet or big eyes or large hands with fingers. Put appropriate items in the cloth bag to correspond with the added body parts.

Another activity could use sound cans filled with rice, beans, sand, large nails, paper clips, and metal washers. For the children to match sounds, use two cans for each item (small film cans or Band-Aid cans). Children first match sounds, then identify sounds.

Develop your own list of activities, using the puppet, that can extend or give practice to the skills or concepts of this activity.

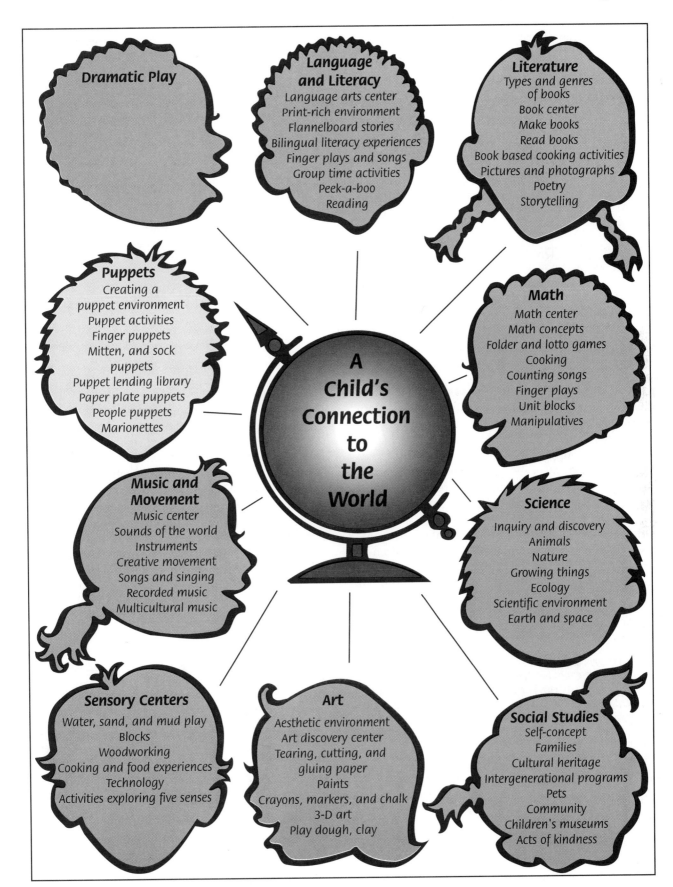

Dramatic Play

Language and Literacy
Language arts center
Print-rich environment
Flannelboard stories
Bilingual literacy experiences
Finger plays and songs
Group time activities
Peek-a-boo
Reading

Literature
Types and genres of books
Book center
Make books
Read books
Book based cooking activities
Pictures and photographs
Poetry
Storytelling

Puppets
Creating a puppet environment
Puppet activities
Finger puppets
Mitten, and sock puppets
Puppet lending library
Paper plate puppets
People puppets
Marionettes

Math
Math center
Math concepts
Folder and lotto games
Cooking
Counting songs
Finger plays
Unit blocks
Manipulatives

A Child's Connection to the World

Music and Movement
Music center
Sounds of the world
Instruments
Creative movement
Songs and singing
Recorded music
Multicultural music

Science
Inquiry and discovery
Animals
Nature
Growing things
Ecology
Scientific environment
Earth and space

Sensory Centers
Water, sand, and mud play
Blocks
Woodworking
Cooking and food experiences
Technology
Activities exploring five senses

Art
Aesthetic environment
Art discovery center
Tearing, cutting, and gluing paper
Paints
Crayons, markers, and chalk
3-D art
Play dough, clay

Social Studies
Self-concept
Families
Cultural heritage
Intergenerational programs
Pets
Community
Children's museums
Acts of kindness

FIGURE 11–17
A curriculum planning web worksheet with puppet activities added.

✳ AFTERVIEW

Through puppets, a child

- 🌐 builds self-esteem.
- 🌐 develops independence.
- 🌐 learns acceptable behavior.
- 🌐 improves listening skills.
- 🌐 learns new ways to express feelings.
- 🌐 learns to share with others and to take turns.

- 🌐 learns to make choices.
- 🌐 develops large and small muscle skills.
- 🌐 practices language skills.
- 🌐 uses creative thinking and imagination.
- 🌐 strengthens problem-solving skills and abstract thinking.
- 🌐 reveals thoughts and attitudes through conversation.

✳ KEY TERMS

hand puppets   puppetry   stick or rod puppets
marionettes   shadow puppets

✳ EXPLORATIONS

1. Select a classmate or colleague as a partner. Share ideas on how a teacher can encourage social, emotional, and language development with puppets.
2. Review the types of puppets discussed in this chapter. Then create a puppet. Share this puppet with a group of children. Use any of the ideas found in this chapter.
3. As a group activity, select a children's book and make puppets to represent the characters in the book. Discuss the criteria for the book selection and carefully choose the materials to use in making the puppets. Upon completion, invite a group of children in to watch the presentation of the story with puppets. Later, discuss the children's reactions to the puppet

story. How did the puppeteers feel about this activity? What will you change and why?
4. Some people can think of puppets only in terms of elaborate stages and complicated marionettes on strings. What are some basics that an early childhood education teacher can follow when introducing puppetry to young children? Does it have to be expensive?
5. Either through research or personal interviews, find out which community resources or agencies present puppet activities or puppet plays and which early education programs offer puppets as part of their learning environment. Share your findings with your classmates or colleagues.

✳ REFERENCES

Borgenicht, D. (1998). *Sesame Street unpaved: Scripts, stories, secrets, and songs.* New York: Children's Television Workshop and Hyperion.

Center for Puppetry Arts. (1994). *Museum guide.* Atlanta, GA: Author.

Esch, G., & Long, E. (2002, January). The fabulously fun finger puppet workshop. *Young Children, 57*(1), 90-91.

Fortson, L. R., & Reiff, J. C. (1995). *Early childhood curriculum.* Boston: Allyn & Bacon.

Henson, C. (1994). *The Muppets make puppets.* New York: Workman Publishing.

Hunt, T., & Renfro, N. (1982). *Puppetry in early childhood education.* Austin, TX: Nancy Renfro Studios.

Jalongo, M. R. (2003, Summer). The child's right to creative thought and expression. *Childhood Education, 79*(4), 218–228.

Raines, S., & Isbell, R. (1994). *Stories: Children's literature in early education.* Clifton Park, NY: Thomson Delmar Learning.

UNICEF in Action. (2007). On-line at: http://www.unicef.org/puppets

✳ ADDITIONAL READINGS AND RESOURCES

Baird, B. (1965). *The art of the puppet.* New York: Macmillan.

Contreras, G. (1995). Teaching about the Vietnamese culture: Water puppetry as the soul of the rice fields. *Social Studies, 86*(1), 25–28.

Dolci, M. (1994, July/August). When the wolf both is and is not a wolf—The language of puppets. *Child Care Information Exchange, 98*, 43–46.

Finch, C. (Ed.). (1993). *Jim Henson: The works—The art, the magic, the imagination.* New York: Random House.

Isenberg, J., & Jalongo, M. J. (2001). *Creative expression and play in the early childhood curriculum* (3rd ed.). Upper Saddle River, NJ: Merrill.

Koralek, D. (2003, July). It's you *we* like: Remembering NAEYC's good friend, Fred M. "Mister" Rogers. *Young Children, 58*(4), 72–73.

Machado, J. M. (2007). *Early childhood experiences in language arts* (8th ed.). Clifton Park, NY: Thomson Delmar Learning.

Mayesky, M. (2006). *Creative activities for young children* (8th ed.). Clifton Park, NY: Thomson Delmar Learning.

Richards, A. (2007). *The story is just the start.* On-line at: http://www.earlychildhoodnews.com

For additional information on early education curriculum, visit our Web site at http://www.earlychilded.delmar.com

CHAPTER 12

DRAMATIC PLAY AND CREATIVE DRAMATICS

OBJECTIVES

AFTER STUDYING THIS CHAPTER, YOU SHOULD BE ABLE TO:

- Define and give examples of dramatic play and creative dramatics.

- Specify developmental stages of dramatic play.

- Identify fantasy and reality understanding in young children.

- Discuss the teacher's role in planning and preparing the environment for dramatic play, including adaptations for special needs children.

- Describe the purpose and process of making prop boxes for dramatic play activities.

- Discuss integrating developmentally appropriate dramatic play into all the curriculum areas.

- Identify the positive and negative aspects of young children imitating superheroes.

OVERVIEW

Play is the natural language of the child. It helps a child observe and respond to the world in which she lives. "The impulse to play, if encouraged, can become a continuing way of learning, a medium of expression, and eventually a creative art" (McCaslin, 1990).

From pat-a-cake to peek-a-boo, a baby watches others and then copies them. "The infant year is spent in close and intense observation of the human species. The baby learns to *read* every expression and gesture of the important adults around her. Toward the end of that first year, imitation begins" (Miller, 2002). The more you can play such pretend games with an infant, the more the infant learns. As the baby coos and babbles, your smiles and hugs give encouragement. When you say a word over and over, the baby will try to say it too. An infant's awareness of human expression, gestures, and sounds is the beginning of creative thinking.

Toddlers love the world of pretend. They will use dishes and pretend to eat and drink. "Toddlers have *object hunger.* They love objects of all kinds and use them in every conceivable way. This shows up in their early pretending. As long as the toy looks like an object they have seen, even if it is not exact, the child will use it in the intended way" (Miller, 2002). They enjoy pretend hellos and goodbyes. As you talk and enter such play, you are helping them learn about the real world. Children learn by repetition. Your willingness to do the same thing over and over is the key that opens the door to their learning. Although toddlers may pretend for short periods of time alone, they need other children and adults to give words and some direction to their play.

Dramatic play is one of the most valuable forms of play in children. "Early childhood educators know the value of dramatic play with preschoolers. Children learn empathy as they practice literally putting themselves in someone else's shoes. Language is enhanced as their play characters express themselves to their peers and social relationships are strengthened" (Miller, 2002). Preschool children love to have stories read to them. They will retell the stories as they play. A few props will get them going on the story. They may give their own twist to the story each time they "play the role." They're trying out new ways to solve problems as well as "trying on" being adults.

Children are fond of imitating people they have seen at the grocery store, the doctor's office, the service station, and the restaurant. Preschoolers like to emulate family members as well as define their own relationships with them. Home relationships are intense, and in dramatic play children graphically show their varying relationships to different family members. This creative play reveals children's pressing needs at the moment. They may seek in play the warmth and affection they fail to get at home. If they are consistently urged toward mature behavior at home, they may seek infantile roles in their role-playing.

Play also handles a child's uniqueness of being little in a world of big people. Through dramatic play, a young child can indicate confusion or misinterpretation of facts, as well as possible fears and attempts to master these fears.

Primary-age children enjoy creating their own activities. They may make them up as they go along. You will see familiar stories in most of their dramatic play. Children's group play usually has "the bestest good guys" and "the baddest bad guys." The good guys will win and often invite the bad ones to be good and win with them.

Children will play out their ideas of death, marriage, parenting, daredevil escapades, superheroes, and everyday life. Although the plots may be complicated, the theme remains the same. That theme of "everything turns out right" adds to a child's feeling of security. With this in mind, it is crucial that we provide an environment that is healing to children in our violent society. "Because very young children are affected by violence, awareness of how to address violence in young children's lives is critical for early childhood professionals" (Jackson, 1997). The dramatic play area offers a safe haven for children to act out their fears and anger, knowing that the teacher will be there to respond to their individual needs.

As we continue through this chapter, we will explore how theorists, researchers, and educators explain the developmental stages of dramatic play and creative dramatics. We will also appropriately plan and prepare the early childhood environment to integrate this fantasy play into the learning centers and curriculum, as we increase children's cooperative interaction skills. David Elkind (1994) explains, "When children are engaged in dramatic play, one of the things they are learning is how to transfer what they learned in one setting and apply it in another. One could hardly wish for a better learning activity than that!"

Dramatic play allows a child to explore and to imitate the people around her. Sometimes, even the teacher gets involved in the fun.

DRAMATIC PLAY AND CREATIVE DRAMATICS DEFINED

dramatic play

A type of creative, spontaneous play in which children use their imaginations to create and dramatize pretend characters, actions, or events.

creative dramatics

The improvised drama of children, age five or six and older.

pantomime

The art of conveying ideas without words.

sociodramatic play

The highest level of symbolic play, young children create their own happenings based on their experiences.

Nellie McCaslin (1990) helps us define *dramatic play, creative dramatics,* and *pantomime* in relationship to the play of young children. She describes **dramatic play** as "the *free play* of the very young child in which he explores his universe, imitating the actions and character traits of those around him." Dramatic play is spontaneous and can be expanded or repeated over and over again just for the fun of it.

Creative dramatics refers to the *improvised* drama of children, age five or six and older, that can emerge from the spontaneous play of children. This process of improvisation is an extension of dramatic play as interpreted by older children. It involves more elaborate situations and imaginative characters. It is child-centered drama used in a "nonperformance" way. You may introduce an idea or theme and set limits for the activity, but then you should "back off" and let the children create.

McCaslin defines **pantomime** as the art of conveying ideas without words. Children enjoy pantomime, and for the young child this is an excellent way to begin creative dramatics. Because many of her thoughts are spoken entirely through the body, the five- or six-year-old finds pantomime a natural means of expression. Simple group pantomimes challenge the imagination and sharpen awareness.

With **sociodramatic play,** the highest level of symbolic play, young children create their own happenings based on their experiences. They imitate the actions and people that they have experienced in their play. They repeat, solve problems, and relive these experiences (Isbell & Raines, 2007).

Researchers believe the *fantasy* element of dramatic play is quite useful. It enables the child to discharge or accomplish through imagination what she is unable to do in reality. Fantasizing relieves tensions and offers a way to interpret and put together the pieces of the complex puzzle that is a child's world. For example, animal play releases aggression, but this is not the only function of this type of dramatic play. A child will often impersonate animals when feeling shy or insecure about verbalizing. I remember such a child, a three-year-old named Michael.

> He came into the classroom growling like an animal. His hands were in the position of paws. Michael entered freely into dramatic play with other children as a dragon, tiger, or wolf. Many times he got the attention of several children when he played the big bad wolf. Morning after morning, The Three Little Pigs was played out. The other children, laughing and chattering happily, hid under the tables to escape the wolf. Michael was capable of expressing himself verbally, but he didn't. Instead, he found peer acceptance in dramatic play. Later, when he was ready to talk and enter into other dramatic play activities, he did so.

A young child invites a teacher to join in his fantasy play.

DEVELOPMENTAL STAGES OF DRAMATIC PLAY

Theorists, researchers, and educators emphasize the importance of *developmental stages of dramatic play* in varying ways. As discussed in Chapter 1, Mildred Parten (1932) categorizes six stages of social play: unoccupied behavior, onlooker behavior, solitary play (infants), parallel play (toddlers), associative play (young preschoolers), and cooperative play (older preschoolers, kindergartners, and primary-age children). Jean Piaget's research (1962) has helped us understand play in terms of cognitive development by presenting play in three stages:

practice play

During Piaget's sensorimotor stage (infancy to two years), infants explore the sensory qualities of objects and practice motor skills.

🜨 **Practice play,** during the sensorimotor stage of development (infancy to two years), in which infants explore the sensory qualities of objects and practice motor skills. This is observable through a child's physical movements and interactions with objects in the environment.

symbolic or dramatic play

A type of play that allows the child to transfer objects into symbols (things that represent something else) and images into people, places, and events within his experiences. Symbolic play occurs during Piaget's preoperational stage (two to seven years). Superhero fantasy play is considered a type of symbolic play for a young child.

games with rules

Children's spontaneous physical and cognitive play that occurs during Piaget's concrete operations stage of development (seven years and older).

functional play

Play that occurs when a child takes on a role and pretends to be someone else.

constructive play

Play that helps children understand their experiences. Involves planning or manipulation of objects or people to create a specific experience.

Symbolic or dramatic play, during the preoperational stage of development (two to seven years), when we see children transfer objects into symbols, things that represent something else. Symbolic thinking is observable during dramatic play when realistic objects such as pots and pans are used for "cooking soup," a block becomes a "real" telephone and the child "talks" into it, and older children, using gestures and actions, pantomime props when there are none.

Games with rules, during the concrete operations stage of development (seven years and older), in which children's spontaneous play develops into games involved with perfecting physical skills and organizing games with rules that are both physical and cognitive. This type of play is observable when it demonstrates children making up their own rules for the games they play, their ability to accept and relate to another person's point of view, and their ability to understand rules to a game that cannot be changed.

Sara Smilansky (1968) divides play into four types of sociodramatic play:

Functional play (infancy through early years) occurs when a child takes on a role and pretends to be someone else. This type of play embodies sensory and motor exploration of the environment and the people in the environment. This is observable when children play in "dress-up clothes," or use props to identify the person they are portraying.

Constructive play (toddlers and preschoolers) helps children understand their experiences. This type of play can occur alone or with others as the child plans the manipulation of objects or people to create a specific experience. This is observable when a child puts keys in a pretend car, starts the motor, adds the sound effects ("Vroooom"), and lets others ride in the car with her.

Dramatic play (toddlers through primary-age children) involves pretending and make believe. This represents a higher level of play behavior and is observable when two or more children take on related roles and interact with one another. (This is demonstrated later in the chapter when specific dramatic play learning centers are discussed.)

Games with rules (older preschoolers and primary-age children) require children to behave according to pre-existing rules. This is observable when children play board games and many outdoor sports.

George Maxim (1997) divides play into two major categories or dimensions. The *social dimension* deals with the ways children progress from solitary pursuits to an interest and skill in collaborating and cooperating with others. The *content dimension* refers to the composition of play—what the children play with, such as sand and blocks, or what they play at, such as serving tea. The key point to remember about the two dimensions is that each is developmental. Review Chapter 1 for other theories and discussions of play and young children.

Understanding of Fantasy and Reality in Young Children

Dramatic play experiences help young children sort out what is make-believe and what is real. "Human beings have a gift for fantasy, which shows itself at a very early age and then continues to make all sorts of contributions to our intellectual and emotional life throughout the lifespan" (Harris, 2002). "Children need ample supplies of fantasy and reality. Gradually children learn to separate fantasy and reality, identify which is which, and travel between them purposefully" (Vail, 1999).

It is both appropriate and developmental that young children try out ways to differentiate fantasy from reality. The younger the child, the more dramatic play is rooted in fantasy. Children confuse fantasy with reality, because they believe what they think is true, whether or not it is true in reality. Read, Gardner, and Mahler (1993) explain further: "Children need help and time to make the distinction between reality and fantasy without having to reject their fantasies. They have a right to imagine and to create fantasies as well as a need to learn to identify reality."

At age five or older, children understand when they are pretending and when they are in the real world. Their understanding is sometimes very sophisticated. "Rather than try to force understanding, which is usually in place by the end of kindergarten, encourage children to use language as a tool to ask questions and explore their thinking. . . . 'Do you think that could really happen?'" (Vail, 1999).

PLANNING AND PREPARING THE ENVIRONMENT

Dramatic play offers many opportunities for supporting a young child's growth and development. Dramatic play produces sheer joy and delight. A child's total being is involved in the activity. Her body, face, language, and emotions mirror enthusiasm for life. To support all of this, you should provide unstructured time, adequate space, flexible materials, and uninterrupted opportunity for the children to enjoy dramatic play. Most important, *let the children have input!* The environment should say, "Pretending is welcome here!"

If you see that a child is not ready to enter freely into dramatic play, your understanding is vitally important. This child needs sufficient time to watch and learn and proceed at her own pace. Perhaps if you pretend with the child at first and then gradually pull away, this will be all that is needed.

> *It takes time to conjure new ideas, and it takes a welcoming and accessible environment for children of all abilities to explore and express the content of their imaginations. . . . [W]hen children know they have an uninterrupted stretch of time, they are more likely to try new roles, take emotional risks, negotiate rich worlds and stories, build tall towers and learn about the properties and possibilities of materials and objects in their environment.* (Haugen, 2002)

The Teacher's Role in Children's Dramatic Play

The following guidelines should help to define the teacher's role in children's dramatic play. Here, as in other curriculum areas, the teacher's role is primarily that of facilitator, so that dramatic play remains a child-initiated activity.

- Provide stimulating props, unstructured time, and adequate space for dramatic play.
- Create curtains, windows, a fireplace, and real plants to make the area home-like, comfortable, and welcoming.
- Monitor the dramatic play area so all children have the opportunity to participate.
- Assist children in learning acceptable kinds of social interaction.
- Allow children to solve their own problems as often as possible.
- Encourage creativity in language and play.
- Keep in mind the children's developmental capabilities.
- Value this type of play.
- Allow children opportunities to "try on" adult roles, both male and female.
- Limit the number of children in the area at one time.
- Introduce props to small groups of children.
- Select props that are authentic and can be used naturally and safely.
- Change props frequently and include ones that reflect different cultures.
- Avoid props and activities that are sexist or racist.
- Serve as a facilitator rather than teacher so dramatic play remains a child-initiated activity.
- Select dress-up clothes and outfits that are simple, durable, and easy to get on or off.

Some teachers keep the home living (housekeeping) area intact as a permanent center and set up a second dramatic play area that expands the theme of the lesson plan. Others, who are limited in classroom space, may choose to have a dramatic play center that changes periodically and sometimes will include the kitchen area or another room in the home. Still others take the dramatic play center outdoors to take advantage of the additional space available.

Change the scene occasionally. Put all the chairs away. Bring in large moving boxes. Hang sheets like a stage curtain, a maze, or a tent. Change rooms with another class. . . . Create discovery kits to take along when you explore new environments. Include a magnifying glass, collecting bags, cameras, and so on. (Haugen, 2002)

The basic equipment for the home living/dramatic play center should be: child-size furniture made of wood or sturdy plastic including tables; chairs; rocking chair; shelves; a "play" sink, stove, and refrigerator; and a full-length mirror. Dolls of both sexes representing differing features and skin coloring, a doll bed or cradle, and a sturdy, nonworking telephone should also be included.

Sometimes, the most creative and appropriate dramatic play area is one that has very little in it and does not have a specific theme. When a special "soft area" is created by adding some pillows, beanbag chairs, and a soft area rug, it becomes a totally child-directed dramatic play area. The children feel relaxed and safe, free to be creative and imaginative. The pillows become props, as needed, or the children can bring in props from around the room.

ADAPTATIONS FOR SPECIAL NEEDS CHILDREN

 "All children, whatever their physical, cognitive, or emotional level of development, have individual interests and special capabilities" (Isbell & Raines, 2007). The following suggestions, from Isbell and Raines (2007) and Mayesky (2006), are intended to help teachers include children with special needs in dramatic play:

In the home living center, children can imitate many different roles in a safe environment.

1. Apply only those rules that are really needed for the child to play safely.
2. Let the child take the lead. This may involve some patient waiting for the child to choose something to do.
3. To encourage the child to play with others, define the space where the children can play, and keep it small at first.
4. Encourage verbalization during play by asking questions and encouraging communication with other children.
5. Offer dramatic play materials that are familiar and part of a child's daily life experiences.
6. Provide some dress-up clothes that are simple to get on or off.
7. Sharing ideas with peers helps children with developmental delays see how things work and how they are to be done.
8. Some children with developmental delays fatigue very easily. Make sure that the child has supportive seating. Some children need chair inserts or standing aids.

SHARING WITH FAMILIES: MAKING PROP BOXES

prop box
A collection of actual items related to dramatic play activities that focuses on a specific theme or lesson plan.

A vital part of the planning and preparing process for dramatic play activities is the creation of prop boxes. A **prop box** is a collection of actual items related to the development and enrichment of dramatic play activities focused on a specific theme or lesson plan. These items should be collected for easy accessibility and placed in sturdy boxes that can be stacked for storage (empty cardboard boxes with lids make great prop boxes).

Label each prop box clearly for identification. A picture or drawing on the outside can suggest what is inside. Cover the boxes with colored contact paper to give them an uncluttered and uniform appearance.

The props selected for the dramatic play areas should stimulate interest, encourage creative expression, create opportunities for problem solving, relate to and expand the experiences of the children, and represent many cultures. These props can be found anywhere and everywhere: in the parents' and staff's closets and garages; at surplus stores, thrift stores, and garage sales; and at local businesses and offices that have used and throwaway items. Invite the children to bring appropriate props from home that represent their interests, hobbies, lifestyles, or current theme.

Maxim (1990) suggests that teachers fix some special prop boxes for the children to take home for specific periods of time. "Children and parents can sign-out for them. Encourage children to talk about their play when they return the boxes. This will stimulate others to want to take them home."

Clothes for the Dramatic Play Center

Clothing that helps children "dress-up" in various roles is an important part of dramatic play. The clothes should be easy for children to put on and take off, as well as attractive, durable, and washable. Wash and dry donated clothing before sharing them with the children. Hem the garments to make sure the children can wear them comfortably and safely. Remove long rope belts, or stitch them into place so they cannot be used around children's necks. Replace back zippers with Velcro hook-and-loop fasteners (Parks, 1992). Teenager-size clothes are useful for young children, or (if you do not sew) perhaps there is a parent who will be willing to make some new "dress-up" clothes for the class.

There should be a special place where clothing is displayed or stored. A cardboard box "closet" with a rod placed across at the children's height can hold clothes on hangers. Clothing hooks or a shortened clothes or hat rack are also appropriate. Whatever you select will help the children understand that, after they have used the article of clothing, it should be placed back where they found it.

A variety of cultures should be represented by using clothing fabric that is tie-dyed, batik, madras prints, and kente cloth. The clothing styles should offer saris, kimonos, serapes, ponchos, grass skirts, and dashikis (Allen, McNeill, & Schmidt, 1992). You should research many cultures and consult with parents as you develop your dramatic play center.

Easy-to-Make Clothes

An easy way to create dramatic play clothes is by selecting large pieces of square, rectangular, and triangular fabric. For example, here are two suggestions for using a square yard of fabric (adapted from Parks, 1992).

TO MAKE A SKIRT. Wrap the square of fabric around the child's waist. Adjust the length to the height of the child, and tie a knot at the waist.

TO MAKE A ROBE. Wrap the square of fabric around the child's chest and under one arm. Tie a knot over the opposite shoulder (Figure 12–1). Adjust the length to the height of the child.

FIGURE 12–1
Examples of easy-to-make clothes for the dramatic play center.

INTEGRATING DRAMATIC PLAY INTO THE CURRICULUM

The following examples of dramatic play centers, and the prop boxes to accompany each, have proven to be successful in early education curriculum. They represent developmentally appropriate play areas and offer creative opportunities for individual or small groups of children.

In setting up areas for infants and toddlers, change very little from what they are used to. Add props or change the room arrangement very slowly. The children will guide you by what they will or will not play with. Older children will help you decide when to change, when to add additional props and materials, and what areas of the room need to be expanded for more dramatic play.

Dramatic Play for Infants

- *A doll corner:* Select sock or soft dolls (depicting many cultures) that are easy to launder and simple cardboard beds for the dolls. The clothing on the dolls should be washable and easy to take off and put on.
- *A home living area:* Choose washable household items that the infant can grasp, such as pots, pans, lids, boxes, plastic cups, bowls, and baskets. These will encourage the child to bang, stack, squeeze, and put the objects together.
- *An area (indoor and/or outdoor) for push-and-pull toys:* This should include doll buggies, wagons, wheelbarrows, and trucks.
- *An area for crawling and climbing:* Provide a rocking boat, short tunnel, climbing steps, and slide.

Dramatic Play for Toddlers

- *Home living area:* In addition to all types of dolls and child-size furniture, add empty food boxes of all sizes and shapes that represent what the children eat at home. This should include empty food boxes with print in different languages on them to represent foods from diverse cultures.
- *Dress-up clothes:* Include items that relate to community helpers. Toddlers love sunglasses with plastic lenses, gloves, purses, and clothing that fits them.
- *Prop box:* Fill it with shopping bags, lunch boxes, toy telephones, keys, pots, pans, small cars, and trucks. (Miniature animals and people can be added to the block center prop box as well. This is discussed fully in Chapter 9.)

A corner for puppet and mask play: This should offer glove puppets, finger puppets, and people puppets; as well as animal masks with eyes, mouth, and nose cut out and a handle under the chin for easy manipulation, as described in Chapter 11.

A beauty/barber shop: Provide washable black, brown, blond, and red wigs, both male and female styles; curlers; empty plastic shampoo bottles; and old hair dryers with the plugs and cords cut off. (Note: Wash or spray wigs and hats often with diluted bleach—one-half teaspoon bleach to one quart of water.)

Dramatic Play for Preschoolers

The dramatic play center in the three-, four-, and five-year-old classroom can start with one specific theme. The concept can be expanded to include adjacent space as more children become involved.

Travel agency: Set up a ticket counter and chairs. The prop box for this activity can include tickets, maps, brochures, posters, pens, pencils, flight schedules, boat schedules, and car and hotel information. The tickets, maps, schedules, and information sheets can also be made by the children.

Ship: All it takes is a balance beam becoming the gangplank, cardboard boxes becoming the outer part of the ship, and "water" (painted by the children) surrounding the ship. Let the children help you add to this adventure by deciding where the ship will land. This is a wonderful opportunity to expand the dramatic play into various ports and countries, such as Hawaii, Africa, Mexico, Alaska, and the Caribbean. Set up prop boxes for each country. Selecting what goes in each is both creative and educational and helps children develop problem-solving skills. Packing small suitcases or briefcases with clothing for warm climates (straw hats, beach toys, suntan lotion, sunglasses, and short-sleeved shirts) and clothing for colder areas (gloves, earmuffs, muffler, stocking caps, and sweaters) helps start this dramatic play.

Train station and train, or airport and airplane: This can expand the travel agency dramatic play or add to the lesson plan relating to transportation. As with the ship theme, develop a prop box for each, including appropriate clothing. Plan the destination with maps and brochures.

Supermarket/grocery store/farmer's market/mercado: Fill the prop box with a toy cash register, calculator, play money (or money the children make), price tags, sales slip pad, empty food containers (some with print in different languages on them to represent foods from diverse cultures), artificial fruit and vegetables, grocery boxes, shopping bags, small shopping carts, brown paper bags, telephone, coupons, and shopping lists. Make signs in several languages and with pictures to explain what is for sale.

This child enjoys making props for the dramatic play area.

Picnic: This is fun for indoors or outdoors and is an excellent dramatic play activity to plan for snack or lunch time. The children decide what to take on the picnic and place the items in a picnic basket. They can wear "dress-up" clothes and use props from the prop box, such as plastic or paper cups, plates, tableware, tablecloth, napkins, eating utensils, aprons, and blankets.

 Ants at a picnic: Put several large picnic baskets in the dramatic play area. Add play food. Then, make a tunnel by taking the ends out of boxes. Line the boxes up, and tape them together to form a tunnel. You can use a cloth tunnel, if you already have one, to have more than one tunnel for the "ants." The children can pretend to be ants taking the "food" from the picnic basket to their home through the tunnels. Continue to add items that the children want to use.

Other suggestions for dramatic play centers are restaurant, florist shop, pet shop, post office, library, book store, music shop, musical instrument store, recording studio, health center, doctor or dentist office, gymnasium, campsite, shoe store, fix-it shop, and apartments in the loft and lower level of the dramatic play area.

Dramatic Play for Primary-Grade Children

Any of the dramatic play suggestions listed for the preschoolers can be expanded or adapted for older children. Give them the list of acceptable themes and allow them the freedom to make choices and select their own activities. For example, if they choose to visit another country as they play, the children may "discover the rain forest" or "go on a safari in Africa." This child-initiated form of dramatic play encourages the older child to take an interest in the wider world, and it is exciting to watch as it unfolds. Some children get involved with one aspect and tackle it as an independent project. Others make the theme a special event or a cooperative venture.

Creative dramatics is a more mature form of the spontaneous dramatic play of young children. Group activities such as story improvisations, body movement, and pantomime give older children a chance to articulate their thoughts and feelings and to socialize and work together toward a goal (Blau, Brady, Bucher, Hiteshew, & Zavitkovsky, 1985).

The following are a few examples of creative dramatics exercises and activities that are appropriate for school-age children:

 Rag doll tin man marionette: Have the children perform simple warm-up exercises by being as limp as a rag doll; they can bend from the waist and bob up and down and swing their shoulders. As stiffened tin men, let them discover how their movements change. Expand this activity and have the children choose a partner. One becomes a marionette and the other becomes the puppeteer. The puppeteer stands in front of the marionette and moves the strings attached to the various parts of the marionette's body. The marionette responds with the proper movement.

 Paper exploration: Give each child a piece of 9 × 12-inch construction paper. Have them balance the paper on different parts of the body. Run with the paper on the palm of their hand. Try putting paper on their feet and raising and lowering the legs.

 The imaginary machine: First, one child will form a "machine-part shape" with her body and add a made-up sound to fit that shape. Each successive child connects to the shape last made with her own unique shape and sound until all of the children are involved in the imaginary machine. Slow the machine down and speed it up. To demonstrate the importance of the parts on the whole, "break" one of the parts. What happens to the machine?

 Mirror images: Each child chooses a partner. They face each other, always keeping each other in full view. One child becomes a mirror that reflects what she sees her partner doing. Perhaps the child puts on clown makeup, exercises, or puts on a tie. After a while, the partners change places, with the other partner becoming the mirror.

Dramatic Play and Other Learning Centers

Dramatic play and creative dramatics lend themselves to every aspect of the curriculum.

Language and literacy development, socialization, exploration of feelings and fears, and problem solving are ongoing components of these activities. Music and rhythmic movement become dramatic and creative when a child makes use of them to become someone or something other than herself.

Math and science concepts can be applied. Charlesworth and Lind (2007) offer some examples:

- One-to-one correspondence can be practiced by exchanging play money for goods or services.
- Sets and classifying are involved in organizing each dramatic play center in an orderly manner.
- Counting can be applied to figuring out how many items have been purchased and how much money must be exchanged.
- Comparing and measuring can be used to decide if clothing fits, or to determine the weight of fruits and vegetables purchased.
- Spatial relations and volume concepts are applied as items purchased are placed in bags, boxes, and/or baskets and as children discover how many passengers will fit in the space shuttle or can ride on the bus.
- Number symbols can be found throughout dramatic play props, such as on price tags, play money, telephones, cash registers, and scales.

As you select the theme, brainstorm using the curriculum planning web worksheet in Chapter 2. Develop your lesson plan, integrate the learning centers, and gather supplies and materials to discover how to meet your goals and objectives through the use of dramatic play.

WHY I TEACH YOUNG CHILDREN

The first year I taught preschool, a young child was very happy to tell me that his mother was going to have a baby. For most of the year the class got regular reports about how things were progressing: mother threw up breakfast, mother is sleepy, mother's feet hurt, and mother cannot sit on the floor anymore. Finally, the baby was born. I asked, "What did mother bring home from the hospital that she did not take with her?" The child thought for a few seconds, smiled, and answered "Flowers."

—Diane B. Ratner

This child enjoys pretending to be a firefighter.

TIPS FOR TEACHERS

The appearance of television or movie heroes may change children's dramatic play. When you hear these heroes' names, you will want to observe the children's play more closely. Sometimes the stunts on television and in movies are dangerous when children try to do them. Violence may become too much a part of the play as they pretend to be superheroes. Your observation will give you an opportunity to teach better ways to solve problems without violence.

Beaty (1992) suggests there are both positive and negative aspects of children's imitation of superheroes.

> *The superhero is a good character who is good-looking, strong, loyal, helpful, unselfish, ready to fight against evil, and always the winner. The bad character is evil-looking, strong, selfish, disloyal, underhanded, sneaky, always challenging the good character, and always the loser. . . . Children are going to attempt superhero play whether or not it is allowed. . . . [S]uperheroes are powerful symbols, indeed, to young children. When you understand that such symbols can represent positive values in our society, then you may want to consider allowing superhero dramatic play in the classroom if it can be controlled and directed into prosocial channels.*

Let us think about how we can deal effectively with the superhero characters in an early education setting. One of the first things to do is to become familiar with *what* is available for the children to watch on television, videos, and the movies. Second, think about *why* the children are imitating these characters. Ask questions of the children and talk to them about other, more appropriate, choices for play. *It's important to establish limits ahead of time.*

Slaby, Roedell, Arezzo, and Hendrix (1995) explain further:

> *Because young children have relatively little real-world experience by which to evaluate the relation of media violence to real life, they stand to benefit greatly from discussing these connections with adults. . . . A teacher might say, "He wants to stop that man from doing bad things, but the only way he knows how to do that is to fight him. I'll bet you can think of other ways that he could stop him without fighting."*

According to Levin (1995), children will need help working through the content they are seeing. Besides open discussions with the children, teach conflict resolution skills, and invite real, healthier role models (such as community helpers and family members) to visit the classroom. Help children regain control of their play by changing it from imitative play to creative, imaginative play. And importantly, work with parents, other teachers, and the early childhood community to understand and support each other's efforts to deal with the marketing of violence to children.

The National Association for the Education of Young Children (1997) has these comments:

1. Show children that superheroes are not special just because they are physically powerful. Point out when superheroes show kindness and helpfulness to others, and show appreciation to the children when they do the same.
2. Talk about real heroes and heroines with children. Introduce them to people like Helen Keller and Martin Luther King, Jr., and discuss how everyday people can demonstrate acts of courage and goodness.
3. Help children build on their interests through superhero play. Watching *Star Wars* may lead to learning about space travel, whereas the *Spiderman* movie or comic book may lead to exploring the world of insects. Always keep your eyes open to learning opportunities for children.

DEVELOPMENTALLY APPROPRIATE AND MULTICULTURAL/ANTI-BIAS ACTIVITIES

 The following song and activities ("Humpty Dumpty" by Bea Wolf) show how a finger play activity that is developmentally appropriate for toddlers and three-year-olds can be expanded to a dramatic play activity appropriate for four- and five-year-olds. The "Humpty Dumpty Song" is provided in Figure 12–2.

The song and dramatic play activity "The Doughnut Shop" by Bea Wolf is appropriate for four- and five-year-olds. Think about how you could expand it for other age groups. "The Doughnut Song" is provided in Figure 12–3.

Books and stories can be used to integrate all areas of the curriculum, including dramatic play. The selection of a familiar story such as "Three Billy Goats Gruff" or "The Three Little Pigs" can be the first tale to be acted out. Then add another book, such as *Brown Bear, Brown Bear, What Do You See?* by Bill Martin, Jr. (1983) or *Gilberto and the Wind* by Marie Hall Ets (1978) or *The Talking Vegetables* by Won-Ldy Paye and Margaret Lippert (2006). Put the book away once you and the children are familiar and comfortable with the story. This gives more freedom to add to or change the basic story as you go along. Simple props and settings can add to the dramatic play. Once the children experience the enjoyment of this kind of activity, you can then expand the activity.

Figure 12–4 is the curriculum planning web worksheet with dramatic play activities added. This worksheet with appropriate additions is included in each chapter.

HUMPTY DUMPTY

(finger play activity with song)

(Suitable for Toddlers and Three-Year-Olds)

Before attempting this activity, read or recite the rhyme to the children on several occasions so they become thoroughly familiar with it. If possible, find a colorful illustration to stimulate their interest. Teacher asks children questions while pointing to various features of the illustration:

Teacher: Who is this?

Children: Humpty Dumpty!

Teacher: What is Humpty Dumpty sitting on?

Children: The wall!

(If children are too young to answer, teacher supplies the answers.)

Teacher guides the children in identifying articles of clothing worn by Humpty Dumpty, points out the horses and soldiers and anything else of visual interest. If children are old enough to understand, some discussion may take place about the fact that Humpty Dumpty is an egg and eggs can break. Children are prepared for the activity when they appear well acquainted with the rhyme.

Teacher: Now we're going to tell the story of Humpty Dumpty with our hands. First, make a wall, like this: *(Teacher holds forearm as though looking at a wristwatch.)*
Now, make a fist with your other hand. This is Humpty Dumpty! Set him down on the wall. Is he happy there? Let him sway back and forth.
(Sway fist as though rocking back and forth on forearm.)

Teacher: Now everyone sing (or say):
Humpty Dumpty sat on a wall.
Humpty Dumpty had a great fall—Boom!

FIGURE 12–2

"Humpty Dumpty Song" and activity for young children.

(Bend wrist down so that Humpty Dumpty drops off wall. Establish a rhythm by beating hands on thighs to simulate horses galloping. Sing or chant the next lines to this rhythm:)

All the king's horses and all the king's men
Couldn't put Humpty together again—
Couldn't put Humpty together again!
Why? (Extend hands outward in a large shrug.)

(During the next phrase extended hands slowly rise to meet over head, simulating an egg shape. Fingers meet on the word egg.)

Because he was an egg!

(This activity provides a good opportunity to point out that an egg is oval shaped, and to practice shaping ovals using fingers, hands, and arms.)

Review the nursery rhyme. Conduct a group discussion based on the fact that, once broken, an egg can never be put together again. Many children will have their own experiences to relate regarding this subject.

Announce that we are about to dramatize Humpty Dumpty. Explain that the word dramatize means to act out.

Guide the children in "falling" safely from a seated position to a lying down position on the floor. For this practice, children should already be seated on the floor so there is very little distance to fall. Explain that this is a fake fall, that we are acting, and that everyone must fall softly so as not to be hurt. Allow a very short time for fake fall practice (two or three falls should do it). Then guide children in pretending to be soldiers, or king's men, on horseback. Let them pretend to hold reins and gallop about for a short time; then announce that everyone seems ready to dramatize the story.

Divide the class into two groups. Group 1 consists of Humpty Dumptys, and group 2 of king's men. Instruct the king's men to wait quietly in a designated area until they hear their cue, which is the galloping rhythm the teacher will clap at the appropriate time. Instruct the Humpty Dumptys to sit on their wall, which can be a line on the floor. When everyone is ready, start the Humpty Dumptys swaying back and forth as all sing or say the first two lines of the rhyme. On "had a great fall," all Humpty Dumptys fake-fall on the floor and lie still. The teacher then claps the gallop rhythm. All the king's men then gallop over to the fallen Humpty Dumptys, dismount, and pat them gently, trying to put them together. On "Why?" the Humpty Dumptys sit up and all the children shrug with hands out. On "Because he was an egg," all slowly form an oval shape with arms above heads, fingers meeting on the word egg.

Repeat the dramatization, with group 1 switching roles with group 2.

Reproduced by permission of B. Wolf

*Reproduced by permission of B. Wolf - 1995
Copyright B. Wolf 1993

THE DOUGHNUT SHOP

(dramatic play for four- and five- year olds)*

(Entertainingly illustrates the concept of subtraction)

This activity requires the following cast:

1. A group of children who act as doughnuts.
2. A group of children who each purchase a doughnut.
3. A cashier or shopkeeper.

Begin by selecting the shopkeeper. The teacher can either fill that role herself, delegate it to a child who has earned a special privilege, or select the shopkeeper in some impartial way.

The children who act as doughnuts are seated in a row, on chairs, or on the floor in a designated area. The purchasers, each equipped with an imaginary or simulated coin, sit or stand in a different area. The shopkeeper sits near the doughnuts and operates an imaginary cash register.

The song is sung as many times as there are doughnuts lined up. Each time it is sung, a different child is named from the group of purchasers. That child walks over to the "shop," pays the shopkeeper, and selects a doughnut to take "home" (back to the purchaser area). Between each repetition of the song the teacher asks, "Now, how many doughnuts are left in the shop?"

After the last doughnut has been purchased, children usually wish to repeat the activity, with the groups switching roles.

Reproduced by permission of B. Wolf

FIGURE 12–3

"The Doughnut Song" and activity for young children.

THE DOUGHNUT SONG*

*Reproduced by permission of B. Wolf - 1995
Copyrght B. Wolf - 1993

✳ AFTERVIEW

Through dramatic play, a child

- 🌐 improves socialization skills.
- 🌐 practices social skills through role negotiation and conflict resolution.
- 🌐 develops external expressions of emotions.
- 🌐 chooses safe outlets for aggression and creates a climate for nonviolence.
- 🌐 identifies and empathizes with feelings of others.
- 🌐 develops self-confidence through role-playing.
- 🌐 acts out familiar situations, "tries on" family roles, works out problems and concerns, and experiments with solutions.

- 🌐 distinguishes fantasy from reality.
- 🌐 stimulates imagination and creativity.
- 🌐 improves problem-solving skills.
- 🌐 enhances sensorimotor skills.
- 🌐 develops muscular coordination, listening and oral language skills, and math readiness.
- 🌐 learns to make choices.

✳ KEY TERMS

constructive play
creative dramatics
dramatic play
functional play

games with rules
pantomime
practice play
prop box

sociodramatic play
symbolic or dramatic play

✳ EXPLORATIONS

1. Select an early education classroom and observe for at least one hour. Describe, in writing, several dramatic play activities the children were involved with at the time of your observation. Describe the activities, which learning centers were part of the activities, how props were used, who initiated the play, and how many joined it.

2. Visit a child life center in a local hospital or health facility. Observe how children's dramatic play is the same or different from classroom play. Describe objectively (factually) what you saw. (For example, were the children giving shots to stuffed animals and placing bandages on the hurt places? Were dolls getting casts put on their arms or legs?) Discuss subjectively (opinion) what you felt and learned from this observation.

3. Discuss children's dramatic play on the playground. What are some of the activities that take place? What limits does the teacher place on outdoor activities? Are they different from indoor dramatic play activities? Explain.

4. Select and plan a dramatic play or creative dramatics activity for young children. Specify which age group this activity is planned for: infants, toddlers, preschoolers, or primary-age children. In writing, list objectives, materials needed, step-by-step procedures for presenting this activity, follow-up activities, and evaluation guidelines. (Use the activity plan worksheet in Chapter 2. A blank activity plan worksheet is available in the front-of-the-book CD.) Prepare this activity and demonstrate it during class or with a group of children.

5. Based on the information in this chapter and on your observations of early education environments, select a partner and develop a dramatic play prop box appropriate for a group of young children. Describe the theme of the lesson plan and discuss how the prop box will be used within the context of the curriculum. Present this activity and demonstrate it during class or with a group of children.

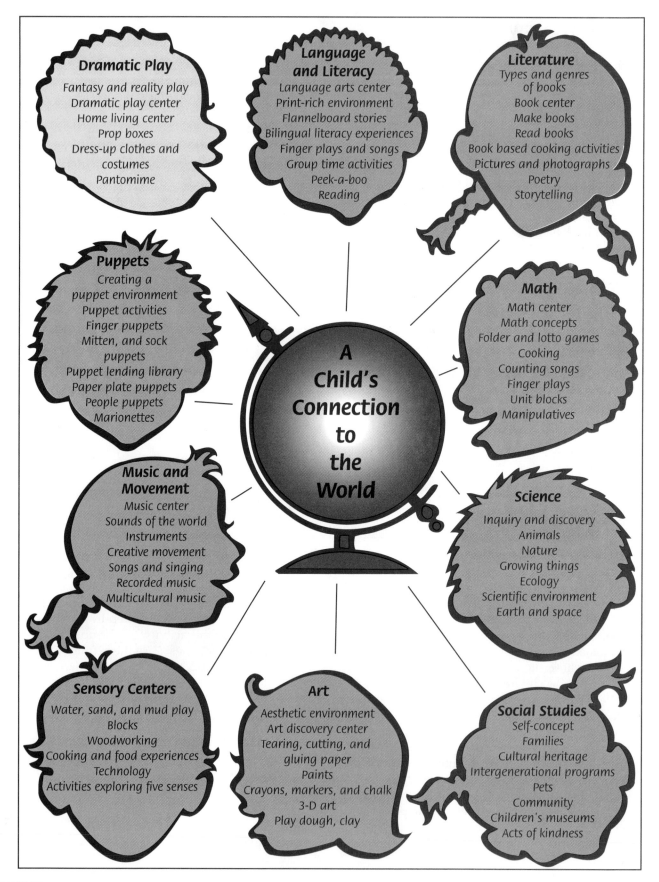

Dramatic Play
Fantasy and reality play
Dramatic play center
Home living center
Prop boxes
Dress-up clothes and
costumes
Pantomime

**Language
and Literacy**
Language arts center
Print-rich environment
Flannelboard stories
Bilingual literacy experiences
Finger plays and songs
Group time activities
Peek-a-boo
Reading

Literature
Types and genres
of books
Book center
Make books
Read books
Book based cooking activities
Pictures and photographs
Poetry
Storytelling

Puppets
Creating a
puppet environment
Puppet activities
Finger puppets
Mitten, and sock
puppets
Puppet lending library
Paper plate puppets
People puppets
Marionettes

Math
Math center
Math concepts
Folder and lotto games
Cooking
Counting songs
Finger plays
Unit blocks
Manipulatives

A Child's Connection to the World

**Music and
Movement**
Music center
Sounds of the world
Instruments
Creative movement
Songs and singing
Recorded music
Multicultural music

Science
Inquiry and discovery
Animals
Nature
Growing things
Ecology
Scientific environment
Earth and space

Sensory Centers
Water, sand, and mud play
Blocks
Woodworking
Cooking and food experiences
Technology
Activities exploring five senses

Art
Aesthetic environment
Art discovery center
Tearing, cutting, and
gluing paper
Paints
Crayons, markers, and chalk
3-D art
Play dough, clay

Social Studies
Self-concept
Families
Cultural heritage
Intergenerational programs
Pets
Community
Children's museums
Acts of kindness

FIGURE 12–4
A curriculum planning web worksheet with dramatic play and creative dramatics activities added.

✳ REFERENCES

Allen, J., McNeill, E., & Schmidt, V. (1992). *Cultural awareness for children*. Menlo Park, CA: Addison-Wesley Publishing Company.

Beaty, J. J. (1992). *Preschool appropriate practices*. New York: Harcourt.

Blau, R., Brady, E. H., Bucher, I., Hiteshew, B., & Zavitkovsky, D. (1985). *Activities for school-age care*. Washington, DC: NAEYC.

Charlesworth, R., & Lind, K. K. (2007). *Math and science for young children* (5th ed.). Clifton Park, NY: Thomson Delmar Learning.

Elkind, D. (1994). A sympathetic understanding of the child, birth to sixteen (3rd ed.). Boston: Allyn & Bacon.

Harris, P. (2002). Imagination is important for children's cognitive development. On-line at: http://www.researchmatters.harvard.edu

Haugen, K. (2002, November–December). Time, trust, and tools: Opening doors to imagination for all children. *Child Care Information Exchange* (148), 36–40.

Isbell, R. T., & Raines, S. C. (2007). *Creativity and the arts with young children*. (2nd ed.). Clifton Park, NY: Thomson Delmar Learning.

Jackson, B. R. (1997, November). Creating a climate for healing in a violent society. *Young Children, 52*(7), 68–70.

Levin, D. E. (1995, March–April). Power Rangers: An explosive topic. *Child Care Information Exchange, 102,* 50–51.

Maxim, G. W. (1997). *The very young* (5th ed.). Upper Saddle River, NJ: Merrill.

Maxim, G. W. (1990). *The sourcebook: Activities for infants and young children* (2nd ed.). Upper Saddle River, NJ: Merrill.

Mayesky, M. (2006). *Creative activities for young children*. (8th ed.). Clifton Park, NY: Thomson Delmar Learning.

McCaslin, N. (1990). *Creative dramatics in the classroom* (5th ed.). New York: Longman.

Miller, K. (2002, November–December). The seeds of dramatic play: Enhanced by adults. *Child Care Information Exchange* (148), 25–26.

National Association for the Education of Young Children (NAEYC). (1997). On-line at: http://naeyc.org/ece/eyly/

Parks, L. (Ed.) (1992, Fall). Easy-to-make clothes for dramatic play. *Texas Child Care, 16*(2), 30–38.

Parten, M. B. (1932). Social participation among preschool children. *Journal of Abnormal and Social Psychology, 27,* 243–269.

Piaget, J. (1962). *Play, dreams and imitation in childhood*. New York: W. W. Norton.

Read, K., Gardner, P., & Mahler, B. (1993). *Early childhood programs: Human relationships and learning* (9th ed.). New York: Harcourt.

Slaby, R. G., Roedell, W. C., Arezzo, D., & Hendrix, K. (1995). *Early violence prevention*. Washington, DC: NAEYC.

Smilansky, S. (1968). *The effects of sociodramatic play on disadvantaged preschool children*. New York: John Wiley & Sons.

Vail, P. L. (1999, January). Observing learning styles in the classroom. *Early Childhood Today, 13*(4), 20–27.

✳ ADDITIONAL READINGS AND RESOURCES

Alexander, N. P. (2001, Winter). Real learning: The joy of discovery. *The Dimensions of Early Childhood, 29*(1), 24.

Bergen, D. (2001, November). Pretend play and young children's development (*ERIC Digest* EDO-PS-01-10).

Berk, L. E. (1994, November). Vygotsky's theory: The importance of make-believe play. *Young Children, 50*(1), 30–39.

Davidson, J. I. (1996). *Emergent literacy and dramatic play in early education*. Clifton Park, NY: Thomson Delmar Learning.

Gowen, J. W. (1995, March). The early development of symbolic play. *Young Children, 50*(3), 75–84.

Greenspan, S. I. (2006). When a child's play themes are violent. *Early Childhood Today*. On-line at: http://content.scholastic.com/browse/article.jsp?id=7759

Grollman, S. (1994, September–October). Fantasy and exploration: Two approaches to playing. *Child Care Information Exchange, 99,* 48–50.

Howell, J., & Corbey-Scullen, L. (1997, September). Out of the housekeeping corner and onto the stage—Extending dramatic play. *Young Children, 52*(6), 82–88.

Kosoff, S., & Doane, A. (1996, January). Creative dramatics. *Early Childhood Today, 10*(4), 18–29.

Lobman, C. (2003, May). The bugs are coming! Improvisation and early childhood teaching. *Young Children, 58*(3), 18–23.

Machado, J. M. (2007). *Early childhood experiences in language arts* (8th ed.). Clifton Park, NY: Thomson Delmar Learning.

McCaslin, N. (1987). *Creative drama in the primary grades: A handbook for teachers*. New York: Longman.

Perlmutter, J. C., & Laminack, J. L. (1993, Summer). Sociodramatic play, a stage for practicing literacy. *Dimensions of Early Childhood, 21*(4), 13–16, 31.

For additional information on early education curriculum, visit our Web site at http://www.earlychilded.delmar.com

APPENDIX A

These sample flannelboard characters and puppet patterns are full-size replications of those mentioned in Chapters 3, 4, 5, 6, and 11.

Use the blank lesson plan worksheets to help you plan appropriate activities for young children in an early childhood setting. Examples of these can be found in Chapter 2 and the front-of-the-book CD.

Lesson plans visually demonstrate the concepts expressed throughout the book. They are only suggestions.

MARIA

MAMÁ

PACO

PAPÁ

APPLE TREE

FALLING APPLE

CAT

SEÑOR WIND

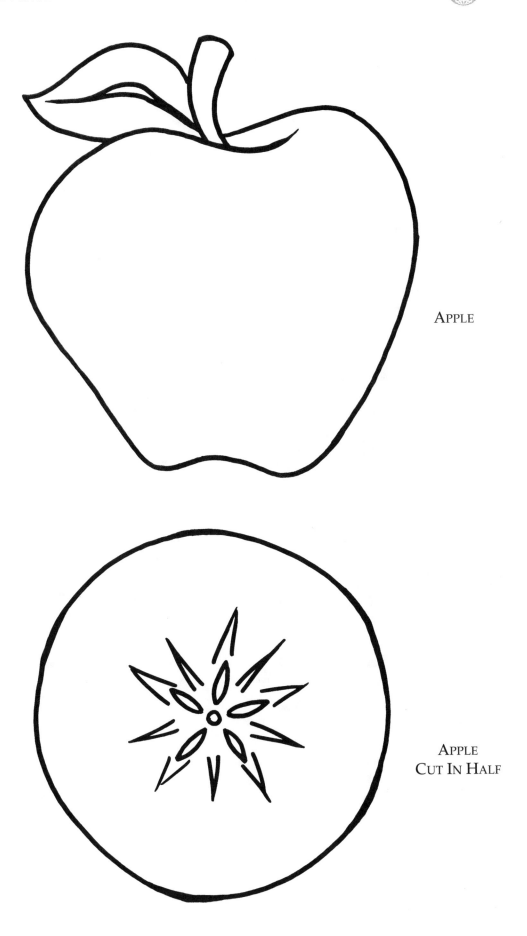

APPLE

APPLE
CUT IN HALF

SUN

FLOWERS

CLOUD

TREES

THUNDERBOLTS

RAINDROPS

Rainbow

CANDLE
(MAKE 10)

BIRTHDAY CAKE

SEED

SEED

SPROUTING
SEED

RAIN CLOUD

RAINDROPS

FLOWER

CARROT

POTATO

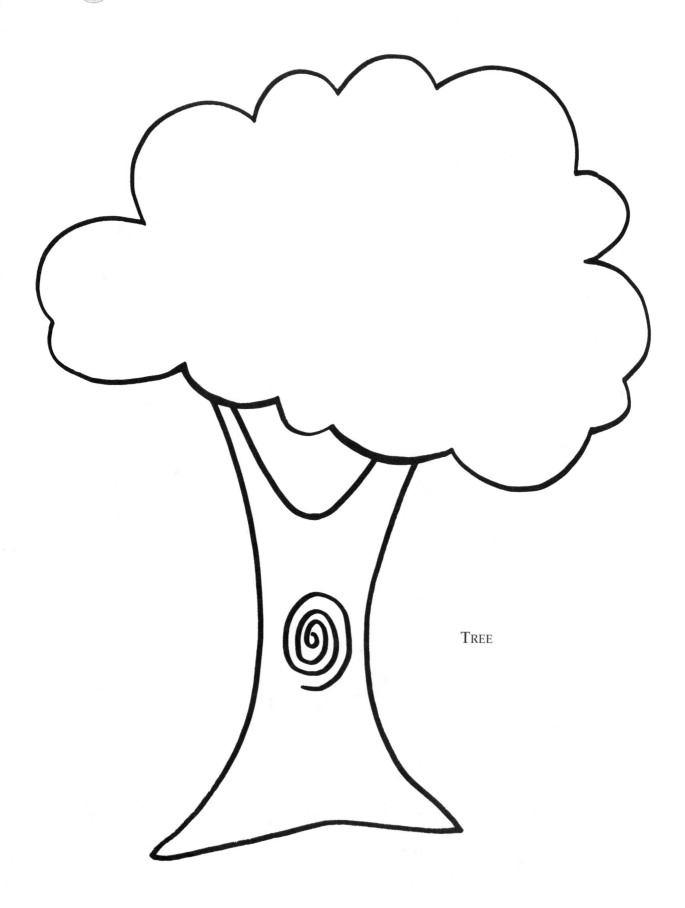

TREE

FINGER PUPPET PATTERNS

FELT FINGER PUPPETS

FOR CHILD HANDS

FOR ADULT HANDS

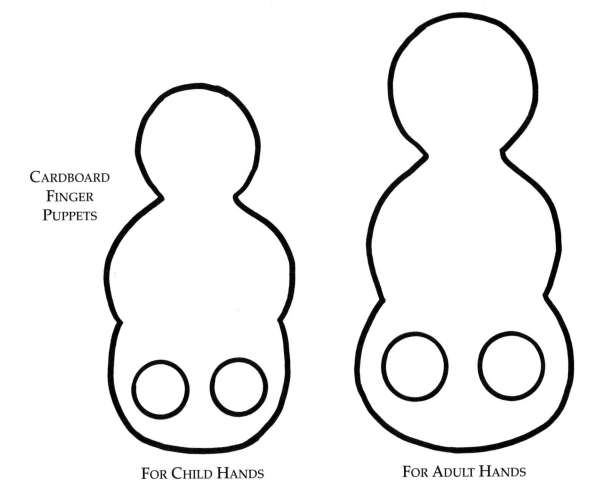

CARDBOARD FINGER PUPPETS

FOR CHILD HANDS

FOR ADULT HANDS

HAND PUPPET PATTERN

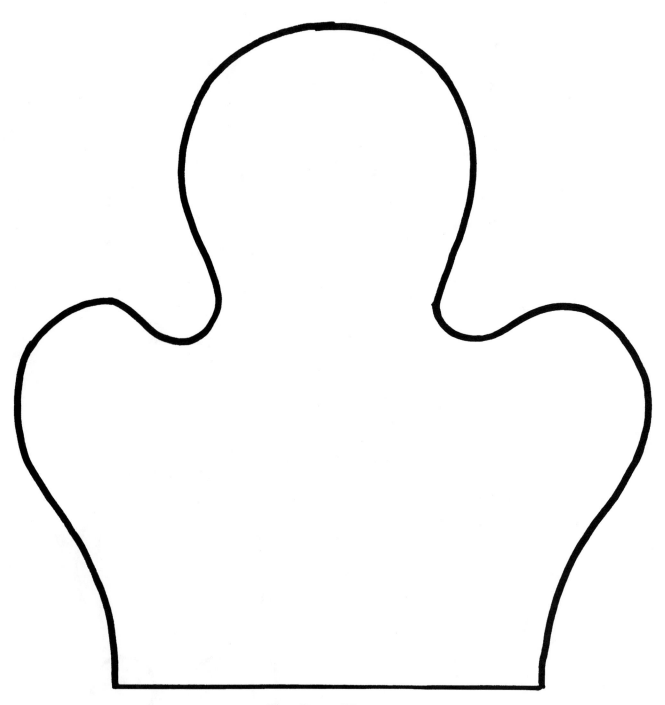

FOR CHILD HANDS

Hand Puppet Pattern

For Adult Hands

PATTERN FOR PEOPLE PUPPETS

INFANT LESSON PLAN

TEACHER(S): _____   DATES: _____   THEME: _____

CENTER / ACTIVITY	MONDAY	TUESDAY	WEDNESDAY	THURSDAY	FRIDAY
SENSORY: ART, MUSIC, TACTILE ACTIVITIES					
COGNITIVE & LANGUAGE ACTIVITIES					
SMALL MUSCLE & LARGE MUSCLE ACTIVITIES					
SELF-AWARENESS, SELF-ESTEEM, SELF-HELP ACTIVITIES					
SPECIAL ACTIVITIES					
BOOKS OF THE WEEK					
SPECIAL NOTES					

TODDLER LESSON PLAN

TEACHER(S):

CONCEPTS:

DATES:

THEME:

SKILLS:

DAY	LARGE GROUP ACTIVITIES	SMALL GROUP ACTIVITIES
MONDAY		
TUESDAY		
WEDNESDAY		
THURSDAY		
FRIDAY		

SENSORY ACTIVITIES	DRAMATIC PLAY / HOME LIVING & PUPPETS	MOVEMENT / OUTDOOR ACTIVITIES
MUSIC ACTIVITIES	SELF-AWARENESS, SELF-ESTEEM, SELF-HELP ACTIVITIES	SMALL MUSCLE / MANIPULATIVE ACTIVITIES
ART ACTIVITIES	LANGUAGE ACTIVITIES	TRANSITIONS
ACTIVITIES / NOTES		BOOKS OF THE WEEK

PRESCHOOL–KINDERGARTEN LESSON PLAN

TEACHER(S):

CONCEPTS:

DATES:

SKILLS:

THEME:

CENTERS & ACTIVITIES	MONDAY	TUESDAY	WEDNESDAY	THURSDAY	FRIDAY
MORNING GROUP ACTIVITY					
AFTERNOON GROUP ACTIVITY					
LANGUAGE & LITERACY					
ART					
MUSIC & MOVEMENT					
DRAMATIC PLAY					
HOME LIVING					
MATH					
MANIPULATIVE					
SCIENCE & DISCOVERY					

BLOCKS	OUTDOOR / LARGE MUSCLE	TRANSITIONS
SENSORY CENTERS	SOCIAL STUDIES	BOOKS OF THE WEEK

SPECIAL ACTIVITIES & NOTES

MY COMMUNITY: INTEGRATED CURRICULUM THEME WITH ACTIVITIES

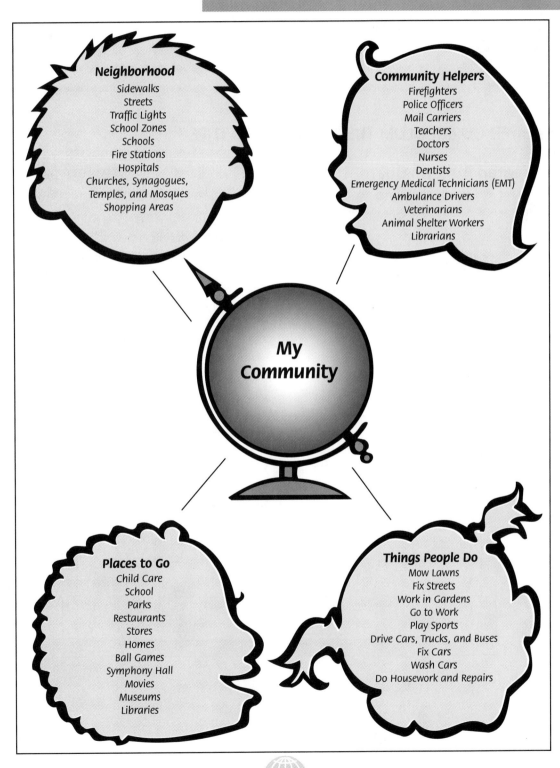

Neighborhood
Sidewalks
Streets
Traffic Lights
School Zones
Schools
Fire Stations
Hospitals
Churches, Synagogues,
Temples, and Mosques
Shopping Areas

Community Helpers
Firefighters
Police Officers
Mail Carriers
Teachers
Doctors
Nurses
Dentists
Emergency Medical Technicians (EMT)
Ambulance Drivers
Veterinarians
Animal Shelter Workers
Librarians

My Community

Places to Go
Child Care
School
Parks
Restaurants
Stores
Homes
Ball Games
Symphony Hall
Movies
Museums
Libraries

Things People Do
Mow Lawns
Fix Streets
Work in Gardens
Go to Work
Play Sports
Drive Cars, Trucks, and Buses
Fix Cars
Wash Cars
Do Housework and Repairs

THEME GOALS

To provide opportunities for children to learn:

1. We all live in a community that is made up of many people.
2. Members of a community work in many different places, such as stores, offices, homes, schools, indoors, and outdoors.
3. Some people wear special clothes or uniforms when they work and use special tools or machines.
4. Family members need to work in the community to buy what the family needs, such as housing, food, clothing, and transportation.
5. We should respect and get along with community members who may think, dress, and act differently than we do.

INTEGRATED CURRICULUM THEME WITH ACTIVITIES

Children-Created Bulletin Board

This bulletin board will keep changing during the time that the "My Community" theme is emphasized. Creating the bulletin board fulfills several purposes: keeping the children interested in their community; offering a space where they can put their drawings, comments, and thank-you notes; and keeping the parents aware of the ongoing community involvement of their children.

- Divide the bulletin board into two sections.
- One area will be for photographs that you and the children take of people from the community who visit the school and for photos you take of community helpers working at their jobs.
- The other section will be for photocopies of the thank-you letters the children send to community helpers and the drawings they create.
- Change the bulletin board every time a new community person is introduced to the children.

Vocabulary Starters

Let the children add additional words.

community—a place where a group of many people live, work, and play together.

neighbors—people who live or work close to your house.

job or occupation—what a person does to earn a living for herself and her family.

community helpers—a man or woman who works at a job that helps the people who live in the community.

respect—treating other people with kindness and understanding.

Language Experiences

Mailboxes

- Collect and make mailboxes out of shoe boxes or milk cartons.
- Have each child make one for himself. Include a box for the teachers.
- Have each child write his name on a box or place a photograph on it for those children who are not yet recognizing their names.
- Provide envelopes and "stamps" (e.g., stickers, Easter Seal stamps, magazine coupon stamps) in the writing center.
- The children can write letters or draw pictures and "send" them to their classmates by placing them in the appropriate classroom mailboxes.

Write Thank-You Letters

- Have the children write thank-you letters or notes to community members who visit the class and to those visited during field trips.
- Younger children can draw pictures to accompany the thank-you note you write.
- Suggestions for people to visit or invite include: firefighter, nurse, doctor, veterinarian, animal caretaker from the zoo, storyteller from the library, museum staff member, doll collector, dance teacher, member of the orchestra, square dance group, and a bell choir.

Letters or Greeting Cards to the Family

- It is fun for the children to write letters or make greeting cards to send to family members.

- Mail them or take a field trip to the post office to mail them.
- Have the children keep track of how long (how many days) it takes mail to get to their houses. Was the family member surprised?

Dramatic Play

Prop Boxes

- In a sturdy box, collect authentic items that represent a certain job or occupation.
- Label each box clearly for identification.

painter—several sizes of brushes, roller, bucket, sandpaper, masking tape, paint-stirring sticks, cap, gloves, old clothes, and a smock or apron. Let younger children paint on boxes with water. Older children can paint with tempera.

baker/chef—hat, apron, spoons, rolling pin, flour, and sifter. See sensory art activities in this theme for a play dough recipe.

firefighter—hats, several pieces of garden hose, raincoats, boots, and gloves.

gardener or florist—plastic flowers, pots with dirt, watering can, garden gloves, and hand shovel.

post office worker or letter carrier—play money (children can make their own with crayons, markers, and scrap construction paper), rubber stamps and stamp pad, postmarked stamps or stickers, envelopes, mail bag (large purse), hat, scrap paper, markers, pencils, and tape.

Telephone Directory

- In the dramatic play/home living area, set up a special place with a small table, a nonworking telephone, a phone message pad and pencil, and a telephone book.
- Make a class telephone directory by having each child write her name, address, and telephone number on a blank piece of paper in a small loose-leaf notebook.
- Add telephone numbers for community services, such as the library, grocery store, and zoo.
- Place this directory by the telephone.
- Suggest to the children that they begin writing down telephone messages and numbers when they "answer the phone" in the dramatic play area.
- An extension of this activity could be to set up a "telephone space" made from a refrigerator box.
- Place another copy of the class telephone directory in the booth along with an actual telephone book or yellow pages.

My Town—My Neighborhood

This activity encourages creativity, observation, problem solving, cooperation, and spatial awareness skills.

- Take a walk around the neighborhood surrounding your center or school.
- Point out buildings, businesses, houses, street names, and roads. In some communities it may be necessary to walk a wider area to find any buildings or businesses.
- For this activity you will need to close some of the centers in the room and expand the dramatic play area.
- Using boxes of varying sizes, construct a community.
- Talk about which buildings are needed, such as houses, apartments, stores, fire and police stations, hospitals, banks, churches, shopping malls, airports, movie theaters, and schools.
- On a large piece of cardboard place the buildings as they are located in your community.
- With the children, name and label the buildings and the streets.
- If you have enough room on your playground, use larger boxes, and make a town that includes cars, buses, and trucks.
- See the math activities in this theme for a further extension of this project.

Puppet Play
Community Helper Puppets

- Cut cardboard circles 8 to 10 inches in diameter or use large paper plates.
- For infants and young toddlers, draw large simple facial features on the cardboard circle.
- Attach a stick, such as a paint stirring stick or tongue depressor, to make a puppet.
- Play peek-a-boo by placing the face in front of an adult's or baby's face.

- Let older children make a set of stick puppet faces by themselves.
- They can add construction paper hats that represent community helpers, such as firefighters, police officers, letter carriers, and construction workers.

Music
The Orchestra

Introduce the children to the concept of a community orchestra. Start with Rubin and Daniel's book, *The Orchestra*, listed in the books section of this theme.

- Play several classical music selections, such as Britten's *A Young Person's Guide to the Orchestra*, Prokofiev's *Peter and the Wolf*, and Saint-Saëns's *Carnival of the Animals*. Choose short excerpts of these to play at any one time.
- Visit your local library for these selections and to find children's books to accompany the music.
- To further develop this activity, add puppets, flannelboard characters, or musical instruments as the children become familiar with the music.

Make Musical Instruments

- Collect bathroom tissue rolls, paper towel tubes, waxed paper, rubber bands, new combs, aluminum pie plates, paper plates and cups, and cereal and oatmeal boxes.
- Guide the children in making and decorating:
  drums—from oatmeal boxes.
  plate shakers—with clothespins or birdseed placed between two aluminum pie plates or paper plates tied together with yarn.
  cup shakers—with dried beans inside two paper cups taped together with masking tape.

flutes—from paper towel tubes. Punch a line of several holes to about two inches from the end. Cover the end with a square piece of waxed paper held in place with a rubber band.

rhythm sticks—from dowel sticks cut to specification at the hardware store.

humming combs—with waxed paper loosely wrapped around a comb, place to the lips and hum.

Movement

Let's Dance

Infants enjoy all kinds of music. Toddlers enjoy dancing to lively music, especially when you tie bells to their shoestrings.
Tie some on your shoes, too.

- Place the infant on his back, hold his ankles, and move the child's feet to the rhythm of the music you are singing or playing.
- Take the baby's hands and move his arms up and down or clap his hands together as the music plays.

Act Out a Story with Dance

- Read a story or poem to the children, such as Stecher's *Max, the Music Maker*, listed in the books section of this theme.
- Let the children be the orchestra. They can play rhythm instruments or the ones they made as you read the book.
- Have the children dance or act out the story by walking quickly and slowly, running in place, tapping along, or moving with scarves or crepe paper streamers.
- Try having half the class be the orchestra while the other half dances.

More Dancing

- Take a field trip to a dance studio or have a dancer visit your class.
- The children enjoy watching a dancer in ballet or tap shoes.
- Have the dance teacher or dancer show the children and you how to do some simple steps.
- Give the children opportunities to repeat these steps over and over again. Try it with different kinds of music.

Sensory Art

Make Play Dough

You will need:

1 cup flour
½ cup salt

1 cup water
1 tablespoon cooking oil
2 teaspoons cream of tartar
vanilla, peppermint, or almond extract

1. Wash hands.
2. Mix all ingredients.
3. Stir over low heat until the mixture forms a ball.
4. Remove from heat, and wrap in waxed paper to cool.
5. Store in an air-tight container.
6. The play dough will last much longer if kept in the refrigerator.
7. You and the children can add food coloring before cooking or wait until after cooking, so the children can see the change from white, to marbled, to the final color.
8. Fragrant extracts, such as vanilla, peppermint, or almond, may be added to the play dough.

Community Telephones

- To make a set of telephones, you will need two empty tin cans, a long piece of string, two toothpicks or nails, and a hammer.
- Punch a hole in the bottom of each can with a hammer and nail.
- Thread the ends of the string through the holes.
- Tie the string around the toothpicks to keep them from coming out of the cans.
- Two children hold the tin can "telephones" and pull the string tight.
- The children then take turns talking and listening.
- For variation, add more phones and create a "community party line."

Woodworking

This activity encourages positive self-esteem, self-motivation, problem-solving, large and small muscle development, hand-eye coordination, and creativity.

- Visit a community hardware store with the children before setting up the woodworking area. This gives the children a firsthand experience seeing many different types of nails, screws, washers, bolts, hammers, screwdrivers, and wood.
- Introduce the children to the woodworking center with its materials, tools, and pictures of houses and buildings under construction at various construction sites.
- Children should be closely supervised, with only two at a time using the tools.
- Collect real tools and materials, such as small claw hammers (8 to 12 ounces), assorted nails, safety goggles (children's swimming masks work well), clamps, a hand drill, wood glue, sandpaper, rulers, pencils, and paper.

- For older children add a cross-cut saw (approximately 18 inches long), screws, and screwdrivers.
- Obtain inexpensive grades of wood from carpenter shops, lumber yards, and do-it-yourself discount stores, or ask parents to contribute.
- In the beginning, children enjoy sanding and gluing the pieces of wood. Add hammering, sawing, and nailing later.

Creative Food Experiences

Eat Rice with Chopsticks

- Begin this project by reading Dooley's *Everybody Cooks Rice*, listed in the books section of this theme.
- Introduce the children to how food connects one neighbor to others in the neighborhood. Recipes using rice are included at the end of Dooley's book.
- To further develop the understanding of other cultures, introduce the use of chopsticks to eat rice.

- Chopsticks are useful tools that are part of Chinese, Japanese, Korean, and Vietnamese cultures.
- Cook rice according to the instructions on the package.
- Give each child a new pair of chopsticks that she can take home after using. Many Asian restaurants give sets of new chopsticks to teachers for the asking.
- Demonstrate to the children how to hold the chopsticks by the thicker end.
- Put one chopstick at the base of the thumb, and hold the other between the thumb, index, and middle fingers. Move only the finger-held chopstick to pick up rice or small pieces of food.
- Many young children find the task easier by holding the chopsticks closer to the end where they are picking up food.

- Explain to the children that it is rude to point with chopsticks. Avoid licking the chopsticks or spearing food with them.

Chicken Soup with Rice

Here is another way to connect language, literacy, and cooking. Read Sendak's *Chicken Soup with Rice*, listed in the books section of this theme.
You will need:

6 cups chicken broth

1 cup chicken, cooked and diced

¾ cup cooked rice

1. Bring broth to a boil.
2. Add chicken and rice.
3. Reheat and eat.

This recipe serves 8.

Math

Partner Tower Building

Tower building promotes math skill development, such as problem-solving, exploration of spatial relationships, and experimentation with weight and balance. Socialization and cooperation are also emphasized.

- In the block center have one child build a tower or shape, and another child duplicate it.
- Let the children continue this activity until they tire of it.
- To vary the activity, have a small group of children build a tower.
- The first child puts a block in place. Each child in the group takes a turn stacking a block on the top of what has been built. Continue taking turns until the tower falls over.
- The children can discuss why they think the tower fell over.
- They may want to experiment with stacking blocks another way.

Mixed-Up People

Older children like to draw pictures of people, such as firefighters, bakers, nurses, cowboys, ballet dancers, and farmers.

- Supply plenty of paper, crayons, markers, and scissors for children to use to make pictures of people.
- Suggest that they cut pictures they have made in three pieces, dividing the picture into body, head, and legs.
- Put the body of one, the head of another, and the legs of another together to make a mixed-up person.
- Make this activity available throughout the theme.

Shape City

- Provide the children with colorful construction paper, scissors, and glue.
- Demonstrate how to cut out all sizes of different shapes. Precut the shapes for younger children.
- The children glue the shapes on a piece of paper to make designs of homes, buildings, vehicles, and people. Younger children enjoy just gluing the shapes everywhere on the page, with no specific design in mind.
- An extension of this activity is for the children to create a shape city on a long piece of butcher paper.

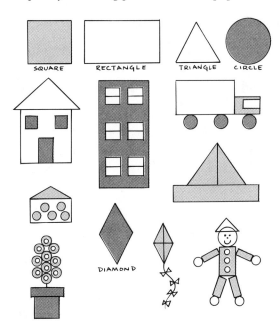

Science

Fire Prevention

- After visiting a fire station or having a firefighter visit the school, reinforce the experience.
- Try STOP (don't run—freeze), DROP (fall to the ground), and ROLL (over and over until the fire is out) to put out fire on clothing.

- Practice what to do to escape from a smoky room. Crawl to the nearest exit. Stay low, because smoke and hot air rise.
- Another vital rule is: If the DOOR is HOT, don't open it! Ask the children what it means if the door is hot.
- Start a list of fire-safety rules on a large sheet of paper or posterboard.
- Ask children to contribute rules you have discussed or ones they learned at home.
- Continue to add to the list. Post it at the children's eye level.

Pulleys

- Ask open-ended questions relating to children's experiences with tall buildings and apartment houses.
- How do the people get from one floor to another?
- Introduce the concept of pulleys and elevators.
- Next, let the children see you set up two chairs to support the ends of a wooden dowel or broomstick.
- Tie heavy string to the handle of a small basket filled with toy animals and people figures from the block center.

- Loop the string over the dowel.
- Ask a child to pull the string down on one side of the dowel. This illustrates how a pulley lifts the basket with toys on the other side.
- Let the children experiment with the pulley.
- Provide materials, and encourage them to make other pulleys.
- Guide them into adding pulleys into the block area with their buildings.

Social Studies

Community Buildings

- Show pictures of all kinds of buildings in communities around the world.
- Obtain the pictures from travel agents, airlines, travel brochures, and magazines such as *National Geographic*. You may want to take some photos as well.

- With the children, compare the similarities and differences of the buildings.
- Ask open-ended questions, such as, "Who do you think works in this building?" "What is her job?" "Why do you think the building is so tall?" "Why is this building so small?" "What country do you think this building is in?" "What city?"
- This discussion can be combined with the Shape City activity in the math section of this theme.

Community Map

- With older children, use a map of your community to show them where their school is. Mark the spot on the map.
- Find some of the streets, roads, houses, and buildings in the neighborhood, and mark these.
- Let the children make a large floor map of the neighborhood and city.
- Provide a large piece of butcher paper, masking tape, construction paper, crayons, and markers. Egg cartons make interesting structures, and paper towel tubes make great tunnels.

Children's Books

Bauer, Judith. (1990). *What's It Like to Be a Doctor?* Mahwah, NJ: Troll Associates.

Bauer, Judith. (1990). *What's It Like to Be a Nurse?* Mahwah, NJ: Troll Associates.

Borden, L. (1990). *The Neighborhood Trucker.* New York: Scholastic.

Butterworth, Nick. (1992). *Busy People.* Cambridge, MA: Candlewick Press.

Darling, David. (1992). *Spiderwebs to Skyscrapers.* New York: Dillon Press.

Dooley, Norah. (1991). *Everybody Cooks Rice.* Illustrated by Peter J. Thornton. Minneapolis, MN: Carolrhoda Books.

Flanagan, Alice K., & Christine Osinski. (1998). *Mrs. Murphy Fights Fires.* San Francisco, CA: Children's Press.

Friend, David. (1992). *Baseball, Football, Daddy, and Me.* New York: Puffin Books.

Henderson, Kathy. (1991). *I Can Be a Basketball Player.* Chicago, IL: Children's Press.

Kuklin, Susan. (1989). *Going to My Ballet Class.* New York: Macmillan.

Merriam, Eve. (1989). *Mommies at Work.* New York: Simon & Schuster.

Patrick, Denise L. (1993). *The Car Washing Street.* Illustrated by John Ward. New York: Scholastic.

Powers, M. E. (1992). *Our Teacher's in a Wheelchair.* Chicago: IL: Whitman.

Pringle, Laurence. (1989). *Jesse Builds a Road.* New York: Macmillan.

Rogers, Fred. (1989). *Going to the Dentist.* New York: Putnam Publishing Group.

Rubin, Mark. (1995). *The Orchestra.* Illustrated by Alan Daniel. Buffalo, New York: Firefly Books.

Sendak, Maurice. (1962). *Chicken Soup with Rice.* New York: Scholastic.

Seymour, Peter. (1990). *Firefighters.* New York: Dutton Children's Books.

Skurzynski, Gloria. (1992). *Here Comes the Mail.* New York: Macmillan Children's Books.

Stecher, Miriam. (1990). *Max, the Music Maker.* Photographs by Alex Meyboom. New York: Lothrop, Lee & Shepard.

Tasky, Sue. (1997). *The Busy Building Book.* New York: Putnam.

Van Laan, Nancy. (1992). *People, People, Everywhere.* New York: Knopf.

Ziefert, Harriet. (1991). *City Shapes.* Illustrated by Susan Baum. New York: HarperCollins.

Family Letter (Primary)

Dear Family,

We are beginning our new theme, "My Community." The children will have opportunities to learn:

- We live in a community made up of many people.
- Members of a community work in many different places.
- Some people wear special clothes or uniforms when they work and use special tools or machines.
- Family members work in the community to buy what the family needs, such as housing, food, clothing, and transportation.
- We should respect and get along with community members who may think, dress, and act differently than we do.

We will be talking about:

- our neighborhood, and who lives and works there
- community helpers
- things that people do
- places to go in the community.

Things to do in the community with your child:

- Take a walk around your neighborhood. Let your child point out things that relate to what he is doing in school.
- Look at ongoing construction sites of homes and buildings.
- Ask about what she is building at school.
- Discuss how specific community helpers have helped your family.
- Eat a dinner using chopsticks, if you have not done so. Let your child show you how.
- Visit a museum, see a play, cheer at a ball game, and enjoy the symphony orchestra in your community.

Come join us for family participation opportunities at school:

- Visit the class and share your occupation with the children.
    Date _____ Time _____

- Join us on our neighborhood walk.
    Date _____ Time _____

- Help us in the woodworking center.
    Date _____ Time _____

On our wish list for this theme are:

nonpostal stamps	milk cartons
envelopes	aluminum pie plates
all sizes of boxes	magazines and catalogs
paper cups and plates	empty oatmeal boxes
tubes from paper towels	

Thanks!

APPENDIX C

The following resources offer publications, educational materials, services, and other resources for teachers. They are listed in association with chapter content. Internet Web sites are also listed for many of the resources.

Internet Disclaimer

The author and Thomson Delmar Learning make every effort to ensure that all Internet resources are accurate at the time of printing. However, due to the fluid, time-sensitive nature of the Internet, Thomson Delmar Learning cannot guarantee that all URLs and Web site addresses will remain current for the duration of this edition.

Chapter 1

- Administration for Children and Families
  U.S. Department of Health and Human Services, Child Care Bureau
  http://www.acf.dhhs.gov
  (Click on "Child Care," then click on "Child Care Bureau")
- Child Care Information Exchange
  (Professional magazine for early childhood administrators and teachers)
  P.O. Box 3249
  Redmond, WA 98073-3249
  http://www.ccie.com
- Council for Professional Recognition (CDA)
  Child Development Associate
  2460 16th Street NW
  Washington, DC 20009-3575
  http://www.cdacouncil.org
- National Association for the Education of Young Children (NAEYC)
  1313 L Street NW, Suite 500
  Washington, DC 20005
  http://www.naeyc.org
  (Write for catalog of publications and membership information)
- National Association for Family Child Care (NAFCC)
  5202 Pinemont Drive
  Salt Lake City, UT 84123
  http://www.nafcc.org
- National Association for Gifted Children
  1707 L Street NW, Suite 550

Washington, DC 20036
http://www.nagc.org
- National Institute on Early Child Development and Education
  U.S. Department of Education
  400 Maryland Avenue SW
  Washington, DC 20202
  http://www.ed.gov
- National Institute for Play
  (Emphasizes the importance of play)
  46 West Garzas Road
  Carmel Valley, CA 03024
  http://www.instituteforplay.com
- *National PTA's Building Blocks: Importance of Children's Play*
  (A collection of information on child's play characteristics by age and types of play activities)
  541 North Fairbanks Court, Suite 1300
  Chicago, IL 60611-3396
  http://www.pta.org
- No Child Left Behind Act
  http://nclb.org
- *Scholastic Early Childhood Today*
  (Professional magazine for early childhood teachers)
  Scholastic Inc.
  555 Broadway
  New York, NY 10012
  http://www.scholastic.com
- School-Age Notes
  (National resource organization for school-age care)
  P.O. Box 476

New Albany, OH 43054
http://www.schoolagenotes.com
- ZERO TO THREE
  (Helping babies and toddlers grow and develop)
  2000 M St. NW, Suite 200
  Washington, DC 20036
  http://www.zerotothree.org

Chapter 2

- American Academy of Pediatrics
  (Committed to the attainment of optimal physical, mental, and social health and well-being for all infants, children, adolescents, and young adults; this Web site has current and helpful information for teachers and parents)
  141 Northwest Point Blvd.
  Elk Grove Village, IL 60007
  http://www.aap.org
- American Dental Association
  (Provides information on good dental health for children, parents, and teachers)
  211 East Chicago Ave.
  Chicago, IL 60611-2678
  http://www.ada.org
- American Montessori Society
  281 Park Avenue South, 6th floor
  New York, NY 10010-6102
  http://www.amshq.org
- Anti-Defamation League of B'nai B'rith
  ADL Resources for Classroom and Community
  823 United Nations Plaza
  New York, NY 10117
  http://www.adl.org
  (Write for information on teacher resources and audio-visual materials that relate to multicultural education; many cities have a local office that also has these materials)
- Association Montessori Internationale/USA
  410 Alexander Street
  Rochester, NY 14607-1028
  http://www.montessori-ami.org
- Bank Street College of Education
  610 West 112th Street
  New York, NY 10025-1898
  http://www.bankstreet.edu
  http://www.bankstreetcorner.com
- Council for Exceptional Children
  (Offers comprehensive information and publications)
  1110 North Glebe Road, Suite 300
  Arlington, VA 22201
  http://www.cec.sped.org
- Early Childhood Educators' and Family Web Corner (NAREA)
  (Lists teacher information programs on many subjects)
  http://www.users.sgi.net/~cokids/teacher.html

- Gryphon House Inc.
  P.O. Box 207
  Beltsville, MD 20704-0207
  http://www.ghbooks.com
- Head Start Information and Publication Center
  U.S. Department of Health and Human Services
  Administration for Children
  http://www.headstartinfo.org
- High/Scope Educational Research Foundation
  600 North River Street
  Ypsilanti, MI 48198-2898
  http://www.highscope.org
- National Child Care Information Center, U.S. Department of Health & Human Services
  Administration for Children & Families
  370 L'Enfant Promenade SW
  Washington, DC 20447
  (A national resource information link to ensure that all children and families have access to high-quality comprehensive services)
  http://nccic.org
- National Dissemination Center for Children with Disabilities (NICHCY)
  (Publications are free; includes *Parent Guide* and publication list)
  P.O. Box 1492
  Washington, DC 20013
  http://www.NICHCY.org
- National Program for Playground Safety (NPPS)
  University of Northern Iowa
  School for Health, Physical Education, and Leisure Services
  Cedar Falls, IA 50614-0618
  http://www.uni.edu/playground
- Project Approach
  (Provides resources for projects with young children)
  http://www.project-approach.com
- Redleaf Press
  (Resources for early childhood professionals)
  10 Yorkton Court
  St. Paul, MN 55117-1065
  http://www.redleafpress.org
- Reggio Emilia
  Web site of North American Reggio Emilia Alliance (NAREA) provides information for educators.
  http://www.reggioalliance.org
  Official Web site for Reggio Children with information in both English and Italian
  http://www.reggiochildren.it
- Tolerance.org
  (A principal on-line destination for people interested in dismantling bigotry and creating communities that value diversity; helpful site for teachers who want to implement anti-bias practices in their classrooms)

c/o The Southern Poverty Law Center
400 Washington Ave.
Montgomery, AL 36104
http://www.tolerance.org

Chapter 3

- American Foundation for the Blind
  11 Penn Plaza, Suite 300
  New York, NY 10011
  http://www.afb.org
  (Go on-line to order *free* teacher and parent resources and posters that explain the Braille alphabet; instead of words and letters printed on a page or in a book, Braille letters and numbers are "bumps" embossed on the page)
- Center for the Study of Books in Spanish for Children and Adolescents
  California State University San Marcos
  Kellogg Library, 5th floor
  333 S. Twin Oaks Valley Road
  San Marcos, CA 92096-0001
  http://www.csusm.edu/csb
- The Children's Book Council (CBC)
  (A nonprofit trade organization dedicated to encouraging literacy and the use and enjoyment of books; CBC is the official sponsor of *Young People's Poetry Week* and *Children's Book Week*)
  12 West 37th Street, 2nd Floor
  New York, NY 10018-7480
  http://www.cbcbooks.org
- Dragon Tales
  (Created especially for preschoolers, Dragon Tales are designed to nurture young children's curiosity and enthusiasm for learning)
  http://pbskids.org
  (click on "PBS Teachers," then type in "Dragon Tales" in the Search box)
- Early Childhood Technology Literacy Project
  (A resource for parents and teachers to share the information gathered and developed during this project; the instructional focus is to integrate technology into instruction while increasing early childhood student skills in reading and writing)
  Montgomery County Public Schools
  Rockville, MD
  http://www.mcps.k12.md.us/curriculum/littlekids
- Early Literacy Advisor (ELA)
  (An assessment system that shapes instruction)
  4601 DTC Blvd., Suite 500
  Denver, CO 80237
  http://www.mcrel.org/programs/literacy/ela/index.asp
- Internet Public Library
  (Offers references, reading zone, books and authors, teacher's and parent's information and activities on art, music, science, math, etc.)

http://www.ipl.org
(Click on either "KidSpace" or "TeenSpace")

- Learning Point Associates
  (Provides professional development resources to help teachers build their knowledge base, apply their expertise to help children meet challenges in reading, and keep abreast of developments concerning literacy education)
  1120 East Diehl Road, Suite 200
  Naperville, IL 60563
  http://www.ncrel.org/litweb
- National Children's Literacy
  (Part of The Soho Center's National Children's Literacy Information Project)
  1564 West Hoover Road
  Madison, VA 22727
  http://www.child2000.org
  (Click on "Yes," then Click on "National Children's Literacy Website™")
- Society of Children's Book Writers and Illustrators
  (Helpful research links that offer literacy and literature Web sites for teachers and parents)
  8271 Beverly Blvd.
  Los Angeles, CA 90048
  http://www.scbwi.org/links/research.htm

Chapter 4

- Bank Street Children's Book Committee
  (Founded 80 years ago to guide librarians, educators, and parents to the best books for children published each year)
  610 West 112th Street
  New York, NY 10025
  http://www.bankstreet.edu/bookcom
  (Publishes *The Best Children's Books of the Year* and *Books to Read Aloud for Children of All Ages*)
- The Children's Literature Web Guide
  (Categorized Internet resources related to books for children and young adults.)
  http://www.acs.ucalgary.ca/~dkbrown/index.html
- Cricket Magazine Group
  Babybug for infants and toddlers
  Ladybug for young children
  Spider for beginning readers
  Cricket for young people
  315 Fifth Street
  Peru, IL 61354
  http://www.cricketmag.com
- Fairrosa Cyber Library of Children's Literature
  (Interesting information on authors, illustrators, articles, reviews, etc. Enter the Reading Room and discover on-line classics, fairy and folk tales, stories and rhymes, magazines, and professional journals.)
  http://www.fairrosa.info

- *Highlights for Children Magazine*
  1800 Watermark Drive
  P.O. Box 269
  Columbus, OH 43216–0269
  http://www.highlights.com
- Let's Find Out Scholastic
  2931 East McCarty Street
  Jefferson City, MO 65101-9957
  http://scholastic.com
- National Center for Family Literacy
  325 W. Main Street, Suite 300
  Louisville, KY 40202-4237
  http://www.famlit.org
- National Children's Book Week (November)
  (Information and classroom "streamers" and posters available from the on-line catalog)
  Children's Book Council
  112 W. 37th St., 2nd Floor
  New York, NY 10018-7480
  http://www.cbcbooks.org
- Reading Is Fundamental (RIF)
  (Information for teachers and parents)
  1825 Connecticut Avenue NW, Suite 400
  Washington, DC 20009
  http://www.rif.org
- *Reading Rainbow*
  http://www.pbs.org
  (Click on "PBS KIDS GO!," then Click on "Reading Rainbow" in the Go box)
- *Stone Soup: The Magazine by Children*
  P.O. Box 83
  Santa Cruz, CA 95063
  http://www.stonesoup.com
- *Weekly Reader*
  3001 Cindel Drive
  Delran, NJ 08075
  http://www.weeklyreader.com
  (See Chapter 4 for other resources on the Internet)

Chapter 5

- Activities Integrating Mathematics and Science (AIMS) Education Foundation
  1595 S. Chestnut Avenue
  Fresno, CA 93702
  http://www.aimsedu.org
- Do math and you can do anything
  (Math challenges for children and families)
  http://www.domath.org
- Helping your child learn math
  (Site for parents—what to do to help your child achieve in math)

http://www.ed.gov/pubs/parents/Math/index.html
- Math Forum@Drexel University
  (Provides resources, materials, activities, person-to-person interactions, and educational products and services that enrich and support teaching and learning)
  3210 Cherry Street
  Philadelphia, PA 19104
  http://mathforum.org
- National Council of Teachers of Mathematics
  1906 Association Drive, Dept. 1-CT
  Reston, VA 20191-1502
  http://www.nctm.org
  (Write for their catalog of resources and publications)
- Texas Instrument Educational Resources
  (Offers a comprehensive collection of math activities for all grades; click on "Educators," "Parents," or "Students" to find resources using math and calculators)
  http://www.ti.com/calc
- Webmath
  (Resource site for children, teachers, and parents—Helps children with math problems they are working on right now; teachers can create a math test on-line)
  http://www.webmath.com

Chapter 6

- *Audubon* Magazine
  National Audubon Society
  700 Broadway
  New York, NY 10003
  http://www.audubon.org
- Bring Birds to Your Backyard
  (A number of government-sponsored booklets are offered to children *free* for the asking: "Homes for Birds" describes the characteristics of various birds and tells the best housing for each; "Backyard Bird Feeding" tells how to attract different species to your house)
  http://www.pueblo.gsa.gov
  (In Site Search box, type in the names of these publications and click on "Go" to download these and other booklets)
  http://www.earthsciweek.org/ (In the Search box, type in "Backyard Birds" and "Bring Birds to Your Backyard")
- EPA—United States Environmental Protection Agency
  (Provides information and services on teaching about the environment, especially designed for classroom use)
  77 West Jackson Blvd.
  Chicago, IL 60604
  http://www.epa.gov/teachers
- Friends of the Environment Foundation—Earth Day Canada
  http://www.ecokidsonline.com
- National Science Teachers Association
  1840 Wilson Blvd.

Arlington, VA 22201
(Information focused on you and your teaching environment)
http://www.nsta.org

- National Wildlife Federation
(Offers several magazines and programs especially for young children)
Some of these are:
1. *Wild Animal Baby*—12 months to 3 years
2. *Your Big Backyard*—ages 3–6
3. *Ranger Rick Magazine*—ages 7–12
11100 Wildlife Center Drive
Reston, VA 20190-5362
(Explore schoolyard habitat, backyard wildlife habitat, and National Wildlife Week on-line)
http://www.nwf.org

- Nature's Classroom (Environmental education programs)
19 Harrington Road
Charlton, MA 01507
http://www.naturesclassroom.org

- Space Day
(Generally held in May and designed to advance science, mathematics, and technology education)
6801 Rockledge Drive
Bethesda, MD 20817
http://www.spaceday.com

- USDA Forest Service
1400 Independence Ave. SW
Washington, DC 20250-0003
http://www.fs.fed.us
(Under Forest Service Home, click on "Just for Kids")

Chapter 7

- Visit children's museums on-line. Here are some Web sites to get you started.
Canadian Children's Museum
http://www.civilization.ca
Children's Discovery Museum of San Jose
http://www.cdm.org
Children's Museum of Boston
http://www.bostonkids.org
Children's Museum of Houston
http://www.cmhouston.org
Children's Museum of Manhattan
http://www.cmom.org
The Eric Carle Museum of Picture Book Art
http://www.picturebookart.org
The New Chicago Children's Museum
http://www.chichildrensmuseum.org
Science Museum of Minnesota
http://www.smm.org

Smithsonian Institution
http://www.si.edu

- National Association for Bilingual Education
1313 L Street NW
Washington, DC 20005
http://www.nabe.org

- National Council for the Social Studies
8555 16th Street, Suite 500
Silver Spring, MD 20910
http://www.ncss.org

- National Geographic Society
1145 17th Street, NW
Washington, DC 20036
(Source for materials about geography, environmental science, and global studies)
http://www.nationalgeographic.com
(In the Search box, Type in "for teachers")

- Social Studies School Service
(Source for materials covering all social studies areas—good selection of posters, videotapes, recordings, and reference materials for teachers)
10200 Jefferson Blvd.
P.O. Box 802
Culver City, CA 90232
http://www.socialstudies.com

- United States Committee for UNICEF
United Nations Children's Fund
333 East 38th Street
New York, NY 10016
http://www.unicefusa.org
(To receive their catalog of cards and gifts, type in "catalog of cards and gifts" in the Search box, then click on the "Order a Catalog" link, and then enter your information)

Chapter 8

- Aline D. Wolf 's "Mommy, It's a Renoir" and four volumes of accompanying art postcards entitled "Child-Size Masterpieces"
Parent Child Press
P.O. Box 675
Hollidaysburg, PA 16648
http://www.parentchildpress.com

- Artsedge
(Supports the place of arts education at the center of the curriculum through the creative and appropriate uses of technology)
The John F. Kennedy Center for the Performing Arts
2700 F Street NW
Washington, DC 20566
http://www.artsedge.kennedy-center.org

- Artsplay
  (An interactive resource from Wolf Trap Institute for Early Learning Through the Arts, an arts-in-education program for the early childhood community; a great resource for teachers)
  1645 Trap Road
  Vienna, VA 22182
  http://www.wolftrap.org
- Barron's Educational Series
  250 Wireless Blvd.
  Hauppauge, New York 11788
  http://www.barronseduc.com
  (Write for their catalog of creative art books)
- Crayola
  http://www.crayola.com
  (Explore this site—it's full of ideas and information for stimulating creativity)
- The Kennedy Center Alliance for Art Education Network
  (Includes 46 state alliance organizations operating in partnership with the Kennedy Center)
  2700 F Street NW
  Washington, DC 20566
  http://www.kennedy-center.org
  (Click on "Education," then type in "National Networks" in the Search box, and then click on "Kennedy Center Alliance for Arts Education Network [state organizations]")

Chapter 9

- Children's Technology Review (CSR)
  (Attempts to help adults leverage the power of technology to support the development of children)
  120 Main Street
  Flemington, NJ 08822
  http://www.childrenstechnology.com
- Kids Food Cyber Club
  (Provides food and nutrition ideas for children)
  http://www.kidsfood.org
- National Dairy Council
  (A leader in nutrition research since 1915, dedicated to providing timely, scientifically sound nutrition information on the health benefits of milk, cheese, and yogurt)
  http://www.nationaldairycouncil.com
- Nutrition Explorations
  10255 West Higgins Road, Suite 900
  Rosemont, IL 60018-5616
  http://www.nutritionexplorations.com
  (This Web site is an excellent resource for children, educators, parents, and school food service personnel)
- USDA
  (Offers a copy of the *Food Guide Pyramid for Young Children* booklet and PDF posters on-line; this pyramid

provides educational messages that focus on children's food preferences and nutrition requirements)
3101 Park Center Drive, 10th Floor
Alexandria, VA 22302-1594
http://www.usda.gov/cnpp

Chapter 10

- Children's Music Network
  (Connecting people who celebrate the positive power of music in children's lives by exchanging ideas, visions, and music)
  P.O. Box 1341
  Evanston, IL 60204-1341
  http://www.cmnonline.org
- Jo Eklof's "Miss Jo's Picture Book Learning Songs" are read-along and sing-along large print picture books, big books, and musical CDs
  Jo Eklof is available to do appearances for child care centers and schools.
  Miss Jo Productions
  6131 Royal Crest Drive
  Dallas, TX 75230
  http://www.missjo.com
- "Music in Motion"
  (A music education and gift catalog for all ages)
  1601 East Plano Parkway, Suite 100
  Plano, TX 75074
  http://www.musicmotion.com
- "Music Together"
  (Program for children, infant to kindergarten, and their adult primary caregivers)
  Kenneth K. Guilmartin, Director
  Center for Music and Young Children
  66 Witherspoon Street
  Princeton, NJ 08542
  http://www.musictogether.com
- National Association of Music Education (MENC)
  1806 Robert Fulton Drive
  Reston, VA 20191
  http://www.menc.org
- PE Central
  (Web site for health and physical education teachers, parents, and students—their goal is to provide the latest information about developmentally appropriate physical education programs for children and youth)
  P.O. Box 10262
  Blacksburg, VA 24060
  http://www.pecentral.org
- West Music
  P.O. Box 5521
  Coralville, IA 52241
  http://www.westmusic.com

- Wolf Trap Institute for Early Learning through the Arts
  (Offers workshops for teachers, parents, and administrators to introduce performing arts activities that will help early childhood educators teach a variety of physical, cognitive, social, and emotional skills to preschool children; these staff development workshops stress the importance of children creating their own stories, songs, and dances, and include material that is appropriate for children with special needs)
  For further information about services, fees, and field trips (for early childhood programs in the Washington, DC, area), write:
  Wolf Trap Institute for Early Learning through the Arts
  1624 Trap Road
  Vienna, VA 22182
  http://www.wolf-trap.org
- ZERO TO THREE
  (Explains the powerful influence of music on a young child's development)
  2000 M St. NW, Suite 200
  Washington, DC 20036
  http://www.zerotothree.org

Chapters 11 & 12

- Center for Puppetry Arts
  1404 Spring Street NW
  Atlanta, GA 30309-2820
  http://www.puppet.org
  (Write for information about the Center for Puppetry Arts Museum, featuring puppets from all over the world and their special "Create a Puppet" workshops)

- FOLKMANIS Puppets
  (Offers many play and create activities plus a wonderful collection of puppets to see or buy)
  http://www.folkmanis.com
- Mister Rogers' Neighborhood
  (Information on training and curriculum materials)
  http://pbs.org
  (In the Search box, type in "Mister Rogers")
- The Puppet Museum
  ("Hello, Hello, Hello!!! I'm Ping Pong, the Panda, and I'm your tour guide here at the museum." This begins a delightful site visit that takes you through the Olde World Puppet Theatre, Ping Pong's Puppet Workshop, puppet Web site links around the world, and many other places.)
  http://www.puppetmuseum.com
- The Puppeteers of America, Inc.
  Joyce and Chuck Berty
  P.O. Box 29417
  Parma, OH 44129
  http://www.puppeteers.org
- The Puppetry Home Page
  (A free resource for the puppetry community and dedicated to helping people connect to the world of puppetry)
  http://www.sagecraft.com/puppetry
- UNICEF
  (Learn about puppets around the world)
  333 East 38th Street
  New York, NY 10016
  http://www.unicef.org/puppets

APPENDIX D

American Library Association (ALA)
50 E. Huron Street
Chicago, IL 60611
http://www.ala.org
(Publishes *American Libraries Booklist*)

American Speech-Language-Hearing Association
10801 Rockville Pike
Rockville, MD 20852
http://www.asha.org

Association for Childhood Education International
(ACEI)
17904 Georgia Avenue, Suite 215
Olney, MD 20832
http://www.acei.org
(Publishes *Childhood Education* and *Journal of Research in Childhood Education*)

Association for Supervision and Curriculum
Development (ASCD)
1703 N. Beauregard Street
Alexandria, VA 22311
http://www.ascd.org
(Publishes *Educational Leadership* and *Journal of Curriculum and Supervision*)

Canadian Association for Young Children (CAYC)
http://www.cayc.ca
(Publishes *Canadian Children*)

Children's Defense Fund
25 E Street NW
Washington, DC 20001
http://www.childrensdefense.org

Children's Foundation
725 15th Street NW, Suite 505
Washington, DC 20005
http://www.childrensfoundation.net
(Publishes *Children's Foundation Child Care Bulletin*)

Council for Early Childhood Professional Recognition
(CDA)
2460 16th Street NW
Washington, DC 20009
http://www.cdacouncil.org
(Publishes *Council Newsletter*)

Council for Exceptional Children (CEC)
1110 North Globe Road, Suite 300
Arlington, VA 22201
http://www.cec.sped.org
(Publishes *Exceptional Children's Journal*)

Families and Work Institute
267 Fifth Avenue, 2nd floor
New York, NY 10016
http://www.familiesandwork.org

International Reading Association Inc.
800 Barksdale Road
Box 8139
Newark, DE 19714
http://www.reading.org
(Publishes *Reading Today*, *The Reading Teacher*, and *Reading Research Quarterly* on-line)

Learning Disabilities Association
4156 Library Road
Pittsburgh, PA 15234
http://www.ldanatl.org
(Publishes *Learning Disabilities Journal*)

National Art Education Association (NAEA)
1916 Association Drive
Reston, VA 20191
http://www.naea-reston.org
(Publishes *Studies in Art Education*, a quarterly journal)

National Association for Bilingual Education (NABE)
1313 L Street NW, Suite 210
Washington, DC 20005

http://www.nabe.org
(Publishes *NABE News Magazine* and *Bilingual Research Journal*)

National Association of Early Childhood Teacher Educators
http://www.naecte.org
(Publishes *Journal of Early Childhood Teacher Education*)

National Association for the Education of Young Children (NAEYC)
1313 L Street NW, Suite 500
Washington, DC 20005
http://www.naeyc.org
(Publishes *Young Children*)

National Association for Family Child Care (NAFCC)
5202 Pinemont Drive
Salt Lake City, UT 84123
http://www.nafcc.org
(Publishes *National Perspective*)

National Association for Gifted Children (NAGC)
1707 L Street, Suite 550
Washington, DC 20036
http://www.nagc.org
(Publishes *Gifted Children Quarterly*)

National Association of Music Education
1806 Robert Fulton Drive
Reston, VA 20191
http://www.menc.org
(Publishes *Music Educators Journal, Teaching Music,* and *General Music Today* on-line)

National Black Child Development Institute (NBCDI)
1313 L Street NW, Suite 110
Washington, DC 20005
http://www.nbcdi.org
(Publishes *Child Health Talk* and *Black Child Care Advocate*)

National Council for the Social Studies
8555 16th Street, Suite 500
Silver Spring, MD 20910
http://www.socialstudies.org

National Council of Teachers of Mathematics (NCTM)
1906 Association Drive
Reston, VA 20191
http://www.nctm.org
(Publishes *Teaching Children Mathematics*)

National Head Start Association
1651 Prince Street
Alexandria, VA 22314
http://www.nhsa.org
(Publishes *Children and Families Magazine*)

National Information Center for Children and Youth with Disabilities (NICHCY)
P.O. Box 1492
Washington, DC 20013
http://www.nichcy.org

National Science Teachers Association (NSTA)
1840 Wilson Blvd.
Arlington, VA 22201
http://www.nsta.org
(Publishes *Science and Children*, E-newsletters, the weekly *NSTA Express*, and monthly *Science Class*)

Save the Children
54 Wilton Road
Westport, CT 06880
http://www.savethechildren.org

Southern Early Childhood Association (SECA)
P.O. Box 55930
Little Rock, AR 72215
http://www.SouthernEarlyChildhood.org
(Publishes *Dimensions of Early Childhood*)

Stand for Children
516 SE Morrison Street, Suite 410
Portland, OR 97214
http://www.stand.org
(Publishes an e-newsletter, *Stand Update*)

Zero to Three—National Center for Infants, Toddlers, and Families
2000 M Street NW, Suite 200
Washington, DC 20036
http://www.zerotothree.org

GLOSSARY

A

accommodation—Piaget's theory of modification of existing cognitive information. Cognitive schemes are changed to accommodate new experiences or information.

advocacy—An attitude that encourages professionals, parents, and other caring adults to work together on behalf of young children.

aesthetic environment—An environment that cultivates an appreciation for beauty and a feeling of wonder and excitement of the world in which we live.

alphabet books—Simple stories based on the alphabet that present letter identification and one-object picture association.

anecdotal record—A brief, informal narrative account describing an incident of a child's behavior that is important to the observer.

anthropology—The study of the way people live, such as their beliefs and customs.

anti-bias—An attitude that actively challenges prejudice, stereotyping, and unfair treatment of an individual or group of individuals.

art—Visual communication through the elements of color, line, shape, and texture instead of words.

assessment—The collection of information or data on young children through observation and recordkeeping of what they do and how they do it as a basis for making educational decisions.

assimilation—Piaget's process of cognitive development, which occurs when a child handles, sees, or otherwise experiences something.

associative play—An activity of a three- or four-year-old child playing with other children in a group; the child drops in and out of play with minimal organization of activity.

astronomy—The study of the universe beyond the earth's atmosphere, such as the sun, moon, planets, and stars.

B

beat—An accent of sound or a continuing series of accents.

beginning-to-read books—Predictable books that are easy to read and present words that are simple and repetitive.

bias—Any attitude, belief, or feeling that results in unfair treatment of an individual or group of individuals.

bicultural—A term used to describe an individual from two distinct cultures.

big books—Oversized books that present extra-large text and illustrations.

board books—First books for infants and toddlers made of laminated heavy cardboard.

C

case study—A way of collecting and organizing all of the information gathered from various sources to provide insights into the behavior of the child studied.

checklist—A record of direct observation that involves selecting from a previously prepared list the statement that best describes the behavior observed, the conditions present, or the equipment, supplies, and materials available.

chemistry—The science dealing with the composition and transformations of substances.

classifying and sorting—Grouping objects by a common characteristic, such as size, shape, or color.

cognitive development—The mental process that focuses on how children's intelligence, thinking abilities, and language acquisition emerge through distinct ages; Piaget's study of children's thinking, involving creating their own mental image of the world, based on encounters with the environment.

concept books—Books that present themes, ideas, or concepts with specific examples. They also identify and clarify abstractions, such as color or shape, and help with vocabulary development.

concept development—The construction of knowledge through solving problems and experiencing the results, while being actively involved with the environment.

constructive play—Play that helps children understand their experiences. Involves planning or manipulation of objects or people to create a specific experience.

cooperative play—A type of play organized for some purpose by the four-year-old and older child. It requires group membership and reflects a child's growing capacity to accept and respond to ideas and actions not originally her own.

counting books—Books that describe simple numeral and picture associations, and often tell a story. They show representations of numbers in more than one format and vary from simple to complex.

crayon resist—A type of art for older children that involves drawing a picture in light-colored crayons then covering the picture with watercolors or thin tempera paint. The paint will cover all but the crayon drawing.

crayon rubbings—Duplicating an object of texture by placing it under paper and rubbing over it with a crayon.

creative dramatics—The improvised drama of children, age five or six and older.

creativity—The process of doing, of bringing something new and imaginative into being.

culture—The sum total of a child's or family's ways of living: their values or beliefs, language, patterns of thinking, appearance, and behavior. These are passed or learned from one generation to the next.

curator—The person who decides what art to display and how to display it.

curriculum—A multileveled process that encompasses what happens in an early education classroom each day, reflecting the philosophy, goals, and objectives of the early childhood program.

curriculum web—A visual illustration or process that integrates various learning activities and curriculum areas.

D

development—Systematic and adaptive changes in the body and mind.

developmentally appropriate practice—The curriculum planning philosophy expressed by NAEYC that recognizes that each child learns and develops differently in physical, intellectual, cultural, emotional, and social growth.

developmental theories—Principles that examine children's growth, behavior, and process of learning.

dramatic play—A type of creative, spontaneous play in which children use their imaginations to create and dramatize pretend characters, actions, or events.

E

early childhood education and early education—The curriculum, programs, and settings that serve young children, from birth through the eighth year of life.

earth and space science—The study of earth materials, objects in the sky, and changes in the earth and sky.

ecology—The study of living things in relation to their environment and to each other.

economics—The study of the production, distribution, and consumption of goods and services.

egocentric—Individuals who think about the world only in relation to themselves.

emergent curriculum—A curriculum that emerges out of the interests and experiences of the children.

emergent literacy—A process of developing awareness about reading and writing before young children can read or write.

environment—In an early childhood setting, the environment represents the conditions and surroundings affecting children and adults.

equilibrium—A balance of one's cognitive schemes and information gathered from the environment; assimilation and accommodation.

evaluation—The process of determining whether the philosophy, goals, and objectives of the early childhood program have been met.

F

flannelboard—Used as a prop to tell or extend a story effectively.

folk literature—Tales that come from the oral tradition of storytelling that appeal to the child's sense of fantasy.

format—The overall arrangement of the way a book is put together, such as size, shape, paper quality, colors, and content of each page.

functional play—Play that occurs when a child takes on a role and pretends to be someone else.

G

games with rules—Children's spontaneous physical and cognitive play that occurs during Piaget's concrete operations stage of development (seven years and older).

genre—Category used to classify literary works, usually by form, technique, or content.

geography—The study of the earth's surface and resources and the concepts of direction, location, and distance.

geology—The study of the earth, such as rocks and shells.

geometry—The area of mathematics that involves shape, size, space, position, direction, and movement.

goals—The general overall aims or overview of an early childhood program.

H

hand puppets—Puppets that are put on the hand; come in many types and varieties and are easy for young children to make and manipulate.

hardware—The physical components of the computer system, such as the monitor, keyboard, mouse, and printer.

history—The study of what has happened in the life of a country or people.

hollow blocks—Wooden blocks larger than unit blocks and opened on the sides.

I

inclusion—Reflective of the blending of practices from early childhood education and early childhood special education.

inclusive curriculum—A curriculum that underscores the importance of individual differences and cultural diversity among young children.

informational books—Books that offer nonfiction for emergent readers by providing accurate facts about people and subject matter.

inquiry—A questioning process that encourages curiosity and exploration. The opposite of rote learning.

integrated curriculum—A curriculum that encourages young children to transfer knowledge and skills from one subject to another while using all aspects of their development.

interaction books—Books used to stimulate imagination by using some device for involving young readers, such as pop-ups, fold-outs, scratch and sniff, pasting books, puzzle pictures, humor, and riddles.

K

kinesthetics—The use of the body to learn about physical capabilities and to develop body awareness.

L

language—Human speech, the written symbols for speech, or any means of communicating.

language development—The developmental process of a predictable sequence that includes both sending and receiving information. It is related, but not tied, to chronological age.

learning—Change in behavior or cognition that occurs as children construct knowledge through active exploration and discovery in their physical social environments.

learning centers—Curriculum centers (sometimes called interest centers or activity centers) that are well-defined areas where materials and supplies are combined around special groupings and common activities.

lesson plan—An outgrowth of theme selection, brainstorming/webbing, and the selection of projects and activities. Involves making a series of choices based on the developmental stages, learning styles, and interests of the children; goals and objectives of the program; and availability of materials, supplies, and resources.

life science—The study of living things, people, plants, and animals.

literacy—The ability to read and write, which gives one the command of a native language for the purpose of communicating.

literacy development—A lifelong process that begins at birth and includes listening, speaking, reading, and writing.

literature—All the writings (prose and verse) of a people, country, or period, including those written especially for children.

locomotor movement—The ability to move the whole body from one place to another.

Logico-Mathematical knowledge—Includes relationships constructed in order to make sense out of the world and to organize information, such as counting and classification.

M

manipulative movement—Large (gross) motor movements demonstrated by pulling, lifting, throwing, or kicking an object.

manipulatives—Toys and materials that enable young children to gain the fine motor control they need to accomplish tasks important to their growth and development.

marionettes—Puppets controlled by strings that offer an extra range of expression and full body movement.

measurement—Finding the length, height, and weight of an object using units like inches, feet, and pounds.

melody—A sequence of tones of varying pitches organized in a rhythmically meaningful way.

meteorology—The science of weather and atmosphere.

Mother Goose nursery rhyme books—Books passed from generation to generation and known by children all over the world. These are often a child's first introduction to literature.

multicultural books—Books that develop awareness of and sensitivity to other cultures. They also help to increase positive attitudes toward similarities and differences in people.

multiple intelligences—Gardner's theory that one form of intelligence is not better than another; all eight are equally valuable and viable.

N

nonlocomotor movement—Occurs when the feet remain stationary (as in standing, kneeling, or sitting), while other parts of the body move.

number sense—A concept that develops over time as children think about, explore, and discuss mathematical ideas.

nutrients—The chemical substances with specific uses in the body.

nutrition—The study of food and how it is used in the body.

O

objectives—The specific purposes or teaching techniques that interpret the goals of planning, schedules, and routines. These objectives are designed to meet the physical, intellectual, social, emotional, and creative development of young children.

object permanence—A mature state of perceptual development. According to Piaget's theory, a baby thinks that objects, including people, cease to exist the moment he stops seeing them. An older child starts to search for the missing object or person.

observation—The process of observing various aspects of an early childhood program by taking in information and interpreting it for meaning.

one-to-one correspondence—The pairing of one object to another object or one group of objects to another group of equal number.

onlooker play—The play of young children introduced to new situations that focuses on an activity rather than the environment.

P

pantomime—The art of conveying ideas without words.

parallel play—Observable play in the older toddler and young three-year-old that emphasizes being near another child while playing with an object rather than playing with a child.

pattern—A sequence of colors, objects, sounds, stories, or movements that repeats in the same order over and over again.

perceptual development—A type of development in which children use their senses to learn about the nature of objects, actions, and events.

philosophy—In an early childhood program the philosophy expresses the basic principles, attitudes, and beliefs of the center or school or individual teacher.

phoneme—The smallest unit of speech.

phonemic or phonological awareness—The ability to hear and identify individual sounds and spoken words.

phonics—The relationship between the letters of the written language and the sounds of spoken language.

physical development—A type of development involving children using large muscles, manipulating small muscles, developing eye-hand coordination, and acquiring self-help skills.

physical knowledge—Learning about objects in the environment and their characteristics, such as color, weight, and size.

physical sciences—The sciences (physics, chemistry, geology, meteorology, and astronomy) that relate to nonliving materials.

picture books—Books written in a direct style that tell a simple story with illustrations complementing the text.

pitch—The highness or lowness of a tone on a musical scale.

play—A behavior that is self-motivated, freely chosen, process-oriented, and enjoyable.

poetry—A form of literature that contributes imaginative rhyme, rhythm, and sound.

portfolio—A collection of a child's work over time and a record of the child's process of learning.

portfolio assessment—An evaluation method based on a systematic collection of information about a child and the child's work gathered by both the child and teacher over time from all available sources.

practice play—During Piaget's sensorimotor play (infancy to two years), infants explore the sensory qualities of objects and practice motor skills.

predictable books—Books that contain familiar and repetitive sequences.

prejudice—An attitude, opinion, or idea that is preconceived or decided, usually unfavorably.

process skills—The abilities to process new information through concrete experiences.

project—An in-depth investigation of a topic.

prop box—A collection of actual items related to dramatic play activities that focuses on a specific theme or lesson plan.

psychology—The study of the mind, emotions, and behavioral processes.

psychosocial theory—Erikson's eight stages that describe the interaction between an individual's social-emotional condition and the interpersonal environment.

puppetry—The art of making or operating puppets or producing puppet shows.

R

rational counting—Requires matching each numeral name, in order, to an object in a group.

realistic literature—A form of literature that helps children cope with common, actual experiences by offering positive solutions and insights.

rebus chart—Visual pictures, such as signs, illustrations, and directions, to help children make sense of any activity.

reference books—Books that emphasize individualized learning through special topic books, picture dictionaries, and encyclopedias.

reflective log or diary—A teacher or administrator's record of the most significant happenings, usually made at the end of the day or during an uninterrupted block of time.

rhyming—The ability to auditorily distinguish two words that end the same way.

rhythm—A sense of movement and patterns in music created by beats, the duration and volume of sounds, and the silences between sounds.

rote counting—The ability to recite names of numerals in order.

routines—The events that fit into the daily time frame of an early childhood program.

S

scaffolding—The adjustable support the teacher offers in response to the child's level of performance.

schedule—The basic daily timeline of an early childhood program.

schema—An integrated way of thinking or of forming mental images.

self-help skills—In early childhood, a child's ability to care for oneself, such as dressing, feeding, and toileting.

self-regulation—A child's natural ability to exercise control over physical and emotional behavior in the face of changing circumstances.

sensory experiences—Experiences that offer opportunities for free exploration in a variety of curriculum areas.

seriation—Ordering of objects based on the ability to place them in a logical sequence, such as smallest to largest or shortest to tallest.

series books—Books written for primary-grade children and that are built around a single character or group of characters.

shadow puppets—Puppets held from rods against a translucent screen lit from behind. These puppets offer a visual dimension that other types do not.

social and emotional development—A type of development consisting of children developing positive images of themselves, expressing personality and individualism, representing imagination and fantasy, establishing enjoyable relationships with others, and expressing feelings.

social sciences—The core of social studies: anthropology, sociology, history, geography, economics, and psychology.

sociocultural theory—Vygotsky's theory that emphasizes that a child's learning development is affected by culture and family environment.

sociodramatic play—The highest level of symbolic play wherein young children create their own happenings based on their experiences.

sociology—The study of group living, cooperation, and responsibilities.

software—A set of instructions used to direct a computer to perform some activity.

solitary play—Independent play behavior of a child without regard to what other children or adults are doing.

spatial sense—Comparisons that help children develop an awareness of themselves in relation to people and objects in space, such as exploration using blocks and boxes.

stereotype—An oversimplified generalization about a particular group, race, or sex, often with negative implications.

stick or rod puppets—Puppets controlled by a single stick, such as a tongue depressor, dowel rod, paper towel roll, craft stick, or ice cream stick.

string painting—A type of painting that involves moving string dipped in paint around on paper to make a design.

symbolic or dramatic play—A type of play that allows the child to transfer objects into symbols (things that represent something else) and images into people, places, and events within his experiences. Symbolic play occurs during Piaget's preoperational stage (two to seven years). Superhero fantasy play is considered a type of symbolic play for a young child.

symbolic thinking—The formation of symbols or mental representations, allowing children to solve problems by thinking before acting.

T

teacher- and child-made books—Books made by the teacher or child that encourage self-esteem, creativity, and the sharing of ideas. They also encourage children to articulate experiences.

tempo—A sense of slowness or rapidity in music.

theme—A broad concept or topic that enables the development of a lesson plan and the activities that fit within this curriculum plan.

theory—A systematic statement of principles and beliefs that are created to explain a group of facts that have been repeatedly tested or widely accepted.

three-dimensional art—Any art form that has three sides. Play dough and clay are examples of three-dimensional materials.

timbre—The unique tone quality of a voice or musical instrument.

tone—An individual musical sound.

transitions—Activities or learning experiences that move children from one activity to another.

U

unit—A section of the curriculum based on the unifying theme around which activities are planned.

unit blocks—Hardwood blocks used in early education environments, especially in block center play.

unoccupied behavior—Refers to a child (infant or toddler) who occupies herself by watching anything of momentary interest.

V

volume—The softness or loudness of sound.

W

whole language—A view of literacy and learning that builds on what children already know about oral language, reading, and writing while emphasizing meaningful language rather than isolated skill development.

woodworking center—An activity center providing many different sensory and three-dimensional experiences.

wordless picture books—Books that tell a story with visually appealing illustrations. These books promote creativity by encouraging a child to talk about experiences and use his or her imagination.

word wall—An alphabetically arranged display or chart of words that children have experienced throughout the school year.

Z

zone of proximal development—The range of potential each child has for learning, with that learning being shaped by the social environment in which it takes place.

INDEX